BUILDING

INTERNET APPLICATIONS WITH DELPHI™ 2

que®

BUILDING

INTERNET APPLICATIONS WITH DELPHI™ 2

Written by Davis Chapman with

Saleh W. Igal • William R. Beem • Kevin Sadler
Dan Dumbrill • Dean Thompson • David Medinets

Building Internet Applications with Delphi 2

Library of Congress Catalog Number: 95-72597

ISBN: 0-7897-0732-2

99 98 97 96   6 5 4 3 2 1

Interpretation of the printing code: The rightmost double-digit
number is the year of the book's printing; the rightmost single-digit
number, the number of the book's printing. For example, a printing
code of 96-1 shows that the first printing of the book occurred in
1996.

All terms mentioned in this book and the CD that are known to be
trademarks or service marks have been appropriately capitalized.
Que cannot attest to the accuracy of this information. Use of a term
in this book should not be seen as affecting the validity of any trade-
mark or service mark.

Screen Reproductions in this book were created by using Collage
Plus from Inner Media, Inc., Hollis, New Hampshire.

Credits

PRESIDENT AND PUBLISHER
Roland Elgey

ASSOCIATE PUBLISHER
Joseph P. Wikert

EDITORIAL SERVICES DIRECTOR
Elizabeth Keaffaber

MANAGING EDITOR
Sandy Doell

DIRECTOR OF MARKETING
Lynn E. Zingraf

SENIOR SERIES DIRECTOR
Chris Nelson

TITLE MANAGER
Bryan Gambrel

ACQUISITIONS EDITOR
Angela C. Kozlowski

PRODUCT DIRECTOR
Nancy D. Price

PRODUCTION EDITOR
Andy Saff

ASSISTANT PRODUCT MARKETING MANAGER
Kim Margolius

TECHNICAL EDITORS
Bob Reselmen
Dan Dumbrill

TECHNICAL SPECIALIST
Nadeem Muhammed

ACQUISITIONS COORDINATORS
Angela C. Kozlowski
Bethany Echlin

OPERATIONS COORDINATOR
Patty J. Brooks

EDITORIAL ASSISTANTS
Michelle Newcomb
Andrea Duvall

BOOK DESIGNER
Kim Scott

COVER DESIGNER
Dan Armstrong

PRODUCTION TEAM
Jason Carr
Chad Dressler
Jenny Earhart
Bryan Flores
Amy Gornik
Jason Hand
Sonja Hart
Daryl Kessler
Bob LaRoche
Michelle Lee
Kaylene Riemen
Laura Robbins
Bobbi Satterfield
Todd Wente
Paul Wilson

INDEXER
Tim Tate

Composed in *Century Old Style* and *Franklin Gothic* by Que Corporation.

About the Authors

Davis Chapman first began programming computers while working on his master's degree in Music Composition. While writing applications for computer music, he discovered that he enjoyed designing and developing computer software. It wasn't long before he realized that he stood a much better chance of eating if he stuck with his new-found skill and demoted his hard-earned status as a "starving artist" to a part-time hobby. Since then, Davis has striven to perfect the art of software design and development, with a strong emphasis on the practical application of client/server technology. He has been with the Dallas, Texas-based consulting firm B. R. Blackmarr and Associates for the past six years. You can reach him at **davischa@onramp.net**.

Saleh W. Igal is Vice President of Enterprise Network Infrastructure at B. R. Blackmarr and Associates. He specializes in the design, implementation, and troubleshooting of corporate client/server networks, and has managed many large-scale network migration projects. Saleh also teaches seminars on Internet security and Transmission Control Protocol/Internet Protocol (TCP/IP), and is a regular in several of the **com.dcom.*** and **comp.os.*** newsgroups. You can reach Saleh at **saleh@brba.com**.

William R. Beem is a Systems Engineer specializing in network, database, and application design and development. He is the author of many magazine articles on computer and financial industry topics. He was a columnist for Ziff-Davis' *Corporate Computing,* and has also written articles for *PC Magazine, PC Computing, LAN Magazine,* and *DataBased Advisor.* He is a self-employed consultant based in Orlando, Florida and a Certified OS/2 Engineer.

Kevin Sadler, who has a degree in Computer Applications and Information Systems from New York University, is a commercial software developer based in Riverside, California. He has written many currently deployed production Windows network applications in C++, Delphi, and Visual Basic. Kevin is currently focusing on Internet World Wide Web (WWW)-related applications based on the Windows NT server platform, using Delphi and Visual C++ as his programming tools of choice. He is presently working with Internet OLE Controls, Java, and other interactive server solutions. His Internet address is **kevin@pacg.com**.

Dan Dumbrill is the Senior Software Developer for Learning Tools, Inc. A full-time programmer since 1982, Dan studied Computer Science at the University of Wyoming. His varied background includes developing the Wyoming State Fair system, a real-time tracking and data acquisition system for the 2.3-meter University of Wyoming Infrared telescope, and a special education management system. Dan has been developing in Delphi since its inception and has taught various classes for Delphi user's groups. Dan's first and foremost love is his wife Stephanie, whom he married in 1990 after meeting on CompuServe. You can reach Dan at **Dumbrill@CompuServe.com**.

Dean Thompson started programming at the age of 13 with the TRS-80 Color Computer. He now works as a consultant in Dallas, programming in many languages, including Delphi, C++, PowerBuilder, Visual Basic, 80-86 Assembler, and SmallTalk. His focus has been on communication between midrange systems and PCs, but he also is avidly interested in computer gaming, Fuzzy Logic, and neural networks.

David Medinets has been programming since 1980, when he started with a Radio Shack Model 1. He still fondly remembers the days when he could cross-wire the keyboard to create funny-looking characters on the display. Since those days, he has spent time debugging emacs on UNIX machines, working on VAXen, and messing around with DOS microcomputers. David lives in Flanders, New Jersey with his wife Kathy and his two computers. He works at Prudential Insurance in Roseland, New Jersey, producing reams of printed output. His prior work has included coauthoring *Special Edition Using Turbo C++ 4.5 for Windows,* and creating CD-ROMs, Windows Help files, and electronic books. You can reach David at **medined@planet.net**.

Dedication

To my wife, Dore, without whose patience and understanding this book would never have been written.—Davis Chapman

Acknowledgments

Many people made it possible for me to write this book. Unfortunately, if I thanked everyone individually, I would end up with a 20-page acknowledgment that no one would ever read, so I will keep this short and to the point. I thank my wife and family for allowing me the time to write this book, and for putting up with my ignoring them over the holidays while I was racing to meet deadlines. I thank Angela, Fred, Nancy, and everyone at Que for talking me into writing this book when I really didn't have the time (you owe me an entire holiday season) and for coaching me through the entire process. Thanks to Fred Slone for getting involved at key points and making his insightful comments and recommendations. I also thank Bob Reselman for his great job as technical editor. He was unrelentingly brutal in pointing out the areas where I wasn't being crystal clear in my explanations, and this book wouldn't have been half as good without the great job that he did. Finally, I thank all of my cowriters for doing such a great job with the subjects that they covered.

I would love to hear from you and get your feedback on how we did. You can find my Web page at **http://rampages.onramp.net/~davischa/** or send me e-mail at **davischa@onramp.net**.

—Davis Chapman

We'd Like To Hear from You!

As part of our continuing effort to produce books of the highest possible quality, Que would like to hear your comments. To stay competitive, we *really* want you, as a computer book reader and user, to let us know what you like or dislike most about this book or other Que products.

You can mail comments, ideas, or suggestions for improving future editions to the address below, or send us a fax at (317) 581-4663. For the online-inclined, Macmillan Computer Publishing has a forum on CompuServe (type **GO QUEBOOKS** at any prompt) through which our staff and authors are available for questions and comments. The address of our Internet site is **http://www.mcp.com** (World Wide Web).

In addition to exploring our forum, please feel free to contact me personally to discuss your opinions of this book: on CompuServe, I'm at **75703,3504**, and on the Internet, **kozlowski@que.mcp.com**.

Thanks in advance—your comments will help us to continue publishing the best books available on computer topics in today's market.

Angela C. Kozlowski
Acquisitions Editor
Que Corporation
201 W. 103rd Street
Indianapolis, Indiana 46290
USA

Contents at a Glance

Table of Contents

II | Building Basic Internet Applications

Introduction

The Internet is not by any means new, but it is growing in popularity at an enormous rate. The original online service, the Internet is about to overtake all the other online services. The primary reason for this increased popularity is that affordable individual Internet connections have just recently become widely available. Another reason is the explosive growth of the World Wide Web, spurred on largely by the arrival of graphical browsers from companies like Netscape, Microsoft, and Spry.

Simultaneously with the boom in personal use of the Internet, business use of the Internet is growing at a tremendous rate. Companies are discovering that leasing Internet connections for each of their facilities is more cost-effective than building and maintaining their own wide area networks (WANs). Furthermore, corporations are taking a close look at Internet technology as a possible solution to some of the more labor-intensive portions of client/server application development and deployment.

Many applications are readily available to serve all your individual Internet needs. Plenty of electronic mail (e-mail), File Transfer Protocol (FTP), newsgroup, and Web browsers are easily available. But what if you want to incorporate some Internet application functionality into a non-Internet-based application, or if you think up a way to enhance an existing Internet application? You need to know how these applications work.

You couldn't choose a better language with which to build Internet applications than Delphi. Until now, most Internet application development has been done in C and C++ (with a growing number created using Visual Basic). The reason for this is that, until relatively recently, most computers connected to the Internet have been UNIX systems. Only recently have Windows-based computers began connecting to the Internet in large numbers. Around the same time that the WinSock specification became available, easy-to-use programming tools like Visual Basic became available. Delphi is one of the few languages that combine the power and flexibility of C and C++ with the easy user-interface design and rapid development of Visual Basic and PowerBuilder. And now, with the release of Delphi 2.0, Delphi is the programming language that makes the most sense to use for programming on all Windows platforms, no matter what your intended application's needs might be. ■

Who Should Use This Book?

This book is intended for programmers already experienced with Delphi. If you are looking for a book to instruct you on how to place controls on a window and attach code to those controls, this isn't the book for you. This book assumes that you already know and understand Delphi fundamentals, including how to allocate memory, manipulate pointers, and work with record structures. The emphasis is on the internal elements and structures that drive basic Internet applications, including network communications using WinSock. In many of the examples, the basic application functionality is assumed and not included in the book itself. In such cases, you can examine the code for the basic application functionality by looking up the source code on the companion CD.

This book tries to walk a very fine line between supplying enough understanding of the principles of Internet application programming and supplying sufficient practical examples of these principles at work. To succeed at developing Internet applications, you have to understand several fundamental principles. At the same time, no theoretical understanding does much good unless you see first hand how to turn your understanding of these principles from theory into working applications. You can combine this theoretical understanding of Internet application programming with all of the different ways in which you can use Delphi in Internet application development—and almost anything is possible, from building the client applications, to extending Web servers and browsers, to replacing the servers.

The Internet is growing and changing very quickly. A single book cannot possibly cover all the topics related to Internet application programming. If this book attempted to do so, it would be at least three or four times bigger than it already is.

This book tries to cover a lot, but it is no more than a starting point from which you can gain an understanding of the fundamentals of Internet programming and how you can apply those principles using Delphi. This starting point includes a basic understanding of network communications and the principles of multicomputer application programming. If you choose to continue down the path of Internet application development, great! If that is not your intention, but you instead want to gain an understanding of how these applications work, that's good too. What you do with the understanding that you gain from reading this book is up to you. We hope that this book gives you enough of an understanding to reach your goal.

What Hardware and Software Do You Need?

Most of the examples in this book were designed for portability between the new 32-bit version Delphi 2.0 and the 16-bit Delphi 1.0 (which comes bundled with Delphi 2.0). On the rare occasions that an example is not compatible between the two versions, we explain why it is not. (If we have missed an incompatibility between the two versions, we apologize for the oversight.) The version of Delphi doesn't affect the validity of this book's content. You can just as easily build and compile most of this book's examples by using the Desktop or Developer versions as well as the Client/Server version.

You also need an Internet connection or a network running the Transmission Control Protocol/Internet Protocol (TCP/IP) network protocol. The connection can be a dial-up Internet connection that uses Point-to-Point Protocol (PPP) or Serial Line Internet Protocol (SLIP). You need this connection when coding the client applications. For the server applications, you will probably want to have an actual network running TCP/IP with either Domain Name Service (DNS), Windows Internet Name Service (WINS), or fully configured host files, so that you can refer to servers by their machine name rather than their TCP/IP address. This network does not have to be extensive. It can consist of two systems with a simple thin-wire Ethernet cable running between them.

Along with the TCP/IP network protocol, you must ensure that you have the appropriate WINSOCK.DLL or WSOCK32.DLL in your WINDOWS\SYSTEM directory. TCP/IP vendors usually supply the WINSOCK.DLL. If you are running Windows NT, the operating system supplies the TCP/IP protocol, the WINSOCK.DLL, and the WSOCK32.DLL. If you are running Windows 95, the WinSock DLLs and the TCP/IP network protocol are readily available with the operating system.

> **CAUTION**
>
> Be careful about which WinSock DLLs you are using in your computer. It is important to use the WinSock DLLs that your TCP/IP vendor supplies. These DLLs have hooks into the TCP/IP implementation and cannot be used with another vendor's TCP/IP implementation. If you have ever tried to switch between multiple versions and manufactures of TCP/IP software, you have probably experienced what many developers call "WinSock Hell."

How Is This Book Organized?

This book is organized into four parts. Each part covers a different area of Internet application programming and related topics. Part I, "Introduction to Internet Applications Programming," provides some background on the Internet, the various applications that have been synonymous with the Internet, the TCP/IP network protocol, and how application communications are performed over that network protocol. The chapters in Part I consist of the following:

■ Chapter 1, "Introduction to Internet Applications Programming," provides a brief overview of Internet application programming and where it currently looks like it is going in the near future.

■ Chapter 2, "The Basic Internet Application Suite," discusses the various applications that have been considered an integral part of the Internet. This chapter also discusses why certain applications are falling out of common usage, and which applications are taking their places.

■ Chapter 3, "Internet Connectivity," discusses the TCP/IP networking protocol and how you provide services over this protocol. The chapter also discusses how dial-up connections can run the TCP/IP network protocol through PPP and SLIP. Also discussed are the differences between the two types of dial-up connections.

■ Chapter 4, "Internet Communications Protocols," takes a close look at the TCP/IP protocol stack and the Open Systems Interconnect (OSI) networking model. The chapter explains how the underlying networking protocols provide for interapplication communications.

■ Chapter 5, "The Principles of Socket Communications and Programming," explains the basic principles behind application communications using the socket mechanism. This chapter examines the TCP port services and how server applications use these services to provide the client applications a socket with which to connect and hold a conversation.

■ Chapter 6, "Socket Programming with Delphi Using WinSock," examines the Windows Socket (WinSock) implementation and how you can use it with Delphi. The chapter takes you step-by-step through the process of building a basic socket framework and then using that framework in a simple Internet application.

Part II, "Building Basic Internet Applications," covers the primary Internet applications and how they work. You examine how an Internet standard is developed and then use those standards to build the applications in the basic Internet application suite. Part II consists of the following chapters:

■ Chapter 7, "Internet Development Standards," provides an overview of the Request for Comment (RFC) process that is used to develop Internet standards. The chapter also explains where you can find these RFC documents and how you can create and file your own RFC to establish new standards.

■ Chapter 8, "Developing an FTP Client and Server," builds your understanding of the File Transfer Protocol (FTP) standard. You then put this understanding to use in building both FTP client and server applications.

■ Chapter 9, "Developing SMTP and POP Mail Clients," takes a look at the Simple Mail Transport Protocol (SMTP), the Post Office Protocol (POP), and the Multipurpose Internet Mail Extensions (MIME). You learn how to combine these two protocols (SMTP and POP) and message format (MIME) to create a full-featured Internet mail client. You then put this knowledge to use by building an SMTP mail client that creates and sends mail, and a POP mail client that receives mail.

■ Chapter 10, "Developing an Internet News Client/Reader," looks at the Usenet Network News Transport Protocol (NNTP) and how you use it to retrieve and examine newsgroup messages. The chapter then takes you through the process of using the NNTP protocol to build a news client.

■ Chapter 11, "Building a UUEncoder/Decoder," takes a close look at two of the most popular encoding schemes used in Internet mail and Usenet News: standard encoding (UUEncoding) and base-64 encoding (from the MIME specification). The chapter examines how these schemes work and why they are used. You then use these encoding algorithms to build an encoding/decoding utility that you can use with most encoded files that you find on the Internet.

Part III, "World Wide Web Programming," deals exclusively with the World Wide Web and the various ways in which you can use Delphi to build and extend Web application functionality. In this part of the book, you examine the various components found on the Web and explore how they all work together. You then look at using Delphi as a Common Gateway Interface (CGI) programming tool to provide additional functionality to Web pages. Next, you examine the Hypertext Transfer Protocol (HTTP) that provides the communications between Web browsers and servers. With this knowledge of HTTP, you then build your own Web client and server applications. Next, you explore how to use Delphi to extend the functionality of both Web browsers and servers in a newly emerging area of Web programming. Finally, you explore security and the Web, examining how various encryption schemes are competing for recognition as a security standard on the Web. You also see how to incorporate these schemes into Delphi applications. Part III consists of the following chapters:

■ Chapter 12, "The Web—HTTP, HTML, and Beyond," looks at all the parts that comprise the World Wide Web. The chapter examines the various protocols and languages that are in use, and where each of them fits in the overall picture.

■ Chapter 13, "Using Delphi with CGI," looks at how you can use Delphi with CGI to provide extended functionality to Web pages created with HTML. The chapter demonstrates the data communications that take place between the Web server and the CGI application and how the CGI application can deliver its results to the client application.

■ Chapter 14, "Using a Database in a CGI Application," looks at how you can use Delphi with CGI to populate Web pages with dynamic data from an online database.

■ Chapter 15, "Building a Web Robot To Verify Link Integrity," explores HTTP. In this chapter, you also take a cursory glance at HTML to see how you can combine it with HTTP in a Web client application to verify the links embedded within a Web page.

■ Chapter 16, "Building a Web Server with Delphi," takes a more thorough look at HTTP. You look at the commands and message formatting as well as the difference between HTTP 0.9 and HTTP 1.0. You then use this information to build a working Web server.

■ Chapter 17, "Internet Security, RSA Encryption, SSL, STT, PCT, and WinSock," examines the current means of providing security and message encryption through Web applications, and how you can use these with Delphi applications.

■ Chapter 18, "The Netscape API—Incorporating Delphi with the Netscape Browser and Server," looks at the new application program interfaces (APIs) that are built in to the newest versions of the Netscape browsers and servers. The chapter also demonstrates how you can use Delphi to extend the functionality of both the Netscape browser and server.

Finally, the appendixes consist mostly of reference material. The appendixes include the complete command sets for the Internet applications examined in this book, header fields for the Internet Message Format, listings of all the available RFCs, and other useful information. This book provides the following appendixes:

- Appendix A, "Internet Application Command Sets," provides complete listings of the command sets used in the FTP, SMTP, POP, NNTP, and HTTP protocols. The appendix also provides the response codes that these commands might send.

- Appendix B, "The Internet Message Format," provides a brief overview of the message format used by Internet mail, Usenet News, and HTTP 1.0. For each of these applications, the appendix shows the various header fields, explains the information in each field, and identifies who adds each of the header fields to the message.

- Appendix C, "RFC Standards Documents," lists many of the available RFC documents and indicates the subject of each.

- Appendix D, "Converting from C and C++ to Object Pascal," provides an overview of how applications written in C and C++ can be translated into Delphi. Currently, most Internet applications are written in C or C++.

- Appendix E, "Browsing the CD-ROM," examines the applications and utilities included on the CD-ROM that accompanies this book.

Conventions Used in This Book

This book presents a variety of code, message (and HTML) text, commands, and response codes. To distinguish these elements clearly from the rest of this book's text, the code, message text, commands and response codes appear in a special monospaced font. For example, when this book displays a few lines of code, it looks similar to the following:

```
function TIntro.AddTwoNumbers(x, y: Integer): Integer;
begin
    AddTwoNumbers := x + y;
end;
```

However, a more extensive code listing is presented in a formal listing, such as Listing 0.1.

Listing 0.1 TSOCKETC.PAS—an Example of a Code Listing

```
function _TSocket.InitializeSocket: Boolean;
var
    lw_SocketVersion: Word;
    li_ErrorReturn: Integer;
    lsp_WinSockInfo: LPWSADATA;
begin
    lw_SocketVersion := $0101;
    li_ErrorReturn := WSAStartup(lw_SocketVersion, @isp_WinSockInfo);
    case li_ErrorReturn of
        WSAEINVAL: InitializeSocket := FALSE;
        WSASYSNOTREADY: InitializeSocket := FALSE;
        WSAVERNOTSUPPORTED: InitializeSocket := FALSE;
```

```
    else
        InitializeSocket := TRUE;
    end;
end;
```

Even though this book contains a large amount of code, you don't have to type it all. The CD that accompanies this book provides all demonstrated code (along with the pieces that aren't shown in the text).

As you read this book, you will come across icons and boxes that mark off separated sections of text. These are notes, tips, and cautions that are not necessarily part of the subject under discussion, but related pieces of important information. Some examples of these elements follow.

 N O T E Notes provide additional information about the subject that you are reading about. ■

TIP Tips provide important information about using the features that you are reading about.

CAUTION

Cautions present information that you want to be aware of to avoid any unnecessary mishaps.

Introduction to Internet Applications Programming

Introduction to Internet Applications Programming

- How Internet application communications work, and how this communication model is quite similar to the current state of client/server technology

- How you can use Delphi in just about all areas of Internet application development, and why Delphi is such a good fit for each type of development

- What the current directions are for Internet applications, and why these directions have vast implications for the entire business computing industry (and have all the client/server development tool vendors running scared)

The term *Internet* brings to mind images of speeding through space while sitting in front of a computer, going places and meeting people at close to light speed. Or it could bring to mind the image of a global village, where national boundaries no longer matter and everyone enjoys the right to free speech, no matter where they live. Or it could bring even more images to mind, each vastly different than the ones just described.

Regardless of the images that spring to mind, the Internet has become an integral part of the computing community. From its meager beginnings as ARPAnet, it has grown into a global means of communicating and conducting business. Currently, the Internet is projected to be central to the future of both business and consumer computing. Many people, even the most casual of computer users, already have electronic mail (e-mail) addresses, and many World Wide Web users who do not already have a home page are racing to learn how to build one.

The current growth of the Internet, and in particular the World Wide Web, is influencing everything in the computing industry. Feeling caught off-guard, a significant number of software companies—including Lotus, Microsoft,

Borland, IBM, and Macromedia—are scrambling to build Internet capabilities into their current offerings. The current conventional wisdom is that if your applications do not at least coexist with the Internet, they'll soon be left behind.

As far as programming tools and languages go, Borland International's Delphi is in excellent position to take advantage of this Internet explosion. Long the domain of C programmers, Internet application programming fits well within the Delphi programming paradigm. This book explains how you can use Delphi to build the various components that make up the Internet application suites, which you can combine into an integrated application much like that which major Web browser manufacturers develop. When you consider some of the more advanced features, such as multithreading and the capability to link using standard .OBJ files, you find that Delphi is one of the few rapid application development tools powerful and flexible enough to develop the server side of Internet applications.

This chapter provides an overview of Internet application programming and explains how Delphi fits into the picture. ▨

Internet and Client/Server Application Communications

The Internet is the platform on which the first widely distributed computing applications were developed and deployed. The communications models used in today's client/server computing model, where application processing is distributed over two or more computers to take advantage of the cumulative computing power, were first developed to accommodate the Internet. So it's no surprise that the communications model used in most Internet applications closely resembles that of the client/server computing model. In a sense, the Internet is both the past and future of client/server computing.

This communication model is quite elegant in its simplicity. First, the client connects to the server. Next, the client and the server hold a conversation in which the client sends a request to the server, and the server responds with the appropriate reply to the request. This conversation continues for as long as the client has requests to make. After the client and server finish their conversation, the client disconnects from the server and the session ends.

Most Internet applications conduct such conversations by using ASCII-readable, text-based commands and replies. Few Internet applications use any sort of binary command/reply model, where the commands and replies are sent in binary form to minimize the amount of data that is sent between the two computers (for that matter, few client/server applications use a binary model), although the data sent or returned with the command or reply is often binary.

Most client/server and all Internet applications assume an underlying layer of Transmission Control Protocol/Internet Protocol (TCP/IP) as the network protocol in use (although any one of several other network protocols could be in use instead). This protocol provides for application-level communications using *sockets*. Sockets provide a means of sending and receiving data over a network connection without having to dig down to the level of formatting packets and managing buffers. Sockets give programmers a suite of network communications functions that are much like the functions available to read, write, and manage files on your computer disk. You learn the details of TCP/IP and socket communications in Chapters 4, "Internet Communications Protocols," and 5, "The Principles of Socket Communications and Programming."

Sockets were first developed with BSD UNIX (Berkley Software Distribution UNIX) as an interprocess communications mechanism. Sockets enable programs running on separate computers, or even on the same computer, to communicate directly and easily. They also enable the programmer to implement this communication without having to delve into the low-level network protocol. Sockets have become synonymous with TCP/IP application programming.

With the advent of Windows came the eventual appearance of the Windows socket interface and application programming interface (API), also known as *WinSock*. Developed as a collaboration among all the various personal computer (PC) TCP/IP vendors, the WinSock specification is intended to provide developers with a consistent socket implementation. This standardization frees developers from worrying about which TCP/IP version the client PC is running (prior to the WinSock standardization, each TCP/IP vendor had a unique programming API for building network applications), and thus lit the fuse for the explosion of Windows-based TCP/IP applications. The consistency of WinSock programming also paved the way for Windows to dominate as the client (and sometimes the server) operating system for client/server and Internet applications.

Using Delphi as an Internet Application Programming Tool

For each Internet application development task that you need to perform, you can choose to use various tools and languages. With the dominance of Windows on the client desktop, and the growing prominence of Windows NT on the server platforms, Delphi is one of the few tools that you can seriously consider for just about all of these development tasks. You can easily use Delphi to build the following:

- Client applications for most Internet application services (such as File Transfer Protocol [FTP], Mail, and News)
- Common Gateway Interface (CGI) scripts to provide additional functionality to Web pages, including database connectivity
- World Wide Web client and server applications
- Extensions to Netscape and Microsoft browsers and servers through their published APIs
- Support for the functionality and applications necessary to organize and manage Internet-based applications and operations

Using Delphi To Build Client Applications

Delphi lends itself quite well to building Internet client applications, and (as you'll see in Chapter 8, "Developing an FTP Client and Server") also to building a Windows-based server. This is because Delphi works well with the WinSock API. As you'll see in later chapters, you can easily build a client application that sends the appropriate request messages to a server, receives the response, and then analyzes the response. Combine this with how easily you can build a user-friendly interface, and you have a quick, powerful tool for building Internet client applications, and the processing horsepower to build a new generation of "intelligent" client applications.

Using Delphi To Provide CGI Process Functionality

The Common Gateway Interface (CGI) is the mechanism by which most Web servers provide functionality to Web pages. By embedding the address of an executable program within a Web page, you can enable a user viewing the page to send data to a database through the Web server. This same application can return data from the database to be displayed in a Web page that is created dynamically. These applications can also provide such functionality as randomly (or not so randomly) changing messages or pictures. In every usage of CGI applications, the data being passed to the CGI application, and the data being returned from the CGI application to the Web browser, is passed through the Web server.

N O T E   Most early Web servers ran on UNIX systems. A common practice on these servers was to build CGI applications using one of the various scripting languages available on most UNIX systems (such as Perl, Awk, and Korn Shell). Because of this, CGI applications are commonly referred to as *CGI scripts*.

Most of the Windows-based Web servers were originally designed to be capable of using Visual Basic 3.0 as the primary CGI scripting tool. The interaction between the Web server and Visual Basic provided this capability by writing initialization and data files that the Visual Basic application could then read as it is starting up. An application can read in data from the server even better with Delphi than with Visual Basic. Delphi provides several advantages over Visual Basic; for example, Delphi has no run-time environment (or the associated overhead), and enables you to access databases through direct connections rather than through the cumbersome Open Database Connectivity (ODBC) interface. (To learn about the use and implications of ODBC in Internet programming, see Chapter 14, "Using a Database in a CGI Application.") Combine Delphi's "stand-alone" nature and easy database access with Delphi's computational power and executable speed, and you have a powerful, flexible tool for building and performing CGI processing.

Using Delphi To Build World Wide Web Applications

Delphi is one of only two or three languages that you could use to make a serious attempt at building a Web browser (although you would probably have to delve much deeper into image and graphics processing than this book can cover). It is also one of the few tools that you could use to build a full-function Web server. Include in this list of Internet tools and applications all the other Web-based tools (HTML editors, Web robots, Web search engines, and so on) and you find that Delphi is one of the most capable programming tools available for performing all these programming tasks. Delphi's capability to work seamlessly with the WinSock API and to process both ASCII and binary data, combined with its multithreading capabilities, makes Delphi a good tool for developing Web applications.

Using Delphi To Extend Netscape Functionality

With each new version of the Netscape browsers and servers, Netscape has added more avenues for customizing and extending its applications' functionality. Whether used through dynamic data exchange (DDE) and object linking and embedding (OLE) or through the Netscape Plug-Ins API, Delphi is an ideal tool for building extensions to the Netscape browser. On the server side, Netscape has opened up their Web server for extensions using the Netscape Server API (NSAPI, also called Internet Server API or ISAPI). Using Delphi 2.0 with the Windows NT version of the Netscape Server, you can easily and quicky extend the server functionality in many ways.

Microsoft has announced that it is enhancing its Web browser and server technology by building in the capability to add extensions, much like Netscape has done. However, Microsoft is adding a twist: Its extensions will probably use OCXs extensively. Using an OCX to extend a Web browser is a shortcoming for Delphi. Although you can use OCXs in your applications when you use Delphi 2.0, Borland hasn't announced the capability to use Delphi to build OCXs. (Borland might add this capability in its next version of Delphi, or a third-party vendor might develop an easy-to-use tool for bundling Delphi-built objects into OCXs.)

Using Delphi To Build Internet Support Applications

Using Delphi also makes sense when building support programs, functionality, and utilities for Internet applications. Although such programs might not interact with the Internet directly, they provide support for other programs that do. The following are examples of such support applications:

- Encoding and decoding of utilities and functions
- Logging and log analysis of server statistics
- Analysis of data received from Web browsers that post data to a Web page

Delphi is one of the few tools that can easily handle all these support applications. Like C and C++, Delphi has the computational horsepower to churn through the encoding and decoding of files to be transferred over the Internet. However, unlike C or C++, Delphi is a truly visual object-oriented programming paradigm; Delphi is also easier to learn and use than C and C++. Like more data-oriented languages such as Visual Basic or PowerBuilder, Delphi also has the data-manipulation capabilities to rip through server logs to analyze and report on server usage (the data-manipulation capabilities of C and C++ are clumsy at best). Most programming languages and tools currently on the market can handle these functions and capabilities, but Delphi is one of the few that make programming in all these areas easy.

The Direction of Internet Computing

The state of Internet application technology is currently changing at a phenomenal rate. New technology appears and is outdated in what often seems like a matter days. Keeping up with this rate of change is difficult, and staying on top of these continuous changes is even more so.

Currently, Internet computing seems to be moving in several different directions. The more glamorous direction is toward multimedia, incorporating sound and video into Web pages and other, mostly proprietary, interactive services. Multimedia and Web-based interactivity require a large amount of bandwidth, both in the Internet connection and on the client desktop.

Internet technology is also moving toward the use of components. A *component* is an active object with its own encapsulated functionality. Components are presenting themselves on the Internet as small data-entry and data-retrieval objects in a three-tier client/server-over-the-Internet architecture. Components are also appearing both locally on the desktop and globally on the Internet as animated objects that can exist alone on a Web page or provide animation services to other Web pages. Animation objects—as well as their cousins, virtual reality components—require either a lot of bandwidth or a user with the patience to tolerate the long download time or increased usage on the client computer.

Yet another major direction for Internet technology is toward Java, an increasingly popular programming language that produces applets. An *applet* is a small, self-contained special-purpose application that is transferred to a desktop computer through a Web page in which a reference for the application is embedded (in the same way that graphic images are currently embedded within Web pages). An applet can perform tasks by itself or by communicating over the Internet to the server to which it is connected. Once again, this technology is cumbersome to load over the Internet and must run on a powerful desktop system. The advantage is that Java is compiled into a secure, executable form consisting of pseudocode (p-code). This code can run on just about any platform, but is not affected by anything outside of the client desktop's browser, and thus cannot transport undesirable elements (such as viruses) to the client computer.

The preceding directions of the Internet are all technology-oriented. But in which direction is the Internet's content and usage heading? Here the Internet is rapidly growing in at least two different directions.

The first direction is toward the growing usage of the Internet and Internet technology as a business tool. Businesses are using Internet and Web technology as the heir-apparent to both client/server and groupware (Lotus Notes and workflow) types of applications. All the client/server and groupware vendors are scrambling to incorporate Internet and Web capabilities into their products. Almost all have announced support for Java, and several have announced new technology that enables developers to convert into Web pages any applications built with the vendor's tools.

The other primary direction is toward the use of the Internet for personal and entertainment purposes. Individual Internet accounts are getting cheaper each day, and a personal account is the latest status symbol. If you don't have an Internet e-mail address, you just aren't hip, cool, or "with it."

So where is Internet application technology heading? Anything that this section prognosticates will probably be obsolete by the time that this book reaches the shelves of your local bookstore. What is hot today will be cold tomorrow. Today's most popular applications and utilities will be old news by next week. With the increase in ISDN and T1 connections, the use of rapidly expanding bandwidth probably will greatly increase. This means that there will be more multimedia and animated Web pages. The ongoing research in encryption technology will result in a corresponding increase of online commerce. The digitization of major libraries and publications will increase the usage of the Internet for research and news purposes, all of which will require supporting programs for maintaining subscriptions and registrations. Finally, the increase in database integration will result in more traditional business applications that use Internet technologies to provide quicker support for the rapidly changing business environment.

From Here...

In this chapter, you've briefly looked at the communication model used in Internet applications, and how this model is similar to that of most client/server computer systems. You also briefly examined the different kinds of Internet applications development in which you can use Delphi as a development tool, and what makes Delphi a good choice for each type of application development. Finally, you explored the current directions in Internet application technology and usage.

To understand what's involved in building the next generation of Internet applications, you first need a more in-depth understanding of where Internet applications have come from and which Internet applications are still popular. You then need to look even more closely at the direction in which the technology's logical evolution is heading. You also need a basic understanding of the networking protocol on which all these applications are built, and how that protocol affects the design and development of Internet applications. Then you can take a close look at the internal workings of some of the most popular Internet applications, building your own versions of each of these applications as you go along. From here you might want to explore the following chapters:

- To get a more thorough understanding of the evolution of Internet applications, see Chapter 2, "The Basic Internet Application Suite."
- To understand the various components involved in Internet connectivity, how one computer finds another using a system name, or how these computers can run an Internet connection over a phone line, see Chapter 3, "Internet Connectivity."
- To understand how the TCP/IP network protocol works, and how it affects the applications built on top of it, see Chapter 4, "Internet Communications Protocols."
- To see how an application running on one computer can connect to a specific application running on another computer and hold a conversation, see Chapter 5, "The Principles of Socket Communications and Programming."
- To bypass all this theoretical stuff and jump right into programming, see Chapter 6, "Socket Programming with Delphi Using WinSock."

CHAPTER 2

The Basic Internet Application Suite

- Understand the major functions in the WinSock API that you will be using—how they work and what they do

- Create a WinSock object, to abstract the socket communication functions into simpler functions that you can easily use in your applications

- Build a simple application to test your WinSock object and interface definition

Although the Internet supports literally thousands of different services, a few key functions provide for the majority of needs for many users. This basic Internet application suite lays the foundation for what most users know as the Internet. A thorough understanding of this basic suite will prepare you to develop for a wide range of existing and future Internet services.

This chapter starts by providing a brief overview of the client/server model that is the framework for all Internet services. Next, the chapter summarizes four of the most important Internet application services:

- The File Transfer Protocol (FTP)

- Electronic mail

- Usenet News

- The World Wide Web

This chapter also discusses other less critical services. The chapter finishes by making some predictions about services that will shape the Internet's future growth. ■

The Client/Server Model

The "information superhighway" is an appropriate metaphor for the Internet. Much like a regular highway transports a wide variety of traffic—such as motorcycles, cars, vans, and trucks—the Internet carries a wide variety of services, acting as a transport for file transfer, terminal emulation, and electronic mail.

A car that has a new feature, such as fuel injection, can still use the same road as a Model T and reach the same destinations. Similarly, new services can be transported across the Internet as soon as they are developed.

This flexibility has fueled the unique explosion of innovation and growth on the Internet. The source of this flexibility is the *client/server* model.

This model divides application programs into two parts: the *client* program, with which the user interacts, and the *server* program, which coordinates activities with clients. In the most simple case, these two programs can run on the same computer. More commonly, a PC local area network (LAN) or the Internet connects the client and server computers, and the application can run regardless of the hardware's physical location.

Client/server applications are, by necessity, founded on common specifications agreed on in advance, known as *protocols*. Most Internet protocol specifications are recorded in RFC (Request for Comment) documents. Anyone can write and submit an RFC; if Internet users think that an RFC has sufficient merit, it will be widely implemented, such as RFC 959, the File Transfer Protocol. Many protocols are defined but rarely used, such as RFC 1097, the Telnet Subliminal-Message Option. Others are obsolete, such as RFC 114, the initial File Transfer Protocol specification. Throughout this book you will see references to RFC documents; the companion CD-ROM's \RFC directory includes these documents.

The open design of the protocol specifications gives Internet applications independence from the method used to carry data, and thus enables a wide variety of clients to access a standard server. For example, although a proprietary cc:Mail server supports only proprietary cc:Mail clients, an Internet mail server can support hundreds of different client software packages. You can connect a Windows PC to a mail server by using Microsoft Exchange, Eudora, Z-Mail, and many other programs. Because these programs all use a common specification, they can interoperate; although the programs are from different software developers, they can all exchange messages with each other.

Client programs using different computers and operating systems can also connect to the same server, if both the client and server programs use the same protocol. A Macintosh that uses System 7, a UNIX workstation, and a mainframe computer can all connect to the same mail server.

Most Internet protocols are relatively simple. For example, the Daytime service simply passes one string—the time—from the server to the client; the first project in this book is a Daytime client. The power of the Internet comes from the actual data that the protocols carry, not the protocols themselves. Although the Hypertext Transport Protocol (HTTP)—the protocol that carries World Wide Web traffic—supports only a few basic commands, it can carry a wide variety of data, from ASCII text to video.

The File Transfer Protocol (FTP)

FTP, the File Transfer Protocol, was one of the first Internet services, and many of FTP's specifications have not changed since the early 1970s. Because of this longevity, FTP provides the most widely accessible way to transfer files among network-connected computers. FTP clients are available on almost every computer platform, from an 8086-based DOS PC to multimillion dollar supercomputers. Unfortunately, FTP's age shows in its inability to prioritize traffic or resume failed transfers.

Many companies store software update and technical support files on FTP servers, such as **ftp.microsoft.com** or **ftp.novell.com**. Publicly accessible servers such as **ftp.coast.net** provide large repositories with thousands of shareware and freeware files.

Some operating systems and integrated Internet access packages include poor FTP clients. For example, Microsoft Windows 95 includes an awkward command-line based FTP client, illustrated in Figure 2.1. The client forces the user to drop from a full-featured graphical environment to a command-line interface, and includes only a basic summary of commands for online help.

FIG. 2.1

The Microsoft FTP client included with Windows 95 provides a primitive command-line interface.

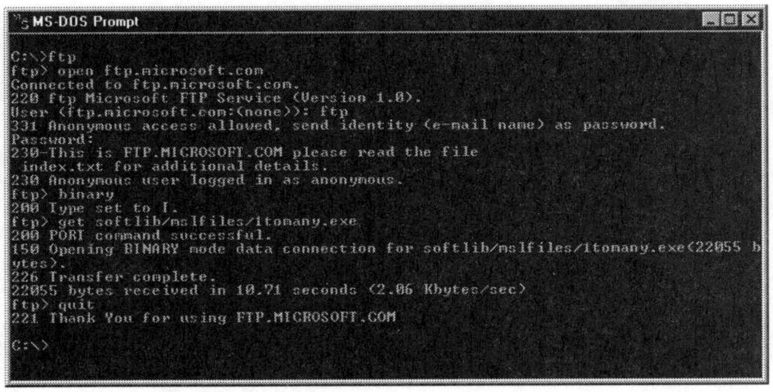

At the other end of the spectrum, some applications include full-blown FTP clients integrated with software designed primarily for other functions, such as file management or World Wide Web access. Figures 2.2 and 2.3 show examples of such applications.

FIG. 2.2

Symantec Norton
Navigator integrates FTP
access into its File
Manager application.

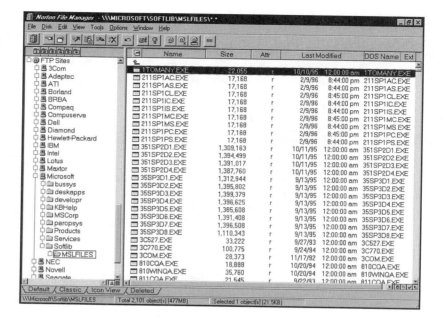

FIG. 2.3

Netscape Navigator
integrates FTP access
with a World Wide Web
browser.

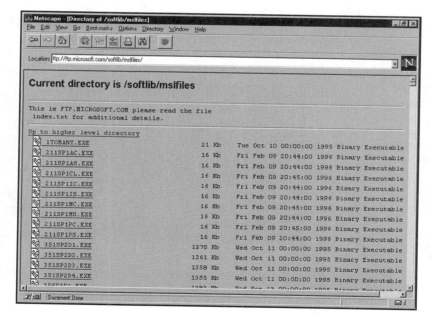

Chapter 8, "Developing an FTP Client and Server," discusses the details of the FTP protocol as
you build an FTP client and FTP server. With this knowledge, you can integrate FTP services
into future applications that you develop.

Electronic Mail

Around 1971, two programmers at Bolt, Baranek, and Newman (BBN), the company contracted to build the first version of the Internet, started sending each other messages rather than just data. From those humble roots, Internet electronic mail, or *e-mail,* has grown to be the essential backbone for global interpersonal communication. Figure 2.4 shows a running e-mail client program.

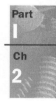

FIG. 2.4

Microsoft Exchange is one example of an Internet e-mail client.

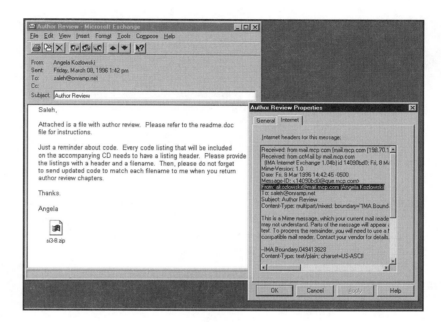

E-Mail Protocols

Internet mail was originally implemented as a feature of FTP. In 1980, Suzanne Sluizer and Jon Postel did the preliminary work on what would come to be known as the Simple Mail Transfer Protocol (SMTP). Still an essential component of Internet mail delivery, the SMTP protocol delivers data between Internet hosts.

However, SMTP was designed with the assumption that big, multiuser time-sharing mainframe host computers would exchange mail, and did not account for PCs that had only occasional connectivity. In 1984, Post Office Protocol (POP) addressed this limitation. As originally defined, POP had two basic functions: to retrieve all messages and keep them on the server, or to retrieve all messages and delete them from the server. The current version, POP3, adds a few new features but keeps much of the same structure as the original version. In Chapter 9, "Developing SMTP and POP Mail Clients," you learn the details of the SMTP and POP protocols as you build an e-mail client and server.

Although SMTP and POP are responsible for transporting mail, they support only a stream of ASCII text and do nothing to standardize the content of mail messages—that is, these protocols do not support rich contents, such as graphics and binary file attachments, as they require binary transmission. To work around this limitation, early Internet users relied on *UUEncode* and *UUDecode*. These programs, supplied with the UNIX operating system, convert binary files to and from a specially coded ASCII format that can be sent through Internet mail. UUEncode converts a binary file into an ASCII format that can be transmitted through Internet mail, and UUDecode reverses the process, changing the text back into a binary file. In Chapter 11, "Building a UUEncoder/Decoder," you build routines to handle the UUEncode and UUDecode process.

UUEncode

Before Internet access was widely available, many UNIX based computers relied on the UNIX to UNIX copy program, or *uucp*. Because uucp was limited to readable ASCII characters, UUEncode and UUDecode were developed to allow the transmission of binary files between UNIX computers. Later, this encoding was adopted for use on the Internet.

In 1992, the Multipurpose Internet Mail Extensions (MIME) standardized the format of messages to contain more than just ASCII text. MIME supported, for the first time, Internet e-mail containing languages other than English, and multimedia attachments with graphics, sound, video, and other user-defined data types. Applications other than e-mail also use MIME support; for example, the World Wide Web would be limited to ASCII text without it. Chapter 3, "Internet Connectivity," describes MIME further.

E-Mail Applications

Besides using e-mail for its traditional purpose—sending messages between users—you can build entire applications on top of the Internet mail structure. For example, mailing list servers send messages to groups of subscribed users. The index at **http://www.neosoft.com/ internet/paml/** catalogs thousands of publicly accessible mailing lists.

To use a mailing list, you usually send an e-mail subscription request to the person or program maintaining the list. For instance, if your name is John Doe and you want to subscribe to the **xyz-l** list at **bigbiz.com**, you might send an e-mail message with a body of SUBSCRIBE xyz-l John Doe to **listserv@bigbiz.com**. From then on, any e-mail message that you sent to **xyz-l@bigbiz.com** would be passed on to all list subscribers, and you would receive copies of all messages sent to that address.

Another class of application built on e-mail is the mail robot, which performs an action based on a mail message. For example, by using the robot at **ftpmail@decwrl.dec.com**, users who have only e-mail access to the Internet can transfer files. This enables the millions of such users to exchange files with remote sites.

Finally, some businesses use e-mail as an application-to-application data transport, supporting remote offices and mobile users. The standard mail protocols provide a powerful tool that you can harness in your application programs.

Usenet News

Usenet News provides a group conferencing facility similar to that provided by many bulletin board systems. The key difference is that because Usenet News is a client/server Internet-based system, it supports messaging from users all over the world.

Usenet is one of the most useful applications on the Internet. If you don't know where to look for information on an obscure topic, or if you have an advanced question that stumped a vendor's technical support department, you can post the question on Usenet and perhaps receive a reply from someone else who has the same problem.

Usenet News clients are usually known as *newsreaders*. More advanced than FTP or the e-mail protocols, Usenet News protocols transport more complex data, making a newsreader a relatively difficult development project. In Chapter 10, "Developing an Internet News Client/Reader," you learn more about Usenet News as you develop a newsreader. Figure 2.5 shows Agent, a commercial newsreader.

FIG. 2.5

The Agent newsreader enables you to read and respond to newsgroup articles.

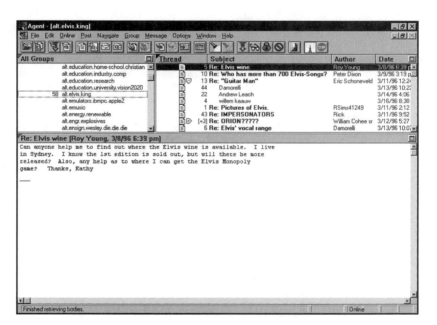

The World Wide Web

The World Wide Web (WWW, or the *Web* for short) is the newest and most powerful information service on the Internet. To many Internet users, the WWW service is synonymous with the Internet. Most of the growth and innovation on the Internet centers around extending the Web's capabilities.

The Web uses the HTTP to deliver information. Web clients, known as *browsers,* also usually support other protocols, providing WWW, FTP, e-mail, and Usenet News in a single integrated application.

The cargo that HTTP transports can include an unlimited number of data types. A single Web page can include hypertext (written in HTML, the Hypertext Markup Language), images, sound, and video. An advanced data type, Java, lets the client run specialized programs locally, blurring the distinction between browser and operating system. Chapter 12, "The Web—HTTP, HTML, and Beyond," describes the basics of how the Web works, explains HTTP and HTML, and summarizes other closely related technologies such as Java.

Most Web pages are static, displaying a fixed topic each time, but much of the Web's power comes from its capability to enable users to fill in information in the blanks of a form. Server programs linked to the Common Gateway Interface (CGI) process this information. Besides being capable of processing forms, CGI lets you add advanced capabilities, such as simple animation and pages built on-the-fly. Chapter 13, "Using Delphi with CGI," introduces CGI and its interaction with Delphi. In Chapter 14, "Using a Database in a CGI Application," you build an application that queries a database and dynamically builds a Web page to respond to the user. Figure 2.6 shows a form that uses CGI.

FIG. 2.6

The Lycos search server lets you enter search information on a form.

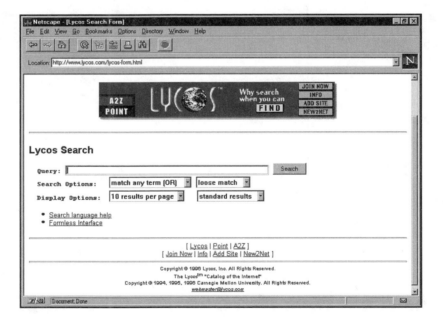

Web Applications

One downside to the Web is that it lacks a central index. Web pages are added and changed daily, but no central registration process exists for recording an index to the pages. Another problem is the lack of tools to manage hypertext links. After you build a WWW site, the hyperlinked structure is often difficult to maintain. For example, a dozen pages at a site might have links pointing to a common page. If that page's name changes, and only some of the links are updated, remote users get a URL not found or similar error message when trying to access that link.

You can solve both of these problems with Web robots (also known as *spiders*). In Chapter 15, "Building a Web Robot To Verify Link Integrity," you build a Web robot to verify the integrity of links at your site. This exercise should also give you greater insight to the inner workings of large Web robots such as Lycos, AltaVista, and Webcrawler.

Many businesses now focus attention on using Internet technology as a means of deploying applications. *Intranets*—internal internets designed to meet the specialized needs of a single enterprise (such as a business or nonprofit organization)—enable those organizations to roll out complex applications to thousands of users in a matter of days rather than the months required for most software.

Another new application for Web service is collaboration software, which enables users scattered around the globe to cooperate on a single project. Lotus Notes and Collabra Share are two examples of such collaboration software. Both intranet and collaboration applications are beyond the realm of most traditional Web server packages; to build these applications, you must custom-develop HTTP server software. In Chapter 16, "Building a Web Server with Delphi," you learn the details of the HTTP protocol as you develop a Web server.

Full-featured Web servers and browsers, such as Netscape Commerce Server and Netscape Navigator, are major software development projects that require years of work and thus are far beyond the scope of this book. Fortunately, you can build custom functions into existing servers and browsers by using API calls. Chapter 18, "The Netscape API—Incorporating Delphi with the Netscape Browser and Server," introduces the Netscape APIs.

Security Concerns

Security was not a major issue when the Internet started as a network connecting technicians and researchers. However, as the Internet grows as a resource for international business, security is becoming a greater concern. Electronic commerce—the capability to exchange money over the Internet—is an essential Internet service. Unfortunately, when you exchange money over the Internet, other users can intercept or modify the data stream, which provides big opportunities for fraud. Also, many businesses want to use the Internet to send private information to their remote offices without the risk of competitors intercepting it.

Several schemes exist for securing Web services. Chapter 17, "Internet Security, RSA Encryption, SSL, STT, PCT, and WinSock," explains the RSA public key algorithm, which currently is the basis for most data security schemes. The chapter also details the Secure Sockets Layer (SSL), Secure Transaction Technology (STT), and Private Communication Technology (PCT) protocols.

Other Services

Most Internet traffic is from FTP, e-mail, Usenet News, and the Web, but many other services are still commonly used.

When the Internet's predecessor, ARPAnet, was built, one of the first services required, in addition to file transfer, was terminal emulation. The Telnet protocol, which transports terminal emulation sessions, is still widely used. Figure 2.7 shows a sample Telnet session.

FIG. 2.7

With the Telnet server at **internic.net**, you can see who owns a domain name.

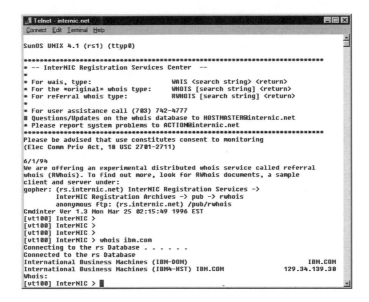

Utility service is one important class of services. Most Internet servers support a range of these services, including the following:

- *Chargen* generates a continuous stream of ASCII characters. By connecting to the Chargen service and verifying that the correct characters are received, you can quickly diagnose network problems from the server to the client.

- *Echo* simply echos characters back to the client. This service is useful for diagnosing network problems from the client to the server. A simple test program can send a stream of characters to Echo and verify the reply.

- *Daytime* simply provides the server time in a formatted string.

Chapter 6, "Socket Programming with Delphi Using WinSock," explains how to use the standard utility services to test your client software.

Internet Application Directions

As the Internet continues to expand, its growth has several implications. Although a few new services are generating much excitement, a revolution is going on behind the scenes: More applications are integrating Internet support as basic product functionality. Already, mail-enabled word processors and FTP-enabled file managers are becoming common. This growth will continue until standard applications completely hide some Internet services. For example, Lotus InterNotes publishes information stored in Notes databases to the Web, without requiring user intervention.

Also, as people become more familiar with the Internet, applications that bypass traditional telecommunications will become more common. Several software packages provide an "Internet phone" capability, enabling their users to place international phone calls for the cost of local Internet access. By enabling you to print to a laser printer across the country just as easily as a printer on your LAN, the Internet can act as a high-quality replacement for fax service.

The Java language, which enables Web browsers to support powerful programs, is already blurring the distinction between a browser and an operating system. Java implements full applications, so the entire model of purchasing software could possibly change; Java support, combined with the capability of online commerce to bill in small increments, might make it practical to rent software by the minute instead of buying it. This could make very specialized applications more readily available and more affordable. In reality, although such efforts are technically possible, issues such as training might put a damper on them.

One limiting factor to the Internet's growth is simply cost. A PC capable of connecting to the Internet, combined with a modem and software, costs at least $1,500. Several companies are now in the early stages of producing low-cost *Web terminals* that can access the Web but cannot run traditional PC applications. At least three companies are working on *set top boxes,* which are even cheaper Web terminals that connect to a television set. As the cost of Web access falls to a few dollars per month, and the Internet's explosive growth continues, the market will fund more powerful and complex applications than are available now.

Bandwidth

Bandwidth is the carrying capacity of a network; the higher the bandwidth, the higher the network's capacity. If the Internet is the information superhighway, bandwidth represents the width of the roads. Bandwidth is measured in kilobits per second (Kbps) or megabits per second (Mbps).

Another critical problem of the current Internet is limited bandwidth. Most users connect to the Internet at 28.8 Kbps or less, a speed that is hardly adequate for sending a graphics-rich Web page, much less sound or video. ISDN access, at 56 to 144 Kbps, promises to provide better access to current services, and is finally available in most parts of the United States, for as little as $30 per month.

ISDN

The Integrated Services Digital Network (ISDN) is an all-digital system that provides two to five times the bandwidth of a modem connection. It uses existing phone lines and works much like a traditional dial-up modem connection. ISDN uses a device called a terminal adapter rather than a modem.

Many pilot projects and trials are now under way to provide much higher speed access to the Internet. Cable modems, which rely on cable television systems' existing infrastructure, and ADSL technology promise several megabits per second access to every home; this data rate can support television-quality video. As the Internet backbone networks are upgraded to 600 Mbps speed and higher, and new access technologies provide fast Internet access, the increased bandwidth provided on future networks may make video servers as common as Web servers are now.

ADSL

Asymmetrical Digital Subscriber Loop (ADSL) is a new technology that promises to deliver 1.5 to 6.1 Mbps of bandwidth over existing phone lines. The technology's asymmetrical aspect is that, while your home computer can retrieve data from the Internet at over 200 times the speed of a modem, it can send data to the Internet at only 16 Kbps to 64 Kbps.

From Here...

This chapter introduced the Internet's basic, founding technologies. You learned about the client/server model and four important Internet services: FTP, e-mail, Usenet News, and the Web. Finally, you learned about some of the future directions of Internet applications. If you haven't used the Internet before, this would be a good time to set the book aside and try it for yourself.

To learn more about related topics, see the following chapters:

- For more technical information on the foundations of Internet connectivity, see Chapter 3, "Internet Connectivity."

- To learn the details of communications protocols underlying the Internet services, see Chapter 4, "Internet Communications Protocols."

- If you are interested primarily in programming for the Web, but not the low-level details required to build other client software, jump ahead to Chapter 12, "The Web—HTTP, HTML, and Beyond."

CHAPTER 3

Internet Connectivity

In Chapter 2, "The Basic Internet Application Suite," you learned how a variety of applications support the Internet's functionality. This chapter delves into the technical details required to develop Internet applications.

- How Internet addressing identifies computers connected to the Internet

- How a subnet mask enables organizations to subdivide their internal networks

- How special addresses support unique functions and make troubleshooting easier

- How TCP/IP and related protocols lay the foundation for Internet communication

- How the Domain Name Service (DNS) translates easy-to-remember names to Internet Protocol (IP) addresses

- How the Serial Line Internet Protocol (SLIP) and Point-to-Point Protocol (PPP) support dial-up access to the Internet

IP Addressing

Every device connected to the Internet has a unique 32-bit identifier, its *IP address*. The address is divided into four eight-bit values, or *octets*. The term *byte* usually is not used in reference to the Internet protocols, because not all computer architectures rely on the concept of an eight-bit byte; for example, computers based on the TI990 processor rely on four-bit *nibbles*. The value is usually written in dotted decimal notation, resulting in the *123.123.123.123* format with which you might be familiar.

Address Classes

Every IP address has two parts: a network address, and a host address within that network. Depending on the first octet's value, the IP address falls into one of five classes: Class A, B, C, D, or E.

The high-order bits of the first octet have special significance: They divide IP addresses into the five classes, as shown in Table 3.1. For example, the network address 128.1.2.3 translates to 10000000.00000001.00000010.00000011 in binary. Because the high-order bits (the first bits of the first octet, reading from left to right) are 10, this IP address is a Class B address.

Table 3.1 IP Address Classes

Class	First Octet Binary	First Octet Decimal	Number of Networks	Hosts per Network
Class A	00000001–01111110	1–126	126	16 million
Class B	10000000–10111111	128–191	16,382	65,534
Class C	11000000–11011111	192–223	2 million	254
Class D	11100000–11101111	224–239	Multicast	Multicast
Class E	11110000–11110111	240–247	Experimental	Experimental

In a Class A address, the first bit is 0, the next seven bits identify the network, and the last 24 bits identify the host on the network. With seven bits for the network portion of the address, minus the two special network numbers 0 and 127, there can be only 126 Class A networks ($2^7 - 2 = 126$), but each can have $2^{24} - 2$, or over 16 million hosts. Thus, Class A addresses are used primarily by very large businesses, the military, and research organizations. General Electric, the Defense Intelligence Agency, AT&T Bell Laboratories, and Massachusetts Institute of Technology (MIT) are some of the few organizations that have Class A addresses.

If the first two bits of the address are 10, it is a Class B address. The first two bits indicate the class, the next 14 bits are the network address, and the last 16 bits signify the host. More common than Class A addresses, Class B addresses are often used by corporations, universities, and Internet service providers.

The first three bits of a Class C address are 110. In a Class C address, the first three bits signify class, the next 21 bits indicate the network address, and the last eight bits identify the host. Class C addresses are the most common, used by most organizations with 250 or fewer Internet-connected devices.

Class D addresses, starting with bits 1110, have only recently been put into use. This class supports the special Internet multicasting service. These addresses are for groups of computers that share a common protocol rather than groups of computers that share a common network. The Internet's multicast backbone is still in the experimental stages, but might provide the foundation for the future replacements for such current broadcast technology as television and radio.

The MBONE

The multicast backbone, or *MBONE,* relies on IP multicast-based routing. It provides time-critical real-time communications over the Internet, and permits a single data stream to be transmitted to tens of thousands of users simultaneously. For more information, see **www.mbone.com**.

Class E addresses start with bits 11110. Reserved for future expansion, these addresses currently are used only on an experimental basis.

When users first connect to the Internet, one of the most common questions is how to get an address. If you are using a dial-up connection, your service provider usually assigns the IP address automatically. If you connect to a local area network (LAN) that is attached to the Internet, the network administrator might assign addresses manually or use the Dynamic Host Configuration Protocol (DHCP) to assign addresses automatically. Figure 3.1 shows Windows 95 being configured for DHCP address assignment.

FIG. 3.1
By choosing the IP Address page's Obtain an IP Address Automatically option, you enable Microsoft TCP/IP to use DHCP to acquire an IP address.

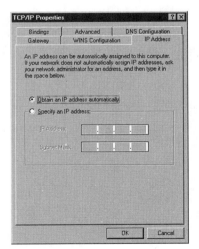

If you are connecting a LAN to the Internet, you should begin by contacting your Internet service provider, who usually will already have a block of addresses available. If the provider cannot meet your needs (for example, if you have thousands of PCs and must have a Class B address), you can contact the Internet Network Information Center (InterNIC) and fill out some forms to obtain a network address. You can contact the InterNIC by the World Wide Web at **www.internic.net**, by File Transfer Protocol (FTP) at **ftp.internic.net**, and by e-mail at **hostmaster@internic.net**.

One obstacle to the continued growth of the Internet is address depletion. Few Class A or Class B addresses are still available, so the InterNIC will not assign a new one unless you can prove that you need it. Also, because it has already assigned more than half of the Class C address space, the InterNIC usually will encourage you to use an address from your service provider instead of assigning you a new one.

Subnet Masks

Obviously, a corporation with a Class B address will not necessarily have a single LAN with over 60,000 machines on it; such an organization is more likely to have its own internal internetwork, spreading LANs across multiple sites. A *subnet mask* breaks a network into smaller networks, known as *subnets*. By using a subnet mask, the Internet supports a three-tier network/subnet/host hierarchy rather than the two-tier network/host model.

The subnet mask defines a "dividing line" between the network address bits and host address bits. The subnet is known only locally; the rest of the Internet still interprets the address in the standard manner.

If you are connecting to the Internet through a LAN, it is important to use the correct subnet mask. Like the IP address, a subnet mask might be assigned manually or be acquired automatically through DHCP.

Most corporate networks that have a Class B network address have subnetted it to accommodate multiple sites. Table 3.2 shows the effect of the subnet mask on dividing a Class B network.

Table 3.2   Class B Subnetting

Mask	Number of Subnets	Hosts per Subnet
255.255.192.0	2	16,382
255.255.224.0	6	8,190
255.255.240.0	14	4,094
255.255.248.0	30	2,046
255.255.252.0	62	1,022
255.255.254.0	126	510

Mask	Number of Subnets	Hosts per Subnet
255.255.255.0	254	254
255.255.255.128	510	126
255.255.255.192	1,022	62
255.255.255.224	2,046	30
255.255.255.240	4,094	14
255.255.255.248	8,190	6

Some organizations, especially businesses that have many small sites (such as retailers and banks), have multiple Class C network addresses divided into small subnets. Table 3.3 shows the subnet possibilities on a Class C address.

Table 3.3   Class C Subnetting

Mask	Number of Subnets	Hosts/Subnet
255.255.255.192	2	62
255.255.255.224	4	30
255.255.255.240	14	14
255.255.255.248	30	6

Technical Details

Tables 3.2 and 3.3 summarize subnet mask values and their effects on Class B and Class C addresses. However, you might be interested in the inner workings of a subnet mask.

In binary, a subnet mask is a value that consists of series of ones followed by a series of zeros, 32 bits long. This value is then masked, using a bitwise AND operation, to split the subnet and host portions of the network address.

For example, if a network has a network number of 172.20.0.0 and a subnet mask of 255.255.224.0, it is broken into six subnets, as shown in Table 3.4.

Table 3.4   A Subnet Mask of 255.255.224.0 Divides a Class B Network into Six Subnets

Description	Decimal	Binary
Network number	172.20.0.0	10101100.00010100.00000000.00000000
Subnet mask	255.255.224.0	11111111.11111111.**111**00000.00000000

continues

Table 3.4	Continued	
Description	**Decimal**	**Binary**
Subnet 1	172.20.32.0	10101100.00010100.**001**00000.00000000
Subnet 2	172.20.64.0	10101100.00010100.**010**00000.00000000
Subnet 3	172.20.96.0	10101100.00010100.**011**00000.00000000
Subnet 4	172.20.128.0	10101100.00010100.**100**00000.00000000
Subnet 5	172.20.160.0	10101100.00010100.**101**00000.00000000
Subnet 6	172.20.192.0	10101100.00010100.**110**00000.00000000

Table 3.4 highlights each subnet number's subnet portion in boldface. Any host with an IP address of 172.20.32.1 (binary 10101100.00010100.**001**00000.00000001) through 172.20.63.254 (binary 10101100.00010100.**001**11111.11111110) is a member of subnet 1. A host with an address of 172.20.64.1 through 172.20.95.254 is a member of subnet 2, and so on.

For additional details on how subnetting works, see RFC 950, "Internet Standard Subnetting Procedure."

Special Addresses

You might have noticed that Table 3.1 doesn't list Class A network numbers 0 and 127. Network 0 designates a *default route*, which simplifies the routing information that IP has to handle. Network 127 is actually the *loopback address*, a special reference to the loopback network. The loopback network takes a computer's network information and, as the name implies, sends it back to the transmitting computer.

Ping

The *ping* utility, included with almost all TCP/IP software packages, verifies the operation of a remote host. It sends a packet of information that the remote host returns if it is operational.

The loopback network enables both a client application and its server to reside on the same computer without incurring actual network traffic. Such a network is quite useful for testing client/server applications, and also good for checking Internet software configuration. A basic troubleshooting technique is to ping 127.0.0.1 before pinging remote hosts; a successful response ensures proper operation of the local TCP/IP software.

You also might have noticed that a Class B network has 65,534 addresses and a Class C network has 254 addresses, not the 65,536 and 256 that you might expect. Also, Class B networks have two fewer subnets and two fewer hosts per subnet than you might expect. The first and last network, subnet, and host have special meaning and cannot be used.

Any of the network, subnet, or host portions of an address that consist of only zeros means "this," as in "this network" or "this host." For example, you can interpret the address 0.0.0.12 as referring to host 12 on this network, and the address 172.16.0.0 as referring to network 172.16.

An "all ones" network address is reserved as a *broadcast address*; by sending information to 172.16.255.255 (binary 10101100.00010000.11111111.11111111), you send that information to every device on every subnet of Class B network 172.16. In some cases, the local network administrator might filter broadcasts for security reasons.

The "Special Addresses" section of RFC 1700, "Assigned Numbers," defines the special addresses.

IP addresses solve only the problem of uniquely identifying a host and its network. The low-level Internet protocol relies on the address to transport information between hosts. Now that you know how IP addressing identifies the computers on the Internet, you can learn how the Internet protocols use this addressing to communicate.

Part
I
Ch
3

The Transmission Control Protocol/Internet Protocol (TCP/IP)

As TCP/IP's name implies, TCP and IP are two separate but closely related protocols. The term *TCP/IP* has also come to indicate the existence of some other supporting protocols, including the User Datagram Protocol (UDP) and the Internet Control Message Protocol (ICMP).

Almost any data communications network transmits data in small chunks, usually referred to as *packets* or *datagrams*. A datagram is simply a specific number of bytes that are grouped together and sent at one time.

Networks break continuous data streams into smaller datagrams for several reasons:

- *Sharing.* The entire concept of a network is based on the capability of multiple logical data streams to share a physical connection. By breaking a data stream into datagrams and labeling those datagrams with a destination and return address, a single network enables multiple computers to share it.

- *Error handling.* If an error corrupts a single bit, only a single datagram must be re-sent. Otherwise, if one bit were corrupted in a file that the network was transferring in a continuous stream, the network would have to re-send the entire file.

- *Isolating failures.* If a network always sends a data stream over the same series of physical connections, and one of those connections fails, the communications link also fails. In a packet-based network such as the Internet, routers can direct datagrams around a failed component, providing better reliability.

Routers

A router is a specialized network device that receives a datagram and forwards it towards the datagram's final destination. All Internet service providers have a router, which is in turn connected to other routers. If the Internet is the information superhighway, routers are the Internet's on-ramps and interchanges.

The Internet, like any network, is based on protocol *layers*, commonly assembled into a *protocol stack*. The *Open System Interconnect (OSI) Reference Model* is an architectural model that provides a common reference for discussing communications layers and stacks.

Internetworking requires different services from various hardware and software components. A *layer* is an entity that gathers related functions, reducing a large number of responsibilities to a small number of layers. The layer might be implemented in hardware (a modem and phone line are one implementation of TCP/IP's network access layer) or in software (in Windows, WINSOCK.DLL usually implements TCP/IP's application layer).

The OSI Reference Model consists of seven layers that define individual functions of data communications protocols. Each layer represents a function that is performed when data is transferred across a network. Table 3.5 defines the OSI Reference Model by briefly describing each layer.

Table 3.5   The OSI Reference Model Defines the Layers in a Network Protocol Stack

Layer	Description
Application	Consists of application programs that use the network
Presentation	Standardizes data presentation to the applications, such as the format of floating point numbers
Session	Manages connections between cooperating applications
Transport	Provides error detection and correction through the entire network path
Network	Manages connections across the network, isolating upper-layer protocols from the details of the network
Data link	Delivers data across the media supplied by the underlying physical layer
Physical	Defines such physical characteristics as voltage levels and cable or fiber specifications

TCP/IP is based on a simpler architecture. It totally eliminates certain functions, such as those in OSI's presentation layer, and combines other functions by merging session and transport services. Although there is no universal agreement on how many layers are in the TCP/IP architecture, for the purpose of this book, it is best defined as the four-layer model shown in Table 3.6.

Table 3.6   TCP/IP's Architecture Consists of Four Layers

Layer	Description
Application	Consists of application programs that use the network
Transport	Provides error detection and correction through the entire network path
Internet	Defines datagrams and routes data through the internetwork
Network access	Specifies the physical link and delivers data across the specified link

Developed after TCP/IP was in use, the OSI model was designed to be a general architectural model. For this reason, OSI and TCP/IP do not correspond exactly. For example, in the OSI model, the presentation layer handles the translation between different numeric formats, but under TCP/IP, this task is the application's responsibility. TCP/IP's transport layer handles both session-management and error-correction functions, so this layer corresponds to the OSI model's transport layer plus the session layer. Figure 3.2 illustrates the correspondence between the OSI and TCP/IP models.

Part

I

Ch

3

FIG. 3.2
You can map the OSI model layers to TCP/IP's architecture.

OSI layers	TCP/IP layers
Application layer	Application layer
Presentation layer	
Session layer	Transport layer
Transport layer	
Network layer	Internet layer
Data link layer	Network access layer
Physical layer	

OSI separates the data link and physical layers, so the model differentiates Ethernet over twisted pair from Ethernet over fiber or Ethernet on coaxial cable. TCP/IP is concerned only with the data link specification, not the physical Ethernet media.

Ethernet

Ethernet is a networking scheme that supports data transmission with a bandwidth of 10 Mbps and 100 Mbps. It can run on a wide variety of physical cabling including twisted pair (similar to phone wire), coaxial cable (similar to that used by cable television), and fiber-optic cable. See **wwwhost.ots.utexas.edu/ethernet** for more information.

You usually don't have to worry about exactly what occurs in each layer; the important concept is that you can replace a layer in the stack, and as long as the layers directly above and below the replaced layer can still interface to it, communications can occur. For example, you can use Ethernet, Token Ring, Fiber Distributed Data Interface (FDDI), or serial lines as the supporting network access layer, enabling TCP/IP to run on a wide variety of networks. NetManage Chameleon, FTP OnNet, and Microsoft TCP/IP-32 all provide a common interface at the application layer, although they use different DLLs and drivers to provide transport and internet layer services.

The other key concept is that each layer is responsible for only a limited set of functions and passes on any other required functions to other layers.

As data passes down the protocol stack, each layer adds control information to ensure proper delivery. This control information, a *header*, is placed in front of the data to be transmitted. Each layer treats the information that it receives from the layer above as data, putting its own header at the beginning. Figure 3.3 illustrates this *encapsulation* process. The procedure is reversed on the receiving end, as each layer strips off its header before passing data to the layer above.

FIG. 3.3
To build a datagram, a network passes the data down through the layers, each of which encapsulates the data and adds its own header.

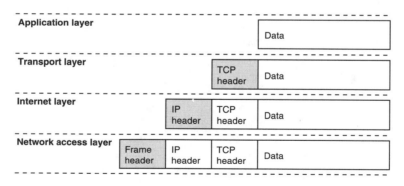

Each layer has its own data structures and is unaware of the data structures used in the layers above and below it; TCP does not directly interact with IP, and IP does not directly manipulate Ethernet's low-level data structures. The data transferred from application to application does not have any headers and is thus seen as a continuous stream of information.

For example, when a browser retrieves a Web page from a server, the server sends a continuous stream of data to the browser. The server, as it passes the stream down through each layer, chops up the data stream into smaller pieces and tags those pieces with headers. The headers enable the client to reassemble the pieces into a continuous data stream. A Web page might take the following sample path:

1. Based on a request that the client sends, the server sends the page to WINSOCK.DLL, which defines the TCP/IP application interface. This moves the data into the *application layer*.

2. WINSOCK.DLL passes the data to a lower-level TCP driver, moving it into the *transport layer*. The data is split into *segments*, which are variable-sized containers for the data. For each segment, a TCP header is generated. This header includes such information as the checksum for data in that segment, and the source port, destination port, and sequence number fields to identify the segment uniquely.

3. The TCP driver then passes the data to the IP driver, which might chop the segment up further into datagrams. Each datagram gets a header with, among other fields, the source and destination IP addresses for the datagram, the length of the datagram, and the type of protocol used. The driver moves the data into the *internet layer*.

    In most Windows TCP/IP implementations, a single driver handles both TCP and IP. Thus, steps 2 and 3 usually occur within a single DLL or DRV.

4. The IP driver then passes the data to a network card driver or SLIP/PPP driver, which actually changes the voltage levels on the wire, at the *network access layer*.

5. A router senses the voltage changes on the wire. The datagram at the internet layer examines the destination address in its IP header and then returns the datagram to the *network access layer* on an interface that is connected to another router that is one step closer to the destination. This step repeats, usually 10 to 40 times, as the datagram moves toward the client.

6. The client notices a voltage change on the wire. From this network access layer information, the client builds a datagram at the *internet layer*.

7. IP, at the internet layer, has now done its job. The datagram passes to TCP at the *transport layer*. TCP has a buffer in which it reassembles datagrams into a segment, even if the datagrams are not received in the correct order. If a segment's checksum is incorrect, TCP throws away the segment and requests a retransmission. TCP then passes the data to the application layer, WINSOCK.DLL.

8. The TCP destination port number field distinguishes the browser from other networked applications running on the client machine. Based on the port number, the *application layer* WINSOCK.DLL passes the reassembled data stream to the *browser application*.

Now that you understand the general process by which data passes over a network, you can next examine the specifics of the TCP/IP protocol.

The Internet Protocol (IP)

IP is the foundation of the Internet. Its responsibilities include the following:

- Defining the datagram, which is the fundamental transmission unit of the Internet

- Specifying the Internet addressing scheme, as described in the section "IP Addressing," earlier in this chapter

Part
I

Ch
3

- Routing datagrams—steering data through the Internet
- Providing *best effort delivery*—trying its best to transmit data through the Internet
- Providing fragmentation and reassembly—breaking data streams into smaller pieces and reassembling them on the receiving end

IP has a clearly defined scope. The protocol does not handle the following:

- A *connectionless* protocol, IP does not exchange control information before transmitting data. The protocol simply throws some datagrams on the network and hopes that each gets to its destination and is accepted once it gets there. IP relies on higher-level protocols, such as TCP, to handle connections.
- An *unreliable* protocol, IP has no error detection or recovery. That doesn't mean that you cannot rely on IP to deliver data accurately, but simply that the protocol doesn't check whether the data was correctly received. When reliable delivery is required, other layers of the TCP/IP protocol provide it.

As Figure 3.3 indicates, an IP header is attached to each datagram. The IP header carries—in addition to the IP source and destination address—other information required to enable the Internet to do its duty, such as the datagram's length, data about fragmentation, and an indicator about the protocol that the datagram is carrying (such as TCP, UDP, or ICMP).

In Windows, one particularly problematic IP parameter is the time-to-live (TTL) counter. While passing through each router, an IP datagram is decremented. This decrementing ensures that an ill-formed datagram cannot roam freely throughout the Internet until the end of time. Most TCP/IP implementations set the TTL at 60 or higher, meaning that the datagram can pass through as many as 60 routers, or *hops*, to reach its final destination.

Microsoft's TCP/IP protocol stacks set the TTL to only 32. But even within the United States, many sites are 35 to 40 hops away. In fact, depending on the varying topology of the Internet, a given site might be 30 hops away some days (in which case everything works) but 35 hops away other days (which will cause sporadic problems). For example, a connection between Dallas and Chicago might usually be routed through San Francisco using 30 hops; if the San Francisco network were unavailable or exceedingly slow, the connection might be routed through Washington, D.C., with 35 hops. In Windows 95 and Windows NT, the following registry key sets the default TTL:

```
Hkey_Local_Machine\System\CurrentControlSet\Services\VxD\MSTCP\DefaultTTL
```

If you change this registry key to 64, you can avoid TTL problems.

For additional details about IP, see RFC 791, "Internet Protocol."

The Transmission Control Protocol (TCP)

While IP carries a datagram across the Internet, TCP is responsible for transport services, making sure that the data inside the datagram makes it to its destination safely. TCP is a *reliable, connection-oriented, byte-stream* protocol:

- *Reliable.* TCP provides reliability by re-sending data until it receives a positive acknowledgment from the remote system. The unit of data that TCP exchanges is a *segment*, which IP's fragmentation capability can actually split into multiple datagrams.

- *Connection-oriented.* TCP establishes a logical end-to-end connection between hosts. The TCP conversation begins with a *handshake*, which synchronizes the connection between the two hosts. At the end of the conversation, TCP sets a flag that indicates that the sender has no more data and terminates the connection.

- *Byte-stream.* TCP handles data as a continuous stream of bytes, not as independent packets. The protocol uses a sequencing mechanism to ensure that it delivers data in the proper order.

As this chapter stated previously, TCP is responsible for transport services, including the following:

- *Error detection.* IP's best effort delivery does not detect errors in the datagram's application data. TCP has a checksum to detect whether a datagram has been garbled in transmission.

- *Retransmission.* IP does not detect errors, so it cannot know when it must retransmit a datagram. TCP retransmits lost or corrupted datagrams.

- *Sequencing.* IP does not guarantee that packets will arrive in the order that they were sent. Datagrams numbered 1, 2, 3, and 4 might be received as 1, 3, 2, and 4. TCP automatically reassembles the datagrams into the correct order.

- *Acknowledgment and flow control.* The receiving TCP sends an *acknowledgment segment* to confirm several functions. First, the segment provides positive acknowledgment, indicating that a series of segments were received properly. The acknowledgment segment also returns a *window*, indicating the available buffer space remaining on the receiving host. After transmitting the number of bytes that the window indicates, the sender waits for the receiver to catch up before sending again.

- *Delivery to the correct application.* Each TCP segment has a source and destination *port number* that uniquely identifies the session. Without TCP ports, two Internet-connected computers could have only a single conversation at a time.

Chapters 4 and 5 provide additional details about the TCP protocol, particularly focusing on how TCP ports support multiple application conversations. For the technical details, see RFC 793, "Transmission Control Protocol."

The User Datagram Protocol (UDP)

UDP is a no-frills transport protocol. This unreliable, connectionless datagram protocol specifies only source and destination ports, the data length, and a header checksum.

Because UDP doesn't provide much, you might wonder why it exists. The protocol is used in a variety of special-purpose situations:

- When transmitting a small amount of data, the overhead of establishing and tearing down a TCP connection can be excessive, making UDP a more efficient choice.

■ "Query/response" applications, which transmit a query and expect a response within a fixed time period, are another good UDP candidate. The response indicates a positive acknowledgment of the query.

■ Some compression schemes for audio and video transmission can accept a certain amount of packet corruption or loss, and thus can use UDP.

■ Some applications provide their own reliable data delivery and thus don't require it from the transport layer. These applications can use UDP more efficiently than TCP. Some commonly used Internet protocols, such as the Network File System (NFS), rely on UDP in this manner.

RFC 768, "User Datagram Protocol," defines UDP.

The Internet Control Message Protocol (ICMP)

ICMP relies on IP to provide diagnostic and control services. Whenever you issue a `ping` command or get a `Destination Unreachable` message, ICMP is doing its job.

The most common user-oriented function that ICMP provides is to check on remote hosts. A host can send the ICMP *Echo* message to a remote system to see whether it is operational. When a server receives this message, it sends the same packet back to the client system. The `ping` and `tracert` utilities, included with most Windows TCP/IP packages, rely on this function to diagnose network connections as shown in Figure 3.4.

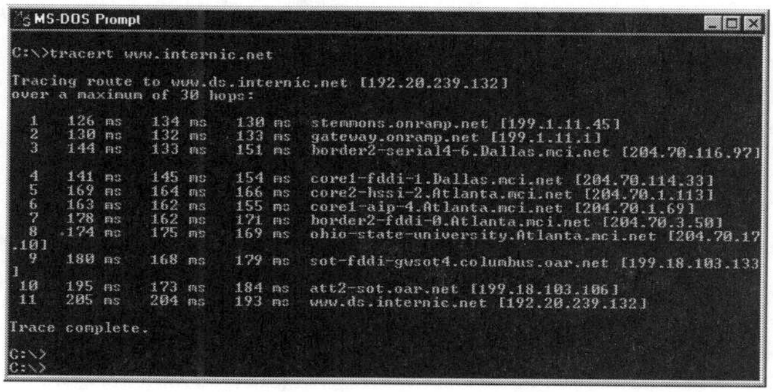

FIG. 3.4

The `tracert` command uses ICMP Echo message to trace the route from your computer to a specified destination.

```
 MS-DOS Prompt                                                    _ □ ×
C:\>tracert www.internic.net

Tracing route to www.ds.internic.net [192.20.239.132]
over a maximum of 30 hops:

  1    126 ms    134 ms    130 ms  stemmons.onramp.net [199.1.11.45]
  2    130 ms    132 ms    133 ms  gateway.onramp.net [199.1.11.1]
  3    144 ms    133 ms    151 ms  border2-serial4-6.Dallas.mci.net [204.70.116.97]
  4    141 ms    145 ms    154 ms  core1-fddi-1.Dallas.mci.net [204.70.114.33]
  5    169 ms    164 ms    166 ms  core2-hssi-2.Atlanta.mci.net [204.70.1.113]
  6    163 ms    162 ms    155 ms  core1-aip-4.Atlanta.mci.net [204.70.1.69]
  7    178 ms    162 ms    171 ms  border2-fddi-0.Atlanta.mci.net [204.70.3.50]
  8   .174 ms    175 ms    169 ms  ohio-state-university.Atlanta.mci.net [204.70.17
.10]
  9    180 ms    168 ms    179 ms  sot-fddi-gwsot4.columbus.oar.net [199.18.103.133
]
 10    195 ms    173 ms    184 ms  att2-sot.oar.net [199.18.103.106]
 11    205 ms    204 ms    193 ms  www.ds.internic.net [192.20.239.132]

Trace complete.

C:\>
C:\>
```

ICMP also provides network flow control. If datagrams arrive at a host faster than the system can process them, it sends an *ICMP Source Quench* message back to the sender. This message tells the sender to stop sending data temporarily.

The dreaded "destination unreachable" warning is yet another ICMP responsibility. A system that detects a problem, usually a router, sends the *ICMP Destination Unreachable* message to the datagram's source (see Fig. 3.5).

FIG. 3.5
An ICMP Destination
Unreachable message
indicates that a host is
currently unavailable.

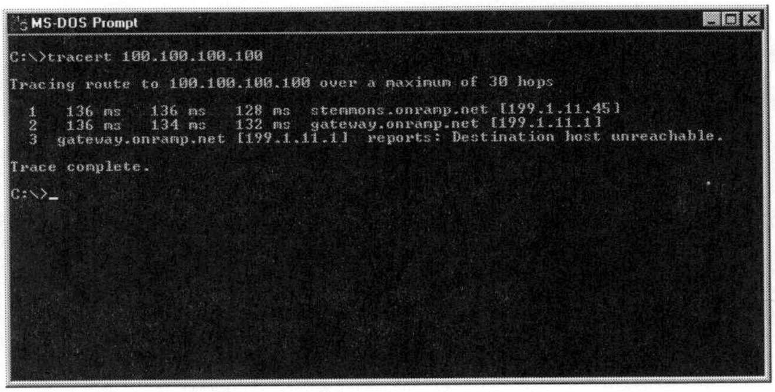

```
C:\>tracert 100.100.100.100

Tracing route to 100.100.100.100 over a maximum of 30 hops

  1   136 ms    136 ms    128 ms  stemmons.onramp.net [199.1.11.45]
  2   136 ms    134 ms    132 ms  gateway.onramp.net [199.1.11.1]
  3  gateway.onramp.net [199.1.11.1]  reports: Destination host unreachable.

Trace complete.

C:\>_
```

ICMP also can redirect routes. If a host has multiple paths from its LAN to the Internet, an *ICMP Redirect* message can signal the host to use a different path.

Other ICMP messages handle such conditions as exceeding the time-to-live parameter and signaling the rejection of messages with poorly formatted IP headers. Although you rarely interact with ICMP directly, your program must be capable of appropriately handling such ICMP conditions as Destination Unreachable. RFC 792, "Internet Control Message Protocol," lists all ICMP messages and provides usage details.

The Domain Name Service (DNS)

Although the section "IP Processing" at the beginning of this chapter describes Internet addressing in detail, it might not have described what you thought of as an Internet address. Many Internet users consider a DNS name to be an Internet address, as **www.whitehouse.gov** is referred to much more often than 198.137.240.91. DNS is the Internet protocol that translates the more memorable name to a cryptic network address.

Before DNS, hosts relied on a data file, the *host table*, to translate host names into addresses. For this reason, the Network Information Center (NIC) placed names and addresses for all Internet sites into a single file. Unfortunately, this solution does not scale well, and quickly became an inefficient way to convert host names to IP addresses. Besides the scalability problem, there was no technique to distribute information automatically about newly registered hosts; you could not access such hosts until NIC distributed its host table.

DNS was developed to address these problems. This program scales well; instead of relying on a single large table, DNS is a distributed database system, now providing information on approximately a million hosts. DNS also solves the distribution problem, guaranteeing that new host information is disseminated to the rest of the internetwork as needed.

DNS is a distributed hierarchical system for resolving host names into IP addresses. A truly distributed database, DNS does not rely on a central database with all the Internet host information; instead, DNS distributes its information across thousands of name servers. At the top of the DNS hierarchy, a group of *root servers* serve a root domain.

Part
I

Ch
3

Just as you find files in DOS by tracing a path from the root directory, through subdirectories, and to the target file, you find information about a host by following a path from the root domain, through subordinate domains, and to the host itself.

Directly under the root domain are top-level domains that are divided into organizational and geographic types. Geographic domains have been established for every country in the world, identified by a two-letter code. Within the United States, the top-level domains are usually organizational—that is, based on the type of an organization to which a system belongs.

The following are examples of top-level domains:

- UK: The United Kingdom geographic domain.
- JP: The Japan geographic domain.
- US: The United States geographic domain. Most second-level domains under the US domain are states (for example, US.TX). The US domain and the organizational domains are not related.
- COM: Commercial organizations, primarily businesses in the United States.
- EDU: Educational institutions, mainly United States universities.
- GOV: Government agencies, such as state governments and divisions of the federal government.
- MIL: Military organizations.
- NET: Network support organizations, such as Internet service providers.
- ORG: Miscellaneous organizations, such as nonprofit organizations.

Under the top-level domains, second-level domains further divide the hierarchy. For example, **whitehouse.gov** defines a second-level domain of the White House in the first-level domain of the government.

DNS distributes information quite efficiently by disseminating information only to those who are interested. When connecting to the Internet, each domain registers its main DNS servers with the InterNIC. The servers with primary responsibility for a domain are known as *authoritative servers*. On receiving a request for information about a host that it doesn't yet know about, a DNS server forwards the request to an authoritative server that is responsible for maintaining accurate information about the domain that the user is querying. When the authoritative server answers, the local server caches the entry for future use. The next time that the local server receives the same request, it returns the cached information.

DNS also relies on recursive queries, passing a query to a server that might know the answer. For example, not even the root servers have complete information about all domains, but they do have pointers to the servers for second-level domains and relay information as appropriate.

To register a new domain name, you contact the InterNIC, just as you do when obtaining an IP address. Because of previous abuses, the InterNIC now charges $50 per year to register a name. This fee is partly intended to avert the legal battles that occur when, for example, a competitor registers **mcdonalds.com** before McDonald's does.

When developing PC software that relies on the Internet, you will often use functions to translate DNS names into IP addresses, but you shouldn't usually have to worry about the details of how DNS handles the translation. If you do want more information, RFC 1034, "Domain Names—Concepts and Facilities," and RFC 1035, "Domain Names—Implementation and Specification," document DNS.

Modem Access to the Internet through SLIP and PPP

Earlier in this chapter, the section "The Transmission Control Protocol/Internet Protocol (TCP/IP)" explained that network layering enables TCP/IP to run over a wide variety of physical media. One of the most popular ways to connect to the Internet is through a dial-up modem connection, using the *SLIP* or *PPP* protocols.

Part

I

Ch

3

The Serial Line Internet Protocol (SLIP)

SLIP (Serial Line Internet Protocol) was developed first. This basic protocol enables isolated hosts, often single-user PCs, to link through TCP/IP over the telephone network. SLIP defines a method for framing datagrams for transmission across a serial connection, signifying when one datagram ends and the next one begins.

SLIP sends datagrams across the serial link as a series of bytes, using the following two special characters to control the data flow:

- SLIP END, a single byte with the decimal value of 192, marks the end of a datagram. On receiving the END character, SLIP knows that it has a complete datagram and delivers it to IP.
- SLIP ESC, a single byte with the decimal value of 219, is used to escape the SLIP control characters. On encountering a character with a value of 192 or 219 in the series of bytes being sent, the sending SLIP converts that character to a two-byte sequence. The SLIP converts the SLIP END character to a two-byte sequence with the decimal values 219 220, and the SLIP ESC character to the two-byte sequence 219 221. On encountering these special two-byte sequences, the receiving SLIP converts them back to their single-byte values.

SLIP was actually used before an RFC was defined. The RFC clearly lists four of SLIP's deficiencies:

- *Addressing*. Both computers in a SLIP link must know each other's IP addresses for routing purposes. Also, when a host uses SLIP to dial up a router, the addressing scheme might be dynamically defined, requiring the router to inform the dialing host of the host's IP address. SLIP does not provide a mechanism for hosts to communicate addressing information over the SLIP connection.
- *Type identification*. SLIP has no type field and thus cannot run multiple protocols simultaneously over the same link. For example, a PC using SLIP cannot connect through a communications server to both a NetWare server using IPX and the Internet using TCP/IP.

- *Error detection and correction.* A major problem when the RFC was published in 1988, this deficiency has been eliminated with advances in modem technology. The modem itself usually detects and corrects errors. If not running an error-correcting protocol, a modern modem can re-send a packet more than 10 times as quickly as modems commonly could in 1988.

- *Compression.* Although today's modems have data-compression functions, companies developing dial-up software achieve even better compression capabilities tuned specifically for the TCP/IP protocol. Usually, streams of packets in a single TCP connection have few changed fields in the IP and TCP headers, so a simple compression algorithm can just send the changed parts of the headers rather than the complete headers. The Van Jacobsen header compression technique relies on the fact that, usually, only the sequence number changes for consecutive IP datagrams.

SLIP is described in RFC 1055, "Nonstandard for Transmission of IP Datagrams over Serial Lines: SLIP."

The Point to Point Protocol (PPP)

SLIP is adequate for establishing a basic dial-up link to the Internet, but its addressing, type identification, and compression deficiencies make the protocol inflexible, slow, and hard to configure. To address these flaws, PPP was developed as an Internet standard.

PPP addresses SLIP's limitations with a three-layer protocol:

- *Data link layer protocol.* PPP uses a slightly modified version of High-Level Data Link Control (HDLC), an international standard for sending data across serial communications lines. PPP adds a protocol field that enables it to pass traffic for multiple network layer protocols. Besides addressing the type identification issue, PPP's reliance on HDLC solves the error detection and correction problem.

- *Link control protocol.* This protocol provides control information for the serial link. It is used to establish the connection, configure communication parameters, manage and debug the link, and close the connection. During link establishment, PPP can negotiate compression and assign IP addresses, solving those problems.

- *Network control protocols.* These individual protocols are customized for each network layer protocol. Network control protocols are defined for IP and also for IPX, DECnet, AppleTalk, Banyan Vines, Open Systems Interconnection (OSI), and several other network protocols. RFCs 1171 and 1172 define the IP Control Protocol (IPCP), which supports IP.

PPP is technically superior to SLIP and is rapidly surpassing SLIP's popularity. However, some older communications servers and dial-in hosts support only SLIP. When choosing a dial-up protocol, use PPP if at all possible, but use SLIP if you have no other choice.

Several extensions to PPP have been developed, such as the option to supply DNS server addresses, provide secure user identification, and even combine multiple serial connections into a single logical connection with higher bandwidth. These new innovations, and many others, provide good prospects for PPP.

PPP is defined in RFC 1171, "The Point-to-Point Protocol for the Transmission of Multi-Protocol Datagrams over Point-to-Point Links," and RFC 1172, "The Point-to-Point Protocol (PPP) Initial Configuration Options."

From Here...

In this chapter, you learned some of the low-level details that enable the Internet to function. You learned how Internet addresses are defined, and what influence subnet masks and special cases have on those addresses. You learned how TCP/IP and related protocols lay the foundation for the Internet, and how DNS, SLIP, and PPP make use of that foundation.

To learn about related topics, see the following sources:

- For additional details on many of the topics, see the referenced RFCs. In particular, RFCs 791, 792, and 793 describe IP, ICMP, and TCP in detail, providing a thorough portrait of the Internet's technical underpinnings.

- To find hundreds of sites with additional details about the Internet, see **http://www.yahoo.com/Computers_and_Internet/Internet**. The Web is one of the best sources of Internet information.

- For more information on how higher-level functions, such as file transfer and Web service, depend on the low-level TCP/IP functionality, see Chapter 4, "Internet Communications Protocols."

Internet Communications Protocols

In Chapters 2 and 3, you learned about the basic Internet applications and some fundamental concepts about how computers communicate using the Internet. In this chapter, you learn how conversations between clients and servers support almost all Internet activities. You also analyze sample conversations generated by six useful protocols:

■ TIME
■ Simple Mail Transfer Protocol (SMTP)
■ Post Office Protocol version 3 (POP3)
■ File Transfer Protocol (FTP)
■ The Network News Transfer Protocol (NNTP)
■ Hypertext Transfer Protocol (HTTP)

This information should give you a better feel for what actually goes "across the wire" on the Internet. ■

Anatomy of an Internet Conversation

In a *connectionless* environment, such as the User Datagram Protocol (UDP) described in Chapter 3, "Internet Connectivity," conversations are based on a strict request/response model, illustrated as follows:

Client:	Request
Server:	Response
Client:	Request
Server:	Response

Each request is a stream of output bytes from the client application. That byte stream is transmitted to the server over TCP/IP, where it acts as input to the server program. A response takes the opposite route; the server outputs a byte stream, which acts as input to the client.

Although this model provides a simple exchange of data, it has some severe limits and is inappropriate for most client/server activity. These limitations include the following:

- *The lack of a continuous connection.* Because the model does not include the concept of a continuous connection, the server application must maintain state information about all clients that are using it and thus must have a table to track every client conversation.

- *Unreliability.* Because UDP does not guarantee that an application will be informed if a datagram doesn't reach its destination, each application must handle those details.

- *Insufficient security.* Because UDP does not rely on a continuous connection, it is generally more difficult to use a *firewall* to add security. Also, because state information is often saved at the client, a wrongdoer who knows that state information can often successfully pretend to be another client.

Firewall

A firewall is a computer or router running software to filter network data so that it complies with locally defined security policies. For example, if a site doesn't allow inbound Web access, the firewall might filter all inbound HTTP requests.

Most of the protocols that rely on UDP are either very simple or extremely complex. For example, the TIME service, which just requests the time from a server, can run over UDP. At the other end of the scale, NFS (Network File System) provides file service, but is a relatively complex protocol.

As stated in Chapter 3, the Transmission Control Protocol (TCP) is connection-based and thus addresses the limitations of UDP. For this reason, most Internet protocols are TCP-based, so this chapter focuses on TCP's connection-based client/server conversations.

The basic flow of a *connection-based* client/server conversation follows:

The client establishes the connection with the server.

Server: OK, connection established

Client: Request

Server: Response

Client: Request

Server: Response

Client: Close connection

Server: Goodbye

The server closes the connection.

Note that four major steps occur in this conversation process:

1. *Open.* The client opens a connection with the server. Depending on the protocol, the server might return a greeting.
2. *Request.* The client sends requests to the server.
3. *Response.* The server responds to the requests. Steps 2 and 3 repeat for the duration of the connection.
4. *Close.* The client requests that the server close the connection, and the server closes it.

This four-step process occurs millions of times each day on the Internet. Every time that you view a Web page, retrieve a file with FTP, send an e-mail message with SMTP, or retrieve an e-mail message with POP3, this four-step process is used.

Be sure to distinguish the difference between a datagram and a request or response message. A single message can be split across multiple datagrams, and a single datagram can contain multiple lines of the message. The following two conversations are functionally equivalent:

Client Datagram: USER bob**\<CRLF\>**

Server Datagram: +OK Password required for bob. **\<CRLF\>**

Client Datagram: PASS bobpass**\<CRLF\>**

Server Datagram: +OK

Server Datagram: bob has 1 message(s) (698 octets). **\<CRLF\>**

Client Datagram: US

Client Datagram: ER b

Client Datagram: ob**\<CRLF\>**

Server Datagram: +OK Password

Server Datagram: required fo

Server Datagram:	`r bob. <CRLF>`
Client Datagram:	`PASS bobpass<CRLF>`
Server Datagram:	`+OK bob has`
Server Datagram:	`1 message(s)`
Server Datagram:	`(698 octets`
Server Datagram:	`). <CRLF>`

N O T E In this example, <CRLF> indicates a carriage-return/line-feed pair. The remainder of this chapter shows client/server messages, not datagrams, so <CRLF> is implied at the end of each line. ▓

When programming with Delphi on top of Windows Sockets, you almost always are concerned solely with the messages that pass across what appears to be a continuous data stream. Although TCP/IP actually splits up the data stream into datagrams, the Windows Sockets API helpfully hides the tedious details of what travels in each datagram.

The remainder of this chapter presents sample conversations generated by six useful protocols, starting with the elementary TIME protocol, and proceeding in complexity to the protocols that support e-mail, file transfer, Usenet News, and the World Wide Web.

The TIME Protocol

TIME is probably the least complicated protocol commonly employed on the Internet. This simple service retrieves the date and time from a TIME server. Although you can run TIME over either UDP or TCP, this section focuses on running the service over the more commonly used TCP.

The TIME protocol represents the most simple case of the client/server model; the client can only make a connection, not issue requests, and the server returns only a single line of data before closing the connection. A TIME client/server conversation flows as follows:

Client:	*Establishes the connection with the server*
Server:	*Returns, in binary, the number of seconds since January 1, 1900*
Server:	*Closes the connection*

Under the client/server model, the client, on receiving the server's response, can perform any action that seems appropriate for that response. The TIME client can display the server time, set the client computer's clock, time-stamp a message, or perform any of several other activities.

The first Internet program that you will build is a TIME client. RFC 868 documents the TIME protocol.

The Simple Mail Transfer Protocol (SMTP) Protocol

Moving up a level in complexity, the SMTP protocol handles e-mail communication. SMTP is more sophisticated than TIME. After a session is established, the client sends SMTP commands and data, and the server sends simple response messages confirming proper operation or signaling errors. When the session is complete, the client sends a QUIT message and the server closes the connection.

Although the SMTP protocol has about a dozen commands, only four basic client commands are required to send an e-mail message:

- MAIL FROM starts a new mail message, resetting the server's buffers, such as recipients and mail data. It also specifies the message sender's mail address, which can be used to report such errors as the inability to deliver mail.
- RCPT TO identifies one recipient. You can repeat this command to send a single message to multiple recipients.
- DATA starts the message contents; all succeeding lines are considered the message text. The message text includes header items, such as Date, Subject, To, Cc, and From. The message text ends with a line consisting of a single period.
- QUIT closes an SMTP session.

Each time that the client sends a command, the server returns a response, which starts with a numeric code. Codes in the range 200–399 indicate a success or informative response, and those in 400–599 range indicate a warning or failure.

Here are the response codes used in the following examples:

- 220 <domain> Service ready. The server returns a 220 message immediately after a successful connection to an SMTP server.
- 221 <domain> Service closing transmission channel. The server returns a 221 message in response to the QUIT command, ending the session.
- 250 Requested mail action okay, completed. A 250 response indicates success, such as the successful acceptance of a mail message.
- 354 Start mail input; end with <CRLF>.<CRLF>. A 351 message indicates that the server is waiting for message data.

The following is a sample SMTP conversation. In this conversation, **tom@org.com** sends a sample e-mail message to **bill@org.com** and **susan@bigstate.edu**.

The client establishes the connection to the server, and the server responds with a prompt message.

Server: 220-mail.org.com Sendmail 8.6.12/8.6.5 ready at Mon, 8 Jan 1996
16:09:27 -0600

The client sends a MAIL FROM message, starting a new session.

Client: MAIL FROM:tom@org.com

The server responds with a success code.

Server: 250 tom@org.com... Sender OK

*The client addresses the mail contents to **bill@org.com** and **susan@bigstate.edu**.*

Client: RCPT TO:bill@org.com

Server: 250 bill@org.com... Recipient ok

Client: RCPT TO:susan@bigstate.edu

Server: 250 susan@bigstate.edu... Recipient ok

The client sends the DATA message, followed by the mail contents.

Client: DATA

Server: 354 Enter mail, end with "." on a line by itself

Client: Subject: Sample message

Client: This is the first line of the message.

Client: This is the second line of the message.

To end the message, the client sends a period (.) on a line by itself.

Client: .

The server responds that it successfully accepted the message.

Server: 250 QAA21540 Message accepted for delivery

The client closes the session.

Client: QUIT

Server: 221 mail.org.com closing connection

The server closes the connection.

Most SMTP servers have no security, making it a trivial matter to forge messages, as the following example demonstrates:

*The client establishes the connection to **www.nasa.gov**.*

Server: 220 bolero.gsfc.nasa.gov Sendmail 5.65 (1.1.8.2/08Sep94-1133PM)
               Mon, 8 Jan 1996 17:32:23 -0500

The client forges a mail message from the space shuttle program's supervisor.

Client: MAIL FROM:shuttle_supervisor@nasa.gov

Server: 250 shuttle_supervisor@nasa.gov... Sender ok

*The client addresses the mail message to **tom@org.com**.*

Client: RCPT TO:tom@org.com

Server: 250 tom@org.com... Recipient ok

The forged message is entered.

Client: DATA

Server: 354 Enter mail, end with "." on a line by itself

Client:	Subject: Welcome to the space shuttle program
Client:	Your application to the space shuttle program has been accepted, and you have
Client:	been selected for the next mission. Please contact us immediately for
Client:	important top secret mission plans.
Client:	
Client:	Congratulations, and good luck.
Client:	.

The server blindly accepts the message and delivers it.

Server:	250 Ok
Client:	QUIT
Server:	221 bolero.gsfc.nasa.gov closing connection

The server closes the connection.

Note that system administrators can trace forged messages by using the log files generated by mail relays, so don't make your plans for world domination quite yet. SMTP is documented in RFC 821, which provides the full list of commands and return codes.

Designed in the early 1980s, SMTP makes some assumptions appropriate for that time: Computers are constantly powered on, always have an Internet connection, and have the multitasking capability to run a background mail-delivery process. With the advent of PCs and dial-up links, you can no longer take these assumptions for granted, so a separate protocol, POP3, handles delivery of mail to PCs.

The Post Office Protocol, Version 3 (POP3)

POP3 is optimized for a single task: delivery of e-mail to single-user computers. The protocol can transfer messages only from a server to the client; it assumes that you are using SMTP to send messages from the client to the server.

POP3 relies heavily on the concept of a maildrop. Much like a maildrop in a post office provides some storage space where the postal service can deliver your mail until you can physically retrieve it, a maildrop on a POP3 server provides some storage space to save your e-mail until your client program can retrieve it.

In operation, the POP3 protocol is slightly more complex than SMTP, partly because it relies on *states*. Immediately after you establish a connection, the POP3 server is in the *authentication state*, waiting for a user name and password. After the user is validated, the server makes a transition to the *transaction state*, processing mail requests from the client. Finally, after issuing a QUIT command in the transaction state, the server goes into an *update state*, clearing messages that were flagged for deletion.

Depending on the server's state, a single command can have multiple meanings. In the authentication state, the QUIT command closes the connection; in the transaction state, it moves the server to the update state.

When the client establishes a connection, the server is in the authentication state. In this state, only three commands are required:

- USER passes the user name from the client to the server.
- PASS provides the user's password to the server.
- QUIT closes the connection.

After the client sends valid USER and PASS information, the server attempts to make the transition to the transaction state. When entering the transaction state, the POP3 server acquires an exclusive-access lock on the maildrop, to prevent users from modifying or removing messages before the session enters the update state. If the POP3 server successfully locks the maildrop, it enters the transaction state, assigning a message number to each message and noting the size of each message.

The transaction state is where most of the action happens in POP3. Because POP3 is designed to support PC clients using interactive programs to retrieve mail, it relies on flexible commands. Of the eight transaction state commands valid in a full POP3 implementation, five are particularly important:

- STAT returns a single-line "drop listing" for the maildrop, returning the number of messages in the maildrop and the total size of the maildrop.
- LIST returns a "scan listing" for the maildrop, returning the message number and size of each message in the maildrop.
- RETR retrieves messages from the maildrop.
- DELE marks messages as deleted.
- QUIT moves from the transaction state to the update state.

Note the important distinction that the DELE command does *not* delete messages, but instead marks them as deleted. The POP3 designers realized that failures (such as communications and application errors) should not cause a user to lose e-mail. QUIT in the transaction state is absolutely required to enter the update state. If a failure occurs, marked messages are not cleared from the server.

The POP3 server remains in the update state only long enough to delete marked messages and unlock the maildrop. It then releases any resources acquired during the transaction state and says goodbye. The server then closes the TCP connection.

The following is a sample POP3 session:

*The client connects to the server **mailhost**.*

Server: +OK QUALCOMM Pop server derived from UCB (version 2.1.4-R3) at
                mailhost starting.

The server starts in the authentication state. The client logs in with a user name of bob and a password of bobpass.

Client: USER bob

Server: +OK Password required for bob.

Client: PASS bobpass

As a courtesy, the server responds that bob has one new message. The server has now made the transition to the transaction state.

Server: +OK bob has 1 message(s) (698 octets).

The client sends the STAT command for a message summary.

Client: STAT

The server responds that bob has one new message, which is 698 octets long. This response is in a standard format.

Server: +OK 1 698

The client issues the LIST command, which lists the message ID and size of each message.

Client: LIST

Server: +OK 1 messages (698 octets)

The server responds that message number one has 698 octets.

Server: 1 698

Server: .

The client sends a command to retrieve message number 1.

Client: RETR 1

The server transmits it.

Server: +OK 698 octets

Server: Received: from server1.org.com (server1.org.com [199.1.154.24])
          by mailhost.org.com (8.6.12/8.6.5) with SMTP id AA14992 for
          <bob@org.com>; Mon, 8 Jan 1996 20:41:03 -0600

Server: Received: by server1.org.com with Microsoft Mail id
          <01BADE09.6B31AEC0@server1.org.com>; Mon, 8 Jan 1996 20:39:34 -0600

Server: Message-ID: <01BADE09.6B31AEC0@server1.org.com>

Server: From: "Tom Thompson" <tom@org.com>

Server: To: "'Bob Bobson'" <bob@org.com>

Server: Subject: Test message

Server: Date: Mon, 8 Jan 1996 20:39:32 -0600

Server: MIME-Version: 1.0

Server: Content-Type: text/plain; charset="us-ascii"

Part

I

Ch

4

Server: Content-Transfer-Encoding: 7bit

Server:

Server: This is a short sample message.

Server: It is two lines long.

Server:

A single line with only a period (.)ends the message.

Server: .

The client issues the DELE command to delete message number one. Note that the message is not deleted yet; if the connection failed now, the message would still be on the server.

Client: DELE 1

Though the server responds that the message has been deleted, it is technically not true.

Server: +OK Message 1 has been deleted.

The client issues the QUIT command to enter the update state and sign off. This is when the message is actually deleted.

Client: QUIT

Server: +OK Pop server at mailhost signing off.

The server closes the connection.

POP3 supports advanced capabilities, such as clearing the delete flag, retrieving only the top lines of a message, uniquely identifying messages, and supporting continuous authentication without sending sensitive password information with every connection. RFC 1725 lists the commands to support POP3's advanced features.

In Chapter 9, "Developing SMTP and POP Mail Clients," you build an e-mail client that uses SMTP to send messages and uses POP3 to retrieve messages.

The File Transfer Protocol (FTP)

FTP is the most common way to transfer files on the Internet. Although the protocol is over 15 years old, it provides the basic functionality that most users require of a file transfer service.

Compared to other Internet protocols, FTP is relatively unique in that it actually relies on two simultaneous connections: a *control connection* and a *data connection*.

The control connection, which is based on the Telnet terminal emulation protocol, is used for the exchange of commands and replies. An experienced user can actually open a terminal emulation session to the FTP control connection and manually command a file transfer. In practice, FTP relies on a small subset of the Telnet protocol, making it relatively easy to hide from the user such raw FTP commands as GET and CWD.

The data connection is a full-duplex connection over which data is transferred. Based on commands passed in the control connection, the data connection is dynamically created and destroyed.

Full-Duplex

A full-duplex communication channel enables data to be transmitted and received simultaneously. Although the FTP protocol technically allows a single data channel to transmit and receive data simultaneously, few implementations support this scenario.

The following are some of the most essential FTP commands:

- USER passes the user name from the client to the server.
- PASS provides the user's password to the server.
- PORT passes to the server some information telling it how to establish the data connection back to the client.
- CWD acts much like the DOS CD command, changing the client's working directory on the server.
- RETR retrieves a file from the server to the client.
- STOR stores a message from the client to the server.
- QUIT closes the connection.

In the following sample conversation, the client at network address **199.199.199.101** retrieves the file TEST.DOC from directory /PUBLIC/SAMPLES:

> *The client control opens a connection to the server control.*

Server control: 220 Service Ready

> *The client specifies a user name and password to log in.*

Client control: USER bob

Server control: 331 User name ok, need password

Client control: PASS bobpass

Server control: 230 User logged in

> *The client issues a CWD command, which changes the directory to /PUBLIC/SAMPLES.*

Client control: CWD /public/samples

Server control: 250 CWD command successful.

> *The client creates a data connection and tells the server to use that data connection on host 199.199.199.101, port 1180 (4*256+156).*

Client control: PORT 199,199,199,101,4,156

Server control: 200 PORT command successful

Client control: RETR test.doc

Server control: 150 File status okay; about to open data connection

> *The server opens the data connection and transmits the file's contents.*

Server data: This is line 1 of file test.doc.

Server data: This is line 2.

Server data: The file is three lines long. This is the last line.

> *The server tells the client that the transmission is complete and closes the data connection.*
>
> **Server control:**   226 Transfer complete, closing data connection
>
> *The client requests that the control connection be destroyed.*
>
> **Client control:**   QUIT
>
> **Server control:**   221 Goodbye
>
> *Finally, the server closes the control connection.*

Notice that the client uses a PORT command to tell the server where to establish the data connection: host **199.199.199.101**, port 1180 (4*256+156). Chapter 5, "The Principles of Socket Communications and Programming," discusses the port number's significance. Also note that, much like the SMTP protocol, return messages start with three-digit numeric codes; this convention is common among many Internet protocols.

The dual-connection nature of FTP supports some exceptional capabilities. For example, a client can open control connections with two servers and command the servers to transfer data between each other without flowing through the client. The client does this by sending a PASV command to one server, forcing it to listen passively for requests, and sending a PORT command to the second server, specifying the first server's address and port from the PASV command.

Although the example shows a simple file retrieval, FTP has several commands that perform directory listings, append to server files, rename and delete files, create and remove directories, and perform many other functions. RFC 959 fully defines the FTP protocol, with its various commands and operating modes. In Chapter 8, "Developing an FTP Client and Server," you develop an FTP client and learn additional details about the FTP protocol.

The Network News Transfer Protocol (NNTP)

NNTP transfers Usenet News from server to server as well as from server to client, and thus is relatively complex. Also, News is inherently more complicated than many other applications that must run on the Internet; an FTP session must communicate between only two known hosts, but NNTP must allow for the newsgroup list, cross-posting of articles, expiration of aged messages, and other elaborate features.

Another reason for NNTP's complexity is the fact that News provides optional modes of interaction, such as several different ways for a client to retrieve News messages from a server.

In Chapter 10, "Developing an Internet News Client/Reader," when you build a newsreader, you learn some more of the subtleties of NNTP. The following are the most useful and basic NNTP commands and options:

- LIST returns a list of newsgroups, along with the numbers of the last and first articles in the newsgroup and a flag indicating whether the user can post to the newsgroup. This command does not list the groups in any particular order.
- NEWGROUPS specifies a date and time; only groups created after that time are listed.

- GROUP selects a newsgroup, returning the article numbers of the first and last articles in the group, along with an estimated number of articles on file for the group.
- HEAD retrieves an article's header.
- BODY retrieves an article's body text.
- ARTICLE retrieves an article's header and body text.
- POST posts an article. The data supplied after a POST command is in a special format, described by RFC 850, that provides such information as the newsgroups to which to post the message, the message's subject, and the e-mail address of the user who sent the message.
- QUIT closes the NNTP connection.

The following is a sample NNTP session. The client first retrieves the full list of newsgroups, and then the list of groups created since January 1, 1996. Next, the client selects the group TX.TEST and demonstrates the HEAD, BODY, and ARTICLE retrieval commands. Finally, the client posts an article and quits.

*The client connects to the server **news.org.com***

Server: 200 news.org.com InterNetNews NNRP server INN 1.4 22-Dec-93 ready (posting ok).

The client requests a list of all newsgroups.

Client: LIST

Server: 215 Newsgroups in form "group high low flags".

***alt.1d**, **alt.2600**, and **alt.3d** are the first few of thousands of newsgroups. **alt.1d** was established as a joke to discuss one-dimensional graphics, **alt.2600** is a hacker newsgroup, and **alt.3d** is for discussions of three-dimensional graphics and animation.*

Server: alt.1d 0000031399 0000031344 y

Server: alt.2600 0000163276 0000159344 y

Server: alt.3d 0000020133 0000020019 y

...and so on. The list ends with a period (.) on a line by itself.

Server: .

The client requests the list of newsgroups that have changed since January 1, 1996. 960101 is simply that date written in YYMMDD *format.*

Client: NEWGROUPS 960101 000000

The server returns a 231 success response, followed by the list of newsgroups created since that date.

Server: 231 New newsgroups follow.

Server: comp.os.linux.m68k 74 1 y

Server: comp.os.ms-windows.apps.utilities.win3x 23 1 y

Server: comp.os.ms-windows.networking.win95 201 1 y

Server: comp.os.ms-windows.apps.utilities.win95 125 1 y

Server: comp.os.ms-windows.apps.compatibility.win95 64 1 y

Server: comp.os.ms-windows.setup.win3x 76 1 y

Server: comp.os.ms-windows.setup.win95 161 1 y

...and so on. The list ends with a period (.) on a line by itself.

Server: .

*The client selects the group **tx.test**, a group for test messages in Texas.*

Client: GROUP tx.test

The server replies with a success response, 211, and indicates that the group has an estimated 13 messages. The first available message is number 1196, and the last message is number 1208.

Server: 211 13 1196 1208 tx.test

The client requests the header of message 1208.

Client: HEAD 1208

The server replies with a success response, 221. The message number is 1208.
<4cvest$phu@news.org.com> specifies a unique identifier for the message.

Server: 221 1208 <4cvest$phu@news.org.com> head

Server: Path: news.org.com!usenet

Server: From: bob@org.com (Bob Bobson)

Server: Newsgroups: tx.test

Server: Subject: Sample message

Server: Date: Wed, 10 Jan 1996 04:21:47 GMT

Server: Lines: 3

Server: Message-ID: <4cvest$phu@news.org.com>

Server: NNTP-Posting-Host: lbj70.org.com

Server: X-Newsreader: Forte Free Agent 1.0.82

Server: .

The client requests the body of article 1208.

Client: BODY 1208

The response does not include the header.

Server: 222 1208 <4cvest$phu@news.org.com> body

Server: This is a sample message. It has three lines.

Server: Line 2.

Server: The third and last line.

Server: .

The client requests article 1208, including the header and the body of the article.

Client: ARTICLE 1208

Server: 220 1208 <4cvest$phu@news.org.com> article

Server: Path: news.org.com!usenet

Server: From: bob@org.com (Bob Bobson)

Server: Newsgroups: tx.test

Server: Subject: Sample message

Server: Date: Wed, 10 Jan 1996 04:21:47 GMT

Server: Lines: 3

Server: Message-ID: <4cvest$phu@news.org.com>

Server: NNTP-Posting-Host: lbj70.org.com

Server: X-Newsreader: Forte Free Agent 1.0.82

Server:

Server: This is a sample message. It has three lines.

Server: Line 2.

Server: The third and last line.

Server: .

The client issues a POST command, to post a new article.

Client: POST

Server: 340 Ok

*The client posts the new article. Notice that **path**, **from**, **newsgroups**, and **subject** are specified in the article, formatted as specified by RFC 850.*

Client: Path: news.org.com!usenet

Client: From: bob@org.com (Bob Bobson)

Client: Newsgroups: tx.test

Client: Subject: Yet another sample message

A blank line separates the article header from the article body.

Client:

Client: This is yet another sample message. It has four lines.

Client: Line 2.

Client: Line 3.

Client: The fourth and last line.

The body is finished with a period (.) on a line by itself.

Client: .

The server responds that the article was successfully posted.

Server: 240 Article posted

The client requests that the NNTP session be closed.

Client: QUIT

Server: 205

The server closes the connection.

RFC 977 documents NNTP, and RFC 850 documents the format of articles.

Part

I

Ch

4

The Hypertext Transfer Protocol (HTTP)

Although the Web is arguably the most powerful service on the Internet, most of its power comes from the data transported through the Web, not from the Hypertext Transport Protocol that supports it. In fact, you probably will find HTTP downright boring after exploring the complexity of FTP and NNTP.

HTTP relies on only three commands, which the specifications call *methods*:

- HEAD tells the server to return only the header of whatever the requested URL identifies. The method is often used for testing hypertext links for validity, accessibility, and recent modification.

- GET tells the server to send whatever information the requested Universal Resource Identifier identifies, including the item's header and body.

- POST is used to post information to a server. The method supports such features as annotating existing resources, posting messages to bulletin boards and newsgroups, and returning data provided by forms.

The following sample HTTP conversation shows the retrieval of the header and then the full contents of a draft of the HTTP version 1.0 specification from **www.ics.uci.edu**:

*The client connects to the server **www.ics.uci.edu** and issues the HEAD command to get the document header.*

Client: HEAD /pub/ietf/http/draft-ietf-http-v10-spec-03.html HTTP/1.0

A blank line is required.

Client:

The server returns the document header, including the HTTP version and success code...

Server: HTTP/1.0 200 OK

...the server's date and time...

Server: Date: Mon, 25 Mar 1996 03:48:38 GMT

...the server type...

Server: Server: Apache/0.8.14

...the content type of the requested document...

Server: Content-type: text/html

...the length of the document...

Server: Content-length: 132624

...and the date that the document was modified.

Server: Last-modified: Wed, 06 Sep 1995 02:33:55 GMT

The client requests the document itself.

Client: GET /pub/ietf/http/draft-ietf-http-v10-spec-03.html HTTP/1.0

A blank line is required.

Client:

The server returns the requested document. What follow are the contents of the document itself.

Server: `<HTML>`

The following line is the HTML `<HEAD>` formatting command. Don't confuse it with the HTTP `HEAD` request command presented earlier.

Server: `<HEAD>`

Server: `<TITLE>Hypertext Transfer Protocol — HTTP/1.0</TITLE>`

Server: `<LINK rev=Made href="mailto:http-wg@cuckoo.hpl.hp.com">`

Server: `</HEAD>`

Server: `<BODY>`

Server: `<PRE>`

Server: `HTTP Working Group          T. Berners-Lee, MIT/LCS`

Server: `INTERNET-DRAFT              R. Fielding, UC Irvine`

Server: `&lt;draft-ietf-http-v10-spec-03.html&gt; H. Frystyk, MIT/LCS`

Server: `Expires March 4, 1996          September 4, 1995`

Server: `</PRE>`

Server:

Server: `<CENTER>`

Server: `<H1>Hypertext Transfer Protocol — HTTP/1.0</H1>`

Server: `</CENTER>`

Server:

Server: `<H2>Status of this Memo</H2>`

Server:

Server: `This document is an Internet-Draft. Internet-Drafts are working`
`                documents of the Internet`

Server: `Engineering Task Force (IETF), its areas, and its working groups.`
`                Note that other groups may`

Server: `also distribute working documents as Internet-Drafts.`

Server: `<P>`

...and so on...

Server: `</BODY>`

Server: `</HTML>`

The server closes the connection.

Figure 4.1 shows the data sent in this conversation presented in a browser.

FIG. 4.1

The HTML data sent in the example conversation, as displayed in Netscape.

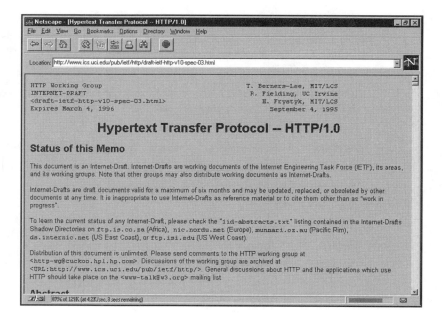

An RFC does not yet support HTTP; it is a draft standard. However, you can get information, directly from the HTTP working group, regarding the latest version of the HTTP standard. To do so, you point your Web browser to **http://www.ics.uci.edu/pub/ietf/http/** (as you probably guessed from the preceding example).

From Here...

In this chapter, you learned how conversations between clients and servers support Internet activities. You also saw the details of the TIME, SMTP, POP3, FTP, NNTP, and HTTP protocols.

For additional information on related topics, see the following sources:

- For detailed information on the protocols, see the related RFCs, or in the case of HTTP, the latest draft specifications on **http://www.ics.uci.edu/pub/ietf/http/**.

- To learn the details of the HTTP protocol, and the HTML-formatted data that it carries, see Chapter 12, "The Web—HTTP, HTML, and Beyond."

- To go through the process of developing FTP, e-mail, Usenet News, and Web applications, see Chapters 8 ("Developing an FTP Client and Server"), 9 ("Developing SMTP and POP Mail Clients"), 10 ("Developing an Internet News Client/Reader"), and 16 ("Building a Web Server with Delphi"). However, be prepared to check Chapters 5 ("The Principles of Socket Communications and Programming") and 6 ("Socket Programming with Delphi Using WinSock"), which present the technical details required to understand Internet application development fully.

- To learn about sockets, the key component of Internet applications, see Chapter 5, "The Principles of Socket Communications and Programming."

The Principles of Socket Communications and Programming

▬ **N**ow that you know how IP addressing identifies hosts on the Internet, and how Transmission Control Protocol/Internet Protocol (TCP/IP) conversations support data communications across the Internet, you might wonder how each host supports multiple conversations simultaneously. Some large Internet servers support thousands of concurrent users, tracking every conversation, and a personal computer (PC) can retrieve a Web page while receiving electronic mail yet never garble the information between the two sources.

This chapter explains how TCP/IP uses protocol numbers and port numbers to provide this capability, by combining data from multiple processes, shipping it over the Internet, and then splitting the incoming data apart on the client. ▬

Multiplexing and Demultiplexing Data

After routing data through the Internet and delivering the data to the proper host, you must deliver the data to the correct process. As data moves down TCP/IP protocol layers, the system *multiplexes* data, combining data streams from many applications into a few transport protocols, and further merging those transport protocols into the IP. When data arrives from the network, you must *demultiplex* the data, dividing the data for delivery to multiple processes.

To attain multiplexing/demultiplexing functionality, IP uses protocol numbers to identify transport protocols, and the transport protocols use port numbers to identify application processes.

Understanding TCP/IP Protocols

In Chapter 3, "Internet Connectivity," you learned that the TCP/IP protocol suite actually includes several other protocols, such as the User Datagram Protocol (UDP) and the Internet Control Message Protocol (ICMP). To sort out which protocol a given datagram is carrying, IP uses a *protocol number*, defined by a single byte in each datagram's IP header.

When you are using Microsoft's TCP/IP software or most other packages, the PROTOCOL file defines the protocol numbers. The PROTOCOL file is simply a table that lists the protocol name and the protocol number associated with that name. Alias protocol names and comments are also allowed. The following is an excerpt from the standard Windows 95 PROTOCOL file:

```
# <protocol name>  <assigned number>  [aliases...]   [#<comment>]
ip      0     IP      # Internet protocol
icmp    1     ICMP    # Internet control message protocol
ggp     3     GGP     # Gateway-gateway protocol
tcp     6     TCP     # Transmission control protocol
egp     8     EGP     # Exterior gateway protocol
pup     12    PUP     # PARC universal packet protocol
udp     17    UDP     # User datagram protocol
```

N O T E The location and layout of the PROTOCOL file depend on the version of TCP/IP that you are using. If you are running Windows 95 and using the native Microsoft TCP/IP, you can find the PROTOCOL file in your WINDOWS directory. If you are using a third-party TCP/IP (such as Trumpet TCP/IP), you probably can find the PROTOCOL file in one of the TCP/IP directories. By convention, the PROTOCOL file has no extension on the file name, but this might not always be the case. Like the file name and location, the actual file layout depends on the version of TCP/IP that you are using. The examples used here are taken from the native Microsoft Windows 95 TCP/IP implementation. ■

This table does not provide a complete listing of every protocol; RFC 1700, "Assigned Numbers," lists many other protocols. However, a system must include only the protocol numbers that it actually uses, not every possible protocol. If the PROTOCOL file lists some protocols that aren't in use, that causes no harm. The preceding table excerpt, for example, lists GGP and EGP, which are used only by core Internet systems, and would probably never actually be used on a Windows 95 PC.

Because TCP/IP technically relies on protocol numbers, not names, the PROTOCOL file is not actually required. However, many utilities, such as netstat, use the information in PROTOCOL to look up protocol names, providing a more user-friendly display of information.

When an IP datagram arrives at a host, the IP layer on that host is responsible for delivering the datagram to one of the transport protocols above it. To decide the transport protocol to which to deliver the datagram, IP looks at the datagram's protocol number. As listed in the preceding table, datagrams with protocol number 1 are delivered to ICMP, those with protocol number 6 are delivered to TCP, and so on.

Understanding TCP/IP Ports

After IP uses the protocol number to pass data to the proper transport protocol, the transport protocol must pass the data to the correct application process. These application processes, also known as *network services*, are tracked with *port numbers*—16-bit values that uniquely identify each network service.

The *source port* number identifies the process that sent the data, and the *destination port* number identifies the process that should receive the data. The port number resolution comes at the transport layer, not the Internet layer, as illustrated in Figure 5.1.

FIG. 5.1
The IP protocol number field and TCP destination port demultiplex incoming data.

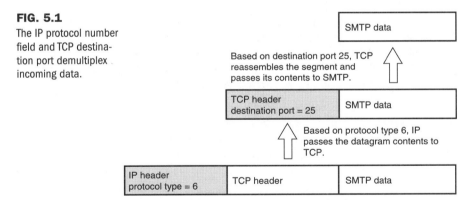

Part
I

Ch
5

Transport protocols do not share port numbers. For example, TCP port 513 offers remote login service, but UDP port 513 offers the "who" service. The combination of protocol and port number, not just the port number itself, is required to uniquely identify the process to which to deliver the data. TCP and UDP assign some of the same port numbers, but usually to similar services. For example, TCP port number 7 identifies the TCP echo service, and UDP port 7 identifies the UDP echo service. As a result, you cannot assume that the first port number found for a particular service is the correct one for the protocol that you are using. When looking up port numbers, you need to be sure and match the protocol as well as the service.

N O T E The WinSock functions (discussed in Chapter 6, "Socket Programming with Delphi Using WinSock") for looking up port numbers—WSAAsyncGetServByName and getservbyname — both take the protocol name as an optional argument, so that the correct port can be found. If the protocol name is not passed to these functions, they return the first match that is found in the services table, regardless of the protocol. ▨

There are only a few transport layer protocols, with TCP and UDP doing most of the work. However, there are hundreds of network services. In fact, if you build an application program that relies on a new service, you must assign it a unique port number. For instance, if you develop a new Internet application to replace the World Wide Web, you would have to find a TCP port that no other Internet applications are currently using. After finding an unused TCP port, you could assign this port to your new application, enabling the client applications to know how to connect to and use your wonderful new Internet service.

Port numbers are divided into several ranges. Port numbers below 256 are reserved for *well-known services* such as File Transfer Protocol (FTP), Simple Mail Transport Protocol (SMTP), Post Office Protocol version 3 (POP3), and Hypertext Transport Protocol (HTTP). Ports from 256 to 1023 are used for *UNIX-specific services* that were originally developed for UNIX systems. However, most of the UNIX-specific services no longer actually depend on UNIX. For example, the talk service, which enables two or more users to converse interactively, is on UDP port 517, but Windows and Macintosh talk clients are widely available.

Ports 1024 through 65535 are *high-numbered ports*. Although user processes usually allocate these ports dynamically, some of these ports carry server applications; Lotus Notes, Microsoft SQL Server, Microsoft SNA Server, and Windows Internet Name Service all inhabit the high-numbered ports. Ports in the range of 1024 and higher that are reserved for specific services (such as those previously mentioned) are known as *reserved ports*.

With Microsoft's TCP/IP stack, as well as most others, the SERVICES file specifies both TCP and UDP port numbers. The format of SERVICES is similar to that of the PROTOCOL file. Each entry lists the service name, the port number/protocol pair for that service, and optional aliases and comments. The following is an excerpt from the standard Windows 95 SERVICES file:

```
# <service name>   <port number>/<protocol>  [aliases...]   [#<comment>]
echo              7/tcp
echo              7/udp
discard           9/tcp      sink null
discard           9/udp      sink null
systat           11/tcp
systat           11/tcp      users
daytime          13/tcp
daytime          13/udp
netstat          15/tcp
qotd             17/tcp      quote
qotd             17/udp      quote
chargen          19/tcp      ttytst source
```

```
chargen          19/udp      ttytst source
ftp-data         20/tcp
ftp              21/tcp
telnet           23/tcp
smtp             25/tcp      mail
time             37/tcp      timserver
time             37/udp      timserver

pop             109/tcp      postoffice
pop2            109/tcp                  # Post Office
pop3            110/tcp      postoffice

nntp            119/tcp      usenet      # Network News Transfer

snmp            161/udp      snmp

biff            512/udp      comsat
exec            512/tcp
login           513/tcp
who             513/udp      whod
shell           514/tcp      cmd         # no passwords used
syslog          514/udp
printer         515/tcp      spooler     # line printer spooler
talk            517/udp
```

N O T E As with the PROTOCOL file, the SERVICES file's location and layout depend on the version of TCP/IP that your computer uses. The one used in the preceding example is the SERVICES file from the native Windows 95 version of TCP/IP and can be found in the WINDOWS directory. Like the PROTOCOL file, the SERVICES file, by convention, has no extension on the file name. ▪

This information, combined with that in the PROTOCOL file, provides everything necessary to deliver data to the correct application.

The SERVICES file lists dozens to hundreds of ports, although few computers actually support every listed service. Listing unused services in this file does no harm.

Many Internet protocols rely on simple seven-bit ASCII messages, so you can often use your knowledge of port numbers to manipulate client applications for purposes other than those for which they were designed. For example, if you use a Telnet terminal emulation application to connect to a server port running the Daytime service, you will see the time in the terminal emulator window. Figure 5.2 shows the connecting of the Daytime service on **www.nist.gov**, and Figure 5.3 shows this action's output.

Because the Daytime service immediately closes the connection after delivering the time, Telnet loses the connection, as shown.

As shown in Figure 5.4, even a Web browser can connect to the same Daytime port, which the browser interprets as a text message. Note closely the URL **http://www.nist.gov:13**, in which *13* is the Daytime service's port number. The Web browser sees the port as a text message.

FIG. 5.2
To use Telnet to connect to other services (such as the echo or daytime services), specify the service port name or number.

FIG. 5.3
Telnetting to the Daytime port returns the current date and time and then closes the connection.

FIG. 5.4
Netscape Navigator connecting to the Daytime port.

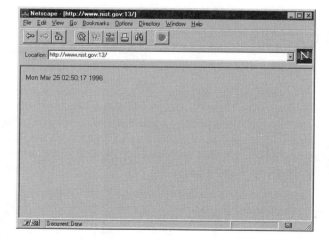

You can use Telnet to test or manipulate almost any service that is based on seven-bit ASCII messages. Most Internet applications use text-based commands and responses, so using Telnet enables you to type the commands and see the response from the server. If you use Telnet to connect to the HTTP port on a server, you can type HTTP request messages to the server and receive HTTP response messages from it, which is an ideal way to check whether the HTTP server that you just developed is working properly.

Understanding TCP/IP Sockets

The well-known ports provide the consistency needed for a client program to access the appropriate program on a server. Because the sender and receiver agree in advance which services are offered on which ports, the well-known ports facilitate the connection process. Given the unique combination of an IP address and TCP port number, a client application can establish communications with the exact server process required.

This unique combination of an IP address and TCP port number is called a *socket*. For example, port 37 on host 192.5.41.41 is a socket that uniquely defines the TIME service on the U. S. Directorate of Time's time server (**192.5.41.41** is the TCP/IP address of the United States Directorate of Time's server computer, and port 37 is the service port of the TIME service or function). All systems that offer the TIME service offer it on port 37.

A socket uniquely identifies a single network process within the entire Internet. However, a socket based on a well-known port handles only half of a conversation: the client to the server. For meaningful communications to occur, the server must be capable of returning data to the client.

In addition to well-known and reserved ports, there are ports known as *dynamically allocated ports*. As their name implies, these ports are assigned on demand. The TCP/IP software tracks the ports that are in use to ensure that two processes do not have the same port number, and that the assigned port number is above the range of standard port numbers. Applications that are connecting to another application (usually on another computer) often use dynamically allocated ports. The application does not need to use a specific port because other applications are not trying to find and connect to it.

Dynamically allocated ports enable client computer systems to connect to multiple servers simultaneously. Figure 5.5 shows the ports in use when connected to multiple services at multiple sites. In this case, Exchange is retrieving mail from **mailhost.onramp.net**, a Telnet session is open to **internic.net**, and Netscape Navigator has four Web connections to **www.microsoft.com**.

Part
I
Ch
5

FIG. 5.5
The netstat command shows which ports the local PC is using.

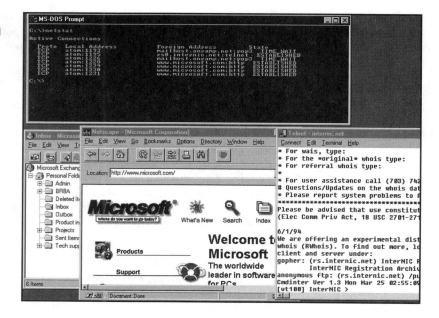

In Figure 5.5, the client is using dynamic ports 1193 and 1226 for its e-mail connection to **mailhost.onramp.net**, port 1195 for its terminal emulation connection to **internic.net**, and ports 1228 through 1231 for its connection to **www.microsoft.com**. The netstat command displays the dynamic ports in use on the client.

Figure 5.6 shows the exchange of port numbers during an HTTP session. The client randomly generates a source port—in this case 3456—and sends a segment with that source port and a destination port of 80, which is HTTP's well-known port. TCP/IP then splits the segment across multiple datagrams and sends them across the Internet. Next, the server reassembles the datagrams into a segment and passes it to the Web server.

FIG. 5.6
An HTTP conversation passing port numbers.

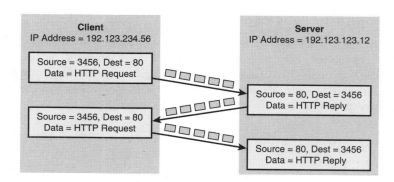

In response, the HTTP server builds a TCP segment, using 80 as the segment's source port and 3456 as its destination. The server splits the segment into datagrams and sends them to the client.

While supporting a conversation to **192.123.234.56** on port 3456, the HTTP server might also support conversations to the same host on ports 3457, 3458, and 3459, as a single browser might open multiple HTTP communication channels to enhance performance. The same server might also send data to **192.234.56.78** on ports 5678 and 5679, as well as to hundreds of other clients.

Understanding User-Defined TCP/IP Ports

As mentioned earlier, if you write an application that offers a new service, you must define a new port on which it can reside. On a Windows-based host, you can define a service to reside on any port, even overriding well-defined ports. If you are building a server that relies on an experimental application layer protocol, see RFC 1700, "Assigned Numbers," for a list of the registered port numbers, and use a new port number that has not yet been assigned. If your service can be adopted for widespread use, register a port number with the Internet Assigned Number Authority at **http://www.isi.edu/div7/iana/**.

Using TCP/IP Ports To Troubleshoot Network Connections

You probably didn't recognize some of the first few names on the list of well-known ports, because echo, discard, and chargen don't usually have dedicated client programs. However, these three services are valuable testing tools. All three of these services are defined for both TCP and UDP. This section describes the TCP versions, but the UDP versions work in a similar, albeit connectionless, manner.

Testing Connectivity with the Echo Service

The echo service simply echos, byte for byte, the data stream that you send to it. Echo is a transport layer testing tool, while PING, which uses ICMP echo messages, is more of an Internet layer testing tool.

Why you would want to use the echo service? Suppose, for example, that a retailer is having a problem with a store application continuously allocating more ports and never freeing them. Because the PING command uses an ICMP message, not a TCP message, the server could respond to the PING command and still seem to be operational while TCP was actually locked. Before fixing the application itself, you could write a small testing tool that checks the operation of each server's echo service to see whether TCP is really operational.

N O T E   PING is a TCP/IP utility that sends a small packet to a specified TCP/IP address and waits for a response. The receiving computer responds by returning the same packet to the original computer. This utility is commonly used to verify that two computers can talk to each other over a network connection. If the receiving computer does not respond to the PING command, it can mean one of several things:

- The receiving computer is turned off.

- The receiving computer is not running the TCP/IP network protocol.

- The network connection between the two computers is broken. This can be a simple matter of an unplugged network cable, or it could mean that there is a malfunctioning network router, hub, or gateway. ■

Testing Connectivity with the Discard Service

The discard service simply throws away data that you send to it. The service's primary use is for testing whether you can establish a TCP session with a server.

Testing Connectivity with the Chargen Service

The chargen service generates a continuous stream of ASCII characters, as shown in Figure 5.7. The service is useful for stressing a network connection to see whether it drops data under a continuous heavy load.

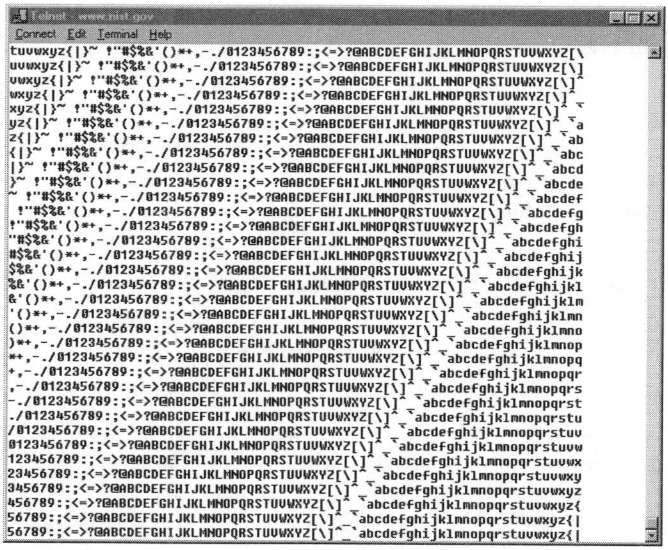

FIG. 5.7

The chargen service generates a continuous stream of ASCII characters.

N O T E Each of these three diagnostic services may or may not be available on a given server; vendors aren't required to implement any of them. Don't assume that a given server has one of these services until verifying it. For example, although Windows NT provides the echo, discard, and chargen services, Windows 95 does not. ▨

From Here...

In this chapter, you looked at the basic components that enable applications running on computers across the Internet to find and connect to each other. You saw how the protocol identifier tells the TCP/IP network drivers how to process and direct incoming data packets. Next, you looked at TCP/IP ports, and how you can use them to enable a client application to identify and connect to a specific server application running on another computer. You then examined TCP/IP sockets and learned how you can use them to identify a computer and application with which a client application wants to exchange data packets. Finally, you looked at how you can use three specific TCP/IP services to diagnose and troubleshoot network connection and communication problems.

So far, this book has concentrated on the fundamental concepts that enable the Internet to exist. A series of numbers—the network number, the subnet number, the host number, the protocol number, and the port number—come together as a socket, the unique identifier on the Internet. To apply this understanding, and use it to build working Internet applications, you must first examine the Windows Socket Application Programming Interface (WinSock API). After you are familiar with the WinSock set of functions, you can begin using them to build Internet applications. The following chapters take you through the basics of WinSock programming and building basic Internet applications:

- ▨ To understand the Windows Socket interface and how to use it in building applications, see Chapter 6, "Socket Programming with Delphi Using WinSock."

- ▨ To learn how Internet applications are defined and standardized, see Chapter 7, "Internet Development Standards."

- ▨ To understand the FTP client/server conversation and how to turn such a conversation into a working application, see Chapter 8, "Developing an FTP Client and Server."

- ▨ For an explanation of SMTP and POP conversations and how to turn those conversations into working applications, see Chapter 9, "Developing SMTP and POP Mail Clients."

- ▨ To understand how to build your own Usenet newsreader, see Chapter 10, "Developing an Internet News Client/Reader."

Part

I

Ch

5

CHAPTER 6

Socket Programming with Delphi Using WinSock

- Understand the major functions in the WinSock API that you will be using—how they work and what they do

- Create a WinSock object, to abstract the socket communication functions into simpler functions that you can easily use in your applications

- Build a simple application to test your WinSock object and interface definition

Before jumping into writing full-fledged Internet applications, you need to build the basic foundation on which you will base all application communications. As you learned in Chapter 5, "The Principles of Socket Communications and Programming," the programming mechanism known as a *socket* is the primary means used to perform inter-application communication over the Internet. The Windows version of the socket mechanism is known as a *Windows Socket,* or *WinSock.* The WinSock specification provides several socket-related functions that use several standardized record structures and constant values. These functions, structures, and constants are readily available in header files for C programmers, and with the introduction of Delphi 2.0, they are also readily available for Delphi programmers (before this release of Delphi, you had to perform your own translation of the C header file for all these function and structure definitions).

You can make your programming task easier by abstracting the WinSock functions further by encapsulating a substantial amount of the basic socket interactions into a WinSock interface object. This object can handle much of the socket-creation and address-binding functionality, and perform most of the necessary error checking within a simple function call. In short, in this chapter you create a WinSock interface that you can use in your applications.

Although in this chapter you do not build a complete WinSock object (you add only the basic functionality that you need to start your initial Internet application programming; in subsequent chapters, you expand on it as you need additional functionality), the object provides the basic functionality on which you construct your Internet applications throughout the rest of this book.

The high-level abstraction that you build in to your WinSock object is available from some commercial Transmission Control Protocol/Internet Protocol (TCP/IP) objects for use with Delphi. These are available as Delphi VCLs or VBXs (and you soon will see some OCXs). You could choose to use one of those prebuilt objects to build your Internet applications, in which case you could skip the material in this chapter. If you have no previous experience building socket applications, whether as Internet or intranet applications, this chapter's material will still help you to understand what is going on "under the covers" of your commercial object. ■

Understanding the WinSock API

To succeed in building Internet applications, you need a basic understanding of the WinSock API. Although an exhaustive examination of the WinSock API and services is beyond what is reasonable to cover in a single chapter (entire books have been written on this subject), this chapter takes a high-level look at the major functions, what they do, and how they work. This will give you enough of an understanding of the WinSock API to enable you to build just about any Internet application. For a more thorough look at the WinSock API, the WinSock 1.1 specifications are included on this book's companion CD.

 TIP All the following WinSock functions, unless specified otherwise, return a numeric status code as the integer return value. This status code is usually either 0 if no errors occurred, or SOCKET_ERROR if something went wrong. If a function returns an error indicator, then you can call the WinSock error functions to learn which error occurred. These error functions are discussed later in this section.

Initializing and Shutting Down WinSock Services

Before you can call any other WinSock functions, you must initialize the WinSock services. This is a simple matter of calling the WSAStartup() function, which initializes the WinSock services and returns to your application some information on the state of the WinSock services.

You have to pass two parameters to the WSAStartup() function. The first parameter is the WinSock version number that your application needs. For most applications, this is simply a matter of passing the value $0101. The second parameter is a pointer to a record structure called TWSAData (in this case PWSAData). This record holds various information about the WinSock implementation and operating system. The following are some of the key elements in this structure:

- wVersion is the WinSock version that is running
- szDescription is the WinSock vendor description of the WinSock implementation
- szSystemStatus is the operating system version that is currently running
- iMaxSockets is the maximum number of sockets currently available for use by the application (this can be a global pool reflecting the total number of sockets currently available to all applications)
- iMaxUpdDg is the maximum buffer size allowable for User Datagram Protocol (UDP) (connectionless) sockets

Listing 6.1 shows the entire record structure definition.

Listing 6.1 WINSOCK.PAS—the *TWSAData* Record Structure Definition

```
type
  PWSAData = ^TWSAData;
  TWSAData = packed record
    wVersion: Word;
    wHighVersion: Word;
    szDescription: array[0..WSADESCRIPTION_LEN] of Char;
    szSystemStatus: array[0..WSASYS_STATUS_LEN] of Char;
    iMaxSockets: Word;
    iMaxUdpDg: Word;
    lpVendorInfo: PChar;
  end;
```

The definition for WSAStartup() is as follows:

```
function WSAStartup(wVersionRequired: word; var WSData: IWSAData): Integer;
```

Before closing your application, you should shut down WinSock. This is a simple matter of calling the WSACleanup function, which does not require any parameters. The following is the definition for WSACleanup:

```
function WSACleanup: Integer;
```

Part
I

Ch
6

Before calling WSACleanup, you should cancel any outstanding blocking by using the WSACancelBlockingCall function. If you haven't used any blocking functions, the WSACancelBlockingCall function doesn't have anything to do, but it is good practice to call this function regardless of whether it is really needed. Therefore, your WinSock shutdown process will look like the following:

```
WSACancelBlockingCall;
WSACleanup;
```

N O T E Theoretically, you should capture and check the return value from both of these functions to see whether an error occurred, but the possible errors that these functions might return will tell you that either the WinSock services were never initialized (that WSAStartup() was not called) or that the network is not running. Neither of these is much of a concern when you are shutting down your application. ■

As you can probably tell from the preceding code excerpt, the definition for WSACancelBlockingCall is as follows:

```
function WSACancelBlockingCall: Integer;
```

Creating a Socket

Before you can use a socket, you have to create one. This is no different than opening a file or any other input/output (I/O) device that you can write to or read from. To create a socket, you use the socket() function. socket() creates and returns a socket descriptor of type TSocket, which is defined as an unsigned integer as follows:

```
TSocket = u_int;
```

The socket that is returned should be captured and used in much the same way that you would capture and use a file descriptor returned from a FileOpen function call. You pass this socket to all the WinSock functions that are performing any I/O functions, such as sending or receiving data or connecting to another computer.

The socket() function requires three parameters that tell it what type of socket to create. The first parameter specifies which network protocol to use (currently TCP/IP is the only one allowed, but others will be allowed with the arrival of the WinSock 2.0 specification). As long as you are using WinSock 1.1, this network protocol is the constant PF_INET (for Internet Protocol).

The second parameter that is passed to the socket() function specifies which type of socket to create. Listing 6.2 defines the available socket types.

Listing 6.2   WINSOCK.PAS—the Socket Type Definitions

```
SOCK_STREAM     = 1;          { stream socket }
SOCK_DGRAM      = 2;          { datagram socket }
SOCK_RAW        = 3;          { raw-protocol interface }
SOCK_RDM        = 4;          { reliably delivered message }
SOCK_SEQPACKET  = 5;          { sequenced packet stream }
```

All the applications you build that use sockets will use stream sockets, so SOCK_STREAM is the only socket type that you need to know. Of the other socket types, SOCK_DGRAM (UDP) is the only one that WinSock implementations reliably support. Support for the SOCK_RAW socket type is recommended in the WinSock specification, but not required, so don't count on such support.

N O T E Because you deal with stream sockets in this book's applications, most of the functions discussed in this section are for use with stream sockets and do not necessarily apply to datagram sockets. ■

The UDP socket type is a connectionless socket. Because it doesn't maintain a connection to the other computer, it doesn't guarantee packet delivery, or that packets will arrive in any particular order. This makes UDP sockets appropriate for applications that must send and receive short bursts of data very quickly. They are also appropriate for broadcast applications, which do not have to send data to a specific computer.

The stream socket type is a connection-based socket. To be able to send and receive data through the socket, each application socket must be connected to a corresponding socket in another application on another computer. You cannot use a stream socket to send a broadcast message to any computers on a network. For all the overhead associated with establishing and maintaining a connection to another computer, stream sockets do have guaranteed packet delivery in the original packet order. This makes stream sockets more fitting for applications that must send large amounts of data to another application on another computer.

The last parameter that you need to pass to the socket() function is the protocol that you are using. In most applications, you use the Internet Protocol (IP), which is defined as 0 in the WinSock definition, so you can hard-code that value for your purposes.

The socket() function can return any value that it wants to assign to a newly created socket. The socket values are not defined in the specification. However, if a new socket cannot be created, the value INVALID_SOCKET is returned. If the socket() function returns the INVALID_SOCKET value, be sure to check which problem occurred, by using WSAGetLastError() (which this chapter looks at later). The definition for socket() is as follows:

```
function socket(af, struct, protocol: Integer): TSocket;
```

Assigning an Address to a Socket

If your application is going to be connecting to other computers, you don't have to worry about which address your socket is using on your computer. However, you do need to know this address if your application needs to allow another application to connect to it. This is particularly important if you are building a server application. Other computers need to know where to find your application.

By default, your socket is automatically assigned an address when you try to connect to another system, but if you want it to use a specific address, you have to `bind()` the socket to the desired address. The `bind()` function is defined as follows:

```
function bind(s: TSocket; var addr: TSockAddr; namelen: Integer): Integer;
```

Of the three parameters that are passed to the `bind()` function, the first and third are pretty straightforward. The first parameter is the socket descriptor that is to be bound to the address specified. The `socket()` function returns this socket. This socket cannot have already been connected to any other computer, because after connecting to another computer, the socket is already assigned an address and cannot be changed.

The third parameter is the length of the socket address record that is being passed as the second parameter. This is a simple matter of calling the `SizeOf` function to retrieve the record size of the `TSockAddr` record.

The second parameter is where things begin to get interesting. The function definition for the `bind()` function shows that the second parameter is a pointer to a record structure called `TSockAddr`. Listing 6.3 defines this record as a redefinition of the TSockAddrIn record, which can be found in listing 6.4.

Listing 6.3   WINSOCK.PAS—the *TSockAddr* Record Definition

```
PSockAddr = ^TSockAddr;
TSockAddr = TSockAddrIn
```

In this record, the `sa_family` variable is the address type (in this book's applications, it is always `PF_INET` for the Internet address family). Unfortunately, this variable specifies only the address type, not the address to be used. The actual address goes into the `sa_data` variable, which doesn't indicate which address value goes into which position in the character array. This is because you never really use this record structure. Instead, you use a record structure called `TSockAddrIn`. The `TSockAddrIn` record redefines the `TSockAddr` record so that the `sa_data` variable is defined as three variables that hold specific values. Listing 6.4 defines the `TSockAddrIn` record.

Listing 6.4   WINSOCK.PAS—the *TSockAddrIn* Record Definition

```
PSockAddrIn = ^TSockAddrIn;
TSockAddrIn = packed record
    case Integer of
        0: (sin family: u short;
           sin port: u short
           sin addr: TInAddr;
           sin zero: array [0..7] of Char);
        1: (sa family: u short;
           sa data: array [0..13] of Char)
    end;
```

In the TSockAddrIn record structure, the sin_family variable is the same as the sa_family variable in the TSockAddr record. You are mainly interested in the rest of the variables that occupy the portion defined as the sa_data variable in the TSockAddr record. Actually, you are interested only in the first two of these variables; the third, sin_zero, is not used in this record structure (it is an unused filler area whose primary purpose is to make this record size match the TSockAddr record size).

The second variable, sin_port, is the TCP port to which this socket is to be bound. This port can be hard-coded, if you know beforehand which port your application will be using; alternatively, you can look up the port to be used at run time by using the getservbyname() function.

TIP You must use the htons() function to convert port numbers from Intel byte order to Internet byte order before placing the value in the sin_port record variable. This is because of the difference in the byte order used on Intel-based computer systems and the byte order used by most Internet server systems. This issue is examined more closely in the section "Dealing with Numbers (Internet Byte Order)," later in this chapter.

The third record variable, sin_addr, keeps things interesting in this record structure. The variable is defined not as a regular data type but as another record structure. Listing 6.5 defines the TInAddr record structure. This structure provides three different ways to access and manipulate the Internet address to be used for this application.

Listing 6.5   WINSOCK.PAS—the *TInAddr* Record Definition

```
PInAddr = ^TInAddr;
TInAddr = packed record
    case integer of
        0: (S_un_b: SunB);
        1: (S_un_w: SunW);
        2: (S_addr: u_long);
    end;
```

If you were going to run your application on a computer that has two or more network cards installed, you might be concerned about whether your application is using the appropriate address. But you most likely will want your application to use the default address configured for the computer on which your application will run. You can specify this address very easily by setting the TInAddr record's S_addr variable to the defined constant INADDR_ANY. This constant tells the bind() function to assign the passed socket to the Internet address already in use by the computer on which it is running.

Connecting to Another System

Most of the applications that you create in this book that use sockets connect to applications running on other computers. In such circumstances, you use the connect() function. The definition for the connect() function is much like the definition for the bind() function. connect() uses the same three parameters, as you can see in the function definition:

```
function connect(s: TSocket; var name: TSockAddr; namelen: Integer): Integer;
```

The main difference is that in the connect() function, you don't care which address you want to use for the socket on your end of the connection; instead, you are concerned with the address of the socket on the other end of the connection. Therefore, you must populate the TSockAddrIn record that you pass as the second parameter with the other computer's address and port.

If you have the TCP/IP address of the computer to which you want to connect, and you are holding it as a string (in the standard ###.###.###.### format used for TCP/IP addresses), you can use the inet_addr() function to convert the string to the format needed to place it directly into the sin_addr.S_addr record variable. The inet_addr() function is defined as follows:

```
function inet_addr(cp: PChar): u_long;
```

If the connect() function returns an error, you can check the error status to determine whether the error was WSAETIMEDOUT, which tells you that the connection timed out before reaching the other computer; WSAENETUNREACH, which tells you that the network is unreachable; or WSAECONNREFUSED, which tells you that the other computer rejected your connection request. Most of the other errors that might occur point to programming errors within your application.

Waiting for Another Computer To Connect to You

If you are building a server application, you need to tell your socket to "listen" for other computers requesting to connect to your application. To do so, you use the listen() function. The listen() function tells the socket passed to it to wait for an incoming connection and then notify the application that a connection is waiting to be serviced. The definition for the listen() function is as follows:

```
function listen(s: TSocket; backlog: Integer): Integer;
```

The first parameter passed to the listen() function is the socket that is to be used for listening for incoming connections. You must bind this socket to a specific address and TCP port before calling the listen() function.

The second parameter specifies the number of connection requests that can be queued; after this number is reached, any additional requests are rejected. The valid values for this parameter are 1 through 5. If you set this value at the maximum of five queued connection requests and a sixth connection request arrives before any of the others can be serviced, the request is rejected and the computer on the other end receives the WSAECONNREFUSED connect error. If you attempt to set the number of queued connections to any value less than 1 or greater than 5, the value automatically defaults to the closer of the two limits (for example, if you specify seven queued connection requests, the value defaults to five connection requests).

The socket can inform the application that an incoming connection request is waiting by using three methods. The first method is to try to service the incoming connection request on a blocking socket. This method halts processing in the active thread until an incoming connection is available to service. The second method is to check at the socket occasionally to see whether an incoming connection is available. This method wastes computing cycles on performing potentially unnecessary tasks. The third method is to have the listening socket trigger an application event when an incoming connection request is available for servicing. This is the most practical method for detecting an incoming connection request. You examine this method in the section "Asynchronous Mode—Letting the Socket Trigger Events," later in this chapter.

Accepting a Connection from Another Computer

When the listening socket informs your application of an incoming connection request, the application has to accept the request before any data can be sent or received through the connection. To accept the request, you use the accept() function. The accept() function takes the listening socket as an argument and creates a new socket that is identical to the listening socket, except that the computer with the first connection request in the queue is connected to the other end of the new socket. The listening socket continues listening and remains unchanged. The definition of the accept() function is as follows:

```
function accept(s: TSocket; var addr: ISockAddr; var addrlen: Integer): TSocket;
```

The parameters passed to the accept() function look much like those that you pass to the connect() and bind() functions. However, there are some differences. The first parameter is the listening socket. This is how the application knows which incoming connection to accept (an application can have multiple sockets listening for incoming connection requests). The third parameter, which is treated the same as in the previous functions, is specified as the length of the TSockAddr record.

The second parameter, however, differs somewhat from what you have seen in the previous functions. The record is the same as that which you have used to specify the address to be used for either the listening socket or for the socket on another computer to which you want to connect. The difference in the accept() function, however, is that you do not need to worry about filling in any values in the record. The function automatically fills this record with the connecting computer's address. You can then verify that this address is acceptable (for those situations in which only certain address ranges are to be allowed to connect to an application).

NOTE Notice that the listening socket continues to listen for incoming connections. When you are shutting down your application, you must close this socket just like all the connected sockets. ■

Closing a Socket

After you finish with a socket, you must close it. (Remember that a socket is much like a file; after you finish reading from or writing to a file, you must close it also.) This is a relatively simple process of calling the function closesocket() on any socket that needs to be closed. The closesocket() function looks almost like a file-closing function, as you can see in the following function definition:

```
function closesocket(s: TSocket): Integer;
```

The `closesocket()` function is quite simple. You pass the socket that you want to close, and the function closes the socket. Unfortunately, using the function isn't always so simple. Under most circumstances, you must shut down a socket before closing it. To do so, you use the `shutdown()` function.

The `shutdown()` function tells the socket to stop sending or receiving data, depending on the shutdown method specified. Table 6.1 lists the allowed methods.

Table 6.1   Socket Shutdown Methods

Value	Method
0	Receives are no longer allowed. This shutdown method is not recommended because it does not prevent the lower-level protocols from receiving more data. As a result, the buffers for the socket can continue to be filled with incoming data, but your application cannot empty them by receiving the data.
1	Sends are no longer allowed. This is the recommended method of shutting down a socket connection. This way, the connected computer knows that your application will not be sending any more data, so it can send any data that it feels it must send before closing the connection. After calling this shutdown method, your application must continue receiving data until there is no more to be received; then the connection is closed.
2	Sends and receives are no longer allowed. This is sometimes the required shutdown method for certain WinSock implementations.

The `shutdown()` function is defined as follows:

```
function shutdown(s: TSocket; how: Integer): Integer;
```

Sending Data through a Socket

After establishing a socket connection with another computer, you want to be able to send data through that connection. This is a simple matter of using the `send()` function. The `send()` function is defined as follows:

```
function send(s: TSocket; buf: PChar; len, flags: Integer): Integer;
```

N O T E   The definition of the send () function as listed above is not the same as the definition that you will find in the WINSOCK.PAS source code that is included with Delphi 2.0. The reason is that, in the Delphi code, the send () function is defined with the *buf* parameter defined as a variable parameter. This is wrong, and it prevents any data from being sent to the other computer. Because of this, most of the examples included on the CD include a module called NWINSOCK.PAS. This is nothing more than the Delphi WINSOCK.PAS with this one correction. If you are planning on doing any datagram socket programming, you will probably need to make this same change to the sendto() function. ▪

The first parameter passed to the send() function is the socket connection through which to send the data. The second parameter is a pointer to a buffer that contains data to be sent. This buffer might be a regular PChar string passed directly to the function, or it might be a pointer to a larger buffer that contains the greater part of a file that must be transferred. The third parameter is the size of the buffer being sent. If the buffer is a regular PChar string, you can determine this size by using the StrLen function; if the buffer is a file buffer, the size allocated for the buffer should be specified. The last parameter being passed to the send() function is a flag that tells the socket how to send the data. In this book, you do not build any applications that need any special sending instructions, so this flag is always 0.

The send() function returns the number of bytes that were sent, unless an error occurred. If an error occurred, the send() function returns the SOCKET_ERROR result code.

Receiving Data through a Socket

Receiving data works much like sending data. To receive data, you use the recv() function, which is defined as follows:

```
function recv(s: TSocket; var Buf; len, flags: Integer): Integer;
```

The primary difference between the send() and recv() functions is that the buffer pointer passed to the recv() function should point to an empty buffer, with the buffer-length parameter specifying how much memory was allocated for the buffer. One of the available flags, MSG_PEEK, enables the application to examine the incoming data without removing it from the WinSock buffers. This flag is quite useful if you are using blocking sockets and want to check whether there is any data to be received. If there is no data to be received, this flag doesn't bring your application to a halt. However, if there is data to be received, you must call the recv() function again (without the MSG_PEEK flag) to flush this data from the WinSock buffers, and you then must examine this data because more might have been received since you called recv() with the MSG_PEEK flag.

Like the send() function, the recv() function returns the number of bytes that were received. If an error occurs, the function returns SOCKET_ERROR.

Checking for Errors

When an error occurs, you can find out which error it is simply by calling the WSAGetLastError function. This function has no parameters to pass and returns an error code of the last error that occurred. The function's definition is as follows:

```
function WSAGetLastError: Integer;
```

The WinSock services do not maintain a stack of errors that occurred, so when you call the WSAGetLastError function, you receive the error code of only the last error that occurred. Therefore, if you are building a multithreaded application, you must call WSAGetLastError immediately after an error occurs, before another error has a chance to occur.

When an error occurs, WSAGetLastError() maintains that error code and returns it each time that it is called, until a different error occurs. However, you can specify an error code for it to return. To do so, you use the WSASetLastError() procedure, which is defined as follows:

```
procedure WSASetLastError(iError: Integer);
```

This procedure causes WSAGetLastError() to return whatever error code you specified using WSASetLastError() until another error occurs. Therefore, you can use the WSAGetLastError() function to build a single error-handling routine to handle all errors, including both WinSock and internal application errors.

Asynchronous Mode—Letting the Socket Trigger Events

Several of the WinSock functions that you have examined are, by default, blocking functions. This means that when you use the connect() function to connect your socket to another computer, your program comes to a halt while waiting for the connection to be made, or until it times out, whichever comes first. If you are building a multithreaded application in which each socket has its own thread that is completely independent from the user interface, this effect might not be so undesirable.

Unfortunately, the likelihood of each of your Internet applications being complex enough to make it worthwhile to pursue a multithreaded design is not great. You are more likely to build single-threaded applications than multithreaded ones. It would be preferable to have the socket trigger events that tell you when the connection has been established, or when incoming data is available for receiving. Fortunately, there is a way to make a socket trigger such events.

The WSAAsyncSelect() function places the socket into asynchronous mode, causing it to trigger an event whenever certain things happen. The definition for the WSAAsyncSelect() function is as follows:

```
function WSAAsyncSelect(s: TSocket; HWindow: HWND; wMsg: u_int;
                        lEvent: Longint): Integer;
```

The WSAAsyncSelect() function places only one socket into asynchronous mode: the one that is passed as the first parameter. The second parameter is the handle for the window or object that is to receive the event message. The third parameter is the event message that is to receive the window specified in the previous parameter. The fourth parameter is a series of flags that specify on which events the socket is to send an event message to the specified window. Listing 6.6 specifies these event flags.

Listing 6.6   WINSOCK.PAS—the *WSAAsyncSelect()* Notification Event Flags

```
FD_READ      = $01; {Incoming data is available for receiving}
FD_WRITE     = $02; {Outgoing data buffers are available for sending}
FD_OOB       = $04; {Out-Of-Band data (not used in this book)}
FD_ACCEPT    = $08; {An incoming connection request is available for
                           accepting}
FD_CONNECT   = $10; {The connection with the remote computer is
                           complete}
FD_CLOSE     = $20; {The connection has been closed}
```

To enable the socket to send the specified event message for multiple events, you can combine the event flags by using a bitwise OR in the function call, as in the following example:

```
WSAAsyncSelect(OpenSocket, handle, UWM_SOCKETEVE        NT, FD_CONNECT or
                             FD_READ or FD_WRITE or FD_CLOSE);
```

This function call causes the OpenSocket socket to send the user-defined UWM_SOCKETEVENT event message to the window in which this function is enclosed whenever the socket is connected to another computer, closed by the other computer, has incoming data available for receiving, or has out-bound buffer space available for sending data.

How does the user event handler know which of these events caused the UWM_SOCKETEVENT event message to be sent? The event flag that triggered the event is placed in the LParamLo attribute of the TMessage object. If an error occurred, the SOCKET_ERROR indicator is placed in the LParamHi attribute of the TMessage object. Therefore, you write an event handler for the user-defined UWM_SOCKETEVENT event message that looks like the one shown in Listing 6.7.

Listing 6.7 A User-Defined Socket Event Handler

```
procedure TMyWindow.UWMSocketEvent(var Msg: TMessage);
begin
   {Did an error occur?}
   if (Msg.LParamHi = SOCKET_ERROR) then
      PerformErrorHandling
   else
   begin
      {No error, so perform the appropriate task}
      case Msg.LParamLo of
          FD_CONNECT: PerformConnectionTask;
          FD_READ: PerformDataReceiveTask;
          FD_WRITE: PerformDataSendingTask;
          FD_CLOSE: PerformConnectionCloseTask;
      end;
   end;
end;
```

You can call WSAAsyncSelect() on a socket once, when creating the socket, and need not ever call this function again. However, sometimes you want to change or even cancel a particular socket's asynchronous behavior. You can call WSAAsyncSelect() at any time for any socket, but the changes affect only calls to the appropriate WinSock function that follow the WSAAsyncSelect() change. If you want to cancel all asynchronous behavior for a socket, you call WSAAsyncSelect(), passing 0 for the event message and the event flags, and thus turning off asynchronous behavior for any functions that follow (outstanding asynchronous functions will still trigger the event handler).

The most important and most misunderstood part of using the WSAAsyncSelect() function is the meaning of each of the event messages. Table 6.2 provides this information.

Part
I

Ch
6

Table 6.2 *WSAAsyncSelect()*'s Event Message Actions

Event Message	Meaning
FD_CONNECT	This event message is sent after the connect() function finishes. If WSAAsyncSelect() is called with the FD_CONNECT flag before the connect() function was called, the connect() function returns immediately, even though the connection has not been completed. When the connection is completed, the connect() function sends the FD_CONNECT event message so that the appropriate post-connection action can be taken. If the FD_WRITE event message is enabled along with the FD_CONNECT event message, both are sent after the connection is completed.
FD_ACCEPT	A listening socket sends this event to inform your application that an incoming connection request is waiting to be accepted. This message should be followed with the accept() function to complete the connection and begin the interaction with the computer on the other end of the connection.
FD_READ	This event informs your application that incoming data is ready to be received. You can use this message in two ways. First, you can call the recv() function before the FD_READ event message is received, in which case the FD_READ event message is informing your application that the buffer passed to the recv() function has been populated with incoming data. Second, you can wait until you receive the FD_READ event message, at which time you must call the recv() function to populate your input buffer with the incoming data. The second method enables you to capture the result value from the recv() function, so that you are informed of how much data was received.
FD_WRITE	This event informs your application that the outbound WinSock buffers are available for sending data through the socket connection. This message informs you that the previous send() function has completed.
FD_CLOSE	This event informs your application that the socket connection has been closed.

Looking Up Another Computer's Address

The WinSock API includes several database functions. You can use these functions to look up computer addresses by using the computer name, service ports based on a service name, and so on. Each of these functions has regular versions that are direct translations from the BSD sockets implementation. (*BSD* stands for Berkeley Software Distribution, which is based at the University of California at Berkeley. BSD developed the BSD UNIX operating system.) Unfortunately, each of these functions is a blocking function and causes your application to halt until the function completes its task. Fortunately, asynchronous versions of each of these functions have been implemented as Windows extensions (any WinSock API function that begins with *WSA* is a Windows extension to the BSD socket API).

One of these database extension functions that you will use extensively is the
WSAAsyncGetHostByName() function, which is defined as follows:

```
function WSAAsyncGetHostByName(HWindow: HWND; wMsg: u_int;
  name, buf: PChar; buflen: Integer): THandle;
```

You pass five parameters to the WSAAsyncGetHostByName() function. The first parameter is the
window handle of the window that is to receive the event message that informs your application
that the host address has been retrieved. The second parameter is the event message to send
to the windows specified in the first parameter. The third parameter is the name of the other
computer. The fourth parameter is the buffer into which the address is to be placed, and the
last parameter is the length of the buffer passed as the fourth parameter. The buffer is passed
as a PChar pointer, but is actually a pointer to the THostEnt record structure, which Listing 6.8
defines.

Listing 6.8 WINSOCK.PAS—the *THostEnt* Record Structure Definition

```
PHostEnt = ^THostEnt;
THostEnt = packed record
    h_name: PChar;
    h_aliases: ^PChar;
    h_addrtype: Smallint;
    h_length: Smallint;
    h_addr_list: ^PChar;
  end;
```

The THostEnt record contains several variables. The first, h_name, is the official name for the
computer requested. The second variable, h_aliases, is an array of alternative names for the
same computer. The third variable, h_addrtype, is an indicator for the other computer's address type. For Internet or TCP/IP addresses, the address type should always be PF_INET.
The fourth variable, h_length, is the address length, which should always be 4 for Internet
addresses. The fifth variable, h_addr_list, is an array of addresses (if a computer has multiple
network cards, it will have multiple addresses). The sixth and final variable, h_addr, is a pointer
to the first address in the list of addresses, which is the primary address that you will need to
use. The addresses that populate this record are in Internet Byte order, so you cannot simply
read them as a long integer value; see the section "Dealing with Numbers (Internet Byte Order)," later in this chapter.

The WSAAsyncGetHostByName() function's return value is a handle that identifies the host
lookup request. On triggering the specified event message on the specified window, the query
handle returns in the TMessage object's HParam variable. You can compare these handles to
determine which lookup query has been completed. The applications in this book are not
going to perform multiple database queries, so you don't have to worry about capturing
the returned handle and comparing it to the handle passed with the event message. Like the
WSAAsyncSelect() function, WSAAsyncGetHostByName() passes any error indicators to the
event handler in the TMessage object's LParamHi variable.

The WSAAsyncGetHostByName() function is one of an entire family of functions for retrieving various information from the host and service databases. These functions are WSAAsyncGetHostByAddr(), WSAGetServByName(), WSAGetServByPort(), WSAGetProtoByName(), and WSAGetProtoByNumber(). All these functions work basically the same, with the primary difference being the record structure used to return the requested information.

Getting Your Own Address

Sometimes you need to know your own socket's address, either to pass this information to another computer to inform it of the address to use, or to manipulate the address in some way. To find this address, you use the getsockname() function, which is defined as follows:

```
function getsockname(s: TSocket;  var name: TSockAddr;
                var namelen: Integer): Integer;
```

The getsockname() function looks similar to the bind() function. However, getsockname() is actually the opposite of the bind() function. Whereas you passed the bind() function a TSockAddr record populated with the address and port that you wanted to use for the specified socket, in the getsockname() function, you pass an empty TSockAddr record that the function populates with the address and port that the socket is using. As with the bind() function, you have to recast the TSockAddr record as a TSockAddrIn record before you can read the address and port that it contains.

Likewise, another function, getpeername(), is exactly like getsockname() except that it populates the TSockAddr record with the address and port in use by the computer connected to the other end of the specified socket. The getpeername() function is defined as follows:

```
function getpeername(s: TSocket; var name: TSockAddr;
                var namelen: Integer): Integer;
```

Dealing with Numbers (Internet Byte Order)

Most Windows machines run Intel processors or Intel-compatible processors. One of the peculiarities of Intel processors is that they use a byte order known as *little endian*. This means that, for any multibyte numeric value, the bytes are ordered from right to left. Although there are valid processor architecture reasons for taking this approach, the byte order introduces a problem: the order is the reverse of the defined standard for byte order on the Internet. RFC 1700, "Assigned Numbers," specifies that the standard byte order is *big endian,* which is the reverse of the byte order that most Windows computers use. Therefore, you must convert all numeric values into Internet byte order before using them in any WinSock API functions.

This actually isn't much of a problem, because the WinSock API provides four functions specifically for this purpose. These functions—htonl(), htons(), ntohl(), and ntohs()—perform the conversions for you. These functions are defined as follows:

```
function htonl(hostlong: u_long): u_long;
function htons(hostshort: u_short): u_short;
function ntohl(netlong: u_long): u_long;
function ntohs(netshort: u_short): u_short;
```

The first two, `htonl()` and `htons()`, convert numbers from Intel byte order (the order in which you need them to be for use in your applications) to Internet byte order. The first, `htonl()`, converts long integer values to Internet byte order and the second, `htons()`, converts regular integers to Internet byte order. The last two, `ntohl()` and `ntohs()`, do the opposite. They convert long and regular integers from Internet byte order back to Intel byte order.

 TIP You should convert any numeric value before using it in a WinSock function, or after receiving it from a WinSock function. One of the most common causes for a connection to result in the WSAECONNREFUSED error is the failure to convert either the address or port values into Internet byte order.

 TIP The DLL name for these external functions depends on the version of Delphi that you are using. In the 16-bit version, these functions are all in the WINSOCK DLL; the 32-bit versions are in the WSOCK32 DLL. The index numbers are consistent across implementations and are part of the specification.

N O T E Many of the socket exercises in this book were written prior to the release of Delphi 2.0, and thus did not have the WinSock API record structures that are defined within. Instead, I created my own translation of the WinSock API and record structures from the C definitions. To avoid having to rework the examples extensively to bring the record names in line with the Delphi record names, I instead added a section at the beginning of each source code file that defines many of the record type names as equaling the Delphi WinSock record names. This provides the level of compatibility necessary to enable the examples to work with the new WinSock API definition. ■

Creating a Wrapper Object to the WinSock Interface

By encapsulating the WinSock functions within a socket wrapper object, you can enable your applications to deal with socket communications on a high level, keeping the low-level implementation details hidden from view. In this section, you begin constructing the object; you enhance it as needed in subsequent chapters.

Initializing and Shutting Down Your Socket

You first must initialize your WinSock interface. To do so, you use the `WSAStartup` function. This function takes two parameters: the WinSock version number (which currently is 1.1) and a pointer to a `WSADATA` record.

If WinSock can initialize itself, it populates the `WSADATA` record with some information that you will want to look at (and possibly use). The first two data elements in the record are the WinSock version number (for now, this number should be the same as that which you passed to the `WSAStartup` function). The third element (`szDescription`) describes the WinSock implementation in use (the vendor name and any other descriptive information that the WinSock vendor chooses to give you). The fourth element (`szSystemStatus`) is a textual description of the current WinSock network (and operating system) status. The next element, `iMaxSockets`, is the number of sockets currently available for use (if WinSock applications are already running on the system, this number might be less than the total number available in the system). The next-to-last element, `iMaxUdpDg`, is the maximum size allowed for a UDP datagram packet (if this value is zero, the size is unlimited). The WinSock vendor can choose to use the final element (`lpVendorInfo`) for whatever information the vendor chooses. You shouldn't use `lpVendorInfo` because the data that it returns is likely to change as your applications run on different vendors' WinSock implementations.

In your application, the procedure that initializes your WinSock interface is `InitializeSocket` (see Listing 6.9).

Listing 6.9   TSOCKET.PAS—the *InitializeSocket* Procedure

```
function _TSocket.InitializeSocket: Boolean;
var
   lw_SocketVersion: Word;
   li_ErrorReturn: Integer;
begin
   lw_SocketVersion := $0101;
   li_ErrorReturn := WSAStartup(lw_SocketVersion, isp_WinSockInfo);
   case li_ErrorReturn of
       WSAEINVAL: InitializeSocket := FALSE;
       WSASYSNOTREADY: InitializeSocket := FALSE;
       WSAVERNOTSUPPORTED: InitializeSocket := FALSE;
   else
       InitializeSocket := TRUE;
   end;
end;
```

When shutting down your WinSock applications, you must perform the appropriate cleanup operations. These operations usually consist of two function calls, `WSACancelBlockingCall` and `WSACleanup`. The first function cancels any lingering blocking calls, and the second performs the actual cleanup and shutdown operations. The `ShutdownSocket` procedure contains these functions (see Listing 6.10).

Listing 6.10   TSOCKET.PAS—the *ShutdownSocket* Procedure

```
procedure _TSocket.ShutdownSocket;
begin
    WSACancelBlockingCall;
    WSACleanup;
end;
```

CAUTION

Before trying to run or debug any WinSock applications, you must have your TCP/IP stack loaded and the network running. If the TCP/IP stack that you are using is a PPP or SLIP connection and you try to run your application from within the Delphi development environment, a message displays warning you that the application cannot run. If you set a breakpoint and try to run the application, you get a General Protection Fault (GPF). This error occurs because the WinSock DLL cannot be loaded into memory unless the TCP/IP protocol is running and active.

Looking Up the Host Address

Next, you probably will have to look up the Internet address of the host computer that the user (or other source) has specified. The GetHostAddress procedure performs this task (see Listing 6.11). The procedure looks up this address by using the WSAAsyncGetHostByName function. You need to pass this function the host name (as a null-terminated string), a pointer to a buffer into which to place the address information, and the size of the buffer. This function performs an asynchronous lookup, so you also must tell the function which window to notify when it finishes and which event to trigger.

Listing 6.11 TSOCKET.PAS—the *GetHostAddress* Procedure

```
procedure _TSocket.GetHostAddress(hWnd: THandle;  wMsg: Word;
              lsHostName: String; NewState: Integer);
var
   ltHandle: THandle;
begin
   StrDispose(ispHostName);
   ispHostName := StrAlloc(Length(lsHostName) + 1);
   StrPCopy(ispHostName, lsHostName);
   StrDispose(icp_Buffer);
   icp_Buffer := StrAlloc((MAXGETHOSTSTRUCT + 1));
   ii_SocketState := NewState;
   ltHandle := WSAAsyncGetHostByName(hWnd, wMsg, ispHostName, icp_Buffer,
                        (MAXGETHOSTSTRUCT + 1));
   if (ltHandle = 0) then
      ShowMessage(SocketError);
end;
```

After you finish looking up the address, you use the ProcessHostAddress function to process the returned information (see Listing 6.12). You first cast the buffer as a HostEnt record and then check the address length specified in the HostEnt record. If the specified address length is zero (or less), you know that you didn't retrieve a valid address. If the specified address length is good, you check the address list's length. If the address list is invalid, you catch the exception and assume that the host address was not found. (If you are performing your own event handling, you could check the error status to see whether an error was returned indicating that the host was not found in the TMessage object's lParamHi attribute.) If the address list is valid, you copy it into a character array that holds the list, translates it into text, and so on.

Part
I

Ch
6

Listing 6.12   TSOCKET.PAS—the *ProcessHostAddress* Function

```
function _TSocket.ProcessHostAddress: Boolean;
var
   llLength: LongInt;
begin
   ihe_HostEntry := PHostEnt(icp_Buffer);
   if (ihe_HostEntry^.h_length <= 0) then
      ProcessHostAddress := FALSE
   else
   begin
      try
         llLength := StrLen(ihe_HostEntry^.h_addr_list^);
         StrDispose(isp_HostAddressList);
         if (llLength < ihe_HostEntry^.h_length) then
            isp_HostAddressList := StrAlloc(llLength)
         else
            isp_HostAddressList := StrAlloc(ihe_HostEntry^.h_length + 1);
         StrLCopy(isp_HostAddressList,
                  PChar(ihe_HostEntry^.h_addr_list^),
                  ihe_HostEntry^.h_length);
         isp_HostAddressList[ihe_HostEntry^.h_length] := Char(0);
         ProcessHostAddress := TRUE;
      except
         ProcessHostAddress := FALSE;
      end;
   end;
end;
```

If you look through the WinSock function reference, you will find that one function converts an Internet address to a string and vice versa. However, for this application, you implement your own function to illustrate the difference between Internet and Intel byte order.

Different computer architectures store binary data (except specific file formats, such as executables, archive files, and images) in differing orders. The Internet and all non-Intel flavors of UNIX store binary data sequentially (1, 2, 3, 4, and so on). Intel-based computers reverse the bytes (2, 1, 4, 3 for 16-bit values, and 4, 3, 2, 1 for 32-bit values). To process these values properly, you must translate them from their current state to the state in which you want them. Therefore, when preparing to send a packet out onto the Internet, you must convert the binary values from Intel to Internet byte order. Likewise, when you receive a binary value (such as an Internet address), you must convert it to Intel byte order if you want to use the value.

For this application, you simply want to display the Internet address as a string. If you were to convert the address to Intel byte order, you would have to convert it back as soon as you tried to use it to connect to the specified computer. You don't need to do anything with the value other than display it as a string, so you write your own function, GetHostAddressString, to perform the string conversion (see Listing 6.13).

TIP The WinSock API includes functions to perform these conversions. The htonl() and htons() functions convert 32- and 16-bit values respectively from Intel byte order to Internet byte order. ntohl() and ntohs() perform the 32- and 16-bit conversions from Internet to Intel byte order.

Listing 6.13 TSOCKET.PAS—the *GetHostAddressString* Function

```
function _TSocket.GetHostAddressString: String;
var
    lsHostAddress: String;
begin
    lsHostAddress := IntToStr(Integer(isp_HostAddressList[0])) + '.' +
                     IntToStr(Integer(isp_HostAddressList[1])) + '.' +
                     IntToStr(Integer(isp_HostAddressList[2])) + '.' +
                     IntToStr(Integer(isp_HostAddressList[3]));
    GetHostAddressString := lsHostAddress;
end;
```

Now you have the Internet address for the host computer to which you want to connect. You're all set to move on to the next step.

Creating, Connecting, and Closing Your Socket

Before you can use a socket to connect to another system, you must create a socket to use for that purpose. Creating a socket is quite simple and straightforward. The socket() function creates and returns a new socket of the type specified, if the function can create one. The primary reasons that you might not be able to create a new socket are that the system has run out of available sockets or system resources, or that a problem has arisen with the TCP/IP network protocol stack. Another reason that you might not be able to create a socket is that you are attempting to create a socket type that your TCP/IP vendor does not support. (An example of this occurs if you try to create a raw socket to implement a network diagnosis utility. Not all WinSock implementations support raw sockets.)

N O T E The maximum number of sockets available that the WSAStartup() function returns can be a global number of sockets, depending on the WinSock implementation. If other applications are running on the system that also are using WinSock communications, all are eating into this resource and depleting the number of available sockets much faster than if your applications were the only ones using sockets. ▨

The socket() function requires three parameters to describe the type of socket that you want to create (see Listing 6.14). The first parameter is the address type specifier. This value is always PF_INET (the ARPA Internet address format) because that is the only address type that the WinSock specification currently supports. The second value is the type of socket that you want to create. Most Internet applications (and all the ones that you create in this book) are stream sockets. Other socket types include datagram (used for UDP communications) and raw (used to create PING- and traceroute-type utilities). The third parameter passed to the socket() function is the protocol to be used with the socket. If you do not want to specify a particular protocol, you can use 0. If unable to create the socket, socket() returns the invalid socket value.

Part

I

Ch

6

N O T E   Datagram sockets do not guarantee delivery. They are implemented as a lower-level communications mechanism and thus do not have the built-in overhead to check for delivery or packet order. Therefore, if you write applications that use datagram sockets, you must be extra careful to verify the data that you receive and the order in which you receive it, and to look for packets that failed to arrive at their destination. Issue retries in the case of a dropped packet. Stream sockets, on the other hand, do guarantee delivery. After you establish a stream socket, all you need to worry about (other than network failure) is whether one of the systems involved disconnects from the other.

You cannot depend on raw sockets being available with your WinSock implementation. The WinSock specification does not require support for them (although the specification does recommend such support), and Microsoft, for example, does not support them in its WinSock implementation. ■

Listing 6.14   TSOCKET.PAS—the *CreateSocket* Function

```
function _TSocket.CreateSocket: _SOCKET;
var
   NewSock: _SOCKET;
begin
   NewSock := socket(PF_INET, SOCK_STREAM, 0);
   if (NewSock = INVALID_SOCKET) then
   begin
        ShowMessage(SocketError);
   end;
   CreateSocket := NewSock;
end;
```

If you have a valid socket and are creating a client application, you want to connect to the computer for which you retrieved the address. Before you can connect your socket to another computer, you must fill a Sockaddr_in record with all the appropriate information about the other system. The socket uses this record to determine which computer to connect to, which port to use, and so on. First, you must specify that the address family is in the AF_INET family (the Internet address family). Next, you specify the port on the other computer to which you want to connect, and thus to which service you are connecting (note that you are converting the port number from Intel to Internet byte order). Then you use the inet_addr() function to convert the host address string to an Internet address (okay, so I lied earlier when I said that you weren't going to do anything else with the host address). Finally, you zero out the sin_zero array. (You need to ensure that this array has a null string in it before using the record to connect to another computer. Although the purpose of this array is rather obscure, it probably is used for padding the address record to a specific length that is necessary for some of the connection process.)

After populating the sockaddr_in record, and before actually calling the connect() function, you call the WSAAsyncSelect() function to tell WinSock that you want the connection to happen asynchronously. The parameters to WSAAsyncSelect() are the socket that you want to operate asynchronously, the window to signal when the socket has connected, the event that you want to trigger on that window, and the socket event that you want to cause WinSock to send the event message. In this case, FD_CONNECT tells WSAAsyncSelect() to signal your window when the specified socket is connected (or timed out) to the other computer.

> **TIP**
>
> The WSAAsyncSelect() function places a particular socket into nonblocking mode (it doesn't cause the application execution to stop until the requested function has completed). The function also returns a socket into blocking mode by passing 0 for the last two parameters (the window event and the socket event).

After placing the socket into asynchronous mode, you call the connect() function to establish the connection to the other computer (see Listing 6.15). The connect() function receives three parameters: the socket to use, the address of the sockaddr_in record, and the length of the host name (the sockaddr_in record). You have placed this socket into nonblocking mode, so the connect() function (and most other functions that you will call from this point on) returns an error condition. On checking the error code, you find that the error condition is WSAEWOULDBLOCK (the socket is marked as nonblocking). You can ignore this error condition.

Listing 6.15 TSOCKET.PAS—the *OpenSocketConnection()* Function

```
function _TSocket.OpenSocketConnection(hWnd: THandle;  wMsg: Word;
            NewState: Integer; ConnectPort: Integer): _SOCKET;
var
   NewSocket: _Socket;
   lcAddress: PChar;
   lsAddress: String;
   llAddress: LongInt;
begin
   NewSocket := CreateSocket;
   if (NewSocket <> INVALID_SOCKET) then
   begin
      isa_SocketAddress.sin_family := AF_INET;
      isa_SocketAddress.sin_port := htons(ConnectPort);
      lsAddress := GetHostAddressString;
      lcAddress := StrAlloc(Length(lsAddress) + 1);
      StrPCopy(lcAddress, lsAddress);
      llAddress := inet_addr(lcAddress);
      StrDispose(lcAddress);
      isa_SocketAddress.sin_addr.s_addr := llAddress;
      isa_SocketAddress.sin_zero[0] := Char(0);
      WSAAsyncSelect(NewSocket, hWnd, wMsg, FD_CONNECT);
      ii_SocketState := NewState;
      if (connect(NewSocket, isa_SocketAddress, 16) = SOCKET_ERROR) then
      begin
         if (WSAGetLastError <> WSAEWOULDBLOCK) then
            ShowMessage(SocketError);
      end;
   end;
   OpenSocketConnection := NewSocket
end;
```

Part

I

Ch

6

Eventually, after wrapping up the conversation that it is holding with the other computer, your application must disconnect. You accomplish this through a simple call to the `closesocket()` function, passing it the socket to close (see Listing 6.16). This function also releases the socket descriptor. If you want to establish another connection, you must start by creating another socket.

Listing 6.16   TSOCKET.PAS—the *CloseSocketConnection()* Procedure

```
procedure _TSocket.CloseSocketConnection(SocketToClose: _SOCKET);
begin
    closesocket(SocketToClose);
end;
```

Sending and Receiving on Your Socket

The last two functions to implement send and receive the data. These functions are pretty simple to perform. Most data transfers between Internet applications in ASCII format, so you will assume (for now) that you are receiving a string to send through your socket. After copying the string into a null-terminated string (all strings passed between Internet applications are null-terminated, never Pascal-style strings), you reset the socket into nonblocking mode. The socket is still in nonblocking mode from the first time that you set it, so all you are really doing is changing which socket events will cause WinSock to send the application window the event that you specified. This time you tell WinSock to signal you each time that it finishes sending or receiving data.

After resetting the socket to the mode that you need, you call the `send()` function to send the buffer that you have filled (see Listing 6.17). The `send()` function receives four parameters: the socket to use, the buffer to send, the size of the buffer, and any flags to use when sending the buffer (such flags specify not to route data, not to send out-of-band data, and so on). You enclose the `send()` function within a procedure called `SocketSend()`, which converts the string that you send into a null-terminated character string, performs some basic error checking, and so on.

Listing 6.17   TSOCKET.PAS—the *SocketSend()* Procedure

```
procedure _TSocket.SocketSend(SendSocket: _SOCKET; hWnd: THandle;
              wMsg: Word; sSendStr: String; NewState: Integer);
var
    liBytesSent: Integer;
begin
    ii_SocketState := NewState;
    StrDispose(icp_Buffer);
    icp_Buffer := StrAlloc(1024);
    StrPCopy(icp_Buffer, sSendStr);
    WSAAsyncSelect(SendSocket, hWnd, wMsg, FD_READ + FD_WRITE);
    liBytesSent := send(SendSocket, icp_Buffer, StrLen(icp_Buffer), 0);
```

```
      if (liBytesSent = SOCKET_ERROR) then
         if (WSAGetLastError <> WSAEWOULDBLOCK) then
            ShowMessage(SocketError);
   end;
```

The recv() function takes the same four parameters as send() (see Listing 6.18). The primary difference is that you let the application pass in the buffer into which to place the data packet received. You can build a procedure, SocketReceive(), around the recv() function to perform your error checking and reset the socket state flag.

Listing 6.18 TSOCKET.PAS—the *SocketReceive()* Procedure

```
procedure _TSocket.SocketReceive(RecvSocket: _SOCKET;
                 hWnd: THandle; wMsg: Word; sBuffer: PChar;
                 BufSize: Integer; NewState: Integer);
var
   liBytesReceived: Integer;
begin
   WSAAsyncSelect(RecvSocket, hWnd, wMsg, FD_READ + FD_WRITE);
   liBytesReceived := recv(RecvSocket, sBuffer, BufSize, 0);
   if (liBytesReceived = SOCKET_ERROR) then
      if (WSAGetLastError <> WSAEWOULDBLOCK) then
         ShowMessage(SocketError);
   ii_SocketState := NewState;
end;
```

That completes your WinSock wrapper object for now. You have implemented the basic functions that you will need the object to perform for most client applications. You expand this object as you get to some of the various Internet applications that need additional functionality that you haven't yet implemented.

Using the Standard Port Services To Test Your Socket Client

Now that you've built a basic socket object, you might want to build a simple application to test it. This test application needs to do the following:

- Initialize the WinSock interface
- Look up a host computer's Internet address
- Create a socket for use
- Connect to the host computer
- Perform a simple conversation with the host computer
- Disconnect from the host computer
- Shut down the WinSock interface

This is a simple enough series of steps. But to which service port should your test application connect? By choosing a service port, you determine the nature of the conversation that takes place between your client test application and the host computer to which you are connecting.

The Standard Socket Ports

There are several standard socket ports that you can use to test your socket implementation (as well as to test network status, host status, and so on):

- The echo port (port 7)
- The discard port (port 9)
- The Telnet port (port 23)
- The time server port (port 37)

By using one of these standard ports, you can conduct a simple conversation that consists of no more than sending a couple of messages back and forth.

The Echo Port   The echo port simply returns to the client application exactly what it received from the client. To test using this port, you send the host a string of characters (the contents of the string do not matter; it can consist of completely random characters) and then receive the host's reply string. After receiving the complete string from the host, compare it to the string that you sent. If the strings match, you have a working socket implementation. If the two strings don't match, examine your socket implementation closely, looking for the possible culprit.

If the string that you received from the host does not match, but either begins or ends in a partial match, start looking at how you are assembling the received strings. The reply might not arrive as a single string but as many that have to be combined. If you are using a stream socket type, the string portions are guaranteed to arrive in order, but not in one piece.

If you are using a datagram socket type, the portions aren't guaranteed to arrive in order. You would need to check the identifiers on the packets to be sure that you reassemble them in the correct order.

The Discard Port   You can use the discard port to test connecting and sending only. If you connect to this port, you never receive any packets back from the host. All strings that you send to the host are thrown away (thus the port name). This is basically the socket service equivalent of the UNIX null device.

The Telnet Port   You use the Telnet port to run interactive terminal sessions. On connecting to the Telnet port, your client application should receive a login prompt. If you send the host a login ID, your application should receive back a password prompt. If you have a valid login ID and password to use on the server to which you are connecting, you can then issue a few commands and observe the results that return to your application.

The Time Server Port   When you connect a client to the time server port, it takes action immediately. The port sends a message to the client computer with the current system time and date, then promptly disconnects from the client system. The time and date sent is in the format used by the operating system (the C type `time_t` is defined as a long integer). On receiving the system time back from the host, you must convert the data into a string that you can display for the user.

Using the Time Service Port To Test Your Socket

For your test application, you connect to the time server port on the host computer that the user specifies (see Fig. 6.1). You define a simple state table for controlling the order in which to execute the various steps that you have to take (see Listing 6.19). You also define a custom event to trigger on completion of any socket functions.

Listing 6.19   SOCKET.PAS—the Time Server Test Application State and Event Constants

```
const
  SKT_NOOP = 0;
  SKT_GETHOSTADDR = 1;
  SKT_CONNECTTOHOST = 2;
  SKT_SENDPACKET = 3;
  SKT_RECVPACKET = 4;
  UWM_SOCKETEVENT = WM_USER + 500;
```

FIG. 6.1
Your completed socket test application getting the current system time from the **whitehouse.gov** Internet server.

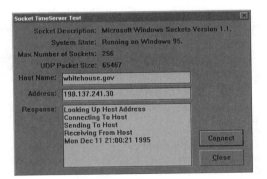

As you can see, your test application can be in one of five states at any particular time:

- Getting the host's Internet address
- Connecting to the host computer
- Sending a message to the host
- Receiving a message from the host
- Waiting for the user to trigger an action (such as connecting to a specified host or closing the application)

Part

I

Ch

6

The user starts the whole process by clicking the Connect button. Listing 6.20 shows the cbConnectClick() procedure that this button invokes. It first checks whether the user has entered a host name in the Host Name text box. If the user has specified a host name, the procedure clears the response/process stage display and initializes it with a message stating that the application is looking up the host address. Finally, the procedure calls the GetHostAddress() function that you built in to your socket object.

Listing 6.20   SOCKET.PAS—the *cbConnectClick()* Procedure

```
procedure TForm1.cbConnectClick(Sender: TObject);
begin
   if Length(HostName.text) > 0 then
   begin
      HostResponse.Clear;
      HostResponse.Lines.Add('Looking Up Host Address');
      NetSocket.GetHostAddress(Handle, UWM_SOCKETEVENT,
          HostName.text, SKT_GETHOSTADDR);
   end;
end;
```

After the WinSock interface finds the host Internet address, you must act on the address that it found. You first have your socket object process the returned address. If you received a good Internet address, you display the address in the Host Address text box. After receiving an address, you can create a socket and connect to the host's time server port. The ProcessHostLookup procedure performs these steps (see Listing 6.21).

Listing 6.21   SOCKET.PAS—the *ProcessHostLookup* Procedure

```
procedure TForm1.ProcessHostLookup;
begin
   if (NetSocket.ProcessHostAddress = TRUE) then
   begin
      HostResponse.Lines.Add('Connecting To Host');
      hostAddress.text := NetSocket.GetHostAddressString;
      isConnectionSocket := NetSocket.OpenSocketConnection(Handle,
          UWM_SOCKETEVENT, SKT_CONNECTTOHOST, IPPORT_TIMESERVER);
   end
   else
      HostResponse.Lines.Add('Cannot Find Host Address');
end;
```

Once connected to the host, you need not send anything to the host. All you have to do is advance the state table and post a socket event message, as shown in Listing 6.22.

Listing 6.22   SOCKET.PAS—the *ProcessHostConnect* Procedure

```
procedure TForm1.ProcessHostConnect;
var
   lsErrorString: String;
begin
```

```
    HostResponse.Lines.Add('Sending To Host');
    NetSocket.SetSocketState(SKT_SENDPACKET);
    PostMessage(Handle, UWM_SOCKETEVENT, 0, 0);
end;
```

You need to request your socket to receive any incoming packets, as shown in Listing 6.23.

Listing 6.23 SOCKET.PAS—the *ProcessHostSend* Procedure

```
procedure TForm1.ProcessHostSend;
var
    liBytesReceived: Integer;
begin
    HostResponse.Lines.Add('Receiving From Host');
    NetSocket.SetSocketState (SKT_RECVPACKET);
end;
```

On receiving a packet, you must ensure that it is valid (often the host computer initially sends an empty packet). If you receive an empty packet, place another request to your socket to receive any incoming packets. If you received a valid packet, you must use the ntohl() function to convert the data from Internet byte order to Intel byte order. Next, you convert the system time into a text string that you can display. Finally, you close your socket. The ProcessHostReceive procedure performs each of these tasks (see Listing 6.24).

Listing 6.24 SOCKET.PAS—the *ProcessHostReceive* Procedure

```
procedure TForm1.ProcessHostReceive;
var
    lsRetnStr: PChar;
    llINetTime, llIntelTime: LongInt;
begin
recv(isConnectionSocket, ilINetTime, size of (LongInt), 0);
    if (ilINetTime<> = 0) then
    begin
        llIntelTime := ntohl(ilINetTime);
        lsRetnStr := InTime(llIntelTime);
        lsRetnStr[(StrLen(lsRetnStr) - 1)] := #0;
        HostResponse.Lines.Add(StrPas(lsRetnStr));
        NetSocket.SetSocketState(SKT_NOOP);
        NetSocket.CloseSocketConnection(isConnectionSocket);
    end;
end;
```

Part

I

Ch

6

The missing piece here is your state table processing function, which the UWM_SOCKETEVENT message triggers (see Listing 6.25). This function checks the current socket state and calls the appropriate process function.

Listing 6.25 SOCKET.PAS—the *UWMSocketEvent()* Procedure

```
procedure TForm1.UWMSocketEvent(var Msg: TMessage);
begin
    case NetSocket.GetSocketState of
        SKT_GETHOSTADDR: ProcessHostLookup;
        SKT_CONNECTTOHOST: ProcessHostConnect;
        SKT_SENDPACKET: ProcessHostSend;
        SKT_RECVPACKET: ProcessHostReceive;
    end;
end;
```

The last detail is the InTime() function. This function converts the host system time into a null-terminated string that you can display for the user (see Listing 6.26). Delphi does not seem to provide a function that converts a system time to a Delphi type without dipping into inline assembly and triggering interrupts (a combination that you want to avoid), so you instead write a DLL that uses C to perform the conversion.

Listing 6.26 INTIME.C—the *InTime()* DLL Function

```
char * far PASCAL _export InTime(long inettime)
{
    long llTime;
    char *lsTimeStr;

    llTime = inettime - DATE_TIME_REF_POINT;
    lsTimeStr = ctime((time_t *)&llTime);
    return(lsTimeStr);
};
```

N O T E No matter which time zone the server to which you are connecting is in, the system time returned is usually fairly close to the system time showing on your computer. This is because the system time is sent as Greenwich Mean Time (GMT), and the ctime() C function performs the conversion to the local time, based on the time zone defined in your operating system configuration. If you want the host time to differ from your local time, change the time zone (or system time) configuration in your client computer configuration. ■

At this point, all that you need to implement for your socket test application is the screen layout, startup and shutdown processing, and all the other pieces that you have to deal with regardless of the nature of the application that you are developing. After these pieces are in place and complete, you should have a working WinSock application.

You could add several enhancements to your WinSock test application. For example, you could check whether the user has entered an Internet address rather than the host name. With this enhancement, you could look up the host name and fill in that piece of information instead of handling the task the other way around. You could enable the application to send strings to the host's echo server port, receive the return string, and display both for examination. You can probably think of dozens of other enhancements that you could add until eventually you have an extensive connection/host status test application.

Creating a Socket Server Application

You have just spent a good deal of time building a WinSock client application. The only difference between a WinSock client application and a WinSock server application is in the way that you make the socket connection with the other computer.

On creating the initial socket, the server calls the `listen()` function to check the queue of sockets waiting to connect. You use the `accept()` function to connect to the server the first socket waiting in the queue.

The `accept()` function creates a new socket with the same characteristics as the listening socket. You connect this new socket to the client socket, returning the original socket to the listen state. This enables server applications to handle multiple socket connections simultaneously. In a multithreading environment, the server application often spins off a new thread to handle the conversation with each client socket connection.

From Here...

In this chapter, you built the foundation on which you can build the other WinSock-based applications that you explore throughout this book. In building this foundation, you first implemented a basic WinSock interface by translating the C WinSock header file into Object Pascal. After completing the interface, you built an object wrapper around the interface to abstract and simplify the WinSock functions that you need to perform. Finally, you built a simple client application to test your WinSock objects.

Now that you have a basic working WinSock implementation, what should you do with it? You next need to understand how Internet applications work, how their conversations proceed, and how you can turn this knowledge into simple, working Internet applications. The following chapters will help your understanding of these issues:

- For an explanation of how the Internet application conversations are defined, how to understand them, and where to find this documentation, see Chapter 7, "Internet Development Standards."

- To understand the FTP client/server conversation and how to turn such a conversation into a working application, see Chapter 8, "Developing an FTP Client and Server."

- For an explanation of SMTP and POP conversations and how to turn those conversations into working applications, see Chapter 9, "Developing SMTP and POP Mail Clients."

- To understand how to build your own Usenet newsreader, see Chapter 10, "Developing an Internet News Client/Reader."

Part

I

Ch

6

Building Basic Internet Applications

Internet Development Standards

Developers are familiar with standards. After all, we have so many of them. The reasons for these standards vary, from presenting a common user interface to ensuring that one application can communicate with another. Like all areas of application development, developing Internet applications requires adherence to a variety of standards. The protocols implemented on the Internet provide a common communication interface that applications must use. ∎

Application-Level Communications

Before delving into the Internet standards themselves, you need to understand how your applications communicate with the various Internet services. The Internet applications that you develop sit on top of the transport layer of the Open System Interconnect (OSI) Reference Model. Various Internet programs, such as a newsreader or File Transfer Protocol (FTP) client, require that you implement and manage the session, presentation, and application layers of the OSI Reference Model. This section addresses the issues that you must consider to provide communications between your application and the Internet.

Addressing

Transport protocols usually expose different address formats to each type of application. The Windows Sockets header file defines the address formats and structures used in WinSock programming. Delphi 2.0 ships with a file called WINSOCK.PAS, which is the Delphi translation of the standard C WINSOCK.H header file. You can find it in the Delphi 2.0\SOURCE\RTL\WIN subdirectory. Listing 7.1 shows the address family definitions. The transport protocol uses socket address structures specified in the *address family* (*af*) argument to the socket() function.

Listing 7.1   The Address Family Definitions

```
{ Address families. }

    AF_UNSPEC       = 0;                  { unspecified }
    AF_UNIX         = 1;                  { local to host (pipes, portals) }
    AF_INET         = 2;                  { internetwork: UDP, TCP, etc. }
    AF_IMPLINK      = 3;                  { arpanet imp addresses }
    AF_PUP          = 4;                  { pup protocols: e.g. BSP }
    AF_CHAOS        = 5;                  { mit CHAOS protocols }
    AF_IPX          = 6;                  { IPX and SPX }
    AF_NS           = 6;                  { XEROX NS protocols }
    AF_ISO          = 7;                  { ISO protocols }
    AF_OSI          = AF_ISO;             { OSI is ISO }
    AF_ECMA         = 8;                  { european computer manufacturers }
    AF_DATAKIT      = 9;                  { datakit protocols }
    AF_CCITT        = 10;                 { CCITT protocols, X.25 etc }
    AF_SNA          = 11;                 { IBM SNA }
    AF_DECnet       = 12;                 { DECnet }
    AF_DLI          = 13;                 { Direct data link interface }
    AF_LAT          = 14;                 { LAT }
    AF_HYLINK       = 15;                 { NSC Hyperchannel }
    AF_APPLETALK    = 16;                 { AppleTalk }
    AF_NETBIOS      = 17;                 { NetBios-style addresses }
    AF_VOICEVIEW    = 18;                 { VoiceView }

    AF_MAX          = 19;
```

The Windows Sockets header file also specifies the function calls that you use and their associated parameters. You must open all Transmission Control Protocol/Internet Protocol (TCP/IP) sockets, including both TCP and User Datagram Protocol (UDP) sockets, with the AF_INET address family. Several WinSock functions take socket addresses as input or output parameters, including the following functions:

- `accept()` enables a client to access your computer.
- `bind()` assigns a name to a newly created socket.
- `getpeername()` retrieves the Internet address of a system connected to a local socket.
- `getsockname()` retrieves the current name for the specified socket.
- `recvfrom()` receives a UDP protocol packet.
- `sendto()` sends a UDP protocol packet.

Your socket address is like your telephone number. The `bind()` function enables you to assign a name that refers to the socket address. It makes an assignment for your program that enables the `connect()` function to say "Call Tracy" rather than "Call 555-1212."

Applications must fill in a socket address when calling `bind()` to a local address, or `connect()` to a remote address.

Some WinSock functions return a socket address as a parameter. Your applications must be capable of interpreting the socket address returned from functions like `accept()`, `getpeername()`, `getsockname()`, `recvfrom()`, and `sendto()`. For example, the socket address returned from the `accept()` function tells you who is signing on your computer. The concept is similar to the caller ID services that most phone companies offer.

Data Delivery

Enormous amounts of data constantly travel across networks, but how much of the data sent across the Internet actually reaches its destination? Most networks are inherently unreliable. To the network, data is nothing more than electrical impulses traveling along a wire, through some switches, and beamed through satellites. If you were to watch automotive traffic from a distance, you wouldn't notice how many people got lost every day; likewise, you never notice how much data loses its way on a network.

The difference between freeway and network traffic is that drivers can figure out that they're lost and eventually find the right road. Data packets do not have any intelligence; when they get lost, they stay lost. That's why application developers put so much effort into checking whether packets have arrived at their destination.

Some transport protocols, such as TCP, handle this task themselves, relieving the application that uses the protocol of the burden of keeping track of its own data. These protocols use their own mechanisms to ensure that data is delivered in the correct order and without loss, corruption, or duplication. TCP is considered a reliable protocol, but the overhead necessary to make it such often means that it's slower than its less-reliable counterparts.

Other protocols, like IP, don't guarantee delivery at all. IP and other inherently unreliable protocols are like an open road on which data can travel quickly. They are speedy, but lack any integrity checks. Such checks are left to the applications themselves. This unreliable transport is like a mail chute in a large building. You know that the chute provides a path from the top floor to the bottom, but you never know whether your mail got to its destination at the bottom or got stuck along the way by some oversized envelope. A mail chute provides no feedback or delivery guarantees, but if all works well, it's fast. Certainly, dropping your mail into a chute is much faster than having to carry it down to the mailbox on the first floor by taking the stairs or the elevator; however, if you instead drop your mail down the chute, your mail's delivery is not as certain.

To program effectively for the Internet, you need to understand the concepts of connection-oriented and connectionless transport protocols and how they relate to reliability.

Connection-Oriented Transport Protocols   The Internet is a busy web of connections. You can always get where you want from where you are—the question is which path you'll take. It's feasible to send a single message that gets fragmented and delivered over multiple different paths to the same source. The receiver must reassemble the fragments before it can read the message.

Connection-oriented transport protocols—such as TCP on the Internet, or SPX in a NetWare environment—require applications to establish a *virtual circuit* before transferring data. In a virtual circuit, the link between client and server appears to be a dedicated point-to-point connection. In practice, this virtual circuit exists temporarily—only for the duration of your connection—and helps ensure reliable communications. The data traveling along virtual circuits can physically take very diverse paths, but the virtual circuit logically appears to your program as a dedicated data path.

To establish a virtual circuit, a server must first inform the transport protocol that it can accommodate incoming transmissions by executing the listen() function. A client must initiate the circuit with a connect() function. The server then obtains a socket for the circuit with the accept() function. After establishing the circuit, both parties can transfer data with the send() and recv() functions. The WinSock specification defines each of these functions. How you implement them in your application depends on the service that you want to perform. Later chapters demonstrate how to use each of these functions. During the communication process, connection-oriented transport protocols acknowledge transmissions, so the sender can gauge what it delivers. Sometimes the sender can speed up or slow down its transmissions based on feedback from the receiver. Keep in mind that it takes two to tango—the client actually initiates the circuit by attempting to connect to the server, but the server must first be there to listen. The client takes an active role, while the server's role is passive.

Connection-oriented transport protocols can operate as either a message-oriented or stream-oriented protocol. Message-oriented transport protocols send or receive each block of data as a single block. In other words, such a protocol never breaks a message into fragments that the receiver must reassemble.

N O T E This rule has one exception. If a message is larger than the physical network's Maximum Transport Unit (MTU), the network forces the fragmentation of a message even if the protocol is message-oriented. Nevertheless, the network also reassembles the message at the endpoint. The fragmentation is transparent to the application. ■

Stream-oriented transport protocols transmit data as a continuous stream without any message boundaries. In other words, the data is simply a stream of bytes. Stream-oriented transport protocols, such as Finger, do not involve record structures. The transport protocol is free to fragment the message as necessary. The application has no control over this process, and doesn't receive any notice about it.

Connectionless Transport Protocols   Connectionless transport protocols, such as IP and UDP, are unreliable. They do not establish circuits with the destination, so they do not receive any feedback about the transmission process. Connectionless applications need only bind() to a socket before it starts using sendto() and recvfrom() functions to move data.

Connectionless transport protocols often support broadcasts. Any bound socket can send a broadcast if the SO_BROADCAST flag is set.

N O T E The send() and sendto() functions support flags that modify a socket's behavior. In this case, the SO_BROADCAST flag enables a socket to send broadcasts. The WINSOCK header file defines additional flags. ■

UDP and IP protocols deliver broadcasts to a socket only if the broadcast is sent to the same port to which the socket is bound.

Broadcast messages place a high load on the network because they force every host on the network to deal with them. As a result, the capability to send broadcast packets is limited to sockets that explicitly serve them. Broadcasts are usually unwelcome because of the load that they place on system resources.

Out-of-Band Data

Some connection-oriented transport protocols support out-of-band, or urgent, data. Data sent with the MSG_OOB flag in the send() function gets delivered as quickly as possible. One unfortunate side effect is that the data often arrives fragmented and out of order. You have to prepare your application to expect this consequence and handle it by reassembling the fragments before opening the message. Avoid out-of-band data unless you have a specific need and your applications on both ends of the connection know how to deal with the data.

The Internet Applications Standards Process

The individuals and organizations responsible for shaping the Internet do a wonderful job of administering disparate concepts and shaping them into standard specifications that work on multiple platforms all over the world. In this section, you explore the organizations involved and how a proposal becomes an Internet standard.

Part

II

Ch

7

General Development Concepts

Creating a set of standards for a worldwide phenomenon is not an easy task. The Internet finds a way to link different computer platforms that were never intended to communicate with each other when first developed. Delphi programmers tend to concentrate on the things that they know, such as IBM-compatible personal computers. Consider some of the issues that you face when developing an application for this machine. Should it run under DOS or Windows? Which version of Windows—3.1, Windows 95, or Windows NT? What about OS/2, or maybe one of the UNIX variants? Each of these operating systems has its own unique way of dealing with programmers and users.

Next, consider who will use your application. Can you guarantee that your users will speak the same language as you? What about symbols or measurements? Are you willing to reduce your market to English-speaking users living in the United States? Perhaps. The guardians of the Internet don't have that luxury, though.

Internet standards face a daunting task of trying to make something that actually works well for many different people and platforms. Consider some of the obstacles that the standards groups must face:

- Standards must work on different types of hardware and operating systems.
- Users around the world do not all speak the same language.
- Developers might not choose the same programming language or tools.

Internet Authorities   Several principal groups help guide the Internet and define its standards:

- The Internet Society (ISOC)
- The Internet Engineering Task Force (IETF)
- The Internet Engineering Steering Group (IESG)
- The Internet Architecture Board (IAB)
- The World Wide Web Consortium (W3C)

These groups represent interested individuals and organizations from all over the globe. Most of them represent an arm of the IETF, and they often work together to formalize standards for different parts of the Internet.

The Internet Society (ISOC)   The ISOC is an international organization that facilitates global cooperation and coordination for the Internet, its technologies, and applications. The group consists of individuals, corporations, nonprofit organizations, and government agencies.

The society has many specific goals, but its main purpose is to provide maintenance and growth for the Internet itself and the technologies that comprise the Internet. The following are some of the society's specific goals:

- The development, maintenance, evolution, and dissemination of standards for the Internet and its internetworking technologies and applications

- The growth and evolution of the Internet architecture
- The maintenance and evolution of effective administrative processes that are necessary for operating the global Internet
- Education and research related to the Internet and the process of internetworking
- The harmony of actions and activities at international levels to facilitate the Internet's development and availability
- The collection and dissemination of information related to the Internet, including historical archives
- Technological assistance for government, organizations, and private citizens of developing nations in implementing their Internet infrastructure and use
- A liaison with other organizations, governments, and the general public for coordination, collaboration, and education toward achieving the preceding goals

As you can see, the ISOC considers itself the guardian of the Internet's fate. The society is the glue that binds different organizations and governments together with respect to this cause.

The ISOC announced its founding in June 1991 at an international conference in Copenhagen. The society was formally established in January 1992 and settled in Reston, Virginia. Although the society has many regional and local chapters, its guiding force is its international Board of Trustees and International Networking Conferences. The board consists of 18 members from all over the world, most of whom were instrumental in creating different components of the Internet and its technology.

The Internet Engineering Task Force (IETF)   The IETF is the Internet's protocol engineering and development arm. The task force does most of its work through mailing lists, but holds meetings three times a year. The IETF does its actual technical work in its *working groups,* which the task force has organized into different technical areas:

- Applications
- IP: Next Generation
- Internet
- Network Management
- Operational Requirements
- Routing
- Security
- Transport
- User Services

The area directors handle the IETF's internal management. The Internet Engineering Steering Group (IESG) consists of the area directors and the IETF's chairperson. You can learn more about the IETF by reviewing its meeting notes, available on the **ds.internic.net** FTP server under the /IETF directory.

Part
II

Ch
7

The Internet Engineering Steering Group (IESG)   With the support of the ISOC, the IESG manages the Internet standards process. A subsidiary of the ISOC, the IESG ensures that the proposed standards of the IETF adhere to the ISOC's principles.

Like the IETF, the IESG keeps its minutes available to the public. You can find them on the **ds.internic.net** server under the /IESG directory.

The Internet Architecture Board (IAB)   The ISOC's technical advisory group, the IAB provides a variety of services to ISOC, IETF, and IESG. The IAB performs the following services:

- Appoints the IETF chair
- Selects all IESG candidates from a list provided by the IETF nominating committee
- Oversees the architecture for the protocols and procedures that the Internet uses
- Oversees the process used to create Internet standards
- Serves as an appeal board for complaints of improper execution of the standards process
- Provides editorial management and publication of the RFC document series that defines Internet standards
- Administrates the various Internet assigned numbers
- Represents the ISOC as a liaison to other standards organizations relevant to the Internet
- Advises the ISOC's board and officers

Like the other groups, the IAB publishes its meeting notes. You can find them on the World Wide Web (WWW) at **http://info.internet.isi.edu** in the /IAB directory.

The World Wide Web Consortium (W3C)   The W3C is a vendor-neutral group that develops common standards for the evolution of the World Wide Web. The Laboratory for Computer Science and the Massachusetts Institute of Technology (MIT) operate the W3C as an industry consortium. These two groups, along with the European Laboratory for Particle Physics (CERN), manage the W3C from France. Membership is open to any organization that signs an agreement. The W3C provides the following to the public:

- A reference code implementation to embody and promote standards
- Various prototype and sample applications that demonstrate the use of new technology
- A repository of information about the World Wide Web for developers and users, including Web-related specifications

You can reach the W3C at **http://www.w3c.org**.

Platform-Independent Concerns   Most developers enjoy a luxury that they take for granted: They can concentrate on developing systems for a single platform. As a Delphi developer, you probably are concerned only with developing for one of the Windows platforms. This mind-set is actually beneficial for an application developer, so that you can concentrate more on the subject of your application and less on the distractions of its platform. Of course, the Internet is a system, not an application. Therefore, anyone who wants to develop a specification for the Internet as a whole must operate in a platform-independent world. Transfer protocols must work on every conceivable operating system and hardware platform.

Defining a standard that works on every system is difficult if you don't narrow the parameters as you develop that standard. To make the development process easier, the standards groups use some *de facto* standards of their own. All the documents that you review about Internet standards have some common elements. Actually, these standards grew out of the close-knit community that characterized the Internet back when it still consisted of academics and researchers in the United States alone. Although the documents use these common elements, they still operate with suitable replacements. This section discusses some of these *de facto* standard elements.

The Internet as a Community   As this chapter previously mentioned, the Internet is a world-wide phenomenon. You can imagine the language barriers that this imposes, particularly if everyone were to use his or her native tongue when submitting standards proposals. Because the Internet began in the United States, English is the common, *de facto* language for all Internet standards documentation.

The de Facto Programming Language   Internet developers share code with one another quite openly. Learning what other programmers do with computers on different platforms is a good way to promote interoperability. At the same time, the use of different programming languages can potentially disrupt the communications process. Internet developers need a common language that works on multiple platforms.

The C language arose as the *de facto* standard language for developing Internet applications. This does not preclude developers from working in other languages, though. (If that were the case, this would be a very short book.) Because C is the Internet standards documentation's *de facto* language, you must translate its C examples into Delphi code.

You need some familiarity with C code to translate the examples to Delphi. Most of the conversions are fairly simple data-type exchanges. The difficulties that you might face most likely revolve around C's use of pointers. You might need to perform some typecasts to overcome a few issues.

Despite these potential difficulties, nothing should prevent you from implementing any Internet programming standard in Delphi.

The de Facto Operating System   UNIX is the Internet's *de facto* operating system. UNIX became popular for much the same reason as C—because the system works on many different hardware platforms.

The most common application program interface (API) used in Internet application development on UNIX is the Berkeley Sockets API. As a Windows programmer, you're in luck: You can use the API calls, plus some Windows extensions, by using the WinSock API discussed in Chapter 5, "The Principles of Socket Communications and Programming."

The Request for Comments (RFC) Documents

The RFC documents are the official documents representing Internet standards. If a specification is not in an RFC document, it's not an official Internet standard. RFCs possess a wealth of information about the Internet and its technology. Finding the RFC that you want, like finding much of the information on the Internet, is sometimes a tedious exercise. Many of the old technologies still have RFCs in the library, so much of material is now irrelevant due to new technologies. Still, RFCs are the motherload of information for people who want to implement Internet technology.

This section discusses the RFC process. You might never have the opportunity to define and submit your own proposal for a standard, but understanding the process can help you keep track of new technologies as they arise. For example, consider the security standards discussed in Chapter 17, "Internet Security, RSA Encryption, SSL, STT, PCT, and WinSock."

Where To Begin The RFC process has strict guidelines for submitting proposals. Proposals are called Internet-Drafts. Anyone can create an Internet-Draft and submit it to the IETF by electronic mail at **internet-draft@cnri.reston.va.us.** Internet-Drafts are rough drafts in the format of an RFC. RFC 1543 specifies the format. Suffice to say that the drafts must be in ASCII text.

> **N O T E** The IAB and IETF allow PostScript versions to accompany the ASCII version, so you can include figures, charts, or diagrams. ■

An Internet-Draft is generally a specification for a new service that meets the following criteria:

- Provides a new and useful service on the Internet
- Has a design that works properly
- Is technically capable (doesn't specify anything beyond the current technology)
- Can be implemented on various platforms and provides a method that enables them to interact
- Has the support and interest of the Internet community

The RFC Development Process The RFC development process is not a speedy one. The IETF requires as much time as it feels is necessary to review Internet-Drafts and solicit feedback from interested parties. The process itself is rigid and standardized, but the many nuances of evaluation can cause significant delays. Proposed software and standards don't always work as their creators advertise them. The IETF must decide whether a proposal has merit and is worthy of modification, or that the proposal should die on the vine.

Development is a finicky process, and technical documentation is no exception. The IETF must mold the specification to work on the Internet without conflicting with existing services. The document usually requires charts, graphs, and diagrams. Sample programs and demonstration code must work without error. The process is a loop of review and refinement.

There are also legal issues to consider. Many Internet-Drafts include algorithms and technologies that might have patent or copyright protection. Vendors in particular tend to guard their developments with sharp legal hounds. Any number of ownership issues can also sink a proposal before it becomes an RFC.

The basic process of moving an Internet-Draft to an RFC consists of the following steps:

1. Create and organize an Internet-Draft.
2. Review the Internet-Draft.
3. Publish the Internet-Draft.
4. Revise the Internet-Draft.
5. Gain acceptance for the Internet-Draft.

Now take a look at each step in this process.

Creating and Organizing an Internet-Draft   Anyone can write a proposal and submit it for review. Sometimes a vendor-sponsored technology, such as Hewlett-Packard's VG100 AnyLAN, becomes an Internet-Draft on its way to RFC status. The IETF working groups typically initiate most Internet-Drafts. This group consists of the people who are most intimately familiar with what the Internet needs within a given area. If you have an interest in a particular Internet field, pay attention to the IETF working group that handles it.

Reviewing the Internet-Draft   The IESG reviews the submitted Internet-Draft to determine whether it deserves an independent technical review. The IESG typically assigns the review process to an existing working group. In some cases, the IESG creates a new and independent technical working group to review the document, particularly when a proposed standard significantly alters Internet operations. The new working group then analyzes the technical merit of the Internet-Draft, and also evaluates its consequences on the Internet as it exists.

Publishing the Internet-Draft   After granting preliminary approval, the IESG authorizes the publication of the document to the Internet community as a proposed standard. Anyone on the Internet can review the Internet-Draft documents through FTP on the **ds.internic.net** server under the /INTERNET-DRAFT directory.

Internet-Drafts are valid for up to six months. During that time, the working group can update, replace, or remove the document at any time. Nothing more than documentation of a work in progress, Internet-Drafts have no official status.

Revising the Internet-Draft   As people read and comment on the published Internet-Draft, its contents usually change. During this time, the IESG and the Internet community evaluate the changes and how the proposal will affect different parts of the Internet. If the implications of changes implemented in a new proposal become too extreme, the IESG might either extend the evaluation period or declare the document significantly and return it to the start of the standards evaluation track. Extensive changes often significantly delay approval of a standard. Although the Internet-Draft period is six months, some standards, due to various delays and revisions, take years to complete the RFC process.

Part
II

Ch
7

Gaining Acceptance for the Internet-Draft After the Internet-Draft completes its review period, the IETF decides whether it becomes an Internet standard. If the IETF reaches a consensus to approve the Internet-Draft, it becomes an RFC. The RFC then goes to the RFC Editor. Chartered by the ISOC and Federal Network Council (FNC), the RFC Editor publishes RFCs and is responsible for the final editorial review of the documents. (The FNC acts as a forum for networking collaborations among federal agencies to meet their research, educational, and operational needs.)

At this point, developers can implement the standards defined in the RFC. Of course, the Internet doesn't stand still, even for approved RFCs. Sometimes revising or retiring an existing RFC becomes necessary due to new technology. RFC revisions go through the same process as new proposals. When a new version is complete, the older version receives the title `Obsolete`.

Finding Specifications and Sample Code

After deciding to implement an RFC, you should do two things. Of course, you want to obtain the RFC and review it thoroughly. Next, you contact other developers on the Internet to see how they're implementing the RFC. The best way to learn how to implement a standard is to read someone else's source code, even if that code is in another programming language. Sometimes the dry text leaves you feeling unsure about a specific function. Seeing the actual code that the text describes gets you beyond the "aha" stage (as in, "Aha! So that's how you do it!").

One of the first places to look for sample code is the IETF working group that originated the proposal for an RFC. Those code samples probably were written in C and work on UNIX machines. Even so, the samples enable you to connect through Telnet to a host computer to run the program.

Another place that you can start searching is the various Usenet groups dedicated to implementing specific RFCs. You might find some helpful information posted at the various **comp.infosystems** newsgroups, which include the following:

- **comp.infosystems.wais**
- **comp.infosystems.www.announce**
- **comp.infosystems.browsers.ms-windows**
- **comp.infosystems.servers.ms-windows**

Other newsgroups include the following:

- **comp.internet.library**
- **comp.internet.net-happenings**
- **comp.os.ms-windows.programmer.tools.winsock**
- **info.rfc**
- **nersc.rfc.software**

Life doesn't stop with Usenet, though. One of the most powerful publishing platforms on the Internet is the World Wide Web. As you might expect, several sources of sample code are available. Many of the WWW home pages also have links to FTP servers. The following are some starting pages for source code on the Web:

- The ISOC home page at **http://info.isoc.org/home.html**
- The IETF home page at **http://www.ietf.cnri.reston.va.us/home.html**
- The InterNIC doc page at **http://ds.internic.net/ds/dspg0intdoc.html**
- The InterNIC standards index at **http://www.internic.net/std/**
- The Sockets page at **http://www.sockets.com**
- The Stardust page at **http://www.stardust.com**

Keep in mind that many of the RFC samples that you find use C language for examples. Use that to your advantage. With the powerful search engines available on the Web, such as Yahoo or Webcrawler, try searches that combine different elements that you find in whatever you want to find. Mix keywords like *RFC, C,* and *SOURCE* to find a C source code sample for RFCs. Try the same thing with Delphi, Visual Basic, COBOL, or even FORTRAN. You never know who may have written the most helpful sample source code, or which language they might have used to write the code.

 If you have a CompuServe account, try visiting the Delphi forum (**GO CIS:DELPHI**) and the Internet Developer's forum (**GO CIS:INETDEV**). On either forum you can meet people or find libraries of source code that can help you achieve your goal.

From Here...

In this chapter, you've learned a little about the standard function calls and data elements that WinSock provides. You've also learned about the procedures necessary to develop an idea into a recognized Internet standard. Now that you understand the Internet standards process, you're probably anxious to investigate some of the RFCs and find out how to implement them. Be sure to investigate the following chapters, which discuss these topics:

- Chapter 8, "Developing an FTP Client and Server," shows you how to develop applications that transfer files both as a requester and as a provider.
- Chapter 9, "Developing SMTP and POP Mail Clients," explains how to build your own e-mail program as well as an Internet post office.
- Chapter 10, "Developing an Internet News Client/Reader," shows you how to retrieve messages posted on the Usenet News service.
- Chapter 12, "The Web—HTTP, HTML, and Beyond," shows you how to create your own Web server or to surf the net with your own browser.

Part
II

Ch
7

Developing an FTP Client and Server

- How an FTP client and server communicate and cooperate

- What data types FTP supports for transferring files

- What format controls the differing data types support

- What data structures you can transfer using FTP

- What transmission modes are available in the FTP protocol

- How to implement an FTP client by using the communications model and command set

- What is involved in building an FTP server

The File Transfer Protocol (FTP) has been in use since the early days of ARPAnet. The primary means of sharing files between computers and users, FTP, combined with the Telnet remote login capabilities, provided users with distributed processing capability during the early days of the Internet. Today, FTP's use is limited primarily to moving files between systems, but it is also often used as a means of serving World Wide Web pages and services. Although an FTP server does not provide as much functionality as a Web server, it can still provide most of the basic services necessary to serve Web pages.

FTP provides a program or user with file- and directory-management capabilities on a remote system. FTP also enables two computer systems to transfer files back and forth, controlled from either system or even from a third computer system. ■

How FTP Works

Part of the purpose for creating the FTP protocol was to allow the interchange of files from one system to another while shielding the user from any differences in the underlying file structure of the two (or more) systems involved. Considering the varied computer systems among which the original users needed to exchange files, this goal was no simple task. To provide this level of platform independence while also providing for reliable file transportation, the designers came up with the FTP communications model, which is described in RFC 959.

The FTP Communications Model

The basic FTP communications model uses two communication pipelines between the client and server systems (see Fig. 8.1). The first communications pipe passes commands and replies between the client and server. The second communications pipe transfers files and other data from one system to the other. The first (*command*) pipe is open throughout the FTP session and passes messages both ways. The second (*data*) pipe is open only when transferring data from one system to the other and passes data in one direction only (although the direction can be either from server to client or from client to server).

FIG. 8.1
The FTP communications model provides separate communications and data pipelines between the client and server applications.

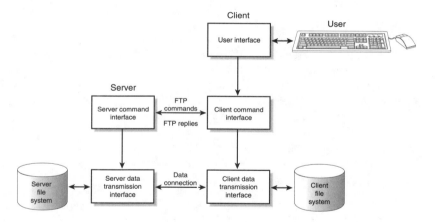

The first connection, the command pipe, is initiated by the FTP client. The client connects to the server on Transmission Control Protocol (TCP) port 21, gives the server a login and password, and then proceeds with the FTP session. Most of the simple communications between the client and the server take place on this first socket connection. If the client issues a simple command that requires a single-line response from the server, this command pipe transmits the reply.

When the client issues a command that requires more than a single, simple response (such as a directory listing) or requests to send or receive a file, the second communications pipe comes into play. To establish this second connection, you have three options. By default, the server initiates the second connection by creating a socket on TCP port 20 and connecting to a second socket on the client, using the same address and port as the first socket on the client. However, the client can specify a different address or port to be used for the data transfer connection, in which case the server then attempts to connect to the client by using the new address (this address or port can also be used to transfer files between the server and a third computer system). The third option is for the client (or third system) to initiate the data transfer connection by telling the server to go into passive mode. The server responds with an address and port to use for the data transfer connection (if the client is initiating the data connection, the server uses a third port, not ports 20 or 21).

As soon as the data transfer is complete, the data communications connection closes. It reopens the next time that the client issues a command that requires that the connection be open.

Data Types

When transferring files between systems, you can use four data types. Of these, only two are commonly used today, although the other two should still be supported (under appropriate circumstances). The systems on both ends of the FTP conversation must provide the support necessary for each of the following data types:

- The *ASCII* (American Standard Code for Information Interchange) type is the default data type for all FTP sessions. It is intended for use when transferring text files. If you attempt to transfer binary files (such as images or executables) through an FTP session without changing the data type, the file will be transferred as an ASCII file, thus totally scrambling the file's contents. The RFC defines the ASCII data type as standard eight-bit NVT-ASCII (Network Virtual Terminal ASCII, defined in the Telnet protocol, RFC 854). The NVT specification dictates that you use the carriage return and line feed character combination as an end-of-line marker.

- The *EBCDIC* (Extended Binary Coded Decimal Interchange Code) data type is used for transferring text files between two or more host systems that use EBCDIC as their internal character set. Technically, the ASCII and EBCDIC data types are the same except for the character set that they use.

- The *Image* data type is the one most commonly used to transfer binary files such as images and applications (and .ZIP files, Word .DOCs, and so on). Transferred as a sequential stream of bytes, this data type makes no assumptions about the target platform and the internal word structure that the platform uses. All FTP implementations should support this data type as well as the default ASCII data type.

- The *Local* data type is a byte-based format specific to the local host. The format must make it possible for another system to reconstruct the data according to the original format. For instance, if the first system transfers a file that contains 36-bit floating-point numbers to a 32-bit based server, the server must store the file in a local format that accommodates the original format (for example, the server might store 36-bit floating-point numbers as 64-bit floating-point numbers). This data type is not widely used, and is primarily used by applications that use the FTP protocol to transfer data from one system to another. You need to implement the Local data type only if you are going to transfer data files (with binary or packed numerical values) between unlike systems—a scenario that is becoming more rare each day.

NOTE When developing your applications, you can ignore most of the following two sections on data formats and structures, especially if you are working with a Windows-based system. The default data format and structure are all that you will ever need (at least for the foreseeable future). All these formats and structures were originally defined long before manufacturers began to strive for compatibility among systems. ■

Format Control

The ASCII and EBCDIC data types might have a second optional parameter to specify additional constraints on the data type. When used, this parameter is an additional option included with the data type specification. These additional formatting constraints depend on the intended usage of the file being transferred. Is the file going to be printed, viewed, or fed into a process as input data? The formatting of the file can differ for each of these destinations. The following data formats are being used less frequently (other than the default) as dumb terminals and line printers slowly fall out of usage:

■ The *Non-Print* format is the default for the ASCII and EBCDIC data types. This file format contains no formatting information. You should assume that the format uses standard values for spacing and margins.

■ The *Telnet* format is used for files that a terminal screen is to display. The format contains terminal formatting control characters (such as carriage return, line feed, newline, vertical tab, and form feed) that format the file on the computer display or printer.

■ The *Carriage Control* format contains IBM printer vertical format control characters (see RFC 740). In this format, the first character of each line is not printed. Instead, this character determines the vertical movement of the paper that should take place before the line or record is printed.

Data Structures

The FTP protocol allows for transferring files constructed with three different file structures. These structures are primarily to allow for exchanging files among systems that have different storage structures. Of these three, the first one, the File structure, is the most prevalent and often the only one that most FTP implementations support. Here are the three file structures:

■ The *File* structure treats the file as one continuous sequence of data bytes with no internal structure. This is the default data structure and often the only data structure supported.

■ The *Record* structure is used for files that consist of sequential records. This structure is often used in IBM host systems, but is rarely seen on anything else (these days).

■ The *Page* structure is used for files that are broken into objects of differing sizes, possibly with other information mixed in. The Page Structure includes a header structure that defines the size of each page, followed by the page itself. The page headers contain such information as the logical page number of the data page that it accompanies, but that page number does not necessarily designate the transmitted page sequence.

Transmission Modes

Three modes are used to transfer data between two systems. The first mode is simply the default transmission mode, but the other two make transmissions efficient and recoverable:

■ *Stream,* the default transmission mode, sends the file as a sequential series of bytes; the FTP server or client does not format the file. Because no formatting is involved, the file source has no way to send an end-of-file marker (because the source can make no assumptions about the file structure). To solve this problem, the end of the file is designated by the closing of the data connection.

■ The *block* transmission mode breaks the file into a series of blocks preceded by one or more header bytes. The header bytes contain a count, indicating the number of bytes in the block, and a descriptor code, which can indicate that a particular block is the last in the transmission. This transmission mode allows for recovery of interrupted file transmissions by having the client indicate to restart the transmission at a certain block count (the last one received). For more information on the header formatting and error recovery within FTP, see RFC 959.

■ The *compressed* transmission mode attempts to compress the file to be transmitted by using a simple run-length encoding algorithm. The algorithm reduces repeated characters (bytes) into two sequential bytes. The first byte indicates that the following (second) byte is compressed and the number of times that it should be repeated on expansion. To indicate the compression, the first bit in the control byte (the first byte) is set to one.

If set to zero, the first bit in the control byte indicates that the following bytes are uncompressed. The rest of the control byte specifies the number of uncompressed bytes that follow it. Therefore, the benefits that you gain by compressing repeated characters are not lost on the unrepeated characters.

N O T E Although the least reliable of the three transmission modes, the stream mode is often the only one that FTP implementations support. Stream mode does not provide for any internal retry or error recovery, and depends on the retry and error recovery built in to the sockets' implementation. Therefore, this transmission mode has to assume that packet receipt is in sequential order, and that the end of transmission is indicated by the closing of the data socket connection. ■

Building an FTP Client

The FTP client that you build in this chapter is by no means complete. It simply is a framework that lays the basic foundation and instills an understanding of working with the FTP protocol. You can then extend this framework to develop a complete FTP client application.

This client enables the user to specify an FTP server to which to connect, the user ID to use for logging in (the default is anonymous) and the password to use. On initiating the connection, the FTP client logs in to the specified FTP server, using the specified user ID and password, and displays the current directory and directory listing from the FTP server. The user can then send or receive files to and from the server. On choosing to connect to an FTP server, the FTP client takes the following steps:

1. Connects to the FTP server.
2. Receives a greeting from the server.
3. Sends the USER message with the specified user ID to the server and waits for the response.
4. After receiving the response to the USER command, sends the PASS command with the specified password.
5. After receiving a positive response to the PASS command, requests the current directory name and path by sending the PWD command to the server.
6. After receiving the response to the PWD command, parses the directory and path from the response message and displays it for the user. You then want to display to the user the directory contents, so you have to issue a couple of other commands to prepare to receive the directory listing. The first command that the client issues is the TYPE command, which specifies the ASCII data transfer type.
7. After receiving the response to the TYPE command, places the server into passive mode, so that the client can initiate the data connection. To do so, the application issues the PASV command.
8. After receiving the response to the PASV command, parses the response message to extract and assemble the TCP address and service port to use. The client uses this address and port when creating and connecting the client data socket.
9. After creating the data socket and connecting it to the address specified in the response to the PASV command, sends the LIST command, to get a directory listing from the server.
10. As the data socket receives the directory listing, adds the received text to a list box in which you display the listing to the user.
11. After receiving the positive completion of the directory listing, becomes idle, waiting for the user to select an action to execute.
12. If the user double-clicks the directory listing from the FTP server, examines the selected line to determine whether the user selected a directory or a file. If the user selected a directory, the client sends the server the CWD command, with the directory into which to move.

After receiving the positive response from the CWD command, the client repeats the preceding steps starting with step 5 (issuing the PWD command to the server).

13. If the user selects a file, begins sending a series of commands to the server in preparation for retrieving the selected file. The first of these steps involves sending the TYPE command to the server, specifying the Image data type, then sending the PASV command to the server.

   After the server enters the passive state and the client has established a data socket connection, the client sends the RETR command, specifying the file to retrieve.

   After receiving the preliminary response from the RETR command, the client saves into the specified file all data received over the data connection.

   After receiving the entire file, the client closes the file and data socket and returns to an idle state.

14. If the user selects a file to send to the server, follows much the same steps as in retrieving a file. Instead of sending the RETR command, the client sends the STOR command to the server.

   After receiving the preliminary response to the STOR command, the client opens the selected file and sends it over the data socket connection.

   After sending the entire file, the client closes the data connection and returns to the idle state.

15. If the user presses the Quit button, sends the QUIT command to the server.

16. After receiving the QUIT command, closes the connection.

N O T E   Appendix A, "Internet Applications Command Sets," provides complete explanations of all
FTP commands, including those used in this chapter's example application. ■

In this example, you use the same procedures for looking up the server address and initiating the connection as you used in the previous example in Chapter 6, "Socket Programming with Delphi Using WinSock." Check Chapter 6 to find listings and explanations of any procedures and functions not covered in this chapter. Table 8.1 lists the files used in this project.

Table 8.1   FTP Client Project Files

File	Description
DFTP.DPR	The FTP client Delphi project file.
TFTPC.DFM	The FTP client window.
TFTPC.PAS	The FTP client code.
TSOCKETC.PAS	The TSocket WinSock abstraction class (first developed in Chapter 6 and extended in this chapter).
NWINSOCK.PAS	The WinSock application program interface (API) definition.

In Chapter 6, you began developing the TSocket class, which is an abstraction of the WinSock interface. In building the FTP client application, you add a simple extension to the TSocket object class. Next, you define constants for each of the possible FTP commands that you might issue, so that you can maintain a command designator flag that tells you the command for which you are receiving a response.

Extensions to the *TSocket* Object

The first area to examine consists of a couple of simple extensions to the TSocket object class. The first extension is a function called GetLine(), which traces through the receive buffer and copies the first line of text to another buffer (see Listing 8.1). The function then moves the rest of the receive buffer's contents forward in the buffer, making the next line of text the first line in the receive buffer. Both buffers are null-terminated strings, with a null character (#0) marking the end of each. After moving the data, GetLine() returns a Boolean value indicating whether a complete string was copied into the target buffer (an incomplete string should be completed with the next buffer of data received from the server).

Listing 8.1 TSOCKETC.PAS—the *GetLine()* Function Returns the First Line of Text from the Receive Buffer.

```
function _TSocket.GetLine(TargetString, SourceString: PChar): Boolean;
var
   liCurPos: Integer;
   liCarRetnPos: Integer;
   liCopyPos: Integer;
begin
   {Initialize the position pointer}
   liCurPos := 0;
   {Scan the SourceString buffer until the first carriage-return or
   null character is found, copying the characters into the
   TargetString buffer as you scan}
   while ((SourceString[liCurPos] <> Char(13)) and
          (SourceString[liCurPos] <> Char(0))) do
   begin
      TargetString[liCurPos] := SourceString[liCurPos];
      Inc(liCurPos);
   end;
   {Terminate the TargetString buffer with a null character}
   TargetString[liCurPos] := Char(0);
   {Did you find a carriage-return?}
   if (SourceString[liCurPos] = Char(13)) then
   begin
      {Move everything after the newline character forward, removing
      the copied line from the SourceString buffer}
      liCopyPos := 0;
      if (SourceString[(liCurPos + 1)] = Char(10)) then
      begin
         liCurPos := (liCurPos + 2);
         while (SourceString[liCurPos] <> Char(0)) do
         begin
```

```
            SourceString[liCopyPos] := SourceString[liCurPos];
            Inc(liCurPos);
            Inc(liCopyPos);
        end;
        {Terminate the SourceString buffer}
        SourceString[liCopyPos] := Char(0);
        {Return TRUE to indicate that you are returning a complete line}
        GetLine := TRUE;
    end
    else
    begin
        {The first character after the carriage-return was not a
        newline character, so return FALSE, to indicate that you are
        not returning a complete line}
        SourceString[0] := Char(0);
        GetLine := FALSE;
    end;
  end
  else
  begin
    {You ended on a null character, return FALSE to indicate that you
    are not returning a complete line}
    SourceString[0] := Char(0);
    GetLine := FALSE;
  end;
end;
```

The primary reason for the GetLine() function is to break a large text buffer into single lines of text that (you hope) are small enough to fit within a string variable (255 bytes). After separating each line of text, you can easily examine its contents, manipulate them, and do whatever else you want by using all the string-manipulation routines available in Delphi.

The next extension isn't actually to the TSocket object, but into the basic window framework that you use for several examples to follow (you could easily build this function in to the TSocket object). This function, ClearBuffer(), is quite simple (see Listing 8.2). It travels through a data buffer and cleans all bytes, setting each to the null character (#0). This provides a clean buffer that you can use to retrieve data. Because a null character automatically marks the end of the received data, you don't have to worry about how to find the amount of data that you receive from the server (as long as the expected data is ASCII text).

**Listing 8.2   TFTPC.PAS—the *ClearBuffer()* Procedure Cleans the Receive
Buffer before Receiving More Data from the Server**

```
procedure TFtp.ClearBuffer(DirtyBuffer: Pchar; BufLength: Integer);
var
    liCurPos: Integer;
    lcNullChar: Char;
begin
    {Initialize the position pointer to 0}
    liCurPos := 0;
    {Create a null character}
```

continues

Listing 8.2 Continued

```
   lcNullChar := Char(0);
   {Loop through the entire buffer passed in, setting each character
   equal to the null character}
   while (liCurPos < BufLength) do
   begin
      DirtyBuffer^ := lcNullChar;
      Inc(liCurPos);
      Inc(DirtyBuffer);
   end;
end;
```

Constant and Variable Declarations

To define the constants that maintain this application's state table, you continue to declare the socket state constants (SKT_) and add constants for each of the FTP commands that you want to implement (FTP_). You also want to define a small set of constants to maintain a simple state table for the data connection (FTPD_) defining the small set of states in which the connection might find itself.

Finally, you want to define three user events that various actions trigger (see Listing 8.3). You continue to maintain the SOCKET event, and add a DATASOCKET event, for events that the data connection socket triggers, and add a third ADDRSOCKET event to trigger when an address lookup is complete. If you continued to use the socket states as you did in the example in Chapter 6, you wouldn't need to define a separate event for the address lookup; however, to enable the event handlers to determine which event triggered them, you want them to examine the information that the WinSock interface passes.

Listing 8.3 TFTPC.PAS—Constant Declarations for the FTP Client Application

```
const
{Constant declarations to represent FTP commands. These commands
keep track of the command last issued, so that the server's responses
can be directed to the appropriate procedure}
  FTP_NOOP = 0;
  FTP_CONNECT = 1;
  FTP_USER = 2;
  FTP_PASS = 3;
  FTP_CWD = 4;
  FTP_CDUP = 5;
  FTP_REIN = 6;
  FTP_QUIT = 7;
  FTP_PORT = 8;
  FTP_PASV = 9;
  FTP_TYPE = 10;
  FTP_STRU = 11;
  FTP_MODE = 12;
  FTP_RETR = 13;
```

```
FTP_STOR = 14;
FTP_STOU = 15;
FTP_APPE = 16;
FTP_REST = 17;
FTP_RNFR = 18;
FTP_RNTO = 19;
FTP_ABOR = 20;
FTP_DELE = 21;
FTP_RMD = 22;
FTP_MKD = 23;
FTP_PWD = 24;
FTP_LIST = 25;
FTP_NLST = 26;
FTPD_NOOP = 0;
FTPD_WAITFORCONN = 1;
FTPD_SEND = 2;
FTPD_RECV = 3;
FTPD_RECVDISP = 4;
{User-defined event declarations, for socket events. The first
is used for the primary socket, the second for the data socket,
and the third for address lookup notifications}
  UWM_SOCKETEVENT = WM_USER + 500;
  UWM_DATASOCKETEVENT = WM_USER + 501;
  UWM_ADDRSOCKETEVENT = WM_USER + 502;
```

In the variable declarations, you need to declare two sockets: one for the command connection and another for the data connection. For the main client application, you use two status indicators: one to indicate the current command being processed and the other to indicate the eventual target command (because to issue some commands, you must first issue one or more intermediate commands). You also declare a status indicator for the data connection, as well as status indicators to maintain the data transfer type and to indicate whether the data file is open.

Other declarations are the event handlers for the three socket events that you defined in the constants section, and three data buffers for sending and receiving data over the socket connections. The last declaration of interest is the file handle, which is the input and output file for all the application's file transfer operations. Listing 8.4 shows all these declarations.

N O T E Only the two buffers that the sockets use directly are actually necessary; the third could be a local variable within the functions and procedures that use it. You declare this third buffer to ensure that if a function or procedure declares a large array as a local variable, that array can fill and trash the program stack (especially if you are using the 16-bit version of Delphi). ■

Listing 8.4 TFTPC.PAS—the Variable Declarations for the FTP Client Application

```
private
  { Private declarations }
  {The command and data sockets}
  isConnectionSocket: _SOCKET;
```

continues

Listing 8.4 Continued

```
    isDataSocket: _SOCKET;
    {A Boolean flag that indicates whether the connection has been
    established}
    ibConnected: Boolean;
    {The command status flag, used to keep track of the last command
    so that responses can be routed to the correct processing
    procedure}
    iiFtpStatus: Integer;
    {The next variable is a command status flag that indicates which
    command the application is going to be issuing. Use this flag
    when you have to send some commands to the server to prepare for
    the command that this variable holds.}
    iiFtpWorkingToward: Integer;
    {The data connection status flag}
    iiDataConnStatus: Integer;
    {The data type of the data connection}
    isDataConnType: Char;
    {A flag to indicate whether the transfer file is open
    (for either sending or receiving)}
    ibFileOpen: boolean;
    {The name of the file being sent or received}
    isFileName: String;
    {The amount of data in the data transfer buffer}
    iiBufferAmt: Integer;
    {The socket event handlers}
    procedure UWMSocketEvent(var Msg: TMessage);
                message UWM_SOCKETEVENT;
    procedure UWMDataSocketEvent(var Msg: TMessage);
                message UWM_DATASOCKETEVENT;
    procedure UWMAddrSocketEvent(var Msg: TMessage);
                message UWM_ADDRSOCKETEVENT;
public
    { Public declarations }
    {The TSocket object}
    NetSocket: _TSocket;
    {Your receive and transfer buffers}
    ReceiveBuffer: array[0..8192] of Char;
    TempBuffer: array[0..8192] of Char;
    TransferBuffer: array[0..8192] of Char;
    {The file being transferred}
    TransferFile: File of Byte;
    {The Internet address and port of the server's data socket}
    DataAddress: String;
```

Data Communications Support

Before getting involved in the command communications, you build the supporting structure for the data channel communications. To start, you implement a special-purpose extension to the TSocket object. This extension creates a data communications socket using the same address and port as the communications socket that is already open.

Creating the Data Communications Socket The `CreateDataSocket()` function creates your data communications socket (see Listing 8.5). The function starts by using the `getsockname()` WinSock function to get the address and port that the command socket uses. Next you create a new socket for the data communications channel. `CreateDataSocket()` gets the socket option (using the `getsockname()` WinSock function) on the new socket that specifies whether the socket can be bound to an address already in use. Then you use the `setsockopt()` WinSock function to set that same option to enable you to bind it to an address that is in use. As soon as you can, you use the WinSock `bind()` function to bind the new socket to the same address and TCP port as the command socket is using. If any errors have occurred, you close the new socket and display the appropriate error message. If everything succeeds, you set the new socket into asynchronous mode by telling the `WSAAsyncSelect()` WinSock function to trigger the event that was passed to the window whose handle was passed on just about every available event.

Listing 8.5   TSOCKETC.PAS—the *TSocket* Object Function Creates the Data Communications Socket

```
function _TSocket.CreateDataSocket(CommandSocket: _SOCKET; hWnd: Thandle;
   wMsg: Word): _SOCKET;
var
   NewSock: _SOCKET;
   liSockaddrSize: Integer;
   lsSockVal: array[0..10] of Char;
   liSockValLen: Integer;
begin
   liSockaddrSize := SizeOf(sockaddr);
{Get the address and port that the command socket is using}
   if (getsockname(CommandSocket, isa_sockaddr,
        liSockaddrSize) = 0) then
   begin
      {Create a new socket to use as the data socket}
      NewSock := CreateSocket;
      if (NewSock <> INVALID_SOCKET) then
      begin
         liSockValLen := 10;
      end;
   end
   else
      {You couldn't get the command socket address}
      NewSock := INVALID_SOCKET;
   {Return the data socket}
   CreateDataSocket := NewSock;
end;
```

Now you implement the equivalent function in the FTP client application (see Listing 8.6). This function, however, is much simpler than its predecessor. It calls the `TSocket` `CreateDataSocket()` function—passing the command socket, the window handle, and the `DATASOCKET` event identifier—and lets that function do all the work. Once the function returns, you check the result (to ensure that the socket is valid) and set the data communications status into the "waiting for a connection" state.

Listing 8.6   TFTPC.PAS—the *CreateDataSocket()* Function Creates the Data Communications Socket

```
function TFtp.CreateDataSocket: boolean;
begin
  {Create the data socket}
  isDataSocket := NetSocket.CreateDataSocket(isConnectionSocket, handle,
   UWM_DATASOCKETEVENT);
  {Did you get a valid socket?}
  if (isDataSocket = INVALID_SOCKET) then
     {No, return FALSE}
     CreateDataSocket := FALSE
  else
  begin
     {Yes, set the data socket status to show that it is waiting for a
     connection, then return TRUE}
     iiDataConnStatus := FTPD_WAITFORCONN;
     CreateDataSocket := TRUE;
  end;
end;
```

N O T E   To comply completely with the FTP definition, you must set the data socket into "listen" mode and wait for the FTP server to connect to it. To accept this connection, you would use the accept() WinSock function. Instead, to simplify the implementation of this FTP client, you use "passive" mode for all the application's data channel communications. Therefore, your data communications socket performs all the connections between the client and server. ■

Opening the Data Communications Connection   Your application connects the data socket to the port that the server specifies, so you need to implement another extension to the TSocket object to make this connection. This function is almost identical to the OpenSocketConnection()function that you implemented in Chapter 6, but assumes either that the socket is already in asynchronous mode or that the socket doesn't need to be in that mode (see Listing 8.7).

Listing 8.7   TSOCKETC.PAS—the *OpenDataSocketConnection()* Procedure Opens the Data Communications Connection

```
procedure _TSocket.OpenDataSocketConnection(hWnd: THandle;  wMsg: Word;
   NewSocket: _SOCKET; HostAddr: String; ConnectPort: Integer);
var
   lcAddress: PChar;
   llAddress: LongInt;
begin
   {Check to ensure that you have received a valid socket}
   if (NewSocket <> INVALID_SOCKET) then
```

```
  begin
    {Specify the connection protocol, port, and address}
    isa_SocketAddress.sin_family := AF_INET;
    isa_SocketAddress.sin_port := htons(ConnectPort);
    lcAddress := StrAlloc(Length(HostAddr) + 1);
    StrPCopy(lcAddress, HostAddr);
    llAddress := inet_addr(lcAddress);
    StrDispose(lcAddress);
    isa_SocketAddress.sin_addr.s_addr := llAddress;
    isa_SocketAddress.sin_zero[0] := Char(0);
    {Connect the socket to the data socket on the FTP server}
    if (connect(NewSocket, isa_SocketAddress, 16) = SOCKET_ERROR) then
    begin
      {If you received an error, inform the user}
      if (WSAGetLastError <> WSAEWOULDBLOCK) then
        ShowMessage(SocketError);
    end;
  end;
end;
```

The FTP client's equivalent function, OpenDataConnection(), is longer but much simpler
(see Listing 8.8). The function's first part parses the address string. The server returns
this string when the function sends the application into passive mode. The function
reassembles the string as a standard notation Internet address that you can pass to the
OpenDataSocketConnection() procedure. The function's next part parses the port
number and assembles it into an integer value. The function's final action is to call the
OpenDataSocketConnection() procedure, passing it the data communication socket, server
address, and port number to use. The application triggers the DATASOCKET event after making
this connection.

**Listing 8.8 TFTPC.PAS—the *OpenDataConnection()* Procedure Opens the
Data Socket Connection with the FTP Server**

```
procedure TFtp.OpenDataConnection(ConnectionAddr: String);
var
   liPort: Integer;
   lsAddress: String;
   lsPortHigh, lsPortLow: String;
   liPosComma: Integer;
begin
   {Convert the server data socket address into a usable address}
   {First, convert the first four numbers into the standard
    ###.###.###.### notation}
   liPosComma := Pos(',', ConnectionAddr);
   if (liPosComma > 0) then
   begin
      lsAddress := Copy(ConnectionAddr, 1, (liPosComma - 1)) + '.';
      ConnectionAddr := Copy(ConnectionAddr, (liPosComma + 1),
                Length(ConnectionAddr));
```

continues

Listing 8.8   Continued

```
   end;
   liPosComma := Pos(',', ConnectionAddr);
   if (liPosComma > 0) then
   begin
      lsAddress := lsAddress + Copy(ConnectionAddr, 1,
                 (liPosComma - 1)) + '.';
      ConnectionAddr := Copy(ConnectionAddr, (liPosComma + 1),
                 Length(ConnectionAddr));
   end;
   liPosComma := Pos(',', ConnectionAddr);
   if (liPosComma > 0) then
   begin
      lsAddress := lsAddress + Copy(ConnectionAddr, 1,
                 (liPosComma - 1)) + '.';
      ConnectionAddr := Copy(ConnectionAddr, (liPosComma + 1),
                 Length(ConnectionAddr));
   end;
   liPosComma := Pos(',', ConnectionAddr);
   if (liPosComma > 0) then
   begin
      lsAddress := lsAddress + Copy(ConnectionAddr, 1, (liPosComma - 1));
      ConnectionAddr := Copy(ConnectionAddr, (liPosComma + 1),
                 Length(ConnectionAddr));
   end;
   {Now take the last two numbers and combine them into the port number}
   liPosComma := Pos(',', ConnectionAddr);
   if (liPosComma > 0) then
   begin
      {The first number is the high byte, the second is the low}
      lsPortHigh := Copy(ConnectionAddr, 1, (liPosComma - 1));
      lsPortLow := Copy(ConnectionAddr, (liPosComma + 1),
                 Length(ConnectionAddr));
      {Combine the two, shifting the high byte to the left 8 bits}
      liPort := (StrToInt(lsPortHigh) shl 8) + StrToInt(lsPortLow);
   end;
   {Open the data socket connection, using the address and port
    that you just extracted from the message that the server returned}
   NetSocket.OpenDataSocketConnection(handle, UWM_DATASOCKETEVENT,
              isDataSocket, lsAddress, liPort);
end;
```

Closing the Data Communications Connection   The last connection procedure that you need to implement for the data socket is CloseDataConnection() (see Listing 8.9). This procedure calls the WinSock shutdown() function to clean up and flush any residual buffers that haven't been sent yet. When shutdown() returns, CloseDataConnection() calls the TSocket procedure CloseSocketConnection() to close the data socket. Therefore, you must re-create the data socket the next time that you need it for a subsequent data transfer. After shutting down the data socket, you check whether the transfer file is open. If so, you close it. Your file transfer is then complete.

Listing 8.9 TFTPC.PAS—the *CloseDataConnection()* Procedure Closes the Data Communications Connection

```
procedure TFtp.CloseDataConnection;
begin
  {Shut down the data socket}
  shutdown(isDataSocket, 2);
  {Close the data socket}
  NetSocket.CloseSocketConnection(isDataSocket);
  {If you are working with an open file, close it}
  if ((iiDataConnStatus = FTPD_SEND) or
     (iiDataConnStatus = FTPD_RECV)) then
  begin
     if ibFileOpen then
     begin
        CloseFile(TransferFile);
        ibFileOpen := FALSE;
     end;
  end;
end;
```

Initiating the Data Transfer After making the data connection, you must trigger the command for which you initiated the data connection. To do so, you check the iiFtpWorkingToward status indicator. You then send the appropriate command and trigger a receive on the command socket. For instance, if you want a directory listing from the server, you would establish the data connection and then send the LIST command to the server. You would do the same to send a file with the STOR command, or to receive a file with the RETR command. Listing 8.10 shows the ProcessDataConnection procedure, which performs each of these tasks.

Listing 8.10 TFTPC.PAS—the *ProcessDataConnection* Procedure Initiates the Data Transfer over the Data Communications Channel

```
procedure TFtp.ProcessDataConnect;
var
   lsReplyMsg, lsRetnCode: String;
   lbProceed: boolean;
   liAddrStart, liAddrEnd: Integer;
begin
   {What command do you want to send?}
   case iiFtpWorkingToward of
      {You want to send a LIST command}
      FTP_LIST:
      begin
         {Set the command status flag to LIST and send the LIST command
         to the server}
         iiFtpStatus := FTP_LIST;
         NetSocket.SocketSend(isConnectionSocket, handle,
            UWM_SOCKETEVENT,'LIST', SKT_SENDPACKET);
```

continues

Listing 8.10 Continued

```
            end;
            {You want to send an NLST command}
            FTP_NLST:
            begin
               {Set the command status flag to NLST and send the NLST command
               to the server}
               iiFtpStatus := FTP_NLST;
               NetSocket.SocketSend(isConnectionSocket, handle,
                  UWM_SOCKETEVENT,'NLST', SKT_SENDPACKET);
            end;
            {You want to send an RETR command}
            FTP_RETR:
            begin
               {Set the command status flag to RETR and send the RETR command
               to the server}
               iiFtpStatus := FTP_RETR;
               NetSocket.SocketSend(isConnectionSocket, handle,
                  UWM_SOCKETEVENT,'RETR ' + isFileName, SKT_SENDPACKET);
            end;
            {You want to send a STOR command}
            FTP_STOR:
            begin
               {Set the command status flag to STOR and send the STOR command
               to the server}
               iiFtpStatus := FTP_STOR;
               NetSocket.SocketSend(isConnectionSocket, handle,
                  UWM_SOCKETEVENT, 'STOR ' + isFileName, SKT_SENDPACKET);
            end;
         end;
      {Clear the receive buffer}
      ClearBuffer(ReceiveBuffer, 8192);
   end;
```

Sending the Data The `ProcessDataSend` procedure is relatively simple (see Listing 8.11). This procedure is triggered by the completion of the previous send. You read in a suitable amount from the file being sent into the transfer buffer, then pass the buffer to the `TSocket` `SocketSendBuffer` procedure (which is essentially the same as the `SocketSend` procedure, except that it doesn't affect the socket's asynchronous mode and doesn't add an end-of-line marker to the end of the buffer).

Listing 8.11 TFTPC.PAS—the *ProcessDataSend* Procedure Reads Data from the Local File and Sends It to the Server over the Data Communication Channel

```
procedure TFtp.ProcessDataSend;
var
   liCurByteCount: Integer;
   lcCurByte: Byte;
   lpTransferDataPointer: PChar;
```

```
begin
    {Is the data file open?}
    if ibFileOpen then
    begin
        {Initialize the counter to keep track of how much you have sent}
        liCurByteCount := 0;
        {Are you at the end of the file?}
        if (not Eof(TransferFile)) then
        begin
            {No, clear the data transfer buffer}
            ClearBuffer(TransferBuffer, 8192);
            {Read the next 4,096 bytes from the file into the transfer
            buffer}
            while ((liCurByteCount < 4096) and (not Eof(TransferFile))) do
            begin
                Read(TransferFile, lcCurByte);
                TransferBuffer[liCurByteCount] := Char(lcCurByte);
                Inc(liCurByteCount);
            end;
            {Send to the server the data transfer buffer's contents}
            NetSocket.SocketSendBuffer(isDataSocket, handle,
                    UWM_DATASOCKETEVENT,
                    TransferBuffer, liCurByteCount, SKT_SENDPACKET);
        end
        else
            {You are at the end of the file, so close the data connection}
            CloseDataConnection;
    end;
end;
```

Receiving the Data The only major procedure left to implement for the data communications channel is that which receives data from the server. This procedure must work in either ASCII or Image (or binary) mode.

You need not worry about capturing how much data you have received because the amount of data that was received is easy to determine. If you receive data in ASCII mode, the first null character (#0) that you find in the data buffer helps you easily determine how much data you have received. Therefore, the procedure enables you to perform an asynchronous data transfer in which you trigger this procedure each time that the transfer buffer receives any data to store.

If you are receiving data in Image mode, however, the same rules do not apply. Any bytes being transferred can be the null character, so you cannot use that character as your indicator. Your easiest option is to take the data socket out of asynchronous mode and use a blocking recv() WinSock call to receive all your data. This function returns the number of bytes that were loaded into the data buffer, so you know how many bytes to write out to the file. After receiving an empty buffer, you can reasonably assume that you have received all the file and can close the data socket. (To be sure, you should probably check with the result code that the command socket sends, or you can check whether the server closed the data socket. In Appendix A, you can find the appropriate result codes listed with the FTP commands.)

Listing 8.12 shows `ProcessDataReceive`, the procedure that receives data from the server for your application.

 If you take the time to implement this procedure using the ideal design, you would spin off the data communications as a separate thread. Then you could use blocking socket functions as much as you want, without affecting the user's ability to interact with the command-level interface or other applications that the computer might be running. This approach is possible only with the Delphi 2.0 32-bit version. Multithreading is not available under Windows 3.1. For information on building multithreading applications, read the documentation for the `TThread` component in the Delphi 2.0 documentation. You can probably also learn about threaded application development in some of the newer Delphi 2.0 books on the market.

Listing 8.12   TFTPC.PAS—the *ProcessDataReceive* Procedure Reads Data from the Receive Buffer and Writes It to a File or List Box

```
procedure TFtp.ProcessDataReceive;
var
   lsTempStr: String;
   liTempBytes: Integer;
   liRecvBytes: Integer;
begin
{Is your data connection in ASCII mode?}
   if (isDataConnType = 'A') then
   begin
      {Yes, you are probably going to be sending this data to the display
      so that the user can view it}
      {Did you receive any data?}
      if (TransferBuffer[0] <> Char(0)) then
      begin
         {Until you reach the end of the received data, extract each line
         from the received data}
         while (NetSocket.GetLine(TempBuffer, TransferBuffer)) do
         begin
            {Convert the line into a Pascal string and add it to the
            list box so that the user can view it}
            lsTempStr := Strpas(TempBuffer);
            if (iiDataConnStatus = FTPD_RECVDISP) then
            begin
               lbHostFiles.Items.Add(lsTempStr);
               lbHostFiles.Update;
            end;
         end;
         {Clear the data transfer buffer}
         ClearBuffer(TransferBuffer, 8192);
      end
      else
      begin
         {You didn't receive anything, so close the connection and send
         the application into idle mode}
         CloseDataConnection;
```

```
                    iiDataConnStatus := FTPD_NOOP;
                    {Send an ABOR command to abort the transfer}
                    iiFtpStatus := FTP_ABOR;
                    NetSocket.SocketSend(isConnectionSocket, handle,
                        UWM_SOCKETEVENT, 'ABOR', SKT_SENDPACKET);
                    {Clear the command transfer buffer}
                    ClearBuffer(ReceiveBuffer, 8192);
                end;
        end
        else
        begin
            {You must have your data connection in IMAGE mode.
             Is is the transfer file open?}
            if ibFileOpen then
            begin
                {Set the data socket into synchronous mode}
                WSAAsyncSelect(isDataSocket, handle, 0, 0);
                {Receive the first set of data}
                liRecvBytes := recv(isDataSocket, TransferBuffer, 8192, 0);
                {Did you receive anything?}
                if (liRecvBytes >= 0) then
                begin
                    {As long as you continue to receive data, loop}
                    while (liRecvBytes > 0) do
                    begin
                        {Write what you have received to the file}
                        for liTempBytes := 0 to (liRecvBytes - 1) do
                        begin
                            Write(TransferFile, Byte(TransferBuffer[liTempBytes]));
                        end;
                        {Clear the data transfer buffer}
                        ClearBuffer(TransferBuffer, 8192);
                        {Receive the next set of data}
                        liRecvBytes := recv(isDataSocket, TransferBuffer,
                            8192, 0);
                    end;
                end;
                {Close the data socket connection}
                CloseDataConnection;
                iiDataConnStatus := FTPD_NOOP;
            end;
        end;
    end;
```

Implementing the Event Handler The only thing left in your data communications model is the DATASOCKET event handler (see Listing 8.13). If you read carefully the WSAAsyncSelect function documentation (in the companion CD's WinSock specification), you notice that the event ID that triggered the event is passed in the low half of the LParam. This enables you to implement this event handler by building a case statement off of the LParamLo element of the Msg object that the procedure received.

Listing 8.13   TFTPC.PAS—the *UWMDataSocketEvent()* Procedure Handles the *DATASOCKETEVENT* Event

```
procedure TFtp.UWMDataSocketEvent(var Msg: TMessage);
begin
   {Which data socket event message did you receive? Call the appropriate
   procedure to handle the event}
   case Msg.LParamLo of
      FD_READ: ProcessDataReceive;
      FD_WRITE: ProcessDataSend;
      FD_OOB: ;
      FD_ACCEPT: AcceptDataConnection;
      FD_CONNECT: ProcessDataConnect;
      FD_CLOSE: CloseDataConnection;
   end;
end;
```

CAUTION

The WSAAsyncSelect() documentation (in the companion CD's WinSock specification) states that the socket connection event sends two event messages to the event handler: an FD_CONNECT and an FD_WRITE event message. If you are using the debugger to step through this case statement in the event handler, you see only the FD_CONNECT message, because it arrives first and the debugger loses the FD_WRITE message. The FD_WRITE message arrives while you are stepping through code and is no longer in the message queue when you press the run button. If you immediately press the run button when stopping for the FD_CONNECT message, you probably will see the FD_WRITE message arrive. Don't ignore these two event messages. You must code your FD_WRITE event-handling routines to handle this initial event before your application sends any messages to the server. (Note that the ProcessDataSend procedure in Listing 8.11 includes checks to ensure that the transfer file is open.)

Command Communications Support

Now that you have finished your data communications channel, you need to turn your attention to implementing the command channel. The data channel discussion ended with the data socket event-routing routine. This discussion of the command channel begins with the corresponding procedures. Most of the basic event procedures remain unchanged from the first example, in Chapter 6. The connect and send procedures are basically unchanged, and you use synchronous mode for sending commands, then switch back into asynchronous mode to receive the replies. The command messages that you send are quite small, so sending a message should not take a noticeable amount of time. Although the replies that you receive are still small, receiving them could take a while (especially if the server is far away over the Internet).

The FD_READ event determines the appropriate procedure for processing the received response. You use a simple implementation model that uses a case statement built on the client application's current command state. This way, you can call the appropriate routine to process the reply that you receive from the server without overcomplicating your code. Listing 8.14 shows the WinSock event handler and the FD_READ processing procedure.

Part
II

Ch
8

Listing 8.14 TFTPC.PAS—the *ProcessHostReceive* and *SOCKETEVENT* Event-Processing Procedures Handle the Incoming WinSock Event Message and Route the Application Processing to the Appropriate Procedure

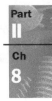

```pascal
procedure TFtp.ProcessHostReceive;
var
   lsRetnStr: String;
   liCarRetnPos: Integer;
begin
   try
      {Receive the incoming data}
      liCarRetnPos := recv(isConnectionSocket, ReceiveBuffer, 8192, 0);
      ReceiveBuffer[liCarRetnPos] := char(0);
      {Have you received anything?}
      if (ReceiveBuffer[0] = Char(0)) then
      begin
         {No, be sure and clear the command receive buffer}
         ClearBuffer(ReceiveBuffer, 8192);
      end
      else
      begin
         {What was the FTP command to which this is a response? Call the
         appropriate procedure to process the response}
         case iiFtpStatus of
            FTP_NOOP: ProcessHostNOOP;
            FTP_CONNECT: ProcessHostWelcome;
            FTP_USER: ProcessHostLogin;
            FTP_PASS: ProcessHostPassword;
            FTP_CWD: ProcessHostCWD;
            FTP_CDUP:;
            FTP_REIN:;
            FTP_QUIT: ProcessHostQuit;
            FTP_PORT: ProcessHostPort;
            FTP_PASV: ProcessHostPasv;
            FTP_TYPE: ProcessHostType;
            FTP_STRU:;
            FTP_MODE:;
            FTP_RETR: ProcessHostRetr;
            FTP_STOR: ProcessHostStor;
            FTP_STOU:;
            FTP_APPE:;
            FTP_REST:;
            FTP_RNFR:;
            FTP_RNTO:;
            FTP_ABOR: ProcessHostAbort;
            FTP_DELE:;
            FTP_RMD:;
            FTP_MKD:;
            FTP_PWD: ProcessHostPWD;
            FTP_LIST: ProcessHostList;
            FTP_NLST: ProcessHostNList;
         end;
      end;
   except
```

continues

Listing 8.14   Continued

```
        {Clear the receive buffer}
        ClearBuffer(ReceiveBuffer, 8192);
    end;
end;

{This is the command socket event handler}
procedure TFtp.UWMSocketEvent(var Msg: TMessage);
begin
    {What command socket event message did you receive? Call the
    appropriate procedure to handle the event}
    case Msg.LParamLo of
        FD_READ: ProcessHostReceive;
        FD_WRITE: ProcessHostSend;
        FD_CONNECT: ProcessHostConnect;
        FD_CLOSE: ;
    end;
end;
```

The SOCKET event handler in Listing 8.14 is essentially the same as the one that you use for the DATASOCKET event handler. The major difference is that you omit the FD_ACCEPT event; you don't need this event in this event handler because you will always be initiating the connections.

Login and Logout Processing

The ProcessHostWelcome event-handling routine establishes a functional format that you use for most of the rest of the command-response routines. The routine first parses the response code. You then pass the response code through a case statement of all of that command's possible reply codes and set flags based on the response. The routine initiates the appropriate follow-up action based on the flags' values. Often, this follow-up action is to send another command to the server and tell the command socket to wait for the response.

ProcessHostWelcome is concerned with only one condition: whether you were connected or rejected (see Listing 8.15). If connected, you must follow up by beginning the login procedure. To do so, you send the USER command to the server.

Listing 8.15   TFTPC.PAS—the *ProcessHostWelcome* Procedure Verifies That the Connection Has Been Made and Initiates the Login Procedure

```
procedure TFtp.ProcessHostWelcome;
var
    lsWelcomeMsg, lsRetnCode: String;
begin
    {Convert the response into a Pascal string}
    lsWelcomeMsg := StrPas(ReceiveBuffer);
    {Extract the response code}
    lsRetnCode := Copy(lsWelcomeMsg, 1, 3);
    {What response code was received, are you connected?}
```

```
   case StrToInt(lsRetnCode) of
      120: ibConnected := FALSE;
      220: ibConnected := TRUE;
      421: ibConnected := FALSE;
   end;
   iiFtpStatus := FTP_NOOP;
   {Display the response message}
   stStatus.Caption := lsWelcomeMsg;
   stStatus.Update;
   {Are you connected?}
   if ibConnected then
   begin
      {Send the USER command with the user ID
       that the application's user supplied}
      iiFtpStatus := FTP_USER;
      NetSocket.SocketSend(isConnectionSocket, handle, UWM_SOCKETEVENT,
         'USER ' + sleLogin.Text, SKT_SENDPACKET);
      {Clear the receive buffer}
      ClearBuffer(ReceiveBuffer, 8192);
   end;
end;
```

The login procedure continues receiving the response to the USER command. You can either continue logging in using the same USER name, in which case you probably must send a password next, or you simply cannot proceed, in which case you might as well disconnect until the user enters a new user ID and restarts the connection process.

 NOTE Appendix A includes a reference section that lists all the available FTP commands that the FTP client can issue, including those discussed in the following implementations. ■

If you find yourself logged in with an acceptable user name and password, you probably next want to determine where you are in the server file system. To do so, you issue the PWD command and await the response (see Listing 8.16).

Listing 8.16   TFTPC.PAS—the *ProcessHostLogin* and *ProcessHostPassword* Procedures Ensure That the User Is Logged into the FTP Server and Then Request the Current Working Directory

```
procedure TFtp.ProcessHostLogin;
var
   lsReplyMsg, lsRetnCode: String;
   lbProceed: boolean;
begin
   lbProceed := FALSE;
   {Convert the response into a Pascal string}
   lsReplyMsg := StrPas(ReceiveBuffer);
   {Extract the response code}
   lsRetnCode := Copy(lsReplyMsg, 1, 3);
```

continues

Listing 8.16   Continued

```
      {What response code was received? Was the command successful?}
      case StrToInt(lsRetnCode) of
         230: lbProceed := TRUE;
         331: lbProceed := TRUE;
         332: ibConnected := FALSE;
         421: ibConnected := FALSE;
         500:;
         501:;
         530:;
      end;
      iiFtpStatus := FTP_NOOP;
      {Display the response message}
      stStatus.Caption := lsReplyMsg;
      stStatus.Update;
      {Was the command successful?}
      if lbProceed then
      begin
         {Send the PASS command with the password
          that the application's user supplied}
         iiFtpStatus := FTP_PASS;
         NetSocket.SocketSend(isConnectionSocket, handle, UWM_SOCKETEVENT,
             'PASS ' + slePassword.Text, SKT_SENDPACKET);
         {Clear the receive buffer}
            ClearBuffer(ReceiveBuffer, 8192);
         end;
      {If you are no longer connected, close the socket}
      if not ibConnected then
         NetSocket.CloseSocketConnection(isConnectionSocket);
end;

procedure TFtp.ProcessHostPassword;
var
   lsReplyMsg, lsRetnCode: String;
   lbProceed: boolean;
begin
   lbProceed := FALSE;
   {Convert the response into a Pascal string}
   lsReplyMsg := StrPas(ReceiveBuffer);
   {Extract the response code}
   lsRetnCode := Copy(lsReplyMsg, 1, 3);
   {What response code was received? Was the command successful?}
   case StrToInt(lsRetnCode) of
      202: lbProceed := TRUE;
      230: lbProceed := TRUE;
      332: ibConnected := FALSE;
      421: ibConnected := FALSE;
      500:;
      501:;
      503:;
      530:;
```

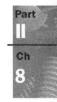

```
   end;
   iiFtpStatus := FTP_NOOP;
   {Display the response message}
   stStatus.Caption := lsReplyMsg;
   stStatus.Update;
   {Was the command successful?}
   if lbProceed then
   begin
      {Send the PWD command}
      iiFtpStatus := FTP_PWD;
      NetSocket.SocketSend(isConnectionSocket, handle, UWM_SOCKETEVENT,
         'PWD', SKT_SENDPACKET);
      {Clear the receive buffer}
         ClearBuffer(ReceiveBuffer, 8192);
   {end;
   {If you are no longer connected, close the socket}
   if not ibConnected then
      NetSocket.CloseSocketConnection(isConnectionSocket);
end;
```

N O T E If you are logging into an FTP server as an anonymous user, the server is likely to request that you use your e-mail address as your password. The system captures and logs this address to give the system administrator a record of who has been connecting to the server. If the server does not allow anonymous logins, it will reject the USER command. The command connection will still be active and you can resubmit the USER command with a valid user login name. ■

Getting a Server Directory Listing

After receiving the response to the PWD command, you want to parse the directory path and display it to the user. Then you will probably want to display a listing of the directory contents. You want to issue a couple of other commands before issuing the LIST or NLST command, so you set the "working toward" flag to indicate that you want eventually to issue the desired one of these two commands. Meanwhile, you issue the TYPE command to ensure that the data connection is in ASCII mode. Listing 8.17 shows the ProcessHostPWD procedure, which performs these tasks.

N O T E Requesting the directory listing is one of the first actions that your FTP client performs after successfully connecting to an FTP server. Technically, you need not issue the TYPE command at that time because the default data type is ASCII. Keep in mind, however, that you can reissue the LIST or NLST command after performing other transactions that might set the data type to one of the other available types. Therefore, you want to issue the TYPE command to ensure that you are in ASCII mode. ■

Listing 8.17   TFTPC.PAS—the *ProcessHostPWD* Procedure Displays the Current Working Directory and Starts the Process of Retrieving the Directory Contents

```
procedure TFtp.ProcessHostPWD;
var
    lsReplyMsg, lsRetnCode: String;
    lbProceed: boolean;
    liDirStart, liDirEnd: Integer;
begin
    lbProceed := FALSE;
    {Convert the response into a Pascal string}
    lsReplyMsg := StrPas(ReceiveBuffer);
    {Extract the response code}
    lsRetnCode := Copy(lsReplyMsg, 1, 3);
    {What response code was received? Was the command successful?}
    case StrToInt(lsRetnCode) of
        257: lbProceed := TRUE;
        421: ibConnected := FALSE;
        500:;
        501:;
        502:;
        550:;
    end;
    iiFtpStatus := FTP_NOOP;
    {Display the response message}
    stStatus.Caption := lsReplyMsg;
    stStatus.Update;
    {Was the command successful?}
    if lbProceed then
    begin
        iiFtpStatus := FTP_NOOP;
        {Parse the directory name and path from the response message and
        display it for the user}
        liDirStart := Pos('"', lsReplyMsg);
        if (liDirStart > 0) then
        begin
            lsRetnCode := Copy(lsReplyMsg, (liDirStart + 1),
                        Length(lsReplyMsg));
            liDirEnd := Pos('"', lsRetnCode);
            if (liDirEnd > 0) then
                lsRetnCode := Copy(lsRetnCode, 1, (liDirEnd - 1));
            stHostPath.Caption := lsRetnCode;
        end;
        {Send the TYPE command, specifying ASCII data type}
        iiFtpStatus := FTP_TYPE;
        {You eventually want to send want to send a LIST command}
        iiFtpWorkingToward := FTP_LIST;
        isDataConnType := 'A';
        NetSocket.SocketSend(isConnectionSocket, handle, UWM_SOCKETEVENT,
            'TYPE A', SKT_SENDPACKET);
        {Clear the receive buffer}
```

```
            ClearBuffer(ReceiveBuffer, 8192);
    end;
    {If you are no longer connected, close the socket}
    if not ibConnected then
        NetSocket.CloseSocketConnection(isConnectionSocket);
end;
```

After setting the data type to ASCII, you want to do two things: create your data socket and request that the server enter passive mode. You want the server to be in passive mode so that the client application can initiate the data socket connection. Otherwise, the server tries to initiate the connection to the client. It doesn't matter which of these things you do first. The ProcessHostType procedure creates your data socket first, though, so that if something goes wrong and you cannot create the socket (perhaps because you are out of available sockets), you won't place the server into passive mode unnecessarily (see Listing 8.18).

N O T E The primary reason that you place the server into passive mode is that when this example application was tested with a Point-to-Point Protocol (PPP) connection to an Internet access provider, the FTP server failed connect to the client. The FTP server example later in this chapter was tested over a Transmission Control Protocol/Internet Protocol (TCP/IP) network and did not encounter the difficulties in listening for and accepting an incoming connection. The PPP configuration probably caused the problems with this client example; the same set of code works fine on a direct network connection. ■

Listing 8.18   TFTPC.PAS—the *ProcessHostType* Procedure Handles the Response to Setting the Data Type for File Transfers

```
procedure TFtp.ProcessHostType;
var
    lsReplyMsg, lsRetnCode: String;
    lbProceed: boolean;
begin
    lbProceed := FALSE;
    {Convert the response into a Pascal string}
    lsReplyMsg := StrPas(ReceiveBuffer);
    {Extract the response code}
    lsRetnCode := Copy(lsReplyMsg, 1, 3);
    {What response code was received? Was the command successful?}
    case StrToInt(lsRetnCode) of
        200: lbProceed := TRUE;
        421: ibConnected := FALSE;
        500:;
        501:;
        504:;
        530:;
    end;
    iiFtpStatus := FTP_NOOP;
```

continues

Listing 8.18 Continued

```
    {Display the response message}
    stStatus.Caption := lsReplyMsg;
    stStatus.Update;
    {Was the command successful?}
    if lbProceed then
    begin
        iiFtpStatus := FTP_PASV;
        {Create the data socket}
        if CreateDataSocket then
        begin
            {Get the socket address (this is legacy code from when you were
            trying to enable the server to establish the data connection)}
            lsRetnCode := NetSocket.GetSockAddr;
            {Send the PASV command}
            NetSocket.SocketSend(isConnectionSocket, handle,
                UWM_SOCKETEVENT, 'PASV', SKT_SENDPACKET);
            {Clear the receive buffer}
            ClearBuffer(ReceiveBuffer, 8192);
        end
        else
            {You couldn't create the data socket, so place the
            application into idle mode}
            iiFtpStatus := FTP_NOOP;
    end;
    {If you are no longer connected, close the socket}
    if not ibConnected then
        NetSocket.CloseSocketConnection(isConnectionSocket);
end;
```

Now that the server is in passive mode, the ProcessHostPasv procedure must parse the address that the server provided for your data connection (see Listing 8.19). The address returns in the format ###,###,###,###,###,###, where the first four sets of numbers are the TCP address, and the last two are the TCP port of the server's data socket. (See Appendix A for more information on the response to the PASV command.) You can then tell the data socket to connect to the server at the specified address and port.

Listing 8.19 TFTPC.PAS—the *ProcessHostPasv* Procedure Handles the Server's Response to a *PASV* Command

```
procedure TFtp.ProcessHostPasv;
var
    lsReplyMsg, lsRetnCode: String;
    lbProceed: boolean;
    liAddrStart, liAddrEnd: Integer;
begin
    lbProceed := FALSE;
    {Convert the response into a Pascal string}
    lsReplyMsg := StrPas(ReceiveBuffer);
    {Extract the response code}
```

```
    lsRetnCode := Copy(lsReplyMsg, 1, 3);
    {What response code was received? Was the command successful?}
    case StrToInt(lsRetnCode) of
        227: lbProceed := TRUE;
        421: ibConnected := FALSE;
        500:;
        501:;
        502:;
        530:;
    end;
    iiFtpStatus := FTP_NOOP;
    {Display the response message}
    stStatus.Caption := lsReplyMsg;
    stStatus.Update;
    {Was the command successful?}
    if lbProceed then
    begin
        {Find the parentheses that enclose the server data socket address}
        liAddrStart := Pos( '(', lsReplyMsg);
        liAddrEnd := Pos( ')', lsReplyMsg);
        {Extract the server data socket address from the response message}
        DataAddress := Copy(lsReplyMsg, (liAddrStart + 1),
                     (liAddrEnd - (liAddrStart + 1)));
        {Open the data socket connection, using the Internet address
         that you received}
        OpenDataConnection(DataAddress);
    end;
    {If you are no longer connected, close the socket}
    if not ibConnected then
        NetSocket.CloseSocketConnection(isConnectionSocket);
end;
```

As you might recall from your data socket implementation, after the data socket is connected, it issues the desired command over the command socket (refer to Listing 8.10). Therefore, you must to be prepared to start receiving the response to the LIST command. Initially you should receive one of the 100 level response codes, which inform you that the socket is ready to start the data transfer. You initiated the data connection, so you can start receiving data over the data socket. You want to set the data socket to the RECVDISP state so that it displays onscreen all data that it receives (refer to Listing 8.12). Next you tell the data socket to start receiving data, and then tell the command socket to start looking for incoming data.

After receiving all data sent over the data channel, the data socket then closes itself. After sending all the data, the command socket receives a second reply code in response to the LIST command, indicating the success or failure of the data transfer. You don't want to issue any command after LIST, so you put the FTP client application into idle mode and wait for the user to select another action. Listing 8.20 shows ProcessHostList, the procedure that processes the server's response to a LIST command.

Listing 8.20—TFTPC.PAS—the *ProcessHostList* Procedure Processes the Server's Response to a *LIST* Command

```pascal
procedure TFtp.ProcessHostList;
var
   lsReplyMsg, lsRetnCode: String;
   lbProceed: boolean;
   lbDoAccept: boolean;
   lbDone: boolean;
begin
   lbProceed := FALSE;
   lbDone := FALSE;
   lbDoAccept := FALSE;
   {Convert the response into a Pascal string}
   lsReplyMsg := StrPas(ReceiveBuffer);
   {Extract the response code}
   lsRetnCode := Copy(lsReplyMsg, 1, 3);
   {What response code was received? Was the command successful?}
   case StrToInt(lsRetnCode) of
      125: lbProceed := TRUE;
      150:
      begin
         lbDoAccept := TRUE;
         lbProceed := TRUE;
      end;
      226: lbDone := TRUE;
      250: lbDone := TRUE;
      421: ibConnected := FALSE;
      425: lbDone := TRUE;
      426: lbDone := TRUE;
      450: lbDone := TRUE;
      451: lbDone := TRUE;
      500:;
      501:;
      502:;
      530:;
   end;
   {Display the response message}
   stStatus.Caption := lsReplyMsg;
   stStatus.Update;
   {Was the command successful?}
   if not lbProceed then
   begin
      iiFtpStatus := FTP_NOOP;
      lbDone := TRUE;
   end
   else
   begin
      {If the data socket is waiting}
      if ((iiDataConnStatus = FTPD_NOOP) or
```

```
              (iiDataConnStatus = FTPD_WAITFORCONN)) then
        begin
          {Clear the server directory listing list box}
          lbHostFiles.Clear;
          iiDataConnStatus := FTPD_RECVDISP;
          {Clear the transfer buffer}
          ClearBuffer(TransferBuffer, 8192);
        end;
        {Clear the receive buffer}
        ClearBuffer(ReceiveBuffer, 8192);
    end;
    {Are you done?}
    if lbDone then
    begin
        {Close the data socket and wait for the user to decide what to do
        next}
        CloseDataConnection;
        iiFtpStatus := FTP_NOOP;
    end;
    {If you are no longer connected, close the socket}
    if not ibConnected then
        NetSocket.CloseSocketConnection(isConnectionSocket);
end;
```

Sending a File

You now must examine two primary actions: sending and receiving files. Start by sending a file
to the server. After the user specifies the file to send, you probably want to use the TYPE command to set the transmission data type to Image. After you choose this setting, most of the
command path is already built automatically, so about all you have to do is strip the file system
path from the file name and then set the "working toward" flag to the STOR command. (The
"working toward" command flag is a reminder of which command you want to send to the
server after you finish with the commands that you have to send in preparation for your target
command.) After doing these two things, you issue the command that tells the server to set the
data type to Image. You then let the structure already in place handle things until you get to the
response to the initial STOR command. Listing 8.21 shows this sequence of events being triggered with a double-click in the list of files on the client computer.

**Listing 8.21 TFTPC.PAS—the *FileListBox* Double-Click Event-Handling
Procedure Initiates the Process for Sending Files**

```
procedure TFtp.FileListBox1DblClick(Sender: TObject);
var
    lsFile: String;
    lbIsDir: Boolean;
    liSlashChar: Integer;
```

continues

Listing 8.21   Continued

```
begin
   {What is the selected file's name?}
   lsFile := FileListBox1.FileName;
   {Remove all the directory and path information from the file name.
   You do so by looking for each slash character and removing all text
   in front of it (including the slash character)}
   liSlashChar := Pos('\', lsFile);
   while (liSlashChar > 0) do
   begin
      lsFile := Copy(lsFile, (liSlashChar + 1), Length(lsFile));
      liSlashChar := Pos('\', lsFile);
   end;
   {Tell the user that you are sending the selected file}
   stStatus.Caption := 'Sending File - ' + lsFile;
   stStatus.Update;
   isFileName := lsFile;
   {Send the TYPE command, specifying IMAGE data type}
   iiFtpStatus := FTP_TYPE;
   {Set the working toward flag so that you have a reminder
    that you want to send the STOR command after taking
    care of the preparations}
   iiFtpWorkingToward := FTP_STOR;
   isDataConnType := 'I';
   NetSocket.SocketSend(isConnectionSocket, handle, UWM_SOCKETEVENT,
      'TYPE I', SKT_SENDPACKET);
   {Clear the receive buffer}
   ClearBuffer(ReceiveBuffer, 8192);
end;
```

Now that the server has given you the "go ahead" to send the selected file, you need to open the file and then start sending the file through the data socket. To do so, you directly call the ProcessDataSend procedure (refer to Listing 8.11). You then tell the command socket to wait for another response and let the data socket do its job. After the transfer is complete and the data socket is closed, the server sends a second reply to the STOR command, indicating the success or failure of the file transfer. At this point, you return to idle mode and wait for the user to specify another action to perform. Listing 8.22 shows the ProcessHostStor procedure, which initiates the file transfer from the client to the server.

Listing 8.22   TFTPC.PAS—the *ProcessHostStor* Procedure Initiates the Process of Sending Files over the Data Channel

```
procedure TFtp.ProcessHostStor;
var
   lsReplyMsg, lsRetnCode: String;
   lbProceed: boolean;
   lbDoAccept: boolean;
   lbDone: boolean;
```

```
begin
   lbProceed := FALSE;
   lbDone := FALSE;
   lbDoAccept := FALSE;
   {Convert the response into a Pascal string}
   lsReplyMsg := StrPas(ReceiveBuffer);
   {Extract the response code}
   lsRetnCode := Copy(lsReplyMsg, 1, 3);
   {What response code was received? Was the command successful?}
   case StrToInt(lsRetnCode) of
      110: lbProceed := TRUE;
      125: lbProceed := TRUE;
      150:
      begin
         lbDoAccept := TRUE;
         lbProceed := TRUE;
      end;
      226: lbDone := TRUE;
      250: lbDone := TRUE;
      421: ibConnected := FALSE;
      425: lbDone := TRUE;
      426: lbDone := TRUE;
      450: lbDone := TRUE;
      451: lbDone := TRUE;
      452: lbDone := TRUE;
      500:;
      501:;
      530:;
      532:;
      551:;
      552:;
      553:;
   end;
   {Display the response message}
   stStatus.Caption := lsReplyMsg;
   stStatus.Update;
   {Was the command successful?}
   if not lbProceed then
   begin
      iiFtpStatus := FTP_NOOP;
      lbDone := TRUE;
   end
   else
   begin
      {Is the data socket waiting?}
      if ((iiDataConnStatus = FTPD_NOOP) or
          (iiDataConnStatus = FTPD_WAITFORCONN)) then
      begin
         {Set the data socket status to sending}
         iiDataConnStatus := FTPD_SEND;
         {Open the selected file}
         OpenSendFile;
         {Send the file}
         ProcessDataSend;
      end;
```

continues

Listing 8.22   Continued

```
      {Clear the receive buffer}
      ClearBuffer(ReceiveBuffer, 8192);
   end;
   {Have you sent the entire file?}
   if lbDone then
   begin
      {Close the data socket and wait for the user to decide what to
      do next}
      CloseDataConnection;
      iiFtpStatus := FTP_NOOP;
   end;
   {If you are no longer connected, close the socket}
   if not ibConnected then
      NetSocket.CloseSocketConnection(isConnectionSocket);
end;
```

Receiving a File

When the user selects a file to send from the server to the client, the client first must analyze the file name (and listing line) to determine whether the selected file is actually a file or a directory. If the selection is a directory, you probably must issue a CWD command to move to that directory on the server. If the selection is in fact a file, you need to place the file name into a variable so that the data channel can use it to create the file on the local system, and specify that you are "working toward" the RETR command so that, after preparing the data socket, you know that you want to retrieve a file from the server. You then issue the TYPE command just as you did for the STOR command. Listing 8.23 shows the client initiating either a file retrieval or a directory change when the user double-clicks in the server directory listing.

**Listing 8.23   TFTPC.PAS—the Double-Click Event Handler for the *HostFiles*
List Box Initiates the File Retrieval (or Directory Change) Process**

```
procedure TFtp.lbHostFilesDblClick(Sender: TObject);
var
   lsFile: String;
   lbIsDir: Boolean;
   liSpaceChar: Integer;
begin
   {Get the selected line from the list box}
   lsFile := lbHostFiles.Items[lbHostFiles.ItemIndex];
   lbIsDir := FALSE;
   {Is it a directory? This handles UNIX and Windows NT FTP servers
   ONLY. If you want to handle other operating systems, you must
   extend this to handle the directory listings of those operating
   systems}
```

```
if ((Copy(lsFile, 1, 1) = 'd') or
    (Pos('<DIR>', lsFile) > 0)) then
begin
    {The user selected a directory}
    lbIsDir := TRUE
end;
{Trim everything from around the file name}
liSpaceChar := Pos(' ', lsFile);
while (liSpaceChar > 0) do
begin
    lsFile := Copy(lsFile, (liSpaceChar + 1), Length(lsFile));
    liSpaceChar := Pos(' ', lsFile);
end;
{Is it a directory?}
if lbIsDir then
begin
    {Tell the user that you are changing the directory on the server}
    stStatus.Caption := 'Changing Working Directory to ' + lsFile;
    stStatus.Update;
    {Send the CWD command, specifying the directory to which to move}
    iiFtpStatus := FTP_CWD;
    NetSocket.SocketSend(isConnectionSocket, handle, UWM_SOCKETEVENT,
        'CWD ' + lsFile, SKT_SENDPACKET);
    {Clear the receive buffer}
    ClearBuffer(ReceiveBuffer, 8192);
end
else
begin
    {Tell the user that you are receiving the selected file}
    stStatus.Caption := 'Retrieving File - ' + lsFile;
    stStatus.Update;
    isFileName := lsFile;
    {Send the TYPE command, specifying the IMAGE data type}
    iiFtpStatus := FTP_TYPE;
    {Set the working toward flag so that you have a reminder
     that you want to send the RETR command after taking
     care of the preparations}
    iiFtpWorkingToward := FTP_RETR;
    isDataConnType := 'I';
    NetSocket.SocketSend(isConnectionSocket, handle, UWM_SOCKETEVENT,
        'TYPE I', SKT_SENDPACKET);
    {Clear the receive buffer}
    ClearBuffer(ReceiveBuffer, 8192);
end;
end;
```

After receiving the initial reply to the RETR command, you must open the file to be retrieved (on the client computer) using the file name that you captured from the user selection, and then call the ProcessDataReceive procedure to retrieve the data. After the file transfer is complete (remember that the data socket is receiving the Image data type synchronously), you can tell the command socket to look for another response from the server. This response should indicate the success or failure of the file transfer. You then want to place the client back into idle mode and wait for the user to do something. Listing 8.24 shows ProcessHostRetr, the procedure that handles the server's response to an RETR command.

Listing 8.24 TFTPC.PAS—the *ProcessHostRetr* Procedure Handles the Server's Response to an *RETR* Command

```
procedure TFtp.ProcessHostRetr;
var
   lsReplyMsg, lsRetnCode: String;
   lbProceed: boolean;
   lbDoAccept: boolean;
   lbDone: boolean;
begin
   lbProceed := FALSE;
   lbDone := FALSE;
   lbDoAccept := FALSE;
   {Convert the response into a Pascal string}
   lsReplyMsg := StrPas(ReceiveBuffer);
   {Extract the response code}
   lsRetnCode := Copy(lsReplyMsg, 1, 3);
   {What response code was received? Was the command successful?}
   case StrToInt(lsRetnCode) of
      110: lbProceed := TRUE;
      125: lbProceed := TRUE;
      150:
      begin
         lbDoAccept := TRUE;
         lbProceed := TRUE;
      end;
      226: lbDone := TRUE;
      250: lbDone := TRUE;
      421: ibConnected := FALSE;
      425: lbDone := TRUE;
      426: lbDone := TRUE;
      450: lbDone := TRUE;
      451: lbDone := TRUE;
      500:;
      501:;
      530:;
      550:;
   end;
   {Display the response message}
   stStatus.Caption := lsReplyMsg;
```

```
        stStatus.Update;
        {Was the command successful?}
        if not lbProceed then
        begin
           iiFtpStatus := FTP_NOOP;
           lbDone := TRUE;
        end
        else
        begin
           {Is the data socket waiting?}
           if ((iiDataConnStatus = FTPD_NOOP) or
               (iiDataConnStatus = FTPD_WAITFORCONN)) then
           begin
              iiDataConnStatus := FTPD_RECV;
              {Create and open the file to receive}
              OpenReceiveFile;
              {Clear the transfer buffer}
              ClearBuffer(TransferBuffer, 512);
              {Begin receiving the file}
              ProcessDataReceive;
           end;
           {Clear the receive buffer}
           ClearBuffer(ReceiveBuffer, 8192);
        end;
        {Are you done?}
        if lbDone then
        begin
           {You are, so close the data socket and wait for the user to decide
           what to do next}
           CloseDataConnection;
           iiFtpStatus := FTP_NOOP;
        end;
        {If you are no longer connected, close the socket}
        if not ibConnected then
           NetSocket.CloseSocketConnection(isConnectionSocket);
     end;
```

The last command response implementation in this example is the response from the CWD command (see Listing 8.25). If the command succeeds, you probably want to issue the PWD command to refresh the display with the new path name and directory contents. If the command fails, you want to place the client application back into idle mode.

Listing 8.25 TFTPC.PAS—the *ProcessHostCWD* Procedure Handles the Server's Response to a Change Directory Command

```
procedure TFtp.ProcessHostCWD;
var
   lsReplyMsg, lsRetnCode: String;
   lbProceed: boolean;
```

continues

Listing 8.25 Contiued

```
begin
   lbProceed := FALSE;
   {Convert the response into a Pascal string}
   lsReplyMsg := StrPas(ReceiveBuffer);
   {Extract the response code}
   lsRetnCode := Copy(lsReplyMsg, 1, 3);
   {What response code was received? Was the command successful?}
   case StrToInt(lsRetnCode) of
      250: lbProceed := TRUE;
      421: ibConnected := FALSE;
      500:;
      501:;
      502:;
      530:;
      550:;
   end;
   iiFtpStatus := FTP_NOOP;
   {Display the response message}
   stStatus.Caption := lsReplyMsg;
   stStatus.Update;
   {Was the command successful?}
   if lbProceed then
   begin
      {Send the PWD command}
      iiFtpStatus := FTP_PWD;
      NetSocket.SocketSend(isConnectionSocket, handle,
         UWM_SOCKETEVENT, 'PWD', SKT_SENDPACKET);
      {Clear the receive buffer}
         ClearBuffer(ReceiveBuffer, 8192);
   end;
   {If you are no longer connected, close the socket}
   if not ibConnected then
      NetSocket.CloseSocketConnection(isConnectionSocket);
end;
```

You now have an FTP client application with basic functionality. Figure 8.2 shows the application in action. To achieve a commercial-quality FTP implementation, you would still have to build in much more functionality. However, the functionality that you've just provided is a good start and gives you familiarity with the FTP command set and communications model. For a more thorough understanding of the FTP command set, you can find the entire set of commands in Appendix A.

FIG. 8.2
The FTP client
application in action.

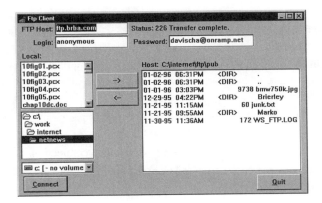

Building an FTP Server

Building an FTP server requires a different approach than building a client application. First, although the client application is quite active, sending messages to the server about what it wants to do, the server is a quite passive application. The server waits for a client to tell it what to do. This difference in attitude makes a world of difference in the approach that you must take in designing a server application. Whereas the client is proactive, the server is quite reactive. The client issues commands and requests, the server responds to commands and requests.

The FTP server that you build in this chapter enables an FTP client to connect and issue several basic commands. The server supports only one active connection at any time, promptly rejecting any additional connection requests. You limit the server to supporting only a few basic FTP commands. A connected client can send and receive a file, and receive the current directory name and contents. The rest of the implementation is up to you; you could easily implement most of the other FTP commands.

After starting, your FTP server takes the following steps:

1. Creates a listening socket and binds it to TCP port 21 (the FTP default).
2. Places the socket into listen mode, waiting for incoming connection requests.
3. After receiving a connection request, accepts the connection and creates a new socket.
4. If the server already has a socket connection open, sends a rejection message to the new connection and then immediately closes the connection.
5. If the server does not already have an active connection, sends a greeting message to the client. After sending the response to the client, the server becomes idle, waiting for the client to make the next request.

6. Returns a response message. If the server receives the USER command, it returns a successful response message. If the server receives a PASS command, it sends a positive response message.

7. Waits to receive a command from the client. The commands that the server receives are PORT, TYPE, MODE, RETR, STOR, PWD, XPWD, LIST, NLST, and QUIT. The server responds to all other commands with an error message.

8. On receiving the LIST, NLST, STOR, or RETR commands, creates a data socket, connects it to the client, then starts the data transfer.

9. After completing the data transfers, closes the data connection.

10. After receiving the QUIT command from the client, sends a goodbye message and closes the connection.

N O T E Appendix A provides complete explanations of all FTP commands, including those used in this server application. ■

In this application, you use the same procedures as you used in the previous examples (in Chapter 6 and the client application earlier in this chapter) to look up the server address and initiate the connection. Any procedures and functions that you use in the client application that this section does not list or explain are covered in Chapter 6 or this chapter's discussion of the client application. Table 8.2 lists the files that you use in the server project.

Table 8.2   FTP Server Project Files

File	Description
FTPS.DPR	The FTP server Delphi project file.
TFTPS.DFM	The FTP server window.
TFTPS.PAS	The FTP server code.
TSOCKETC.PAS	The TSocket WinSock abstraction class (first developed in Chapter 6 and extended earlier in this chapter)
NWINSOCK.PAS	The WinSock application program interface (API) definition.

TIP If you are using a Point-to-Point Protocol (PPP) or Serial Line Internet Protocol (SLIP) connection to an Internet access provider to run and test these examples, you probably will have trouble with this application. For the easiest time running and testing this or any other server application, you should be running on a network environment. This environment can be as simple as two PCs with a single Ethernet connection between them. As long as the computers are running TCP/IP as one of the protocol stacks, with host files or correctly configured Domain Name Service (DNS) or Windows Name Service (WINS) to resolve host names, you should have no problems (other than bugs that might be introduced into the client or server applications that you are using).

Waiting for a Connection

The first thing that any server does is wait. It waits for a client to come along. The server is much like a waiter in a restaurant. The waiter must wait until a client enters the restaurant and sits at the waiter's table. The waiter then receives requests from the clients, and does his best to serve those requests. Like the waiter, the FTP server waits for a client to serve, then does its best to fulfill every request that the client makes. But before it can begin waiting, the server must provide an open socket to which the client application can connect. This socket listens for incoming connection requests and then accepts those requests by creating a dedicated socket for each of the incoming connections. To accommodate this newly needed functionality, you extend your TSocket class with a few additional functions.

Listening for a Connection To enable a client to connect, a server application creates a socket that listens for an incoming connection. The application creates this listening socket just as any other stream socket—by using the socket() function. The listening socket is treated differently only after it is created.

Before asking a socket to listen for incoming connections, you must tell it the port on which to listen (see Listing 8.26). To do so, you use the bind() WinSock function. However, before calling the bind() function, you must populate a sockaddr_in record with the address and port on which the socket should be listening. This populating works essentially the same as it did when you were binding the data socket in your FTP client to the same address and port as the command socket. The primary difference is that you don't already have a connected socket from which to grab your address (unconnected sockets don't know their address). You can get around this problem by filling the address portion with the INADDR_ANY constant (as in Listing 8.26). This tells the socket to use the host address of the computer on which it is running, regardless of what that address might be. When you ask the socket for its address immediately after telling it to use the machine address, the socket still doesn't know its own address.

N O T E If you are building a server application to run in a machine with more than one network card, and you want the application to use one specific card, you must bind the socket to a specific address. In such a case, you should store the TCP/IP address so that it is used in a configuration file that your server application reads before binding any sockets to an address. Remember that the bind() function (as discussed in Chapter 6) binds the socket not just to a specific port, but also to a specific address. ■

After binding the socket to a specific address and port, you must put it into asynchronous mode, specifying which events should result in the socket notifying you. The only event in which you are really interested is the FD_ACCEPT event (because that event alerts you to waiting connection requests from client applications), but you ask the socket to inform you about all available events.

Now you can tell the socket to listen for new connections. To do so, you create the CreateListenSocket() function, which uses the listen() WinSock function (see Listing 8.26). The listen() function requires two parameters: the socket and the number of waiting connections that you will allow to queue. By limiting the number to one socket requesting connections, you tell the socket to respond quickly to the connection requests. This provides a socket that waits patiently for a client to connect and begin issuing requests.

Listing 8.26 TSOCKETC.PAS—the *CreateListenSocket()* Function Creates a Socket That Listens for New Connections

```
function _TSocket.CreateListenSocket(hWnd: THandle; wMsg: Word;
                                     aiPort: Integer): _SOCKET;
var
   NewSock: _SOCKET;
   liSockaddrSize: Integer;
   lsa_sockaddr: sockaddr_in;
begin
   liSockaddrSize := SizeOf(sockaddr);
   {Create a new socket}
   NewSock := CreateSocket;
   {Specify the Internet Address family, the port passed as a function
   argument, and INADDR_ANY for the address. This causes bind() to
   use the computer TCP/IP address for binding}
   lsa_sockaddr.sin_family := PF_INET;
   lsa_sockaddr.sin_port := htons(aiPort);
   lsa_sockaddr.sin_addr.S_addr := INADDR_ANY;
   if (NewSock <> INVALID_SOCKET) then
   begin
      {Bind the socket to the address that you just specified}
      if (bind(NewSock, lsa_sockaddr, liSockaddrSize) = 0) then
      begin
         {Get the socket name (and address). This might return only zeros
         for the TCP/IP address}
         getsockname(NewSock, isa_sockaddr, liSockaddrSize);
         {Place the socket into asynchronous mode, telling it what event
         to trigger if one of the specified events occurs}
         WSAAsyncSelect(NewSock, hWnd, wMsg, FD_CONNECT or FD_ACCEPT or
                        FD_READ or FD_WRITE or FD_CLOSE);
         {Tell the socket to listen for incoming connection requests}
         if (listen(NewSock, 1) = SOCKET_ERROR) then
         begin
            {If an error occurred, tell the user}
            ShowMessage(SocketError);
            closesocket(NewSock);
            NewSock := INVALID_SOCKET;
         end;
      end
      else
      begin
         {If an error occurred, tell the user}
         ShowMessage(SocketError);
         closesocket(NewSock);
```

```
        NewSock := INVALID_SOCKET;
      end
    end;
    {Return the new socket}
    CreateListenSocket := NewSock;
  end;
```

Accepting an Incoming Connection When a client requests a connection to a listening socket (by using the connect() function), the new connection must be accepted. To accomplish this, you create the AcceptConnectingSocket() function, which uses the accept() WinSock function (see Listing 8.27). The accept() function creates and returns a new socket that is an exact duplicate of the listening socket with the client connected to the other end. The accept() function receives a sockaddr_in record, which it also populates with the address of the client attached to the new socket (this populating enables the server to connect the data socket to this address and port to perform file transfers). You reset the asynchronous state on your new socket, not because the socket no longer operates asynchronously but to change the event that the socket triggers. The new socket should use its own event handler, not that of the listening socket. The listening socket automatically continues listening and waiting for the next connection request.

Listing 8.27 TSOCKETC.PAS—the *AcceptConnectingSocket()* Function Accepts the Client Connection Request Socket

```
function _TSocket.AcceptConnectingSocket(ListenSocket: _SOCKET;
                        hWnd: THandle;  wMsg: Word): _SOCKET;
var
   NewSock: _SOCKET;
   liSockaddrSize: Integer;
begin
   liSockaddrSize := SizeOf(sockaddr);
   {Accept the incoming connection request, creating a new socket}
   NewSock := accept(ListenSocket, isa_sockaddr, liSockaddrSize);
   {Reset asynchronous mode on the new socket, changing which event
   it triggers}
   WSAAsyncSelect(NewSock, hWnd, wMsg, FD_CONNECT or FD_ACCEPT or
                                 FD_READ or FD_WRITE or FD_CLOSE);
   {Did you receive a valid socket?}
   if (NewSock = INVALID_SOCKET) then
      if (WSAGetLastError <> WSAEWOULDBLOCK) then
         ShowMessage(SocketError);
   {Return the new socket}
   AcceptConnectingSocket := NewSock;
end;
```

Building the FTP Server Framework

As you examine the private variables that you've declared for your FTP server, you might have noticed that this application has defined not one or two sockets, but four sockets (see Listing

8.28). You can get away with this because you are implementing an incomplete FTP server. If you were to implement the passive command, you would need at least one additional socket, for listening on the data port. Most of the other variables are those that you would expect (and many of those that you used in the FTP client application) with a couple of additions.

Listing 8.28   TFTPS.PAS—the Variable Declarations for the FTP Server

```
private
    { Private declarations }
    {The primary command connection socket}
    isConnectionSocket: _SOCKET;
    {The data connection socket}
    isDataSocket: _SOCKET;
    {The listening socket (waiting for connection requests from clients)}
    isListenSocket: _SOCKET;
    {The rejection socket, used to accept connections long enough to send
    a rejection message}
    isRejectSocket: _SOCKET;
    {Are you connected to a client?}
    ibConnected: Boolean;
    {Is the data socket connected to a client?}
    ibDataConnected: Boolean;
    {The FTP command status flag}
    iiFTPStatus: Integer;
    {The holding buffer}
    isHoldBuffer: String;
    {The data port for the client}
    iiAltPort: Integer;
    {The number of current client connections}
    iiNumConnected: Integer;
    {Flag to indicate whether a rejection message has been sent to a
    client}
    ibRejectSent: Boolean;
    {The message to send to the client}
    isSendMsg: String;
    {The status of the data socket connection}
    iiDataConnStatus: Integer;
    {The type of the data connection}
    isDataConnType: Char;
    {Is the transfer file open?}
    ibFileOpen: boolean;
    {The transfer file name}
    isFileName: String;
    {The amount in the transfer buffer}
    iiBufferAmt: Integer;
    {The client TCP/IP address}
    isClientAddr: String;
{User-defined event declarations, for socket events. The first is
for the primary command socket, the second for the data socket
connection, the third for the listening socket, and the last
for the socket connection that is being rejected)
    procedure UWMSocketEvent(var Msg: TMessage); message UWM_SOCKETEVENT;
    procedure UWMDataSocketEvent(var Msg: TMessage);
                                    message UWM_DATASOCKETEVENT;
```

```
procedure UWMListenSocketEvent(var Msg: TMessage);
                           message UWM_LISTENSOCKETEVENT;
procedure UWMRejectSocketEvent(var Msg: TMessage);
                           message UWM_REJECTSOCKETEVENT;
```

The first addition is the counter to keep track of the number of current connections. Most FTP servers have a limit to the number of concurrent connections that it can support at one time. The user can usually configure this number, and the administrator can adjust it as necessary. For your server application, you limit the number of concurrent connections to one. You could increase this number, but that would require either spinning off an independent thread for each connection or adding several more sockets to accommodate the additional connections (using multiple threads is the more elegant of the two options).

The other additional variable is a simple flag that indicates whether you have sent a rejection message to a client that has requested a connection after your server has already reached its limit of concurrent connections. The server sends this message as soon as the reject socket triggers its event handler with the FD_SEND event, indicating that it is ready to send a message. By using this flag to indicate whether the socket has sent this message, you can ensure that you have sent the entire message before closing the socket, disconnecting the client (and guaranteeing that the client cannot receive any additional message from your server until it reconnects).

Starting To Listen with the Server Startup Whenever your server application is running, it needs to listen for connecting clients, so it should begin the listening when it is started up. For this reason, you modify your otherwise consistent application startup procedure. Now, after successfully initializing the WinSock interface, you create the listening socket by calling the CreateListenSocket() function that you created earlier in Listing 8.26. Listing 8.29 shows the FormCreate() procedure that includes CreateListenSocket().

Listing 8.29   TFTPS.PAS—the *FormCreate()* Procedure Creates the Listening Socket at the Same Time as the Window

```
procedure TFTPServe.FormCreate(Sender: TObject);
begin
   {Initialize the various variables}
   ibConnected := FALSE;
   ibDataConnected := FALSE;
   ibRejectSent := FALSE;
   iiFTPStatus := FTP_NOOP;
   iiNumConnected := 0;
   {Create the TSocket class object}
   NetSocket := _TSocket.Create;
   {Initialize the WinSock interface}
   if not NetSocket.InitializeSocket then
      Close
   else
   begin
```

continues

Listing 8.29 Continued

```
      {Create the listening socket, looking for clients requesting
      a connection}
      isListenSocket := NetSocket.CreateListenSocket(handle,
                     UWM_LISTENSOCKETEVENT, IPPORT_FTP);
      if (isListenSocket = INVALID_SOCKET) then
         Close
      else
      begin
         {Display the socket address for the user}
         stAddress.Caption := NetSocket.GetSockAddr;
         stAddress.Update;
      end;
   end;
end;
```

Adapting the Data Connection Functionality The ways in which both the server and the client handle the data connection are mostly the same, so you can plug your FTP client's data connection functionality directly into your FTP server application. You can remove the functionality to send a received file directly to the screen, but that minor change isn't necessary—leaving that functionality in the server application doesn't hurt anything. The primary functionality that you must modify is the sequence of events that you trigger when establishing the data socket connection. You aren't implementing passive mode, so you can immediately begin the file transfer when connected. Therefore, the ProcessDataConnect procedure opens the appropriate file and starts receiving or sending data (see Listing 8.30).

Listing 8.30 TFTPS.PAS—the *ProcessDataConnect* Procedure Opens the Appropriate File and Starts Receiving or Sending Data

```
procedure TFTPServe.ProcessDataConnect;
var
   lsReplyMsg, lsRetnCode: String;
   lbProceed: boolean;
   liAddrStart, liAddrEnd: Integer;
begin
   {What is your data socket connection status?}
   case iiDataConnStatus of
      {You are sending a file}
      FTPD_SEND:
      begin
         {Open the file and send it}
         OpenSendFile;
         ProcessDataSend;
      end;
      {You are receiving a file}
      FTPD_RECV:
      begin
         {Open the file target, clear the transfer buffer, and receive
         the file}
         OpenReceiveFile;
```

```
        ClearBuffer(TransferBuffer, 512);
        ProcessDataReceive;
      end;
    end;
end;
```

Accepting the Requesting FTP Clients When notified that a client is requesting a connection (through the FD_ACCEPT event for the listening socket), your server must accept that connection. What you do with that incoming connection after accepting it depends on how many connections you already have. Based on the number of current connections (this application's available concurrent connections are limited to one, but you could easily write this application to accept hundreds of concurrent connections), you can accept the connection (by using the AcceptConnectingSocket() function in Listing 8.27) as the isConnectionSocket or the isRejectSocket. If you accept the connection as the primary connection socket, you must increment the connection count, set the state flag (used primarily for determining which message to send), and grab and hold on to the connecting client's address.

If you accept the connecting socket as the rejection socket, you must send the connecting client a rejection message and then disconnect. The rejection socket's FD_WRITE event triggers both of these actions. The first time that this event occurs, you send the rejection message. The second occurrence tells you that the rejection message has been sent and thus that you can close the connection and disconnect the client. Listing 8.31 shows how the server decides whether to accept or reject the connections based on how many connections are currently active.

Listing 8.31   TFTPS.PAS—the *ProcessListenAccept* and *SendConnectReject* Procedures Decide Whether To Accept or Reject the Connections Based on How Many Connections Are Currently Active

```
procedure TFTPServe.ProcessListenAccept;
begin
    {Are there no current connections?}
    if (iiNumConnected = 0) then
    begin
        {Yes, accept this connection and send a greeting}
        isConnectionSocket := NetSocket.AcceptConnectingSocket(
                      isListenSocket, handle, UWM_SOCKETEVENT);
        if (isConnectionSocket <> INVALID_SOCKET) then
        begin
            {Increment the number of current connections}
            Inc(iiNumConnected);
            iiFTPStatus := FTP_CONNECT;
            {Get the client address}
            isClientAddr := NetSocket.GetSockAddr;
            {Clear the display}
            mleReceived.Clear;
            mleSent.Clear;
        end;
```

continues

Listing 8.31 Continued

```
      end
      else
      begin
        {You have too many connections already, so accept the connection
         with the rejection socket}
        isRejectSocket := NetSocket.AcceptConnectingSocket(isListenSocket,
                          handle, UWM_REJECTSOCKETEVENT);
      end;
  end;

  {This procedure sends a rejection message to a client application, then
  disconnects the client}
  procedure TFTPServe.SendConnectReject;
  begin
    {Has the rejection message been sent yet?}
    if (not ibRejectSent) then
    begin
      {Send the rejection message}
      NetSocket.SocketSend(isRejectSocket, handle, UWM_REJECTSOCKETEVENT,
          '421 Unable to open connection at this time', SKT_NOOP);
      ibRejectSent := TRUE;
    end
    else
    begin
      {Close the connection}
      NetSocket.CloseSocketConnection(isRejectSocket);
      ibRejectSent := FALSE;
    end;
  end;
```

Sending the Appropriate Message Finally, the server framework needs a mechanism that enables you to send the appropriate message to the client easily. All the messages that you will send will have an associated status code, so you can build this mechanism around those codes. To do so, you create a simple procedure, SendMsg(), that uses a case statement to assign the appropriate message string to a variable and then sends that message with any additional special message text appended to it. You can enhance this procedure by adding a second procedure, SendContextMsg, that calls the SendMsg() procedure with a default response code for each of the possible commands that a client might send. Listing 8.32 shows both of these procedures.

Listing 8.32 TFTPS.PAS—the *SendMsg()* and *SendContextMsg* Procedures Ensure That the Server Sends the Appropriate Message

```
procedure TFTPServe.SendMsg(aSendSock:_SOCKET;
         iMsg, iNewState, aiEvent: Integer; asAdditionalMsg: String);
var
    lsMsgStr: String;
begin
    {Which message needs to be sent}
    case iMsg of
```

```
     {Default messages for each FTP response code}
     110: lsMsgStr := '110 Restart Marker ';
     120: lsMsgStr := '120 Service not ready';
     125: lsMsgStr :=
              '125 Data connection already open, starting transfer';
     150: lsMsgStr := '150 File OK, About to open data connection';
     200: lsMsgStr := '200 ';
     202: lsMsgStr := '202 Command not needed at this site';
     211: lsMsgStr := '211 ';
.
.
.

     552: lsMsgStr := '552 Action aborted, storage allocation exceeded';
     553: lsMsgStr := '553 File name not allowed';
  end;
  {Send the default message with any additional message to the client}
  NetSocket.SocketSend(aSendSock, handle, aiEvent,
            lsMsgStr + asAdditionalMsg, SKT_NOOP);
  {Display the message for the user to see}
  mleSent.Lines.Add(lsMsgStr + asAdditionalMsg);
  iiFTPStatus := iNewState;
end;

{This procedure sends the appropriate message and response code for
commands that the client has sent}
procedure TFTPServe.SendContextMsg;
begin
  {Which command did you received?}
  case iiFTPStatus of
     {Send the appropriate response}
     FTP_NOOP:;
     FTP_CONNECT: SendMsg(isConnectionSocket, 220, FTP_NOOP,
                                     UWM_SOCKETEVENT, isSendMsg);
     FTP_USER: SendMsg(isConnectionSocket, 230, FTP_NOOP,
                                     UWM_SOCKETEVENT, isSendMsg);
     FTP_PASS: SendMsg(isConnectionSocket, 230, FTP_NOOP,
                                     UWM_SOCKETEVENT, isSendMsg);
     FTP_CWD: SendMsg(isConnectionSocket, 550, FTP_NOOP,
                                     UWM_SOCKETEVENT, isSendMsg);
     FTP_CDUP: SendMsg(isConnectionSocket, 550, FTP_NOOP,
                                     UWM_SOCKETEVENT, isSendMsg);
     FTP_REIN: SendMsg(isConnectionSocket, 502, FTP_NOOP,
                                     UWM_SOCKETEVENT, isSendMsg);
.
.
.

     FTP_OK: SendMsg(isConnectionSocket, 200, FTP_NOOP,
                                     UWM_SOCKETEVENT, isSendMsg);
     FTP_SYST: SendMsg(isConnectionSocket, 215, FTP_NOOP,
                                     UWM_SOCKETEVENT, isSendMsg);
     FTP_UNKWN: SendMsg(isConnectionSocket, 500, FTP_NOOP,
                                     UWM_SOCKETEVENT, isSendMsg);
  end;
  isSendMsg := '';
end;
```

Serving the Client

Now that you've got much of the supporting functionality in place, you need to enable your FTP server to respond to the commands sent by a client. You want to keep each of these actions as simple as possible so that your server responds quickly with the appropriate reply.

Sending the Working Directory One way that you can take advantage of what Delphi provides is to have the Visual Components do as much processing work as possible. Even if no user will interact with these controls, they can still serve your purposes. For example, if the client sends the PWD command to your application, you can place a few API calls to determine which directory your FTP server is currently using, or you can place a TFileListBox component on the window and let it do all the work. Then all you have to do is grab the directory attribute and call the procedure that sends the context message (see Listing 8.33).

Listing 8.33 TFTPS.PAS—the *SendWorkingDirectory* Procedure Sends the Context Message

```
procedure TFTPServe.SendWorkingDirectory;
begin
   {Get the current directory from the TFileListBox control}
   isSendMsg := flbCurDir.Directory;
   {Send the appropriate message to the client}
   SendContextMsg;
end;
```

Setting the Data Connection Mode Unfortunately, you can't always use Delphi components to do all your work. But by limiting the available options on certain data connection attributes, you can greatly simplify your implementation. By limiting the available transfer modes to only the stream mode, you reduce your response to the MODE command to sending a positive or negative response, without having to worry about formatting the data file as it is being sent or received through the data socket connection. Listing 8.34 shows the server checking the transfer connection type that was requested, to determine which response to send.

Listing 8.34 TFTPS.PAS—the *CheckModeRequest()* Procedure Checks the Requested Transfer Connection Type To Determine Which Response To Send

```
procedure TFTPServe.CheckModeRequest(asMode: String);
begin
   {Is the requested mode "Stream"?}
   if (asMode = 'S') then
   begin
      {Yes, send a success response message}
      isSendMsg := 'Stream Mode Enabled';
      SendContextMsg;
   end
   else
   begin
      {No, send an error response message}
```

```
      isSendMsg := 'Mode ' + asMode + ' not supported';
      SendMsg(isConnectionSocket, 502, FTP_NOOP, UWM_SOCKETEVENT,
         isSendMsg);
   end;
end;
```

Sending a Directory Listing By placing the Delphi Visual Components on the server window, you can use them to navigate between directories and provide the client with directory listings. Instead of building a directory listing to send to the client when it sends a LIST command, you can save the TFileListBox's contents to a temporary file and then treat it as if it were any other file that the client requested (see Listing 8.35). You can expand this functionality by setting the mask to any file pattern that you might receive from the client as an argument to the LIST or NLST commands.

N O T E The method provided for sending the directory contents to the client is quite suitable as a response to the NLST command, but inappropriate as a response to the LIST command. To fulfill the LIST command properly, you must provide a native operating system directory listing. Therefore, you should issue a DOS DIR command, capturing the output and sending the resulting directory listing to the client.

Listing 8.35 TFTPS.PAS—the *SendDirectoryList()* Procedure Sends the Client a Listing of the Current Directory

```
procedure TFTPServe.SendDirectoryList;
begin
   {Send the "preparing to connect data socket" message}
   SendMsg(isConnectionSocket, 150, FTP_NOOP,UWM_SOCKETEVENT, isSendMsg);
   {Save the TFileListBox control's contents to a temporary file}
   isFileName := '\tmp.lst';
   flbCurDir.Items.SaveToFile(isFileName);
   {Create the data socket}
   isDataSocket := NetSocket.CreateDataSocket(isConnectionSocket,
                   handle, UWM_DATASOCKETEVENT);
   iiDataConnStatus := FTPD_SEND;
   {Open the data socket connection so that you can send the file}
   OpenDataConnection(isClientAddr);
end;
```

Sending and Receiving Files As you could probably tell from the directory listing procedure, the mechanism to initiate the sending and receiving of files is much simpler in the server inplementation than in the client implementation. The mechanism is a simple series of steps that you could easily combine into a single procedure with a flag passed as an argument to indicate which function to perform.

Listing 8.36 shows the procedures that send and receive files. To initiate the sending and receiving of files, you first send to the client a message that signals the client that you are about to open the data socket. Next, you set the transfer file name with the one that the client's command specifies. Then you create the data socket. The next step is the only difference between the two procedures: You set the data connection status to indicate whether you are sending or receiving a file. Finally, you open the data connection to the client. From this point, the data connection functionality takes care of the rest of the file transfer processing.

Listing 8.36   TFTPS.PAS—the *SendRecvFile()* and *ReceiveStoreFile()* Procedures Send and Receive Files

```
procedure TFTPServe.SendRecvFile(asFileName: String);
begin
   {Send the "preparing to connect data socket" message}
   SendMsg(isConnectionSocket, 150, FTP_NOOP,UWM_SOCKETEVENT, isSendMsg);
   {Place the received file name into the transfer file name variable}
   isFileName := asFileName;
   {Create the data socket}
   isDataSocket :=    NetSocket.CreateDataSocket(isConnectionSocket,
                  handle, UWM_DATASOCKETEVENT);
   iiDataConnStatus := FTPD_SEND;
   {Open the data socket connection so that the file can be sent}
   OpenDataConnection(isClientAddr);
end;

procedure TFTPServe.ReceiveStoreFile(asFileName: String);
begin
   {Send the "preparing to connect data socket" message}
   SendMsg(isConnectionSocket, 150, FTP_NOOP,UWM_SOCKETEVENT, isSendMsg);
   {Place the received file name into the transfer file name variable}
   isFileName := asFileName;
   {Create the data socket}
   isDataSocket := NetSocket.CreateDataSocket(isConnectionSocket,
                  handle, UWM_DATASOCKETEVENT);
   iiDataConnStatus := FTPD_RECV;
   {Open the data socket connection so that the file can be received}
   OpenDataConnection(isClientAddr);
end;
```

Parsing the Received Command   The next functionality is probably the most complex portion of the server's command response functionality. When you receive a message from the client, you must parse it into two different portions: the command and the arguments. Before you can parse the received command message, you must retrieve it from the socket. If you receive any data from the socket, you send it to the GetLine() function, to parse the command line from any other data that might be in the receive buffer. After extracting the command line from the receive buffer, you can begin parsing the command from its arguments.

You parse the command from its arguments by looking for the first space character before the end of the string. If you find a space, the portion of the string in front of the space is parsed as the command, and the portion after the space is parsed as the command's arguments. If the string has no space character, you assume that the entire string is a command with no arguments. You then pass these two strings to a procedure that determines which command you have received and calls the appropriate procedure to respond to it.

Part

II

Ch

8

The ReadCommandMsg procedure provides all this command-parsing functionality (see Listing 8.37).

N O T E Note that this entire FTP server application doesn't call the WinSock recv() function until after it receives the FD_READ event message. There are two ways to use the FD_READ event message with the recv() function, and the method that this example demonstrates is actually the more elegant of the two, although the WinSock documentation might lead you to believe that you should use the recv() and WSAAsyncSelect() functions differently.

The WinSock documentation (supplied on the companion CD) seems to suggest that a previously executed recv() function call triggers the FD_READ event by placing data in the receive buffer. This is not entirely true, and isn't the intended usage of these two functions. The correct usage is to use the FD_READ event message as the signal that the recv() function is likely to succeed because data is sitting in the WinSock buffer ready to be placed into a receive buffer. By calling recv() after receiving the FD_READ message, you know exactly how much data WinSock has placed into your receive buffer. The FD_READ event message actually tells you that the buffer has received data and that you can call the recv() function to retrieve the data.

Likewise, the FD_WRITE event message does not signal the completion of the previous send, but that the WinSock buffer is empty and thus available to send data to the connected system using the send() function. This part of the WinSock documentation often misleads many programmers, regardless of their BSD socket programming experience. The fact that the "incorrect" usage does work only adds to the confusion over the correct usage of these functions. ▨

Listing 8.37   TFTPS.PAS—the _ReadCommandMsg_ Procedure Parses a Received Command from Its Arguments

```
procedure TFTPServe.ReadCommandMsg;
var
   lsCommand: String;
   lsMessage: String;
   liCmdLength: Integer;
   liMsgLength: Integer;
begin
   {Receive the incoming data}
   liMsgLength := recv(isConnectionSocket, ReceiveBuffer, 8192, 0);
   {Did you receive anything?}
   if (liMsgLength = SOCKET_ERROR) and
         (WSAGetLastError <> WSAEWOULDBLOCK) then
      ShowMessage(NetSocket.SocketError)
   else
   begin
      {Get the first line}
      if NetSocket.GetLine(TempBuffer, ReceiveBuffer) then
      begin
         {Add the received line to the display}
```

continues

Listing 8.37 Continued

```
      mleReceived.Lines.Add(StrPas(TempBuffer));
      {Is there anything in the hold buffer that you need to add
      in front of this line?}
      if (Length(isHoldBuffer) > 0) then
         lsMessage := isHoldBuffer + StrPas(TempBuffer)
      else
         lsMessage := StrPas(TempBuffer);
      {Reset the hold buffer}
      isHoldBuffer := '';
      {Find the end of the command}
      liCmdLength := Pos(' ', lsMessage);
      if (liCmdLength = 0) then
      begin
         {The entire line is the command}
         liCmdLength := Length(lsMessage);
         lsCommand := lsMessage;
         lsMessage := '';
      end
      else
      begin
         {Separate the command from the arguments}
         lsCommand := Copy(lsMessage, 1, (liCmdLength - 1));
         lsMessage := Copy(lsMessage, (liCmdLength + 1),
                                      Length(lsMessage));
      end;
      {Send the command and its arguments to the CheckCommandMsg
      procedure}
      CheckCommandMsg(lsCommand, lsMessage);
   end
   else
   begin
      {You have an incomplete line. Place it in the hold buffer and
      wait for the rest of the command line to arrive}
      if (Length(isHoldBuffer) > 0) then
         isHoldBuffer := isHoldBuffer + StrPas(TempBuffer)
      else
         isHoldBuffer := StrPas(TempBuffer);
   end;
   end;
end;
```

Determining Which Command You Received After parsing the command from its arguments, you can build a simple procedure, CheckCommandMsg, to determine which command you received and how to respond (see Listing 8.38). To build this procedure, you use a series of if...then statements, each comparing the command string to a specific command to see whether they match. After finding a match, you set a flag to indicate that you found a match (if you don't find a match, you respond with a message indicating that the message was not understood). Then you call the appropriate procedure, passing the arguments wherever the command expects to receive arguments.

Listing 8.38   TFTPS.PAS—the *CheckCommandMsg()* Procedure Checks the Parsed Command and Determines the Server's Next Action

```
procedure TFTPServe.CheckCommandMsg(asCommand, asArguments: String);
var
   lbCmdFound: Boolean;
begin
   lbCmdFound := FALSE;
   {Did you receive a NOOP command?}
   if (asCommand = 'NOOP') then
   begin
      lbCmdFound := TRUE;
      iiFTPStatus := FTP_OK;
      SendContextMsg;
   end;
   {Did you receive a USER command?}
   if (asCommand = 'USER') then
   begin
      lbCmdFound := TRUE;
      iiFTPStatus := FTP_USER;
      {Validate the login ID}
      ValidateLogin(asArguments);
   end;
   .
   .
   .
   {Did you receive an NLST command?}
   if (asCommand = 'NLST') then
   begin
      lbCmdFound := TRUE;
      iiFTPStatus := FTP_NLST;
      {Send the directory listing}
      SendDirectoryList;
   end;
   {Did you receive a SYST command?}
   if (asCommand = 'SYST') then
   begin
      lbCmdFound := TRUE;
      iiFTPStatus := FTP_SYST;
      SendContextMsg;
   end;
   {Did you recognize the command?}
   if (not lbCmdFound) then
   begin
      iiFTPStatus := FTP_UNKWN;
      SendContextMsg;
   end;
end;
```

Handling the Socket Events

Finally, you add the socket event handlers (see Listing 8.39). Notice that the listen and reject sockets have only a single event message to which you must respond, and the command socket responds only to the read and write messages. The only socket that needs all the possible event messages is the data socket. If you wanted to build a robust, commercial-quality application, you would have to handle a few additional event messages (in particular, the Out-Of-Band event message), but the following procedures cover the basics.

Listing 8.39   TFTPS.PAS—the Socket Event-Handler Procedures

```
procedure TFTPServe.UWMSocketEvent(var Msg: TMessage);
begin
   {What socket event was received? Call the appropriate procedure}
   case Msg.LParamLo of
      FD_READ: ReadCommandMsg;
      FD_WRITE: SendContextMsg;
      FD_ACCEPT:;
      FD_CONNECT:;
      FD_CLOSE:;
   end;
end;

procedure TFTPServe.UWMDataSocketEvent(var Msg: TMessage);
begin
   {What socket event was received? Call the appropriate procedure}
   case Msg.LParamLo of
      FD_READ: ProcessDataReceive;
      FD_WRITE: ProcessDataSend;
      FD_OOB:;
      FD_ACCEPT: AcceptDataConnection;
      FD_CONNECT: ProcessDataConnect;
      FD_CLOSE: CloseDataConnection;
   end;
end;

procedure TFTPServe.UWMListenSocketEvent(var Msg: TMessage);
begin
   {What socket event was received? Call the appropriate procedure}
   case Msg.LParamLo of
      FD_READ:;
      FD_WRITE:;
      FD_OOB:;
      FD_ACCEPT: ProcessListenAccept;
      FD_CONNECT:;
      FD_CLOSE:;
   end;
end;

procedure TFTPServe.UWMRejectSocketEvent(var Msg: TMessage);
begin
   {What socket event was received? Call the appropriate procedure}
   case Msg.LParamLo of
      FD_READ:;
      FD_WRITE: SendConnectReject;
      FD_ACCEPT:;
      FD_CONNECT:;
      FD_CLOSE:;
   end;
end;
```

Understanding the Minimum FTP Server Implementation Requirements

Now that you have built the basic foundation for your FTP server, you need to consider the required minimum functionality that you should actually implement. RFC 959 lists the following requirements as the minimum FTP server implementation to make the FTP server workable without generating an unreasonable number of error messages:

Commands	USER, QUIT, PORT, TYPE, MODE, STRU, RETR, STOR, and NOOP
Type	ASCII Non-Print
Mode	Stream
Structure	File and Record

The entire example implementation on this book's companion CD covers almost all these minimum requirements. The only missing command is the STRU (structure) command and the corresponding processing involved for the record file structure.

Figure 8.3 shows the application as it is serving a connected client. The application displays in the upper memo area the commands that the client sent, and displays in the lower memo area the server's responses.

FIG. 8.3

The FTP server application in action, serving a connected client. The upper memo area displays the commands that the client sent, and the lower memo area displays the server's responses.

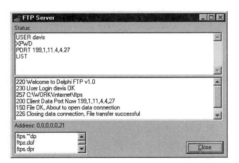

From Here...

In this chapter, you took a good look at the FTP protocol model, including the communications model and the ways in which you use the two socket connections to send various types of information back and forth. You examined the various data types and formats that you use to send files between two systems, and spent a little time noting which of these types and formats are widely used and which are not. Then you explored the command set that controls an FTP session. After looking at all these elements, you used this information to build a basic FTP client application and FTP server application.

You can expand these FTP applications, building in support for all the omitted functions. You can also add multithreading capabilities so that the file-retrieval functionality does not interfere with the command processing or with other applications running on the system. You could also make the error handling much more robust, so that the client handles the various response codes with much more specific actions, and so that the server handles the various errors much more gracefully than it currently does (try requesting a file that doesn't exist and see for yourself how ungracefully the server responds). You could build in to the client some file system analyses and displays that ensure that the underlying file system and operating system that the server is running are transparent to the user, and have the user interface present a single uniform display of the file system contents. Finally, you could convert the data socket to perform listen and accept actions on the socket connection instead of placing the server into passive mode. The basic code for this enhancement is already included with the sample code on the companion CD.

Once you feel comfortable with the FTP protocol and communications model, you can dig into the other Internet communications protocols by exploring the following chapters:

- To familiarize yourself with the other widely used Internet applications, see Chapter 2, "The Basic Internet Application Suite."
- To better understand the principles of socket communications, the usage of TCP ports, and connection-based communications, see Chapter 5, "The Principles of Socket Communications and Programming."
- To understand the SMTP and POP mail protocols, see Chapter 9, "Developing SMTP and POP Mail Clients."
- To understand the Usenet Internet News protocol, see Chapter 10, "Developing an Internet News Client/Reader."

Developing SMTP and POP Mail Clients

- SMTP's commands and communication model

- The Internet Message Format, the standardized e-mail message format that enables SMTP to know what to do with a particular message

- The Multipurpose Internet Mail Extensions (MIME) to the Internet Message Format, which enable users to embed binary objects into e-mail messages

- POP, which enables a mail client, which is not always connected to the Internet, to retrieve messages from a mail server that is storing the messages until they can be retrieved

These days, almost everybody knows all about electronic mail, and just about everyone has an e-mail address. I have an e-mail address. My wife has an e-mail address. My neighbor's dog has an e-mail address. (Okay, that last example might be a slight exaggeration.) It's getting harder every day to find someone who doesn't have an e-mail address.

It wasn't always like this. In the early days of the Internet, there was no reliable means of sending e-mail from one host to another. Most of the host systems had various e-mail implementations, but they didn't have a standard communication protocol that they could use to exchange messages. Also, there wasn't a unified message format that mail servers could pass among one another.

A reliable means of exchanging e-mail among users, no matter where they might be located, was important to the usage of the Internet, so a standard for exchanging e-mail messages among hosts was developed. This mail protocol is independent of the mail system that operates within a host. Created strictly to enable hosts to exchange e-mail messages reliably, this message-exchange protocol, the Simple Mail Transport Protocol (SMTP), is still widely used.

The SMTP protocol worked well as long as servers with several users logged in did most of the computing. As people began using more single-user computers, logging in to the host servers only to exchange data and retrieve messages, the need grew for a mail protocol that expected the receiving computer to be connected only for short, irregular intervals. To address this need, the Post Office Protocol (POP) was developed. Today, most Internet Mail clients use a combination of SMTP (for sending messages) and POP (for receiving messages). ■

The Simple Mail Transport Protocol (SMTP)

SMTP (described in RFC 821) was originally designed to enable two mail servers to exchange mail messages. The primary mail exchange mechanism used to route e-mail messages around the Internet, SMTP works on a simple store-and-forward model in which the client holds the messages that need to be passed to the server and issues to the server commands that tell it how to process each message. The mail client can be another mail server that has one (or more) messages that it must pass to another mail server. Most Internet mail clients use the SMTP protocol to send messages.

The Internet Message Format

Part of the SMTP specification is the message format that is to be used. RFC 822 describes this format, which is called the Internet Message Format. In addition to its use for Internet mail, the Internet Message Format is also the standard message format used by the Usenet Internet News.

The Internet Message Format specifies a message header that contains much information that SMTP uses to determine where and how to send a message, as well as how to read it. The format also specifies a message ID and how to generate it so that each Internet message has a unique identifier that the various mail and news servers and clients use to specify which messages they already have received and which messages they need to receive.

The basic format consists of a header and the message body. The header section is at the top of each message, with an empty line separating the header from the message body. The entries in the header consist of a header name followed by a colon (:), and the header body appropriate for the header name. The available header names are standardized; you should not vary them, because most e-mail and news applications depend on a specific wording for the header names. Table 9.1 lists some of the common header names.

Table 9.1   Common Internet Message Format Header Names

Name	Description
From:	The sender's e-mail address and/or alias.
To:	The message's primary recipient(s). You can list multiple recipients by separating them with commas.

Name	Description
Cc: and Bcc:	The recipients to receive a carbon copy or blind carbon copy of the message. As with the primary recipients, you can specify multiple carbon copy recipients, each separated by a comma, on a single line.
Subject:	A descriptive line stating the message's subject.
Date:	The date that the message was created and passed to the system.
Message-ID:	A unique identifier, usually formatted using the originating system time and date followed by the system name.
Reply-To:	A secondary address (in addition to the address specified in *From:*) to which the recipient can send replies to the message.
References:	The message ID (from the Message ID header field) of the message to which the recipient is responding.

Several other header names can be included in the message format. The mail and news servers add several more header names as the message is routed along its way. Appendix B, "The Internet Message Format," lists most of the common header names.

The SMTP Communications Model

The SMTP communications model is a one-way path from the message sender to the message receiver. According to this model, an SMTP server contacts another SMTP server only when it has one or more mail messages that the first server needs to pass to the second. The sending server does not receive any mail messages back from the receiving server during this session (see Fig. 9.1). If the receiving server has any mail messages that it needs to pass to the sending server, it must reverse the roles and initiate a second session with the first server.

FIG. 9.1

The SMTP communications model. Mail messages travel from the sending computer to the receiving computer. The receiving computer cannot send mail messages back to the sending computer without reversing the roles and becoming the sending computer.

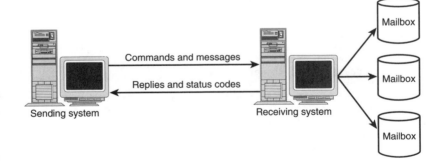

After receiving all the messages from the sending server, the receiving SMTP server—if it has received messages that must be passed to another SMTP server—then initiates an SMTP session with a third server. In this scenario, the receiving server becomes the sending server, and the third server is the receiving server. If the receiving server has any mail messages that go into mailboxes on its file system, it distributes the messages accordingly.

The Multipurpose Internet Mail Extensions (MIME)

Since SMTP was put in place, the types of data that users need to be capable of sending by e-mail have diversified extensively. In the early days, the data was all text-based. If you needed to send something, you would usually send it as program source code or as raw data in textual format. These days, the data that you send is more likely to be a word processing document, a graphic image, or a sound or video clip.

To accommodate these diverse file and object types, the Internet Message Format had to be greatly extended. The Multipurpose Internet Mail Extensions (MIME) were developed for this purpose. RFCs 1521 and 1522 document these extensions.

The Basic MIME Message Structure

The MIME specification is not for a new e-mail application protocol, but for a new message format compatible with the older Internet Message Format (RFC 822). This format allows for the extension of the capabilities of Internet e-mail while keeping the existing transport applications and infrastructure. As an extension of the RFC 822 message format, the MIME format maintains the basic message structure with a header and body sections. The header section contains the same elements as the RFC 822 message format, with a few additions. The following is an example of a MIME message:

```
{This is the message header section}
From - Wed Mar 06 22:43:32 1996
Received: from bullfrog.brba.com (dal22.onramp.net [199.1.11.122]) by
mailhost.onramp.net (8.7.3/8.6.5) with SMTP id WAA07611 for
<davischa@onramp.net>; Wed, 6 Mar 1996 22:45:26 -0600 (CST)
Message-ID: <313E6964.5500@onramp.net>
Date: Wed, 06 Mar 1996 22:43:16 -0600
From: Davis Chapman <davischa@onramp.net>
X-Mailer: Mozilla 2.0GoldB1 (Win95; I)
{This next line specifies that it is a MIME message}
MIME-Version: 1.0
To: davischa@onramp.net
Subject: Book CD
{This next line specifies that it is a mixed type message and that
the sections are divided by the specified boundary marker}
Content-Type: multipart/mixed; boundary="-----------6B9767D111AE"
X-Mozilla-Status: 0001
{End of the header section}

This is a multipart message in MIME format.

{The first boundary marker, marking the first section of the message}
--------------6B9767D111AE
{This section is plain text, using the US-ASCII character set}
```

```
Content-Type: text/plain; charset=us-ascii
Content-Transfer-Encoding: 7bit
{End of the section header}

Davis,

I am enclosing the QUE permission agreement. You will need to pull
it into Word and make the appropriate modifications for your company
name, date, and product (as appropriate). Please return it and a
copy of what you want included on the CD to Angela Kozlowski at the
address in the agreement.

Thanks,
Davis

{The next section boundary marker}
--------------6B9767D111AE
{The next section is a binary file, encoded using base 64 encoding}
Content-Type: application/octet-stream
Content-Transfer-Encoding: base64
Content-Disposition: attachment; filename="Sublic2.doc"
```

```
0M8R4KGxGuEAAAAAAAAAAAAAAAAAAAAAPgADAP7/CQAGAAAAAAAAAAAAABAAAAAQAAAAA
AAAAEAAAAgAAAAEAAAD+////AAAAAAAAAD///////////////////////////////////
//////////////////////////////////////////////////////////////////
.
.
.
AAACAAAAAQAAAP7///8AAAAAAAAAP////////////////////////////////////////
////////////////////////////////////////////////////////////////////
////////////////////////////////////////////////////////////////////
///////////////////////////////////
```

```
{The final boundary marker}
--------------6B9767D111AE--
```

The MIME Version Header   The MIME version header identifies a message as a MIME message, and specifies the version of the MIME standard to which the message complies. If this header is not found, the mail client should treat the message as an RFC 822 formatted message (for information on the Internet message format defined in RFC 822, see Appendix B). The current MIME version is 1.0. The MIME version header syntax is as follows:

```
MIME-Version: 1.0#13#10
```

N O T E   In the preceding example (and many to follow), the #13#10 on the end of each line indicates that each of these lines ends with the carriage-return and line-feed characters. When you build Pascal strings, you add these to the line as #13#10, so these examples were built using this notation for consistency with the Delphi Pascal language.

This header field is included in the standard Internet message header section. This additional field has been added to indicate that the message has been formatted using MIME extensions to the standard Internet message format.

The Content Type Header   The content type header identifies the file format of the embedded objects. The header tells the MIME reader how to display or manipulate the message's body. The content type header consists of the header name followed by a MIME type. The MIME type consists of two type names separated by a forward slash character (/). The first name is the type name, and the second is the subtype name. The following are a few examples of the content type header:

```
Content-Type: image/jpeg#13#10
Content-Type: image/gif#13#10
Content-Type: image/bmp#13#10
Content-Type: video/mpeg#13#10
Content-Type: application/octet-stream#13#10
```

In the first three of the preceding examples, the object type is image, with the subtype being jpeg, gif, and bmp. These three image files are embedded within the message. The fourth line is an mpeg video, and the last is a program or file archive.

Following the type and subtype names can be a set of parameters. Each parameter consists of a parameter name followed by an equal sign (=) and then the parameter value. These parameters are separated from the type and subtype, as well as any other parameters, by semicolons. The following is an example of such a set of parameters:

```
Content-Type: text/plain; charset=us-ascii#13#10
```

This object type marker tells the message reader that the following section is plain text using the United States English character set. The marker could easily specify a different character set, and if the reader can display the specified language, the reader displays the message in the specified language and character set.

This header is completely optional. If it is not included, the message is treated as straight ASCII text.

The Content Transfer Encoding Header   The content transfer encoding header identifies the encoding scheme used to convert the object embedded in the message body. To embed into a mail message a binary object of any type (such as a graphic image, audio file, or document), you must convert the object into ASCII so that it complies with the RFC 822 message format. The content transfer encoding header informs the mail reader which of these mechanisms you used to encode the object, so that the reader can properly decode the object. The following is the syntax for the content transfer encoding header:

```
Content-Transfer-Encoding: Base64
```

The MIME documentation defines five encoding types, but three (seven-bit, eight-bit, and binary) indicate that the object has no encoding, but that the message contents are of one of these three data types. The seven-bit encoding is normal for text areas within a MIME-formatted message. The other two, eight-bit and binary, are used only when the mail transport is not SMTP, because SMTP allows only seven-bit ASCII characters. The other two encoding schemes—quoted-printable and base-64—do convert objects from a binary format to ASCII (and back).

The Quoted Printable Encoding Scheme   The quoted-printable encoding scheme is designed to make an encoded object fairly readable to the recipient. Each byte of data is represented by an equal sign (=) followed by two hexadecimal digits that represent the value of the byte. Bytes with values that fall within the range of printable ASCII characters are represented as those characters. The following is an example of a readable object:

```
Date: Sat, 16 Mar 96 16:55:23 CST
From: Davis Chapman <davischa@onramp.net>
To: davischa@onramp.net
Subject: Quoted Printable MIME Example
Message-ID: <0239847361.0@onramp.net>
MIME-Version: 1.0
X-Mail-Agent: Delphi SMTP Mail Client
Content-Type: text/plain; charset=iso-8859-1
Content-Transfer-Encoding: quoted-printable

This is an example of a quoted-printable message. The following
word "praticit=E0" means usefulness in Italian. The last letter is
an a with a backward accent over it.
```

The quoted-printable encoding scheme is primarily used to encode text messages that include extended ASCII (eight-bit) characters. This scheme is often used to encode textual messages in non-English languages that use extended ASCII characters in their character set. For a full explanation of the quoted-printable encoding scheme, see RFC 1521.

The Base-64 Encoding Scheme   The base-64 encoding scheme translates mostly binary data into ASCII text. The scheme divides every three bytes into four six-bit characters, then uses a cross-reference table to represent these as printable ASCII characters. Chapter 11, "Building a UUEncoder/Decoder," examines this encoding scheme in detail.

The Multipart MIME Message Structure

One of the MIME format's more popular capabilities is that of having multiple-part messages. By using multiple-part messages, you can embed both graphics and sound with a textual message, or build a simple application that displays animation that illustrates the message subject and includes all the various supporting files necessary to run the application.

The multipart message structure consists of multiple messages combined in one message body, each with its own header information indicating the content type and encoding scheme. The sections are separated by boundary markers that the main message header defines. For an in-depth discussion on multipart message structure, see RFC 1521.

N O T E   When sending and receiving MIME mail messages with large embedded objects, the messages can become quite large. Some Internet access providers place limits on the message size that can be sent or received through their systems. Because of this limitation, you might not receive complete messages if the message size is larger than the limitation that the access provider has defined. In fact, if the mail message exceeds the size limitations, some access providers don't deliver the message at all. You should keep this potential problem in mind when choosing your access provider. ■

The Post Office Protocol (POP)

You can send mail using SMTP, and you can embed any type of object into the mail messages using the MIME message format. However, you are still missing one important part of e-mail functionality. With SMTP, the server to receive mail messages must contact the client and send all mail messages that are destined for the client. Therefore, you must register the client machine as the machine name in the recipient's Internet address.

The sending computer (the mail server) has to know about the receiving computer (the mail client, most likely your PC). The sending computer has to know how (and when) to connect to the receiving computer, so that it can send the mail messages that it is holding. In other words, the sending computer has to call your computer. The receiving computer also must have a host name registered with Domain Name Service (DNS) servers across the Internet. All mail messages would be sent with the receiving computer name rather than the mail server machine name (for example, my mail address would probably be **davischa@bullfrog.ind** rather than **davischa@onramp.net**). Furthermore, the mail server at your access provider would keep the mail messages for only a few days before returning them as undeliverable. Unless you plan on keeping your computer on and connected to the Internet all the time, this scenario is rather impractical. The scenario is more suitable for a computer that is serving multiple people as a shared mail host, not an individual computer used by a single person.

SMTP was designed back in the era when users spent all their time connected to some sort of host and running a terminal session. The protocol is not designed for the more prominent situation of today, in which most e-mail users connect only briefly to the mail server that holds their mailboxes. You must maintain the mail messages on the server and transfer them to the client when it requests them. This is the purpose for which the Post Office Protocol (POP) was designed.

POP was designed to compensate for SMTP's shortcomings, which are in the receiving of messages, not in the sending. For this reason, the designers of POP didn't include functionality to send messages, assuming that SMTP would continue to be used to perform that function. With the POP protocol, the receiving computer initiates the connection. The receiving computer connects to the mail server, logs in, and retrieves any waiting messages. Therefore, the sending computer doesn't have to know anything about the receiving computer except whether it used a login and password that correspond to a valid mailbox. Today, almost every Internet mail client that you might use employs a combination of SMTP (to send messages) and POP (to receive messages).

The POP Communications Model

RFC 1725 describes the POP communications model in detail. In this simple store-and-forward model, the local mail server stores messages until the client retrieves them. The POP client connects to the server on TCP port 110. To log in to the server, the client uses an account ID and password. After successfully logging in to the server, the client can query the server about the availability of new messages, retrieve any messages that the server currently is holding, or delete any messages from the server.

The POP communications model uses three transaction states to provide this functionality to the POP client:

- The authorization state, in which the server verifies that the client is logging in to a valid mailbox

- The transaction state, in which the client can retrieve and delete messages

- The update state, which the model enters immediately when the client issues the QUIT command

The update state is that in which any actions to manipulate messages (primarily deletions) are committed. As long as the client remains in the transaction state, it can issue a reset command to undo any message deletions that it performed.

Building an SMTP Send Mail Client Application

To keep things as simple as possible in this chapter's example applications, you implement a separate SMTP Send Mail client and POP Retrieve Mail client. Although you could incorporate both of these functions into a single Internet Mail client, the difference is minimal.

The SMTP mail client that you build in this section enables the user to specify a recipient of the message, the user's return address, and the mail server to which to connect. The user can then type in a message to send. On entering all this information, the user can send the message to the designated recipient. This application cannot save the messages that it sends into any storage files so that you can retrieve messages for later review. When the user chooses to send the message, your SMTP client takes the following steps:

1. Connects to the SMTP mail server.

2. Receives a greeting from the server.

3. Sends the HELO message to the server and waits for the response.

4. On receiving the response to the HELO command, informs the server of the message sender by using the MAILFROM command.

5. On receiving the response to the MAILFROM command, uses the RCPTTO command to tell the server to whom you are sending the message.

6. On receiving the response to the RCPTTO command, if a CC recipient is specified, tells the server about this recipient by using the RCPTTO command.

7. If no additional recipients are specified, sends the DATA command to tell the server that the message follows.

8. On receiving the initial response to the DATA command, sends to the server the message header followed by the message body.

9. On receiving the final response to the DATA command, logs out from the server by sending the QUIT command.

10. On receiving the response to the QUIT command, closes the connection.

N O T E In Appendix A, "Internet Applications Command Sets," you can find complete explanations of all the SMTP commands used in this example, as well as any SMTP commands that this example does not use. ▩

In this example, you use the same procedures for looking up the server address and initiating the connection that you used in the previous examples (see Chapters 6 and 8). Any procedures and functions that this chapter does not list and explain are covered in these previous chapters. Table 9.2 lists the files used in this project.

Table 9.2 SMTP Mail Client Project Files

File	Description
NETMAIL.DPR	The SMTP mail client Delphi project file.
TMAIL.DFM	The SMTP mail client window.
TMAIL.PAS	The SMTP mail client code.
TSOCKETC.PAS	The TSocket WinSock abstraction class (first developed in Chapter 6, and expanded in Chapter 8).
NWINSOCK.PAS	The WinSock application program interface (API) definition.

Declaring the SMTP Command State Table

You begin your SMTP client by declaring the state table constants for each of the SMTP commands that you might issue (see Listing 9.1). These constants maintain a variable that specifies the command last issued to the SMTP server. This variable enables you to determine easily the command to which the server is responding, and to direct the response message to the appropriate procedure to process that response.

Listing 9.1 TMAIL.PAS—the SMTP Mail Client Constant Declarations

```
const
{Constant declarations to represent SMTP commands. These keep
track of the command last issued so that responses received
from the server can be directed to the appropriate procedure}
  MAIL_NOOP = 0;
  MAIL_CONNECT = 1;
  MAIL_HELO = 2;
  MAIL_MAILFROM = 3;
  MAIL_RCPTTO = 4;
  MAIL_RCPTCC = 5;
  MAIL_DATA = 6;
  MAIL_RSET = 7;
  MAIL_SEND = 8;
  MAIL_SOML = 9;
```

```
      MAIL_SAML = 10;
      MAIL_VRFY = 11;
      MAIL_EXPN = 12;
      MAIL_HELP = 13;
      MAIL_TURN = 14;
      MAIL_QUIT = 15;
      MAIL_SENDINGHEADER = 16;
      MAIL_SENDINGMESSAGE = 17;
   {User-defined event declarations for socket events. The first is to be
   used for the primary socket, the second is to be used for address
   lookup notifications}
      UWM_SOCKETEVENT = WM_USER + 500;
      UWM_ADDRSOCKETEVENT = WM_USER + 501;
```

Receiving the SMTP Server Greeting

After connecting to the SMTP server, you receive a greeting from the server. You want to respond to the greeting by sending a HELO command with your system name. Use the WinSock gethostname() function to retrieve your system name, which you send to the server as the parameter with the HELO command. Listing 9.2 shows the ProcessHostWelcome procedure, which receives the greeting and sends your response.

Listing 9.2   TMAIL.PAS—the *ProcessHostWelcome* Procedure Receives the Server's Greeting and Sends the Client's Response

```
procedure TSMTPClient.ProcessHostWelcome;
var
   lsWelcomeMsg, lsRetnCode: String;
   lsHostName: array[0..79] of Char;
begin
   {Convert the received message to a Pascal string}
   lsWelcomeMsg := StrPas(ReceiveBuffer);
   {Copy the response code into the lsRetnCode variable}
   lsRetnCode := Copy(lsWelcomeMsg, 1, 3);
   {Check to see what was returned}
   case StrToInt(lsRetnCode) of
      {Positive Response, you are connected}
      220: ibConnected := TRUE;
      {Negative Response, you are not connected}
      421: ibConnected := FALSE;
   end;
   {Set the command status flag to NOOP}
   iiMailStatus := MAIL_NOOP;
   {Display the response message}
   stStatus.Caption := lsWelcomeMsg;
   stStatus.Update;
   {If you are connected}
   if ibConnected then
   begin
```

continues

Listing 9.2 Continued

```
      {Set the command status flag to indicate that you sent a HELO}
      iiMailStatus := MAIL_HELO;
      {Get the name of the computer on which you are running}
      if (gethostname(lsHostName, sizeof(lsHostName)) = SOCKET_ERROR)
        then ShowMessage(NetSocket.SocketError)
      else
      begin
        {Send HELO command to mail server, telling it who you are}
        NetSocket.SocketSend(isConnectionSocket, handle,
         UWM_SOCKETEVENT, 'HELO ' + StrPas(lsHostName), SKT_SENDPACKET);
        {Clear the receive buffer}
        ClearBuffer(ReceiveBuffer, 8192);
      end;
    end;
  end;
end;
```

Telling the SMTP Server Who Is Sending the Message

After receiving the server response to the HELO command (yes, that is the correct spelling for the command, not a misspelling of the word *hello*), you can begin sending messages. Before sending a message, however, you must tell the server who is sending the message. To do so, you send a MAIL command, with the return address as part of the parameters. You must enclose the return address within angled brackets (< and >) as in the following example:

```
MAIL FROM <davischa@onramp.net>
```

Listing 9.3 shows the ProcessHostHelo procedure, in which the client examines the server's response to the HELO command and determines which command to issue next.

Listing 9.3 TMAIL.PAS—the *ProcessHostHelo* Procedure in Which the Client Examines the Server's Response to the *Helo* Command and Determines Which Command To Issue Next

```
procedure TSMTPClient.ProcessHostHelo;
var
   lsWelcomeMsg, lsRetnCode: String;
   lbContinue: boolean;
begin
   {Initialize the continue flag to FALSE, so that you have to alter it
   only in the event of a positive response from the server}
   lbContinue := FALSE;
   {Convert the received message to a Pascal string}
   lsWelcomeMsg := StrPas(ReceiveBuffer);
   {Copy the response code into the lsRetnCode variable}
   lsRetnCode := Copy(lsWelcomeMsg, 1, 3);
   {Check to see what was returned}
```

```
      case StrToInt(lsRetnCode) of
         {Positive Response, set the continue flag to TRUE}
         250: lbContinue := TRUE;
         {Some sort of Negative Response}
         421: ;
         500: ;
         501: ;
         504: ;
      end;
      {Set the command status flag to NOOP}
      iiMailStatus := MAIL_NOOP;
      {Display the response message}
      stStatus.Caption := lsWelcomeMsg;
      stStatus.Update;
      {If you are continuing}
      if lbContinue then
      begin
         {Set the command status flag to indicate that you sent a MAIL FROM}
         iiMailStatus := MAIL_MAILFROM;
         {Send the MAIL command to the mail server,
         telling it who the sender is}
         NetSocket.SocketSend(isConnectionSocket, handle, UWM_SOCKETEVENT,
            'MAIL FROM:<' + sleLogin.text + '>', SKT_SENDPACKET);
         {Clear the receive buffer}
         ClearBuffer(ReceiveBuffer, 8192);
         {Prepare for receiving the response from the server}
      end;
   end;
```

Telling the SMTP Server to Whom To Send the Message

When you receive the response to the MAIL command, you must tell the server to whom to send the message. To do so, you pass the RCPT command with the recipient address as part of the parameters (enclosed in angled brackets, as in the return address), as in the following example:

```
RCPT TO: <davischa@onramp.net>
```

Listing 9.4 shows ProcessHostMailFrom, the procedure that tells the server where you are sending the message.

Listing 9.4   TMAIL.PAS—the *ProcessHostMailFrom* Procedure Tells the Server to Whom To Send Your Message

```
procedure TSMTPClient.ProcessHostMailFrom;
var
   lsWelcomeMsg, lsRetnCode: String;
   lbContinue: boolean;
```

continues

Listing 9.4 Continued

```
begin
    {Initialize the continue flag to FALSE, so that you have to alter it
    only in the event of a positive response from the server}
    lbContinue := FALSE;
    {Convert the received message to a Pascal string}
    lsWelcomeMsg := StrPas(ReceiveBuffer);
    {Copy the response code into the lsRetnCode variable}
    lsRetnCode := Copy(lsWelcomeMsg, 1, 3);
    {Check to see what was returned}
    case StrToInt(lsRetnCode) of
        {Positive Response, set the continue flag to TRUE}
        250: lbContinue := TRUE;
        {Some sort of Negative Response}
        421: ;
        451: ;
        452: ;
        500: ;
        501: ;
        552: ;
    end;
    {Set the command status flag to NOOP}
    iiMailStatus := MAIL_NOOP;
    {Display the response message}
    stStatus.Caption := lsWelcomeMsg;
    stStatus.Update;
    {If you are continuing}
    if lbContinue then
    begin
        {Set the command status flag to indicate that you sent an RCPT TO}
        iiMailStatus := MAIL_RCPTTO;
        {Send the RCPT command to the mail server, telling it to whom
        to send the message}
        NetSocket.SocketSend(isConnectionSocket, handle, UWM_SOCKETEVENT,
            'RCPT TO:<' + sleTo.text + '>', SKT_SENDPACKET);
        {Clear the receive buffer}
        ClearBuffer(ReceiveBuffer, 8192);
    end;
end;
```

Telling the SMTP Server of Any Additional People to Whom To Send the Message

After receiving the server's response to the RCPT command, you must issue additional RCPT commands to specify any additional recipients on either the *Send To:*, *CC:*, or *BCC:* lines. If you have specified all the recipients, you must issue the DATA command to tell the server that you are ready to send the message text. The `ProcessHostRcptTo` procedure specifies additional recipients and issues `DATA` (see Listing 9.5).

> **N O T E**   In the example implementation, the user can specify only a single *To:* and *CC:* address. To enable the user to specify multiple recipients on either the *To:* or *CC:* lines, you must parse each line into the separate address and issue an `RCPT` command for each address specified. For example, consider a mail message that has the following *To:* and *CC:* lines:
>
> ```
> TO: bob@somewhere.com
> CC: davischa@onramp.net, bclinton@whitehouse.gov, billg@microsoft.com
> ```
>
> Your SMTP mail client would have to issue the following four `RCPT` commands:
>
> ```
> RCPT TO: <bob@somewhere.com>
> RCPT TO: <davischa@onramp.net>
> RCPT TO: <bclinton@whitehouse.gov>
> RCPT TO: <billg@microsoft.com>
> ```

Listing 9.5   TMAIL.PAS—the *ProcessHostRcptTo* Procedure Specifies Additional Recipients and Tells the Server That You Are Ready To Send Your Message Text

```
procedure TSMTPClient.ProcessHostRcptTo;
var
   lsWelcomeMsg, lsRetnCode: String;
   lbContinue: boolean;
begin
   {Initialize the continue flag to FALSE, so that you have to alter it
   only in the event of a positive response from the server}
   lbContinue := FALSE;
   {Convert the received message to a Pascal string}
   lsWelcomeMsg := StrPas(ReceiveBuffer);
   {Copy the response code into the lsRetnCode variable}
   lsRetnCode := Copy(lsWelcomeMsg, 1, 3);
   {Check to see what was returned}
   case StrToInt(lsRetnCode) of
      {Positive Response, set the continue flag to TRUE}
      250: lbContinue := TRUE;
      251: lbContinue := TRUE;
      {Some sort of Negative Response}
      421: ;
      450: ;
      451: ;
      452: ;
      500: ;
      501: ;
      503: ;
      550: ;
      551: ;
      552: ;
      553: ;
   end;
```

continues

Listing 9.5   Continued

```
{Display the response message}
stStatus.Caption := lsWelcomeMsg;
stStatus.Update;
{If you are continuing}
if lbContinue then
begin
    {Do you have a CC address to which to send this message?}
    if ((Length(sleCC.Text) > 0) and (iiMailStatus = MAIL_RCPTTO)) then
    begin
        {If you have a CC address, tell the server about it}
        {Set command status flag to indicate that you sent RCPT TO}
        iiMailStatus := MAIL_RCPTCC;
        {Send the RCPT command to the mail server, telling it whom
        to send the message}
        NetSocket.SocketSend(isConnectionSocket, handle, UWM_
            SOCKETEVENT, 'RCPT TO:<' + sleCC.text + '>', SKT_SENDPACKET);
        {Clear the receive buffer}
        ClearBuffer(ReceiveBuffer, 8192);
    end
    else
    begin
        {No one else to whom to send the message, so send the message}
        {Set the command status flag to indicate that you sent a DATA}
        iiMailStatus := MAIL_DATA;
        {Send the DATA command to the mail server, telling it that you
        are about to send the message}
        NetSocket.SocketSend(isConnectionSocket, handle,
            UWM_SOCKETEVENT, 'DATA', SKT_SENDPACKET);
        {Clear the receive buffer}
        ClearBuffer(ReceiveBuffer, 8192);
    end;
end;
end;
```

Sending the Message Header

After sending the mail message, you have to start the header section. Pascal imposes a limit on the length of its strings, so you have to break the header into one or two header line pieces and send these pieces as a series of messages. Remember that the Internet Message Format specifies that an empty line separate the message header section from the body. Therefore, the first empty line sent is interpreted as the end of the header section and the beginning of the body section. Before sending any strings that it has received, the TSocket object's SocketSend() function adds a carriage-return and line-feed character combination to the end of each string. For this reason, you must ensure that you add such a character combination to the end of only the last header string that you are sending. You can embed as many of these character combinations in the midst of the line as long as none of them are next to each other with nothing between them. Listing 9.6 shows the SendMessageHeader procedure, which assembles and sends the message header.

N O T E With the release of version 2.0, Delphi no longer limits the size of Pascal strings. However, in this book's examples, the length of all Pascal strings is limited to maintain compatibility with Delphi 1.0. This compatibility is important if you still need to produce 16-bit applications. ■

Part
II

Ch
9

Listing 9.6   TMAIL.PAS—the *SendMessageHeader* Procedure Assembles and Sends the Message Header

```
procedure TSMTPClient.SendMessageHeader;
var
   lsHeader: String;
begin
   {Build the TO header line, adding a carriage return and line feed to
   the end of the line}
   lsHeader := 'To: ' + sleTo.Text + #13#10;
   {Add the FROM header line. This is the end of what you are sending as
   one packet, so you need to be sure not to add on carriage-return and
   line-feed characters, or else the mail servers and readers will think
   this is the end of the message header}
   lsHeader := lsHeader + 'From: ' + sleLogin.Text;
   {Send the two header lines already assembled to the server}
   NetSocket.SocketSend(isConnectionSocket, handle, UWM_SOCKETEVENT,
                        lsHeader, SKT_SENDPACKET);
   {Build the SUBJECT header line. You have to assume that the line
   could be long, so you don't want to add anything else to this
   header line. Because you are not adding anything else, you need
   to be sure not to add the carriage-return and line-feed characters
   because you are not finished with the header section}
   lsHeader := 'Subject: ' + sleSubject.Text;
   {Send the Subject line to the server}
   NetSocket.SocketSend(isConnectionSocket, handle, UWM_SOCKETEVENT,
                        lsHeader, SKT_SENDPACKET);
   {Build a couple of header lines stating which mailer created this
   message. These header lines are not standard, but are user-defined
   extensions, as has become fairly common practice. These lines
   are the end of the message header, so you want to add the
   carriage-return and line-feed characters to the end of each line.
   Therefore, when the SocketSend procedure adds another carriage-
   return and newline pair, it is seen as the separator between
   the message header and body}
   lsHeader := 'X-Sender: ' + #13#10;
   lsHeader := lsHeader + 'X-Mailer: Delphi SMTP Mailer v1.0' + #13#10;
   {Send the last two lines of the message header}
   NetSocket.SocketSend(isConnectionSocket, handle, UWM_SOCKETEVENT,
                        lsHeader, SKT_SENDPACKET);
   {Call the SendMessageText procedure, to send the message body}
   SendMessageText;
end;
```

Sending the Message Body

Now that you have sent the header section, the SendMessageText procedure sends the message body (see Listing 9.7). To fit the message into Pascal strings (so that you can use the SocketSend() function), the procedure parses the message into 245-byte blocks. (If you were building a polished application, you would want to handle this message parsing differently, because this method is likely to perform some interesting reformatting on long messages.) SendMessageText sends each message block until it reaches the end of the message. You then send the end-of-message marker (#13#10 + '.' + #13#10). The procedure then calls the WinSock recv() function to get the server response to the entire message, and calls ProcessHostData to verify that the message has been sent successfully.

Listing 9.7   TMAIL.PAS—the *SendMessageText* Procedure Sends the Body of the Message

```
procedure TSMTPClient.SendMessageText;
var
   lsText: String;
   liTextPos, liBufPos, liTextLength: Integer;
   lpcMessBuf: PChar;
   lpcBufArray: Array[0..245] of Char;
begin
   {Get the message body length}
   liTextLength := mleMessage.GetTextLen;
   {allocate a Pchar buffer to hold the entire message}
   lpcMessBuf := StrAlloc((liTextLength + 1));
   {Copy the message from the TMEMO field into the allocated buffer}
   mleMessage.GetTextBuf(lpcMessBuf, (liTextlength + 1));
   {Is the message longer than 245 characters long? The reason for the
   245 character limit is to ensure that the strings can be converted
   to Pascal strings and passed to the SocketSend function, so that
   you don't have to build a new send function. The 245 character limit
   leaves enough room to add the carriage-return and line-feed
   characters to the end of each line}
   if (liTextLength > 245) then
   begin
      {If so, you need to break it up into multiple messages}
      liTextPos := 0;
      {Loop until you reach the end of the message}
      while (liTextPos < liTextLength) do
      begin
         {Copy the text into the smaller buffer, limiting the copied text
         to 245 character strings}
         liBufPos := 0;
         while ((liBufPos < 245) and (liTextPos < liTextLength)) do
         begin
            lpcBufArray[liBufPos] := lpcMessBuf[liTextPos];
            Inc(liBufPos);
            Inc(liTextPos);
         end;
         {Mark the end of the copied string with a NULL character}
         lpcBufArray[liBufPos] := #0;
```

```
            {Convert the string into a Pascal string}
            lsText := StrPas(lpcBufArray);
            {Send the string to the server}
            NetSocket.SocketSend(isConnectionSocket, handle,
                UWM_SOCKETEVENT, lsText, SKT_SENDPACKET);
        end;
        {You have reached the end of the message; send the message-
        termination string}
        NetSocket.SocketSend(isConnectionSocket, handle,
            UWM_SOCKETEVENT, #13#10 + '.' + #13#10, SKT_SENDPACKET);
    end
    else
    begin
        {The message is shorter than 245 characters; send it with
        the message-termination string on the end}
        lsText := StrPas(lpcMessBuf) + #13#10 + '.' + #13#10;
        NetSocket.SocketSend(isConnectionSocket, handle,
            UWM_SOCKETEVENT, lsText, SKT_SENDPACKET);
    end;
    {Release the memory allocated for holding the message body}
    StrDispose(lpcMessBuf);
    {Clear the receive buffer}
    ClearBuffer(ReceiveBuffer, 8192);
    {Set the socket into synchronous mode, so that the following recv()
    will wait until a response is received from the server}
    WSAAsyncSelect(isConnectionSocket, handle, 0, 0);
    {Receive the response to the message body from the server}
    liTextLength := recv(isConnectionSocket, ReceiveBuffer, 8192, 0);
    {Did you receive anything?}
    if (liTextLength > 0) then
        {If so, call ProcessHostData to process the response}
        ProcessHostData
    else
    begin
        {if you didn't receive anything, try again}
        liTextLength := recv(isConnectionSocket, ReceiveBuffer, 8192, 0);
        {Did you receive anything this time?}
        if (liTextLength > 0) then
            {If so, call ProcessHostData to process the response}
            ProcessHostData
        else
        begin
            {You still didn't receive a response from the message}
            {Set the command status flag to indicate that you sent a QUIT}
            iiMailStatus := MAIL_QUIT;
            {Send the QUIT command to the mail server, telling the server
            that you have finished your session}
            NetSocket.SocketSend(isConnectionSocket, handle,
                UWM_SOCKETEVENT, 'QUIT', SKT_SENDPACKET);
            {Clear the receive buffer}
            ClearBuffer(ReceiveBuffer, 8192);

        end;
    end;
end;
```

Sending the Message to the SMTP Server

After receiving the response to the DATA command, you call SendMessageHeader to send the actual message header. That procedure, in turn, calls SendMessageText to send the message body. After the application finishes sending the message, you again call ProcessHostData to check the server response code to verify that you sent the message successfully (see Listing 9.8). If so, you send the server the QUIT command to end the session.

Listing 9.8 TMAIL.PAS—the *ProcessHostData* Procedure Verifies That the Application Sent Your Message Successfully

```
procedure TSMTPClient.ProcessHostData;
var
    lsWelcomeMsg, lsRetnCode: String;
    lbContinue: boolean;
    lbDone: boolean;
begin
    {Initialize the continue flag to FALSE, so that you have to alter it
    only in the event of a positive response from the server}
    lbContinue := FALSE;
    lbDone := FALSE;
    {Convert the received message to a Pascal string}
    lsWelcomeMsg := StrPas(ReceiveBuffer);
    {Copy the response code into the lsRetnCode variable}
    lsRetnCode := Copy(lsWelcomeMsg, 1, 3);
    {Check to see what was returned}
    case StrToInt(lsRetnCode) of
        {Positive Response, set the continue flag to TRUE}
        250:
        begin
            lbContinue := TRUE;
            {250 also means that the server has received the complete
            message. You are finished and can end this session}
            lbDone := TRUE;
        end;
        354: lbContinue := TRUE;
        {Some sort of Negative Response}
        421: ;
        451: ;
        452: ;
        500: ;
        501: ;
        503: ;
        552: ;
        554: ;
    end;
    {Set the command status flag to NOOP}
    iiMailStatus := MAIL_NOOP;
```

```
{Display the response message}
stStatus.Caption := lsWelcomeMsg;
stStatus.Update;
{If you are continuing}
if lbContinue then
begin
    {Are you finished sending the message?}
    if lbDone then
    begin
      {Set the command status flag to indicate that you sent a QUIT}
      iiMailStatus := MAIL_QUIT;
      {Send the QUIT command to the mail server, telling the server
      that you have finished your session}
      NetSocket.SocketSend(isConnectionSocket, handle,
          UWM_SOCKETEVENT, 'QUIT', SKT_SENDPACKET);
      {Clear the receive buffer}
      ClearBuffer(ReceiveBuffer, 8192);
    end
    else
      {No, you haven't sent the message yet, the server is ready to
      receive the message}
      SendMessageHeader;
  end;
end;
```

Part
II

Ch
9

Quitting the SMTP Session

When you receive the server's response to the QUIT command, the ProcessHostQuit procedure clears all the message fields and shuts down the socket connection (see Listing 9.9). The
procedure leaves your SMTP client ready to let the user enter another mail message to send to
the same recipient or a different one.

**Listing 9.9   TMAIL.PAS—the *ProcessHostQuit* Procedure Sets Up the Client
To Send Another Mail Message**

```
procedure TSMTPClient.ProcessHostQuit;
var
   lsWelcomeMsg, lsRetnCode: String;
   lbContinue: boolean;
begin
   {Initialize the continue flag to FALSE so that you have to alter it
   only if the server returns a positive response}
   lbContinue := FALSE;
   {Convert the received message to a Pascal string}
   lsWelcomeMsg := StrPas(ReceiveBuffer);
   {Copy the response code into the lsRetnCode variable}
   lsRetnCode := Copy(lsWelcomeMsg, 1, 3);
   {Check to see what was returned}
```

continues

Listing 9.9 Continued

```
case StrToInt(lsRetnCode) of
  {Positive Response, set the continue flag to TRUE}
  221: lbContinue := TRUE;
  {Some sort of Negative Response}
  500: ;
end;
{Set the command status flag to NOOP}
iiMailStatus := MAIL_NOOP;
{Display the response message}
stStatus.Caption := lsWelcomeMsg;
stStatus.Update;
{Clear all of the message-specific data from the screen}
sleTo.Clear;
sleCC.Clear;
sleSubject.Clear;
mleMessage.Clear;
{If you are connected}
if ibConnected then
begin
{Shut down and close the socket connection to the server}
  shutdown(isConnectionSocket, 0);
  NetSocket.CloseSocketConnection(isConnectionSocket);
end;
end;
```

Directing the SMTP Server Responses to the Appropriate Procedure

The `ProcessHostReceive` procedure is essentially the same as that which you have built for your other applications (see Listing 9.10). The procedure checks the SMTP conversation's current state and calls the appropriate response-processing procedure. The rest of the SMTP mail client is just the usual window-painting and application overhead.

Listing 9.10 TMAIL.PAS—the *ProcessHostReceive* Procedure Checks the Conversation's State and Initiates the Appropriate Response

```
procedure TSMTPClient.ProcessHostReceive;
var
   lsRetnStr: String;
   liCarRetnPos: Integer;
begin
   try
{Receive any incoming data}
liCarRetnPos := recv(isConnectionSocket, ReceiveBuffer, 8192, 0);
ReceiveBuffer[liCarRetnPos] := Char(0);
      {You have received an FD_READ event, so check whether you
      received anything}
      if (ReceiveBuffer[0] = Char(0)) then
```

```
begin
   {Clear the receive buffer}
   ClearBuffer(ReceiveBuffer, 8192);
end
else
begin
   {You received data, so check which command you issued and
   call the appropriate procedure}
   case iiMailStatus of
      MAIL_NOOP: ;
      MAIL_CONNECT: ProcessHostWelcome;
      MAIL_HELO: ProcessHostHelo;
      MAIL_MAILFROM: ProcessHostMailFrom;
      MAIL_RCPTTO: ProcessHostRcptTo;
      MAIL_RCPTCC: ProcessHostRcptTo;
      MAIL_DATA: ProcessHostData;
      MAIL_RSET: ;
      MAIL_SEND: ;
      MAIL_SOML: ;
      MAIL_SAML: ;
      MAIL_VRFY: ;
      MAIL_EXPN: ;
      MAIL_HELP: ;
      MAIL_TURN: ;
      MAIL_QUIT: ProcessHostQuit;
   end;
end;
except
   {Clear the receive buffer}
   ClearBuffer(ReceiveBuffer, 8192);
end;
end;
```

Figure 9.2 shows the SMPT Send Mail client application running.

FIG. 9.2

The SMTP Send Mail
client in action.

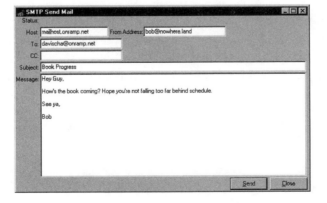

Building a POP Retrieve Mail Client Application

The SMTP Send Mail client application is fairly simple. The POP Retrieve Mail client is a little more complex, but not much.

The POP mail client that you will build enables the user to specify a mailbox, password, and the mail server to which to connect. On connecting to the mail server, the client retrieves the headers from all the mail messages currently on the server. The user can then specify a mail message to retrieve from the server. This application cannot save the messages that it receives into any storage files so that you can retrieve messages for later review. Also, the application does not delete the messages from the mail server, leaving them for future retrieval (with a more feature-complete mail client). To enable this application to download all mail messages, you must implement a local storage system. Because this application does not implement such a system, you retrieve messages only when the user selects them for retrieval. On choosing to connect to the mail server, the POP client takes the following steps:

1. Connects to the POP mail server.
2. Receives a greeting from the server.
3. Sends the USER message to the server, specifying the mailbox that the user wants to use.
4. On receiving the response to the USER command, uses the PASS command to send the password for the specified mailbox.
5. On receiving the response to the PASS command, uses the STAT command to check how many messages are in the mailbox.
6. On receiving the response to the STAT command, uses the TOP command to begin requesting the message headers. This command starts with the first message and loops until all message headers have been retrieved.
7. If no additional message headers remain to be retrieved, becomes idle and waits for the user to specify a message to retrieve.
8. When the user double-clicks a message header, issues the RETR command to retrieve the entire message.
9. On receiving the entire message, returns to the idle state and waits for the user to select another message or to choose to quit the session.
10. If the user chooses to quit the session, sends the QUIT command to the server.
11. On receiving the response to the QUIT command, closes the connection.

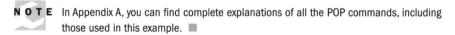

N O T E In Appendix A, you can find complete explanations of all the POP commands, including those used in this example. ■

In this example, you use the same procedures for looking up the server address and initiating the connection as you used in the previous examples (see Chapters 6 and 8). You can find in these previous chapters explanations of any procedures and functions that this chapter does not list or explain. Table 9.3 lists the files used in this project.

Table 9.3 POP Mail Client Project Files	
POPMAIL.DPR	The POP mail client Delphi project file.
TPOP.DFM	The POP mail client window.
TPOP.PAS	The POP mail client code.
TSOCKETC.PAS	The TSocket WinSock abstraction class (first developed in Chapter 6 and expanded in Chapter 8).
NWINSOCK.PAS	The WinSock API definition file.

Defining the POP Command State Table

To start, you define the state table constants for each of the POP commands that you might issue (see Listing 9.11).

Listing 9.11 TPOP.PAS—the POP Client Application's Constant Declarations

```
const
{Constant declarations to represent POP commands. You use these
declarations to keep track of which command was last issued,
so that responses received from the server can be directed to
the appropriate procedure}
  MAIL_NOOP = 0;
  MAIL_CONNECT = 1;
  MAIL_USER = 2;
  MAIL_PASS = 3;
  MAIL_QUIT = 4;
  MAIL_STAT = 5;
  MAIL_LIST = 6;
  MAIL_RETR = 7;
  MAIL_DELE = 8;
  MAIL_RSET = 9;
  MAIL_APOP = 10;
  MAIL_TOP = 11;
  MAIL_UIDL = 12;
{User-defined event declarations for socket events. The first is
for the primary socket, the second for address lookup notifications)
  UWM_SOCKETEVENT = WM_USER + 500;
  UWM_ADDRSOCKETEVENT = WM_USER + 501;
```

Receiving the Greeting from the Server and Sending the Logon

After connecting to the POP mail server, you must capture the greeting and respond by initiating the login process. The ProcessHostWelcome procedure initiates this process by sending the server a USER command with the account name (see Listing 9.12).

Listing 9.12   TPOP.PAS—the *ProcessHostWelcome* Procedure Initiates the Login Process

```
procedure TTPOPClient.ProcessHostWelcome;
var
   lsWelcomeMsg, lsRetnCode: String;
begin
   {Convert the received message to a Pascal string}
   lsWelcomeMsg := StrPas(ReceiveBuffer);
   {Copy the response code into the lsRetnCode variable}
   lsRetnCode := Copy(lsWelcomeMsg, 1, 3);
   {Check to see what was returned}
   if (lsRetnCode = '+OK') then
      {Positive Response, you are connected}
      ibConnected := TRUE
   else
      {Negative Response, you are not connected}
      ibConnected := FALSE;
   {Set the command status flag to NOOP}
   iiMailStatus := MAIL_NOOP;
   {Display the response message}
   stStatus.Caption := lsWelcomeMsg;
   stStatus.Update;
   {If you are connected}
   if ibConnected then
   begin
      {Set the command status flag to indicate that you sent a USER}
      iiMailStatus := MAIL_USER;
      stState.Caption := 'MAIL_USER';
      stState.Update;
      {Send the USER command to the mail server, telling it who you are}
      NetSocket.SocketSend(isConnectionSocket, handle, UWM_SOCKETEVENT,
         'USER ' + sleLogin.Text, SKT_SENDPACKET);
      {Clear the receive buffer}
      ClearBuffer(ReceiveBuffer, 8192);
   end;
end;
```

Receiving the Logon Response and Sending the Password

Now that you have sent the USER command, you need to verify that the account exists on the server. If it does, the ProcessHostUser procedure continues the authentication process by sending the account password with the PASS command as stored in slePassword (see Listing 9.13). If the account doesn't exist, the procedure sends the QUIT command.

Listing 9.13 TPOP.PAS—the *ProcessHostUser* Procedure Verifies That the Specified Account Exists on the Server

```pascal
procedure TTPOPClient.ProcessHostUser;
var
   lsWelcomeMsg, lsRetnCode: String;
   lbContinue: boolean;
begin
   {Initialize the continue flag to FALSE, so that you have to alter it
   only in the event of a positive response from the server}
   lbContinue := FALSE;
   {Convert the received message to a Pascal string}
   lsWelcomeMsg := StrPas(ReceiveBuffer);
   {Copy the response code into the lsRetnCode variable}
   lsRetnCode := Copy(lsWelcomeMsg, 1, 3);
   {Check to see what was returned}
   if (lsRetnCode = '+OK') then
      {Positive Response, set the continue flag to TRUE}
      lbContinue := TRUE;
   {Set the command status flag to NOOP}
   iiMailStatus := MAIL_NOOP;
   {Display the response message}
   stStatus.Caption := lsWelcomeMsg;
   stStatus.Update;
   {If you are continuing}
   if lbContinue then
   begin
      {Set the command status flag to indicate that you sent a PASS}
      iiMailStatus := MAIL_PASS;
      stState.Caption := 'MAIL_PASS';
      stState.Update;
      {Send the PASS command to the mail server,
       telling it your password}
      NetSocket.SocketSend(isConnectionSocket, handle, UWM_SOCKETEVENT,
         'PASS ' + slePassword.Text, SKT_SENDPACKET);
      {Clear the receive buffer}
      ClearBuffer(ReceiveBuffer, 8192);
   end
   else
   begin
      {Set the command status flag to indicate that you sent a QUIT}
      iiMailStatus := MAIL_QUIT;
      stState.Caption := 'MAIL_QUIT';
      stState.Update;
      {Send the QUIT command to the mail server, telling it you have
      finished your session}
      NetSocket.SocketSend(isConnectionSocket, handle, UWM_SOCKETEVENT,
         'QUIT', SKT_SENDPACKET);
      {Clear the receive buffer}
      ClearBuffer(ReceiveBuffer, 8192);
   end;
end;
```

Checking the Mailbox Status

After successfully logging in to the POP server, you want to check the account's status to determine how many messages are in the mailbox. To check this, the ProcessHostPass procedure issues the STAT command (see Listing 9.14). If you failed to log in to the server, the procedure issues the QUIT command and ends the session.

Listing 9.14   TPOP.PAS—the *ProcessHostPass* Procedure Checks How Many Messages Are in the Mailbox

```
procedure TTPOPClient.ProcessHostPass;
var
   lsWelcomeMsg, lsRetnCode: String;
   lbContinue: boolean;
begin
   {Initialize the continue flag to FALSE, so that you have to alter it
   only in the event of a positive response from the server}
   lbContinue := FALSE;
   {Convert the received message to a Pascal string}
   lsWelcomeMsg := StrPas(ReceiveBuffer);
   {Copy the response code into the lsRetnCode variable}
   lsRetnCode := Copy(lsWelcomeMsg, 1, 3);
   {Check to see what was returned}
   if (lsRetnCode = '+OK') then
      {Positive Response, set the continue flag to TRUE}
      lbContinue := TRUE;
   {Set the command status flag to NOOP}
   iiMailStatus := MAIL_NOOP;
   {Display the response message}
   stStatus.Caption := lsWelcomeMsg;
   stStatus.Update;
   {If you are continuing}
   if lbContinue then
   begin
      {Set the command status flag to indicate that you sent a STAT}
      iiMailStatus := MAIL_STAT;
      stState.Caption := 'MAIL_STAT';
      stState.Update;
      {Send the STAT command to the mail server, asking for the mailbox
      status}
      NetSocket.SocketSend(isConnectionSocket, handle,
         UWM_SOCKETEVENT, 'STAT', SKT_SENDPACKET);
      {Clear the receive buffer}
      ClearBuffer(ReceiveBuffer, 8192);
   end
   else
   begin
      {Set the command status flag to indicate that you sent a QUIT}
      iiMailStatus := MAIL_QUIT;
      stState.Caption := 'MAIL_QUIT';
      stState.Update;
      {Send the QUIT command to the mail server, telling it you have
      finished your session}
      NetSocket.SocketSend(isConnectionSocket, handle, UWM_SOCKETEVENT,
```

```
            'QUIT', SKT_SENDPACKET);
        {Clear the receive buffer}
        ClearBuffer(ReceiveBuffer, 8192);
    end;
end;
```

Receiving the Mailbox Status and Requesting the First Message Header

After receiving the response to the STAT command, you must parse the number of messages from the response. If any messages are in the mailbox, the ProcessHostStat procedure starts a loop that issues the TOP command to capture the header information from each message (see Listing 9.15).

> **Listing 9.15 TPOP.PAS—the *ProcessHostStat* Procedure Captures Each Message's Header Information**

```
procedure TTPOPClient.ProcessHostStat;
var
    lsRetnMsg, lsRetnCode: String;
    lbContinue: boolean;
    liSpacePos: Integer;
begin
    {Initialize the continue flag to FALSE, so that you have to alter it
    only in the event of a positive response from the server}
    lbContinue := FALSE;
    {Convert the received message to a Pascal string}
    lsRetnMsg := StrPas(ReceiveBuffer);
    {Copy the response code into the lsRetnCode variable}
    lsRetnCode := Copy(lsRetnMsg, 1, 3);
    {Check to see what was returned}
    if (lsRetnCode = '+OK') then
        {Positive Response, set the continue flag to TRUE}
        lbContinue := TRUE;
    {Set the command status flag to NOOP}
    iiMailStatus := MAIL_NOOP;
    {Display the response message}
    stStatus.Caption := lsRetnMsg;
    stStatus.Update;
    {If you are continuing}
    if lbContinue then
    begin
        {You must parse the returned status message to find out how many
        messages are sitting in the mailbox. You start by locating the
        first space character}
        liSpacePos := Pos(' ', lsRetnMsg);
        if (liSpacePos > 0) then
        begin
            {Trim everything through the first space (the status
            indicator)}
```

continues

Listing 9.15   Continued

```
            lsRetnMsg := Copy(lsRetnMsg, (liSpacePos + 1),
                              Length(lsRetnMsg));
            {Find the next space character}
            liSpacePos := Pos(' ', lsRetnMsg);
            {Everything in front of the next space character is the number
            of messages in the mailbox, so you want to copy and convert that
            into a variable to maintain how many messages to expect}
            if (liSpacePos > 0) then
               iiNumMessages := StrToInt(Copy(lsRetnMsg, 1,
                          (liSpacePos - 1)));
         end;
         {Are there any messages to retrieve?}
         if (iiNumMessages > 0) then
         begin
            {Yes, there are messages to retrieve}
            {Set the command status flag to indicate that you sent a TOP}
            iiMailStatus := MAIL_TOP;
            stState.Caption := 'MAIL_TOP 1 of ' + IntToStr(iiNumMessages);
            stState.Update;
            {Set the message counter to indicate that you are retrieving
            the first message}
            iiCurMessage := 1;
            {Send the TOP command to the mail server, requesting the top
            of the first message}
            NetSocket.SocketSend(isConnectionSocket, handle,
               UWM_SOCKETEVENT, 'TOP 1 1', SKT_SENDPACKET);
            {Clear the receive buffer}
            ClearBuffer(ReceiveBuffer, 8192);
         end
         else
         begin
            {No messages to be retrieved, tell the user}
            ShowMessage('No messages on server.');
            {Set the command status flag to indicate that you sent a QUIT}
            iiMailStatus := MAIL_QUIT;
            stState.Caption := 'MAIL_QUIT';
            stState.Update;
            {Send the QUIT command to the mail server, telling it you are
            finished with your session}
            NetSocket.SocketSend(isConnectionSocket, handle,
                    UWM_SOCKETEVENT, 'QUIT', SKT_SENDPACKET);
            {Clear the receive buffer}
            ClearBuffer(ReceiveBuffer, 8192);
         end;
      end;
   end;
```

Parsing the Message Header and Requesting the Next Message Header

When you receive a message's header (in response to the TOP command), you want to parse the portions of interest and place them in a list box so that the user can select the messages to retrieve. If you retrieve the headers on all the messages, you want to enter an idle state and wait for the user to select a message to retrieve. If you haven't retrieved all the message headers, you want to retrieve the header of the next message by issuing another TOP command. Listing 9.16 shows the ProcessHostTop procedure, which displays the message headers in the list box.

Part
II

Ch
9

Listing 9.16 TPOP.PAS—the *ProcessHostTop* Procedure Displays the Message Headers in a List Box

```
procedure TTPOPClient.ProcessHostTop;
var
   lsRetnMsg, lsRetnCode: String;
   lbContinue: boolean;
   lbComplete: boolean;
   liSpacePos: Integer;
begin
   {Initialize the continue flag to FALSE, so that you have to alter it
   only if the server responds positively }
   lbContinue := FALSE;
   lbComplete := FALSE;
   {Get the first line from the received buffer}
   if (NetSocket.GetLine(TempBuffer, ReceiveBuffer) or
                (isHoldBuffer <> '')) then
   begin
      {Are you holding anything in the Hold buffer from a previous,
      incomplete message?}
      if (isHoldBuffer <> '') then
         {Yes, so set the continue flag to TRUE and skip the status
         code checking}
         lbContinue := TRUE
      else
      begin
         {No, this is the start of a new message}
         {Convert the received message to a Pascal string}
         lsRetnMsg := StrPas(TempBuffer);
         {Copy the response code into the lsRetnCode variable}
         lsRetnCode := Copy(lsRetnMsg, 1, 3);
         {Check to see what was returned}
         if (lsRetnCode = '+OK') then
            {Positive Response, set the continue flag to TRUE}
            lbContinue := TRUE;
         {Set the command status flag to NOOP}
         iiMailStatus := MAIL_NOOP;
         {Display the response message}
         stStatus.Caption := lsRetnMsg;
         stStatus.Update;
```

continues

Listing 9.16 Continued

```
end;
{If you are continuing}
if lbContinue then
begin
   {Is there anything in the Hold buffer?}
   if (isHoldBuffer <> '') then
   begin
      {Yes, add the first line to what is in the Hold buffer}
      lsRetnMsg := isHoldBuffer + StrPas(TempBuffer);
      {Empty the hold buffer, so you won't trigger this section
      again until you need to}
      isHoldBuffer := '';
      {Did you find the message-termination marker?}
      if (lsRetnMsg = '.') then
         {Yes, set the complete flag to TRUE}
         lbComplete := TRUE;
      {Do you have the FROM header field?}
      if (Pos('From:', lsRetnMsg) > 0) then
      begin
         {Yes, copy the field value into the isFrom variable}
         liSpacePos := Pos(' ', lsRetnMsg);
         if (liSpacePos > 0) then
            isFrom := Copy(lsRetnMsg, (liSpacePos + 1),
                        Length(lsRetnMsg));
      end;
      {Do you have the SUBJECT header field?}
      if (Pos('Subject:', lsRetnMsg) > 0) then
      begin
         {Yes, copy the field value into the isSubject variable}
         liSpacePos := Pos(' ', lsRetnMsg);
         if (liSpacePos > 0) then
            isSubject := Copy(lsRetnMsg, (liSpacePos + 1),
                           Length(lsRetnMsg));
      end;
      {You are done with special handling to complete
       the unfinished line held in the Hold buffer}
   end;
   {Loop as long as you can get complete lines from the received
   data and you haven't found the message-termination marker,
   getting the next line from the received data}
   while (NetSocket.GetLine(TempBuffer, ReceiveBuffer) and
            (not lbComplete)) do
   begin
      {Convert the line into a Pascal string}
      lsRetnMsg := StrPas(TempBuffer);
      {Did you find the message-termination marker?}
      if (lsRetnMsg = '.') then
         {Yes, set the complete flag to TRUE}
         lbComplete := TRUE;
      {Do you have the FROM header field?}
      if (Pos('From:', lsRetnMsg) > 0) then
      begin
         {Yes, copy the field value into the isFrom variable}
```

```
           liSpacePos := Pos(' ', lsRetnMsg);
           if (liSpacePos > 0) then
              isFrom := Copy(lsRetnMsg, (liSpacePos + 1),
                           Length(lsRetnMsg));
        end;
        {Do you have the SUBJECT header field?}
        if (Pos('Subject:', lsRetnMsg) > 0) then
        begin
           {Yes, copy the field value into the isSubject variable}
           liSpacePos := Pos(' ', lsRetnMsg);
           if (liSpacePos > 0) then
              isSubject := Copy(lsRetnMsg, (liSpacePos + 1),
                              Length(lsRetnMsg));
        end;
        {Loop back and get the next line from the received data}
   end;
   {Have you received the complete message?}
   if lbComplete then
   begin
      {If so, add the From and Subject information into the
      lbMessages List Box}
      lbMessages.Items.Add(isFrom + ' - ' + isSubject);
      {Are there more messages to retrieve?}
      if (iiNumMessages > iiCurMessage) then
      begin
         {Set the command status flag to indicate that you
         sent a TOP}
         iiMailStatus := MAIL_TOP;
         {Increment the message counter}
         Inc(iiCurMessage);
         {Update the display to indicate which message you are
         retrieving}
         stState.Caption := 'MAIL_TOP ' + IntToStr(iiCurMessage) +
                 ' of ' + IntToStr(iiNumMessages);
         stState.Update;
         {Send the TOP command to the mail server, requesting the
         top of the next message}
         NetSocket.SocketSend(isConnectionSocket, handle,
           UWM_SOCKETEVENT, 'TOP ' + IntToStr(iiCurMessage) + ' 1',
             SKT_SENDPACKET);
         {Clear the receive buffer}
         ClearBuffer(ReceiveBuffer, 8192);
      end
      else
      begin
         {No more messages to retrieve, place the client into
         an idle state, waiting for the user to select an action}
         {Set the command status flag to NOOP}
         iiMailStatus := MAIL_NOOP;
         stState.Caption := 'MAIL_NOOP ' + IntToStr(iiCurMessage)
                 + ' of ' + IntToStr(iiNumMessages);
         stState.Update;
         {Change the default command button from the CONNECT
         button to the RETRIEVE button}
         cbConnect.Default := FALSE;
```

continues

Listing 9.16   Continued

```
                  cbRetrieve.Default := TRUE;
            end;
        end
        else
        begin
          {Set the command status flag to indicate that you sent a TOP}
          iiMailStatus := MAIL_TOP;
          {Update the display to indicate which message you are
              retrieving}
          stState.Caption := 'MAIL_TOP ' + IntToStr(iiCurMessage) +
                          ' of ' + IntToStr(iiNumMessages);
          stState.Update;
          {You haven't received a message-termination marker,
          so you must have an incomplete line. You place it into
          the Hold buffer and add the first line from the next data
          received to it}
          isHoldBuffer := lsRetnMsg;
          {Clear the receive buffer}
          ClearBuffer(ReceiveBuffer, 8192);
        end;
    end;
  end
  else
  begin
    {Set the command status flag to NOOP}
    iiMailStatus := MAIL_NOOP;
    stState.Caption := 'MAIL_NOOP';
    stState.Update;
    {Display the response message}
    stStatus.Caption := 'Top of message not received.';
    stStatus.Update;
  end;
end;
```

Receiving a Mail Message

After issuing an RETR command, you must check the response from the server to verify that the request succeeded. If it did, the ProcessHostRetr procedure parses through the message as it is received, looking for the end-of-message marker (see Listing 9.17). Until reaching the end-of-message marker, the procedure adds each line to the text box so that the user can see and read the message. After finding the end-of-message marker, you place the session back into idle mode and wait for the user to select another message.

Listing 9.17 TPOP.PAS—the *ProcessHostRetr* Procedure Parses the Response to the *RETR* Command and Displays Each Line in the Text Box

```
procedure TTPOPClient.ProcessHostRetr;
var
   lsRetnMsg, lsRetnCode: String;
   lbContinue: boolean;
   lbComplete: boolean;
   liSpacePos: Integer;
begin
   {Initialize the continue flag to FALSE, so that you have to alter it
   only if the server responds positively}
   lbContinue := FALSE;
   lbComplete := FALSE;
   {Get the first line from the received buffer}
   if (NetSocket.GetLine(TempBuffer, ReceiveBuffer) or
          (isHoldBuffer <> '')) then
   begin
      {Are you holding anything in the Hold buffer from a previous,
      incomplete message?}
      if (isHoldBuffer <> '') then
         {Yes, so set the continue flag to TRUE and skip the status
         code checking}
         lbContinue := TRUE
      else
      begin
         {Convert the received message to a Pascal string}
         lsRetnMsg := StrPas(TempBuffer);
         {Copy the response code into the lsRetnCode variable}
         lsRetnCode := Copy(lsRetnMsg, 1, 3);
         {Check to see what was returned}
         if (lsRetnCode = '+OK') then
            {Positive Response, set the continue flag to TRUE}
            lbContinue := TRUE;
         {Set the command status flag to NOOP}
         iiMailStatus := MAIL_NOOP;
         {Display the response message}
         stStatus.Caption := lsRetnMsg;
         stStatus.Update;
      end;
      {If you are continuing}
      if lbContinue then
      begin
         {Is there anything in the Hold buffer?}
         if (isHoldBuffer <> '') then
         begin
            {Yes, add the first line to what is in the Hold buffer}
            lsRetnMsg := isHoldBuffer + StrPas(TempBuffer);
            {Empty the hold buffer, so you don't trigger this section
            again until you need to}
            isHoldBuffer := '';
            {Did you find the message-termination marker?}
            if (lsRetnMsg = '.') then
               {Yes, set the complete flag to TRUE}
```

continues

Listing 9.17 Continued

```
                    lbComplete := TRUE
                else
                    {No, add the line to the mleText Tmemo field}
                    mleText.Lines.Add(lsRetnMsg);
            end;
            {Loop as long as you can get complete lines from the received
            data and haven't found the message-termination marker,
            getting the next line from the received data}
            while (NetSocket.GetLine(TempBuffer, ReceiveBuffer) and
                        (not lbComplete)) do
            begin
                {Convert the line into a Pascal string}
                lsRetnMsg := StrPas(TempBuffer);
                {Did you find the message-termination marker?}
                if (lsRetnMsg = '.') then
                    {Yes, set the complete flag to TRUE}
                    lbComplete := TRUE
                else
                    {No, add the line to the mleText Tmemo field}
                    mleText.Lines.Add(lsRetnMsg);
            end;
            {Have you not received the complete message?}
            if not lbComplete then
            begin
                {Set the command status flag to indicate
                 that you sent an RETR}
                iiMailStatus := MAIL_RETR;
                isHoldBuffer := lsRetnMsg;
                {Clear the receive buffer}
                ClearBuffer(ReceiveBuffer, 8192);
            end;
        end;
    end
    else
    begin
        {You didn't receive anything}
        {Set the command status flag to NOOP}
        iiMailStatus := MAIL_NOOP;
        stState.Caption := 'MAIL_NOOP';
        stState.Update;
        {Display the response message}
        stStatus.Caption := 'Message not received.';
        stStatus.Update;
    end;
end;
```

Receiving the Response to a Session *QUIT* Request

On receiving the server response to the QUIT command, you must clean up, shut down the socket, and close the application. The ProcessHostQuit procedure performs each of these tasks (see Listing 9.18).

Listing 9.18 TPOP.PAS—the *ProcessHostQuit* Procedure Closes the Client Application

```
procedure TTPOPClient.ProcessHostQuit;
var
   lsRetnMsg: String;
begin
   {Convert the received message to a Pascal string}
   lsRetnMsg := StrPas(ReceiveBuffer);
   {Set the command status flag to NOOP}
   iiMailStatus := MAIL_NOOP;
   stState.Caption := 'MAIL_NOOP';
   stState.Update;
   {Display the response message}
   stStatus.Caption := lsRetnMsg;
   stStatus.Update;
   cbRetrieve.Default := FALSE;
   cbConnect.Default := TRUE;
   {If you are connected}
   if ibConnected then
      {Close the application, also closing the socket connection}
      Close;
end;
```

Selecting a Message To Retrieve

When the user selects a message to retrieve, you must determine the message number and pass it to the server with the RETR command. Listing 9.19 shows the procedure that passes this number to the server.

Listing 9.19 TPOP.PAS—the Procedure That Requests the Selected Message

```
procedure TTPOPClient.lbMessagesDblClick(Sender: TObject);
var
   liNumSelected: Integer;
begin
   {Get the message number that was selected for retrieval}
   liNumSelected := lbMessages.ItemIndex;
   {Did the user select a message?}
   if (liNumSelected > 0) then
```

continues

Listing 9.19 Continued

```
begin
  {Yes, clear the message area}
  mleText.Clear;
  {Display the action being started}
  stStatus.Caption := 'Retrieving Message ' +
     IntToStr((liNumSelected + 1));
  stStatus.Update;
  {Set the command status flag to indicate that you sent an RETR}
  iiMailStatus := MAIL_RETR;
  stState.Caption := 'MAIL_RETR';
  stState.Update;
  {Send the RETR command to the mail server, requesting the
  selected message}
  NetSocket.SocketSend(isConnectionSocket, handle, UWM_SOCKETEVENT,
     'RETR ' + IntToStr((liNumSelected + 1)), SKT_SENDPACKET);
  {Clear the receive buffer}
  ClearBuffer(ReceiveBuffer, 8192);
  end;
end;
```

Figure 9.3 shows the POP Mail Client application running.

FIG. 9.3

The POP Mail Client in action.

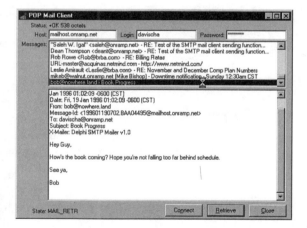

From Here...

In this chapter, you examined SMTP and POP, the primary protocols used for sending and receiving electronic mail over the Internet, how each behaves, and why you need both to provide a complete mail client. You also explored the two primary message formats—the Internet Message Format and MIME—to see how the information in the messages is interpreted and used. The message formats also enable you to examine how you can embed objects of various file types into Internet mail messages. You then applied all this information to build rudimentary versions of the two primary functions—sending and receiving—involved in Internet mail.

Part

II

Ch

9

From here, you could combine your two Internet mail clients into a single, integrated e-mail client. You could add mailbox-management capabilities into the POP mail client and provide additional message formatting and interpreting to make both mail clients MIME-enabled. Also, you could modify the SMTP client so that its sending capabilities are more flexible (for example, you could enable the client to handle more than one recipient and one CC recipient). You could build these applications' functionality in to other applications to make them Internet mail enabled. In short, you could introduce many enhancements to expand your mail clients' current capabilities.

For more information on how you can expand your mail client and what more you can do with Internet applications, see the following chapters:

- To familiarize yourself with the other widely used Internet applications, see Chapter 2, "The Basic Internet Application Suite."

- To understand the Usenet Internet News protocol, see Chapter 10, "Developing an Internet News Client/Reader."

- To become more familiar with the standard encoding schemes used in MIME and standard Internet file encoding, see Chapter 11, "Building a UUEncoder/Decoder."

- To get a glimpse at where Internet applications are going and how to incorporate mail into those future directions, see Chapter 12, "The Web—HTTP, HTML, and Beyond."

- To understand all the SMTP and POP commands, see Appendix A, "Internet Applications Command Sets."

- To gain a better understanding of the Internet Message Format, see Appendix B, "The Internet Message Format."

Developing an Internet News Client/Reader

Do you want to meet other people, express an opinion, or take part in a discussion on any topic imaginable? Then Usenet News might be the place for you. Usenet News is a global bulletin board on which you can post a message on any topic so that people all over the world can read it. The news is organized in groups, where the name of each group indicates the general topic category under discussion (although that category usually does not limit the participants' discussion).

This chapter takes a look at the Usenet News service and the Network News Transport Protocol (NNTP) that the news uses to provide its services to Internet users. ▪

Usenet News

The Usenet News network is a distributed service in which the local news server services each news client. The local server holds all the news articles for a while but eventually deletes them to make room for newer articles. Each news server's system administrator specifies how long an article remains in a particular newsgroup.

When posted to a newsgroup on a news server, an article is distributed throughout the entire Usenet network of news servers, eventually ending up on every news server that carries the newsgroup to which the article was posted. This system of global distribution makes the Usenet News network an attractive forum for discussions on any topic imaginable. No matter what the topic, there is probably someone else, somewhere in the world, who has an interest in the same topic.

N O T E Newsgroups are not what the name might imply. You won't find the daily news or the hot headlines in any of these newsgroups. Instead, you'll find an area of discussion in which many people are voicing opinions and taking part in arguments, usually on a general subject indicated by the newsgroup name, but not always (discussions often stray far afield from the newsgroup subject area). Newsgroups are basically the Internet equivalent of forums on CompuServe, America Online, Prodigy, or any of the many private bulletin board systems currently running around the world. These newsgroups are areas for reading the opinions of people around the world about a particular subject, and for holding group discussions in which everyone is considered equal. Everyone can express his or her opinion, although you do have to be prepared to be *flamed* (angrily denounced) by anyone who strongly disagrees with you. ▨

How Articles Are Distributed

The method used for distributing Usenet articles is fairly simple. Each news server regularly contacts certain other news servers (each server's system administrator determines how often these contacts occur). When the servers are connected, each one gives the other a list of articles that it has received since the two servers last exchanged articles. Each of the two servers then replies with a list of the articles that it wants from the other server. The list is determined by the newsgroups to which each server subscribes, and the articles that the server does not already have. Each server then gives the other the articles requested. Both of these two news servers then perform the same sequence of events with other news servers, passing on those articles that the other servers want and receiving desired articles from the other. When included on a news server's list of articles, that article either originated on that particular news server or was received from another news server.

This distribution method does have a side effect or two. Because of the distribution method, and the different routes by which articles are transported from one server to another, you can often find the responses to a particular article before the original article reaches the news server to which you are connected.

The distribution method requires that each news article have a unique identifier. This identifier consists of an ID unique to the originating news server, along with the name of the originating news server (for example, **<DJuuLE.G3x@news.newsserver.com>**). In addition to assigning this article ID to each article, the news server assigns a sequential number within each newsgroup. The article number, however, is not unique to an article, and might not be the same on any two news servers.

News articles are formatted according to RFC 1036 (which is based on RFC 850). RFC 1036 specifies the contents of the header fields, which include—among other items—the unique message ID, the server path used to get from the sender to your local news server, and the IDs of any other articles that the article is referencing. This last item enables browsers (such as Netscape 2.0) to group articles according to discussion threads. The RFC also specifies that a blank line separate the article header from the body, and that a single period on a line by itself designate the end of the article. The following is an example of a complete Usenet article:

```
{Starting the article header section}
Path: news.onramp.net!newshost.convex.com!cnn.exu.ericsson.se!usenet
From: david@somenet.com (David S. Somebody)
Newsgroups: comp.lang.pascal.delphi.misc,alt.comp.lang.borland-delphi,
alt.lang.delphi,dsmnet.general
Subject: Central Somewhere Delphi Users Group
Date: Fri, 15 Mar 1996 21:23:59 GMT
Organization: Somewhere Internet
Lines: 16
{This next line is the message ID. Notice that the article number is not
part of the article header. The Usenet server maintains this number as a
server-level method of indexing articles}
Message-ID: <4icn3q$h0r@dsm6.dsmnet.com>
NNTP-Posting-Host: 205.217.160.216
X-Newsreader: Forte Free Agent 1.0.82
Xref: news.onramp.net comp.lang.pascal.delphi.misc:27792


ANNOUNCEMENT

Central Somewhere Delphi Users Group

Next Meeting:  Thursday, March 21, 1996, 5:30 - 7:00 p.m.
               Somewhere Computing Association
               2100 24th Avenue, Suite 200
               Somewhere, TX


Please e-mail or telephone for further information:

David S. Somebody
Renegade Software
(214) 555-1212
david@somenet.com.
```

N O T E If a line begins with a period, it is preceded by a second period. This designates that the period is part of the message and does not mark the end of the message.

Part

II

Ch

10

Building an Internet Newsreader

The Usenet news client that you build in this chapter enables the user to specify a Usenet news server to which to connect, download a list of the available newsgroups, select a newsgroup to join, download a list of available articles in the specified newsgroup, and select an article for retrieving. This application cannot save the articles that it receives into any storage files so that you can retrieve articles for later review. Also, this application cannot post articles. Both of these missing functions are standard in most commercial or shareware newsreaders.

In summary, the news client performs the following steps:

1. Connects to the Usenet News server.

2. Receives a greeting from the server and places the application into idle mode, waiting for the user to select an action.

3. If the user requests the list of available newsgroups, issues the LIST command to the server.

4. On receiving the response to the LIST command, begins receiving the list of newsgroups, adding them to a list box for the user to view.

5. On receiving the message-termination marker (a line with a single period character on it), places the application into idle mode to wait for the user to select another action.

6. When the user selects a newsgroup to join, either by double-clicking the group in the list box or typing the newsgroup name into the name TEdit control, issues the JOIN command to join the specified newsgroup.

7. On receiving the response to the JOIN command, parses the response to learn how many articles are in the newsgroup, as well as the first and last article numbers.

8. Sets the current article number to the first article number and uses the HEAD command to request the header of that article.

9. On receiving the article header, parses it and adds the values of the From and Subject header fields into the list box for the user to view. Increments the article counter and requests the next article header.

10. Repeats the previous step until all article headers have been received, then places the application into idle mode, waiting for the user to select another action.

11. When the user selects an article for retrieving, requests the article from the server by using either the ARTICLE command or a combination of the HEAD and BODY commands.

12. On receiving the article, adds it to the TMemo field for the user to view. After retrieving the entire article, places the application into idle mode, waiting for the user to select another action.

13. When the user selects to quit the application, issues the QUIT command to the server.

14. On receiving the response to the QUIT command, closes the connection and exits the application.

Figure 10.1 is a flow chart that shows how all these actions and steps fit together.

FIG. 10.1

The application flow for a Usenet newsreader.

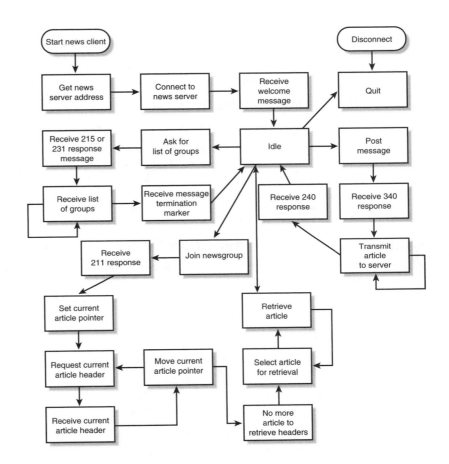

> **N O T E** In Appendix A, "Internet Applications Command Sets," you can find all the Usenet commands, including those used in this example. Appendix B, "The Internet Message Format," describes the message format used in Usenet articles. ▓

In this example, you use the same procedures for looking up the server address and initiating the connection that you used in the previous examples (see Chapters 6, 8, and 9). You should check these chapters for listings and explanations of any procedures and functions not covered in this chapter. Table 10.1 lists the files used in this project.

Table 10.1   Usenet Newsreader Project Files

File	Description
USENET.DPR	The Usenet newsreader Delphi project file.
NEWS.DFM	The Usenet newsreader window.

continues

Table 10.1 Continued	
File	**Description**
NEWS.PAS	The Usenet newsreader code.
POSTMSG.DFM	The beginnings of an article-posting window.
POSTMSG.PAS	The beginnings of an article-posting code.
TSOCKETC.PAS	The TSocket WinSock abstraction class (first developed in Chapter 6, "Socket Programming with Delphi Using WinSock," and then expanded in Chapter 8, "Developing an FTP Client and Server").
NWINSOCK.PAS	The WinSock application program interface (API) definition.

Laying Out the Newsreader State Table

You are almost ready to begin building your own Usenet client. Before you start coding, however, you must plan the state table that you will use when building the application. Begin by specifying the different actions that you want to enable your reader to take from an idle state:

- Connecting to a news server
- Getting a list of newsgroups available on the news server
- Joining a newsgroup, displaying a list of articles in that group, and then selecting and retrieving an article
- Posting a message to one or more newsgroups
- Quitting the session and disconnecting from the news server

Next, you break each of these actions into the individual steps involved. You begin by connecting to the news server as follows:

1. Start the news client application.
2. Get the address for the news server.
3. Connect to the news server.
4. Receive the welcome message.

The remaining three actions are not as simple. The next action is to retrieve the list of available newsgroups:

1. Issue the LIST or NEWGROUPS command to request a list of newsgroups.
2. Receive a response code of 215 or 231 (depending on which command you issued).
3. Begin receiving a list of newsgroups.
4. Loop until you receive the end-of-message marker (or until the connection breaks).

Now post a new article:

1. Issue the POST command, which informs the server that you want to post a new article.
2. Have the server reply with the response code of 340, informing you that it is ready to accept your article.
3. Have the client application enter a loop, sending the article in segments sized according to what the socket buffer can handle, until the client has sent the entire article.
4. Have the client send the end-of-message marker.
5. Have the server respond with the 240 code, indicating that you have posted the article successfully.

The next action is to join a particular newsgroup and retrieve articles from that group:

1. Issue the GROUP command to join a newsgroup.
2. Receive the 211 response code, and then parse the response to get the number of articles in the group and the first and last article numbers.
3. Set the current article pointer (usually to the first article in the group) by using the STAT command.
4. Issue the HEAD command to retrieve the current article header.
5. Receive the current article header.
6. Navigate to the next article (usually by using the NEXT command).
7. Loop through steps 4, 5, and 6 until you have retrieved all article headers.
8. Select an article for retrieval.
9. Retrieve the selected article by using either the ARTICLE command or a combination of the STAT, HEAD, and BODY commands.
10. Loop between steps 8 and 9 until you have retrieved all desired articles.

The final action to outline is to end the session (you want to start by outlining the easy actions). The steps to end the session are the following:

1. If a valid connection to a news server has been established, issue the QUIT command.
2. Close the connection and exit the news client application.

You can now start building your newsreader by defining state codes for each of these states, as shown in Listing 10.1.

Listing 10.1 NEWS.PAS—Constant Declarations for Use in Implementing the Newsreader State Table

```
const
{Constant declarations to represent the socket state}
  SKT_NOOP = 0;
  SKT_GETHOSTADDR = 1;
  SKT_CONNECTTOHOST = 2;
```

continues

Listing 10.1   Continued

```
  SKT_SENDPACKET = 3;
  SKT_RECVPACKET = 4;
{Constant declarations to represent Usenet commands. You use these
declarations to keep track of which command was last issued, so that
responses received from the server can be directed to the appropriate
procedure}
  UNN_NOOP = 0;
  UNN_CONNECT = 1;
  UNN_ASKFORLIST = 2;
  UNN_GETLIST = 3;
  UNN_JOINGROUP = 4;
  UNN_ASKFORHEADER = 5;
  UNN_GETHEADER = 6;
  UNN_GETTINGHEADER = 7;
  UNN_ASKFORMESSAGE = 8;
  UNN_GETMESSAGEHEADER = 9;
  UNN_GETTINGMESSAGEHEADER = 10;
  UNN_GETMESSAGETEXT = 11;
  UNN_GETTINGMESSAGETEXT = 12;
  UNN_ASKTOPOSTMESSAGE = 13;
  UNN_POSTMESSAGE = 14;
  UNN_QUITING = 15;
{User-defined event declarations, for socket events)
  UWM_SOCKETEVENT = WM_USER + 500;
```

Next you declare the variables that you use throughout your newsreader class, as shown in Listing 10.2.

Listing 10.2   NEWS.PAS—Public and Private Variables in Your Newsreader Class

```
  private
    { Private declarations }
{The primary socket to be used in the connection with the server}
    isConnectionSocket: _SOCKET;
{A flag to indicate whether the connection has been made}
    ibConnected: Boolean;
{The command state indicator}
    iiUseNetStatus: Integer;
{The hold buffer for incomplete message lines}
    HoldBuffer: String;
{Variables to hold the author and subject of messages}
    isAuthor, isSubject: String;
{Variables to keep track of how many groups to retrieve, how many
articles to retrieve, the current article, etc.}
    iiNumGroups: Integer;
    iiNumToStop: Integer;
    iiNumArticles: Integer;
    iiFirstArticle: Integer;
    iiLastArticle: Integer;
```

```
    iiCurArticle: Integer;
    iiCurCount: Integer;
    iiNumComplete: Integer;
    iiNumAdditional: Integer;
{The socket event-handler declaration}
    procedure UWMSocketEvent(var Msg: TMessage); message UWM_SOCKETEVENT;
  public
    { Public declarations }
{The TSocket class declaration}
    NetSocket: _Tsocket;
{The receive and temporary buffers}
    ReceiveBuffer: array[0..8192] of Char;
    TempBuffer: array[0..8192] of Char;
```

Part
II
Ch
10

NOTE The variable-naming convention used in this and several other examples throughout this book is a variation on Hungarian notation. In this notation, variables have two (or more in certain data-type circumstances) characters that specify the scope and data type of the variable. The first character indicates the variable scope as follows:

i   Instance variable. These variables are defined at the class level and are available throughout the class methods.

l   Local variable. A specific function or procedure defines these variables, which do not exist outside the scope of that routine.

The second character (or set of characters) indicates the data type of the variable as follows:

i   Integer variable.

l   Long Integer variable.

s   String variable.

This naming convention is followed in most circumstances. In the few instances where it is not applied, the variable is either a large buffer variable, with a scope throughout the class, or another class.

A similar naming convention is used in naming controls on the user interface. A two- or three-character abbreviation of the control type is prefixed to the control name. The following are examples of these control names:

cb Control button (TButton)

sle Single-line edit (TEdit)

These naming conventions have evolved through experience working with multiple rapid application-development tools. Although they do not follow standard Delphi conventions, they do enable a developer to move easily among development tools. ■

Now that you have laid out your state table, you are ready to begin coding your newsreader application.

Connecting to the News Server

The cbConnectClick() procedure begins the entire process by looking up the address for the specified news server (see Listing 10.3).

Listing 10.3   NEWS.PAS—the *cbConnectClick()* Procedure Looks Up the News Server's Address

```
procedure TNews1. cbConnectClick(Sender: TObject);
begin
{Make sure the HostName TEdit control is not blank.}
   if Length(HostName.text) > 0 then
   begin
      {Set the status display and command status flag to indicate
      that the host address is being looked up}
      lStatusDisp.Caption := 'Looking Up Host Address';
      iiUseNetStatus := UNN_CONNECT;
      {Use the GetHostAddress procedure to look up the address of the
      Usenet news server. Chapter 6 covers this procedure.}
      NetSocket.GetHostAddress(Handle, UWM_SOCKETEVENT,
            HostName.text, SKT_GETHOSTADDR);
   end;
end;
```

When you have the news server's address, you can connect to it by using TCP port 119 (the default port for Usenet news service, as defined in RFC 1036). The ProcessHostLockup procedure makes this connection (see Listing 10.4).

Listing 10.4   NEWS.PAS—the *ProcessHostLockup* Procedure Connects Your Newsreader to the News Server

```
procedure TNews1.ProcessHostLookup;
begin
   {Update the display to reflect that you are attempting to connect
   to the server}
   lStatusDisp.Caption := 'Connecting To Host';
   {Call ProcessHostAddress (first written in Chapter 6) to reformat
   the received address so that you can connect}
   if (NetSocket.ProcessHostAddress = TRUE) then
   begin
      {Call OpenSocketConnection (first developed in Chapter 6) to
      create a new socket and open a connection to the host. This
      triggers the socket event when the connection has been
      established}
      isConnectionSocket := NetSocket.OpenSocketConnection(Handle,
            UWM_SOCKETEVENT, SKT_CONNECTTOHOST, 119);
   end
   else
      {The host address was not found, so inform the user}
      lStatusDisp.Caption := 'Cannot Find Host Address';
end;
```

Receiving the Greeting from the Server

After establishing your connection to the news server, you must clear the receive buffer and look for the news server's connection reply. The `ProcessHostConnect` and `ProcessSendHost` procedures perform these tasks (see Listing 10.5).

Listing 10.5   NEWS.PAS—the *ProcessHostConnect* and *ProcessSendHost* Procedures Receive the News Server's Welcome Message

```
procedure TNews1.ProcessHostConnect;
begin
   lStatusDisp.Caption := 'Sending To Host';
   NetSocket.SetSocketState(SKT_SENDPACKET);
   PostMessage(Handle, UWM_SOCKETEVENT, 0, 0);
end;

procedure TNews1.ProcessHostSend;
begin
   {Did you have any errors?}
   if NetSocket.CheckSocketError then
      {If so, display the error message}
      lStatusDisp.Caption := NetSocket.SocketError
   else
   begin
      {Otherwise, receive the greeting from the host}
      lStatusDisp.Caption := 'Receiving From Host';
      {Clear the receive buffer}
      ClearBuffer(ReceiveBuffer, 8192);
      NetSocket.SetSocketSkate (SKT_RECVPACKET);
   end;
end;
```

Directing Server Responses to the Appropriate Procedure

After receiving the news server's response, you need to display the response message and enable the appropriate buttons. You also should check the news server's response to verify that the server didn't reject your connection and to determine whether you have permission to post messages. `ProcessHostReceive` is the application's general procedure for handling all data that the application receives from the news server (see Listing 10.6). Therefore, the procedure also must check the newsreader's state and call the appropriate state-processing function based on the command that the server last sent.

Listing 10.6   NEWS.PAS—the *ProcessHostReceive* Procedure Processes Incoming Packets from the News Server

```
procedure TNews1.ProcessHostReceive;
begin
```

continues

Listing 10.6   Continued

```
try
    {Was any data received? If the first position in the receive
    buffer is null, then no data was received}
    if (ReceiveBuffer[0] = Char(0)) then
    begin
        {No data was received, so prepare for the next set
         of incoming data}
        {Clear the receive buffer}
        ClearBuffer(ReceiveBuffer, 8192);
    end
    else
    begin
        {Data was received, choose the appropriate action based on
         the command sent to the server}
        case iiUseNetStatus of
            UNN_CONNECT:
                begin
                    {You were connecting to the server, so the incoming
                    data is the greeting from the server. Set the various
                    flags to indicate that you are connected and waiting
                    for the user to select an action}
                    ibConnected := TRUE;
                    iiUseNetStatus := UNN_NOOP;
                    {Display the server greeting for the user}
                    lStatusDisp.Caption := StrPas(ReceiveBuffer);
                    {Enable the LIST and JOIN GROUP buttons}
                    cbList.Enabled := TRUE;
                    cbJoinGroup.Enabled := TRUE;
                    cbPost.Enabled := TRUE;
                    {Change the default button from the CONNECT
                    button to the LIST button}
                    cbConnect.Default := FALSE;
                    cbList.Default := TRUE;
                end;
            {The rest of these call the appropriate procedure
            for the action being taken}
            UNN_ASKFORLIST: ParseGroupListString;
            UNN_GETLIST: ParseGroupListString;
            UNN_JOINGROUP: ParseGroupName;
            UNN_ASKFORHEADER: ProcessAskForHeader;
            UNN_GETHEADER: ProcessGetHeader;
            UNN_GETTINGHEADER: ProcessGetHeader;
            UNN_ASKFORMESSAGE: ProcessAskForMessage;
            UNN_GETMESSAGEHEADER: ProcessGetMessageHeader;
            UNN_GETTINGMESSAGEHEADER: ProcessGetMessageHeader;
            UNN_GETMESSAGETEXT: ProcessGetMessage;
            UNN_GETTINGMESSAGETEXT: ProcessGetMessage;
            UNN_ASKTOPOSTMESSAGE: ProcessPostMessage;
            UNN_POSTMESSAGE: ProcessPostComplete;
            UNN_QUITING: ProcessQuit;
```

```
        end;
      end;
    except
      {On an exception, clear the receive buffer and prepare for more
      incoming data}
      ClearBuffer(ReceiveBuffer, 8192);
    end;
  end;
```

Figure 10.2 shows your newsreader connected to a Usenet News server. Notice the server greeting message in the status display at the top of the window. Now that you have established your connection to the news server, you can add the other functionality that you want to implement.

FIG. 10.2
Your newsreader connected to a Usenet News server.

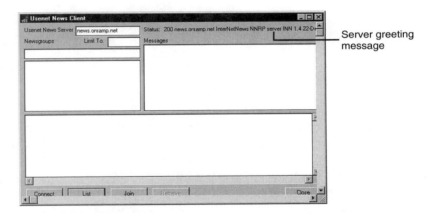

Server greeting message

Disconnecting from the News Server

Next you want to ensure that you can end your session with the news server. First you must verify that you are in an active session with a news server. If you do not have an active session, you get a series of errors complaining that you are trying to send and receive data using an invalid socket. If you do not have an active connection, you simply close the window (and the application). If you do have an active connection, you want to send a QUIT command to the server so that it can sever the connection. The cbCloseClick() procedure follows these steps to begin disconnecting from the server (see Listing 10.7).

Listing 10.7   NEWS.PAS—the *cbCloseClick()* Procedure Initiates the Disconnect Procedure

```
procedure TNews1. cbCloseClick(Sender: TObject);
begin
```

continues

Listing 10.7   Continued

```
   {Are you connected?}
   if ibConnected then
   begin
     {Update the display to reflect that you are quitting
      the application}
     lStatusDisp.Caption := 'Quitting';
     iiUseNetStatus := UNN_QUITING;
     {Invalidate the receive buffer by placing a null character in the
      first position. This isn't really necessary, because you are
      going to call the ClearBuffer procedure in a couple of lines}
     ReceiveBuffer[0] := Char(0);
     {Send the QUIT command to the server}
     NetSocket.SocketSend(isConnectionSocket, handle, UWM_SOCKETEVENT,
                  'QUIT', SKT_RECVPACKET);
     {Clear the receive buffer}
     ClearBuffer(ReceiveBuffer, 8192);
   end
   else
     {You are not connected, so you can just close the application}
     Close;
end;
```

You want to ensure that you wait until you receive the news server's response before closing your application, just in case you receive some kind of error message (although an error is highly unlikely). After receiving the response, you can close the window. The ProcessQuit procedure handles the server's response (see Listing 10.8).

Listing 10.8   NEWS.PAS—the *ProcessQuit* Procedure Processes the Host's Response to the *QUIT* Command

```
procedure TNews1.ProcessQuit;
var
   liSpaceCharPos: Integer;
   lbEndOfStr: Boolean;
   lsTempStr, lsRetnStr: String;
begin
   {Initialize the End of String flag to FALSE}
   lbEndOfStr := FALSE;
   {Place a null character at the end of the receive buffer}
   ReceiveBuffer[8192] := Char(0);
   {Does the command flag indicate that you are quitting?}
   if (iiUseNetStatus = UNN_QUITING) then
   begin
      {Convert the receive buffer into a Pascal string}
      lsRetnStr := StrPas(ReceiveBuffer);
      {Check for a space character}
      liSpaceCharPos := Pos(' ', lsRetnStr);
```

```
      {If the response includes a space, you probably have a
      valid response message}
      if (liSpaceCharPos > 0) then
      begin
         {Copy the first character into a temporary variable}
         lsTempStr := Copy(lsRetnStr, 1, 1);
         {Is the first character a 4? If so, you received
         a command-rejected response}
         if (lsTempStr = '4') then
         begin
            {Set the End of String flag to TRUE and show the user
            the response message}
            lbEndOfStr := TRUE;
            lStatusDisp.Caption := lsRetnStr;
            lStatusDisp.Update;
         end;
      end;
   end;
   {Set the command status to NOOP}
   iiUseNetStatus := UNN_NOOP;
   {Close the application}
   Close;
end;
```

Now that you have taken care of this basic housekeeping, you can get down to your newsreader's actual business.

Getting a List of Newsgroups

To start receiving a list of the available newsgroups on the news server, you issue the LIST command. Before issuing this command, however, you check whether the user entered a limit on the number of newsgroups to retrieve. The cbListClick() procedure retrieves the news server's list (see Listing 10.9).

 TIP

If you are implementing this news client in the 16-bit version of Delphi and loading the newsgroups into a list box, you should limit the number of newsgroups that you retrieve. Retrieving all the available newsgroups takes a long time, but also, when working with the 16-bit version of Delphi, you might find that your system often locks up after retrieving over 5,000 newsgroups (although you also can sometimes retrieve over 6,000 newsgroups with no problem). This problem might be related to the availability of resources.

**Listing 10.9   NEWS.PAS—the *cbListClick()* Procedure Issues the *LIST*
Command To Get a Listing of the Available Newsgroups**

```
procedure TNews1.cbListClick(Sender: TObject);
begin
   {Display for the user that you are issuing a LIST command}
   lStatusDisp.Caption := 'Requesting List of NewsGroups';
```

continues

Listing 10.9 Continued

```
   {Set the command flag to reflect that you are issuing a LIST command}
   iiUseNetStatus := UNN_ASKFORLIST;
   {Invalidate the receive buffer}
   ReceiveBuffer[0] := Char(0);
   {Has the user specified a number of newsgroups to limit the list?}
   if (LimitNum.Text <> '') then
      {If so, convert it to the variable so that you can stop on
      receiving the specified number}
      iiNumToStop := StrToInt(LimitNum.Text)
   else
      {Otherwise, set the limitation variable to 0 to reflect that the
      user wants to retrieve all newsgroups}
      iiNumToStop := 0;
   {Send the LIST command to the server}
   NetSocket.SocketSend(isConnectionSocket, handle, UWM_SOCKETEVENT,
                  'LIST', SKT_RECVPACKET);
   {Clear the receive buffer}
   ClearBuffer(ReceiveBuffer, 8192);
 end;
```

When you receive your first buffer full from the server, you must strip off the first line, because it is the server's response. On this response line, you must change the command state flag to indicate that you do not have to look for the server response (for a discussion and example of the server-response line, see Appendix A) on any of the subsequent buffers (your application uses the ParseGroupListString procedure to process the first received buffer as well as all additional received buffers that contain the list of newsgroups).

From this point until you either run out of buffer or find the end-of-message marker, you strip off each line and parse it to extract the group name. After extracting the current line from the buffer, you check whether any data is left from the previous buffer. If any is left, you paste it to the front of the line that you extracted from the current buffer and then clear the holding buffer.

Next, you check whether the current line is the end-of-message marker. If so, you stop processing the buffer. Otherwise, you parse the group name, extracting everything that precedes the first space character and then adding it to the list of newsgroups.

As you update the number of groups retrieved, you compare it to the number that the user entered to limit how many groups to retrieve. If you have retrieved the number of groups that the user specified, you stop retrieving newsgroups. The easiest way to do so is to disconnect from the server and then reestablish the connection.

If after reaching the end of the buffer you haven't found the end-of-message marker, you retrieve from the server another buffer full of newsgroups. If you reach the end of the message, or at least the limit that the user specified, you reset the application to the idle state and enable the appropriate buttons.

The `ParseGroupListString` procedureperforms all this parsing and processing (see Listing 10.10).

Listing 10.10   NEWS.PAS—the *ParseGroupListString* Procedure Parses and Processes the Initial Response to the *LIST* Command

```
procedure TNews1.ParseGroupListString;
var
   liSpaceCharPos: Integer;
   lbEndOfList: Boolean;
   lsTempStr, lsRetnStr: String;
begin
   {Initialize the End of List flag to FALSE}
   lbEndOfList := FALSE;
   {Place a null character at the end of the receive buffer}
   ReceiveBuffer[8192] := Char(0);
   {Does the command flag indicate that you are receiving the initial
   set of newsgroups?}
   if (iiUseNetStatus = UNN_ASKFORLIST) then
   begin
      {This is your initial set of newsgroups. You must look for the
      server response code, initialize the number-of-groups counter, and
      update the display.}
      iiNumGroups := 0;
      stNumGroups.Caption := IntToStr(iiNumGroups);
      stNumGroups.Update;
      {Get the first line from the receive buffer}
      if NetSocket.GetLine(TempBuffer, ReceiveBuffer) then
      begin
         {Convert the first line to a Pascal string}
         lsRetnStr := StrPas(TempBuffer);
         {Change the command flag to indicate that you have already
         received the initial buffer of newsgroups and no longer
         need to look for the response line}
         iiUseNetStatus := UNN_GETLIST;
         {Display the response line for the user}
         lStatusDisp.Caption := lsRetnStr;
         lStatusDisp.Update;
      end;
   end;
   {Loop as long as there are additional newsgroup lines and you haven't
   received the message-termination marker}
   while ((NetSocket.GetLine(TempBuffer, ReceiveBuffer)) and
         (not lbEndOfList)) do
   begin
      {Convert the line into a Pascal string}
      lsRetnStr := StrPas(TempBuffer);
      {Is there anything in the hold buffer?}
      if (HoldBuffer <> '') then
      begin
         {Yes, this line must be the completion of the line that begins
         in the hold buffer, so add the two together}
         lsRetnStr := HoldBuffer + lsRetnStr;
```

continues

Listing 10.10   Continued

```
            {Empty the hold buffer}
            HoldBuffer := '';
        end;
        {Have you found the message-termination marker (a period on a line
        by itself)?}
        if (lsRetnStr = '.') then
            {Yes, set the End of List flag to TRUE}
            lbEndOfList := TRUE
        else
        begin
            {Otherwise, you must parse the newsgroup name and add it
            to the list box for the user to see}
            {Find the first space in the line}
            liSpaceCharPos := Pos(' ', lsRetnStr);
            {Everything preceding the space is the newsgroup name. Parse it
            and place the name into a temporary string variable (the
            other information in the line is the number of articles in the
            newsgroup, and the beginning and ending article numbers)}
            lsTempStr := Copy(lsRetnStr, 1, (liSpaceCharPos - 1));
            {Add the newsgroup name to the list box}
            lbNewsGroups.Items.Add(lsTempStr);
            lbNewsGroups.Update;
            {Increment the number of newsgroups listed}
            Inc(iiNumGroups);
            {Have you reached your cut-off point?}
            if (iiNumGroups = iiNumToStop) then
            begin
                {Yes, set the End Of List flag to TRUE and sever the
                connection}
                lbEndOfList := TRUE;
                NetSocket.CloseSocketConnection(isConnectionSocket);
                {Reestablish the connection so the user can retrieve
                articles from one of the newsgroups}
                iiUseNetStatus := UNN_CONNECT;
                NetSocket.GetHostAddress(Handle, UWM_SOCKETEVENT,
                                HostName.text, SKT_GETHOSTADDR);
            end;
            {Update the display to reflect the number of newsgroups
            listed}
            stNumGroups.Caption := IntToStr(iiNumGroups);
            stNumGroups.Update;
        end;
    end;
    {You either do not have another complete line of data, or have
    reached the end of the list of newsgroups}
    {Are you at the end of the list of newsgroups?}
    if (not lbEndOfList) then
    begin
        {No, place the portion of a line into the hold buffer}
        HoldBuffer := StrPas(TempBuffer);
        {Clear the receive buffer}
        ClearBuffer(ReceiveBuffer, 8192);
    end
    else
```

```
begin
   {Yes, change the command status flag to indicate that the
   application is idle}
   iiUseNetStatus := UNN_NOOP;
   {Change the default button from the LIST button to the
   JOIN GROUP button}
   cbJoinGroup.Enabled := TRUE;
   cbList.Default := FALSE;
   cbJoinGroup.Default := TRUE;
   end;
end;
```

Figure 10.3 shows the newsreader displaying a list of available newsgroups retrieved from a news server. Now that the user can see which newsgroups are available on the news server to which the application is connected, he or she can select one to join.

FIG. 10.3

The list of available newsgroups retrieved from the news server.

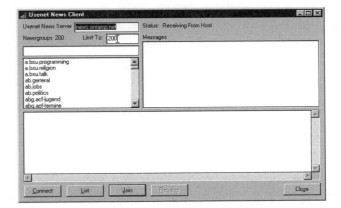

Joining a Newsgroup

After the user either selects a newsgroup in the list of groups retrieved from the server or types the name of a group that the list might or might not include, the application tries to join that group by specifying the group name with the GROUP command (see Listing 10.11). You also want to enable the appropriate buttons so that the user can retrieve the article after selecting it.

Listing 10.11   NEWS.PAS—the *cbJoinGroupClick()* Procedure Issues the Request To Join a Particular Newsgroup.

```
procedure TNews1.cbJoinGroupClick(Sender: TObject);
begin
   {Update the display to reflect that you are joining a newsgroup}
   lStatusDisp.Caption := 'Joining NewsGroup';
```

continues

Listing 10.11 Continued

```
   {Set the command status flag to reflect that you are joining a
   newsgroup}
   iiUseNetStatus := UNN_JOINGROUP;
   {Invalidate the receive buffer}
   ReceiveBuffer[0] := Char(0);
   {Reset which button is the default button}
   cbRetrieve.Enabled := TRUE;
   cbPost.Enabled := TRUE;
   cbList.Default := FALSE;
   cbJoinGroup.Default := FALSE;
   cbRetrieve.Default := TRUE;
   {Send the GROUP command to the server}
   NetSocket.SocketSend(isConnectionSocket, handle, UWM_SOCKETEVENT,
                   'GROUP ' + GroupToJoin.Text, SKT_RECVPACKET);
   {Clear the receive buffer}
   ClearBuffer(ReceiveBuffer, 8192);
 end;
```

When you receive the response to your request to join a particular newsgroup, you parse the response and extract its information. You first examine the response code to verify that you succeeded in joining the specified newsgroup.

If you succeeded, you parse the number of articles in this newsgroup, as well as the first and last article numbers. The last item in the message is the newsgroup name, which you will display in the window status line. RFC 1036 defines this response message format, and Appendix A provides an example.

Now that you have successfully joined the selected newsgroup, you start retrieving the headers of all the articles in the group. To do so, you issue the STAT command with the article number of the group's first article. This command sets the current article pointer to the first article, and you can start requesting headers and navigating with the relational navigation commands, NEXT and LAST.

ParseGroupName is the procedure that parses the response to the GROUP command and begins retrieving article headers (see Listing 10.12).

Listing 10.12 NEWS.PAS—the *ParseGroupName* Procedure Interprets the Response to the *GROUP* Command and Initiates the Retrieval of Article Headers.

```
procedure TNews1.ParseGroupName;
var
   liCarRetnPos: Integer;
   liSpaceCharPos: Integer;
   lbEndOfStr: Boolean;
   lsTempStr, lsRetnStr: String;
```

```
begin
    {Initialize the End of String flag to FALSE}
    lbEndOfStr := FALSE;
    {Place a null character at the end of the receive buffer}
    ReceiveBuffer[8192] := Char(0);
    {Does the command flag indicate that you are joining a newsgroup?}
    if (iiUseNetStatus = UNN_JOINGROUP) then
    begin
        {Convert the first line to a Pascal string}
        lsRetnStr := StrPas(ReceiveBuffer);
        {Check for the first space character}
        liSpaceCharPos := Pos(' ', lsRetnStr);
        {If the response includes a space, you probably have a
        valid response message}
        if (liSpaceCharPos > 0) then
        begin
            {Copy the first character into a temporary variable}
            lsTempStr := Copy(lsRetnStr, 1, 1);
            {Trim off the response code}
            lsRetnStr := Copy(lsRetnStr, (liSpaceCharPos + 1),
                                            Length(lsRetnStr));
            {Is the first character a 4 or a 5? If so, you received
            a command-rejected response}
            if ((lsTempStr = '4') or
                (lsTempStr = '5')) then
            begin
                {Set the End of String flag to TRUE and show the user
                the response message}
                lbEndOfStr := TRUE;
                lStatusDisp.Caption := lsRetnStr;
                lStatusDisp.Update;
            end;
        end;
        {Can you continue?}
        if (not lbEndOfStr) then
        begin
            {Find the next space character}
            liSpaceCharPos := Pos(' ', lsRetnStr);
            if (liSpaceCharPos > 0) then
            begin
                {Parse the next string, which specifies the number
                 of articles currently in the newsgroup}
                lsTempStr := Copy(lsRetnStr, 1, (liSpaceCharPos - 1));
                {Trim off the number of articles}
                lsRetnStr := Copy(lsRetnStr, (liSpaceCharPos + 1),
                                                Length(lsRetnStr));
                {Convert the number of articles into an integer and place it
                into the appropriate variable}
                iiNumArticles := StrToInt(lsTempStr);
            end;
            {Find the next space character}
            liSpaceCharPos := Pos(' ', lsRetnStr);
            if (liSpaceCharPos > 0) then
            begin
```

continues

Listing 10.12   Continued

```
        {Parse the next string, which specifies the number of the
        first article currently in the newsgroup}
        lsTempStr := Copy(lsRetnStr, 1, (liSpaceCharPos - 1));
        {Trim off the first article number }
        lsRetnStr := Copy(lsRetnStr, (liSpaceCharPos + 1),
                                        Length(lsRetnStr));
        {Convert the first article number into an integer and place
        it into the appropriate variable}
        iiFirstArticle := StrToInt(lsTempStr);
    end;
    {Find the next space character}
    liSpaceCharPos := Pos(' ', lsRetnStr);
    if (liSpaceCharPos > 0) then
    begin
        {Parse the next string, which specifies the number
         of the last article currently in the newsgroup}
        lsTempStr := Copy(lsRetnStr, 1, (liSpaceCharPos - 1));
        {Trim off the last article number }
        lsRetnStr := Copy(lsRetnStr, (liSpaceCharPos + 1),
                                        Length(lsRetnStr));
        {Convert the last article number into an integer and place
        it into the appropriate variable}
        iiLastArticle := StrToInt(lsTempStr);
    end;
    {Check the numbers to ensure that the article number range
    matches the specified number of articles. Adjust the number of
    articles if necessary}
    if (((iiLastArticle - iiFirstArticle) + 1) > iiNumArticles) then
        iiNumArticles := ((iiLastArticle - iiFirstArticle) + 1);
    {Set the current article indicator to the first article}
    iiCurArticle := iiFirstArticle;
    {Locate the carriage-return/newline character combination in
    the remaining response line}
    liCarRetnPos := Pos(#13#10, lsRetnStr);
    if (liCarRetnPos > 0) then
    begin
        {Trim off the end-of-line marker; the remainder should be
        the newsgroup name}
        lsTempStr := Copy(lsRetnStr, 1, (liCarRetnPos - 1));
        lsRetnStr := Copy(lsRetnStr, (liCarRetnPos + 2),
                                        Length(lsRetnStr));
    end;
    {Check whether you have a second end-of-line marker}
    liCarRetnPos := Pos(#13#10, lsRetnStr);
    if (liCarRetnPos > 0) then
    begin
        {If so, trim it off and add it to the newsgroup name}
        lsTempStr := lsTempStr + ' ' + Copy(lsRetnStr, 1,
                                        (liCarRetnPos - 1));
    end;
    {Display the newsgroup name for the user to see}
    lStatusDisp.Caption := lsTempStr;
    lStatusDisp.Update;
    {Set the current article count to 0}
```

```
            iiCurCount := 0;
            {Set the command status flag to indicate that you are asking for
            an article header}
            iiUseNetStatus := UNN_ASKFORHEADER;
            {Invalidate the receive buffer}
            ReceiveBuffer[0] := Char(0);
            {Send the STAT command to the server, passing the first article
            number}
            NetSocket.SocketSend(isConnectionSocket, handle,
                        UWM_SOCKETEVENT, 'STAT ' + IntToStr(iiCurArticle),
                        SKT_RECVPACKET);
            {Clear the receive buffer}
            ClearBuffer(ReceiveBuffer, 8192);
        end;
    end;
end;
```

Part
II
Ch
10

When you receive the response to the positioning of the current article pointer, you verify that the command succeeded. If so, the `ProcessAskForHeader` procedure issues a request for the new current article's header (see Listing 10.13).

Listing 10.13 NEWS.PAS—the *ProcessAskForHeader* Procedure Processes the Response To Set the Current Article Pointer and Request the Header for the Current Article

```
procedure TNews1.ProcessAskForHeader;
var
    liSpaceCharPos: Integer;
    lbEndOfStr: Boolean;
    lsTempStr, lsRetnStr: String;
begin
    {Initialize the End of String flag to FALSE}
    lbEndOfStr := FALSE;
    {Place a null character at the end of the receive buffer}
    ReceiveBuffer[8192] := Char(0);
    {Does the command flag indicate that you are requesting an article
    header?}
    if (iiUseNetStatus = UNN_ASKFORHEADER) then
    begin
        {Convert the first line to a Pascal string}
        lsRetnStr := StrPas(ReceiveBuffer);
        {Check for the first space character}
        liSpaceCharPos := Pos(' ', lsRetnStr);
        {If the response includes a space, you probably have a
        valid response message}
        if (liSpaceCharPos > 0) then
        begin
            {Copy the first character into a temporary variable}
```

continues

Listing 10.13 Continued

```
            lsTempStr := Copy(lsRetnStr, 1, 1);
            {Trim off the response code}
            lsRetnStr := Copy(lsRetnStr, (liSpaceCharPos + 1),
                                         Length(lsRetnStr));
            {Is the first character a 4? If so, you received
            a command-rejected response}
            if (lsTempStr = '4') then
            begin
               {Set the End of String flag to TRUE and show the user
               the response message}
               lbEndOfStr := TRUE;
               lStatusDisp.Caption := lsRetnStr;
               lStatusDisp.Update;
            end;
         end;
         {Can you continue?}
         if (not lbEndOfStr) then
         begin
            {Find the first space character}
            liSpaceCharPos := Pos(' ', lsRetnStr);
            {If so, you received a complete response message}
            if (liSpaceCharPos > 0) then
            begin
               {Set the command status flag to indicate that you are asking
               for an article header}
               iiUseNetStatus := UNN_GETHEADER;
               {Invalidate the receive buffer}
               ReceiveBuffer[0] := Char(0);
               {Clear the hold buffer}
               HoldBuffer := '';
               {Send the HEAD command to the server}
               NetSocket.SocketSend(isConnectionSocket, handle,
                      UWM_SOCKETEVENT, 'HEAD', SKT_RECVPACKET);
               {Clear the receive buffer}
               ClearBuffer(ReceiveBuffer, 8192);
            end;
         end;
      end;
   end;
```

After you first retrieve the response to your request for the current article's header, you examine it to verify that the request succeeded. If so, the ProcessGetHeader procedure passes the buffer to the GetHeaderLine function to parse the header and extract the information that you want to display to the user so that he or she can choose which articles to retrieve (see Listing 10.14).

Listing 10.14 NEWS.PAS—the *ProcessGetHeader* Procedure Receives the Current Article's Header Section

```
procedure TNews1.ProcessGetHeader;
var
    liSpaceCharPos: Integer;
    lbEndOfStr: Boolean;
    lsTempStr, lsRetnStr: String;
begin
    {Initialize the End of String flag to FALSE}
    lbEndOfStr := FALSE;
    {Place a null character at the end of the receive buffer}
    ReceiveBuffer[8192] := Char(0);
    {Does the command flag indicate that you are requesting an article
    header?}
    if (iiUseNetStatus = UNN_GETHEADER) then
    begin
        {Convert the first line to a Pascal string}
        lsRetnStr := StrPas(ReceiveBuffer);
        {Check for the first space character}
        liSpaceCharPos := Pos(' ', lsRetnStr);
        {If response includes a space, you probably have a
        valid response message}
        if (liSpaceCharPos > 0) then
        begin
            {Copy the first character into a temporary variable}
            lsTempStr := Copy(lsRetnStr, 1, 1);
            {Is the first character a 4? If so, you received
            a command-rejected response}
            if (lsTempStr = '4') then
            begin
                {Set the End of String flag to TRUE and show the user
                the response message}
                lbEndOfStr := TRUE;
                lStatusDisp.Caption := lsRetnStr;
                lStatusDisp.Update;
            end;
        end;
    end;
    {Does the command flag indicate that you are requesting an article
    header?}
    if ((iiUseNetStatus = UNN_GETHEADER) or
        (iiUseNetStatus = UNN_GETTINGHEADER)) then
        {Are you at the end of the article header?}
        if (not lbEndOfStr) then
            {No, you must get the rest of the article header}
            GetHeaderLine;
end;
```

When you receive the header, you begin looping through the lines of the header, looking for the information of interest. In this case, you look for the article's subject and the message's author. Other information that you might want to keep track of includes the message ID, the article date, and the IDs of the articles to which the current article is responding.

You also look for the end-of-message marker, to verify that you received the entire article header. If you did not receive the entire header, you retrieve an additional buffer to complete the article header. If you receive the entire header, you issue a NEXT command to move the current article pointer to the next article in the newsgroup. The GetHeaderLine procedure parses the article header to find the needed information (see Listing 10.15).

Listing 10.15   NEWS.PAS—the *GetHeaderLine* Procedure Parses the Article Header

```
procedure TNews1.GetHeaderLine;
var
   liSpaceCharPos: Integer;
   lbEndOfStr: Boolean;
   lsTempStr, lsRetnStr: String;
begin
   {Initialize the End of String flag to FALSE}
   lbEndOfStr := FALSE;
   {Loop as long as you can extract full strings from the receive
   buffer and have not found the message-termination marker}
   while ((NetSocket.GetLine(TempBuffer, ReceiveBuffer)) and
         (not lbEndOfStr)) do
   begin
      {Convert the extracted line to a Pascal string}
      lsRetnStr := StrPas(TempBuffer);
      {Is there anything in the hold buffer?}
      if (HoldBuffer <> '') then
      begin
         {Yes. It must be the start of the extracted line, so add it
         to the front of the extracted line}
         lsRetnStr := HoldBuffer + lsRetnStr;
         {Empty the hold buffer}
         HoldBuffer := '';
      end;
      {Is the header field 'From:' in this line?}
      liSpaceCharPos := Pos('From: ', lsRetnStr);
      if (liSpaceCharPos > 0) then
      begin
         {Yes, so extract the value and place it in the
         isAuthor variable}
         lsTempStr := Copy(lsRetnStr, (liSpaceCharPos + 6),
                                          Length(lsRetnStr));
         isAuthor := lsTempStr;
      end;
      {Is the header field 'Subject:' in this line?}
      liSpaceCharPos := Pos('Subject: ', lsRetnStr);
      if (liSpaceCharPos > 0) then
      begin
         {Yes, so extract the value and place it in the
         isSubject variable}
         lsTempStr := Copy(lsRetnStr, (liSpaceCharPos + 9),
                                          Length(lsRetnStr));
         isSubject := lsTempStr;
      end;
```

```
        {Is this the message-termination marker?}
        if (lsRetnStr = '.') then
            {Yes, set the End of String flag to TRUE}
            lbEndOfStr := TRUE;
        {Have you reached the end of the article header?}
        if (lbEndOfStr) then
        begin
            {Yes, add the author and subject to the list box for the user
            to see}
            lbMessages.Items.Add(isAuthor + ' - ' + isSubject);
            {Wipe out the author and subject variable}
            isAuthor := '';
            isSubject := '';
            lbMessages.Update;
            {Increment the article count and update the display}
            Inc(iiCurCount);
            stNumMessages.Caption := IntToStr(iiCurCount) + ' of ' +
                            IntToStr(iiNumArticles);
            stNumMessages.Update;
            {Are there more articles to retrieve?}
            if (iiCurArticle < iiLastArticle) then
            begin
                {Set the command status flag to indicate that you are asking
                for an article header}
                iiUseNetStatus := UNN_ASKFORHEADER;
                {Invalidate the receive buffer}
                ReceiveBuffer[0] := Char(0);
                {Send the NEXT command to the server}
                NetSocket.SocketSend(isConnectionSocket, handle,
                    UWM_SOCKETEVENT, 'NEXT', SKT_RECVPACKET);
                {Clear the receive buffer}
                ClearBuffer(ReceiveBuffer, 8192);
            end;
            {Increment the current article marker}
            Inc(iiCurArticle);
        end;
    end;
    {Have you received the complete header?}
    if (not lbEndOfStr) then
    begin
        {No, you must wait for the rest of the article header}
        {Set the command status flag to indicate that you are asking for
        an article header}
        iiUseNetStatus := UNN_GETTINGHEADER;
        {Place the remaining data into the hold buffer}
        HoldBuffer := StrPas(TempBuffer);
        {Clear the receive buffer}
        ClearBuffer(ReceiveBuffer, 8192);
    end;
end;
```

Figure 10.4 shows the newsreader application listing the selected newsgroup's available articles.

FIG. 10.4

The list of available articles in the selected newsgroup.

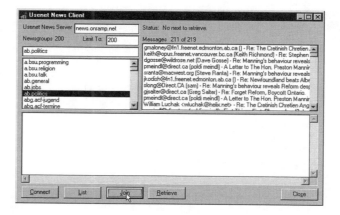

You now have shown the user the articles available in the selected newsgroup, and can enable the user to select and retrieve an article from this newsgroup.

Retrieving an Article

You could retrieve the selected article with a single ARTICLE command, or perform the retrieve in a three-step process using the STAT, HEAD, and BODY commands. For your newsreader application, you use the latter method.

To retrieve the selected article, you must determine either the article number or the article ID for the selected article. If you had captured the article ID when retrieving the headers, you could use it to specify which article to retrieve. However, because you do not capture this ID, the cbRetrieveClick() procedure calculates the article number by adding the selected header's index number to the first article's number (see Listing 10.16). The procedure sets the current article pointer to that article number by issuing the STAT command to the news server.

N O T E To calculate the requested article number, add the first article number to the selected line number from the list box that you populated with the article headers. This method of calculating the selected article number is not entirely reliable. Sometimes article numbers are skipped on the server, which causes them to get out of sync with this method of determining article numbers. A better method is to populate a dynamic structure with the message IDs of the newsgroup articles, so that when the user selects an article, the application can request the article by using the unique message ID, and thus guarantee that the correct article is retrieved. ■

Listing 10.16   NEWS.PAS—the *cbRetrieveClick()* Procedure Initiates the Retrieval of a Particular Article

```
procedure TNews1. cbRetrieveClick(Sender: TObject);
begin
   {Update the display to reflect that you are retrieving an article}
   lStatusDisp.Caption := 'Retrieving Article';
   {Set the command status flag to indicate that you are asking for
   an article}
   iiUseNetStatus := UNN_ASKFORMESSAGE;
   {Invalidate the receive buffer}
   ReceiveBuffer[0] := Char(0);
   {Clear the TMemo field}
   Memo1.Clear;
   {Send the STAT command to the server. You calculate the article number
   by adding the selected line number from the article header list box
   to the first article number}
   NetSocket.SocketSend(isConnectionSocket, handle, UWM_SOCKETEVENT,
                   'STAT ' + IntToStr(iiFirstArticle +
                   lbMessages.ItemIndex), SKT_RECVPACKET);
   {Clear the receive buffer}
   ClearBuffer(ReceiveBuffer, 8192);
end;
```

After receiving the response to your request to position the current article pointer to the selected article, the ProcessAskForMessage procedure verifies that the request succeeded (see Listing 10.17). If so, the procedure requests the header of this article from the news server.

Listing 10.17   NEWS.PAS—the *ProcessAskForMessage* Procedure Positions the Newsreader at the Correct Article and Requests the Article Header

```
procedure TNews1.ProcessAskForMessage;
var
   liSpaceCharPos: Integer;
   lbEndOfStr: Boolean;
   lsTempStr, lsRetnStr: String;
begin
   {Initialize the End of String flag to FALSE}
   lbEndOfStr := FALSE;
   {Place a null character at the end of the receive buffer}
   ReceiveBuffer[8192] := Char(0);
   {Does the command flag indicate that you are requesting an article
   body?}
   if (iiUseNetStatus = UNN_ASKFORMESSAGE) then
   begin
      {Convert the first line to a Pascal string}
      lsRetnStr := StrPas(ReceiveBuffer);
      {Check for the first space character}
      liSpaceCharPos := Pos(' ', lsRetnStr);
      {If the response includes a space, you probably have a
```

continues

Listing 10.17 Continued

```
                valid response message}
                if (liSpaceCharPos > 0) then
                begin
                   {Copy the first character into a temporary variable}
                   lsTempStr := Copy(lsRetnStr, 1, 1);
                   {Trim off the response code}
                   lsRetnStr := Copy(lsRetnStr, (liSpaceCharPos + 1),
                                                    Length(lsRetnStr));
                   {Is the first character a 4? If so, you received
                   a command-rejected response}
                   if (lsTempStr = '4') then
                   begin
                      {Set the End of String flag to TRUE and show the user
                      the response message}
                      lbEndOfStr := TRUE;
                      lStatusDisp.Caption := lsRetnStr;
                      lStatusDisp.Update;
                   end;
                end;
                {Can you continue?}
                if (not lbEndOfStr) then
                begin
                   {Find the first space character}
                   liSpaceCharPos := Pos(' ', lsRetnStr);
                   {If so, you received a complete response message}
                   if (liSpaceCharPos > 0) then
                   begin
                      {Set the command status flag to indicate that you are asking
                      for an article header}
                      iiUseNetStatus := UNN_GETMESSAGEHEADER;
                      {Invalidate the receive buffer}
                      ReceiveBuffer[0] := Char(0);
                      {Clear the hold buffer}
                      HoldBuffer := '';
                      {Send the HEAD command to the server}
                      NetSocket.SocketSend(isConnectionSocket, handle,
                              UWM_SOCKETEVENT, 'HEAD', SKT_RECVPACKET);
                      {Clear the receive buffer}
                      ClearBuffer(ReceiveBuffer, 8192);
                   end;
                end;
             end;
          end;
       end;
```

When the server returns the article header, you process the returned header using much the same functions as you used to process the returned headers when building your list of headers. The primary difference is that in this case you don't look for any specific information from the header; you simply want to extract each line and add it to the memo control that you are using to display the article text.

After receiving all the article header (as designated by the end-of-message marker, a single period on a line by itself), the GetMessageHeadLine procedure uses the BODY command to issue a request for the article's text (see Listing 10.18). Before issuing this request, you add an empty line to the memo control to separate the header from the body of the article.

Listing 10.18   NEWS.PAS—the *GetMessageHeadLine* and *ProcessGetMessageHeader* Procedures Retrieve the Article's Header for Display

```
procedure TNews1.GetMessageHeadLine;
var
   lbEndOfStr: Boolean;
   lsTempStr, lsRetnStr: String;
begin
   {Initialize the End of String flag to FALSE}
   lbEndOfStr := FALSE;
   {Does the command flag indicate that you are requesting an article
   body?}
   if (iiUseNetStatus = UNN_GETMESSAGEHEADER) then
      {Get the first line from the response, which is the response code
      and not part of the message}
      NetSocket.GetLine(TempBuffer, ReceiveBuffer);
   {Loop as long as there are more lines in the receive buffer and you
   haven't found the message-termination marker}
   while ((NetSocket.GetLine(TempBuffer, ReceiveBuffer)) and
         (not lbEndOfStr)) do
   begin
      {Convert the line into a Pascal string}
      lsRetnStr := StrPas(TempBuffer);
      {Is there anything in the hold buffer?}
      if (HoldBuffer <> '') then
      begin
         {Yes, it must be the start of the extracted line, so add it
         to the front of the extracted line}
         lsRetnStr := HoldBuffer + lsRetnStr;
         {Empty the hold buffer}
         HoldBuffer := '';
      end;
      {Is this the message-termination marker?}
      if (lsRetnStr = '.') then
         {Yes, set the End of String flag to TRUE}
         lbEndOfStr := TRUE;
      {Have you reached the end of the message header?}
      if (lbEndOfStr) then
      begin
         {If so, add a blank line to the message display}
         Memo1.Lines.Add('');
         Memo1.Update;
         {Set the command status flag to indicate that you are asking for
         an article body}
         iiUseNetStatus := UNN_GETMESSAGETEXT;
         {Invalidate the receive buffer}
         ReceiveBuffer[0] := Char(0);
```

continues

Listing 10.18 Continued

```
            {Send the BODY command to the server}
            NetSocket.SocketSend(isConnectionSocket, handle,
                UWM_SOCKETEVENT, 'BODY', SKT_RECVPACKET);
            {Clear the receive buffer}
            ClearBuffer(ReceiveBuffer, 8192);
        end
        else
        begin
            {Otherwise, add the header line to the display}
            Memo1.Lines.Add(lsRetnStr);
            Memo1.Update;
        end;
    end;
    {Is there more header to retrieve?}
    if (not lbEndOfStr) then
    begin
        {Set the command status flag to indicate that you are asking for
        an article header}
        iiUseNetStatus := UNN_GETTINGMESSAGEHEADER;
        {Place what is left into the hold buffer}
        HoldBuffer := StrPas(TempBuffer);
        {Clear the receive buffer}
        ClearBuffer(ReceiveBuffer, 8192);
    end;
end;

{The ProcessGetMessageHeader procedure checks for an error response code
before passing the received data to the GetMessageHeadLine procedure}
procedure TNews1.ProcessGetMessageHeader;
var
    liSpaceCharPos: Integer;
    lbEndOfStr: Boolean;
    lsTempStr, lsRetnStr: String;
begin
    {Initialize the End of String flag to FALSE}
    lbEndOfStr := FALSE;
    {Place a null character at the end of the receive buffer}
    ReceiveBuffer[8192] := Char(0);
    {Does the command flag indicate that you are requesting an article
    header?}
    if (iiUseNetStatus = UNN_GETMESSAGEHEADER) then
    begin
        {Convert the first line to a Pascal string}
        lsRetnStr := StrPas(ReceiveBuffer);
        {Check for the first space character}
        liSpaceCharPos := Pos(' ', lsRetnStr);
        {If the response includes a space, you probably have a
        valid response message}
        if (liSpaceCharPos > 0) then
        begin
            {Copy the first character into a temporary variable}
            lsTempStr := Copy(lsRetnStr, 1, 1);
            {Is the first character a '4'? If so, you received
```

```
      a command-rejected response}
      if (lsTempStr = '4') then
      begin
          {Set the End of String flag to TRUE and show the user
          the response message}
          lbEndOfStr := TRUE;
          lStatusDisp.Caption := lsRetnStr;
          lStatusDisp.Update;
      end;
   end;
end;
{Does the command flag indicate that you are requesting an article
header?}
if ((iiUseNetStatus = UNN_GETMESSAGEHEADER) or
   (iiUseNetStatus = UNN_GETTINGMESSAGEHEADER)) then
   {Have you reached the end of the header?}
   if (not lbEndOfStr) then
      {If not, call the GetMessageHeadLine to parse the header
      and add it to the display}
      GetMessageHeadLine;
end;
```

The GetMessageTextLine and ProcessGetMessage procedures use the same method to retrieve and process the selected article's body (see Listing 10.19). You strip off the response line, examine it to verify that the request succeeded, parse the article into individual lines, and add each line into the memo control. You continue until reaching the end-of-message marker.

Listing 10.19 NEWS.PAS—the *GetMessageTextLine* and *ProcessGetMessage* Procedures Retrieve the Article Text

```
procedure TNews1.GetMessageTextLine;
var
   lbEndOfStr: Boolean;
   lsTempStr, lsRetnStr: String;
begin
   {Initialize the End of String flag to FALSE}
   lbEndOfStr := FALSE;
   {Does the command flag indicate that you are requesting an article
   body?}
   if (iiUseNetStatus = UNN_GETMESSAGETEXT) then
      {Get the first line from the response, which is the response code
      and not part of the message}
      NetSocket.GetLine(TempBuffer, ReceiveBuffer);
   {Loop as long as there are more lines in the receive buffer and you
   haven't found the message-termination marker}
   while ((NetSocket.GetLine(TempBuffer, ReceiveBuffer)) and
          (not lbEndOfStr)) do
   begin
      {Convert the line into a Pascal string}
      lsRetnStr := StrPas(TempBuffer);
```

continues

Listing 10.19   Continued

```
      {Is there anything in the hold buffer?}
      if (HoldBuffer <> '') then
      begin
        {Yes, it must be the start of the extracted line, so add it
        to the front of the extracted line}
        lsRetnStr := HoldBuffer + lsRetnStr;
        {Empty the hold buffer}
        HoldBuffer := '';
      end;
      {Is this the message-termination marker?}
      if (lsRetnStr = '.') then
        {Yes, set the End of String flag to TRUE}
        lbEndOfStr := TRUE;
      {Have you reached the end of the message body?}
      if (not lbEndOfStr) then
      begin
        {No, add the message line to the display}
        Memo1.Lines.Add(lsRetnStr);
        Memo1.Update;
      end;
    end;
    {Is there more message to retrieve?}
    if (not lbEndOfStr) then
    begin
      {Set the command status flag to indicate that you are asking for
      an article body}
      iiUseNetStatus := UNN_GETTINGMESSAGETEXT;
      {Place the remainder into the hold buffer}
      HoldBuffer := StrPas(TempBuffer);
      {Clear the receive buffer}
      ClearBuffer(ReceiveBuffer, 8192);
    end;
end;

{The ProcessGetMessage procedure checks for an error-response code before
passing the received data to the GetMessageTextLine procedure}
procedure TNews1.ProcessGetMessage;
var
   liSpaceCharPos: Integer;
   lbEndOfStr: Boolean;
   lsTempStr, lsRetnStr: String;
begin
   {Initialize the End of String flag to FALSE}
   lbEndOfStr := FALSE;
   {Place a null character at the end of the receive buffer}
   ReceiveBuffer[8192] := Char(0);
   {Does the command flag indicate that you are requesting an article
   body?}
```

```
if (iiUseNetStatus = UNN_GETMESSAGETEXT) then
begin
   {Convert the first line to a Pascal string}
   lsRetnStr := StrPas(ReceiveBuffer);
   {Check for the first space character}
   liSpaceCharPos := Pos(' ', lsRetnStr);
   {If the response includes a space, you probably have a
   valid response message}
   if (liSpaceCharPos > 0) then
   begin
      {Copy the first character into a temporary variable}
      lsTempStr := Copy(lsRetnStr, 1, 1);
      {Is the first character a 4? If so, you received
      a command-rejected response}
      if (lsTempStr = '4') then
      begin
         {Set the End of String flag to TRUE and show the user
         the response message}
         lbEndOfStr := TRUE;
         lStatusDisp.Caption := lsRetnStr;
         lStatusDisp.Update;
      end;
   end;
end;
{Does the command flag indicate that you are requesting an article
body?}
if ((iiUseNetStatus = UNN_GETMESSAGETEXT) or
    (iiUseNetStatus = UNN_GETTINGMESSAGETEXT)) then
    {Have you reached the end of the body?}
    if (not lbEndOfStr) then
        {If not, call the GetMessageTextLine to parse the body
        and add it to the display}
        GetMessageTextLine;
end;
```

Figure 10.5 shows the news client after retrieving the selected article.

Part
II

Ch
10

FIG. 10.5

The selected article retrieved into the news client.

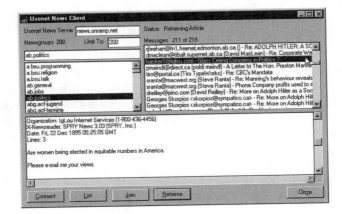

CAUTION

If you are using the 16-bit version of Delphi and attempt to retrieve an article that contains an encoded image (or other suitably large file) into a memo control, you are quite likely to overrun the amount of data that you can insert into a memo control. If you exceed this limit, you encounter a General Protection Fault (GPF). To deal with this error condition, you can use some exception handling and try an alternative to holding the article (such as writing it directly to file). This chapter's newsreader example does not handle the error condition. For information on exception handling, see *Delphi Developer's Guide* (ISBN 0-672-30704-9), from Sams Publishing and Borland Press.

The only functionality left to build in to your Usenet newsreader is the capability to post a new article. Although this chapter doesn't show you exactly how to implement the article post functionality, you should have enough information (and know of enough places to look for more information) that you can implement the article-posting functionality yourself. For more information on the commands and protocols involved, see RFC 977, and for more information on article formatting, see RFCs 1036 and 850.

From Here...

In this chapter, you learned how to use the basic Usenet Network News Transport Protocol (NNTP) to build your own news client. In the process, you took a brief look at how news articles are distributed throughout the Internet, as well as some of the issues that this distribution method raises. You also looked at how to use a subset of the NNTP command set (to become familiar with the commands that you must use to build an NNTP news client, see Appendix A). Finally, to help you plan your simple news client implementation, you outlined the various steps that an NNTP news client executes.

From here you could expand this simple application by fully implementing the article-posting functionality. You could also add the capability to cancel any retrievals from the server in midstream (for group lists and articles, this would mean using the method that cancels the list retrieval at the limit set by the user; for article headers, this means ending the retrieval process). You could replace the memo control with a more robust text editor and display that can handle the largest of news articles. You also could build in the capability to encode and decode files for embedding within news articles.

Then you could convert all this functionality into a different sort of application. For example, you could combine text search functionality to create a news-scanning application. This application would scan the text of articles in selected newsgroups to find and retrieve articles containing references to predefined subjects. You could build an article thread follower that scans the article headers to find and retrieve those that are replying to a particular article (or are replying to a reply to the original, or a reply to a reply to a reply to the original, and so on). After building these applications, you could plug them into a Web server to enable it to search news articles as part of a Web service (either as an Internet or intranet service). The number of possibilities for what this functionality enables you to build is unlimited.

The following chapters cover other Internet protocols that you might want to consider combining with the NNTP protocol:

- To understand how standards for Internet applications and file formats are developed and where to find the documentation, see Chapter 7, "Internet Development Standards."

- To understand the Simple Mail Transport Protocol (SMTP) and build an SMTP client, see Chapter 9, "Developing SMTP and POP Mail Clients."

- To integrate file encoding and decoding into your NNTP client, see Chapter 11, "Building a UUEncoder/Decoder."

- To see how to build a Web server, see Chapter 16, "Building a Web Server with Delphi."

- To understand all the Usenet commands, see Appendix A, "Internet Applications Command Sets."

- To gain a better understanding of the Internet Message Format, see Appendix B, "The Internet Message Format."

Part
II

Ch
10

Building a UUEncoder/Decoder

Now that you've been building all these Internet applications to send and receive e-mail, and you can browse the Usenet newsgroups, you've probably noticed that many files (pictures, utilities, and even word processing documents) are posted in some sort of encoded format. These files are available as ASCII text, which, to the average programmer, looks like complete nonsensical garbage. Unless you have done much programming in lower-level languages, you can't possibly read these files and make any sense of them!

These files are in the format *UUEncoded*. This is a simple type of encryption that allows for the conversion of any binary file type (pictures, applications, and so on) into ASCII text, and back into the original format. The purpose of these encoding schemes is to enable printable ASCII text to represent binary files completely, to simplify the transfer between two (or more) computer systems (printable ASCII being the lowest common denominator between most systems). Although technological advances have minimized the need for this encoding, it is still the primary way to transfer binary files through Internet e-mail, and the only way to post a file to a newsgroup.

The encoding and decoding of binary files into ASCII text is not directly an Internet application, but it is an Internet-related application. Therefore, this chapter takes a look at what is involved in this encoding and decoding routine. ■

Using ASCII as the Common Transfer Format

During the early days of the Internet (and ARPAnet, and possibly even earlier), when the large facilities that started building interconnected networks wanted to be able to exchange files with each other—whether as e-mail, documents, or source code—the system builders found that they had a problem when trying to find a common format that all systems could use. Some systems could transfer 8-bit words, and some 16, but many could transfer only 7-bit words (a *word* being the number of bits that a particular system processor could move about at one time). Ultimately, the one word format that all the systems could send and receive was 7-bit printable ASCII characters.

Therefore, to transfer files back and forth, these Internet pioneers needed an algorithm to convert all non-ASCII files into text so that they could transfer the files to another system, then convert them back again. One of the algorithms that they came up with is known as *standard* or *UUEncoding*. This format has evolved into the most popular format in use for posting files to newsgroups.

N O T E The *UU* prefix on the common name for this encoding format probably derives from the UUCP (UNIX-to-UNIX Communications Package) set of communication utilities. The UUCP suite is used for performing serial communications among UNIX systems. Most earlier versions of the UUCP suite allowed only seven-bit serial communications. Because of this communication limitation, using ASCII encoding was a perfect fit when file transfers were needed.

Much more recently, a new standard was developed for expanding the capabilities of the Simple Mail Transfer Protocol (SMTP) mail system in use throughout the Internet. Instead of only being able to send more than just plain text messages, users needed the capability to attach an image, word processing document, spreadsheet, or other files to the e-mail messages that they were sending across the Internet. To accommodate this need, the Multipurpose Internet Multimedia Extensions (MIME) standard was developed as an extension to the SMTP standard. The MIME standard enabled users to attach any type of file to an e-mail message.

To accommodate this expansion of the capabilities of the Internet mail system without excluding the older systems on the Internet, the developers of the MIME standard included a new encoding algorithm: base-64 encoding. This encoding/decoding algorithm, which is built in to all MIME-compliant e-mail clients, has become quite popular on the Internet for all instances that require encoding.

Understanding the Binary-to-ASCII Conversion

The two most popular encoding methods take the same basic approach to encoding binary data as ASCII text. This method consists of a series of four steps:

1. Break the file into six-bit groups. This limits the available number of bit combinations to 64 distinct values ($2^6 = 64$).

2. Convert these six-bit groups into numbers (0 through 63).

3. Match the numeric value of each group to its corresponding (printable) character in an encoding table.

4. Take the matching character and write it out to the encoded file.

The corresponding decoding process is the reverse of this sequence of steps.

As illustrated in Figure 11.1, both of these encoding schemes take three eight-bit bytes and slice them into four six-bit bytes (padding the two leftmost bits of each new byte with zeros). This reduces the number of possible byte combinations to 64 unique values. Once sliced up in this way, the bytes can be cross-referenced against a table of 64 printable ASCII characters to provide a file that any two systems can easily transfer.

FIG. 11.1
Redividing three bytes into four bytes.

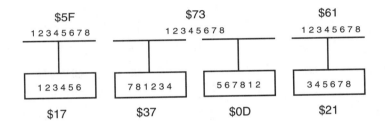

The Standard (UU) Encoding Algorithm

At this point, the two encoding algorithms go separate ways. The standard encoding (UUEncoding) algorithm uses a simple table (see Table 11.1) starting with what should be the space character (usually denoted as the value #20 in the ASCII character set) and uses sequential ASCII values through the underscore character (#5F, again from the ASCII character set). Because the space character is not easily differentiated from nonencoded space characters, the left-angled single quote character (#60 in the ASCII character set) is used in the space character's place. You see how this exception to the table works when you examine the decoding algorithm later in this chapter. Figure 11.2 illustrates the entire encoding process.

Table 11.1 The Cross-Reference Table for Standard UUEncoding

Decimal Value	Hex Value	ASCII Character	ASCII Value	Decimal Value	Hex Value	ASCII Character	ASCII Value
0	$00	'	$60	32	$20	@	$40
1	$01	!	$21	33	$21	A	$41
2	$02	"	$22	34	$22	B	$42
3	$03	#	$23	35	$23	C	$43

continues

Table 11.1 Continued

Decimal Value	Hex Value	ASCII Character	ASCII Value	Decimal Value	Hex Value	ASCII Character	ASCII Value
4	$04	$	$24	36	$24	D	$44
5	$05	%	$25	37	$25	E	$45
6	$06	$	$26	38	$26	F	$46
7	$07	'	$27	39	$27	G	$47
8	$08	(	$28	40	$28	H	$48
9	$09	)	$29	41	$29	I	$49
10	$0A	~	$2A	42	$2A	J	$4A
11	$0B	+	$2B	43	$2B	K	$4B
12	$0C	,	$2C	44	$2C	L	$4C
13	$0D	-	$2D	45	$2D	M	$4D
14	$0E	.	$2E	46	$2E	N	$4E
15	$0F	/	$2F	47	$2F	O	$4F
16	$10	0	$30	48	$30	P	$50
17	$11	1	$31	49	$31	Q	$51
18	$12	2	$32	50	$32	R	$52
19	$13	3	$33	51	$33	S	$53
20	$14	4	$34	52	$34	T	$54
21	$15	5	$35	53	$35	U	$55
22	$16	6	$36	54	$36	V	$56
23	$17	7	$37	55	$37	W	$57
24	$18	8	$38	56	$38	X	$58
25	$19	9	$39	57	$39	Y	$59
26	$1A	:	$3A	58	$3A	Z	$5A
27	$1B	;	$3B	59	$3B	[	$5B
28	$1C	<	$3C	60	$3C	\	$5C
29	$1D	=	$3D	61	$3D	]	$5D
30	$1E	>	$3E	62	$3E	^	$5E
31	$1F	?	$3F	63	$3F	_	$5F

FIG. 11.2

The standard
UUEncoding process.

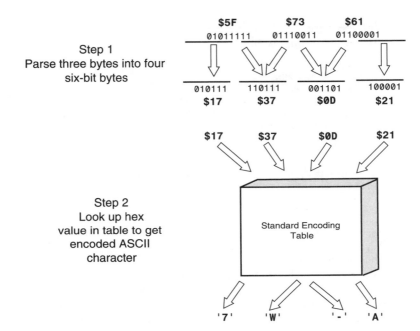

Step 1
Parse three bytes into four
six-bit bytes

Step 2
Look up hex
value in table to get
encoded ASCII
character

When writing the encoded file, the UUEncoding algorithm prefixes each line with an encoded character that, when decoded, specifies the number of unencoded bytes included on that line. This informs the decoder of the number of bytes to attempt to decode on any particular line of the encoded file. By informing the decoding application of the line length, an encoding application has the option of using a nonstandard line length on any or all lines in the encoded file. Usually each line consists of 45 unencoded bytes, or 60 encoded characters (for every three UNEncoded characters, there will be four encoded characters). Therefore, the algorithm prefixes most average lines with the letter *M* (which is #2D in hexadecimal, which equals 45 in decimal values). A normal exception to this standard line length is the last line of most UUEncoded files. This line is normally shorter than the standard length, and begins with a character other than *M* to reflect the actual length.

The beginning and ending of the encoded file are normally designated with standardized markers. The begin marker has the following form:

```
begin mode > filename
```

where *mode* is usually 644 (UNIX file permissions meaning read-write permission for the owner, and read-only permission for everyone else). The end marker consists of a line with a single ' character followed by a line consisting of the word end. Listing 11.1 shows a file with typical begin and end markers.

Listing 11.1   BMW750K.UUE—the Beginning and Ending of a Typical UUEncoded Image File

```
{ Begin Marker. Notice that the file being encoded is bmw75ok.jpg}
Begin 644 bmw750k.jpg
{Binary data encoded in the UU algorithm;
 Notice the M at the beginning of each line.}
M_]C_X"02D9)1@'!'0$!'0$$!L"'$L"'#_VP!#''$'#'0$'P%$04$'&P;'DA0$!P
M!P\(+"PD(,4M'-#0U.D'5%3U%,XY'5%M9FX'+"PD(,4M'=G$4M9F?$Q'Q%P[_
.
.
.
MS,[++Q)8VVJV]]K$>DE_7??(?L_79#O[X^F=@,AK$?1#_Y"]%]^`V!2W<Q9#U*!
21110'4444'%%%'!1110!__9
{end marker begins here}
'
end
```

The encoding table used for standard UUEncoding allows for decoding without the use of a cross-reference table. Actually, you could easily perform the encoding without using a cross-reference table, by adding the ASCII value of the space character to each six-bit byte and then replacing all space characters with the underscore character. Nevertheless, your implementation will use such a table. The algorithm subtracts the ASCII value for the space character ($20) from each character's ASCII value. This subtraction brings most of the characters back down to their original six-bit values. The algorithm ANDs the resulting value with a six-bit mask ($3F) to get rid of any values greater than 63 (this mask reduces the $60 ASCII value back down to zero). At this point, the algorithm recombines every four bytes into the original three bytes by bit-shifting and ORing the resulting values together. This process restores the file to its original format. Figure 11.3 illustrates the decoding process.

The Base-64 (MIME) Encoding Algorithm

The base-64 encoding algorithm attempts to use only letter and number ASCII characters. Unfortunately, there aren't enough letters and numbers to use each exclusively (there are only 62), so the algorithm has to use two additional characters (+ and /). Table 11.2 is the base-64 encoding table, and Figure 11.4 illustrates the entire coding process.

FIG. 11.3

The cross-reference table for standard UUEncoding.

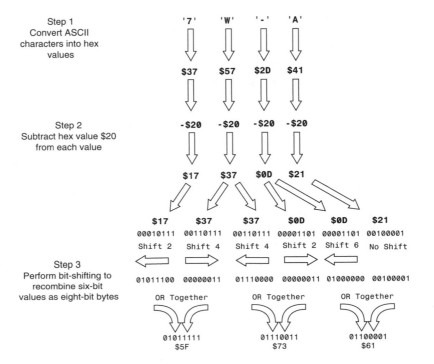

Step 1
Convert ASCII characters into hex values

Step 2
Subtract hex value $20 from each value

Step 3
Perform bit-shifting to recombine six-bit values as eight-bit bytes

Table 11.2 The Base-64 Encoding Cross-Reference Table

Decimal Value	Hex Value	ASCII Character	ASCII Value	Decimal Value	Hex Value	ASCII Character	ASCII Value
0	$00	A	$41	5	$05	F	$46
1	$01	B	$42	6	$06	G	$47
2	$02	C	$43	7	$07	H	$48
3	$03	D	$44	8	$08	I	$49
4	$04	E	$45	9	$09	J	$4A

continues

Table 11.2 Continued

Decimal Value	Hex Value	ASCII Character	ASCII Value	Decimal Value	Hex Value	ASCII Character	ASCII Value
10	$0A	K	$4B	37	$25	l	$6C
11	$0B	L	$4C	38	$26	m	$6D
12	$0C	M	$4D	39	$27	n	$6E
13	$0D	N	$4E	40	$28	o	$6F
14	$0E	O	$4F	41	$29	p	$70
15	$0F	P	$50	42	$2A	q	$71
16	$10	Q	$51	43	$2B	r	$72
17	$11	R	$52	44	$2C	s	$73
18	$12	S	$53	45	$2D	t	$74
19	$13	T	$54	46	$2E	u	$75
20	$14	U	$55	47	$2F	v	$76
21	$15	V	$56	48	$30	w	$77
22	$16	W	$57	49	$31	x	$78
23	$17	X	$58	50	$32	y	$79
24	$18	Y	$59	51	$33	z	$7A
25	$19	Z	$5A	52	$34	0	$30
26	$1A	a	$61	53	$35	1	$31
27	$1B	b	$62	54	$36	2	$32
28	$1C	c	$63	55	$37	3	$33
29	$1D	d	$64	56	$38	4	$34
30	$1E	e	$65	57	$39	5	$35
31	$1F	f	$66	58	$3A	6	$36
32	$20	g	$67	59	$3B	7	$37
33	$21	h	$68	60	$3C	8	$38
34	$22	i	$69	61	$3D	9	$39
35	$23	j	$6A	62	$3E	+	$2B
36	$24	k	$6B	63	$3F	/	$2F

FIG. 11.4

The base-64 encoding process.

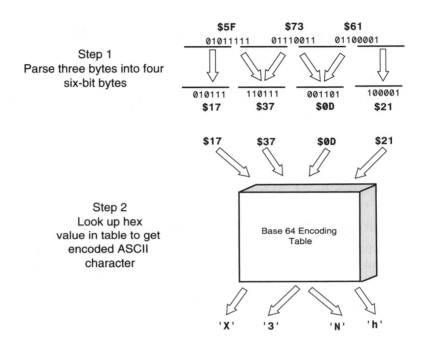

Step 1
Parse three bytes into four six-bit bytes

Step 2
Look up hex value in table to get encoded ASCII character

The other major difference between base-64 and standard encoding is that the base-64 format does not prefix each line with its length. When decoding a base-64 file, the program needs to look for end-of-line markers to know when to quit decoding a particular line. If the last line is too short, the program pads the line with the equal character (=), which extends the line until it is the appropriate length (some decoders insist that this length be 60 characters long, others just insist that the line length be a multiple of four). For example, if the last line consisted of seven unencoded bytes, it would be encoded into 10 characters (the first six bytes would encode to eight characters, the last one would be broken up into two characters). At a minimum, this line would be padded with two equal characters so that the line length is 12 characters long (a nice multiple of four). A finicky decoder might insist that the line be padded with 50 equal characters to make the line a full 60 characters long.

The begin marker is slightly different than that of standard encoding in that base-64 encoding suffixes the word begin with -base64 to designate that the file is a base-64 encoded file. The last difference is that the end marker does not have a zero-length line preceding the line containing the word end. Here's an example of a begin marker:

```
{ Begin Marker. Notice that the file being encoded is bmw75ok.jpg}
begin-base64 644 BMW750K.JPG
{Binary data encoded in the base-64 algorithm}
/9j/4AAQSkZJRgABAQEBLAEsAAD/2wBDAAUDBAQEAwUEBAQFBQUGBwwIBwcH
Bw8LCwkMEQ8SEhEPERETFhwXExQaFRERGCEYGh0dHx8fExciJCIeJBweHx7/
2wBDAQUFBQcGBw4ICA4eFBEUHh4eHh4eHh4eHh4eHh4eHh4eHh4eHh4eHh4e
.
.
```

```
.
zM7LxJY22q2a6jaX0eIkxhmwhHX8DXG0UV0Yei6MeW910E3cKKKK3EFFFFAB
RRRQAUUUUAFFFFABRRRQB//Z===
{end marker begins here}
end
```

Decoding a base-64 encoded file is much easier than decoding a UUEncoded file. The only reasonable way to do so is to use a decoding cross-reference table, such as that shown in Table 11.3. By using the ASCII values of each character, you can use the cross-referenced values to convert each encoded character directly back to its original six-bit value, without using any additional logic (other than discarding characters that don't have a cross-reference value). You can recombine these values into the original eight-bit values from the unencoded file as illustrated in Figure 11.5.

Table 11.3   The Base-64 Decoding Cross-Reference Table

Decimal Value	ASCII Value	ASCII Character	Decode Value	Decimal Value	ASCII Value	ASCII Character	Decode Value
43	$2B	+	$3E	63	$3F		
44	$2C			64	$40		
45	$2D			65	$41	A	$00
46	$2E			66	$42	B	$01
47	$2F	/	$3F	67	$43	C	$02
48	$30	0	$34	68	$44	D	$03
49	$31	1	$35	69	$45	E	$04
50	$32	2	$36	70	$46	F	$05
51	$33	3	$37	71	$47	G	$06
52	$34	4	$38	72	$48	H	$07
53	$35	5	$39	73	$49	I	$08
54	$36	6	$3A	74	$4A	J	$09
55	$37	7	$3B	75	$4B	K	$0A
56	$38	8	$3C	76	$4C	L	$0B
57	$39	9	$3D	77	$4D	M	$0C
58	$3A			78	$4E	N	$0D
59	$3B			79	$4F	O	$0E
60	$3C			80	$50	P	$0F
61	$3D			81	$51	Q	$10
62	$3E			82	$52	R	$11

Decimal Value	ASCII Value	ASCII Character	Decode Value	Decimal Value	ASCII Value	ASCII Character	Decode Value
83	$53	S	$12	103	$67	g	$20
84	$54	T	$13	104	$68	h	$21
85	$55	U	$14	105	$69	I	$22
86	$56	V	$15	106	$6A	j	$23
87	$57	W	$16	107	$6B	k	$24
88	$58	X	$17	108	$6C	l	$25
89	$59	Y	$18	109	$6D	m	$26
90	$5A	Z	$19	110	$6E	n	$27
91	$5B			111	$6F	o	$28
92	$5C			112	$70	p	$29
93	$5D			113	$71	q	$2A
94	$5E			114	$72	r	$2B
95	$5F			115	$73	s	$2C
96	$60			116	$74	t	$2D
97	$61	a	$1A	117	$75	u	$2E
98	$62	b	$1B	118	$76	v	$2F
99	$63	c	$1C	119	$77	w	$30
100	$64	d	$1D	120	$78	x	$31
101	$65	e	$1E	121	$79	y	$32
102	$66	f	$1F	122	$7A	z	$33

Part
II

Ch
11

CAUTION

Although the base-64 encoding format is well documented, it also seems to be quite fragile. The problem is that many MIME-compliant encoders (including mail clients and Usenet news clients) format the base-64 encoded files slightly differently. This often results in the more picky decoders rejecting the file with formatting errors. The most common location for these errors is in the format of the file's last lines.

Another problem, which plagues both formats, is that some encoders omit the begin markers. Although the message header lists the file name and encoding format, the line before the encoding starts does not list them. Both of these variations from the standard cause problems in the less forgiving decoders. The decoder that you will implement forgives incorrect end marker formatting, but doesn't forgive the omission of the begin marker. (You might want to add this enhancement after you start finding messages that use this alternative formatting.)

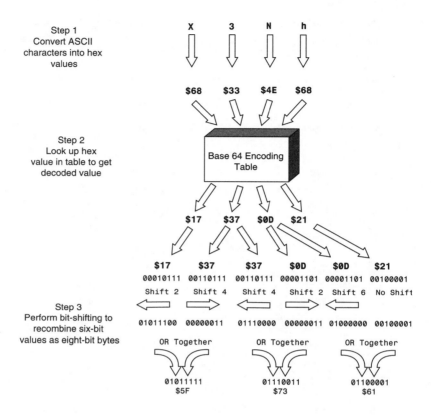

FIG. 11.5
The base-64 decoding process.

Building a UUEncoder

Because of the similarities in the two approaches, you can build an encoding application that can handle both encoding formats within one function. The differences that you must consider are the following:

- Make sure that you are using the correct cross-reference table
- Use the correct format of the begin and end markers
- Insert the line length at the beginning of each line if you are encoding the file with the standard format

Declaring and Loading the Encoding Tables

You begin building you application by defining the file handles for both the encoded and decoded files (see Listing 11.2). You also define an encoding table to use.

Listing 11.2   SDIMAIN.PAS—File Handles and the Encoding Table

```
EncodedFile: TextFile;
DecodedFile: File of Byte;
EncodingTable: array[0..63] of Char;
```

You next need to provide a way to load the encoding table appropriately for the two differing encoding algorithms (see Listing 11.3). You load the table by using a straight assignment of characters to each position in the table.

Listing 11.3   SDIMAIN.PAS—*LoadStdEncodeTable*, the Procedure That Loads the Encoding Table for Both Standard and Base-64 Encoding

```
procedure TSDIAppForm. LoadStdEncodeTable;
begin
   EncodingTable[0] := '`';              { $60 }
   EncodingTable[1] := '!';              { $21 }
   EncodingTable[2] := '"';              { $22 }
   EncodingTable[3] := '#';              { $23 }
   .
   .
   .
   EncodingTable[60] := Char($5C);       { $5C }
   EncodingTable[61] := ']';             { $5D }
   EncodingTable[62] := '^';             { $5E }
   EncodingTable[63] := '_';             { $5F }
end;

procedure TSDIAppForm.LoadBase64EncodeTable;
begin
   EncodingTable[0] := 'A';
   EncodingTable[1] := 'B';
   EncodingTable[2] := 'C';
   EncodingTable[3] := 'D';
   .
   .
   .
   EncodingTable[61] := '9';
   EncodingTable[62] := '+';
   EncodingTable[63] := '/';
end;
```

N O T E   You could use a simpler method for loading these tables by declaring tables of type `EncodingTable` and loading the tables with values in the declaration, as follows:

```
var
Base64Table : EncodingTable = { 'A', 'B', 'C', 'D', 'E', ...'+', '/'};
```

If you used this method, you would either have to declare two encoding tables and a pointer to the appropriate one, or write two separate functions to perform the encoding in the different formats. Although the coding to load the table might be simpler, the method doesn't yield significantly different performance and would require twice as much code. ■

Part

II

Ch

11

Encoding the Input File

The encoding function is quite simple (see Listing 11.4). The value that results from the recombination of bits into six-bit bytes is ANDed with $3F to mask out any unwanted residual bits. The resulting value specifies the table position at which the function finds its return value.

Listing 11.4 SDIMAIN.PAS—*uuENC()*, the Function That Performs the Encoding

```
function TSDIAppForm.uuENC(OutByte: Byte): Char;
begin
   uuENC := Char((EncodingTable[((OutByte) and $3F)]));
end;
```

Now comes the real grunt work. You first open both files and reset them for reading and writing appropriately. You want to include only the input file name in the begin marker line, so you strip any file system path from the file name. Next, you write out the appropriate begin marker line for the encoding algorithm that you are using and then load the encoding table accordingly.

Now you are ready to start performing the actual encoding. First you execute a loop that terminates on reaching the end of the input file. This loop reads in 45 bytes (unless less than 45 bytes are left in the file). Next, you initialize the text line that you are writing to the encoded file. If you are using standard encoding, you encode the number of characters that you read in; otherwise, you start the line with nothing.

Now you encode the set of bytes that you read in. Loop through the bytes three at a time until less than three bytes are left. Use bit-shifting to divide and recombine the bytes. After you have each of the resulting four six-bit bytes, you encode it and add it to the output line. When less than three bytes are left, break out of the loop and fall through a couple of simple if then statements to encode the last one or two bytes. Pad the line with the equal sign, because you are using base-64 encoding.

Finally, tack on the appropriate end marker at the end of the file. Then close both files and clean up after yourself. Listing 11.5 shows all the code that performs this encoding.

Listing 11.5 SDIMAIN.PAS—*PerformEncode*, the Procedure That Performs All Encoding

```
procedure TSDIAppForm.PerformEncode;
var
   CurLine: array[1..45] of Byte;
   CurByte: Byte;
   CurPos: Integer;
   EncodedLine: String;
   NumRead: Integer;
begin
```

```
AssignFile(DecodedFile, InputFileName.Caption);
AssignFile(EncodedFile, OutputFileName.Caption);
Reset(DecodedFile);
Rewrite(EncodedFile);
EncodedLine := InputFileName.Caption;
CurPos := Pos('\', EncodedLine);
while (CurPos > 0) do
begin
  EncodedLine := Copy(EncodedLine, (CurPos + 1), Length(EncodedLine));
  CurPos := Pos('\', EncodedLine);
end;
if (rgEncoding.ItemIndex = 0) then
begin
   WriteLn(EncodedFile, 'begin 644 ' + EncodedLine);
   LoadStdEncodeTable;
end
else
begin
   WriteLn(EncodedFile, 'begin-base64 644 ' + EncodedLine);
   LoadBase64EncodeTable;
end;
while (not Eof(DecodedFile)) do
begin
   NumRead := 0;
   while ((NumRead < 45) and (not Eof(DecodedFile))) do
   begin
      Read(DecodedFile, CurByte);
      Inc(NumRead);
      CurLine[NumRead] := CurByte;
   end;
   if (rgEncoding.ItemIndex = 0) then
      EncodedLine := uuENC(Byte(NumRead))
   else
      EncodedLine := '';
   CurPos := 1;
   while (CurPos <= (NumRead - 2)) do
   begin
      CurByte := (CurLine[CurPos] SHR 2);
      EncodedLine := EncodedLine + uuENC(CurByte);
      CurByte := ((CurLine[CurPos] SHL 4) or
                 (CurLine[(CurPos + 1)] SHR 4));
      EncodedLine := EncodedLine + uuENC(CurByte);
      CurByte := ((CurLine[(CurPos + 1)] SHL 2) or
                 (CurLine[(CurPos + 2)] SHR 6));
      EncodedLine := EncodedLine + uuENC(CurByte);
      CurByte := (CurLine[(CurPos + 2)] and $3F);
      EncodedLine := EncodedLine + uuENC(CurByte);
      CurPos := CurPos + 3;
   end;
   if (CurPos < NumRead) then
   begin
      CurByte := (CurLine[CurPos] SHR 2);
      EncodedLine := EncodedLine + uuENC(CurByte);
      if (CurPos = (NumRead - 1)) then
      begin
```

Part
II

Ch
11

continues

Listing 11.5   Continued

```
              CurByte := ((CurLine[CurPos] SHL 4) and $30);
              EncodedLine := EncodedLine + uuENC(CurByte);
              if (rgEncoding.ItemIndex = 1) then
                  EncodedLine := EncodedLine + '=';
          end
          else
          begin
              CurByte := (((CurLine[CurPos] SHL 4) and $30) or
                          ((CurLine[(CurPos + 1)] SHR 4) and $0F));
              EncodedLine := EncodedLine + uuENC(CurByte);
              CurByte := ((CurLine[(CurPos + 1)] SHL 2) and $3C)
          end;
          EncodedLine := EncodedLine + uuENC(CurByte);
          if (rgEncoding.ItemIndex = 1) then
              EncodedLine := EncodedLine + '=';
      end;
      WriteLn(EncodedFile, EncodedLine);
  end;
  if (rgEncoding.ItemIndex = 0) then
  begin
      EncodedLine := uuENC(0);
      WriteLn(EncodedFile, EncodedLine);
  end;
  WriteLn(EncodedFile, 'end');
  CloseFile(EncodedFile);
  CloseFile(DecodedFile);
end;
```

Now you have an encoding utility that you can use to format images, applications, and anything else that you want to send through Internet mail or post to a Usenet newsgroup. You next must handle the other half of the equation (encoding information does little good unless you can decode it later).

Building a UUDecoder

Unfortunately, the two encoding schemes differ enough to make it difficult to combine the decoding into a single function. You have to split the decoding into two separate functional processes.

Decoding a UUEncoded File

Start with the standard encoding algorithm (see Listing 11.6). You can write a simple function to decode each individual character. You need only subtract the ASCII value for the space character from the encoded character's ASCII value. Then you mask out bits seven and eight (to prevent any garbage from slipping through) and return the resulting byte value.

Listing 11.6   SDIMAIN.PAS—*uuDEC()*, the Standard Decoding Function

```
function TSDIAppForm.uuDEC(InByte: Byte): Byte;
begin
   uuDEC := ((InByte - Byte(' ')) and $3F);
end;
```

Now that you can decode any individual character, you must write a procedure to process and decode the entire file. You first create a loop within which you decode each line until you reach the end of the file. Once in the loop, you read each line into a string buffer. If the string length is longer than two characters, you know that you have a line with some encoded characters.

N O T E   You use the length of two characters because the line that is read usually includes line-termination characters. If a line is only two characters long, it most likely consists of the carriage return and line feed characters. ▓

Once you have a valid line, you must decode the line-length character so that you know how many bytes you are decoding. You then start another loop in which you stay until the line no longer has any characters left to decode. Decode the line three bytes (four encoded characters) at a time, calling the decoding function and then using bit-shifting to recombine the bytes appropriately. When less than three bytes are left, decode the last one or two as appropriate.

If the number of encoded bytes on the current line is specified as zero, you are probably on the last encoded line and can expect the next line to be the encoding end marker. After reaching the end of the file, you close both files and clean up. Listing 11.7 shows the entire standard decoding procedure.

Part
II

Ch
11

Listing 11.7   SDIMAIN.PAS—*StdDecode*, the Standard Decoding Procedure

```
procedure TSDIAppForm.StdDecode;
var
   NumChars: Integer;
   CurPos: Integer;
   CurLine: String;
   CurChar: Byte;
   MoreToRead: Boolean;
   LineEnd: Boolean;
begin
   MoreToRead := TRUE;
   while (MoreToRead = TRUE) do
   begin
      ReadLn(EncodedFile, CurLine);
      if (Length(CurLine) > 2) then
      begin
         NumChars := Integer(uuDEC(Byte(CurLine[1])));
         CurPos := 2;
         if (NumChars > 0) then
         begin
            LineEnd := FALSE;
```

continues

Listing 11.7 Continued

```pascal
            while (NumChars > 0) do
            begin
               if (NumChars >= 3) then
               begin
                  CurChar := ((uuDEC(Byte(CurLine[CurPos])) SHL 2) or
                             (uuDEC(Byte(CurLine[(CurPos + 1)])) SHR 4));
                  Write(DecodedFile, CurChar);
                  CurChar := ((uuDEC(Byte(CurLine[(CurPos + 1)])) SHL 4)
                          or (uuDEC(Byte(CurLine[(CurPos + 2)])) SHR 2));
                  Write(DecodedFile, CurChar);
                  CurChar := ((uuDEC(Byte(CurLine[(CurPos + 2)])) SHL 6)
                            or uuDEC(Byte(CurLine[(CurPos + 3)]))));
                  Write(DecodedFile, CurChar);
               end
               else
               begin
                  if (NumChars >= 1) then
                  begin
                     CurChar := ((uuDEC(Byte(CurLine[CurPos])) SHL 2) or
                                (uuDEC(Byte(CurLine[(CurPos + 1)])) SHR 4));
                     Write(DecodedFile, CurChar);
                  end;
                  if (NumChars >= 2) then
                  begin
                    CurChar := ((uuDEC(Byte(CurLine[(CurPos + 1)])) SHL 4)
                           or (uuDEC(Byte(CurLine[(CurPos + 2)])) SHR 2));
                    Write(DecodedFile, CurChar);
                  end;
               end;
               NumChars := (NumChars - 3);
               CurPos := (CurPos + 4);
            end;
         end
         else
         begin
            ReadLn(EncodedFile, CurLine);
            if (CompareStr(CurLine, 'end' + #13#10) <> 0) then
               ShowMessage(InputFileName.Caption + ': No end line.');
         end;
      end;
      if (Eof(EncodedFile)) then
      begin
         CloseFile(EncodedFile);
         CloseFile(DecodedFile);
         MoreToRead := FALSE;
      end;
   end;
end;
```

Decoding a Base-64 Encoded File

Unlike with the standard encoding scheme, you do need a cross-reference table for use in decoding the base-64 encoded files. Technically, you could have characters ranging in value from 0 to 255, but correctly encoded characters fall only between 43 and 122 (inclusive). You can discard any encoded characters that don't fall within this ASCII value range. Excluding those characters that fall outside the range of allowable characters enables you to build a cross-reference table that is almost as small as the one that you used for the encoding process. Because you declared the decoding table as a local variable, you must load it with the appropriate values before doing anything else.

As in the standard decoding process, you must establish a loop in which you remain, decoding each line of the input file, until reaching the end of the file. Within this loop, you read a line into a string buffer, then decode and write out the decoded file. When you have your line of encoded characters, check whether the first four characters consist of equal signs (end-of-file padding). If not, you can proceed with decoding the line.

At this point, you start another loop to decode the current line. You end this loop either when you find an equal sign (=) or reach the end of the line. Next, you check for end-of-line characters (carriage return or line feed), then any other characters outside of the range of the decoding table, and finally any characters that fall within the decoding table range that are not valid base-64 encoding characters. Next, you decode four characters at a time into the original six-bit values. When you have these four values, you can use bit-shifting to recombine them into the original eight-bit bytes. Continue this process until you reach the end of the input file. When you finish, close both files and exit the procedure. Listing 11.8 shows the entire base-64 decoding procedure.

Listing 11.8 SDIMAIN.PAS—*Base64Decode*, the Base-64 Decoding Procedure

```
procedure TSDIAppForm.Base64Decode;
var
   NumChars: Integer;
   CurPos: Integer;
   CurLineLength: Integer;
   CurLine: String;
   CurChar: Byte;
   MoreToRead: Boolean;
   LineEnd: Boolean;
   base64Table: array[43..122] of Byte;
   c1, c2, c3: Byte;
begin
   LoadBase64Table(@base64Table);
   MoreToRead := TRUE;
   while (MoreToRead = TRUE) do
   begin
```

continues

Listing 11.8   Continued

```
ReadLn(EncodedFile, CurLine);
LineEnd := FALSE;
if (Length(CurLine) > 2) then
begin
   if (CompareStr(Copy(CurLine, 1, 4), '====') <> 0) then
   begin
      CurPos := 1;
      CurLineLength := Length(CurLine);
      while (((base64Table[Integer(CurLine[CurPos])] and $40)
            <> 0) and (CurPos < CurLineLength)) do
      begin
         if ((CurLine[CurPos] = #13) or (CurLine[CurPos] = #10) or
            (CurLine[CurPos] = '=')) then
         begin
            LineEnd := TRUE;
            Exit;
         end;
         Inc(CurPos);
      end;
      if (CurPos = CurLineLength) then LineEnd := TRUE;
      if (not LineEnd) then
      begin
         while ((CurPos < CurLineLength) and (not LineEnd)) do
         begin
            if (Byte(CurLine[CurPos]) < 43) then
               Inc(CurPos)
            else
            begin
               if (Byte(CurLine[CurPos]) > 122) then
                  Inc(CurPos)
               else
               begin
                  if (base64Table[Byte(CurLine[CurPos])] = $7F)
                        then
                     Inc(CurPos)
                  else
                  begin
                     c1 := base64Table[Byte(CurLine[CurPos])];
                     Inc(CurPos);
                     c2 := base64Table[Byte(CurLine[CurPos])];
                     Inc(CurPos);
                     c3 := base64Table[Byte(CurLine[CurPos])];
                     Inc(CurPos);
                     CurChar := ((c1 SHL 2) or (c2 SHR 4));
                     Write(DecodedFile, CurChar);
                     if (CurLine[(CurPos - 1)] <> '=') then
                     begin
                        CurChar := ((c2 SHL 4) or (c3 SHR 2));
                        Write(DecodedFile, CurChar);
                        if (CurLine[CurPos] <> '=') then
                        begin
```

```
                              CurChar := ((c3 SHL 6) or
                                (base64Table[Byte(CurLine[CurPos])])));
                              Write(DecodedFile, CurChar);
                              Inc(CurPos);
                          end
                          else
                              MoreToRead := FALSE;
                      end
                      else
                          MoreToRead := FALSE;
                  end;
                end;
              end;
            end;
          end;
        end;
      if (Eof(EncodedFile)) then
          MoreToRead := FALSE;
  end;
  CloseFile(EncodedFile);
  CloseFile(DecodedFile);
end;
```

Part

II

Ch

11

The decoding table load procedure takes the decoding table address as the parameter that is being passed (see Listing 11.9). This enables you to load the table by loading each value into the address space that the pointer is specifying, then incrementing the pointer to move to the next address.

Listing 11.9 SDIMAIN.PAS—*LoadBase64Table*, the Procedure for Loading the Base-64 Decoding Table

```
procedure TSDIAppForm.LoadBase64Table(PB64Table: PByte);
begin
   PB64Table^ := $3E;
   Inc(PB64Table);
   PB64Table^ := $7F;
   Inc(PB64Table);
   PB64Table^ := $7F;
   Inc(PB64Table);
   .
   .
   .

   PB64Table^ := $31;
   Inc(PB64Table);
   PB64Table^ := $32;
   Inc(PB64Table);
   PB64Table^ := $33;
end;
```

Determining Which Decoding Process To Use

The last procedure determines which of the two encoding schemes was used on a particular file (see Listing 11.10). You must read in each line of the file until you find the begin marker. After finding that line, you can check whether it contains the `-base64` marker, which designates the base-64 encoding scheme. You can also find the original file on the begin marker line. After determining the encoding scheme and the original file name, you can open the decoded file and begin the appropriate decoding procedure.

Listing 11.10   SDIMAIN.PAS—*PerformDecode*, the Procedure for Determining the Encoding Type

```
procedure TSDIAppForm.PerformDecode;
var
    CurLine: String;
    TargetName: String;
    BeginPos: Integer;
    FoundBeginMarker: Boolean;
begin
    FoundBeginMarker := FALSE;
    AssignFile(EncodedFile, InputFileName.Caption);
    Reset(EncodedFile);
    while ((FoundBeginMarker = FALSE) and (not Eof(EncodedFile))) do
    begin
        ReadLn(EncodedFile, CurLine);
        BeginPos := Pos('begin', CurLine);
        if (BeginPos > 0) then
            FoundBeginMarker := TRUE;
    end;
    if Eof(EncodedFile) then
        CloseFile(EncodedFile);
    if (not FoundBeginMarker) then
        ShowMessage(InputFileName.Caption + ': No begin marker found.')
    else
    begin
        BeginPos := Pos('begin-base64', CurLine);
        if (BeginPos = 0) then
            rgEncoding.ItemIndex := 0
        else
            rgEncoding.ItemIndex := 1;
        if (OutputFileName.Caption = '') then
        begin
            if (rgEncoding.ItemIndex = 0) then
                BeginPos := 11
            else
                BeginPos := 18;
            TargetName := Copy(CurLine, BeginPos, Length(CurLine));
            OutputFileName.Caption := TargetName;
        end
```

```
  else
      TargetName := OutputFileName.Caption;
  OutputFileName.Refresh;
  AssignFile(DecodedFile, TargetName);
  Rewrite(DecodedFile);
  if (rgEncoding.ItemIndex = 0) then
      StdDecode
  else
      Base64Decode;
    end;
  end;
```

Now that you have completed your UUEncoder/decoder, you can use it to decode encoded images downloaded from the Usenet newsgroups, as shown in Figure 11.6. This produces easily displayable images as shown in Figure 11.7.

FIG. 11.6
Decoding an image downloaded from the **alt.binaries.pictures. vehicles** Usenet newsgroup.

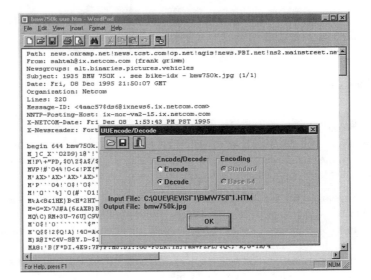

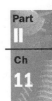

You now have encoding and decoding procedures that you can use in your SMTP mail client to make it MIME-compatible, or for use in posting or retrieving files to and from the Usenet newsgroups. You can easily enhance this application with some of the other encoding algorithms that are in use on the Internet, to make it even more of an all-purpose encoding/decoding utility.

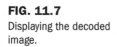

FIG. 11.7
Displaying the decoded image.

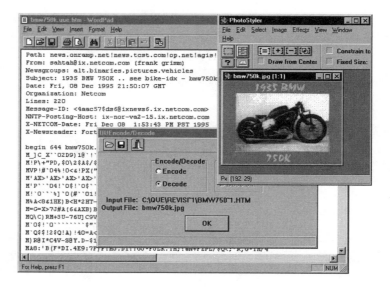

From Here...

This chapter explored the use of encoding files as printable ASCII characters on the Internet. You looked at the reasons for such encoding, why it began, and where it continues to be practiced. Next, you examined two of the primary encoding algorithms in use, and learned how to perform the encoding and to format the algorithms. With this understanding of encoding, you built a working application for encoding and decoding files.

You can embed these functions in the Usenet newsreader to encode files as you post them and to decode them as you retrieve them. You can enhance these routines to read some of the variations on the basic formats and alter the formatting to be more compatible with some of the more fragile decoders. You can extend your SMTP mail client and use the encoding and decoding functions to make your mail client MIME-compatible. Or you could simply use the application to decode the files that you find while searching the Internet. The following chapters will help you with the Internet applications in which you can use these encoding algorithms:

■ To understand how standards for Internet applications and file formats are developed and where to find the documentation, see Chapter 7, "Internet Development Standards."

■ To understand the SMTP protocol and build an SMTP client, see Chapter 9, "Developing SMTP and POP Mail Clients."

■ To integrate the encoder/decoder application with a Usenet newsreader, see Chapter 10, "Developing an Internet News Client/Reader."

■ To see what new encryption methods are being used on the Internet, see Chapter 17, "Internet Security, RSA Encryption, SSL, STT, PCT, and WinSock."

World Wide Web Programming

CHAPTER 12

The Web—HTTP, HTML, and Beyond

- Understand the basic structure of the World Wide Web

- Understand the three components most responsible for the current Web: HTTP, HTML, and CGI

- Understand object-oriented Web technologies such as Java and JavaScript

In Chapter 4, "Internet Communications Protocols," you learned the basics of the Hypertext Transport Protocol (HTTP), but little about how the various components that comprise the Web interact. This chapter details the three components primarily responsible for the current Web: HTTP, Hypertext Markup Language (HTML), and Common Gateway Interface (CGI). Later in the chapter, you see how object-oriented technologies such as Java are now building the foundation for a future generation of Web applications. ■

Understanding the Basic Structure of the Web

The basic structure of the World Wide Web is that the HTTP protocol acts as a generic transport to carry various types of information from the server to the client. Each entity that can be served is uniquely identified with a Universal Resource Locator (URL).

The most common type of data carried across HTTP is HTML. In addition to including basic text-formatting directives, HTML also has directives that provide such capabilities as hypertext links and inline image loading; the hyperlinked resources and inline image files are identified with URLs embedded within the HTML document.

Although some low-end personal Web servers can send only static pages, most HTTP servers support CGI, the Common Gateway Interface specification. With CGI, you can write programs that integrate with the Web, performing such tasks as form processing and database lookups.

CGI is restricted to server-side programs, a serious limitation. For example, using CGI, the only way that you can interact with users is to provide them with simple forms to fill out. Object-oriented technologies such as Java address this limitation, enabling the server to send to the client small programs to execute locally.

HTTP is the core protocol that carries Web traffic, so the next section addresses it first. However, unless you plan on building a Web server or browser, or are just plain interested in the low-level details of the Web, you might want to skip to the section "The Hypertext Markup Language (HTML)."

The Hypertext Transfer Protocol (HTTP)

The HTTP specification describes HTTP 1.1 as follows:

> The Hypertext Transfer Protocol (HTTP) is an application-level protocol for distributed, collaborative, hypermedia information systems. It is a generic, stateless, object-oriented protocol which can be used for many tasks, such as name servers and distributed object management systems, through extension of its request methods (commands). A feature of HTTP is the typing and negotiation of data representation, allowing systems to be built independently of the data being transferred.

Packing about a dozen buzzwords into just three sentences, this abstract provides only the briefest summary of what HTTP is and how it acts as the foundation for the Web. However, an analysis of the abstract sheds a little light on this simple yet powerful protocol:

- *Application-level protocol.* Although usually deployed on top of Transmission Control Protocol/Internet Protocol (TCP/IP), HTTP is also implemented on top of other lower-layer protocols. HTTP presumes only a reliable transport, so you can use any protocol that guarantees that minimum requirement.

- *Distributed, collaborative, hypermedia information systems.* HTTP supports distributed information systems—that is, systems spread across multiple servers. The protocol provides this support through the use of URLs that point to the destination data; a hypertext HTML document usually provides these URLs.

■ *Generic.* HTTP does not dictate the content of data that it transfers; it simply acts as a conduit for moving application-level data. You can transfer any type of data through HTTP. Later in this chapter, you see how advanced data types traveling over HTTP make the Web flexible.

■ *Stateless.* HTTP does not maintain a state. When a transfer is requested over HTTP, the connection is created, the transfer occurs, and then the connection is terminated. The lack of a state is one of HTTP's weaknesses; without state information, each Web page stands alone. For example, it is difficult to develop a Web-based application that enables a user to log in on one page and maintain that login information for as long as the user is actively accessing the site. Every document transferred through HTTP has no context and is completely independent of all documents transferred before it.

■ *Object-oriented,* and *typing and negotiation of data representation.* HTTP is not object-oriented in the same sense as a programming language. This description simply means that HTTP has tags that specify the data type of the data that is about to be transferred over the network, and *methods*, which are commands that specify what should be transferred.

■ *Systems built independently of data being transferred.* Because HTTP just moves data, an HTTP server does not need to know about each data type that it is to transfer. For example, a Web server does not need specific knowledge about the inner workings of the Quicktime video file format to send data with a "video/quicktime" media type.

HTTP messages fall into one of four categories:

■ *Simple request.* A request format compatible with HTTP 0.9. Web browsers should not generate simple requests, but Web servers should be able to understand them, for backward compatibility.

■ *Simple response.* A response format compatible with HTTP 0.9. Web servers should not generate simple responses, except when replying to simple requests.

■ *Full request.* A standard HTTP request.

■ *Full response.* A standard HTTP response.

A simple request consists of the string GET followed by a space, the URL of the request, a carriage return, and a line-feed character. The simple response returns only the *entity body*.

N O T E An *entity* is an object to which a URL refers. For example, an HTML formatted page is one type of entity; a .GIF image is another. An *entity body* is the actual *contents* of the entity, contrasted with an *entity header*, which carries information about the entity, such as the size and type of the entity. ■

Although the HTTP specifications still support the simple message formats, they exclude many of the most important features of HTTP. For example, simple messages are limited to the GET method, and thus cannot support forms. The simple request message format also prevents the client from using content negotiation and keeps the server from identifying the returned entity's media type, so you should avoid using this format.

The following sections describe full request and full response messages.

HTTP Full Request Messages

An HTTP full request message consists of the request line followed by zero or more general headers, request headers, or entity headers.

N O T E HTTP headers are strings in a *name: value* format, separated by carriage returns. For example, the header *Content-length: 10240* specifies that an entity body has exactly 10,240 bytes. ▨

The headers are then followed with a carriage return and line feed, and for some methods, an entity body.

The following conversation illustrates how headers are sent and returned when responding to a full request message:

*The client connects to the server **www.netscape.com**, and requests the header of Netscape's home page. The HEAD method requests only the header. The / refers to the default entity—the home page. HTTP/1.0 specifies the HTML version for a full request message.*
Client: HEAD / HTTP/1.0
Next, the client sends a general header with the e-mail address related to the browser.
Client: From: bob@org.com
*The client also specifies the page that referred it to **www.netscape.com**.*
Client: Referer: http://search.yahoo.com/bin/search?p=netscape
The client follows this with a blank line, as required by HTTP.
Client:
The server responds with the success code 200, which indicates that the message was success-fully interpreted, and that the requested entity exists.
Server: HTTP/1.0 200 OK
The server then responds with the general headers first. This includes the server type...
Server: Server: Netscape-Communications/1.1
...the current date and time...
Server: Date: Thursday, 28-Mar-96 05:30:32 GMT
...and the date and time that the requested entity was last modified.
Server: Last-modified: Wednesday, 27-Mar-96 15:23:10 GMT
The server then sends the entity headers, which specifically apply to the requested entity. This includes its size...
Server: Content-length: 11044
...and type. The content type is specified in Multipurpose Internet Multimedia Extensions (MIME) format.
Server: Content-type: text/html
www.netscape.com *then closes the connection.*

Both full request and full response messages rely on methods, which are humanly readable, single-word commands that control HTTP, such as GET and POST.

The simplest HTTP full request message consists of only a request line. The request line consists of a method, a space, the requested URL, a space, the HTTP version, and a carriage return and line feed. For example, the following is a valid HTTP full request message:

```
GET index.html HTTP/1.1
```

In this message, GET is the method, index.html is the requested URL, and HTTP/1.1 is the version of HTTP.

Unlike the simple request, a full request can use any of a variety of methods. The preceding example shows the most common method, GET. HTTP 1.0 supports only three methods, GET, HEAD, and POST:

- ■ GET retrieves whatever information the requested URL identifies.
- ■ HEAD retrieves only header information, not the body of the requested entity.
- ■ POST sends information from the client to the server. Usually, Web-based forms rely on the POST method to transfer form data to the server.

The HTTP 1.1 specification, which is still in the review process, adds 10 more methods:

N O T E Most HTTP servers do not yet support many of the new HTTP 1.1 methods; they are presented here as an overview of some of the upcoming features in HTTP 1.1. ■

- ■ OPTIONS requests information about the communication options available that affect the retrieval of the requested URL. This method enables the client to determine the options or requirements associated with a resource without actually retrieving it.
- ■ PUT requests that you store the enclosed entity under the supplied URL, enabling you to update a remote Web site.
- ■ PATCH is similar to PUT except that the entity contains a list of differences between the original version of the resource identified by the requested URL and the contents that you want for the resource after you invoke the PATCH action. PATCH must provide a MIME media type (such as application/diff) so that the server knows what to do with the entity after receiving it. For example, a Web browser can specify that a destination URL be patched using the standard *diff* algorithm by generating a PATCH method and then specifying the application/diff MIME type and then the actual patch to apply.
- ■ COPY requests that the resource identified by the requested URL be copied to the location given in the request's URL header field.
- ■ MOVE, DELETE, LINK, and UNLINK work similarly to COPY, performing basic operations on URLs.
- ■ TRACE is a diagnostic method that simply echos the entity data back to the client.
- ■ WRAPPED lets a client encapsulate one or more messages. After encapsulating a message, you can, for example, encrypt it to increase security.

Instead of relying on FTP's approach of using separate communication channels for data and control information, HTTP uses only a single channel. To pass both the entity body, and the

Part

III

Ch

12

control information required to interpret that entity body correctly, HTTP's header fields act as a method's modifiers.

There are three types of header fields:

- *General header fields* are common to both request and response messages. The general header fields control such things as an entity's cacheable status, the date and time that the message originated, and the status of the connection between the message source and destination.

- *Request header fields* are specific to full request messages. These control such things as the MIME media types that the client accepts, the client user's e-mail address, and the URL of the entity that referred the client to make the request (for example, if a link on **www.yahoo.com** refers you to an entity on **www.microsoft.com**, then Microsoft can log it).

- *Entity header fields* are used by both request and response messages. These headers are most commonly associated with response messages, so the next section details them.

The entity body, whether for a request or a response, is simply a stream of octets. HTTP does not restrict the information that flows through this body, but simply provides the mechanism for labeling and transferring that information. The most commonly used request methods, GET and HEAD, do not send an entity from the client to the server, so the entity body usually does not apply to a request message.

HTTP Full Response Messages

An HTTP full response message consists of a status line, followed by zero or more general headers, response headers, or entity headers. The headers are then followed with a carriage return and line feed, and possibly an entity body.

The status line consists of the HTTP version, a space, the status code, a space, a descriptive message, and a carriage return and line feed. The following all-too-common message indicates a *broken link*—a pointer to a page that does not exist:

```
HTTP/1.1 404 Not found
```

As earlier examples implied, each status code consists of three numeric digits. The 200 code, which indicates a successful response, is the most common status code. Chapter 16, "Building a Web Server with Delphi," details the use of response codes in HTTP applications. For the latest list of codes, see the current draft of the HTTP standards at **http://www.ics.uci.edu/pub/ietf/http/**.

The status code is immediately followed by a set of headers and then the entity body.

Response headers provide the exact location of the requested resource, the version of server software, authentication responses, and optional methods that the server supports. As an example of a case in which a response header is useful, a browser can use a value returned in a Server field (for example, Server: Netscape-Communications/1.1) to determine which type of server a site is using.

A response message usually has one or more entity headers that describe the actual entity about to be passed. The following are some of the more important entity headers:

- `Content-Type` is probably the single most important header in all of HTTP. The header specifies, in MIME format, the type of data that the entity contains. For example, `Content-type: text/html` indicates that an entity is an HTML page, and `Content-type: image/gif` specifies a .GIF image.

- `Content-Encoding` enables HTTP to transport data with representations other than ASCII, coordinating the actions between server and client. For example `Content-Encoding: gzip` enables the server to transmit a `gzip` compressed file to the client and have the client decompress the file.

- `Content-Length` specifies the entity's size.

- `Content-MD5`, `Content-Version`, and `Last-Modified` indicate the entity's checksum, version information, and modification date, respectively. A request message with an `Unless` request header field can later use these headers to check whether the entity has changed.

- `Expires` indicates when the entity's information expires. After the expiration date, the client cannot use a cached copy, and must again request the entity from the server.

- `Link` and `Title` work much like the HTML `<link>` and `<title>` elements described in the next section. Because these headers are at the HTTP level, you can use them on all entity types, not just HTML. For example, a .GIF image entity with a header containing `Content-type: image/gif` and `Title: Sample GIF Image` could display the image with an appropriate title.

Although you can specify these and other header fields, programs that rely on HTTP should not assume that any of these headers exist. For example, if a message doesn't specify the `Content-Length`, your client must simply wait for the server to close the connection to end the message. On the other hand, if you are writing a server program, you should usually include as many headers as possible to enable the client to exercise its full functionality. If you can determine an entity's length in advance, send the `Content-Length` header; if you can determine the date that an entity was last modified, send the `Last-Modified` header; and so on.

Part
III

Ch
12

The Hypertext Markup Language (HTML)

Although HTTP provides the means for transporting a wide variety of data, the real power of the Web comes from the actual data that it transports. The data type that has become almost synonymous with the Web is HTML, the Hypertext Markup Language.

HTML is similar in concept to the internal structure of a word processor's file, in that it indicates page formatting. Unlike a word processor file, HTML is based on the *logical* structure of a document, not the *physical* structure. Whereas a word processor might specify that the heading for a new section be specified as 18-point bold text, HTML would indicate only that it is a heading and let the browser interpret the heading as it sees fit.

Because HTML indicates a document's structure instead of indicating its physical layout, you can display HTML documents on many browsers running on many operating systems. For example, the browser LYNX runs on UNIX and VAX/VMS computers with text-only terminals. Whereas a graphical browser might display a heading in large font, LYNX can display the heading only as bold, because the terminal does not support multiple fonts.

HTML relies on *tags,* special commands enclosed in angle brackets, to indicate the context and formatting of a document's text, as well as more interesting things like hypertext references.

The following example shows one of the most basic HTML documents (see Fig. 12.1):

```
<HTML>
<HEAD>
<TITLE>Simple HTML Example 1</TITLE>
</HEAD>
<BODY>
<H1>Level-one heading</H1>
This is a simple example of HTML.
This is the first paragraph.<P>
This is the second paragraph.<P>
</BODY>
</HTML>
```

FIG. 12.1

A simple HTML example as shown in Netscape.

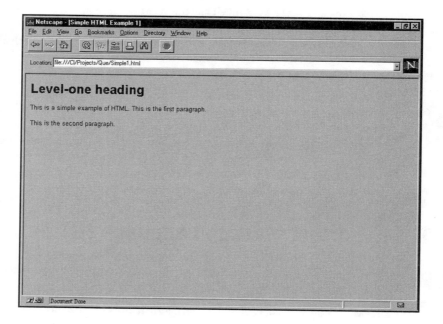

As this example illustrates, HTML documents usually begin with an <HTML> tag, indicating that the document is in HTML format, and end with </HTML>. The <HEAD> tag introduces text that describes an HTML document. Most documents have only a <TITLE> tag in the head section. The <BODY> tag indicates the document's body. It appears after the head section.

Notice that the <TITLE> tag has a corresponding </TITLE> tag to indicate the end of the title, and the <H1> pair works in much the same manner to indicate a first-level heading. Almost all HTML tags work in this manner, with the following format:

```
<tag> tagged item </tag>
```

One exception to this rule is the <P> tag, which indicates the end of a paragraph. It stands alone, with no corresponding </P> tag.

You must use the <P> tag to separate paragraphs. Although the first paragraph of the preceding example is split into two separate lines, it is recognized as a single paragraph and is thus treated as such. The browser ignores indentation and blank lines in the source text. Thus, the following is equivalent to the first example:

```
<TITLE>Simple HTML Example 1</TITLE><H1>Level-one heading</H1>
This is a simple example of HTML. This is the first paragraph.<P>
This is the second paragraph.<P>
```

Whenever you want to break text into multiple paragraphs, you should use <P>.

The <TITLE> tag indicates the document's title, which most browsers display on their window's title bar. The <H1> tag indicates a first-level header, <H2> a second-level header, and so on, to support outline-structured documents.

You might now wonder how to use some of the more advanced tags, such as hypertext links. The anchor tag, <A>, supports hypertext links.

Linking to Other Documents: the <A> Tag

Including an anchor tag in your document requires four steps:

1. Start the anchor with <A, followed by a space.
2. Specify the document to which you want to point, using the HREF="filename" parameter followed by a right angle bracket (>).
3. Enter the text that serves as the hypertext link in the current document.
4. Enter the ending anchor tag: </A>.

To extend the previous example to include an anchor, you expand it as follows:

```
<TITLE>Simple HTML Example 2</TITLE>
<H1>Level-one heading</H1>
This is a simple example of HTML.
This is the first paragraph.<P>
This paragraph has a reference to the
<A HREF="http://www.whitehouse.gov">White House</A>.<P>
```

Figure 12.2 shows this HTML example as displayed in Netscape.

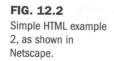

FIG. 12.2
Simple HTML example
2, as shown in
Netscape.

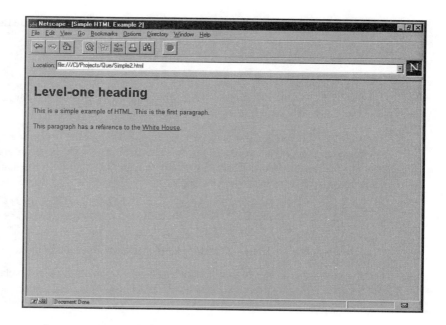

If you have a link on your server, you can shorten the HREF parameter to include only the relative path to the referenced document. Suppose, for example, that your HREF is as follows:

```
HREF=http://"www.org.com"/docs/main1.html
```

You could shorten this parameter to one of the following if the current document is in the DOCS directory:

```
HREF=/docs/main1.html
```

```
HREF=main1.html
```

Note that subdirectories in a URL, as used by the <A> tag, are specified with forward slashes, not backslashes. For example, under DOS you might refer to a file as C:\HTMLDOCS\MAIN\INDEX.HTML, but in a URL, you might specify the same file as /MAIN/INDEX.HTML from within the HTMLDOCS directory.

The <A> tag also enables you to build named anchors to let hypertext links jump to a certain point in a document. The NAME parameter specifies this option, as follows:

```
<TITLE>HTML Example 3</TITLE>
<H1>Level-one heading</H1>
This is the first paragraph.<P>
This paragraph has a reference to a
<A HREF="#ref1">later point</A> in the document.<P>
<P>
<A NAME=ref1>This is the referenced text.</A><P>
```

You can extend the reference to a named anchor to other documents on other servers as well. The following example opens the page WEATHER/USA on server **www.intellicast.com** and jumps to the section of the document that specifies yesterday's high and low temperatures for the United States:

```
<A HREF=" http://www.intellicast.com/weather/usa/#extremes">
```

Supporting Lists: the *<LI>* Tag

HTML supports several types of lists, including bulleted and numbered lists. These two types of lists rely on the <LI> tag to indicate each item. A bulleted list starts with the <UL> tag, and a numbered list starts with the <OL> tag, as shown in the following example:

```
<TITLE>HTML Lists</TITLE>
<H1>Level-one heading</H1>
This is the first paragraph.<P>
Here is a bulleted list:
<UL>
    <LI> First bulleted item
    <LI> Second bulleted item
</UL>
with some text immediately following it.<P>
Here is a numbered list:
<OL>
    <LI> First
    <LI> Second
    <LI> Third
</OL>
This is a nested list:
<UL>
    <LI> Mammals:
        <UL>
        <LI> Hamster
        <LI> Cat
        <LI> Dog
        </UL>
    <LI> Reptiles:
        <UL>
        <LI> Snake
        <LI> Gila Monster
        </UL>
</UL>
```

Figure 12.3 shows HTML lists as displayed in Netscape Navigator.

Although Netscape Navigator happens to format a bulleted list tag by using circular and square bullets, another browser might format the list in a completely different manner. Navigator interprets the *logical* first level <LI> tag and displays it *physically* as a circular bullet. A text mode browser might display the <LI> tag as an asterisk or a dash, and another graphical browser might display it as an arrow.

FIG. 12.3
HTML lists as shown in
Netscape Navigator.

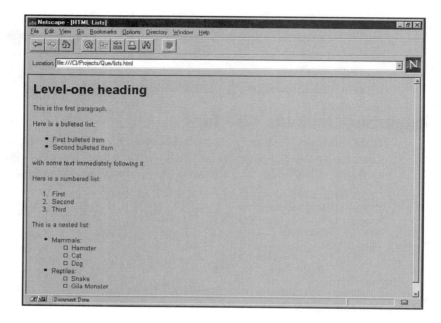

Formatting Characters: Character Style Tags

HTML often offers several ways to display text in exactly the same manner, based on logical styles and physical styles. For example, the physical <B> tag and logical <STRONG> tag display identically as bold text in most browsers.

You should almost always use the logical tags, rather than the physical tags, for formatting. Because the logical tags indicate the document's structure and not just character formatting, they give the user more control over how a document is displayed.

The following are some of the more commonly used HTML logical styles:

- <DFN> indicates a word being defined, usually with italics.
- <EM> emphasizes a term, usually with italics.
- <CODE> is used for short segments of computer code, which are usually displayed in a fixed-width font.
- <STRONG> indicates strong emphasis, and is typically displayed in bold type.

Subject to the warnings to use logical and not physical tags, the physical styles are <B> for bold, <U> for underline, <I> for italics, and <TT> for fixed-width text. All character styles are paired, as in the following example:

```
This is <EM>emphasized</EM> text.
```

Displaying Special Characters

Because HTML itself uses the ampersand, angle brackets, and quotation marks, you have to use the following special codes to display these characters:

- &lt displays the left angle bracket (<)
- &gt displays the right angle bracket (>)
- &amp displays the ampersand (&)
- &quot displays double quotation marks (")

Displaying Inline Images: the *<IMG SRC>* Tag

To reference inline images, you use the <IMG SRC> tag. For example, the following reference displays an image in the browser:

```
<IMG SRC = "UpArrow.gif">
```

<IMG SRC> has several options for aligning and positioning an image within the browser window. One important option for the <IMG SRC> tag is ALT, which specifies the alternative text that a user sees when the browser does not support images, or when image loading is disabled. For example, the following code displays the text *Up* rather than the image:

```
<IMG SRC = "UpArrow.gif" ALT = "Up">
```

Some browsers support advanced formatting options, such as the following:

```
<IMG SRC = "UpArrow.gif" ALT = "Up" BORDER = 2 HSPACE = 10>
```

These options format the image with a two-pixel border and 10 pixels of space on either side of the image.

HTML Summary

By now you should understand that building a basic HTML document is not all that difficult. To build HTML documents, you accomplish most of your work simply by learning the various tags and making sure that you have paired them correctly.

Although this discussion has provided the basic information that you need to build simple HTML pages, newer releases of HTML add advanced formatting features such as tables, support for color, background images, and frames. These features are documented on the Web itself (see **http://www.hotwired.com/surf/special/toolkit/** for a good starting point) and in several books on the subject.

Now that you know the basics of HTML, you might wonder how to build programs that interact with it. The most common method of interacting with HTML on a Web server is by using the Common Gateway Interface, or CGI.

Part
III

Ch
12

The Common Gateway Interface (CGI)

CGI is a standard for interfacing applications with Web servers. Most Web pages are static—that is, they are based on HTML files that don't change. CGI programs, on the other hand, are executed in real-time, and can return dynamic information.

For example, if you want to give Web users access to a database and enable them to query it, you could use CGI. To do so, you would create a CGI program that the Web server would call. This program would process the query, send it to the database engine, and format the results so that you can send them to the client. Although this sounds simple, processing the input data stream and formatting the output data stream can sometimes be difficult.

Because CGI programs just process an input data stream and send an output data stream, you can write them in almost any programming language. In fact, with enough patience, you could build simple CGI scripts from DOS batch files, as in the following example:

```
@echo off
echo Content-type: text/html
echo.
type dochead.1
dir
```

The supporting file DOCHEAD.1 contains the following:

```
<HTML>
<HEAD>
<TITLE>DOS Batch File CGI Example</TITLE>
</HEAD>
<BODY>
<PRE>
```

In this example, the batch file outputs the header file, followed by a directory listing. Because the < and > characters have special meaning in DOS, the tags are isolated into a separate file. The <PRE> tag indicates that the following text has been preformatted and should not be interpreted as HTML.

CGI programs must run on either Windows 95 or Windows NT. Because Windows and Windows for Workgroups are not true multitasking environments, a CGI program could completely take control away from the Web server, keeping it from sending the output of the CGI program back to the client.

Enforcing CGI Security

CGI requires that an executable program run on your Web server, so you need to take some security precautions. By convention, CGI programs reside in a special directory called CGI-BIN; you should ensure that unprivileged Web users cannot write to this directory. Otherwise, users might potentially replace your CGI programs with their own rogue programs.

On UNIX-based systems, CGI programs are often written in Perl or a UNIX command shell. Because scripting languages offer powerful file-manipulation commands, programmers must take special precautions to keep Web users from fooling a CGI script into allowing full control of the server. For example, the UNIX command shells interpret the pipe character (¦) in much the same way as DOS does, redirecting the output of a command as the input of another command. A villainous user could fill in a field of a form as ¦ rm -r *, which the script might interpret much to the same effect that adding ¦ deltree/y *.* would have on a DOS command.

On the Windows platform, this security problem is usually not a big concern, especially if you are running a CGI program written in a compiled language such as Delphi. But including file-manipulation commands in a CGI program without strict security limits is still usually a bad idea. If your Delphi CGI program passes control to batch files or other scripts, consider the effects that rogue input, such as the ¦ or > characters, could have.

Getting Information from the Server

When a client requests the URL that corresponds to your CGI program, the server executes the program. Your program's output flows through the HTTP server to the client.

Information passes to the program through environment variables and the standard input data stream. Note that you do *not* pass data on the command line. For details on how to pass this information into Delphi, see Chapter 13, "Using Delphi with CGI."

You can use two methods to pass form data from the server to your CGI program. The GET method passes form data in the environment variable QUERY_STRING, whereas the POST method passes information through standard input. The GET method is of limited use due to restrictions on the length of environment variables.

Both methods return form data in a special format. The HTML form labels each input item with a NAME tag. The methods return the form data as a stream of *name=value* pairs, as in value1=15. These values are separated by the ampersand character and are URL-encoded—that is, spaces are changed to plus signs, and some characters are encoded in hexadecimal.

Your CGI program must first parse the data, splitting the input stream based on the & characters and then decoding the actual data. After that, the program can do what it wants with the data.

The following is an example of a basic form in HTML. In this example, pay particular attention to the <FORM> tag and its parameters: The tag uses the POST method and passes the form data to a CGI program called CGIDEMO1. To accept the data, the CGI-BIN directory needs a corresponding CGIDEMO1.EXE.

```
<TITLE>Form example</TITLE>
<H1>Form example</H1>
This is a demonstration form. <P>
<HR>
<FORM METHOD="POST" ACTION=
    "http://yourserver.com/cgi-bin/cgidemo1">
First: <INPUT NAME="entry1"> <P>
Second: <INPUT NAME="entry2"> <P>
Third: <INPUT NAME="entry3"> <P>
To submit the query, press this button:
<INPUT TYPE="submit" VALUE="OK"><P>
</FORM>
```

Figure 12.4 shows the form as displayed in Netscape.

FIG. 12.4

The sample form as shown in Netscape.

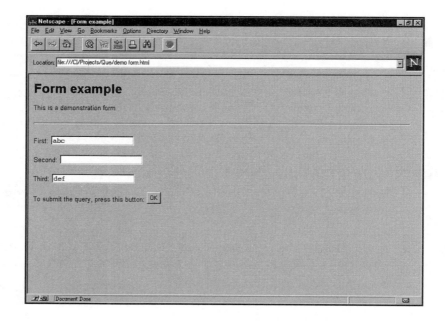

When you enter data as shown in Figure 12.4, the Web server receives the data and passes the following information to the CGI program:

```
entry1=abc&entry2=&entry3=def
```

Because the form is submitted with the POST method, the information passes to the CGIDEMO1 program on standard input. Note that the information is not terminated with an end-of-file character; CGI programs must evaluate the CONTENT_LENGTH environment variable and read the specified number of characters.

Sending Information to the Client

One of the most important parts of developing CGI programs is to format the program's output properly so that the server can correctly interpret it. CGI programs can return many data types, from simple text or HTML documents, to graphics images and audio clips. They can also return references that point to other documents. If your program doesn't correctly inform the server which type of data it is sending, the client might not process the document properly.

For each document or document reference, CGI requires a short header to lead the output. This header is ASCII text followed by a blank line. The document itself then follows in its native format. For example, the line Content-Type: text/html, followed by a blank line, would precede an HTML document.

The simplest example of a header is a basic document reference. If the CGI program outputs the Location: keyword, followed by a relative URL as in Location: /dir1/dir2/sample.htm, or an absolute URL like Location: http://www.whitehouse.gov, the server acts as if the client had not requested your script but had instead requested the specified document. The server automatically looks up the file type and sends appropriate headers. Because this is a CGI output header, it must be followed with a blank line.

For example, the following DOS batch file is a CGI program that forwards a user to the White House's home page:

```
@echo off
echo Location: http://www.whitehouse.gov
echo.
```

Although a CGI program that uses the Location: keyword can reference other static documents, the most interesting programs build dynamic Web pages on the fly. To do so, the program must output a full document with a header specifying a MIME type. For example, to send an HTML document back to the client, your program could output the following:

```
Content-type: text/html

<HTML><HEAD>
<TITLE>Sample CGI Output</TITLE>
</HEAD><BODY>
<H1>Sample CGI Output</H1>
This is a sample of sending HTML formatted output.<p>
Press <A HREF="http://www.whitehouse.gov">this</A>
 to go to the White House.<p>
</BODY></HTML>
```

Note again that CGI requires you to send the Content-type line, followed by a blank line, before the document's body.

Understanding CGI and Context

As stated earlier, HTTP is a stateless protocol—each request is completely independent from those that precede it, so the server has no way to correlate a URL request from previous ones.

There are a few ways around this problem. The most common is to append a question mark (?) followed by some state information to the URL. The question mark acts as a special separator that lets you tag variables to the end of a URL.

For example, suppose that you are building a commerce site in which users have "shopping baskets" of items that they want to buy. Each time that a user chooses an additional item, the site adds it to the list of items in the basket. If the user has bought three of item number 101 and five of item number 202 and was in the process of buying five of item number 123, the URL might look something like the following:

```
http://www.org.com/cgi-bin/shop.html?items=3+101+5+202&add=123&quan=5
```

The first part of the URL, **http://www.org.com/cgi-bin/shop.html**, specifies the actual document. The ? separates the document from the variables. Finally, three variables are specified: items, which has a value of 3+101+5+202; add, which has a value of 123; and quan, which has a value of 5.

The downside of this approach is that the URLs can grow extremely long. For this reason, this method's usefulness is limited.

A better approach is based on a session ID. When the user first connects to the server and logs in, your CGI program can generate a session ID and store it in a file or database. You can then append that session ID to every URL for the duration of the session, as in the following example:

```
http://www.org.com/cgi-bin/shot.html?id=0010F012
```

The CGI program could then create files or database entries based on that session ID, with one record per shopping basket item.

Unfortunately, if you use this second approach, a background process must periodically time out and clear state information. Otherwise, the server fills up to maintain context information that the clients no longer use. In the shopping basket example, a user might choose a few items but then get distracted and move on to another site; you don't want the overhead of maintaining that information until the end of time. Also, if your system allocates inventory when the user puts the item in the shopping basket, you would want to free that inventory when terminating the old context.

Object-Oriented Web Technologies

Internet information services were developed in five general stages:

- *Pre-Web*. Before the Web existed, an information service called *Gopher* enabled Internet users to access information sources. Gopher documents are strictly tree-structured, and don't support hyperlinks. Also, Gopher documents support only text or only graphics on a given page, not mixed text and graphics. For an example of what a Gopher server can support, see **gopher://umn.edu**.

- *Early Web*. Early Web documents lifted Gopher's structural limitations. Documents could be hyperlinked, and could mix text and graphics on a single page. However, if a page changed frequently, it would have to be periodically updated on the server's disk.

- *CGI*. With the advent of CGI, server-based programs could process data entered on forms, and return custom pages built on the fly. However, CGI is limited to request/response interaction, so the user must request a page of information, and the client then receives that static page.

- *Server-to-client programs*. The current state-of-the-art on the Web uses technologies like Java (described later in this chapter) to deliver actual programs from the Web server to the client. The client then runs the program, achieving a higher level of interaction.

- *Client-to-server programs*. In the future, clients might be capable of sending programs to Web servers. As a simple example of how this capability might be useful, a client could send a program to summarize results from a Web server's database on and then send only the results to the client. As an advanced example, one future goal is to enable users to tell a client to find the best price on a new 4G disk drive, and then have the client generate code that flows across multiple servers to gather information.

To accomplish the goals described in the last two stages, the future direction of the Web is based on object-oriented technology. In this technology's initial incarnation (which is also its current incarnation), small applications, known as *applets,* are transmitted from the server to the client to perform local processing. This model may soon be extended to enable clients to send programs to a server that will, for example, perform extended database queries.

The object-oriented Web technology now receiving the most attention is Sun's Java. It has been widely licensed to other companies, including Netscape, Microsoft, IBM, ORACLE, Borland, and Symantec. Java has been heavily touted in computer industry magazines and even prominently mentioned in such nonindustry business publications as *Forbes* and the *Wall Street Journal.* However, although many people are talking about Java, few understand what it really is. This section presents overviews of Java and JavaScript, comparing these two languages to competing object-oriented Web technologies.

Java

Java is a multithreaded, object-oriented language, portable across a wide variety of operating systems and processor architectures. Java programs are compiled into pseudocode, which the Java interpreter runs on the client machine.

To a large extent, Java is just another data type, like a .GIF image or HTML file, albeit a very advanced one. Any HTTP server can serve Java applets, which the server handles the same as any other files. The special action happens when a Java-enabled browser on the client interprets the applet class files.

Although based on C++, Java has several major simplifications. Unlike C++, Java has automatic garbage collection, freeing the programmer from the grief of dealing with storage management. It does not have cumbersome C-style pointers, pointer arithmetic, `malloc`, or `free`. Although Java has a `new` operator, Java automatically tracks an object's status, freeing an object's memory after the object is no longer needed.

Java also omits some of the more complex C++ constructs, such as operator overloading and multiple inheritance. It is superior to C++ in that it supports interfaces, enabling you to plug together software components from different vendors and thus minimize the risk that one vendor's changes will break the other vendors' products. Interfaces work much like properties and methods in a VBX, OCX, or Delphi component.

Unlike C++, Java requires explicit type declarations and relies on true arrays rather than C++'s pointers. These simplifications enable Java compilers to perform extensive checking, making Java programs more robust than those built in most other languages.

Java is designed to support a distributed environment. It has a library of routines, JAVA.NET, for accessing such TCP/IP protocols as HTTP and File Transfer Protocol (FTP). Because Java integrates with Web services, programmers can access objects across the Internet through URLs as easily as most languages enable programmers to access the local file system.

Java is built from the ground up to be a secure environment. Java cannot directly manipulate files on disk, and even protects itself through type safety—a Java program cannot cast a Java integer into an object reference or get at private memory locations to corrupt a Java program. Authentication in Java is based on public key encryption, not on the reusable password system that plagues many Internet protocols such as Telnet and FTP.

Public Key Encryption

Many older services, such as FTP and Telnet, transmit unencrypted passwords over the Internet. If villains capture the low-level network traffic between the client and server, they can reuse the password to gain access.

Public key encryption is akin to having a key and handing out locks to everyone you know. The server sends the client a lock, which is used to encrypt the authentication data in a completely secure manner.

Public key encryption using RSA's patented algorithm is detailed in Chapter 17, "Internet Security, RSA Encryption, SSL, STT, PCT, and WinSock."

Java includes several class and method libraries that developers can use to create multiplatform applications. These libraries include the following:

- JAVA.LANG includes base types that are imported into any program. These types include the declarations for Object (the root of the class hierarchy) and Class, as well as threads, exceptions, and many other fundamental classes.

- JAVA.IO supports streams and random-access files, much like the standard I/O library in C or C++.

- JAVA.NET provides for sockets, Telnet interfaces, and URLs.

- JAVA.UTIL supplies container and utility classes, such as Dictionary, HashTable, and Stack, as well as Date and Time classes.

- JAVA.AWT is the Abstract Windows Toolkit. It provides an abstract layer so that you can easily port Java applications from one window system to another. The toolkit has classes for such components as colors, fonts, buttons, and scroll bars.

The procedure for writing a Java applet is similar to that of any object-oriented language. The following "Hello world" program, a basic example of the Java language in use, looks quite similar to the C++ program that performs the same function:

```
class HelloWorld {
      static public void main(String args[]) {
          System.out.println("Hello world!");
      }
  }
```

The example begins by declaring the HelloWorld class. Within that class, the main() method contains a single method invocation to display the string Hello world! on standard output. The println() method of the out object of the System class actually performs the output operation.

As with any compiled language, the exact method used to compile a Java program depends on the development environment in use. Using the Java Developers Kit, available at **http://**

java.sun.com/JDK-1.0/, you compile a program with the javac compiler and execute it with the Java run-time interpreter.

Java is relatively new, so changes are still being made to the language. For more information on Java, see **http://java.sun.com**.

JavaScript

You can think of JavaScript as Java's little brother, because it is a subset of Java that makes some simplifications to the Java language. Although the syntax of JavaScript is similar to that of Java, JavaScript is a completely interpreted language, embedded directly into HTML pages, not compiled into pseudocode like Java. The difference between the two environments' complexity is much like the difference between other scripting languages, such as dBASE or HyperTalk, and compiled object-oriented languages, such as C++ or Delphi. Just as C++ is more complex and also more powerful than dBASE, JavaScript is more complex and powerful than Java.

JavaScript's scope is smaller than Java's, and JavaScript thus offers a simpler, but more restricted, programming environment. A Java program is based on the full object-oriented model, but JavaScript scripts rely on extensible objects built in to the browser, with no classes or inheritance. JavaScript does not require Java's static typing and strong type checking—variables can be defined on the fly and are dynamically typed. JavaScript supports only a few data types, such as numeric, Boolean, and string values.

JavaScript statements can recognize and respond to user events such as mouse clicks, form input, and page navigation. For example, you could use a JavaScript function to verify the format of a telephone number entered into a form without requiring any network transmission.

JavaScript works with Java by exposing to script authors the useful properties of Java applets. JavaScript statements can use a Java applet's exposed properties to interact with that applet. A likely architecture for future Web-based applications is based on an HTML page with embedded JavaScript commands, supported in turn by Java applets. This environment plays on the strengths of all three environments, using HTML for page formatting and static information, JavaScript for simple event-handling and as interface "glue," and Java for full-blown, compiled programs. Under this arrangement, most developers could use off-the-shelf Java programs and concentrate on simple scripting.

For more information on JavaScript, see **http://www.netscape.com**.

Other Object Technologies

Most of the object-oriented Web attention has focused on Java and JavaScript, but several other competitors are in the race to bring object-oriented features to the Web.

Microsoft Internet Studio, formerly known as Blackbird, is based on sending object linking and embedding (OLE) controls (OCXs) across the Internet. For example, if you click a Web link to download a movie and don't have a viewer program on your client PC, the Web server first sends you an OCX capable of displaying the movie and then sends the movie itself.

The two major criticisms of Microsoft's approach focus on its lack of security and portability. When you click a link that activates an OCX, you have no guarantee that it isn't a virus or a program to erase your hard disk. The lack of portability stems from the fact that OCXs can run only on Windows, not on other platforms such as Macintosh and UNIX-based machines. In fact, unless multiplatform versions are developed, OCXs are limited to Intel processors and won't even run on Windows NT workstations with Alpha, MIPS, and PowerPC processors.

Apple is concentrating on using object orientation to Web-enable existing applications. CyberDog defines a Web object that integrates with OpenDoc (Apple's cross-platform competitor to OLE), letting any document support Web features. This object would support powerful capabilities, such as dynamically updated links to worldwide data sources. Unfortunately, although OpenDoc is generally considered to be technically superior to Microsoft's OLE (and in fact even incorporates OLE), its poor market acceptance may hamper CyberDog's usefulness.

NeXT WebObjects concentrates on the server, enabling it to connect to internal databases and spreadsheets to allow for more complex publishing. Its object orientation makes it more powerful and easier to use and maintain than CGI programming. NeXT's direction is to bring similar object-oriented technology to server-to-client interaction, much like Java, and later extend it to client-to-server interaction. This direction should enable a client to send programs to the server, execute them, and then review the results. For more information on WebObjects, see **http://www.next.com/AboutNeXT/CorpBrochure/WebQA.html**.

General Magic is also addressing the client-to-server model. The company is now retargeting its Telescript language to the Web. Although General Magic originally designed Telescript for personal digital assistants (PDAs), its agent-based concepts offer significant advantages over the other object-oriented languages. For example, a Telescript agent can travel from computer to computer, retaining items in memory, facilitating development of a program that can find the user the best price for a particular item. Contrast this capability with a Java program, which cannot retain its memory when moving across the network. For more information on TeleScript, see General Magic's Web site at **http://www.genmagic.com/**.

From Here...

In this chapter, you learned about the foundations of the Web: HTTP, HTML, and CGI. Also, you discovered how object-oriented Web technologies, such as Java and JavaScript, may quickly change the nature of Web development.

The next five chapters of this book concentrate on applying this knowledge to developing actual Web applications:

- To develop Delphi applications using CGI, see Chapter 13, "Using Delphi with CGI," and Chapter 14, "Using a Database in a CGI Application."
- For an advanced project that requires some HTTP knowledge, see Chapter 15, "Building a Web Robot To Verify Link Integrity."
- For step-by-step instructions on building a Web server in Delphi using the HTTP protocol, see Chapter 16, "Building a Web Server with Delphi."

■ For information on how to integrate Delphi programs tightly with Netscape browsers and servers, see Chapter 18, "The Netscape API—Incorporating Delphi with the Netscape Browser and Server."

Part
III

Ch
12

Using Delphi with CGI

- The Common Gateway Interface (CGI)

- Interaction between Delphi and CGI

- Coding with CGI and Delphi

This chapter covers the basics of the Common Gateway Interface (CGI) and specifically the Windows CGI specification. The chapter demonstrates throughout the relationship between the Web server and Delphi, the application-development tool. You create a custom Internet Delphi component to make coding with CGI in Delphi more productive. You then create several examples that demonstrate the functionality of a programmed Internet Web server. ■

How CGI Works

The Common Gateway Interface (CGI) is a popular method for interfacing a Web server with an external program. You can develop the external applications, which are usually referred to as CGI scripts or programs, in a variety of languages, including Delphi, C and C++, Visual Basic, and Perl. You can implement CGI on many different platforms, including UNIX, Microsoft Windows NT, and Microsoft Windows 95.

The Web server program itself executes CGI programs, usually in response to a user request from an Internet browser. For example, if a user wants to review his checking account balance from a bank's Web page, the following would happen:

1. The user requests a Uniform Resource Locator (URL) that specifies a CGI script/ program (for example, **http://www.bank.com/cgi/checkbal.exe**) and passes user-specific information, such as the user's account number and password with the URL. (Passing parameters is covered later in this chapter.)

2. The bank's Web server gathers the user-specific information and executes the CGI program CHECKBAL.EXE. This program queries a database and produces a result set that represents the user's checking account balance.

3. The CGI program CHECKBAL.EXE formats the information from the result set by using the proper HTTP/HTML wrapper. The program then returns the information to the Web server, which in turn returns the information through the network to the user's browser.

Figure 13.1 illustrates the relationship between the Web server process and the out-of-process (.EXE) CGI program.

FIG. 13.1

The relationship between the Web server process and the out-of-process (.EXE) CGI program.

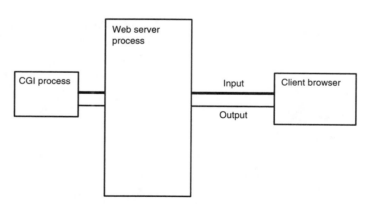

If you're using Delphi for CGI work, you must be using a version of Microsoft Windows as your Web server's platform. The most popular Windows platform for Web servers is Windows NT, although Windows 95 is used in many instances as well. As you might expect, anything that you can do with a Delphi program you can also do with a Delphi CGI program. Popular capabilities include database queries, database manipulation, form-based electronic mail (e-mail), paging, and faxing.

UNIX and Windows have inherent differences, so Robert Denny, author of Website, created a CGI specification, WinCGI, especially for Windows platforms. The specification is available through the Internet at the following URL:

http://website.ora.com/wsdocs/32demo/windows-cgi.html

Throughout this chapter as well as Chapter 14, "Using a Database in a CGI Application," you use the WinCGI 1.3 specification. The examples also use the Web server WebSite 1.0o from O'Reilly and Associates. This 32-bit server runs on the Windows NT and Windows 95 platforms. (Website 1.1 was released as these chapters were being written.)

Given Delphi's object-oriented nature, you can package the nuts and bolts of WinCGI processing to create very functional Delphi components for reuse. Once you understand the underlying process, you can create a basic Delphi CGI component that you can use today!

Interaction between Delphi and CGI

The Windows CGI specification clearly defines the interaction between Delphi and the Web server. Keep in mind that the Web server program starts your CGI program. For this reason, your Delphi CGI program will not be a typical form-based executable. As a matter of fact, because you don't need a graphical user interface (GUI), you need not show the form at all. You create a standard Delphi form and then place all the processing in the form's `Create` procedure. After the `Create` procedure finishes and before the form is visible, you can stop the program's execution.

The Web server passes and retrieves information from your CGI program in two different forms:

- Command-line parameters
- Data files

You start with the command line that the Web server uses to start your CGI program. Windows CGI 1.3 defines one command-line parameter:

`WinCGI-exe cgi-data-file`

`WinCGI-exe` is the full name of your Delphi CGI program, including the path (for example, **c:\website\cgi-win\checkbal.exe**). The `cgi-data-file` parameter is actually a Windows .INI file that contains a tremendous amount of information about the user and environment as well as the actions that you are about to perform. You use .INI files because Windows does not have an easily redirected `stdout` or `stdin` that UNIX platforms utilize in the standard CGI specification. Using .INI files is a great idea because they are well organized, easily readable for debugging purposes, and nothing new to Windows programmers.

Programmers typically read and write to .INI files by using such Windows API functions as the following:

- `GetPrivateProfileString()`
- `GetPrivateProfileInt()`

- ■ WritePrivateProfileString()
- ■ WritePrivateProfileInt()

Fortunately, because you're using Delphi, you can bypass the Windows API and use Delphi objects specifically designed to handle .INI files. If you examine .INI files, you notice that they use a key-value format. Listing 13.1 is an actual snippet of a *cgi-data-file* .INI file.

Listing 13.1 A Snippet from an Actual *cgi-data-file* .INI File

```
[CGI]
Request Protocol=HTTP/1.0
Request Method=POST
Executable Path=/cgi-win/quecgi1.exe
...
[System]
GMT Offset=-28800
Debug Mode=No
Output File=c:\temp\4cws.out
Content File=c:\temp\4cws.inp
...
[Form Literal]
name=John Doe
company=Sun Lighting
...
```

The bracketed items are called *sections*. The other lines contain entries and values. The Windows CGI specification fully details the entire *cgi-data-file* specification and defines what each of its values represents. This section investigates some of the more meaningful entries.

In the [System] section, notice an entry value Output File=c:\temp\4cws.out. This entry gives the file name from which the server retrieves the CGI program response. This is the file that the server returns to the user through the network. In the hypothetical bank balance example (discussed earlier in this chapter), the contents of the Output File might look like the following after the CGI program has finished executing:

```
HTTP/1.0 200 OK
Date: Thursday, 25-Jan-96 16:04:30 GMT
Server: WebSite 1.1
Content-type: text/html
Last-modified: Thursday, 25-Jan-96 16:04:30 GMT
Content-length: 5000

<HTML><HEAD>
<TITLE>Your Checking Balance</TITLE></HEAD>
<BODY>Your Checking Balance is $100.00</BODY></HTML>
```

You use the [Form Literal] section later in this chapter. As you can see in the *cgi-data-file* snippet, this section is where things start to get interesting:

```
[Form Literal]
name=John Doe
company=Sun Lighting
...
```

This section is the most basic area that a browser form uses to pass request-specific data. This data could include such information as a name, address, music selection, shoe size, or anything else that you need to collect.

Understanding the *cgi-data-file* Sections and Their Values

The `cgi-data-file` includes eight different sections and many entries and values. The following descriptions match the WinCGI values with the standard CGI values where applicable.

The *[CGI]* Section   The [CGI] section takes the following values:

- Request Protocol
- Request Method
- Executable Path
- Logical Path
- Physical Path
- Query String
- Request Range
- Referer (the URL address from which the current page was hyperlinked)
- From
- User Agent
- Content Type
- Content Length
- Content File
- Server Software
- Server Name
- Server Port
- Server Admin
- CGI Version
- Remote Host
- Remote Address
- Authentication Method
- Authentication Realm
- Authenticated Username

The *[Accept]* Section   The client browser sends, in the HTTP request header, acceptable data types to the [Accept] section, as in the following example:

```
[Accept]
*/*=Yes
image/gif=Yes
image/x-xbitmap=Yes
image/jpeg=Yes
```

Part
III

Ch
13

The *[System]* Section   The [System] section takes the following values:

- GMT (Greenwich Mean Time) Offset
- Debug Mode
- Output File
- Content File

The *[Extra Headers]* Section   The client browser sends any extra information that appears in the HTTP header to the [Extra Headers] section. Every HTTP response has a header. Some HTTP headers have extra information in them that is useful but not required or defined in the current specification. The server then parses the entries into this section, as in the following example:

```
[Extra Headers]
Connection=Keep-Alive
Host=www.pacg.com
```

The *[Form Literal]* Section   The [Form Literal] section is filled in if the request is from an HTTP form. You use this section more than any of the others. The entries in this section usually correspond to entry fields on an HTTP form, as in the following example:

```
[Form Literal]
name=Michael Jones
company=Sunset Company
address1=200 Devore Street
address2=
city=Elsmere
state=AZ
zip=11111
country=USA
email=fddfd@one.com
phone=888-888-8888
bdate=08/27/33
```

The *[Form External]*, *[Form Huge]*, and *[Form File]* Sections   These sections do not take values.

Reading *cgi-data-file* Information with Delphi's *TIniFile* Object

The Delphi TIniFile object handles reading the information in the *cgi-data-file* quite well. You use only the ReadString() method associated with the TIniFile object, as shown in the GetOutputFile procedure (Listing 13.2).

Listing 13.2   The *GetOutputFile* Procedure Uses the *ReadString()* Method To Read Information from the *cgi-data-file*

```
procedure TForm1.GetOutputFile;
var
    CgiIniFile : TIniFile;
    OutputFileName : String;
```

```
begin
    CgiIniFile := TIniFile.Create(ParamStr(1));
    OutputFileName := CgiIniFile.ReadString('System', 'Output File', '');
    CgiIniFile.Free;
end
```

Although you have declared the TIniFile object, you must allocate memory for it with the Create() method. The ParamStr() function is a Delphi system function that returns a specified command-line parameter. In this case, the function returns the full path of the *cgi-data-file* as the first parameter. At this point, you can use the ReadString() method to read directly from the [System] section and retrieve the full path of the output file name. Finally, for good Windows housekeeping, you should free the memory allocated for the TIniFile object with the Free method.

In the next section, you use these basic principles and build a small Delphi CGI program that demonstrates the preceding concepts.

Coding with CGI

The Delphi CGI program that you create in this chapter is the equivalent of the proverbial "Hello World" example with which you are doubtlessly familiar. The program presents the user with an HTML form page that has one button on it (see Fig. 13.2). The button instructs the server to execute your Delphi CGI program. The CGI program retrieves the name of the server-assigned output file and writes a properly formatted HTTP/HTML message to deliver to the client through the network.

FIG. 13.2
The Delphi CGI "Hello World" application.

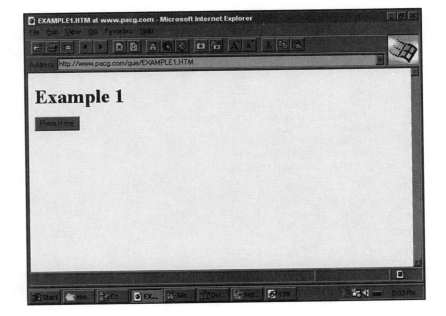

Part

III

Ch

13

Listing 13.3 shows the HTML file for the sample page.

Listing 13.3 EXAMPLE1.HTM—the HTML File for the Sample Page

```
<HTML>
<!—
Author:     Kevin Sadler
Date:       January 20, 1996
URL:        http://www.pacg.com/que/example1.htm

Delphi CGI Coding Example
—>

<BODY>
<H1>Example 1</H1>
<FORM ACTION="/cgi-win/quecgi1.exe" METHOD="POST">
<INPUT TYPE="submit" VALUE="Press Here!">
</FORM>

</BODY>
</HTML>
```

Listing 13.4 shows the actual Delphi CGI program, which is quite straightforward and brief.

Listing 13.4 MAIN.PAS—the QUECGI1 Project's Delphi CGI "Hello World" Program

```
unit Main;

interface

uses
 SysUtils, WinTypes, WinProcs, Messages, Classes, Graphics, Controls,
 Forms, Dialogs, IniFiles;

type
 TForm1 = class(TForm)
 procedure FormCreate(Sender: TObject);
 private
 { Private declarations }
 public
 { Public declarations }
 end;

var
 Form1: TForm1;

implementation

{$R *.DFM}

procedure TForm1.FormCreate(Sender: TObject);
```

```
var
 CgiIniFile : TIniFile;
 OutputFile : TextFile;
 OutputFileName : String;

begin
 CgiIniFile := TIniFile.Create(ParamStr(1));
 application.ProcessMessages;
 OutputFileName := CgiIniFile.ReadString('System', 'Output File', '');
 CgiIniFile.Free;

 AssignFile( OutputFile, OutputFileName);
 ReWrite(OutputFile);

 Writeln(OutputFile, 'HTTP/1.0 200 OK');
 Writeln(OutputFile, 'Date: Thursday, 12-Jan-96 16:04:30 GMT');
 Writeln(OutputFile, 'Server: WebSite 1.0');
 Writeln(OutputFile, 'Content-type: text/html');
 Writeln(OutputFile, 'Last-modified: Thursday, 25-Jan-96 16:04:30 GMT');
 Writeln(OutputFile, 'Content-length: 5000');
 Writeln(OutputFile, '');
 Writeln(OutputFile, '<HTML><HEAD>');
 Writeln(OutputFile, '<TITLE>Example One</TITLE></HEAD>');
 Writeln(OutputFile, '<BODY>Hello World</BODY></HTML>');

 CloseFile(OutputFile);

 Halt;

 end;
 end.
```

Listing 13.5 shows a modification to the Delphi project QUECGI1.DPR file. This modification causes this CGI program not to display its form.

Listing 13.5 QUECGI1.DPR—a Modification That Keeps the Delphi CGI "Hello World" Program from Displaying Its Form

```
program Quecgi1;

uses
 Forms,
 Main in 'MAIN.PAS' {Form1};

{$R *.RES}

begin
 Application.CreateForm(TForm1, Form1);
 {Application.Run;}
 end.
```

Part
III

Ch
13

Note that the line `Application.Run` is commented out. Delphi creates the form in this line:

```
Application.CreateForm(TForm1, Form1);
```

The `FormCreate()` event procedure executes all of the program's code. The last line of the `FormCreate()` actually closes the application. Therefore, the `Application.Run` method is not necessary for your purposes.

Figure 13.3 shows the project's form.

FIG. 13.3

The project contains an empty form with no components.

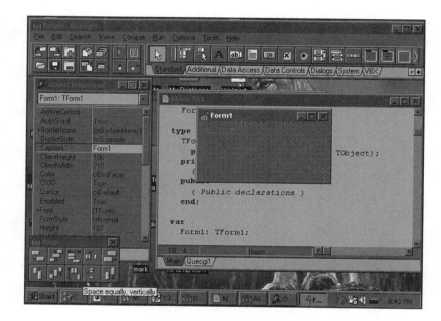

If an application such as this simple one has no GUI, you really have no reason to create a Delphi form. But as you develop more complex CGI applications that need to access databases, process e-mail, fax, use serial communications, and perform a host of other services, you can simply drop all the readily available Delphi components on your form. This adds overhead to the size of the actual executable, but you shorten your development time considerably. Figure 13.4 shows the final result.

You can now enhance your CGI program to do something more interesting. This time, you use information in the [CGI] section of the *cgi-data-file* and then pass that information back to the user. Specifically, you retrieve the request method, the Web server name, and the user's current IP address.

Figure 13.5 shows the Web page that initiates the project's execution.

FIG. 13.4
The result of executing the QUECGI1 example on a WWW browser.

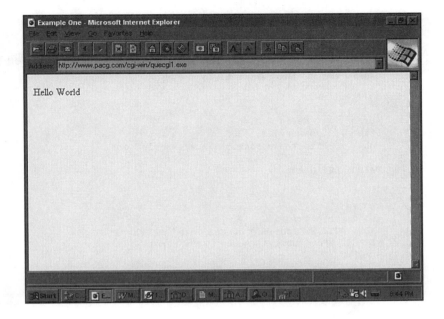

FIG. 13.5
The WWW page that initiates the execution of the QUECGI2 project.

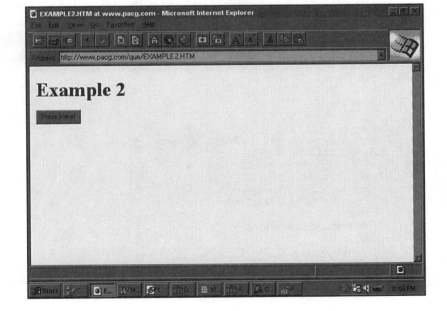

Part
III

Ch
13

Listing 13.6 shows the HTML file for your revised program's sample page.

Listing 13.6   EXAMPLE2.HTM—the HTML File for the Revised Delphi CGI "Hello World" Program's Sample Page

```
<HTML>
<!—
Author:     Kevin Sadler
Date:       January 20, 1996
URL:        http://www.pacg.com/que/example2.htm

Delphi CGI Examples
—>

<BODY>
<H1>Example 2</H1>
<FORM ACTION="/cgi-win/quecgi2.exe" METHOD="POST">
<INPUT TYPE="submit" VALUE="Press Here!">
</FORM>

</BODY>
</HTML>
```

Listing 13.7 shows the Delphi code for your enhanced program.

Listing 13.7   MAIN.PAS—the QUECGI2 Project's Enhancement of the Delphi CGI "Hello World" Program That Passes Additional Information to the User

```
unit Main;

interface

uses
 SysUtils, WinTypes, WinProcs, Messages, Classes, Graphics, Controls,
 Forms, Dialogs, IniFiles;

type
 TForm1 = class(TForm)
 procedure FormCreate(Sender: TObject);
 private
 { Private declarations }
 public
 { Public declarations }
 end;

var
 Form1: TForm1;

implementation

{$R *.DFM}
```

```pascal
procedure TForm1.FormCreate(Sender: TObject);
var
 CgiIniFile : TIniFile;
 CgiIniFileName : String;
 OutputFile : TextFile;
 OutputFileName : String;
 RequestMethod : String; {Variable to hold the retrieved results}
 ServerName : String; { " " }
 RemoteAddress : String; { " " }

begin
 CgiIniFile := TIniFile.Create(ParamStr(1));
 application.processMessages;
 OutputFileName := CgiIniFile.ReadString('System', 'Output File', '');

 {Retrieve the three data items that you want for these examples:
 request method, server name, and the user's IP address/remote address}

 RequestMethod := CgiIniFile.ReadString('CGI', 'Request Method', '');
 ServerName := CgiIniFile.ReadString('CGI', 'Server Name', '');
 RemoteAddress := CgiIniFile.ReadString('CGI', 'Remote Address', '');

 CgiIniFile.Free;

 AssignFile( OutputFile, OutputFileName);
 ReWrite(OutputFile);

 Writeln(OutputFile, 'HTTP/1.0 200 OK');
 Writeln(OutputFile, 'Date: Thursday, 12-Jan-96 16:04:30 GMT');
 Writeln(OutputFile, 'Server: WebSite 1.0');
 Writeln(OutputFile, 'Content-type: text/html');
 Writeln(OutputFile, 'Last-modified: Thursday, 25-Jan-96 16:04:30 GMT');
 Writeln(OutputFile, 'Content-length: 5000');
 Writeln(OutputFile, '');
 Writeln(OutputFile, '<HTML><HEAD>');
 Writeln(OutputFile, '<TITLE>Example Two</TITLE></HEAD>');
 Writeln(OutputFile, '<BODY><HR>Hello Again World, <P>');
 Writeln(OutputFile,
    'The Request Method is <B>' + RequestMethod + '</B>.<BR>');
 Writeln(OutputFile,
    'The Server Name is <B>' + ServerName + '</B>.<BR>');
 Writeln(OutputFile,
    'Your IP Address is <B>' + RemoteAddress + '</B>.<P>');
 Writeln(OutputFile,
    'Sir, the time on deck is <B>' + DateTimeToStr(Now) + '</B><P><HR>');
 Writeln(OutputFile, '</BODY></HTML>');

 CloseFile(OutputFile);

 Halt;

end;

end.
```

In Listing 13.7, QUECGI2.DPR's MAIN.PAS uses the `TIniFile` object's `ReadString()` method to retrieve from the `cgi-data-file` the information that you want. As you retrieve the information, you store it in previously declared string variables.

The area of the code in which you write to the output file demonstrates how to return data to the user. The following line provides an example:

```
Writeln(OutputFile,
     'The Request Method is <B>' + RequestMethod + '</B>.<BR>');
```

This line results in the user browser displaying the following message:

```
The Request Method is POST.
```

Figure 13.6 shows the result as displayed onscreen.

FIG. 13.6

The result of executing the QUECGI2 example on a WWW browser.

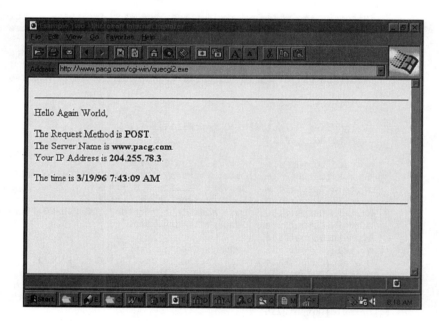

Form-Based Data

So far, you have been dealing with browser- or server-supplied data. Most CGI programs and scripts on the Internet use HTML forms as the primary vehicle for collecting information. Forms provide an extremely convenient way to collect and process information for database queries, guest books, calculations, online ordering, and more.

Processing HTML form data through Windows CGI is not difficult. Such processing is simply an extension of the processing that you have been using. Figure 13.7 shows a simple example.

FIG. 13.7
The HTML file
EXAMPLE3.HTM
presented in a WWW
browser.

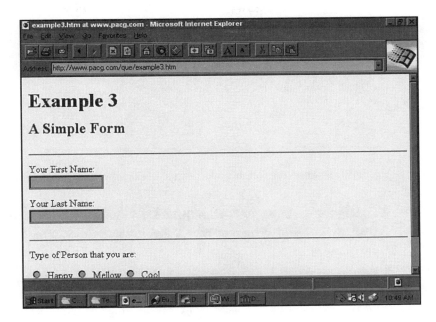

The next modification of your "Hello World" program demonstrates one technique that you can use to collect user-specific information from the browser. Listing 13.8 shows the HTML file for this version of the program.

Listing 13.8 EXAMPLE3.HTM—the HTML File for the Second Revised Delphi CGI "Hello World" Program's Sample Page

```
<HTML>
<!—
Author:    Kevin Sadler
Date:      January 20, 1996
URL:       http://www.pacg.com/que/example3.htm

Delphi CGI Coding
—>

<BODY>
<H1>Example 3</H1>
<FORM ACTION="/cgi-win/quecgi3.exe" METHOD="POST">
<H2>A Simple Form</H2>
<HR>
Your First Name:<BR>
<INPUT TYPE="text" NAME="firstname"><P>
Your Last Name:<BR>
<INPUT TYPE="text" NAME="lastname"><P>
<HR>
Type of Person that you are:<P>
<INPUT TYPE="radio" NAME="typeperson" VALUE="Happy">Happy
```

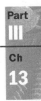

Part
III

Ch
13

continues

Listing 13.8   Continued

```
<INPUT TYPE="radio" NAME="typeperson" VALUE="Mellow">Mellow
<INPUT TYPE="radio" NAME="typeperson" VALUE="Cool">Cool<P>

<INPUT TYPE="submit" VALUE="Press Here!">
</FORM>

</BODY>
</HTML>
```

Listing 13.9 shows the Delphi code for this version of your enhanced program.

Listing 13.9   MAIN.PAS—the QUECGI3 Project's Enhancement of the Delphi CGI "Hello World" Program That Collects Information from the User

```
unit Main;

interface

uses
  SysUtils, WinTypes, WinProcs, Messages, Classes, Graphics, Controls,
  Forms, Dialogs, IniFiles;

type
  TForm1 = class(TForm)
  procedure FormCreate(Sender: TObject);
  private
  { Private declarations }
  public
  { Public declarations }
  end;

var
  Form1: TForm1;

implementation

{$R *.DFM}

procedure TForm1.FormCreate(Sender: TObject);
var
  CgiIniFile : TIniFile;
  CgiIniFileName : String;
  OutputFile : TextFile;
  OutputFileName : String;
  RequestMethod : String;
  ServerName : String;
  RemoteAddress : String;
```

```
    FirstName : String;
    LastName : String;
    TypePerson : String;

begin
    CgiIniFile := TIniFile.Create(ParamStr(1));
    application.processMessages;

    OutputFileName := CgiIniFile.ReadString('System', 'Output File', '');

    {Retrieve the three data items that you want for this example:
    request method, server name, user's IP address/remote address,
    and the form data}

    RequestMethod := CgiIniFile.ReadString('CGI', 'Request Method', '');
    ServerName := CgiIniFile.ReadString('CGI', 'Server Name', '');
    RemoteAddress := CgiIniFile.ReadString('CGI', 'Remote Address', '');

    {The form data that you are retrieving resides in the Form Literal
    section. You have to know something about the HTML that defines
    each field, specifically the name="xxx". You use the xxx to find
    the right entry.}

    FirstName := CgiIniFile.ReadString('Form Literal', 'firstname', '');
    LastName := CgiIniFile.ReadString('Form Literal', 'lastname', '');
    TypePerson := CgiIniFile.ReadString('Form Literal', 'typeperson', '');

    CgiIniFile.Free;

    AssignFile( OutputFile, OutputFileName);
    ReWrite(OutputFile);

    Writeln(OutputFile, 'HTTP/1.0 200 OK');
    Writeln(OutputFile, 'Date: Thursday, 12-Jan-96 16:04:30 GMT');
    Writeln(OutputFile, 'Server: WebSite 1.0');
    Writeln(OutputFile, 'Content-type: text/html');
    Writeln(OutputFile, 'Last-modified: Thursday, 25-Jan-96 16:04:30 GMT');
    Writeln(OutputFile, 'Content-length: 5000');
    Writeln(OutputFile, '');
    Writeln(OutputFile, '<HTML><HEAD>');
    Writeln(OutputFile, '<TITLE>Example Three</TITLE></HEAD>');
    Writeln(OutputFile,
        '<BODY><HR>Hello ' + FirstName + ' ' + LastName + ', <P>');
    Writeln(OutputFile,
        'The Request Method is <B>' + RequestMethod + '</B>.<BR>');
    Writeln(OutputFile,
        'The Server Name is <B>' + ServerName + '</B>.<BR>');
    Writeln(OutputFile,
        'Your IP Address is <B>' + RemoteAddress + '</B>.<P>');
```

Part
III

Ch
13

continues

Listing 13.9   Continued

```
Writeln(OutputFile,
    'Sir, the time on deck is <B>' + DateTimeToStr(Now) + '</B><P><HR>');

Writeln(OutputFile,
    'You are a really <B>' + TypePerson + '</B> individual.');

Writeln(OutputFile, '</BODY></HTML>');

CloseFile(OutputFile);

Halt;

end;

end.
```

You are now very close to treating Internet browser screens like regular computer display monitors. The standard approach that you use on regular desktop applications now can be applied to the World Wide Web. In a regular desktop application, you present the user with a variety of edit boxes, radio buttons, check boxes, and other controls. The user fills in these controls with information. You, as the developer, then read the information in the controls, and typically place the information into variables. After placing the information in internal variables, there really is no limit to the processing that you can do. When your processing is finished, you return a response to the user.

WinCGI is the specification that defines how you retrieve the information from the user and return a response to the user. However, the user might be across the street or across the globe. The network used for the transport probably is the Internet.

```
var
.....
  FirstName : String;
  LastName : String;
  TypePerson : String;

FirstName := CgiIniFile.ReadString('Form Literal', 'firstname', '');
LastName := CgiIniFile.ReadString('Form Literal', 'lastname', '');
TypePerson := CgiIniFile.ReadString('Form Literal', 'typeperson', '');
```

Figure 13.8 shows the result of executing QUECGI3 on a Web browser.

This book's companion CD includes the source code for the Delphi projects for all examples, as well as the HTML files that initiate the requests.

FIG. 13.8
The result of executing the QUECGI3 example on a WWW Browser.

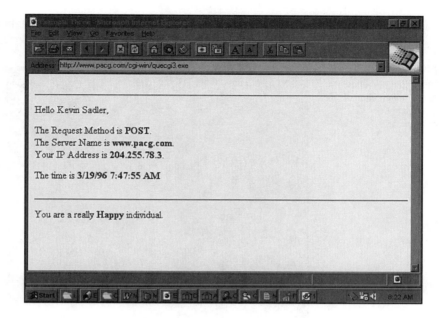

Using Delphi To Create a WinCGI Component

Now take some of the functionality that you've been using and package it into a simple Delphi component. This exercise assumes that you are already familiar with the mechanics and design of creating Delphi components. This component will have the following functionality:

- Initializes the WinCGI environment by determining the *cgi-data-file* and determining and opening the output file, and initializes several WinCGI environment variables
- Provides a standard method for sending a standard HTTP header
- Provides a standard method for returning a line of HTML code to the client
- Provides a standard method for reading form-based values
- Provides standard properties for the *cgi-data-file* name and the output file name to use for testing
- Provides a standard property for the Web server name to use to create the HTTP header
- Provides a private function for formatting a date to GMT format
- Provides a standard method for closing the output file

In a real-world component, you would add features like error checking, data validation, and the capability to read "huge" data. You would also provide component variables for all the CGI environment data and give the user access to it. However, the purpose of this exercise is simply

Part
III

Ch
13

to demonstrate how to create a WinCGI Delphi component. Figure 13.9 shows the Delphi environment while creating the Delphi CGI component.

FIG. 13.9

The Delphi environment during the creation of the Delphi CGI component.

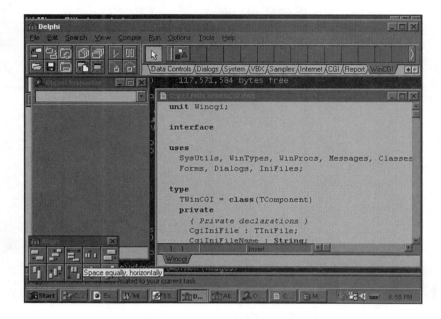

Listing 13.10 shows the Delphi code that creates your WinCGI component.

Listing 13.10   WINCGi.PAS—the Delphi Code That Creates Your WinCGI Component

```
unit Wincgi;

interface

uses
 SysUtils, WinTypes, WinProcs, Messages, Classes, Graphics, Controls,
 Forms, Dialogs, IniFiles;

type
 TWinCGI = class(TComponent)
 private
 { Private declarations }
 CgiIniFile : TIniFile;
 CgiIniFileName : String;
 OutputFile : TextFile;
 OutputFileName : String;
 WebServer : String;

 procedure SetIniFile( testini : String );
 function GetIniFile: String;
```

```
procedure SetOutputFile ( outfile : String);
function GetOutputFile: String;
procedure SetWebServer ( web : String );
function GetWebServer: String;

function OpenOutputFile: Boolean;
function GetGMTTime : String;

protected
{ Protected declarations }
public
{ Public declarations }
REQUEST_METHOD : String;
SERVER_NAME : String;
REMOTE_ADDR : String;

constructor Create(AOwner: TComponent); override;
function InitWinCGI: Boolean;
function CloseWinCGI: Boolean;
function GetLiteral( keyname : String ) : String;
function Send( dataout : String ) : Boolean;
function SendHTTPHeader: Boolean;

published
{ Published declarations }
property OutputDataFile : String read GetOutputFile write SetOutputFile;
property CGIDataIniFile : String read GetIniFile write SetIniFile;
property WebServerName : String read GetWebServer write SetWebServer;
end;

procedure Register;

implementation

constructor TWinCGI.Create(AOwner: TComponent);
begin
 inherited Create(AOwner);
 WebServer := 'Website 1.X';
end;

function TWinCGI.InitWinCGI : Boolean;
begin
 try
 CgiIniFile := TIniFile.Create(ParamStr(1));
 application.processMessages;

 OutputFileName := CgiIniFile.ReadString('System', 'Output File', '');

 {Retrieve the three data items that you want for this example:
 request method, server name, and the user's IP address/remote address}

 REQUEST_METHOD := CgiIniFile.ReadString('CGI', 'Request Method', '');
 SERVER_NAME := CgiIniFile.ReadString('CGI', 'Server Name', '');
 REMOTE_ADDR := CgiIniFile.ReadString('CGI', 'Remote Address', '');
```

continues

Part

III

Ch

13

Listing 13.10   Continued

```
  OpenOutputFile;
  Result := True;
  except
  Result := False;
  end;
end;

function TWinCGI.CloseWinCGI : Boolean;
begin
try
 CgiIniFile.Free;
 CloseFile(OutputFile);
 Result := True;
except
 Result := False;
end;
end;

function TWinCGI.GetLiteral( keyname : String) : String;
begin
 try
 Result := CgiIniFile.ReadString('Form Literal', keyname, '');
 except
 Result := 'Unknown';
 end;
end;

procedure TWinCGI.SetOutputFile ( outfile : String);
begin
 OutputFileName := outfile;
end;

function TWinCGI.GetOutputFile : String;
begin
 Result := OutputFileName;
end;

procedure TWinCGI.SetIniFile ( testini : String);
begin
 CGIIniFileName := testini;
end;

function TWinCGI.GetIniFile : String;
begin
 Result := CGIIniFileName;
end;

procedure TWinCGI.SetWebServer ( web : String);
begin
 WebServer := web;
end;

function TWinCGI.GetWebServer : String;
begin
```

```pascal
 Result := WebServer;
end;

function TWinCGI.GetGMTTime : String;
begin
 Result := FormatDateTime('ddd, dd mmm yyyy hh:nn:ss "GMT"', Now);
end;

function TWinCGI.OpenOutputFile : Boolean;
begin
 if OutputFileName <> '' then
 begin
 try
 AssignFile( OutputFile, OutputFileName);
 ReWrite(OutputFile);
 Result := True;
 except
 Result := False
 end
 end
 else
 Result := False;
end;

function TWinCGI.Send( dataout : String ) : Boolean;
begin
 try
 Writeln(OutputFile, dataout);
 Result := True;
 except
 Result := False;
 end;
end;

function TWinCGI.SendHTTPHeader : Boolean;
begin
try
 Writeln(OutputFile, 'HTTP/1.0 200 OK');
 Writeln(OutputFile, 'Date: ' + GetGMTTime);
    {Thursday, 12-Jan-96 16:04:30 GMT');}
 Writeln(OutputFile, 'Server: ' + WebServer);
 Writeln(OutputFile, 'Content-type: text/html');
 Writeln(OutputFile, '');
 Result := True;
except
 Result := False;
end;
end;

procedure Register;
begin
 RegisterComponents('WinCGI', [TWinCGI]);
end;

end.
```

Notice that this code provides for the three CGI environment variables that you have been using in the previous examples:

```
public
  { Public declarations }
  REQUEST_METHOD : String;
  SERVER_NAME : String;
  REMOTE_ADDR : String;
```

The public declaration means that the user can access these variables in the WinCGI program.

Because the REQUEST_METHOD, SERVER_NAME, and REMOTE_ADDR variables are initialized automatically with your component, you can send the information back to the client with the following code:

```
Send('Request Method is: ' + REQUEST_METHOD + '<P>');
Send('Server Name is: ' + SERVER_NAME + '<P>');
Send('Remote Address is: ' + REMOTE_ADDR + '<P>');
```

The defined methods make it easier for your component to do the routine tasks that every WinCGI program must do:

■ InitWinCGI determines the *cgi-data-file*, reads the name of the output file, reads the three CGI environment variables (REQUEST_METHOD, SERVER_NAME, and REMOTE_ADDR), and opens the output file for your response.

■ CloseWinCGI closes the output file and frees the TInifile object that you use to read from the *cgi-data-file*.

■ GetLiteral(*keyname : String*) reads a value from the [Form Literal] section of the *cgi-data-file*. An HTML form would have passed this value to the server. To determine which entry pair to read, you pass the key name as a parameter.

■ Send(*dataout : String*) writes a line to the output file to be returned to the user's browser. This component performs no content checking.

■ SendHTTPHeader writes a standard HTTP header to the output file. This valid header consists of five lines, including one which properly formats a GMT time and reads a component property for the Web server software name.

The companion CD provides the source and the component for your review.

You can use the WinCGI component in a new program and observe how this component can help improve your productivity. To demonstrate how this could work, Listing 13.11 rewrites the last example, this time using your new component to perform the same functionality as the last example. You will quickly see how you can utilize this component to accomplish much greater things.

Listing 13.11   UNIT1.PAS—the QUECGI4 Project's Revision of the QUECGI3 Project That Returns User Information

```
unit Unit1;

interface

uses
 SysUtils, WinTypes, WinProcs, Messages, Classes, Graphics, Controls,
 Forms, Dialogs, Wincgi, StdCtrls;

type
 TForm1 = class(TForm)
 WinCGI: TWinCGI;
 Label1: TLabel;
 procedure FormCreate(Sender: TObject);
 private
 { Private declarations }
 public
 { Public declarations }
 end;

var
 Form1: TForm1;

implementation

{$R *.DFM}

procedure TForm1.FormCreate(Sender: TObject);
var
 res : Boolean; {Check the return value of your methods}
 FirstName : String;
 LastName : String;
 TypePerson : String;
begin
with WinCGI do
begin
 InitWinCGI;

 FirstName := GetLiteral('firstname');
 LastName := GetLiteral('lastname');
 TypePerson := GetLiteral('typeperson');

 SendHTTPHeader; {Method that sends 5 lines to the server,
 including a properly formatted GMT line
 and a line that reads the WebServerName
 property from your component}

 Send('<HTML><HEAD>'); {Writes a line to output file}
 Send('<TITLE>Example Four</TITLE></HEAD>');
```

continues

Listing 13.11 Continued

```
Send('<BODY BGCOLOR=
    "#FFFFFF"><HR>Hello ' + FirstName + ' ' + LastName + ', <P>');
Send('<H2>Using Our Delphi Component!</H2>');
Send('The Request Method is <B>' + REQUEST_METHOD + '</B>.<BR>');
Send('The Server Name is <B>' + SERVER_NAME + '</B>.<BR>');
Send('Your IP Address is <B>' + REMOTE_ADDR + '</B>.<P>');

Send(
    'The time is <B>' + DateTimeToStr(Now) + '</B><P><HR>');
Send('You are a really <B>' + TypePerson + '</B> individual.');
Send('</BODY></HTML>');

CloseWinCGI; {Method that closes the output file}

Halt; {Stops the program. The Web server takes control and
delivers the output file to the user.}
end;

end;

end.
```

Here's a quick comparison of the two coding styles. The design goal for your component is to reduce redundant coding and provide greater functionality.

Here's the "before" version of the initialization of the WinCGI environment:

```
CgiIniFile := TIniFile.Create(ParamStr(1));
 application.processMessages;

OutputFileName := CgiIniFile.ReadString('System', 'Output File', '');

{Retrieve the three data items that you want for this example:
request method, server name, user's IP address/remote address,
and the form data}

RequestMethod := CgiIniFile.ReadString('CGI', 'Request Method', '');
ServerName := CgiIniFile.ReadString('CGI', 'Server Name', '');
RemoteAddress := CgiIniFile.ReadString('CGI', 'Remote Address', '');

{The form data that you are retrieving resides in the Form Literal
section. You have to know something about the HTML that defines each
field, specifically the name="xxx". You use the xxx to find the
right entry.}

FirstName := CgiIniFile.ReadString('Form Literal', 'firstname', '');
LastName := CgiIniFile.ReadString('Form Literal', 'lastname', '');
TypePerson := CgiIniFile.ReadString('Form Literal', 'typeperson', '');

AssignFile( OutputFile, OutputFileName);
ReWrite(OutputFile);
```

Now here's the "after" version of this initialization code:

```
with WinCGI do
begin
 InitWinCGI;
```

Now compare the code that retrieves the form variables from the Form Literal section. Here's the "before" version:

```
FirstName := CgiIniFile.ReadString('Form Literal', 'firstname', '');
LastName := CgiIniFile.ReadString('Form Literal', 'lastname', '');
TypePerson := CgiIniFile.ReadString('Form Literal', 'typeperson', '');
```

And here's the "after" version:

```
FirstName := GetLiteral('firstname');
LastName := GetLiteral('lastname');
TypePerson := GetLiteral('typeperson');
```

Here's the "before" version of the code that sends an HTTP header:

```
 Writeln(OutputFile, 'HTTP/1.0 200 OK');
 Writeln(OutputFile, 'Date: Thursday, 12-Jan-96 16:04:30 GMT');
 Writeln(OutputFile, 'Server: WebSite 1.0');
 Writeln(OutputFile, 'Content-type: text/html');
 Writeln(OutputFile, 'Last-modified: Thursday, 25-Jan-96 16:04:30 GMT');
 Writeln(OutputFile, 'Content-length: 5000');
 Writeln(OutputFile, '');
```

Compare that code to the "after" version:

```
SendHTTPHeader;
```

Now compare the code that sends the browser response. First, here's the "before" version:

```
Writeln(OutputFile, '<HTML><HEAD>');
Writeln(OutputFile, '<TITLE>Example Two</TITLE></HEAD>');
Writeln(OutputFile,
    '<BODY><HR>Hello ' + FirstName + ' ' + LastName + ', <P>');
Writeln(OutputFile,
    'The Request Method is <B>' + RequestMethod + '</B>.<BR>');
Writeln(OutputFile, 'The Server Name is <B>' + ServerName + '</B>.<BR>');
Writeln(OutputFile,
    'Your IP Address is <B>' + RemoteAddress + '</B>.<P>');

Writeln(OutputFile,
    'Sir, the time on deck is <B>' + DateTimeToStr(Now) + '</B><P><HR>');

Writeln(OutputFile,
    'You are a really <B>' + TypePerson + '</B> individual.');
Writeln(OutputFile, '</BODY></HTML>');
```

And now here's the "after" version:

```
 Send('<HTML><HEAD>'); {Writes a line to output file}
 Send('<TITLE>Example Four</TITLE></HEAD>');
 Send('<BODY BGCOLOR="#FFFFFF"><HR>Hello ' + FirstName + ' ' +
     LastName + ', <P>');
```

```
Send('<H2>Using Our Delphi Component!</H2>');
Send('The Request Method is <B>' + REQUEST_METHOD + '</B>.<BR>');
Send('The Server Name is <B>' + SERVER_NAME + '</B>.<BR>');
Send('Your IP Address is <B>' + REMOTE_ADDR + '</B>.<P>');

Send('Sir, the time on deck is <B>' + DateTimeToStr(Now) +
   '</B><P><HR>');
Send('You are a really <B>' + TypePerson + '</B> individual.');
Send('</BODY></HTML>');
```

Finally, here's the "before" version of the code that closes the output file and cleans up:

```
CgiIniFile.Free;
CloseFile(OutputFile);
```

Figure 13.10 shows the result of executing the QUECGI4 example on a Web browser.

FIG. 13.10

The result of executing
the QUECGI4 example
on a WWW browser.

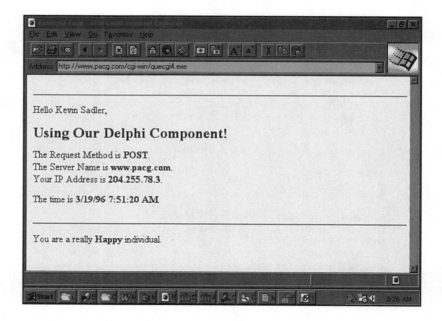

Feel free to enhance, modify, and extend the source code. I would be happy to hear any comments or discuss any ideas that you have regarding the code. You can reach me through the Internet at **kevin@pacg.com**.

All the preceding examples are working on the Pacific Group's Web site at the following URLs:

```
http://www.pacg.com/que/example1.htm
http://www.pacg.com/que/example2.htm
http://www.pacg.com/que/example3.htm
http://www.pacg.com/que/example4.htm
```

N O T E   Delphi 1.0 is a 16-bit development environment that produces 16-bit .EXEs and .DLLs. With no modifications necessary, these executables and DLLs run as WinCGI programs under Windows NT, a 32-bit operating environment. Delphi 2.0, announced early in 1996, produces true 32-bit .EXEs that run much more efficiently in Windows NT. Delphi 2.0 also includes a 32-bit Borland Database Engine. The programs described in this chapter are easily portable to a true 32-bit environment.

An alternative trend in interactive World Wide Web programming promises to increase performance in sites with huge CGI loads. Microsoft has published a specification, the Internet Server Application Program Interface (ISAPI), for its Web Server. O'Reilly and Associates has developed Website Application Program Interface (WSAPI), which follows a similar approach.

These two new APIs utilize "in-process" programs or extensions that run in the same process space as the Web server software. This approach promises greater efficiency and performance, because you do not have to create a new process each time that you call an interactive program. However, only experienced developers should even think about attempting to write a DLL that runs in the same address space as your server. Knowledge of Win32 advanced features such as threading is a necessity.

The good news is that Delphi 2.0 is a development environment that you can use for this approach. Delphi 2.0 supports the complete Win32 API. ▨

From Here...

This chapter covered the basics of Delphi CGI programming. Along the way, you have also encapsulated some of the properties and methods into a working Delphi WinCGI component.

To learn more about related topics, see the following chapters:

- ▨ To examine all the parts that comprise the World Wide Web, see Chapter 12, "The Web—HTTP, HTML, and Beyond."
- ▨ To extend your work to database programming with Delphi and CGI, see Chapter 14, "Using a Database in a CGI Application."
- ▨ To learn about HTTP, see Chapter 15, "Building a Web Robot To Verify Link Integrity."

Part
III

Ch
13

Using a Database in a CGI Application

- Perform the processing that you initiate after collecting information through CGI and before the response returns to the user

- Incorporate database capabilities into a CGI application

- Develop a working database application in steps

Chapter 13, "Using Delphi with CGI," detailed how to use Delphi and WinCGI to communicate with a user's Internet browser. In that chapter, you saw three examples that demonstrate how to read system and environment information, retrieve user input, and display a response to the user. WinCGI defined the protocol that you use to capture the input and return the output to the user. You also saw how to develop a small Delphi WinCGI component that encapsulates much of the repetitive, bare-bones coding of the WinCGI specification. ∎

Developing a Database Application

CGI processing in Delphi is much like standard application programming. CGI defines how you send and receive data. After you receive the data, you can fully use your knowledge of Delphi and the rapid application development (RAD) features for which it is known.

The application that you create in this chapter enables the user to enter data into your database through a Web browser. You also enable the user to query the database with specific criteria and view the results of the query on his or her browser. You use the "raw" WinCGI specification in the first example; for all subsequent examples, you use the CGI component that you developed in Chapter 13.

The first stage is to enable the user to input records into a database through a Hypertext Markup Language (HTML) form. The user enters his or her first name and last name in standard text boxes. To specify the third data item, the user uses radio buttons to select the type of person he or she is.

The next phase is to provide the user with a mechanism to search for a particular record in the database and have the WinCGI program display the desired result, or to display a message explaining that the search failed to find the desired record.

The last phase is to enable the user to search for a group of records and then have the program change the result display's format dynamically, based on the type of data that the user specified.

Your first task is to enable the user to add a record to a database using an HTML form and CGI. The Borland Database Engine that ships with Delphi and other Borland products has drivers that can communicate with virtually every type of database. The drivers are either native or use Open Database Connectivity (ODBC). The programs in this chapter work on local database tables, such as Paradox or dBase, that reside on the same machine as the Web server. The programs also work in client/server environments in which relational database engines reside on completely different machines. Delphi provides to these databases a common programming interface through the TTable, TDatabase, TSession, and TQuery objects.

For these example programs, you use a small dBASE table called PEOPLE.DBF. Table 14.1 shows this table's structure.

Table 14.1 PEOPLE.DBF's Structure

Field Name	Type	Size (Number of Characters)
FIRSTNAME	Character	20
LASTNAME	Character	20
TYPEPERSON	Character	20
GENDER	Character	10

To enable users to add records to the table, you provide the HTML form shown in Figure 14.1. Listing 14.1 shows the code that displays this form, which feeds your CGI program.

FIG. 14.1

The user adds records by using this simple HTML form.

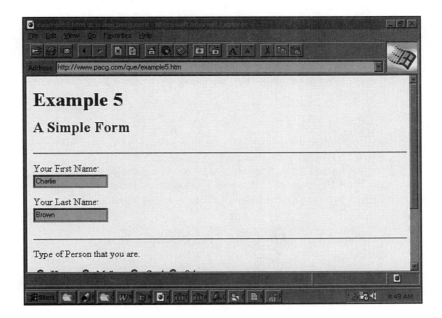

Listing 14.1 EXAMPLE5.HTM—the Web Page That Generates Your Application's Input Form

```
<HTML>
<!—
Author:     Kevin Sadler
Date:       January 20, 1996
URL:        http://www.pacg.com/que/example5.htm

Delphi CGI Coding
—>

<BODY>
<H1>Example 5</H1>
<FORM ACTION="/cgi-win/quecgi5.exe" METHOD="POST">
<H2>A Simple Form</H2>
<HR>
Your First Name:<BR>
<INPUT TYPE="text" NAME="firstname"><P>
Your Last Name:<BR>
<INPUT TYPE="text" NAME="lastname"><P>
<HR>
Type of Person that you are:<P>
<INPUT TYPE="radio" NAME="typeperson" VALUE="Happy">Happy
```

Part
III

Ch
14

continues

Listing 14.1   Continued

```
<INPUT TYPE="radio" NAME="typeperson" VALUE="Mellow">Mellow
<INPUT TYPE="radio" NAME="typeperson" VALUE="Cool">Cool<P>
<INPUT TYPE="radio" NAME="typeperson" VALUE="Other">Other<P>
Your Gender:<P>
<INPUT TYPE="radio" NAME="gender" VALUE="Male">Male
<INPUT TYPE="radio" NAME="gender" VALUE="Female">Female

<INPUT TYPE="submit" VALUE="Press Here!">
</FORM>

</BODY>
</HTML>
```

In this first example program, you program directly to the WinCGI specification and also use the WinCGI component that you developed in Chapter 13. If you did not use the component to write this program, the Delphi CGI code would look like Listing 14.2.

Listing 14.2   UNIT1.PAS—the QUECGI5 Project's Delphi CGI Coding That Generates Your Application's HTML Form, Written without Your WinCGI Component

```
unit Unit1;

interface

uses
 SysUtils, WinTypes, WinProcs, Messages, Classes, Graphics, Controls,
 Forms, Dialogs, IniFiles, DB, DBTables;

type
 TForm1 = class(TForm)
 Table1: TTable;
 Table1FIRSTNAME: TStringField;
 Table1LASTNAME: TStringField;
 Table1TYPEPERSON: TStringField;
 Table1GENDER: TStringField;
 procedure FormCreate(Sender: TObject);
 private
 { Private declarations }
 public
 { Public declarations }
 end;

var
 Form1: TForm1;

implementation

{$R *.DFM}
```

```
procedure TForm1.FormCreate(Sender: TObject);
var
 CgiIniFile : TIniFile;
 CgiIniFileName : String;
 OutputFile : TextFile;
 OutputFileName : String;
 RequestMethod : String;
 ServerName : String;
 RemoteAddress : String;
 FirstName : String;
 LastName : String;
 TypePerson : String;
 Gender : String;

begin
 CgiIniFile := TIniFile.Create(ParamStr(1));
 application.processMessages;

 OutputFileName := CgiIniFile.ReadString('System', 'Output File', '');

 {Retrieve the three data items that you want for this example:
 request method, server name, user's IP address/remote address,
 and the form data}

 RequestMethod := CgiIniFile.ReadString('CGI', 'Request Method', '');
 ServerName := CgiIniFile.ReadString('CGI', 'Server Name', '');
 RemoteAddress := CgiIniFile.ReadString('CGI', 'Remote Address', '');

 {The form data that you are retrieving resides in the Form Literal
 section. You have to know something about the HTML that defines each
 field, specifically the name="xxx". You use the xxx to find the right
 entry.}

 FirstName := CgiIniFile.ReadString('Form Literal', 'firstname', '');
 LastName := CgiIniFile.ReadString('Form Literal', 'lastname', '');
 TypePerson := CgiIniFile.ReadString('Form Literal', 'typeperson', '');
 Gender := CgiIniFile.ReadString('Form Literal', 'gender', '');

 {Add the record to the PEOPLE.DBF table. This is not unlike
 standard Delphi programming. Of course, in a production situation,
 you would do edit checking, check for required fields, etc.}

 Table1.Edit;
 Table1FIRSTNAME.Value := FirstName;
 Table1LASTNAME.Value := LastName;
 Table1TYPEPERSON.Value := TypePerson;
 Table1GENDER.Value := Gender;
 Table1.Post;

 CgiIniFile.Free;

 AssignFile( OutputFile, OutputFileName);
 ReWrite(OutputFile);
```

Part
III

Ch

14

continues

Listing 14.2   Continued

```
Writeln(OutputFile, 'HTTP/1.0 200 OK');
Writeln(OutputFile, 'Date: Thursday, 12-Jan-96 16:04:30 GMT');
Writeln(OutputFile, 'Server: WebSite 1.0');
Writeln(OutputFile, 'Content-type: text/html');
Writeln(OutputFile, 'Last-modified: Thursday, 25-Jan-96 16:04:30 GMT');
Writeln(OutputFile, 'Content-length: 5000');
Writeln(OutputFile, '');
Writeln(OutputFile, '<HTML><HEAD>');
Writeln(OutputFile, '<TITLE>Example Two</TITLE></HEAD>');
Writeln(OutputFile, '<BODY BGCOLOR="#FFFFFF"><HR>Hello ' + FirstName + '
    ' + LastName + ', <P>');
Writeln(OutputFile, 'A record has been added to the database.<P>');
Writeln(OutputFile,
    'The Request Method is <B>' + RequestMethod + '</B>.<BR>');
Writeln(OutputFile,
    'The Server Name is <B>' + ServerName + '</B>.<BR>');
Writeln(OutputFile,
    'Your IP Address is <B>' + RemoteAddress + '</B>.<P>');
Writeln(OutputFile,
    'The time is <B>' + DateTimeToStr(Now) + '</B><P><HR>');
Writeln(OutputFile, 'You are a <B>' + Gender + '</B> and a really <B>'
    + TypePerson + '</B> individual.');


Writeln(OutputFile, '</BODY></HTML>');

CloseFile(OutputFile);

Halt;

end;


end.
```

Figure 14.2 shows the QUECGI Delphi project's form.

EXAMPLE5.HTM accomplishes the following:

■ Captures the user input, following the CGI specification's guidelines

■ Performs a database operation with a standard Delphi TTable component

■ Outputs a response to the user, following the CGI specification guidelines

FIG. 14.2
The QUECGI5 Delphi project.

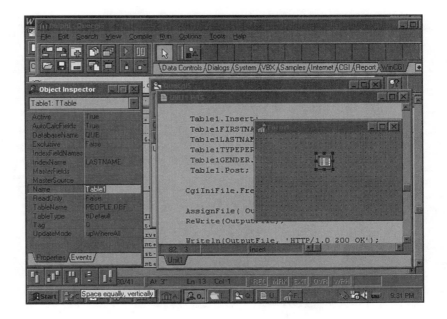

Listing 14.3 shows the same functionality as Listing 14.2, but in this example you use the component that you designed and created in Chapter 13.

Listing 14.3 UNIT1.PAS—the QUECGI5 Project's Delphi CGI Coding That Adds a Database Record to PEOPLE.DBF and Generates Your Application's HTML Response, Written with Your WinCGI Component

```
unit Unit1;

interface

uses
  SysUtils, WinTypes, WinProcs, Messages, Classes, Graphics, Controls,
  Forms, Dialogs, DB, DBTables, Wincgi;

type
  TForm1 = class(TForm)
  WinCGI: TWinCGI;
  Table1: TTable;
  Table1FIRSTNAME: TStringField;
  Table1LASTNAME: TStringField;
  Table1TYPEPERSON: TStringField;
```

Listing 14.3   Continued

```
Table1GENDER: TStringField;
procedure FormCreate(Sender: TObject);
private
{ Private declarations }
public
{ Public declarations }
end;

var
 Form1: TForm1;

implementation

{$R *.DFM}

procedure TForm1.FormCreate(Sender: TObject);
var
 res : Boolean; {Check the return value of your methods}

 FirstName : String;
 LastName : String;
 TypePerson : String;
 Gender : String;
begin
with WinCGI do
begin
 InitWinCGI;

 FirstName := GetLiteral('firstname');
 LastName := GetLiteral('lastname');
 TypePerson := GetLiteral('typeperson');
 Gender := GetLiteral('gender');

 {Add the record to the PEOPLE.DBF table. This is not unlike
 standard Delphi programming. Of course, in a production situation,
 you would do edit checking, check for required fields, etc.}

 Table1.Insert;
 Table1FIRSTNAME.Value := FirstName;
 Table1LASTNAME.Value := LastName;
 Table1TYPEPERSON.Value := TypePerson;
 Table1GENDER.Value := Gender;
 Table1.Post;

 SendHTTPHeader; {Method that sends 5 lines to the server,
 including a properly formatted GMT line
 and a line that reads the WebServerName
 property from your component}

 Send('<HTML><HEAD>'); {Writes a line to output file}
 Send('<TITLE>Example Four</TITLE></HEAD>');
 Send('<BODY BGCOLOR="#FFFFFF"><HR>Hello ' + FirstName + '
    ' + LastName + ', <P>');
 Send('<H2>Using Our Delphi Component!</H2>');
 Send('A record has been added to the database.<P>');
```

```
Send('The Request Method is <B>' + REQUEST_METHOD + '</B>.<BR>');
Send('The Server Name is <B>' + SERVER_NAME + '</B>.<BR>');
Send('Your IP Address is <B>' + REMOTE_ADDR + '</B>.<P>');

Send
  ('The time is <B>' + DateTimeToStr(Now) + '</B><P><HR>');
Send('You are a <B>' + Gender + '</B> and a really <B>'
  + TypePerson + '</B> individual.');
Send('</BODY></HTML>');

CloseWinCGI; {Method that closes the output file}

Halt; {Stops the program. The Web server takes control and
delivers the output file to the user.}
end;

end;


end.
```

Figure 14.3 displays the Delphi project with the CGI component as well as the TTable component.

FIG. 14.3

The Delphi project with the CGI component as well as the TTable component.

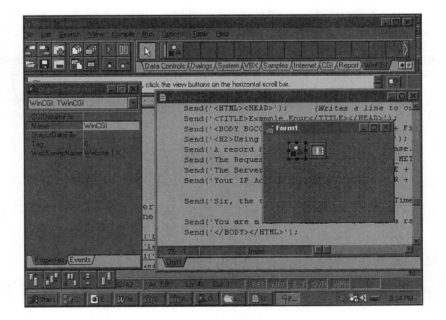

When the Web server software starts this program, you use your CGI component to read the form-related data:

```
FirstName := GetLiteral('firstname');
 LastName := GetLiteral('lastname');
```

```
TypePerson := GetLiteral('typeperson');
Gender := GetLiteral('gender');
```

The variables that you have declared in your program are plain Pascal strings. From this point on, you can interact with the TTable object in the same manner that you would in any other program. As previously discussed, CGI is used only to get the data from the server and to give it back to the server. After you have this data, you use only standard Delphi. The following code stores your four variables into the database:

```
{Add the record to the PEOPLE.DBF table. This is not unlike
 standard Delphi programming. Of course, in a production situation,
 you would do edit checking, check for required fields, etc.}

Table1.Insert;
Table1FIRSTNAME.Value := FirstName;
Table1LASTNAME.Value := LastName;
Table1TYPEPERSON.Value := TypePerson;
Table1GENDER.Value := Gender;
Table1.Post;
```

Figure 14.4 shows an example of the form that this code generates. The response that you return to the user's browser verifies that you have added a record. You also return some useful information that tells the user that the program did indeed read the information correctly. You could also do other creative things, like adding an ID field and incrementing a counter for that field. You could also get a little more adventurous by e-mailing or paging a confirmation back to the user or an administrator.

FIG. 14.4

Your HTML form returns important information to the user.

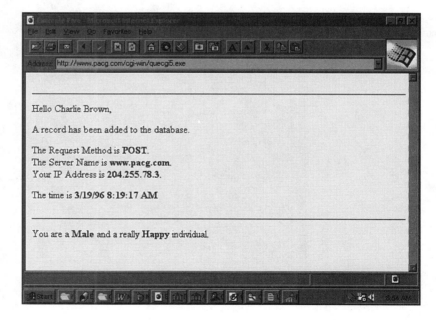

N O T E Don't forget to check for database errors. This is definitely a requirement for production applications. ■

Using Delphi To Provide a Database Search Capability

The next phase of the database project is to enable the user to search the PEOPLE.DBF database for a particular person by specifying that person's last name. In this example, you use the TTable object's FindKey method to find the correct record. If the record is found, the application returns the results to the user through CGI. If the record is not found, you have to tell the user. Figure 14.5 shows the search form.

FIG. 14.5
The search utility's form.

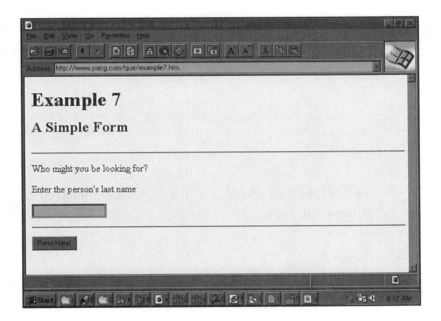

Listing 14.4 shows the HTML file that creates the search form.

Listing 14.4   EXAMPLE7.HTM—the HTML File for Your Application's Search Form

```
<HTML>
<! —
Author:      Kevin Sadler - kevin@pacg.com
Date:        January 20, 1996
URL:         http://www.pacg.com/que/example7.htm
```

continues

Listing 14.4   Continued

```
Delphi CGI Coding
—>

<BODY BGCOLOR="#FFFFFF">
<H1>Example 7</H1>
<FORM ACTION="/cgi-win/quecgi7.exe" METHOD="POST">
<H2>A Simple Form</H2>
<HR>
Who might you be looking for?<BR>
Please enter the person's last name:<BR>

<INPUT TYPE="text" NAME="lastname"><P>

<HR>

<INPUT TYPE="submit" VALUE="Press Here!">
</FORM>

</BODY>
</HTML>
```

For the remaining examples, you use the component that you created in Chapter 13. The processing that you do here is straightforward. You capture the last name search criteria, use FindKey, to determine the result, and return the appropriate response to the server/user.

Listing 14.5 shows the Delphi code for your search utility.

Listing 14.5   UNIT1.PAS—the QUECGI7 Project's Delphi Code To Display the Search Results

```
unit Unit1;

interface

uses
 SysUtils, WinTypes, WinProcs, Messages, Classes, Graphics, Controls,
 Forms, Dialogs, Wincgi, DB, DBTables;

type
 TForm1 = class(TForm)
 Table1: TTable;
 WinCGI: TWinCGI;
 Table1FIRSTNAME: TStringField;
 Table1LASTNAME: TStringField;
 Table1TYPEPERSON: TStringField;
 Table1GENDER: TStringField;
 procedure FormCreate(Sender: TObject);
 private
 { Private declarations }
```

```
    public
    { Public declarations }
    end;


var
  Form1: TForm1;

implementation

{$R *.DFM}

procedure TForm1.FormCreate(Sender: TObject);
var
  res : Boolean; {Check the return value of your methods}
  criteria : String;

begin
with WinCGI do
begin
  InitWinCGI;

  criteria := GetLiteral('lastname');

  {Add the record to the PEOPLE.DBF table. This is not unlike
  standard Delphi programming. Of course, in a production situation,
  you would do edit checking, check for required fields, etc.}

  SendHTTPHeader; {Method that sends 5 lines to the server,
  including a properly formatted GMT line
  and a line that reads the WebServerName
  property from your component}

  Send('<HTML><HEAD>'); {Writes a line to output file}
  Send('<TITLE>Example Four</TITLE></HEAD>');
  Send('<BODY BGCOLOR="#FFFFFF"><HR>');
  Send('<H2>Using Our Delphi Component!</H2>');


  {Here's where you check whether the search is successful or
  not. The page that is returned is entirely dependent on whether
  the record is found and what's in the record - a dynamic page!!}
  if Table1.FindKey([criteria]) then
  begin
  Send('<H2>Found It!</H2>');
  Send('Here''s the rest of the info..<P>');
  Send('First Name: <B>' + Table1FIRSTNAME.Value + '</B><P>');
  Send('Last Name: <B>' + Table1LASTNAME.Value + '</B><P>');
  Send('The person is a <B>' + Table1GENDER.Value + '</B> and a really <B>');
  Send(Table1TYPEPERSON.Value + '</B> person.<P>');
  Send('Thanks for Asking!');
  end
  else
  begin
```

Part
III

Ch
14

continues

Listing 14.5 Continued

```
Send('<H2>Sorry!</H2>');
Send(
 'Couldn''t find anyone with the last name <B>' + criteria + '</B><P>');
Send(
 'Click the BACK button on your browser and try again.<P>');
end;

Send
 ('The time is <B>' + DateTimeToStr(Now) + '</B><P><HR>');
Send('</BODY></HTML>');

CloseWinCGI; {Method that closes the output file}

Halt; {Stops the program. The Web server takes control and
delivers the output file to the user.}
end;

end;

end.
```

The heart of this example that dynamically creates the HTML file starts when the program looks for the record. Notice that you send only the HTML that is appropriate to the result of the search. If the search is unsuccessful, you send a blank response. The search might also generate an exception, in which case you also send the user the appropriate feedback. If the database server is down, you should tell the user so that he or she can try the search later, instead of leading the user to believe that the desired record doesn't exist.

Listing 14.6 shows a snippet in which code is executed on a successful or unsuccessful search.

Listing 14.6 UNIT1.PAS—a Snippet from the QUECGI7 Project in Which Code Is Executed on a Successful or Unsuccessful Search

```
if Table1.FindKey([criteria]) then
 begin
 Send('<H2>Found It!</H2>');
 Send('Here''s the rest of the info..<P>');
 Send('First Name: <B>' + Table1FIRSTNAME.Value + '</B><P>');
 Send('Last Name: <B>' + Table1LASTNAME.Value + '</B><P>');
 Send('The person is a <B>' + Table1GENDER.Value + '</B> and a really <B>');
 Send(Table1TYPEPERSON.Value + '</B> person.<P>');
 Send('Thanks for Asking!');
 end
 else
 begin
 Send('<H2>Sorry!</H2>');
 Send(
  'Couldn''t find anyone with the last name <B>' + criteria + '</B><P>');
 Send('Click the BACK button on your browser and try again.<P>');
 end;
```

Figure 14.6 shows an example of this form returning input information.

FIG. 14.6
Sample output in the HTML form.

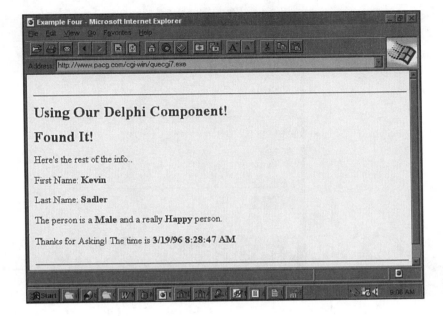

Returning a Data Set to a Web Page

In the final example, you enable the user to ask for all records of a particular type. In this case, the user can ask for all the female records or all the male records (see Fig. 14.7). This example demonstrates the use of the TQuery object in your CGI program to prepare the result set. You also combine standard Delphi programming, such as a While construct, with the CGI specification to return a dynamic result set to the user.

Also, you'll have a little fun with the background based on the search criteria. In the previous example as well as this one, the delineation between the basic steps of CGI programming are not as clear:

1. Get the data (WinCGI).
2. Process the data (standard Delphi).
3. Return the response (WinCGI).

The steps overlap to make a truly dynamic page. Listing 14.7 shows the HTML file for the form page displayed to the user.

Part
III

Ch
14

FIG. 14.7
The Example 8 form enables users to specify whether to display all men or all women in the database.

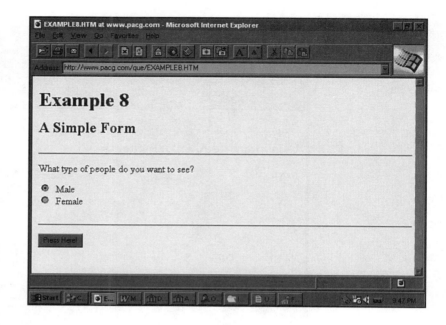

Listing 14.7 EXAMPLE8.HTM—the HTML File for Your Application's Data Set Search Form

```
<HTML>
<!—
Author:     Kevin Sadler
Date:       January 20, 1996
URL:        http://www.pacg.com/que/example8.htm

Delphi CGI Coding
—>

<BODY BGCOLOR="#FFFFFF">
<H1>Example 8</H1>
<FORM ACTION="/cgi-win/quecgi8.exe" METHOD="POST">
<H2>A Simple Form</H2>
<HR>
What type of people do you want to see?<P>

<INPUT TYPE="radio" NAME="gender" value="Male">Male<BR>
<INPUT TYPE="radio" NAME="gender" value="Female">Female<P>

<HR>

<INPUT TYPE="submit" VALUE="Press Here!">
</FORM>

</BODY>
</HTML>
```

The following is the SQL property of the form's TQuery object:

```
SELECT * FROM PEOPLE WHERE GENDER = :gend
```

:gend is a variable that you use for a parameterized query. You set this variable based on data that you collect from the form. For example, if the user clicks the Male radio button, the SQL property executes as follows:

```
SELECT * FROM PEOPLE WHERE GENDER = 'MALE'
```

Listing 14.8 shows EXAMPLE8.HTM's Delphi code.

Listing 14.8   UNIT1.PAS—the QUECGI7 Project's Delphi Code for Your Application's Data Set Search Form

```
unit Unit1;

interface

uses
  SysUtils, WinTypes, WinProcs, Messages, Classes, Graphics, Controls,
  Forms, Dialogs, DB, DBTables, Wincgi;

type
  TForm1 = class(TForm)
  WinCGI: TWinCGI;
  Query1: TQuery;
  Query1FIRSTNAME: TStringField;
  Query1LASTNAME: TStringField;
  Query1TYPEPERSON: TStringField;
  Query1GENDER: TStringField;
  procedure FormCreate(Sender: TObject);
  private
  { Private declarations }
  public
  { Public declarations }
  end;

var
  Form1: TForm1;

implementation

{$R *.DFM}

procedure TForm1.FormCreate(Sender: TObject);
var
  res : Boolean; {Check the return value of your methods}
  criteria : String;

begin
with WinCGI do
begin
```

continues

Part
III

Ch
14

Listing 14.8 Continued

```
InitWinCGI;

criteria := GetLiteral('gender');

{This is where you set up the parameter for the TQuery
that will determine whether you pull the male or
female records}
with Query1 do
begin
close;
ParamByName('gend').AsString := criteria;
open;
end;

SendHTTPHeader; {Method that sends 5 lines to the server,
including a properly formatted GMT line
and a line that reads the WebServerName
property from your component}

Send('<HTML><HEAD>'); {Writes a line to output file}
Send('<TITLE>Example Eight</TITLE></HEAD>');

{If you're showing Males, then send a white background,
If you're showing Females, then send a pink background.}
if criteria = 'Male' then
Send('<BODY BGCOLOR="#FFFFFF"><HR>')
else
Send('<BODY BGCOLOR="#BC8F8F"><HR>');

Send('<H2>Using Our Delphi Component!</H2>');
Send('<CENTER><H2>A List of ' + criteria + 's</H2><CENTER>');


{Here's where you get a little fancy and will
loop through the records and put them in a
table - a dynamic page!!}
if Query1.EOF then
begin
Send('<H2>Sorry!</H2>');
Send('Couldn''t find anyone in the database that is a <B>'
  + criteria + '</B><P>');
Send('Click the BACK button on your browser and try again.<P>');
end
else
begin
Send('<CENTER><TABLE BORDER>');
send('<TR>');
send('<TH>First Name');
send('<TH>Last Name');
send('<TH>Person Type');
```

```
while not Query1.EOF do
begin
send('<TR>');
send('<TD>' + Query1FIRSTNAME.Value);
send('<TD>' + Query1LASTNAME.Value);
send('<TD>' + Query1TYPEPERSON.Value);
Query1.Next;
end;
send('</TABLE></CENTER>');
end;

Send('The time is <B>' + DateTimeToStr(Now) +
  '</B><P><HR>');
Send('</BODY></HTML>');

CloseWinCGI; {Method that closes the output file}

Halt; {Stops the program. The Web server takes control and
delivers the output file to the user.}
end;

end;

end.
```

To retrieve the :gend / criteria value, you use the following code:

```
criteria := GetLiteral('gender');
```

To initialize and execute the TQuery object, you need the following code:

```
with Query1 do
 begin
 close;
 ParamByName('gend').AsString := criteria;
 open;
 end;
```

After executing this code, the application creates a data set based on the SQL statement in the TQuery object's SQL property. At this point, you have the results that you need. Now you need to send these results to the user. By now, you should be quite familiar with this process. First, you check the user's selected criteria and then send a different browser background based on the choice:

```
{If you're showing Males, then send a white background,
 If you're showing Females, then send a pink background.}
 if criteria = 'Male' then
 Send('<BODY BGCOLOR="#FFFFFF"><HR>')
 else
 Send('<BODY BGCOLOR="#BC8F8F"><HR>');
```

Part
III

Ch
14

This example demonstrates the flexibility of Delphi and the CGI specification. Your imagination is the only limiting factor in the process. By overlapping standard Delphi programming with CGI programming, you can pretty much do anything.

Next, you must determine whether you have any records to send, because the database might not have any Male or Female records at all:

```
if Query1.EOF then
 begin
 Send('<H2>Sorry!</H2>');
 Send('Couldn''t find anyone in the database that is a <B>'
    + criteria + '</B><P>');
 Send('Click the BACK button on your browser and try again.<P>');
 end
 else...
```

As you can see, you use the CGI interface to return the appropriate response to the user. Now for the fun part. If there are any records, you format the response in a logical construct for rows of data: HTML tables. This is actually quite easy. You loop through the data set until it is empty. With each record, you send the HTML commands to format the table properly. Listing 14.9 shows the code for this formatting.

Listing 14.9   UNIT1.PAS—the QUECGI8 Project Formats the Response to the Data Set Search

```
Send('<CENTER><TABLE BORDER>');
send('<TR>');
send('<TH>First Name');
send('<TH>Last Name');
send('<TH>Person Type');

while not Query1.EOF do
begin
send('<TR>');
send('<TD>' + Query1FIRSTNAME.Value);
send('<TD>' + Query1LASTNAME.Value);
send('<TD>' + Query1TYPEPERSON.Value);
Query1.Next;
end;
send('</TABLE></CENTER>');
```

Figure 14.8 shows the results of a search for all males in the database, and Figure 14.9 shows the results for all females.

FIG. 14.8
The results of a search for all males in the database.

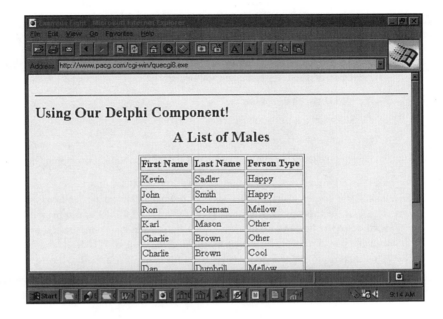

FIG. 14.9
The results of a search for all females in the database.

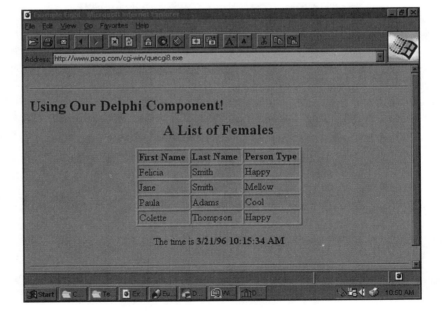

From Here...

In this chapter, you used a Delphi WinCGI component and a database to create some simple examples that use the CGI interface to interact with a database. The CGI programs that you created enable the user to do the following:

- Add records to a table
- Search for a particular record
- Query for a data set
- Dynamically format the page and data presentation based on the data set

To take a look at a real-life example of Delphi WinCGI programs interacting with a database, visit The Peoples Marketplace, an Internet classified ad site, at **http://peoplesmarket.com**. The CGI for this site was written entirely with Delphi using the principles and techniques described in the last two chapters. All the display pages are formatted with CGI work. Other advanced techniques, such as serving large chunks of HTML from text files, were also used. This technique separates the HTML maintenance from the CGI program. HTML writers can modify their code without forcing the developer to modify his or her program code.

This code can apply to a table that resides on IBM DB2 on a mainframe, an ORACLE engine residing on a reduced instruction set computer (RISC) box, or a Paradox table located on the same machine as the Web server and your CGI program. Delphi is a powerful tool for building complex applications on the Internet World Wide Web.

To explore related topics, see the following chapters:

- Chapter 12, "The Web—HTTP, HTML, and Beyond," looks at all the parts that comprise the World Wide Web.
- Chapter 13, "Using Delphi with CGI," looks at how you can use Delphi with CGI to provide extended functionality to Web pages created with HTML.
- Chapter 15, "Building a Web Robot To Verify Link Integrity," explores HTTP.

Building a Web Robot To Verify Link Integrity

If you have spent any time browsing the World Wide Web, you have a pretty good idea how easy it is for a Web link to become broken. The target site moves, shuts down, or becomes unavailable for any number of reasons. Several studies show that one of the most time-consuming aspects of any Webmaster's job is to maintain and verify links. This tedious task begs for automation. In this chapter, you build a Web robot that performs a base level of link verification. ■

- The Uniform Resource Locator (URL), what it consists of, and how to break it down into its various usable components

- A small amount of Hypertext Markup Language (HTML) formatting, in particular the tags that indicate links or embedded objects

- The basic Hypertext Transfer Protocol (HTTP), the communications protocol used between Web browsers and Web servers

- How all these work together to provide the basic navigation functionality of today's Web browsers

Understanding URLs

Uniform Resource Locators (URLs), also known as Web page addresses, are the mechanism by which World Wide Web users find various Web pages as well as many other Internet and internal network resources. This addressing and identifying scheme is very generalized, flexible, and complete. RFC 1738 documents the URL scheme, and RFC 1808 provides some additional documentation regarding relative addressing.

The original design for URLs came from the European Laboratory for Particle Physics (CERN) as the World Wide Web project was starting back in 1990. The original designers needed and came up with a way to embed within an HTML document the address of another document which the current document referenced in some way. This addressing scheme had to identify several elements to enable the browser to link correctly to the referenced document:

- The protocol used by the server on which the referenced document is located. (Originally, about a dozen Internet protocols were used over the Web, but most have been phased out as the demand for full HTTP functionality has increased.)

- The server on which the document resides. This includes the Transmission Control Protocol (TCP) port to which to connect, and possibly the user name and password to use when connecting.

- The directory in which the document can be found (relative to the service's root directory).

- The document file name.

The following is the format for this scheme:

```
protocol://[username:[password]][@]host[:port]/[directorypath/][filename]
```

The only truly required portions in this format are the protocol and host. If you don't specify a port, the default port of the specified protocol is assumed. If you don't specify a file name, index.html or default.html is often assumed.

For your Web robot, you can parse the URL into three parts, using the following steps:

1. Search for the :// marker. The Internet protocol that you are using precedes this marker (in this chapter, you are implementing only the HTTP protocol, so HTTP is the only protocol in which you are interested).

2. Search for the next slash (/) character, to find the end of the host name and port.

3. Look for a colon (:) within the host name. This character is followed by the port that you are using (if the URL is not using the default port).

Whatever is left in the URL is the file or object name that is being requested.

NOTE Although when the Web began it used about a dozen different protocols, that number has slowly diminished to fewer than a half-dozen protocols. The primary ones that you encounter are the following:

- HTTP

- FTP

- NNTP (Usenet News)

- mailto (SMTP Mail)

- file (Local File)

To provide a fairly complete Web robot implementation, you would have to extend the robot that you are building in this chapter with support for these other protocols. You should also support the other protocols as well, so that the robot has complete support for those increasingly rare occasions when the robot might encounter an old Web site that hasn't upgraded to using an HTTP server. ▪

Often, extensions are tacked on to the end of the basic URL. These extensions are often parameters that are passed to the file specified in the URL (if that file is an executable or CGI script). Other times, these extensions are positional commands to the browser, for use in moving the browser display to a specific location within the HTML page.

Parsing the HTML for Links

Now that you have a basic idea of how to interpret URLs, you need to know how to find them within an HTML document (Web page). An extensive examination of HTML formatting, tags, and other sundry topics are beyond the scope of this chapter. Several good books (and also a few not-so-good ones) go into these subjects in extensive depth and detail. But you do need to take a look at the basic HTML formatting so that you can find the embedded links. Then you can check to ensure that the referenced pages exist.

First, you can ignore most of the text included in the HTML documents. The only time that you need to pay any attention to this text is when you can connect to the server on which a particular HTML document or file is supposed to reside, but find that the document or file is not there. In these cases, the server sends a small HTML document stating that the requested HTML document was not found on that server.

You can also build in some intelligence to recognize the basic HTML document that states that the referenced document has been moved to a new location. You could have your robot use this information to generate a report that lists the old URLs with the new URLs, so that the HTML document can be updated.

You're primarily interested in the markup tags that are embedded within HTML pages. Each HTML tag is enclosed within angled brackets (< and >). You need to examine only the text enclosed within these characters. Each enclosure (with a few exceptions, such as image files) has an open and close tag. The open tag starts with the identifier to indicate what the tag begins, and the close tag consists of the opening identifier, preceded with a slash. Everything within an HTML document is enclosed within at least one pair of tags. Usually the document begins with an <HTML> tag and ends with the corresponding </HTML> tag. Therefore, as long as you receive the opening <HTML> tag, you can look for the closing </HTML> tag to mark the end of the page. Occasionally, you encounter a page that doesn't include the <HTML> tags. In such a case, you can look for the closing </BODY> tag that marks the end of the body section (normally, the only thing that follows this is the closing </HTML> tag). The following is an example of a small HTML document:

```
{The <html> tag marks this as the start of an HTML document}
<html>
{The <head> tag marks the beginning of the document header}
<head>
<title>Davis Home Page</title>
{The </head> tag marks the ending of the document header}
</head>
{The <body> tag marks the beginning of the document body}
<body>
{The following are four embedded images followed by some text. Because
there is not a complete URL with the image names, the images are assumed
to be in the same location as this Web page document}
<div align=center><img src="davisred.gif" alt="Davis Chapman's"></div>
<div align=center><img src="homepred.gif" alt="Home Page"></div>
<p><img src="parihd9.gif" align=left >
<img src="parihd2.gif" align=right >A forum for personal commentary,
humor, and information on the current state of the industry and
anything else I feel like commenting about. This is a work in progress,
and will hopefully be in a constant state of evolution.</p>
{The following two lines are hyperlinks to other Web pages}
<p><a HREF="whoami.html">Who am I?</a> </p>
<p><a HREF="pogo.html">Pogo Page</a> </p>
{The </body> tag marks the ending of the document body}
</body>
{The </html> tag marks the ending of the HTML document}
</html>
```

N O T E If you are unfamiliar with HTML, check one of the many books available on developing and maintaining Web pages, such as Que Corporation's *Running a Perfect Web Site* (ISBN 0-7897-0210-x). ▓

Within the HTML document, you are primarily interested in finding the links to other pages or files (known as *anchors*) and embedded images. Both of these have simple identifiers that you can look for in the document tags. The anchors use A, and the images use IMG. After you find these tags, you must scan them to find the URL of the various files. Within the anchor tags, HREF= marks the URL of the linked file. Within the image tags, SRC= marks the file. In both of these cases, you extract the URL that follows the equals sign. You will use these URLs to test the links embedded within the Web page.

To build a commercial-quality Web robot, you would want to grab other HTML tags as well—for example, the background image URL that is usually embedded within the opening BODY tag. You would also need to search for and process appropriately several other extensions. You can find most of the various extensions in documentation available on the Netscape Web site at **http://home.netscape.com/assist/net_sites/index.html** (and now that Microsoft has entered the HTML extensions race, you can probably find other extensions documented at Microsoft's Web site at **http://www.microsoft.com/ie/author/htmlspec/html_toc.htm**).

Understanding Basic HTTP

The Hypertext Transfer Protocol (HTTP) is a very simple communications and transaction protocol. There are no states that you need to monitor. An HTTP conversation consists of four actions:

1. Connect to the Web (HTTP) server.
2. Send a command to the server.
3. Receive a response from the server.
4. Disconnect from the server.

In other words, you connect, request, or send something, wait for the response, and then disconnect. It's a simple single-command transaction. To make things even simpler, HTTP has only three basic commands—GET, HEAD, and POST—and some response codes. (Several more commands are documented, but they aren't widely used yet.)

N O T E HTTP is still an emerging standard. The number and nature of available commands are bound to change. The three commands that you examine in this chapter are the basic ones that you are sure to implement on most all HTTP servers that you develop now and into the foreseeable future. ▓

All three HTTP commands use the same basic syntax:

```
command  URI [protocol version]#13#10
```

N O T E In the preceding example (and many to follow), the #13#10 on the end of each line indicates that each of these lines ends with the carriage-return and line-feed characters. In building the Pascal strings, these characters are added to the line as #13#10, so these examples were built using this notation for consistency with the Delphi Pascal language. ▓

URI stands for Uniform Resource Indicator, which is the URL's file or resource specifier portion. You should specify the protocol version as follows:

```
protocol/version
```

Therefore, if your client were using the HTTP 1.0 protocol, it would look like the following:

```
HTTP/1.0
```

For instance, if you want to retrieve the Web page at **http://rampages.onramp.net/ ~davischa/pogo.html**, you would issue the following command to the HTTP server at **rampages.onramp.net**:

```
GET /~davischa/pogo.html HTTP/1.0
```

N O T E The protocol version number does not have to be on the command line with the HTTP commands. The example Web robot application does not include the number with any of the commands that you send to the HTTP servers, because including the protocol version number would cause more servers to return an error condition than return a successful response. This form of the command syntax (including the protocol version) is the "official" version listed in the specification documents, but few servers currently seem to support it. This might change as the specification becomes more standardized. ■

The *GET* Command

The GET command is the primary command that you will use in your robot. The command requests that the HTTP server respond by sending the file or resource specified with the command. Most of the other HTTP commands (which this chapter doesn't cover) are variations on the GET command.

The *HEAD* Command

The HEAD command is like the GET command, only the server returns just the response header with no document body.

The *POST* Command

The POST command returns values to some sort of CGI script. In these commands, the URI that is passed is the name of the CGI script to be executed, and is often followed with one or more variables that the CGI script uses to perform whatever actions it is supposed to enact. For instance, if a Web page asks visitors to sign a guestbook, the submission might look like the following:

```
POST /cgi-bin/signguest?name=Davis+Chapman HTTP/1.0
```

Response Codes

The HTTP response codes are similar to the response codes that other Internet applications use. Each response code consists of three digits and uses the same basic number encoding that you have seen in several other Internet applications. Table 15.1 lists the HTTP response codes.

Table 15.1   The HTTP Command Response Codes

Code	Description
200	Okay. The command succeeded.
201	Created. HTTP issues this code after a POST command creates a new resource. The textual portion of this response gives the new resource's URL.
202	Accepted. The request was accepted for processing, but the processing is not complete.

Code	Description
203	Partial information. This code is a response to a GET command that does not retrieve the entire object.
204	No response. There is no information to send back.
301	Moved. The requested resource has been moved to a new URI.
302	Found. The resource actually exists under a different URL.
303	Method. This response is in discussion only at this time. Until this response code becomes part of the standard, you shouldn't receive the code from any HTTP servers.
304	Not modified. If the client does a conditional GET, specifying an If-Modified-Since condition, this code is returned.
400	Bad request. The request was incorrectly formatted or otherwise not understandable.
401	Unauthorized. The client does not have proper authorization to retrieve the requested file.
402	Payment required. The requested file requires some form of payment for retrieval to be approved.
403	Forbidden. The requested file is forbidden to the client application.
404	Not found. The requested file was not found.
500	Internal error. The HTTP server had an internal error that prevented it from fulfilling the request.
501	Not implemented. This server has not implemented the command that the client issued.
502	Service temporarily overloaded. Too many clients are currently connected to the server, so no more connections are allowed.
503	Gateway time-out. The server connection was not established before the gateway time-out period was reached.

Creating a Web Robot Application

You want your Web robot application to work by first connecting to a specified HTTP server and then getting the page of HTML specified by the user. The robot must parse URLs for the image and anchor links within that document. After getting all these links, the robot must connect to each specified server and request the appropriate resources. If the specified resource exists and is available, the robot should remove that URL from the list of URLs to verify. If the robot cannot verify one of the URLs—either because the server cannot be reached or the specified URI is not available on that server—then you should leave that URL untouched until you can verify it by other means.

The Web robot that you will build enables the user to specify a Web page to retrieve and verify. The robot will retrieve and analyze this Web page to extract all images and links embedded within it. After extracting the links, the robot can connect to each of the specified HTTP servers and request the specified files, removing the URLs from the display after verifying the link. This process leaves the Web robot with only those links that it could not verify in the display list boxes after it finishes. On choosing to verify the specified Web page, the Web robot takes the following steps:

1. Parses the user-entered URL to determine the HTTP server and file to retrieve.

2. Connects to the specified server and requests the specified Web page.

3. On receiving the requested page, parses it to extract the embedded image file and hyperlinked Web page URLs.

4. Disconnects from the server and waits for the user to choose to verify the extracted links.

5. In response to the user clicking the VERIFY button, parses the first image URL into the server and file names, attempts to connect to the specified server, and requests the image file.

6. If the robot succeeds in retrieving the image file, removes the image URL from the list of image files.

7. If the robot cannot connect to the specified server, or cannot retrieve the specified image file, leaves the file name in the list of image files.

8. Repeats the previous three steps until all image files have been tested, then repeats the previous three steps for all the Web page links.

9. After testing all images and links, returns to an idle state, displaying to the user all the unretrieved image files and Web links.

N O T E   In Appendix A, "Internet Applications Command Sets," you can find all the HTTP commands, including those that you use in this application. ▪

In this application, you use the same procedures for looking up the server address and initiating the connection as you used in the previous examples first introduced in Chapters 6 and 8. You should check these chapters for listings and explanations for any procedures and functions not covered in this chapter. Table 15.2 lists the files that you use in this project.

Table 15.2   Web Robot Project Files

File	Description
WROBOT.DPR	The Web robot Delphi project file.
TROBOT.DFM	The Web robot window.
TROBOT.PAS	The Web robot code.
TSOCKETC.PAS	The TSocket WinSock abstraction class (first developed in Chapter 6, and expanded in Chapter 8).

File	Description
NWINSOCK.PAS	The WinSock application program interface (API) definition.

Declaring the Web Robot Command State Table

You must define your state table with constants for each command that you might need—not just for the primary connection, but for the image and link connections. You use these constants to maintain a variable that indicates which command you last issued to the HTTP server, and which action is currently being undertaken. This variable enables you to determine easily the command to which the server is responding, and direct the response message to the appropriate procedure to process that response. Listing 15.1 shows the constant declarations.

Listing 15.1   TROBOT.PAS—the Constant Declarations for the Web Robot Application

```
const
{Constant declarations to represent HTTP commands and actions to be
taken. These constants keep track of the command last issued,
so that you can direct the server's responses to the appropriate
procedure}
  HTTP_NOOP = 0;
  HTTP_CONNECT = 1;
  HTTP_GET = 2;
  HTTP_HEAD = 3;
  HTTP_POST = 4;
  HTTP_LINKCONNECT = 5;
  HTTP_LINKGET = 6;
  HTTP_LINKHEAD = 7;
  HTTP_LINKPOST = 8;
  HTTP_IMGCONNECT = 9;
  HTTP_IMGGET = 10;
  HTTP_IMGHEAD = 11;
  HTTP_IMGPOST = 12;
{User-defined event declarations, for socket events. The first is
used for the primary socket, the second for address lookup notifications)
  UWM_SOCKETEVENT = WM_USER + 500;
  UWM_ADDRSOCKETEVENT = WM_USER + 501;
```

In the variable definitions, notice that you define a second socket that you use to get the image files (see Listing 15.2). You do so to retrieve just enough of the image file to verify that you are receiving an image. After reaching that point, you want to disconnect the socket and move on to something else. This scheme works fine until you need to receive HTML documents through the same socket immediately after disconnecting from an incoming image. Because of the size of most image files, more image data would still arrive on the socket long after you disconnected and connected it to an HTML link site. (When receiving a large amount of data, a socket connection can continue to receive data well after the connection closes. The server sends all this data before receiving notification that the client has been disconnected.) By moving the image retrievals to their own socket, you enable these problems to clear themselves up.

> **Listing 15.2   TROBOT.PAS—Variable Declarations for the Web Robot Application**

```
private
  { Private declarations }
{The primary socket to be used in the connection with the server}
  isConnectionSocket: _SOCKET;
{The secondary socket to be used in retrieving image files}
  isImageSocket: _SOCKET;
{A flag to indicate whether the connection has been made}
  ibConnected: Boolean;
{The command state indicator}
  iiHTTPStatus: Integer;
{The hold buffer for incomplete message lines}
  isHoldBuffer: String;
{The link test state indicator}
  iiTestStatus: Integer;
{The number of the link being tested}
  iiTestNumber: Integer;
{The port to use (if not the default)}
  iiAltPort: Integer;
{The socket event-handler declarations}
  procedure UWMSocketEvent(var Msg: TMessage); message UWM_SOCKETEVENT;
  procedure UWMAddrSocketEvent(var Msg: TMessage); message
                     UWM_ADDRSOCKETEVENT;
public
  { Public declarations }
{The TSocket class declaration}
  NetSocket: _TSocket;
{The receive and temporary buffers}
  ReceiveBuffer: array[0..8192] of Char;
  TempBuffer: array[0..8192] of Char;
```

Other noteworthy variables in Listing 15.2 include the iiTestStatus variable, which maintains the link test status that is the goal of the current socket connection. The variables also include a counter that keeps track of which link in the list is the current link being tested. Finally, there is the alternative port variable, iiAltPort. For URLs that specify a port number with the host address, you must parse the port and hold it until you try to connect to the server. You cannot leave the port on the host name while looking up the host address, because that would cause the address lookup to fail.

Looking Up the Host Address and Connecting to the HTTP Server

The ProcessHostLookup procedure looks much the same as in previous examples in Chapters 6 and 10 (see Listing 15.3). The difference is in the logic that it uses to determine which of the two sockets to use when connecting to the host. The procedure also differs in that it now checks the port number that the alternative port variable currently holds. If that variable holds the port number zero, ProcessHostLookup replaces that number with the default HTTP port of 80. This differs from the previous examples, in which you always assumed that the default port was being used for each of the services to which you were connecting.

Listing 15.3   TROBOT.PAS—the *ProcessHostLookup* Procedure Looks Up the Host Address

```
procedure TWebRobot.ProcessHostLookup;
begin
   {Update the display to reflect that you are attempting to connect
   to the server}
   stStatus.Caption := 'Connecting To Host';
   stStatus.Update;
   {Check to see whether you  need to connect
    to an alternative service port}
   if (iiAltPort = 0) then
      iiAltPort := 80;
   {Call ProcessHostAddress (first written in Chapter 6) to reformat
   the received address so that you can connect}
   if (NetSocket.ProcessHostAddress = TRUE) then
   begin
      {Call OpenSocketConnection (First developed in Chapter 6) to
      create a new socket and open a connection to the host. This
      triggers the socket event when the connection has been
      established}
      if (iiTestStatus = HTTP_IMGCONNECT) then
         isImageSocket := NetSocket.OpenSocketConnection(Handle,
                        UWM_SOCKETEVENT, SKT_CONNECTTOHOST, iiAltPort)
      else
         isConnectionSocket := NetSocket.OpenSocketConnection(Handle,
                        UWM_SOCKETEVENT, SKT_CONNECTTOHOST, iiAltPort);
   end
   else
   begin
      {The host address was not found, so inform the user}
      stStatus.Caption := 'Cannot Find Host Address';
      stStatus.Update;
   end;
end;
```

The ProcessHostConnect procedure changes slightly from previous versions used in other examples (see Listing 15.4). Instead of looking for an incoming welcome message from the server, you instead go straight to the ProcessHostWelcome procedure, where you issue your one command for this session.

Listing 15.4 TROBOT.PAS—the *ProcessHostConnect* Procedure Passes Control to the *ProcessHostWelcome* Procedure after the Connection Has Been Established

```
procedure TWebRobot.ProcessHostConnect;
begin
  {Update the display to reflect that you are connected}
  stStatus.Caption := 'Receiving Welcome From Host';
  stStatus.Update;
  {Update the command state flags}
  iiHTTPStatus := HTTP_CONNECT;
  stState.Caption := 'HTTP_CONNECT';
  stState.Update;
  {Call ProcessHostWelcome to send the file or page request}
  ProcesshostWelcome;
end;
```

Requesting the Web Page or Image File

The ProcessHostWelcome procedure is probably longer and more convoluted than it needs to be, but it helps illustrate what the robot must do next (see Listing 15.5). This procedure determines which mode the application is in—whether the robot is retrieving the initial HTML page, retrieving an image file, or verifying an HTML page link. In the first and last of these cases, you must parse the file and path sections from the URL. If no file or path name follows the host name, you substitute the file name index.html.

> **N O T E** On the HTML pages with which this application was tested, some servers worked if the file name was index.html, and others worked if the file name was default.html. According to the HTTP specifications, you should be able to pass the server the entire URI (including the host name portion) and expect the server to return the appropriate HTML page. Unfortunately, this does not work as advertised when you use HTTP 0.9-formatted commands (as you are doing in this application). If you send the entire URI, the server returns an error message. To retrieve the correct file, you have to send only the path and file name portion of the URI. Therefore, you have to specify the default HTML file name. To get this to work with every Web site, you have to implement an iterative retrieval that tests both of these Web page names along with the variations that use the .HTM extensions (for NT and Windows Web servers) along with any other default page names that might be configured into the many Web servers on the Internet. Because this iterative testing is not built in to this example application, several URLs fail because of the difference in the default page name. ◼

Listing 15.5 TROBOT.PAS—the *ProcessHostWelcome* Procedure Determines the Robot Application's Mode and Sends the Appropriate Request to the Server

```
procedure TWebRobot.ProcessHostWelcome;
var
  lsWelcomeMsg, lsRetnCode: String;
  lsResource: String;
```

```
                liURIStart, liURIEnd: Integer;
                liNumTrys, liAmtReceived: LongInt;
begin
    {You are connected, there is no response code to check}
    ibConnected := TRUE;
    {Set the command status flag to NOOP}
    iiHTTPStatus := HTTP_NOOP;
    {Display the response message, none in this case}
    stStatus.Caption := lsWelcomeMsg;
    stStatus.Update;
    {Are you connected?}
    if ibConnected then
    begin
        {What is your test status?, NOOP (getting the initial page), IMAGE
        (testing image URLs), or LINK (test Web links)}
        case iiTestStatus of
            { NOOP (getting the initial page)}
            HTTP_NOOP:
            begin
                {Set the command status flag to indicate that you sent a GET}
                iiHTTPStatus := HTTP_GET;
                stState.Caption := 'HTTP_GET';
                stState.Update;
                {Parse the user-entered URL;you want the file name}
                lsResource := sleURL.Text;
                liURIStart := Pos(':/', lsResource);
                if (liURIStart > 0) then
                    lsResource := Copy(lsResource, (liURIStart + 3),
                                Length(lsResource));
                liURIEnd := Pos('/', lsResource);
                if (liURIEnd = Length(lsResource)) then
                    lsResource := '/index.htm'
                else
                    lsResource := Copy(lsResource, liURIEnd,
                            Length(lsResource));
                {Double-check the connection}
                if NetSocket.IsSocketConnected(isConnectionSocket) then
                begin
                    {Update the display to reflect what you are doing}
                    stStatus.Caption := 'Requesting Web Page';
                    stStatus.Update;
                    {Send the GET command to the server}
                    NetSocket.SocketSend(isConnectionSocket, handle,
                                UWM_SOCKETEVENT,
                                    'GET ' + lsResource, SKT_SENDPACKET);
                    {Clear the receive buffer}
                    ClearBuffer(ReceiveBuffer, 8192);
                end
                else
                begin
```

continues

Listing 15.5 Continued

```
                {You are not connected, so tell the user}
                stStatus.Caption := 'Not Connected';
                stStatus.Update;
            end;
        end;
        {LINK (test Web links)}
        HTTP_LINKCONNECT:
        begin
            {Set the command status flag to indicate that you sent a GET
            on a link test}
            iiHTTPStatus := HTTP_LINKGET;
            stState.Caption := 'HTTP_LINKGET';
            stState.Update;
            {Parse the link URL; you want the file name}
            lsResource := lbLinks.Items[iiTestNumber];
            liURIStart := Pos(':/', lsResource);
            if (liURIStart > 0) then
            begin
                lsResource := Copy(lsResource, (liURIStart + 3),
                            Length(lsResource));
                liURIEnd := Pos('/', lsResource);
                if (liURIEnd > 0) then
                begin
                    if (liURIEnd = Length(lsResource)) then
                        lsResource := '/index.html'
                    else
                        lsResource := Copy(lsResource, liURIEnd,
                                        Length(lsResource));
                end
                else
                    lsResource := '/index.html'
            end;
            {Double-check the connection}
            if NetSocket.IsSocketConnected(isConnectionSocket) then
            begin
                {Update the display to reflect what you are doing}
                stStatus.Caption := 'Requesting Web Page';
                stStatus.Update;
                {Is it a CGI request? You don't test those.}
                if (Pos('cgi', lsResource) = 0) then
                begin
                    {Send the GET command to the server}
                    NetSocket.SocketSend(isConnectionSocket, handle,
                                UWM_SOCKETEVENT,
                                'GET ' + lsResource, SKT_SENDPACKET);
                    {Clear the receive buffer}
                    ClearBuffer(ReceiveBuffer, 8192);
                    {You are running in synchronous mode now. You need
                    to loop several times to ensure that the connection
                    has sufficient time to retrieve the link page}
                    liNumTrys := 0;
                    while ((recv(isConnectionSocket, ReceiveBuffer,
                                    8192, 0) < 1) and
                            (liNumTrys < 100000)) do
```

```
                    Inc(liNumTrys);
                  {If you didn't receive anything, place a 'Not Found'
                   page in the receive buffer}
                  if ((liNumTrys = 100000) and
                         (StrLen(ReceiveBuffer) = 0)) then
                    StrPCopy(ReceiveBuffer, '<TITLE>Not Found</TITLE>');
              end;
          end
          else
          begin
              {You are not connected, so tell the user.
               Place a 'Not Found' page in the receive buffer}
              stStatus.Caption := 'Not Connected';
              stStatus.Update;
              StrPCopy(ReceiveBuffer, '<TITLE>Not Found</TITLE>');
          end;
          {Call the ProcessHostLinkGet procedure to analyze the
          received page}
          ProcessHostLinkGet;
       end;
       {IMAGE (testing image URLs)}
       HTTP_IMGCONNECT:
       begin
          {Set the command status flag to indicate that you sent a GET
          on an image link test}
          iiHTTPStatus := HTTP_IMGGET;
          stState.Caption := 'HTTP_IMGGET';
          stState.Update;
          {Parse the link URL; you want the file name}
          lsResource := lbImages.Items[iiTestNumber];
          liURIStart := Pos(':/', lsResource);
          if (liURIStart > 0) then
          begin
              lsResource := Copy(lsResource, (liURIStart + 3),
                                   Length(lsResource));
              liURIEnd := Pos('/', lsResource);
              if (liURIEnd = Length(lsResource)) then
                  lsResource := 'default.htm'
              else
                  lsResource := Copy(lsResource, (liURIEnd + 1),
                               Length(lsResource));
          end;
          {Double-check the connection}
          if NetSocket.IsSocketConnected(isImageSocket) then
          begin
              {Update the display to reflect what you are doing}
              stStatus.Caption := 'Requesting Image';
              stStatus.Update;
              {Send the GET command to the server}
              NetSocket.SocketSend(isImageSocket, handle,
                UWM_SOCKETEVENT, 'GET ' + lsResource, SKT_SENDPACKET);
              {Clear the receive buffer}
              ClearBuffer(ReceiveBuffer, 8192);
```

continues

Listing 15.5   Continued

```
              {You are running in synchronous mode now. You must
                 loop several times to ensure that you receive the
                 entire image}
              while (recv(isImageSocket, ReceiveBuffer,
                  8192, 0) < 1) do;
          end
          else
          begin
            {You are not connected, so tell the user.
             Place a 'Not Found' page in the receive buffer}
            stStatus.Caption := 'Not Connected';
            stStatus.Update;
            StrPCopy(ReceiveBuffer, '<TITLE>Not Found</TITLE>');
          end;
          {Call the ProcessHostLinkGet procedure to analyze the
          received page}
          ProcessHostLinkGet
        end;
      end;
    end;
  end;
```

After parsing the URL's file and path, `ProcessHostWelcome` sends the GET command to the server by using the appropriate socket. Next, the procedure prepares to receive the response from the server. If you are receiving the original HTML page, you do so asynchronously. If you are testing a link, you do so synchronously.

You perform the link tests synchronously so that after disconnecting from a server, you no longer receive data buffers from that connection. If you were to use an asynchronous connection, you might still receive data from the server long after disconnecting.

If `ProcessHostWelcome` does not receive any data, or doesn't have a connection to the server, the procedure fills the data buffer with a header section that indicates that the robot did not find the link. This enables you to send the failure through the same channel as the successful tests, so that you can implement a single routine for controlling the URLs.

Extracting HTML Tags from a Web Page

Because you are examining the original HTML page by extracting the embedded links, you need to extract the HTML tags easily so that you can examine each individually. To do so, you implement a variation of the `GetNextLine` function. This version, `GetHTMLReference()`, parses the next HTML tag from within the data buffer, using the tag to populate the target buffer (see Listing 15.6). The function then returns TRUE or FALSE to indicate whether it returned a complete tag or whether you should find the remainder of the tag in the next buffer full that you receive from the server. This necessitates a different version of this same function that returns only the remaining portion of the current tag. (You could do so by adding another parameter to the first function.)

**Listing 15.6   TROBOT.PAS—the *GetHTMLReference()* Functions Get HTML
Tags from the Buffer**

```pascal
function TWebRobot.GetHTMLReference(TargetString, SourceString: PChar):
            Boolean;
var
   liCurPos: Integer;
   liCurTargetPos: Integer;
   liCarRetnPos: Integer;
   liCopyPos: Integer;
begin
   {Initialize the current position marker to 0}
   liCurPos := 0;
   {Scan the SourceString buffer, looking for the beginning of an HTML
   tag (marked by the left angle character <)}
   while ((SourceString[liCurPos] <> '<') and
          (SourceString[liCurPos] <> Char(0))) do
      Inc(liCurPos);
   {Initialize the target string position marker to 0}
   liCurTargetPos := 0;
   {Copy characters from the source string to the target string until
   either the end of the tag or the end of the source string is found}
   while ((SourceString[liCurPos] <> '>') and
          (SourceString[liCurPos] <> Char(0))) do
   begin
      if (SourceString[liCurPos] <> '<') then
      begin
         TargetString[liCurTargetPos] := SourceString[liCurPos];
         Inc(liCurPos);
         Inc(liCurTargetPos);
      end
      else
         Inc(liCurPos);
   end;
   {Mark the end of the tag with a null character in the target string}
   TargetString[liCurTargetPos] := Char(0);
   {Move the remaining text in the source string forward, so that the
   first character after the current HTML tag is the first character
   in the string; return TRUE if a complete HTML tag was found, return
   FALSE if an incomplete HTML tag was found}
   if (SourceString[liCurPos] = '>') then
   begin
      liCopyPos := 0;
      liCurPos := (liCurPos + 1);
      while (SourceString[liCurPos] <> Char(0)) do
      begin
         SourceString[liCopyPos] := SourceString[liCurPos];
         Inc(liCurPos);
         Inc(liCopyPos);
      end;
      SourceString[liCopyPos] := Char(0);
      GetHTMLReference := TRUE;
   end
   else
```

continues

Listing 15.6   Continued

```pascal
   begin
      SourceString[0] := Char(0);
      GetHTMLReference := FALSE;
   end;
end;

{This function does the same thing as the previous function, only it
assumes that the first character is in the middle of an HTML tag and
only looks for the end of the tag}
function TWebRobot.GetRestHTMLReference(TargetString,
                                  SourceString: PChar): Boolean;
var
   liCurPos: Integer;
   liCurTargetPos: Integer;
   liCarRetnPos: Integer;
   liCopyPos: Integer;
begin
   {Initialize the current position marker to 0}
   {Initialize the target string position marker to 0}
   liCurPos := 0;
   liCurTargetPos := 0;
   {Copy characters from the source string to the target string until
   either the end of the tag or the end of the source string is found}
   while ((SourceString[liCurPos] <> '>') and
          (SourceString[liCurPos] <> Char(0))) do
   begin
      TargetString[liCurTargetPos] := SourceString[liCurPos];
      Inc(liCurPos);
      Inc(liCurTargetPos);
   end;
   {Mark the end of the tag with a null character in the target string}
   TargetString[liCurTargetPos] := Char(0);
   {Move the remaining text in the source string forward, so that the
   first character after the current HTML tag is the first character
   in the string; return TRUE if a complete HTML tag was found, return
   FALSE if an incomplete HTML tag was found}
   if (SourceString[liCurPos] = '>') then
   begin
      liCopyPos := 0;
      liCurPos := (liCurPos + 1);
      while (SourceString[liCurPos] <> Char(0)) do
      begin
         SourceString[liCopyPos] := SourceString[liCurPos];
         Inc(liCurPos);
         Inc(liCopyPos);
      end;
      SourceString[liCopyPos] := Char(0);
      GetRestHTMLReference := TRUE;
   end
   else
   begin
```

```
      SourceString[0] := Char(0);
      GetRestHTMLReference := FALSE;
    end;
end;
```

Analyzing the Retrieved Web Page

After receiving the original HTML page, you must search it for the embedded links and images. To do so, you establish a loop on the `GetHTMLReference()` function. As each tag returns, you can compare it to the tags in which you are interested:

- `</HTML>` or `</BODY>` marks the end of the page.
- `<A ...>` contains a link to another page (or possibly a link to another position on this page, although you aren't checking for that in this example application).
- `<IMG ...>` contains an image.

If you find one of the first two tags (`</HTML>` or `</BODY>`), you finish your parsing because you have reached the end of the HTML page. If you find the anchor tag (`<A ...>`) or the image tag (`<IMG ...>`), you look for the URL contained within each and add the URL to the appropriate list box.

If you reach the end of the data buffer before reaching the end of the page, you look for the next buffer of HTML to arrive. If you reach the end of the HTML page, you can place the application into idle mode so that the user can determine what to do next.

Listing 15.7 shows `ProcessHostGet`, the procedure that searches the HTML page for embedded links.

N O T E The current HTML tag documentation mentions several tags for which this routine should search, such as the parameter for the BODY tag that specifies a background image. However, `ProcessHostGet` doesn't search for all the possible tags because the two tags that you are looking for (hyperlink and image tags) provide sufficient examples to demonstrate the HTML parsing. Also, HTML tags are being added fairly quickly (as quickly as the company adding them can implement them into the latest browser), so there is no way to anticipate all the potential tags that might be in use by the time this book reaches the shelves. You can find the complete HTML specification at the World Wide Web Consortium page at **http://www.w3.org/**. ■

Listing 15.7 TROBOT.PAS—the *ProcessHostGet* Procedure Searches the HTML Page for Embedded Links

```
procedure TWebRobot.ProcessHostGet;
var
    lbComplete: Boolean;
    lsCurRef: String;
    liAddressStart, liAddressEnd: Integer;
begin
```

continues

Listing 15.7   Continued

```
{Are you connected?}
if (ibConnected) then
begin
   {Convert the received string to a Pascal string}
   lsCurRef := StrPas(ReceiveBuffer);
   {Did you get a NOT FOUND response?}
   if (Copy(lsCurRef, 1, 16) = '<TITLE>Not Found') then
   begin
      {Inform the user and shut down the connection}
      stStatus.Caption := 'URL Not Found';
      stStatus.Update;
      shutdown(isConnectionSocket, 0);
      NetSocket.CloseSocketConnection(isConnectionSocket);
      ibConnected := FALSE;
   end
   else
   begin
      {You did not receive a NOT FOUND, so begin parsing it to
      extract the tags in which you are interested}
      lbComplete := FALSE;
      {Is there anything in the hold buffer?}
      if (Length(isHoldBuffer) > 0) then
      begin
         {Yes, it must be an incomplete tag, so get the rest
         of the tag}
         if GetRestHTMLReference(TempBuffer, ReceiveBuffer) then
         begin
            {Add the two tag parts together}
            lsCurRef := isHoldBuffer + StrPas(TempBuffer);
            {Empty the hold buffer}
            isHoldBuffer := '';
            {Do you have either the BODY or HTML end tag? If so, you
            have reached the end of the page}
            if (lsCurRef = '/BODY') then
               lbComplete := TRUE;
            if (lsCurRef = '/HTML') then
               lbComplete := TRUE;
            {Did you find a hyperlink?}
            if (Copy(lsCurRef, 1, 6) = 'A HREF') then
            begin
               {Yes, extract the URL and add it to the display}
               liAddressStart := Pos('=', lsCurRef);
               if (liAddressStart > 0) then
               begin
                  lsCurRef := Copy(lsCurRef, (liAddressStart + 1),
                                   Length(lsCurRef));
                  if (Pos('"', lsCurRef) = 1) then
                     lsCurRef := Copy(lsCurRef, 2, Length(lsCurRef));
                  if (Pos('"', lsCurRef) > 0) then
                     lsCurRef := Copy(lsCurRef, 1,
                                      (Length(lsCurRef) - 1));
               end;
               lbLinks.Items.Add(lsCurRef);
            end;
```

```pascal
      {Did you find an image?}
      if (Copy(lsCurRef, 1, 3) = 'IMG') then
      begin
         {Yes, extract the URL and add it to the display}
         liAddressStart := Pos('SRC=', lsCurRef);
         if (liAddressStart > 0) then
         begin
            lsCurRef := Copy(lsCurRef, (liAddressStart + 5),
                             Length(lsCurRef));
            liAddressEnd := Pos('"', lsCurRef);
            if (liAddressEnd > 0) then
               lsCurRef := Copy(lsCurRef, 1, (liAddressEnd - 1))
            else
               lsCurRef := Copy(lsCurRef, 1,
                                (Length(lsCurRef) - 1));
         end;
         lbImages.Items.Add(lsCurRef);
      end;
   end;
end;
{Clear the Temp Buffer}
ClearBuffer(TempBuffer, StrLen(TempBuffer));
{Loop as long as you find additional tags and haven't
reached the end of the page}
while (GetHTMLReference(TempBuffer, ReceiveBuffer) and
       (not lbComplete)) do
begin
   {Convert the extracted tag to a Pascal string}
   lsCurRef := StrPas(TempBuffer);
   {Do you have the HTML end tag? If so, you
   have reached the end of the page}
   if (lsCurRef = '/HTML') then
      lbComplete := TRUE;
   {Did you find a hyperlink?}
   if (Copy(lsCurRef, 1, 6) = 'A HREF') then
   begin
      {Yes, extract the URL and add it to the display}
      liAddressStart := Pos('=', lsCurRef);
      if (liAddressStart > 0) then
      begin
         lsCurRef := Copy(lsCurRef, (liAddressStart + 1),
                          Length(lsCurRef));
         if (Pos('"', lsCurRef) = 1) then
          lsCurRef := Copy(lsCurRef, 2, Length(lsCurRef));
         if (Pos('"', lsCurRef) > 0) then
          lsCurRef := Copy(lsCurRef, 1, (Length(lsCurRef) - 1));
      end;
      lbLinks.Items.Add(lsCurRef);
   end;
   {Did you find an image?}
   if (Copy(lsCurRef, 1, 3) = 'IMG') then
   begin
      {Yes, extract the URL and add it to the display}
      liAddressStart := Pos('SRC=', lsCurRef);
```

continues

Listing 15.7 Continued

```
                if (liAddressStart > 0) then
                begin
                  lsCurRef := Copy(lsCurRef, (liAddressStart + 5),
                                        Length(lsCurRef));
                  liAddressEnd := Pos('"', lsCurRef);
                  if (liAddressEnd > 0) then
                    lsCurRef := Copy(lsCurRef, 1, (liAddressEnd - 1))
                  else
                    lsCurRef := Copy(lsCurRef, 1, (Length(lsCurRef) - 1));
                end;
                lbImages.Items.Add(lsCurRef);
              end;
              {Clear the Temp Buffer}
              ClearBuffer(TempBuffer, StrLen(TempBuffer));
            end;
            {Have you reached the end of the page?}
            if (not lbComplete) then
            begin
              {No, place the remaining partial tag into the hold buffer}
              if (StrLen(TempBuffer) > 0) then
                isHoldBuffer := StrPas(TempBuffer);
              {Clear the receive buffer}
              ClearBuffer(ReceiveBuffer, 8192);
            end
            else
            begin
              {Yes, inform the user, shut down the connection, and change
              the default button to the TEST button}
              stStatus.Caption := 'Finished Retrieving';
              stStatus.Update;
              shutdown(isConnectionSocket, 0);
              NetSocket.CloseSocketConnection(isConnectionSocket);
              cbConnect.Default := FALSE;
              cbTest.Default := TRUE;
              ibConnected := FALSE;
            end;
        end;
      end;
  end;
```

N O T E Notice that you are checking for an HTML page rather than a response code to determine whether the URL is valid, because this application uses HTTP 0.9 format commands. The response codes are returned only for HTTP 1.0 or greater formatted commands. For a discussion on the differences between HTTP 0.9 and HTTP 1.0, see Chapter 16, "Building a Web Server with Delphi." ■

Directing the HTTP Server Responses to the Appropriate Procedure

The `ProcessHostReceive` procedure is much smaller than in previous examples in Chapters 6, 8, 9, and 10 (see Listing 15.8). You need to call only a few variations on the `GET` command (based on what is being requested) and the `CONNECT` procedure.

Listing 15.8   TROBOT.PAS—the *ProcessHostReceive* Procedure Checks the Conversation's State and Initiates the Appropriate Response

```
procedure TWebRobot.ProcessHostReceive;
var
   lsRetnStr: String;
   liCarRetnPos: Integer;
begin
   try
      {Receive the incoming data}
      liCarRetnPos := recv(isConnectionSocket, ReceiveBuffer, 8192, 0);
      ReceiveBuffer[liCarRetnPos] := Char(0);
      {You have received an FD_READ event, so check whether you
      received anything}
      if (ReceiveBuffer[0] = Char(0)) then
      begin
         {Clear the receive buffer}
         ClearBuffer(ReceiveBuffer, 8192);
      end
      else
      begin
         {You received data, so check which command you issued and
         call the appropriate procedure}
         case iiHTTPStatus of
            HTTP_NOOP:;
            HTTP_CONNECT: ProcessHostWelcome;
            HTTP_GET: ProcessHostGet;
            HTTP_LINKGET: ProcessHostLinkGet;
            HTTP_IMGGET: ProcessHostLinkGet;
         end;
      end;
   except
      {Clear the receive buffer}
      ClearBuffer(ReceiveBuffer, 8192);
   end;
end;
```

Initiating the Connection

The connect command button script is a little more involved than its earlier versions (see Listing 15.9). In this version, you take the URL that the user entered and parse the host name and port. If the URL specifies a port, you must place the specified value into the alternative port variable; otherwise, you must specifically set the port variable to zero (so that the default port of 80 is used). After parsing the host name, you can look up the host address and connect using the same procedures as you used in previous examples in Chapters 6, 8, 9, and 10 by passing that name to the host address lookup function.

Listing 15.9   TROBOT.PAS—the *cbConnectClick()* Procedure Parses the User-Entered URL and Initiates the Host Address Lookup So That a Connection Can Be Established

```
procedure TWebRobot.cbConnectClick(Sender: TObject);
var
   lsHostAddress: String;
   liNameStart, liNameEnd: Integer;
begin
   {Make sure the URL TEdit control is not blank.}
   if (Length(sleURL.Text) > 0) then
   begin
      {Parse the URL to extract the host name}
      lsHostAddress := sleURL.text;
      stURL.Caption := lsHostAddress;
      liNameStart := Pos(':/', lsHostAddress);
      if (liNameStart > 0) then
      begin
         lsHostAddress := Copy(lsHostAddress, (liNameStart + 3),
                                           Length(lsHostAddress));
         liNameEnd := Pos('/', lsHostAddress);
         if (liNameEnd > 0) then
            lsHostAddress := Copy(lsHostAddress, 1, (liNameEnd - 1));
         {Check for an alternative TCP service port}
         liNameEnd := Pos(':', lsHostAddress);
         iiAltPort := 0;
         if (liNameEnd > 0) then
         begin
            iiAltPort := StrToInt(Copy(lsHostAddress, (liNameEnd + 1),
                                        Length(lsHostAddress)));
            lsHostAddress := Copy(lsHostAddress, 1, (liNameEnd - 1));
         end;
      end;
      {Clear the image and link list boxes}
      lbImages.Clear;
      lbLinks.Clear;
      {Set the status display and command status flag to indicate that
      the host address is being looked up}
      stStatus.Caption := 'Looking Up Host Address';
      stStatus.Update;
      iiHTTPStatus := HTTP_CONNECT;
      stState.Caption := 'HTTP_CONNECT';
      stState.Update;
      {Use the GetHostAddress procedure to look up the address of the
      server. Chapter 6 covers this procedure.}
      NetSocket.GetHostAddress(Handle, UWM_ADDRSOCKETEVENT,
            lsHostAddress, SKT_GETHOSTADDR);
   end;
end;
```

Figure 15.1 shows the Web robot after parsing all the links from the specified HTML page.

FIG. 15.1

The Web robot displaying all the links parsed from the specified HTML page.

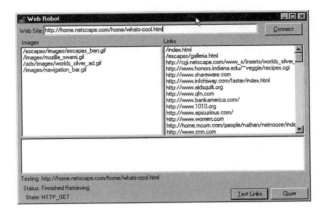

Initiating the Link Verification

You must perform similar URL parsing for the URLs to be tested. You must consider a few differences between these URLs and the original Web page URL that the user entered. If a link or image URL does not include the protocol or host name portions of the URL, you use the protocol and host name of the HTML page in which this URL is embedded. Also, if the URL does not begin with a forward slash (/), you use the current HTML page's path. You must consider all of this when parsing the test link URLs. You first test the image links. If you have no images to test, you start by testing the anchor links. Listing 15.10 shows cbTestClick(), the procedure that begins to test these link URLS.

Listing 15.10   TROBOT.PAS—the *cbTestClick()* Procedure Begins To Test the Link URLs

```
procedure TWebRobot.cbTestClick(Sender: TObject);
var
    lsHostAddress: String;
    liNameStart, liNameEnd: Integer;
begin
    {Initialize the number of links tested}
    iiTestNumber := 0;
    {Are there any images to test?}
    if (lbImages.Items.Count > 0) then
    begin
        {Yes, get the first image URL and parse it to get the host address}
        iiTestStatus := HTTP_IMGCONNECT;
        lsHostAddress := lbImages.Items[0];
        stURL.Caption := lsHostAddress;
        {Is it a complete URL?}
        if (Pos('://', lsHostAddress) = 0) then
        begin
```

continues

Listing 15.10   Continued

```
            {No, get the user-entered URL}
            lsHostAddress := sleURL.text;
        end;
    end
    else
    begin
        {There are no images. Are there any hyperlinks to test?}
        if (lbLinks.Items.Count > 0) then
        begin
            {Yes, get the first link URL and parse it to get the host
            address}
            iiTestStatus := HTTP_LINKCONNECT;
            lsHostAddress := lbLinks.Items[0];
            stURL.Caption := lsHostAddress;
            {Is it a complete URL?}
            if (Pos('://', lsHostAddress) = 0) then
            begin
                {No, get the user-entered URL}
                lsHostAddress := sleURL.text;
            end;
        end;
    end;
    {Do you have a URL to connect to?}
    if (Length(lsHostAddress) > 0) then
    begin
        {Yes, parse the host name and TCP port}
        liNameStart := Pos(':/', lsHostAddress);
        if (liNameStart > 0) then
        begin
            lsHostAddress := Copy(lsHostAddress, (liNameStart + 3),
                                          Length(lsHostAddress));
            liNameEnd := Pos('/', lsHostAddress);
            if (liNameEnd > 0) then
                lsHostAddress := Copy(lsHostAddress, 1, (liNameEnd - 1));
            liNameEnd := Pos(':', lsHostAddress);
            iiAltPort := 0;
            if (liNameEnd > 0) then
            begin
                iiAltPort := StrToInt(Copy(lsHostAddress, (liNameEnd + 1),
                                      Length(lsHostAddress)));
                lsHostAddress := Copy(lsHostAddress, 1, (liNameEnd - 1));
            end;
        end;
        {Set the status display and command status flag to indicate that
        the host address is being looked up}
        stStatus.Caption := 'Looking Up Host Address';
        stStatus.Update;
        iiHTTPStatus := HTTP_CONNECT;
        stState.Caption := 'HTTP_CONNECT';
        stState.Update;
        {Use the GetHostAddress procedure to look up the address of the
        server. Chapter 6 covers this procedure.}
```

```
      NetSocket.GetHostAddress(Handle, UWM_ADDRSOCKETEVENT,
           lsHostAddress, SKT_GETHOSTADDR);
   end;
end;
```

Verifying the Link That You Are Testing

After receiving a buffer full of data from the link that you are currently testing, you must examine the data and check whether the link is valid. The ProcessHostLinkGet procedure starts by examining whether the first few characters indicate that the link was not found or is invalid (see Listing 15.11). If so, the procedure moves to the next link. If the data is valid, you send it to the display window, so that the user can view a sampling of the page that you just retrieved. ProcessHostLinkGet removes the URL from the list box and moves on to the next URL, at which the procedure starts parsing the URL all over again to get the host address.

Listing 15.11   TROBOT.PAS—the *ProcessHostLinkGet* Procedure Checks Whether a Link Is Valid

```
procedure TWebRobot.ProcessHostLinkGet;
var
   lbComplete: Boolean;
   lsCurRef: String;
   lsHostAddress: String;
   liAddressStart, liAddressEnd: Integer;
   liNameStart, liNameEnd: Integer;
begin
   {Are you connected?}
   if (ibConnected) then
   begin
      {Initialize the complete flag to FALSE}
      lbComplete := FALSE;
      ibConnected := FALSE;
      {Are you testing a link or an image?}
      case iiHTTPStatus of
         {You are testing a link}
         HTTP_LINKGET:
         begin
            {Check the initial HTML to verify that you have a valid page}
            lsCurRef := StrPas(ReceiveBuffer);
            if (((Copy(lsCurRef, 1, 14) <> '<TITLE>Invalid') and
               (Copy(lsCurRef, 1, 16) <> '<TITLE>Not Found')) and
               (Pos('Not Found', lsCurRef) = 0)) then
            begin
               {You have a valid page, so remove this link
                from the list box}
               lbLinks.Items.Delete(iiTestNumber);
               lbLinks.Refresh;
               {Decrement the test index number, so that once you
                increment, you return to the same line in the list
                box}
```

continues

Listing 15.11   Continued

```
                Dec(iiTestNumber);
                {Display to the user the page's first few lines}
                mleHTML.Clear;
                mleHTML.Lines.Add(Copy(lsCurRef, 1, 200));
                mleHTML.Refresh;
            end;
            {Are there any untested links remaining?}
            if (lbLinks.Items.Count > (iiTestNumber + 1)) then
            begin
                {Increment the test index number}
                Inc(iiTestNumber);
                {Get the next link URL and parse it to get the host
                address}
                iiTestStatus := HTTP_LINKCONNECT;
                lsHostAddress := lbLinks.Items[iiTestNumber];
                stURL.Caption := lsHostAddress;
                {Is it a complete URL?}
                if (Pos('://', lsHostAddress) = 0) then
                begin
                    {No, get the user-entered URL}
                    lsHostAddress := sleURL.text;
                end;
            end
            else
                {No more links to test}
                lbComplete := TRUE;
            {Turn off all asynchronous behavior}
            WSAAsyncSelect(isConnectionSocket, handle, 0, 0);
            {Continue receiving data until no more is received}
            while (recv(isConnectionSocket, ReceiveBuffer,
                                 8192, 0) > 0) do;
            {Shut down the connection}
            shutdown(isConnectionSocket, 0);
            NetSocket.CloseSocketConnection(isConnectionSocket);
            isConnectionSocket := INVALID_SOCKET;
        end;
        {You are testing an image}
        HTTP_IMGGET:
        begin
            {Check for the beginnings of an HTML tag to see whether
             you are receiving a page rather than an image}
            if (ReceiveBuffer[0] <> '<') then
            begin
                {You have a valid image;
                 remove this URL from the list box}
                lbImages.Items.Delete(iiTestNumber);
                lbImages.Refresh;
                {Decrement the test index number, so that after you
                increment, you return to the same line in the list
                box}
                Dec(iiTestNumber);
                {Display to the user the first few bytes}
                lsCurRef := StrPas(ReceiveBuffer);
```

```
        mleHTML.Clear;
        mleHTML.Lines.Add(lsCurRef);
        mleHTML.Refresh;
    end;
    {Are there any untested images remaining?}
    if (lbImages.Items.Count > (iiTestNumber + 1)) then
    begin
        {Increment the test index number}
        Inc(iiTestNumber);
        {Get the next image URL and parse it to get the host
        address}
        iiTestStatus := HTTP_IMGCONNECT;
        lsHostAddress := lbImages.Items[iiTestNumber];
        stURL.Caption := lsHostAddress;
        {Is it a complete URL?}
        if (Pos('://', lsHostAddress) = 0) then
        begin
            {No, get the user-entered URL}
            lsHostAddress := sleURL.text;
        end;
    end
    else
    begin
        {No more images to test, are there any links?}
        if (lbLinks.Items.Count > 0) then
        begin
            {Yes, get the first link URL and parse it to get the
            host address}
            iiTestStatus := HTTP_LINKCONNECT;
            iiTestNumber := 0;
            lsHostAddress := lbLinks.Items[0];
            stURL.Caption := lsHostAddress;
            {Is it a complete URL?}
            if (Pos('://', lsHostAddress) = 0) then
            begin
                {No, get the user-entered URL}
                lsHostAddress := sleURL.text;
            end;
        end
        else
            {No more links to test}
            lbComplete := TRUE;
    end;
    {Turn off all asynchronous behavior}
    WSAAsyncSelect(isImageSocket, handle, 0, 0);
    {Continue receiving data until no more is received}
    while (recv(isImageSocket, ReceiveBuffer, 8192, 0) > 0) do;
    {Shut down the connection}
    shutdown(isImageSocket, 0);
    NetSocket.CloseSocketConnection(isImageSocket);
    isImageSocket := INVALID_SOCKET;
    end;
end;
```

continues

Listing 15.11 Continued

```
{Have you tested all links and images?}
if (not lbComplete) then
begin
   {No, parse the host name from the next to be tested}
   if (Length(lsHostAddress) > 0) then
   begin
      liNameStart := Pos(':/', lsHostAddress);
      if (liNameStart > 0) then
      begin
         lsHostAddress := Copy(lsHostAddress, (liNameStart + 3),
                                     Length(lsHostAddress));
         liNameEnd := Pos('/', lsHostAddress);
         if (liNameEnd > 0) then
            lsHostAddress := Copy(lsHostAddress, 1,
            (liNameEnd - 1));
         liNameEnd := Pos(':', lsHostAddress);
         iiAltPort := 0;
         if (liNameEnd > 0) then
         begin
            iiAltPort := StrToInt(Copy(lsHostAddress,
                            (liNameEnd + 1), Length(lsHostAddress)));
            lsHostAddress := Copy(lsHostAddress, 1,
                            (liNameEnd - 1));
         end;
      end;
      {Set the status display and command status flag to indicate
      that you are looking up the host address. }
      stStatus.Caption := 'Looking Up Host Address';
      stStatus.Update;
      iiHTTPStatus := HTTP_CONNECT;
      stState.Caption := 'HTTP_CONNECT';
      stState.Update;
      {Use the GetHostAddress procedure to look up the address of
      the server. Chapter 6 covers this procedure.}
      NetSocket.GetHostAddress(Handle, UWM_ADDRSOCKETEVENT,
                            lsHostAddress, SKT_GETHOSTADDR);
   end;
end
else
begin
   {You have tested all images and links, so tell the user}
   stStatus.Caption := 'Finished Testing';
   stStatus.Update;
   iiTestStatus := HTTP_NOOP;
   cbTest.Default := FALSE;
   cbConnect.Default := TRUE;
end;
   end;
end;
```

Figure 15.2 shows the Web robot checking the validity of URLs embedded in the specified HTML page (notice at the bottom of the window the URL of the link currently being tested).

Figure 15.3 shows the remaining URLs after testing (the status display at the bottom of the window has been updated to reflect that all links have been tested).

FIG. 15.2
Checking the validity of URLs embedded in the specified HTML page.

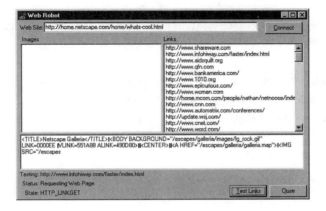

FIG. 15.3
The remaining URLs after testing.

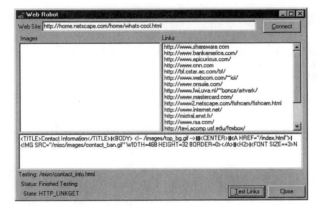

Testing the Socket Connection

Finally, you need an extension to the TSocket object class that determines whether a socket is connected to the host. There is an elegant way to do this, and a not-as-elegant way to do this. The implementation that the Web robot uses is the not-as-elegant way, but it still works fine and fits better with the Web robot's program flow. The correct way to check for a valid connection is to check the error code in the socket event handler on the FD_CONNECT event. If there is an error code, you can examine it to see which kind of error occurred.

NOTE The more elegant method of verifying a connection is to check for an error condition in the socket event handler when the FD_CONNECT event message is received. For more information on this method, see the explanation on the WSAAsyncSelect WinSock function in Chapter 6. ■

After getting past the socket event, you must use a different approach to check whether you are connected. An easy way to do so is to attempt to get the address of the host to which you are supposedly connected, using the WinSock getpeername() function (defined in Chapter 6). If this function returns an error, you can check whether the last error is WSAENOTCONN. If so, you are not connected. IsSocketConnected() is the function that you use to check whether a socket is connected to the host (see Listing 15.12).

Listing 15.12   TSOCKETC.PAS—the *IsSocketConnected()* Function Checks Whether a Socket Is Connected to the Host

```
function _TSocket.IsSocketConnected(TestSocket: _SOCKET): Boolean;
var
   lst_peeraddr: sockaddr;
   li_namelen: Integer;
begin
   {Allocate memory for the other computer's address}
   li_namelen := SizeOf(sockaddr);
   {Request the other computer's address}
   if (getpeername(TestSocket, lst_peeraddr, li_namelen) = 0) then
      {No errors, you must be connected}
      IsSocketConnected := TRUE
   else
   begin
      {You received an error, was it NOT CONNECTED?}
      if (WSAGetLastError <> WSAENOTCONN) then
         ShowMessage(SocketError)
      else
         {You are not connected}
         IsSocketConnected := FALSE;
   end;
end;
```

From Here...

In this chapter, you took a cursory look at the composition of Uniform Resource Locators (URLs) and Uniform Resource Identifiers (URIs). You learned how to parse these into their individual components so that you can use them to fulfill various needs. You also examined a small subset of Hypertext Markup Language (HTML) markup tags, particularly the ones that contain URLs for resources and inline images. You then explored the basic functionality of Hypertext Transfer Protocol (HTTP), how it operates, and the core commands involved. Then you used this information to build a basic Web robot that you can use to test Web pages to verify the links embedded within host pages.

From here, you could build in an iterative test procedure to check and test the various possibilities for the default Web page from a certain site. This procedure would provide a more thorough testing process. You could also build in some logging and reporting capabilities that would log the reason that a particular resource was not verified (whether the resource couldn't connect to the server, couldn't be found, couldn't be moved, and so on). You could also build in support for the other protocols (such as FTP and NNTP) that can be used as Web servers.

To understand the other protocols involved in the Web, as well as other functionality that Delphi can use in Web applications, see the following chapters:

- To understand the FTP protocol and how it operates, see Chapter 8, "Developing an FTP Client and Server."

- To understand the various other components found on the Web, see Chapter 12, "The Web—HTTP, HTML, and Beyond."

- To learn how you can use Delphi as a CGI scripting tool, see Chapter 13, "Using Delphi with CGI."

- To better understand how an HTTP server works, see Chapter 16, "Building a Web Server with Delphi."

- To see how to use Delphi as an extension to the Netscape Navigator Internet browser, see Chapter 18, "The Netscape API—Incorporating Delphi with the Netscape Browser and Server."

- To understand all the HTTP commands, see Appendix A, "Internet Applications Command Sets."

CHAPTER 16

Building a Web Server with Delphi

- How to format HTTP replies and requests, both for HTTP version 0.9 (simple) and 1.0 (full)

- How the HTTP server parses a request into its various components

- How the server processes Common Gateway Interface (CGI) requests and returns the results to the client

- How to build a basic HTTP server that you can extend with all sorts of additional functionality

Throughout the Internet, probably no other area's technology is changing and evolving more rapidly than the World Wide Web. With all these rapid changes, and with the many new ways that users are inventing for applying Web technology, probably one of the most important pieces of Web technology is the Web server. (The most important piece, and the piece most affected by the rapid changes, is the Web browser.)

Currently, the HTTP server is little more than a file server with some rudimentary process-management capabilities. To meet the growing demand for database-based Web applications, the server will evolve to become more of a form of middle-ware (a software application that manages connections and communication between clients and such networked resources as large databases). An HTTP server will become more tightly integrated with the database server and begin pumping out dynamically created HTML documents, based on page templates and database query results. (Currently, database interaction and dynamic HTML are accomplished through the use of CGI scripts and applications.) As Java and Networked OLE (expected to become a reality with Windows NT 4.0) are used more widely, the HTTP server will evolve from a passive server to an active server, running its own server side-applets and components.

So far, the Web server (also known as the *HTTP server*) has remained relatively unaffected by all this evolution in the technology. But that is about to change. As Web technology is used more with (and in place of) client/server systems, the server will become more of a bottleneck in the technology evolution—and that won't be tolerated for long.

But all these developments remain in the near future. To understand how HTTP server technology can, will, and must evolve, you need to examine the current technology, how it works, and its capabilities and shortcomings. This chapter explores how you can incorporate Delphi into the evolution of the Web browsers and servers that you develop in Chapter 18. ■

Understanding the HTTP Protocol and Header Formatting

The HTTP protocol has been in use since 1990, but has gained widespread recognition only within the past couple of years, thanks to the explosion in graphical browsers such as Netscape and Mosaic. Over time, the HTTP protocol has grown and evolved so that the current version now has more formatting and informational requirements than the previous version. However, many of the older version browsers and servers remain in operation, so you should build in to your application compatibility with the older version. These two formats are known as HTTP 0.9 (simple format) and HTTP 1.0 (full format). Work is progressing on the HTTP 1.1 and HTTP-NG protocols, but it appears that these new versions will affect the conversation between the client and server more than the message formats that a client and server pass between them.

N O T E Much of the work on HTTP 1.1 and HTTP-NG relates to converting the HTTP conversation from a single file request to multiple file requests during a single connection to a server. This conversion reduces the connection-establishment overhead and can speed up the delivery of Web pages to Web clients. ■

HTTP 0.9, the Simple Format

When building the Web robot in Chapter 15, "Building a Web Robot To Verify Link Integrity," you used the short request and reply formats. The short request consists of only the command and the resource name. The response to these request messages from the Web client is the requested resource or a small HTML document that explains that the requested resource isn't available. There is nothing more to the simple format. The client either receives the requested file from the server or receives a substitute document.

The HTTP standards drafts stress the need for both browsers and servers to be compatible with older versions of the other. If a server receives a request from an HTTP 0.9 browser (or other Web utility), it must respond with the appropriate HTTP 0.9 reply. Likewise, if a browser comes across an older server, it must communicate with it as an HTTP 0.9 browser.

HTTP 1.0, the Full Format

The HTTP 1.0 message format, unlike the HTTP 0.9 format, provides a substantial amount of information to the server and client about each other, as well as the object that the user requested. The full request and reply formats for HTTP 1.0 are both multiline messages that end with an empty line (so that you end up with two sets of carriage-return and line-feed end-of-line markers together). These message headers inform each other of the HTTP version at which each can communicate, the size and date of a requested object, the object types that a client can accept, the commands that a server supports, and more.

Part

III

Ch

16

N O T E In the previous section, and in subsequent sections, you read about "objects" being requested and served. In this context, an object is usually some type of file. It could be an HTML Web page or an image file, but could also be a video or sound file, or even a Java applet. In short, an "object" is anything that a Web server can serve. ■

The HTTP 1.0 specification began formatting HTTP requests and responses in the Internet Message Format. By using this message format, the client and servers can pass information about what is being requested and returned, enabling the client and server to determine how best to display or process the object that comprises the message body.

The Full Request. The full request consists of at least one HTTP header line, the request line. The request line can be followed by general header lines, request header lines, and entity header lines, all followed by an empty line. This header can be followed with an entity body, depending on the command being issued. The typical minimum request looks like the following:

```
{HTTP version with carriage-return and line-feed characters}
GET / HTTP/1.0#13#10
{Another set of carriage return and line feeds, thus terminating request}
#13#10
```

You rarely find an HTTP 1.0 browser sending such a small message. Instead, the request will probably look more like the following:

```
{GET command asking for the default site page}
GET / HTTP/1.0#13#10
{Pragma directive instructing any routers and pass-through servers
not to serve this request out of any cached copies, but to serve
this request with the master file}
Pragma: no-cache#13#10
{This client accepts bitmap, .GIF, and JPEG images}
Accept: image/x-bitmap, image/gif, image/jpeg#13#10
{The current client date}
Date: Wed, Feb 7, 1996 21:30 CST#13#10
{The client is MIME 1.0-compatible)
MIME-Version: 1.0#13#10
{The requesting user}
From: davischa@onramp.net#13#10
{The location of the hyperlink from which this URL was taken}
Referer: http://rampages.onramp.net/~davischa/#13#10
{The client application}
User-Agent: Delphi HTTP Client v1.0#13#10
#13#10
```

After you get past the request line, the request starts to look much like the Internet Message Format that you first saw when examining Internet mail (for more information on the Internet Message Format and the available HTTP headers, see Appendix B, "The Internet Message Format"). The reason for the similarity is that the format is a variation on the Internet Message Format defined in RFC 822. This standard format has been extended with some additional header fields to accommodate the needs of HTTP applications. These various headers identify the file types that the client application will accept, the user using the application, and the location from which you jumped to this page (or the page that had this object embedded within it). For a detailed look at the various headers available for use in the request, check the Web site at **http://www.w3.org/**. This site is the home page of the organization that is overseeing the Web's evolution, maintaining standards, and managing the development of the next generation of standards. (Although the Web uses several standards defined in RFCs, the basic Web technologies are not being developed through the usual RFC process.)

The Full Response. The format of the full response line is similar to that of the full request. The difference between the two is in the format of the first line, the status line, and the types of message header information that are likely to be returned. The format of the status line is to give the HTTP version information first, followed by a numeric response code, then some text explaining the reason for the status code that was returned (for a full listing of the potential response codes, see Appendix A, "Internet Applications Command Sets"). The HTTP server might send the following status line in response to a successful client request:

```
{The server is responding to the request with an 'OK' response}
HTTP/1.0 200 OK#13#10
```

This initial response line is followed by several lines of message header, providing the client with such information as the file size and file type of the object that the server is about to return, the commands that the server accepts, and whether the server requires authorization information. A typical full response might look something like the following:

```
{This is a positive response to the full request issued by the client
in the previous section. The server is responding with an 'OK' positive
response.}
HTTP/1.0 200 OK#13#10
{The current system time on the server}
Date: Thu, 8 Feb 1996 20:06:43 GMT#13#10
{The MIME-compliance of the following page (this header line is often
misused in HTTP message headers)}
MIME-Version: 1.0#13#10
{The server application}
Server Delphi Web Server v1.0#13#10
{Which commands does the server allow}
Allow: GET, HEAD#13#10
{The requested page is 2,323 bytes long}
Content-Length: 2323#13#10
{The requested page is an HTML document}
Content-Type: text/html#13#10
#13#10
```

This particular header would be immediately followed with the requested HTML file. The requested file would not follow this header only if the client issued the HEAD command, in which case only the header would be returned.

Serving HTML to a Client

Serving an HTML Web page or an image or sound file is mostly a simple matter of checking whether the server can find the file, open it, and send it to the client.

Part

III

Ch

16

> **N O T E** One of the first configuration options that must be part of any HTTP server is the capability to define which portion of the file system is available for browsing. The GET command returns any specified file, regardless of its file type. Therefore, an HTTP server must be configurable to limit access to specifically allocated portions of the server file system. Usually, you provide this capability by defining a directory on the computer file system as the root directory from which all Web pages will be served. This limits the available Web pages and files to those that are in this directory, or in a subdirectory off of this directory.

When a client connects to an HTTP server and issues a GET command, the server first must parse the file name from the request line. However, what if the client provides a path to a directory without specifying a file name? In that case, if the GET command path specification has a name that starts or ends with /, the server needs to have defined a default file name (usually index.html) that it returns. For example, if the requested object is / and the Web file service root is defined as **C:\web**, the HTTP server looks for **C:\web\index.html** (or, on a DOS-based server platform, **C:\web\index.htm**). If the client requests **/info/**, the server looks for **C:\web\info\index.html**. If the client requests a specific file, the server looks for the requested file in the relative location within the file system's Web file service area. For instance, if the client requests **/info/new.html**, the server looks for **C:\web\info\new.html**.

After locating the appropriate file, the server examines various information about the file. This information is for use in the response message header. The information includes the file size and type, so that the server can tell the client what it is about to send. Then the server opens the file and begins to pipe it through the socket connection to the client that requested it, unless the client issued the HEAD command. If the client issued the HEAD command, the server sends only the information about the file (although occasionally the server searches the file to find all the links so that the message header can include that information).

Responding to CGI Requests

It is through CGI requests—issued by the client with either the GET or POST commands—that the functionality of the Web server becomes really interesting and challenging. A CGI request is not the name of a file that the client wants to have returned, but the name of an application that the client wants to run on the server. When the server receives a CGI script request, the server runs another application, often passing some sort of parameters to this other application, and then passes the output to the client. Often, the server has to parse information from the request line that it received from the client, and pass this information to the CGI application (usually called a *CGI script,* due to the preponderance of UNIX `shell`, `awk`, and `perl` scripts that these processes use) in one of many different forms.

Receiving Data from the Client

A client can send data to the server in three ways. The first and most common way is to send it as a Uniform Resource Locator (URL) query string. The URL of the CGI application to which the client is passing the data is followed with a question mark and then the data, as in the following example:

```
http://www.somewhere.com/cgi-bin/search?query-string
```

In this instance, the Web server runs the application or shell script called `search` in the directory CGI-BIN (the traditional CGI executable directory) and passes it the string `query-string`. This form of passing data is fairly straightforward.

A second way that a client might pass data to the server is known as *passing extra path information*. In this case, additional path information is passed on the end of the URL, followed by the question mark and query string. An extra path URL might look like the following:

```
http://www.somewhere.com/cgi-bin/search/dir/filename?query-string
```

In this case, the strings `/dir/filename` and `query-string` pass to the application `search`. Therefore, the server must be prepared to parse what looks like additional path information from the URL when it encounters an executable process in a location at which the URL implies that a directory should be located. In other words, if the server does not find a directory called SEARCH within the CGI-BIN directory, but instead finds an executable program, the server must assume that the remainder of the URL's path information is actually data that is supposed to be passed to the `search` application. For example, suppose that the server receives the following URL:

```
http://www.here.com/cgi-bin/search/dir/phonenum?Chapman
```

The server would then pass the strings `/dir/phonenum` and `Chapman` to the CGI application `search`. This application would probably look for entries for someone with the name `Chapman` in the file /DIR/PHONENUM and return any such entries to the client application.

The third method that a client might use to pass data to the server is within the body of the message that it sends to the server (remember that both the request message from the client and the response message from the server use the standard Internet Message Format). This method is most often used with the `POST` command.

When using the query string formats, the client often passes multiple data values, separated by commas (,) or plus signs (+) (for example, `Gates+McNeeley` specifies a search for documents with both *Gates* and *McNeeley* in the same article, and `89,200` specifies coordinates in an imagemap). The server must parse these values into separate variables to be passed to the CGI script. Another form that data values might take is the variable-name/value form, in which a variable name is followed by the equal sign (=) and then the value. When multiple variables are passed in this format, the ampersand character (&) separates the variables (for example, lname=Chapman&fname=Davis specifies input into a form). For example, if a simple Web form asks a user for a first and last name, so that they could be saved in a database, the URL that is passed to the server might look something like the following:

```
http://www.here.com/cgi-bin/savename?lname=Chapman&fname=Davis
```

However, a request to search for a news article containing the names Gates and McNeeley might return a URL that looks like the following:

```
http://www.here.com/cgi-bin/articlesearch?Gates+McNeeley
```

And when a user clicks an imagemap to jump to a specified Web page represented by a section in the image, the URL returned might look like the following:

```
http://www.here.com/imagemap/first.map?89,200
```

Part
III

Ch
16

Sending Data to the CGI Process

There are three ways that the server process uses to pass data to the CGI process that it is calling. The first of these methods is to pass the data as command-line arguments to the process. This method is practical only when the server is starting up the CGI process and the data is limited to less than 10 elements.

Some CGI processes run constantly, with the server passing information to the process. To do so, the server usually uses the second method, which is to pass the data as input to the CGI process. This method is often used with CGI processes for which starting up or shutting down is so expensive (in either time or resources) that keeping the process running is more practical. Processes that interact with databases or host systems often use this method.

The third way that the server can pass information to the CGI process is used most often when the data is in the form of variables and values. In this case, the server either passes the data as environment variables (usually on UNIX platforms) or as an .INI file (usually on Windows platforms). (Environment variables usually aren't used on DOS and Windows platforms because of the strict limit on the amount of memory that the operating systems allocate for environment variables.)

Returning Data from the CGI Process

After the CGI application receives the data and performs its task, the CGI process must return the results to the client. You can do this in two ways. First, you send the CGI process's results to the server and let the server determine how to format and return them to the client. Alternatively, the CGI process can send its results directly to the client. The implementations of these techniques depend somewhat on the server's type and design. Often, with Windows-based servers, the CGI process writes its output to a file that the server reads and sends to the client. It's even feasible for the server to provide a pass-through input port for the CGI process to use to pass its output directly through the server socket connection to the client. This connection is basically a socket port (or other mechanism) to which the CGI application can connect. The input that the CGI application sends through this socket passes directly to the client application.

One of the newest developments in HTTP server technology is the extendable server. An *extendable server* is one for which the server developer has provided an application programming interface (API) that enables developers to build applications that hook into the server and provide new and additional functionality without the overhead of starting and stopping a separate application (as in CGI applications). Both Netscape and Microsoft are developing new servers into which you can plug additional functionality. You can use such servers to perform tasks that formerly were the domain of CGI scripts (such as database input and output), and thus make such tasks part of the server itself without having to provide any additional processes. Such servers also give the add-ons direct access to the client socket connection, without the overhead involved in passing the CGI output to the client. The field of extendable servers is likely to be one of the hottest areas of new Internet software development over the next few years. Chapter 18, "The Netscape API—Incorporating Delphi with the Netscape Browser and Server," examines this subject in more detail.

Building an HTTP Server

In this section, you build a Web server that has a few limitations. First, like the File Transfer Protocol (FTP) server that you built in Chapter 8, "Developing an FTP Client and Server," this HTTP server allows only a single interactive connection at a time. Second, this server does not accommodate any CGI processing. Finally, because it doesn't allow any CGI processing, the server cannot offer any support for the POST command.

The Web server that you will develop enables the user to specify a root directory, under which should be all the Web files to be served and the name of the default Web page to be served if the Web client requests the / page. This server cannot process any CGI requests, so it doesn't need to support the POST command. This single-threaded application must limit itself to servicing only a single connection at a time. On startup, the Web server takes the following steps:

1. Creates a socket on the default HTTP TCP service port (80) and listens for incoming connection requests.
2. Accepts any received connection requests.
3. If a connection is already active, sends the new connection an unavailable response and disconnects the client. If there are no existing connections, waits for the client to send a request.
4. Analyzes received requests from the client to determine whether the requested file is available.
5. Returns the requested file to the client.
6. Disconnects from the client and waits for the next connection request.

N O T E   In Appendix A, you can find complete explanations of all the HTTP commands, including those used in this application. ■

In this application, you use the same procedures for creating the listening sockets and accepting incoming connections as you used in the previous server example (see Chapter 8, "Developing an FTP Client and Server"). You should check Chapter 8 for listings and explanations of any procedures and functions not covered in this chapter. Table 16.1 lists the files used in this project.

Table 16.1 HTTP Web Server Project Files

File	Description
WEBSERVE.DPR	The HTTP Web server Delphi project file.
WSERVE.DFM	The HTTP Web server window.
WSERVE.PAS	The HTTP Web server code.
TSOCKETC.PAS	The TSocket WinSock abstraction class (first developed in Chapter 6, and expanded in Chapter 8).
NWINSOCK.PAS	The WinSock application program interface (API) definition.

Part
III

Ch
16

Building on What You've Created

You can model this Web server as a combination of the FTP server that you built in Chapter 8 and the Web robot that you built in Chapter 15. Therefore, you don't need to examine in detail the constant or variable declarations, with one minor exception. The way that your server responds to a client's request depends largely on whether the client sent an HTTP 1.0 format request or an HTTP 0.9 format request. Because several areas within the server must know this information, declaring a private variable to track the client's HTTP version makes sense:

```
ibIsFullRequest: Boolean;
```

You can initialize this variable to FALSE when starting the server and then reset it after completing each conversation. When parsing each received request, you can set this variable to TRUE if you find that you have received a request in HTTP 1.0 format.

You take much of the listening and connection-accepting code directly from the FTP server. The primary difference in this portion of the code is that the Web server listens on the HTTP default port of 80 rather than the FTP default command connection port (21). Therefore, your function call to create the listening socket looks like the following:

```
{Create a listening socket on TCP service port 80}
isListenSocket := NetSocket.CreateListenSocket(handle,
                    UWM_LISTENSOCKETEVENT, 80);
```

Reading the Client Request

Because you are incorporating all this existing code (mostly in Chapter 8), you soon reach a point at which you have to handle the incoming request from the client. You begin with the version of the ReadCommandMsg procedure that you created for the FTP server. You add to this procedure a loop through which the procedure retrieves the rest of the received message, even though all you really want is the first line, which should contain the request itself. To parse the request line, the Web server uses essentially the same algorithm as the FTP server, passing the command and the arguments strings to the CheckCommandMsg procedure for processing. Listing 16.1 shows the Web server's version of ReadCommandMsg.

Listing 16.1   WSERVE.PAS—the *ReadCommandMsg* Procedure Reads the Request Sent by the Client

```
procedure TWbServe.ReadCommandMsg;
var
   lsCommand: String;
   lsMessage: String;
   liCmdLength: Integer;
   liMsgLength: Integer;
begin
   {Receive the request from the client, then check for any errors}
   liMsgLength := recv(isConnectionSocket, ReceiveBuffer, 8192, 0);
   if (liMsgLength = SOCKET_ERROR) and
         (WSAGetLastError <> WSAEWOULDBLOCK) then
      ShowMessage(NetSocket.SocketError)
   else
   begin
      {Terminate the received request string}
      ReceiveBuffer[liMsgLength] := Char(0);
      {Get the first (request) line}
      if NetSocket.GetLine(TempBuffer, ReceiveBuffer) then
      begin
         {Add the request line to the display for the user to see}
         mleReceived.Lines.Add(StrPas(TempBuffer));
         {Is there anything in the hold buffer?}
         if (Length(isHoldBuffer) > 0) then
            {If so, add it in front of your new line}
            lsMessage := isHoldBuffer + StrPas(TempBuffer)
         else
            lsMessage := StrPas(TempBuffer);
         {Empty the hold buffer}
         isHoldBuffer := '';
         {Find the space character to determine the end of the command}
         liCmdLength := Pos(' ', lsMessage);
         if (liCmdLength = 0) then
         begin
            {If there is no space character, it is not the command
            line of the header}
            liCmdLength := Length(lsMessage);
            lsCommand := lsMessage;
            lsMessage := '';
         end
         else
```

```
      begin
         {Separate the command from the rest of the request}
         lsCommand := Copy(lsMessage, 1, (liCmdLength - 1));
         lsMessage := Copy(lsMessage, (liCmdLength + 1),
                     Length(lsMessage));
      end;
      {Pass the command and parameter to the CheckCommandMsg procedure}
      CheckCommandMsg(lsCommand, lsMessage);
   end;
   {Any additional lines are of no concern in this application, so
   pass them directly to the display}
   while NetSocket.GetLine(TempBuffer, ReceiveBuffer) do
   begin
      mleReceived.Lines.Add(StrPas(TempBuffer));
   end;
   {Is there any left over? If so, place it into the hold buffer.}
   if (Length(StrPas(TempBuffer)) > 0) then
   begin
      if (Length(isHoldBuffer) > 0) then
         isHoldBuffer := isHoldBuffer + StrPas(TempBuffer)
      else
         isHoldBuffer := StrPas(TempBuffer);
   end;
 end;
end;
```

Analyzing the Request

Now that you've separated the command and its arguments, you want to scan the arguments to see whether the HTTP 1.0 marker is included. If it isn't, you know that you have an HTTP 0.9 request and must use an HTTP 0.9 formatted response (as specified by the HTTP 1.0 specification). If you find the marker, you must trim it from the rest of the arguments (the URI).

So far in this server, you have not added any support for CGI processing or the POST command, so you can assume that the remaining URI is the requested object's file name. You call the ConvertFileNameToDos procedure to convert the file name into something with which you can work. Next, you need to look at which command was received (HEAD or GET). If you received the GET command, you call the appropriate procedure (SendShortObject or SendFullObject) to send the requested object. If you received the HEAD command, you call the appropriate procedure (SendShortHeader or SendFullHeader) to send the requested object's header. If you received any other request, you send a message informing the client that the request was either an unknown or unsupported command. Then, if the command is anything other than GET or HEAD, you close the connection (because the current HTTP protocol does not allow multiple requests during a single connection).

N O T E The current version (and previous versions) of HTTP allows only a single command to be issued per connection. This limitation might change in future versions. Current research into potential new versions of the HTTP protocol seeks to allow multiple commands during a single connection. This advancement will speed up the serving of objects (from the client's perspective) but complicate the connection conversation. The protocol will probably utilize an FTP model in which the commands use one connection while the data is transferred over another connection. For information on this research, check with the W3 organization Web site at **http://www.w3.org/**. ■

Part
III

Ch
16

As you convert the requested URI into a DOS file name, you must add the configured root directory to the beginning of the file name, thus limiting the source from which the client can request files (although this scheme still has shortcomings; for example, the client might request a file in the parent directory of the configured root directory, or might request the default page in a subdirectory). If the requested URI is simply /, you substitute the configured default file name.

Listing 16.2 shows the CheckCommandMsg() procedure, which checks which command the server received.

Listing 16.2   WSERVE.PAS—the *CheckCommandMsg()* Procedure Determines Which Command the Application Received

```
procedure TWbServe.CheckCommandMsg(asCommand, asArguments: String);
var
    lbCmdFound: Boolean;
    liSpacePos: Integer;
begin
    {Initialize the command found flag to FALSE}
    lbCmdFound := FALSE;
    {Is the HTTP 1.0 indicator included?}
    if (Pos('HTTP/1.0', asArguments) > 0) then
    begin
        {Yes, mark this request as a full (HTTP 1.0) request}
        ibIsFullRequest := TRUE;
        {Now trim the HTTP 1.0 indicator from the file name}
        liSpacePos := Pos(' ', asArguments);
        if (liSpacePos > 0) then
            isFileName := Copy(asArguments, 1, (liSpacePos - 1));
    end
    else
    begin
        {No HTTP 1.0 indicator, so you must treat this request
         as an HTTP 0.9 request}
        ibIsFullRequest := FALSE;
        isFileName := asArguments;
    end;
    {Was the default page requested?}
    if (isFileName = '/') then
        isFileName := sleDefPage.Text
    else
        {No, add the root directory to the requested file name}
        isFileName := sleDefDir.Text + isFileName;
    {Call the ConvertFileNameToDos procedure to convert the file name into
    the DOS format so that you can use it}
    ConvertFileNameToDos;
    {Did the client send a GET command?}
    if (asCommand = 'GET') then
```

```
begin
   {Yes, is it a full or short request (HTTP 1.0 or 0.9)?}
   lbCmdFound := TRUE;
   iiHTTPStatus := HTTP_GET;
   if (ibIsFullRequest) then
      SendFullObject
   else
      SendShortObject;
end;
{Did the client send a HEAD command?}
if (asCommand = 'HEAD') then
begin
   {Yes, is it a full or short request (HTTP 1.0 or 0.9)?}
   lbCmdFound := TRUE;
   iiHTTPStatus := HTTP_HEAD;
   if (ibIsFullRequest) then
      SendFullHeader
   else
      SendShortHeader;
end;
{Did the client send a POST command?}
if (asCommand = 'POST') then
begin
   {Yes, send the client a NOT SUPPORTED response}
   lbCmdFound := TRUE;
   iiHTTPStatus := HTTP_POST;
   SendContextMsg;
   {Close the connection}
   CloseConnection;
end;
{Did you find a matching command?}
if (not lbCmdFound) then
begin
   {No, send a COMMAND UNKNOWN response}
   iiHTTPStatus := HTTP_UNKWN;
   SendContextMsg;
   {Close the connection}
   CloseConnection;
end;
end;
```

Sending a Response to an HTTP 0.9 Client

If the server has been contacted by an HTTP 0.9 client that happens to issue the HEAD request, the server informs the client that the HEAD command is not allowed (for HTTP 0.9 clients). To do so, you format a small HTML document that explains the situation, and then send the document to the client. After graciously informing the client that the server doesn't support the HEAD command, you close the connection, ending the conversation and preventing the client from attempting to argue about the validity of its request. Listing 16.3 shows SendShortHeader, the procedure that sends the rejection message.

Listing 16.3 WSERVE.PAS—the *SendShortHeader* Procedure Sends a Rejection Message to an HTTP 0.9 Client

```
procedure TWbServe.SendShortHeader;
var
   isShortHeaderMsg: String;
begin
   {Build the response document informing the client that the HEAD
   command is not allowed in the HTTP 0.9 protocol}
   isShortHeaderMsg := '<TITLE>Operation Not Allowed</TITLE>';
   {Send the message to the client}
   NetSocket.SocketSend(isConnectionSocket, handle, UWM_SOCKETEVENT,
                                          isShortHeaderMsg, SKT_NOOP);
   {Add the message to the display}
   mleSent.Lines.Add(isShortHeaderMsg);
   {Close the connection}
   CloseConnection
 end;
```

If the HTTP 0.9 client issues the GET command, the server must determine whether the client requested a valid file. If the server checks whether the file exists and finds that it doesn't, the server sends a short HTML document explaining that the requested file doesn't exist and then promptly closes the connection. If the requested file does exist, the server opens and sends it. Listing 16.4 shows SendShortObject, the procedure that sends the requested file to the client. This procedure lets the ProcessDataSend procedure close the connection, because otherwise SendShortObject doesn't know when it is finished sending the object. The object, in this case, is the file that the procedure is sending.

Listing 16.4 WSERVE.PAS—the *SendShortObject* Procedure Sends the Requested Object to an HTTP 0.9 Client

```
procedure TWbServe.SendShortObject;
var
   isShortObjectMsg: String;
begin
   {Does the requested file exist?}
   if FileExists(isFileName) then
   begin
      {Yes, open and send it}
      OpenSendFile;
      ProcessDataSend;
   end
   else
   begin
      {No, build an HTML document stating that the requested file
      was not found}
      isShortObjectMsg := '<TITLE>Not Found</TITLE>';
      {Send the message to the client}
      NetSocket.SocketSend(isConnectionSocket, handle, UWM_SOCKETEVENT,
                                             isShortObjectMsg, SKT_NOOP);
```

```
      {Add the message to the display}
      mleSent.Lines.Add(isShortObjectMsg);
      {Close the connection}
      CloseConnection;
   end;
end;
```

Sending a Response to an HTTP 1.0 Client

If the client is an HTTP 1.0 client, you have to deal with it a little differently. If the client sends a HEAD command, you can respond with the information that the client wants. To get the first piece of information, you determine whether the requested object actually does exist. If it doesn't, you send a 404 response (which indicates that the object was not found) and close the connection. If the file does exist, you open it to get some information about the file. After opening the file, you can send the client a 200 response message that includes all the desired information and then close the connection. Listing 16.5 shows SendFullHeader, the procedure that sends a response header to the client.

N O T E In Appendix A, you can find descriptions of the 404 and 200 response codes, as well as all other response codes that you are sending to the client. ▨

Listing 16.5 WSERVE.PAS—the *SendFullHeader* Procedure Sends a Response Header to an HTTP 1.0 Client

```
procedure TWbServe.SendFullHeader;
begin
   {Does the requested file exist?}
   if FileExists(isFileName) then
   begin
      {Yes, open the file and send the full header message, passing the
      FileHeader function as the additional message string parameter to
      the SendFullMsg procedure}
      OpenSendFile;
      SendFullMsg(isConnectionSocket, 200, HTTP_NOOP, UWM_SOCKETEVENT,
                         FileHeader);
      {Close the connection}
      CloseConnection;
   end
   else
   begin
      {No, send a full message informing the client that the requested
      file does not exist on this server}
      SendFullMsg(isConnectionSocket, 404, HTTP_NOOP, UWM_SOCKETEVENT,
                         isFileName);
      {Close the connection}
      CloseConnection;
   end;
end;
```

If the client issues a GET command, the SendFullObject procedure takes the same action as SendFullHeader takes in response to the HEAD command, with one exception (see Listing 16.6). If the file does exist, instead of closing the connection after sending the message header, you must send the requested file. To send the file, SendFullObject calls the ProcessDataSend procedure rather than the CloseConnection procedure.

Listing 16.6 WSERVE.PAS—the *SendFullObject* Procedure Sends the Requested Object to an HTTP 1.0 Client

```
procedure TWbServe.SendFullObject;
begin
   {Does the requested file exist?}
   if FileExists(isFileName) then
   begin
      {Yes, open the file and send the full header message, passing the
      FileHeader function as the additional message string parameter to
      the SendFullMsg procedure}
      OpenSendFile;
      SendFullMsg(isConnectionSocket, 200, HTTP_NOOP, UWM_SOCKETEVENT,
                        FileHeader);
      {Now, send the file}
      ProcessDataSend;
   end
   else
   begin
      {No, send a full message informing the client that the requested
      file does not exist on this server}
      SendFullMsg(isConnectionSocket, 404, HTTP_NOOP, UWM_SOCKETEVENT,
                        isFileName);
      {Close the connection}
      CloseConnection;
   end;
 end;
```

If the client sends a POST command or some other unknown command, you must respond with the appropriate message to inform the client that the server either doesn't support the requested command or doesn't understand the requested command. Listing 16.7 shows SendContextMsg, the procedure that sends this message.

As you can see in Listing 16.7, SendContextMsg does not distinguish between HTTP 0.9 and HTTP 1.0 clients when responding to POST and unknown commands. This is a shortcoming of the current implementation. In the spirit of tolerance for older clients that is strongly encouraged in HTTP development, you should expand the following procedure to make this distinction and send the appropriately formatted reply. To do so, you must format the HTTP 0.9 messages as HTML pages without the response code numbers.

Listing 16.7 WSERVE.PAS—the *SendContextMsg* Procedure Sends the Client an Invalid Command Response

```
procedure TWbServe.SendContextMsg;
begin
  {What is the requested command?}
  case iiHTTPStatus of
    {NOOP, GET, and HEAD, don't do anything}
    HTTP_NOOP:;
    HTTP_GET:;
    HTTP_HEAD:;
    {POST and Unknown, send 401 and 400 responses accordingly}
    HTTP_POST: SendFullMsg(isConnectionSocket, 401, HTTP_NOOP,
                    UWM_SOCKETEVENT, '');
    HTTP_UNKWN: SendFullMsg(isConnectionSocket, 400, HTTP_NOOP,
                    UWM_SOCKETEVENT, '');
  end;
end;
```

Converting the Requested File Name

Before you can check for and open any requested files, ConvertFileNameToDOS must ensure that you have converted them into file names and paths that your server can understand (see Listing 16.8). By convention, URLs use UNIX file names and paths, so this should be a simple process of substituting the DOS backslash character (\) for the UNIX slash character (/).

> **CAUTION**
>
> The ConvertFileNameToDos procedure does not correctly convert long file names into DOS-readable file names. If you use the 16-bit version of Delphi and a client passes the implementation a long file name, you will have problems.

Listing 16.8 WSERVE.PAS—the *ConvertFileNameToDOS* Procedure Converts the Requested File Name into a DOS File Name

```
procedure TWbServe.ConvertFileNameToDos;
var
  liSlashPos: Integer;
begin
  {Find the first slash character}
  liSlashPos := Pos('/', isFileName);
  {Loop as long as there are more slash characters}
  while (liSlashPos > 0) do
  begin
    {Copy the file name, replacing the slash character with the
    backslash character}
    isFileName := Copy(isFileName, 1, (liSlashPos - 1)) + '\' +
        Copy(isFileName, (liSlashPos + 1), Length(isFileName));
    liSlashPos := Pos('/', isFileName);
  end;
end;
```

Standardizing the Response Codes

Most of the messages that you send to the client contain the same information in the same format, so simplifying the sending and formatting of this information is important. To do so, you create a single procedure, SendFullMsg, for sending the message header (see Listing 16.9). The two most important elements that you pass to this procedure are the response number and the additional message information string. The response number determines the response line that you will send to inform the client of the success or failure of its request. The additional message string contains any additional lines of information that the message header must include. If the client requests a valid file, this additional message string contains the header lines that contain the file information that you need to include in your response header (in Listings 16.5 and 16.6, notice that the full message header and object procedures include a procedure call to FileHeader). After determining the response line, you also send header lines giving the server date and time, MIME version, server implementation type, and any additional information that the message header is to include.

Listing 16.9   WSERVE.PAS—the *SendFullMsg()* Procedure Sends Standard Messages to an HTTP 1.0 Client

```
procedure TWbServe.SendFullMsg(aSendSock:_SOCKET;
            iMsg, iNewState, aiEvent: Integer; asAdditionalMsg: String);
var
   lsMsgStr: String;
begin
   {Initialize the message with the specified response code}
   case iMsg of
      200: lsMsgStr := 'HTTP/1.0 200 OK' + #13#10;
      201: lsMsgStr := 'HTTP/1.0 201 Created' + #13#10;
      202: lsMsgStr := 'HTTP/1.0 202 Accepted' + #13#10;
      204: lsMsgStr := 'HTTP/1.0 204 No Content' + #13#10;
      301: lsMsgStr := 'HTTP/1.0 301 Moved Permanently' + #13#10;
      302: lsMsgStr := 'HTTP/1.0 302 Moved Temporarily' + #13#10;
      304: lsMsgStr := 'HTTP/1.0 304 Not Modified' + #13#10;
      400: lsMsgStr := 'HTTP/1.0 400 Bad Request' + #13#10;
      401: lsMsgStr := 'HTTP/1.0 401 Unauthorized' + #13#10;
      403: lsMsgStr := 'HTTP/1.0 403 Forbidden' + #13#10;
      404: lsMsgStr := 'HTTP/1.0 404 Not Found' + #13#10;
      500: lsMsgStr := 'HTTP/1.0 500 Internal Server Error' + #13#10;
      501: lsMsgStr := 'HTTP/1.0 501 Not Implemented' + #13#10;
      502: lsMsgStr := 'HTTP/1.0 502 Bad Gateway' + #13#10;
      503: lsMsgStr := 'HTTP/1.0 503 Service Unavailable' + #13#10;
   end;
   {Add the current date and time}
   lsMsgStr := lsMsgStr + 'Date: ' +
            FormatDateTime('ddd, d mmm yyyy hh:mm:ss "CST"', Now());
   {Send what you have so far, then add them to the display}
   NetSocket.SocketSend(aSendSock, handle, aiEvent, lsMsgStr, SKT_NOOP);
   mleSent.Lines.Add(lsMsgStr);
```

```
{Build two more header lines, telling the client what server software
is servicing this request}
lsMsgStr := 'MIME-Version: 1.0' + #13#10;
lsMsgStr := lsMsgStr + 'Server: Delphi Web Server v1.0' + #13#10;
{Send these two lines, plus what was passed in as the additional
header information lines, and add them to the display}
NetSocket.SocketSend(aSendSock, handle, aiEvent,
          lsMsgStr + asAdditionalMsg, SKT_NOOP);
mleSent.Lines.Add(lsMsgStr + asAdditionalMsg);
{Reset the current command status flag to the specified state value}
iiHTTPStatus := iNewState;
end;
```

Sending the Requested File

Opening the requested file is straightforward. The OpenSendFile procedure opens and resets the file and then notes the file's size (see Listing 16.10). You then are prepared to send the client the information about the file, and to send the file itself.

Listing 16.10 WSERVE.PAS—the *OpenSendFile* Procedure Opens the Requested File and Checks Its Size

```
procedure TWbServe.OpenSendFile;
begin
   {Set the FILE OPEN flag to TRUE}
   ibFileOpen := TRUE;
   {Assign the file name to the file handle}
   AssignFile(TransferFile, isFileName);
   {Reset and open the file for reading}
   Reset(TransferFile);
   {Read the file size into the file size variable}
   ilFileSize := FileSize(TransferFile);
 end;
```

Now that you have the file open, you can format all the information about the file that you need to send to the client. Listing 16.11 shows a series of functions that you implement to format this information automatically. The first function, FileSizeHeader, formats and returns the content-length header line, providing the client with the file's length. The second, FileTypeHeader, determines from the file extension the type of file that the server has requested and opened. This function is by no means complete. FileTypeHeader defines only three types of files; it does not include all the possible file types that browsers know and display for the user. The last of these functions, FileHeader, grabs the results from the first two functions (FileSizeHeader and FileTypeHeader) and prefixes them with the header line informing the client which commands are allowed, and returns the message header section to the calling procedure. When an HTTP 1.0 client requests a file that does exist, the SendFullMsg procedure calls this function as its additional message string portion.

Listing 16.11 WSERVE.PAS—the *FileSizeHeader*, *FileTypeHeader*, and *FileHeader* Functions Provide the File Information Lines of the Response Header

```
function TWbServe.FileSizeHeader: String;
begin
   {Build the file size message header line}
   FileSizeHeader := 'Content-Length: ' + IntToStr(ilFileSize) + #13#10;
end;

function TWbServe.FileTypeHeader: String;
var
   lsFileExt: String;
   lsFileType: String;
   liPosPeriod: Integer;
begin
   {Specify a default file type of HTML text}
   lsFileType := 'text/html';
   {Locate the extension in the file name}
   liPosPeriod := Pos('.', isFileName);
   if (liPosPeriod > 0) then
   begin
      {Is it a .GIF or JPEG file?}
      lsFileExt := Copy(isFileName, (liPosPeriod + 1), 3);
      if ((lsFileExt = 'gif') or (lsFileExt = 'GIF')) then
         lsFileType := 'image/gif';
      if ((lsFileExt = 'jpg') or (lsFileExt = 'JPG')) then
         lsFileType := 'image/jpeg';
   end;
   {Build the file content-type header line}
   FileTypeHeader := 'Content-Type: ' + lsFileType + #13#10;
end;

function TWbServe.FileHeader: String;
var
   lsHeaderStr: String;
begin
   {Put all three of these lines together into a message header section}
   lsHeaderStr := 'Allow: GET, HEAD' + #13#10;
   lsHeaderStr := lsHeaderStr + FileSizeHeader + FileTypeHeader;
   FileHeader := lsHeaderStr;
 end;
```

The `ProcessDataSend` procedure is basically the same one that you used in your FTP server (see Listing 16.12). The most important difference is that this version sends the file through the primary connection socket rather than a separate data socket, which as you might remember is a fundamental feature of the FTP protocol architecture. The procedure reads and sends one buffer of data at a time. On reaching the end of the file, you close the connection.

Listing 16.12   WSERVE.PAS—the *ProcessDataSend* Procedure Sends the Requested Object to the Client

```
procedure TWbServe.ProcessDataSend;
var
   liCurByteCount: Integer;
   lcCurByte: Byte;
   lpTransferDataPointer: PChar;
begin
   {Is the requested file open?}
   if ibFileOpen then
   begin
      {Initialize the byte counter}
      liCurByteCount := 0;
      {Are you at the end of the file?}
      if (not Eof(TransferFile)) then
      begin
         {No, clear the transfer buffer}
         ClearBuffer(TransferBuffer, 8192);
         {Read 4,096 bytes from the file into the transfer buffer}
         while ((liCurByteCount < 4096) and (not Eof(TransferFile))) do
         begin
            Read(TransferFile, lcCurByte);
            TransferBuffer[liCurByteCount] := Char(lcCurByte);
            Inc(liCurByteCount);
         end;
         {Send what you've read from the file}
         NetSocket.SocketSendBuffer(isConnectionSocket, handle,
                  UWM_SOCKETEVENT,
                  TransferBuffer, liCurByteCount, SKT_SENDPACKET);
      end
      else
         {You've sent the entire file, so close the connection}
         CloseConnection;
   end;
end;
```

Closing the Connection

Finally, you need a procedure to close the connection (see Listing 16.13). If you are holding the requested file open, you also must close the socket connection. Then you need to decrement the number of connections that you currently have open and are processing.

Listing 16.13 WSERVE.PAS—the *CloseConnection* Procedure Closes the Connection to the Client

```
procedure TWbServe.CloseConnection;
begin
  {Before closing the socket connection, shut it down}
  shutdown(isConnectionSocket, 2);
  {Close the socket connection and destroy the socket}
  NetSocket.CloseSocketConnection(isConnectionSocket);
  {If the requested file is open, close it}
  if ibFileOpen then
  begin
    CloseFile(TransferFile);
    ibFileOpen := FALSE;
  end;
  {Decrement the number of current connections, so that more incoming
  connection requests can be accepted}
  Dec(iiNumConnected);
end;
```

You now have a simple, working Web server. Figure 16.1 shows it in action, and Figure 16.2 shows the server receiving a Web page. You can connect to the server by using any Web browser, as long as the server name is registered with your Domain Name Server (DNS) or is in your hosts file.

FIG. 16.1

The simple Web server in action.

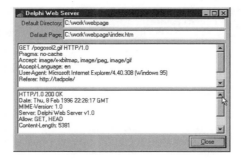

FIG. 16.2
Receiving a Web page from the Web server.

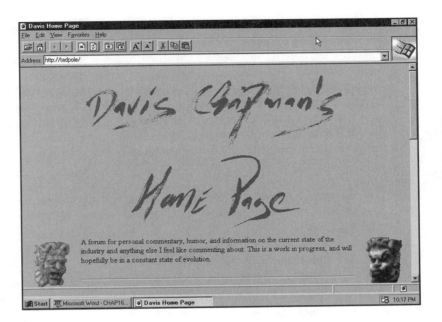

From Here...

In this chapter, you looked at the current functionality that a Web server is expected to provide, and what that functionality entails. You learned the difference between HTTP 0.9 and HTTP 1.0 message formats for both requests and responses. You looked into what is involved in providing CGI support within a Web server, how the server has to parse and pass data sent from the client to the CGI process, and how the server has to enable the CGI process to return data to the client. Then you used all this information to build a basic HTTP server with limited functionality.

From here, you could do much to expand your understanding and experience with Web servers and HTTP applications in general. Using what you have learned about the HTTP 1.0 message formats, you could modify the Web robot that you built in Chapter 15. For example, you could enable the robot to use and receive full message formats so that it can receive response codes that indicate the success or failure of links, or request only the message headers of the links that it is testing.

You could also expand the Web server to fix some of the shortcomings that were pointed out as you were building it (such as adding support for HTTP 0.9 responses for POST and unknown messages, and determining the file content type of more file types). If you feel ambitious, you could convert the server into a multithreading server application, so that more than one connection can be active at the same time, or you could add support for CGI processing. If you feel even more ambitious, you could create your own HTTP/CGI extensions and convert your Web server into a database/Web server, taking advantage of Delphi's database connectivity to provide for Web-based client/server applications. Finally, you could add security features and support for client authentication and communication encryption.

To get more information on these possibilities, see the following chapters:

- For an understanding of Internet addressing, and how a client is able to convert a server name into an Internet address, see Chapter 3, "Internet Connectivity."

- For an understanding of how a client can choose which of many applications running on a server computer to which to connect, see Chapter 5, "The Principles of Socket Communications and Programming."

- For a glimpse at where the Web came from and where it is going, see Chapter 12, "The Web—HTTP, HTML, and Beyond."

- For an understanding of the various things that you can do with CGI processes, and the various ways that they can process requests and return data to the client, see Chapter 13, "Using Delphi with CGI," and Chapter 14, "Using a Database in a CGI Application."

- For an understanding of Internet security and encryption, and how you can incorporate them into Web browsers and servers, see Chapter 17, "Internet Security, RSA Encryption, SSL, STT, PCT, and WinSock."

- For a look at how the new generation of Web servers is allowing for extended functionality through tools like Delphi, see Chapter 18, "The Netscape API—Incorporating Delphi with the Netscape Browser and Server."

- For a list of all the possible HTTP commands, see Appendix A, "Internet Applications Command Sets."

- For a list of all the possible HTTP message header entries, see Appendix B, "The Internet Message Format."

Internet Security, RSA Encryption, SSL, STT, PCT, and WinSock

- What types of security are available on the Internet

- How encryption protects documents and files

- Why security is essential to electronic commerce

- The difference between security specifications and their implementations

- What security proposals are forthcoming on the Internet

The term *Internet security* is almost an oxymoron. The purpose behind the Internet is to provide an open communication platform among a cooperative collection of users. The Internet most certainly is not an entity designed to protect or conceal anything. No regulating body or government has absolute control over who can access the Internet. Anyone can enter it as a user or provider. Any computer attached to the Internet is almost a blatant advertisement for someone to meander inside the network and take a peek.

This model of universal, unrestricted access served Internet users quite well for many years. The fairly recent commercialization of the Internet brings forth an entirely new set of users with different objectives and concerns. Their entry brings forth a heightened sense of overcrowding, and with it, a need for privacy. The increasing number of personal computer users brings, unfortunately, increasing occurrences of computer crime. Given this increase of "cyber-crime," it's only natural that commercial entities want to protect their assets.

The same is true for individual users who want to practice legitimate, lawful commerce on the Internet. Such users see the Internet as a place to gather and exchange information as well as a new, alternative way to purchase products and services. Using current Internet technology, a company can provide information about its specific products to any consumer at any time. Also, current credit card transaction technology makes it possible for users to send their credit card numbers over the Internet and receive their purchases almost immediately. Attracted by advertised products and the ease of buying items with a credit card, consumers can easily be lured into making immediate, impulsive purchases. The immediacy of electronic communication thus becomes a strong enticement to buy a product now!

Sounds nice, doesn't it? However, this cyber-marketplace has the same dangers as the physical marketplace. A criminal who knows that you have money will feel compelled to relieve you of its burden. As you become increasingly comfortable sending money to vendors by using robot programs, criminals will surely create their own robot programs that can mug your robot and steal your money.

N O T E The knowledge that commerce is the driving force that provides jobs for programmers is what provides value. Organizations interested in protecting their assets on the Internet will hire programmers who understand the needs of commercial enterprises and how to protect them with Internet security techniques. You won't make a dime off some idealist who thinks all information yearns for freedom. On the other hand, a programmer who can show a business how to safely tap into a new distribution channel by implementing secure transaction methods can make a tremendous profit.

Suppose that a computer vendor posts a Web page that enables consumers to custom-tailor their new computers with specific peripherals, software, and accessories. To a customer, this idea is intriguing. Add security, however, and the situation changes. Instead of an intriguing idea, a Web page is now a viable incentive for the customer to place an order immediately with a credit card transaction. Adding security helps assuage a customer's fears of some unscrupulous individual stealing a credit card number as it travels across the Internet. The concept of providing secure transactions isn't limited to large corporations like IBM. Before long, everyone from Sears to Krazy Achmed's ComputoRama will want developers to help them establish a presence on the Internet. Learn how to secure business transactions on the Internet and then raise your rates. ■

Two types of people are interested in Internet security: those who must protect information and those who want to get it. You probably can learn more valid security information from the criminal hackers than from security professionals. After all, the hacker likes to disseminate information whereas security professionals prefer to conceal information. Keep this in mind when browsing for additional information about security. This chapter provides information on the prevalent Internet security topics in action today and those in the design stages for tomorrow. ■

Internet Security

The topic of Internet security covers two distinct areas:

- ■ Network security
- ■ Transaction security

Most people probably think of network security foremost. Network security is an organization's ability to protect its assets from unauthorized users. Such assets include the computer's physical components (the CPU, storage, printers, and so on) as well as its logical components (user IDs and passwords).

Transaction security addresses how two or more entities conduct a private communication process or transaction. When you write a check and pass it to someone else, your signature verifies that the check is authentic. Transaction security provides a set of rules to perform the same task. As electronic commerce grows, transaction security is becoming as important as network security.

Network Security

Implementing network security isn't as simple as locking a door. Organizations must take several steps to protect their computers and data from users who do not have rightful access. Such unauthorized users, or *attackers,* often gain access when the protector overlooks a simple yet essential security component.

Network security consists of three aspects:

- Physical—preventing physical access to the hardware, such as a locked computer room or closet.
- Procedural—procedures are the actions computer users take that add security.
- Logical—software security measures, such as password validation.

Think of these three aspects as a triangle. If you remove any one of them, the entire structure collapses. As a programmer, you can do very little to implement physical security. Perhaps you can make recommendations in your documentation, but a program won't save anything if the user leaves the door unlocked and a program signed on with full rights while strolling down the hall for a cup of coffee. Leaving a door open might also spill over into a violation of procedures.

However, programmers have some control over procedural methods. After all, developing an application is a process of automating procedures. Specifications tell programmers what goal they need to accomplish, but not always how to accomplish the goal. That's why some programs written to the same specification do not perform with identical results; the specifications leave some room for interpretation.

When you design your application, the procedures that you include or omit can determine the amount and type of security that the users' information has. An attacker gaining illicit access to a computer system "through a back door" often is the result of the software designer failing to address a potential security flaw that the attacker can exploit. Although a specification might give you some latitude on *how* you implement security features, you should not pick and choose *which* security features to implement. Failure to implement all security features properly, as specified, can provide the open back door that an attacker needs to gain access. Bear this in mind as you read the sections ahead that cover specific Internet security specifications.

The logical aspect of network security is where programmers have the most control. The degree of quality and integrity of logical network security depends on your specific implementation of a security specification. Suppose that a specification has a procedure that states that you should allow access only to user accounts that begin with *XYZ*. That is a procedural specification. When you write the code and it executes on your server, the security aspect changes to a logical one.

Firewalls   Perhaps the most common implementation of logical network security is a *firewall*. A firewall is a single point of contact between a private and public network. An organization's internal network is an example of a private network, whereas the Internet is a public network. If you connect the two networks, the device (usually a router or server) that implements the connection is your firewall. What you do, or fail to do, with that firewall determines your security's integrity. The following are the three most common types of firewalls:

- Bastion
- Screening filter
- Dual-homed gateway

Bastion Firewalls   A bastion firewall is a machine placed between the private network and the Internet. The bastion's basic purpose is to deny access to anyone who is not on a user-defined list of authorized users. The bastion relays messages to or from other authorized users on the list. Bastions operate at the application layer of the Open System Interconnect (OSI) Reference Model (Chapter 3, "Internet Connectivity," describes the OSI Reference Model). Continual interaction with the application layer impedes overall network performance when the network environment must support many users. A bastion firewall lets all users on the internal network access the public network, and then enforces security rules at the application or user level. This type of firewall is vulnerable when an attacker impersonates an authorized user to gain access to the network.

Screening Filter Firewalls   A screening filter firewall uses a router to connect the private network to the Internet. This type of firewall controls Internet access by examining each packet that flows through the router. Screening filters operate at the network layer of the OSI Reference Model. The implication of operating at this layer is that screening filters can control access to machines and ports on the private network, but cannot control anything in higher layers of the OSI Reference Model. Screening filters are vulnerable to spoofing. *Spoofing* is a process in which an attacker "fools" a network connection into thinking that the attacker is a legitimate user. If an attacker can spoof past the screening filter, the applications and data files are wide open to misuse.

Dual-Homed Gateway Firewalls   A dual-homed gateway firewall combines the elements of screening filter and bastion firewalls to offer protection at the network and application layers. Depending on the implementation, this type of firewall can utilize one or many computers to perform the firewall function. A dual-homed gateway firewall protects the network from general access while letting some applications work from outside the private network. This type of firewall is quite flexible, enabling you to choose which resources to protect with one or both of the methods at its disposal.

Firewall Theory   If you have information to protect, or know someone who does, you're probably thinking that firewalls are a good idea. You first have to consider what type of program you need to write to implement a firewall. This section discusses some of the common security techniques involved in creating a working firewall.

Secure IP Tunnels   An Internet Protocol (IP) tunnel is a path between two firewalls that uses the Internet as a transport device. Packets that traverse the Internet Protocol tunnel are subject to any prying eyes along the way. Hence, the need for security arises for private communication. Here's how an Internet Protocol tunnel works.

Secure IP tunnels encapsulate IP packets and their headers into an encrypted IP packet. The firewall on the sending side of the tunnel encloses the sender's information in the encrypted packet and forwards it through the Internet toward the receiving end. The receiving firewall removes the encapsulation, decrypts the message, and routes it to the proper address inside its private network.

Both ends of the secure IP tunnel must agree on the method of encapsulation and encryption, the levels of protection, and which ports will communicate. Otherwise, these encrypted packets become excess chatter on the Internet. Secure IP tunnels are an effective means of implementing security. They enable network administrators to set security policy without bothering the users with security details.

IP Filters   You might have seen old movies in which someone tried to get inside the Paramount Movie lot, only to have a guard tell them that they couldn't get in because they weren't on the list. IP filters are nothing more than an automated version of the guard.

IP filters allow or deny IP packets at a firewall between the Internet and the private network. At the base level, IP filters refuse all packets moving in either direction. An administrator must define which packets to allow or discard based on some criteria, such as an application or user network address. IP filters can also filter based on direction, such as whether the packet is incoming or leaving the private network. To perform this task, IP filters rely on address information stored in the router's routing tables.

By itself, IP filtering is insufficient as a firewall, but does provide a basic infrastructure for building further security measures. Attackers often investigate the routing tables to learn valid addresses. If they can spoof one of these addresses, they can bypass the IP filter security, because no passwords operate at this level.

Proxy Servers   A proxy is a person authorized to act on another's behalf. Proxy servers extend this concept by acting as a bastion and relaying communications to known users (that is, users defined on the internal network) that the server deems acceptable. Users in the private network access an application in the proxy server. This server requires users to authenticate themselves before giving them access to the Internet.

Proxy servers let administrators determine which pieces of the Internet are available to the users on the private network. An organization might implement proxy servers if it finds that users are spending too much time browsing the World Wide Web instead of working. It's proof that firewalls work in both directions. A firewall not only can prevent external users from entering an internal network, but can also prevent internal users from entering an external network. Proxy servers also prevent unauthorized data from leaving the premises through the Internet. At the very least, they record who sent what to whom.

One disadvantage of proxy servers is the overhead that they incur on communication. Proxy servers are time-consuming and slow a system's performance noticeably. The advantage of a proxy server is that it does not require users to run a special program. Once the authentication passes, they can use whatever Telnet, File Transfer Protocol (FTP), or other Internet application they want.

SOCKS Servers   SOCKS servers operate much the same as proxy servers, but do not require users to authenticate themselves directly. Instead, the SOCKS servers require SOCKS-compatible versions (called *SOCKSified* clients) of client software. The SOCKSified client sends its requests to the server's SOCKS port. The server automatically authenticates the client and allows the outbound communication.

SOCKS servers definitely have disadvantages. Like proxy servers, the SOCKS servers provide a firewall that imposes overhead on the system. To work with a SOCKS server, clients must use specific SOCKSified versions of programs. Finally, a SOCKS server works only on outbound connections to the Internet. It does not provide services for incoming security, so it doesn't allow incoming sessions to communicate with the private network.

Transaction Security

A transaction is the process of conducting business. In most cases, such a transaction involves moving something of importance from one location to another. The amount of security that you choose depends on how much value is attached to the items involved in the transaction. If you're sending a message to someone else, the value that you place on the message determines whether you send an open postcard, a letter in a sealed envelope, or perhaps a package with a dedicated courier service. The degree and type of transaction security that you use for sending data over the Internet is much the same as sending a letter.

Most electronic mail (e-mail) is much like a post card. It travels from one location to the next, stopping at various points along the path. Any network administrator could read your message without any resistance or any way for you to detect that it is being read. Should such indiscriminate access to data be unacceptable to you or those to whom you send the data, you might find yourself in need of transaction security.

Before deciding on a method of transaction security, it helps to define the elements necessary to secure a transaction. The following list might help you decide what's best for your situation:

- *Transactions must be confidential.* Your transaction should remain private and unavailable to others as it travels the Internet. Encryption is the best way to ensure that your transactions remain confidential.

- *The transaction must retain integrity.* This means that your transaction arrives in the same state that you sent it. Nothing along the path should alter or affect the contents of your transaction. If you send $10 in a financial transaction, you don't want it to arrive with a zero cash balance. Encryption helps retain integrity. Installing some form of authentication, such as a checksum or digital signature, is also wise.

■ *Both the sender and receiver must be accountable.* Both parties should agree on the transaction and offer some form of acknowledgment when sending or receiving the transaction.

■ *Both parties must be authenticated.* Some communication protocols use a series of Acknowledgment and Negative Acknowledgment codes to communicate the status of a transaction. The codes verify whether the transaction made it in one piece, but don't verify that the right person is sending or receiving the transaction. Authentication ensures that the parties are who they say they are.

Encryption   Encryption is the process of transforming a message so that only the intended receiver can restore the message to its original, readable form. A random pattern can easily scramble a message. However, the problem with random patterns is that because of the unpredictable nature of the scrambling process, nobody—not even the message's originator—knows how to unscramble the message so that the receiver can use it again. A valid scheme must use a regular pattern to encrypt the message so that the receiver can decrypt it. However, such a scheme must retain some secrecy so that others cannot decrypt the message.

These patterns are called *keys*. The size and type of a key determines how difficult it is for someone to crack the encryption code and reassemble the message. Keys are bit codes. Computers can easily perform a repetitive search until it finds the correct key to decode the encrypted message. The longer the bit code, the more difficult and time-consuming it is to crack it. The shorter the bit code, the easier it is to crack, especially with the assistance of modern computer technology. Many Internet servers use only 40-bit keys that, although difficult to decipher, are still vulnerable to decoding. A larger bit code increases the number of possible bit combinations and therefore greatly diminishes the likelihood of unauthorized access. Some products use a 128-bit key to make unauthorized decryption practically impossible.

N O T E   To calculate the number of possible bit combinations in a given set of bits, raise 2 to a power X, where X is the number of bits in the set. For example, a two-bit set has four possible combinations because $2^2 = 4$. The possible combinations are (in binary notation) 00 01 10 11. An eight-bit set has 256 possible combinations because $2^8 = 256$. A 40-bit set has 1,099,511,627,776 possible combinations because $2^{40} = 1,099,511,627,776$. ■

CAUTION

The United States government considers encryption schemes to be a form of munitions. Therefore, the exporting of encryption-capable applications falls under heavy scrutiny. The government allows as much as 40-bit key encryption for export. Any key using an encyption over a 40-bit code must remain within the United States. Violation of this policy is subject to criminal penalty.

There are two types of keys: symmetric and asymmetric. A symmetric key is one in which the sender and receiver use the same key to encrypt and decrypt a message. Using only a single key is the major weakness of symmetric key encryption schemes. In a symmetric key encryption scheme, the key code must travel unencrypted so that the receiver can use it to decrypt the message. If an attacker gets this key code, he can decrypt your messages, regardless of how many bits you have used to encrypt them.

The United States government defined and endorses the Data Encryption Standard (DES), which is a symmetric, secret-key encryption scheme. Both the sender and receiver must know the same secret key code to encrypt and decrypt messages with DES. The DES standard operates on 64-bit blocks with a 56-bit key. DES operates rather quickly and works well for encrypting large data sets. So far, no one has ever broken into a DES-encrypted file, although many researchers have tried. A pair of researchers proposed a theory that could break the DES encryption scheme, but they still consider DES a secure standard due to the resources and time required to crack a DES-encrypted file. One of these researchers, Adi Shamir, is also one of the creators of the RSA public-key encryption system. The section "RSA Encryption," later in this chapter, covers that encryption system.

Asymmetric key encryption schemes use a public and a private key. Anyone who wants to receive an encrypted message must have both keys. The receiver provides the public key, and the sender then uses it to encrypt the message. The only way to decrypt the message is with a combination of the receiver's public and private key. Even the sender can't decrypt the message, because the sender doesn't know the receiver's private key. Asymmetric encryption schemes soon turn into a web of public keys. In small groups, this process is reasonable, but it becomes unmanageable in large environments with many users.

RSA is an example of a public-key encryption system. The section "RSA Encyption," later in this chapter, covers this system in detail.

Authentication   Authentication is a process that assures a document's recipient of the sender's validity and the document's integrity. The authentication process verifies that a transaction is original and unmodified. The process yields a digital signature created from a *message digest,* which is a unique string of bits based on the message's contents. A signature is an unforgeable data string that authenticates that a specific person created or agreed with the document's contents. A sender creates the message digest and encrypts it with a private key. The message digest accompanies the message. The receiver decrypts the message digest and compares it to the message. If the two agree, the authentication process is valid. You can encrypt and sign a message at the same time.

Another authentication process relies on digital certificates. These digital certificates contain the following:

- A public key
- A *Distinguished Name* (name and address information)
- Issue data and expiration data
- The digital signature of a certifying authority (CA)

The CA is a trusted authority, such as VeriSign, that creates digital certificates. The CA usually charges for this service. A CA publishes its public key and Distinguished Name for other people to add to Web browsers or servers as part of their trusted root (a directory not available to users logged on the server—typically \ETC\HOSTS). Users who want to authenticate a digital certificate use the CA's public key to verify the CA's signature in the certificate.

RSA Encryption

RSA is an algorithm for asymmetric encryption. Named after its inventors—Ron Rivest, Adi Shamir, and Leonard Adleman—the algorithm, owned by Public Key Partners (PKP) of Sunnyvale, California, received a patent in 1983. RSA's use is subject to the approval, and possible license, of its owners. Anyone in North America must obtain a royalty-based license from PKP to use the RSA algorithm in a commercial endeavor. Fortunately, PKP usually allows free noncommercial use of RSA for personal, academic, or intellectual reasons, with written permission. The United States government can use RSA without a license, because the algorithm was developed at the Massachusetts Institute of Technology (MIT) with some government funding. The patent does not apply outside North America.

Part
III

Ch
17

RSA is well established as a *de facto* standard. As the most widely implemented public-key encryption system, it is a safe choice for implementing encryption schemes in applications. RSA's common use makes it easier to exchange digital signatures. This standard is entrenched in the financial transaction protocols being developed for electronic commerce. This endorsement alone confirms that RSA carries much weight as a secure standard.

RSA and DES

RSA is a complement to, rather than a replacement for, DES encryption. Each scheme has benefits that the other lacks. DES is a fast encryption scheme and works well for bulk encryption. Although RSA is fine for encrypting small messages, DES is a better choice for larger files because of its speed. RSA provides digital signatures and secure key exchange without requiring a prior exchange of secret codes.

A single user protecting files for personal use probably won't need RSA. For such use, a single key-encryption scheme like DES usually suffices because there's no danger involved in passing the key to anyone else. RSA becomes important when you must share messages with others.

Combining the two encryption schemes is like sending a coded message in a secure envelope. A typical RSA digital envelope transaction with another party might operate as follows:

1. Encrypt the message with a random DES key.
2. Encrypt the DES key with RSA.
3. Send the combined DES/RSA encrypted document through the Internet.

As mentioned before, RSA also creates digital signatures. When authentication is as important as concealment, you must use RSA in place of or in conjunction with DES encryption.

How Does RSA Work?

RSA starts with two large primes: p and q. The product of p and q is n, the modulus. You might find some documentation pertaining to RSA that recommends choosing a key pair with *strong* prime numbers. A strong prime is one with properties that make the product (n) hard to factor with certain methods.

N O T E A *modulus* is the mathematical process of dividing two operands and returning the remainder. ▪

N O T E *Factoring* is the process of splitting an integer into a small set of integers (*factors*) which, when multiplied, yields the original integer. Prime factorization requires splitting an integer into factors that are prime numbers. Multiplying two prime integers is easy, but factoring the product is much more difficult. That's why prime integers are such prize candidates for encryption schemes. Reversing the process of multiplication using prime numbers is extremely difficult. This is called a *one-way function*—one that is easy to perform in the forward direction, but far more difficult to compute in the inverse direction. ▪

Due to new factoring methods, the common-knowledge method of choosing strong primes is no longer an advantage. The new methods have just as much success on strong primes as with the weak ones.

Another concern with choosing your primes is the size of modulus that you want. There's a bit of a trade-off: A larger modulus creates a more secure encryption scheme, but also slows the encryption process. Choose your modulus length based on your security needs, or perhaps based on the resources that an attacker might use to crack your encrypted message. Here's some research trivia to help guide your decision: Rivest's estimates suggest that an attacker can factor a 512-bit modulus with an $8.2 million effort. If you require a 512-bit modulus, each of your primes should be approximately 256 bits long.

Next, choose a number, called e, that is less than the value of n and also relatively prime to (p-1)(q-1). Next, find its inverse value, d, (mod(p-1)(q-1)). That means that (ed = 1 mod(p-1)(q-1)).

The variables e and d are, respectively, the public and private exponents. The public key pair is (n,e). The private key is d. You should keep factors p and q confidential, or else destroy them.

Before you start writing your own code, pay attention to this next part, because it reveals the Achille's heel of RSA encryption.

Trying to determine the private key from the public key combination (n,e) is practically impossible. Now look at those variables (p and q) that you want to hide or destroy. If you factor n into p and q, you can discover the private key (d).

The RSA encryption algorithm follows these steps:

1. Create two variables, P and Q. Create another variable, N.
2. Choose two large prime numbers and assign one to P and the other to Q.
   N is the modulus of P and Q (n := P mod Q).

3. Create a variable, E.

4. Choose a number to assign to E that is less than the value of N and also relatively prime to the results of the formula ((P-1) (Q-1)).

5. Create a variable, D.

6. Find the inverse value of E with the formula (mod(P-1) (Q-1)). Assign that value to variable D.

Keeping in mind how much an attacker would love to have your p and q primes, carefully consider which method to use to generate primes. If you select a predictable pattern, an attacker might duplicate it and render your machinations useless. It's best to obtain random numbers from a physical process. Some computers use dedicated peripheral cards just for this purpose. One example is the FedWire II system that many American banks use. FedWire II is an encrypted communication network that performs monetary wire transfers between banks and the Federal Reserve. You probably want a less expensive solution. Try timing some of the various input devices connected to your computer (such as your mouse, keyboard, or serial device) and use the time difference between inputs as a random number generator. If you choose an algorithm based on a random seed, try to select a seed that isn't obvious to someone who can duplicate your efforts, or at least a seed that is truly random.

RSA Authentication

RSA authentication is a specific method for creating a digital signature. A digital signature holds a unique advantage over a handwritten signature. With a handwritten signature, you can alter a document's contents without invalidating the signature. You cannot do this with a digital signature, because the document's contents comprise the digital signature itself.

N O T E A digital signature failure doesn't always mean that someone tampered with your document. If you are transmitting the document over the Internet or other network lines, a digital signature failure might also suggest a corrupted file transfer. ■

You obtain your digital signature from a message digest. A message digest is the result of a hash function. A *hash function* is a mathematical algorithm that reads some input data source, usually a message or some kind of document, and returns a compact binary output that represents the source. Some other types of programs, such as databases, use hash functions as an index to the data source for quick searches.

N O T E A hash function uses a variable-size input and returns a fixed-size string, called the *hash value*. ■

Hash functions that are difficult to invert are specifically useful for creating message digests. A message digest is a concise representation of the message used to create the digest. Any change in the message itself yields a different message digest string, thus making it useful as a digital signature.

Part
III

Ch
17

Several well-known message digest functions are in use, but MD5 is perhaps the best function to implement as a digital signature. MD5 is secure, reasonably fast, and publicly available for unrestricted use. For more details on the MD5 function, see RFC 1321.

One significant issue with digital signatures is a legal matter rather than a technical one. Digital signatures might not have the same legal status as a handwritten signature. No one has yet challenged the validity of a digital signature in court, so there is no legal precedent. The National Institute of Standards and Technology (NIST) has, however, requested an opinion from the United States General Accounting Office (GAO) regarding the legal status of digital signatures. The GAO opinion is that digital signatures meet the legal standards of handwritten signatures.

Current Security Specifications

The previous sections discussed theories, concepts, and algorithms as they pertain to Internet security. This section provides an overview of some security specifications that put these theories into motion. Specifications are the guidelines for implementations of a concept. For example, Netscape Communications has a Secure Sockets Layer (SSL) specification that it implements in its products, Netscape Navigator and Netscape Commerce Server. The specifications that this section discusses are instructions to build your own implementation; the final products are the implementation.

Whenever you want to implement any specification or RFC, either for personal or business reasons, you should always investigate ownership issues of the algorithms used in the specification. Some algorithms are in the public domain, others perhaps free for personal or academic use. If you decide to implement a protocol in a business application or commercial product, you might have to pay royalties to the owner.

Another item that you should consider is how different specifications overlap to resolve a similar problem. Perhaps you need one or more methods to resolve your particular problem. Several Internet-Drafts propose to resolve the problem of security on the Internet. Each of these standards attacks the same problem. Each proposed standard uses some methods, such as encryption, that are common to the others. Then again, each security proposal offers something unique. Competing standards often cause more work for developers. Until a standards war settles on a victor, you might have to implement each of these specifications so that your application's users can conduct transactions with users of other programs. Perhaps the author of another program didn't have your foresight and implemented only one secure protocol. That puts the burden on you to accommodate the other author's program or leave your application's users in the cold.

The Secure Sockets Layer (SSL)

The SSL is a public domain Internet security technology developed by Netscape Communications. SSL combines the elements of an Internet transfer protocol with modern encryption and authentication techniques. The result is a secure communication environment for transactions on an unsecured, public network. SSL implements RSA encryption to ensure private and authenticated communications over the Internet.

The SSL protocol provides three basic properties:

- Symmetric cryptography to ensure a private connection. The encryption activates after an initial protocol exchange to define a secret key code.
- Asymmetric cryptography to authenticate the connection.
- Reliable connections in which a secure hash function, such as MD5, checks message integrity.

SSL is application protocol independent. A higher-level protocol can layer itself on top of the SSL protocol transparently. The SSL protocol does not interfere with the higher-level protocol's performance, even when communicating with an insecure source. Because SSL is a layered protocol, messages at each layer can include fields for length, description, and content. The SSL protocol fragments messages into manageable blocks. SSL can compress the data before adding a signature and encryption. When this compression process is complete, SSL transmits the message. A client decrypts and decompresses the fragments, reassembles the fragments in order, and then delivers the message to higher-level applications. An SSL session can include multiple secure connections.

The SSL Record Protocol, a subset of the SSL protocol, encapsulates higher-level protocols, such as the SSL Handshake Protocol. The SSL Handshake Protocol enables the server and client to authenticate one another and negotiate an encryption process. Unfortunately, the SSL handshake process is a potential weakness in the entire security process. The client authentication process is independent of the cipher strength used in the session. In other words, the cipher strength that the process uses to determine the key process is weaker than the cipher strength used in later communications with the key. An attacker's best chance to beat SSL security is to crack the weak cipher code that contains the key and then use that key to decrypt the transaction.

Part of the handshake process includes coordinating the states of the client and server. The state of either machine can be *operating* or *pending*. This coordination allows both sides to operate consistently, even if not in parallel states. When the handshake is complete, the client and server can exchange cipher specification messages.

N O T E   A cipher specification defines the bulk data encryption algorithm and a message digest algorithm. It also defines cryptographic attributes, such as the hash size. ■

SSL requires a reliable transport protocol, such as Transmission Control Protocol (TCP). The layer above TCP is the SSL Record Protocol. The SSL record layer receives uninterpreted data from clients in arbitrarily sized blocks. SSL compresses all records using the compression algorithm defined in the current session state. You must use a lossless compression algorithm.

N O T E Lossy compression is irreversible. It provides the highest degree of compression, but at the cost of lost information. Lossy compression makes guesses about which information it can sacrifice while still maintaining a close resemblance to the original data source.

Lossless compression, however, is reversible. It doesn't provide as much compression as a lossy scheme, but doesn't lose any information and provides a method to restore the original data source. ▨

Although the SSL protocol itself is rather complex, you should not have much difficulty implementing it in your applications. That's because WinSock 2.0 offers some additions for SSL support. As a Delphi programmer, you will doubtlessly use WinSock to write your Internet applications. The developers of the WinSock 2.0 specification recognize the need for secure transmission and the ubiquitous nature of Netscape Communications and its SSL protocol. Therefore, WinSock 2.0 supports new constant definitions and record structures to accommodate developers who need to implement the SSL protocol.

Private Communication Technology (PCT)

Microsoft developed the Private Communication Technology (PCT) protocol to prevent electronic eavesdropping in client/server applications. The protocol is compatible with SSL, but claims to correct or improve on several weaknesses of SSL.

PCT's purpose is to provide a private communication path between a client and server. The protocol adds authentication for the server and also provides the same option for clients. Like SSL, PCT requires a reliable transport protocol such as TCP. Also like SLL, PCT is an application-protocol-independent protocol, so higher-level application protocols such as Hypertext Transport Protocol (HTTP) or FTP can layer above it and operate transparently.

PCT begins connections by performing a handshake to negotiate an algorithm and symmetric encryption key and then authenticating the server. The difference between PCT and SSL at this point is that, during this handshake, PCT uses certified asymmetric public keys. This step helps PCT eliminate one of SSL's potential security problems. The PCT protocol doesn't specify any details regarding certification verification. Instead, PCT expects the programmer to provide a function that rules on the validity of a received certificate. Providing your own validation rules is actually a benefit, because it gives you the option to choose the certificate system based on your needs, not those of a secure transport protocol. After the handshake, PCT encrypts all data transmission using the session key negotiated during the handshake.

PCT differs from SSL mainly in the handshake phase. Beyond that, the security is much the same. The following list identifies the chief differences between PCT and SSL:

- ▨ PCT's message structures are significantly shorter than SSL's. A reconnected session without client authentication requires only one message in each direction.
- ▨ PCT provides a wider choice of protocol characteristics for negotiated encryptographic algorithms and formats. In addition to the cipher type and server certificate type negotiated in SSL sessions, PCT also negotiates a hash function type and key exchange

type. If client authentication is necessary, PCT also negotiates a client signature type and certificate type.

■ Message authentication uses different keys than those used as encryption keys. This allows longer authentication keys, and thus a much more secure authentication process.

■ PCT's client authentication challenge/response sequence uses the type of cipher negotiated for the session. SSL's client authentication uses a weaker cipher that is independent of the type negotiated for the session.

Much of the PCT protocol specification is similar to the SSL protocol specification. Both protocol specifications are merely Internet-Drafts at this point. An *Internet-Draft* is merely a working document of the Internet Engineering Task Force (IETF), which means that it is not an approved or authorized specification. However, odds are good that the IETF will grant some form of approval to one or both of these specifications. Until then, expect revisions and changes that might invalidate your code and infuriate you.

Secure Transaction Technology (STT)

If you have any doubt that electronic commerce drives the need for Internet security, this section should open your eyes. The Secure Transaction Technology (STT) protocol is a joint development between Visa and Microsoft to provide a method to secure bankcard transactions over open networks such as the Internet.

N O T E   Visa and Microsoft developed STT as an open specification for the industry. Meanwhile, MasterCard, IBM, and others worked on another open specification for the industry: Secure Electronic Payment Protocol (SEPP).

On February 1, 1996, MasterCard International and Visa International joined together to announce a technical standard for safeguarding payment-card purchases made over the Internet. They call the new specification Secure Electronic Transactions (SET), which combines both efforts.

The SET details were to be published late in February 1996. ■

Earlier sections of this chapter discussed the growing trend of electronic commerce and the need for secure financial transactions. Breaking into an encrypted file is a daunting task, and people always take the path of least resistance. Cracking an encrypted transaction is the modern equivalent of blowing up the bank to steal its money. To say the least, it's not subtle. Besides, a criminal must decide whether the contents are worth the effort. If the prize inside an encrypted file is nothing more than a collection of Charlie Brown movies in AVI format, it's probably not worth the effort required to crack the file.

Suppose that an attacker wants to steal your funds. Instead of attacking your secure file, he might instead set up a Web server that claims to represent a legitimate business. With a little creative programming, the attacker's site could let you browse an electronic catalog of goods. After you decide to make a purchase, you engage your super-secret encryption scheme and send off a payment to the server. After a nice run of collecting credit card numbers, the server closes down. You're left anxiously awaiting a package that never arrives—and as you wait, the attacker is trashing your credit history. This kind of nightmare is exactly what bankcard holders want to avoid. They already spend millions of dollars to combat credit card fraud.

With the aim of fighting such scams, STT has the following objectives:

- Ensuring confidentiality of payment information
- Authenticating cardholders and merchants
- Preserving the integrity of payment data

Bankcard providers certainly want to encourage commerce on the Internet. An analysis of past mail order and telephone order transactions shows that customers strongly prefer paying with bankcards rather than with checks, wire transfers, or any other type of payment. Credit cards fit better with the nature of electronic communications than any other payment medium.

The STT protocol specifications, like other security specifications, can address only a portion of the protocols necessary for electronic commerce. Standard Internet protocols (such as TCP/IP and HTTP) already exist to provide the transport mechanism, communication services, and application interface necessary for commerce. STT differs from the protocols previously discussed in this chapter in that it concentrates exclusively on the security aspects that pertain to bankcard transactions. The following aspects of bankcard transactions are within the scope of the STT protocol:

- The application of cryptographic algorithms, like RSA and DES
- Credential messages and object formats
- Purchase messages and object formats
- Authorization messages and object formats
- Message protocols between client and server

Clearing and settlement is the process by which a merchant receives payment for a transaction using a bankcard. The merchant authorizes the transaction and then later requests payment from the cardholder's financial institution. Internet commerce poses the same danger to merchants as they face from other sources: credit card fraud.

The clearing and settlement process differs depending on the card used and the relationship defined between the merchant and the financial institution. As such, STT does not modify the clearing and settlement process. The merchant is responsible for clearing and settling electronic commerce transactions in the same manner in which it processes other transactions. The clearing terms depend on the merchant's agreement with its bank.

STT brings forth a new application of digital signatures by requiring dual signatures. Electronic commerce requires two sets of authorizations. Suppose that you want to send an offer to a vendor to buy an item. You would include a digital signature to authenticate yourself as a customer and otherwise validate the message. At the same time that you send your message to the vendor, you send another message to your financial institution that authorizes it to release the funds that you specify *if* the vendor accepts your offer. You need not disclose the details of the offer to the financial institution. All the financial institution needs is your instruction to release funds if it meets a specified condition.

To process the offer automatically, the vendor sends a request for payment, including your digital signature, to your financial institution. The financial institution matches signatures. If it verifies that both are the same, it transfers the funds to your vendor. The transaction, from a financial perspective, is then complete.

A dual signature concatenates the message digests from your letters to the vendor and the financial institution. STT then computes another message digest from the concatenated result and encrypts it with the signer's private signature key.

One key element necessary for authorization is a credential for cardholders and merchants alike. The financial institution provides a credential for cardholders. In theory, you cannot alter these credentials and only the financial institution can generate them. Likewise, the merchant's financial institution issues the merchant's credential.

N O T E In this case, a credential is a binary file that acts as the bank's seal of approval for financial transactions. The binary file is actually a digital signature like those discussed earlier in the chapter. ▣

Part
III

Ch
17

From Here...

Encryption is an age-old technology that works quite well. Its application in electronic commerce is still in its infancy, however. Each of the Internet security specifications discussed in this chapter is still under revision. Some products, particularly those from Netscape and Microsoft, already implement the concepts, even though the specifications are nothing more than working drafts. Perhaps that's why people still don't trust their cards to these schemes.

Nevertheless, the market for such technology continues to grow. If you're a programmer who works as an independent contractor, this is an excellent field to enter on the ground floor. With billions of dollars in purchasing power at stake, vendors clamor for space on the Internet. As this happens, they spend a lot of money on developers who can ensure the safety of their dollars, as well as that of their customers.

In the meantime, here are some Web sites that might help you find more information:

- RSA Data Security at **http://www.rsa.com/**
- The Internet Engineering Task Force at **http://www.ietf.cnri.reston.va.us/home.html**
- The IBM Home Page at **http://www.ibm.com**
- Microsoft at **http://www.microsoft.com**
- Netscape Communications at **http://www.netscape.com**
- The Internet Spec List at **http://www.graphcomp.com/info/specs/**
- InterNIC Specifications at **http://ds.internic.net/ds/dspg0intdoc.html**
- Raptor Systems Security at **http://www.raptor.com/./library/library.html**
- Stardust Technologies at **http://www.stardust.com/wsresource/wsresrce.html**

- WinSock Development Info at **http://www.sockets.com/**
- MasterCard at **http://www.mastercard.com**
- Visa at **http://www.visa.com**

This chapter gives you a bird's eye view of Internet security concepts and techniques. You can browse some of the preceding Web pages for more information on security topics. Then, you might want to try implementing security in some of the protocols discussed in previous chapters:

- Consider making your mail a little more private by adding encryption to the SMTP and POP mail protocols, as discussed in Chapter 9, "Developing SMTP and POP Mail Clients."
- Consider merging SSL or PCT with a Web browser discussed in Chapter 12, "The Web—HTTP, HTML, and Beyond."
- Try adding SSL or PCT to the Web server that you built in Chapter 16, "Building a Web Server with Delphi."

The Netscape API—
Incorporating Delphi
with the Netscape
Browser and Server

- Control the Netscape browser using Dynamic Data Exchange (DDE) from a Delphi application

- Control the Netscape browser using Object Linking and Embedding (OLE) Automation from a Delphi application

The world of the Internet is changing rapidly. In many cases, software hasn't been able to keep up with the pace. Even with teams of programmers working on a single package, the needs of the marketplace often exceed the capability of a rapidly changing product. When users need features, they often cannot or will not wait until the next revision of the package.

Software developers have several choices to make when their domain is dynamic and swiftly changing. The first choice is to create a static, closed system that the marketplace simply passes by. The alternative is to create an open system that enables developers to add new features when users start demanding them. The latter alternative is the focus of this chapter. Netscape has chosen to make its programs extensible. Programmers can extend the functionality of the Netscape browser and server software by programming to the Netscape application program interface (API).

By publishing the Navigator API, Netscape enables programmers to treat the browser as an open system. When a user's needs exceed the browser's capabilities, a programmer can add functionality to the browser by using the API. The converse is also true: If you need to Internet-enable an existing program, you can use the Navigator API to extend that program's functionality.

This chapter not only deals with extending the Netscape browser, but also with using the browser as a tool to Internet-enable a new or existing program. Microsoft CEO Bill Gates says that "an Internet browser is a trivial piece of software." At most levels, programmers would tend to agree with this assertion. However, most programmers don't have weeks or months to invest in creating a browser if their application must duplicate existing browser functionality. In general, programmers, when given a choice, will try not to "reinvent the wheel." Netscape provides a powerful interface that enables programmers to treat the Netscape browser as a module and therefore save a lot of programming time. ▄

Netscape Browser Automation Using DDE and Delphi

DDE is one method of program intercommunication. DDE uses shared memory to exchange data between two programs. Unlike OLE, DDE is fairly unstructured. It enables each program to determine how DDE is used. Some programs use DDE only to exchange data; other programs, such as Netscape's Navigator, can use DDE as a way to enable another program to control them remotely.

Netscape provides a rich DDE programming interface that enables programmers to control many desirable aspects of the Netscape browser from another program. To help you with your program development, Delphi provides a simple set of DDE components, which you can find, starting with DDEClientConv, on the System tab of the Delphi palette. Figure 18.1 shows the available Delphi components for using DDE.

The DDE communication process consists of six parts: server, client, service name, topic, arguments, and return value.

The Server

In the traditional computing sense of the word, the *server* is the program that receives and acts on a *DDE request,* which is a message from a client program requesting data or an action from the server. In this chapter's discussion, the Netscape browser is the server.

The Client

The *client* is the program that initiates the *DDE conversation,* which is the interaction between the two cooperating programs. The client initiates the conversation by sending the server commands or requests. In most cases when using the Netscape DDE API, the Delphi program acts as the client.

FIG. 18.1
The Delphi DDE
components.

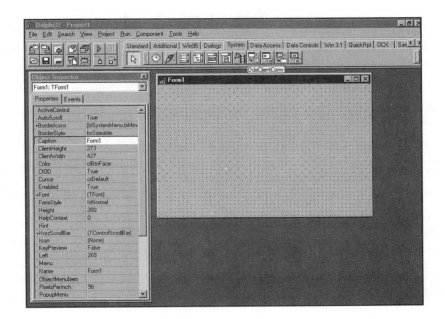

 N O T E With DDE, both participating programs can be a client, a server, or both. If both programs
are servers, messages can continually pass back and forth. An example of continually
passing messages is the Delphi program asking the Netscape browser to load a large Web page; the
browser then continually sends progress messages to the Delphi program for display. ■

The Service Name

The *service name* or *service* tells Windows the program with which your Delphi program will
communicate. In the case of the Netscape browser, the service is NETSCAPE.

The Topic

The *topic* identifies the type of request that the client sends to the server. The topic might refer
to data that the service is requesting or a command that the program should execute.

The Arguments

Arguments are the details for whatever topic is selected. Arguments enable specific pieces of
information to be passed to the target of the DDE message, usually the DDE server. In the
case of an Internet browser, arguments might include a file name or Uniform Resource Locator
(URL).

The Return Value

The *return value* retrieves information that the DDE server sends. In the case of DDE, the return value is usually a pchar (a pointer to a zero-terminated character string), but can be a pointer to other data types.

A Brief Overview of the Netscape Server DDE Topics

When learning a new API, getting a quick overview of its capabilities is often useful. This section provides just such an overview of the Netscape DDE server capabilities. Topics of interest include WWW_OpenURL, which might request that Navigator open and display a Web page, and WWW_WindowChange, which tells Navigator to change the position and/or the size of its display window. Delphi simplifies the task of using DDE, as the following code snippet demonstrates:

```
if NetscapeDDE.SetLink( 'NETSCAPE', 'WWW_OpenURL' )
 then
   NetscapeDDE.RequestData( 'HTTP://WWW.MCP.COM',0xFFFFFFFF,0x1,,,,' );
```

The call to SetLink() identifies the DDE server, NETSCAPE, and the topic, WWW_OpenURL. The method RequestData() sends the needed arguments to Navigator. Detailed descriptions of each topic and its arguments follow the overview sections.

Table 18.1 lists the topics for which the Netscape Navigator acts as a server.

Table 18.1   The Topics for Which the Netscape Navigator Acts as a Server

Topic	Purpose
WWW_Activate	Requests that the Netscape Navigator activate a particular window or create a new window. If the request succeeds, the Netscape window becomes the topmost window and gets the input focus.
WWW_CancelProgress	Asks the browser to cancel a specified transaction. The browser can have multiple windows open, with each downloading, so the client must specify which transaction to cancel.
WWW_Exit	Causes the Netscape browser to close all windows and exit.
WWW_GetWindowInfo	Returns the URL and the specified browser window's current title.
WWW_ListWindows	Returns an array of Netscape window IDs that the Netscape browser currently has open.
WWW_OpenURL	Requests that Netscape load a given URL.
WWW_ParseAnchor	Returns a fully qualified URL when passed an absolute URL and a relative URL.
WWW_QueryURLFile	Returns a URL when passed a path to a local file.

Topic	Purpose
WWW_RegisterProtocol	Registers a protocol that the DDE server should handle.
WWW_RegisterURLEcho	Registers a DDE server with the browser for echoing URLs.
WWW_RegisterViewer	Registers a new viewer for a given Multipurpose Internet Multimedia Extensions (MIME) type. Whenever Navigator is about to display the specified MIME type, the data is passed to the registered viewer instead.
WWW_RegisterWindowChange	Requests that Netscape notify the DDE server whenever a change occurs to a browser's window.
WWW_ShowFile	Directs the Netscape browser to display a local file.
WWW_UnRegisterProtocol	Cancels a protocol's registration.
WWW_UnRegisterURLEcho	Stops the Netscape browser from echoing the URL to a DDE server.
WWW_UnRegisterViewer	Cancels a previously defined view registration.
WWW_UnRegisterWindowChange	Cancels the notification that is being sent whenever a change to one of Navigator's windows occurs.
WWW_Version	Requests that the Netscape browser return the current API version.
WWW_WindowChange	Tells the Netscape browser to make the stated changes to one of its windows.

Part
III

Ch
18

A Brief Overview of the Netscape Client DDE Topics

Table 18.2 lists the topics for which the Netscape Navigator acts as the DDE client and sends a message to a DDE server. Topics in this section require that the Delphi program be set up as a DDE server to receive status messages or data directly from Navigator.

Table 18.2   The Topics for Which the Netscape Navigator Acts as a Client

Topic	Purpose
WWW_Alert	Requests that a DDE server respond to a Netscape message.
WWW_BeginProgress	Tells the DDE server that Netscape is starting to send progress messages.
WWW_EndProgress	Notifies the DDE server that the loading of a URL has finished.

continues

Table 18.2   Continued

Topic	Purpose
WWW_MakingProgress	Notifies the DDE server of the progress of a loading URL.
WWW_OpenURL	Sends a request from Netscape that the DDE server is to load a URL.
WWW_QueryViewer	Queries the DDE server for a file name in which to place the currently loading URL.
WWW_SetProgressRange	Tells the DDE server the maximum percentage of progress that will be reported.
WWW_URLEcho	Identifies to the DDE server the currently loading URL.
WWW_ViewDocFile	Tells the DDE server the location of the file that the register viewer is to display.
WWW_WindowChange	Sends to a DDE server the changes to a browser window.

Detailed Descriptions of the Netscape DDE Server Topics

This section goes into details to describe each of the DDE server topics. The details include the topic, a detailed description of each of the arguments, and a description of the value that the browser returns in response to the topic.

> **N O T E**   When sending a message to a DDE server, these topics use two transaction types:
> REQUEST and POKE. The transaction type tells the programmer whether to use the Delphi method RequestData or PokeData. Topics that use the POKE transaction type do not return a value. Each of these topics uses the REQUEST transaction unless its description specifies otherwise. ■

The *WWW_Activate* Topic

Arguments: Window, Flag

Window identifies the Netscape window to activate. If the value of Window is 0xffffffff, the most recently active browser window is activated or new window is created if none are open.

> **CAUTION**
> Window, when used as an argument to a topic, refers to an identifier that Netscape returns. The argument is in no way related to a Windows handle. The Window argument simply identifies which of Navigator's open windows is the topic's target.

Although `Flag` is currently not used, it isn't optional. You must use a value of 0x0.

Returns: `Window`

`Window` is a pointer to a long integer, the identifier of the activated browser window.

The *WWW_CancelProgress* Topic

Argument: `Transaction`

`Transaction` is the transaction identifier that a `WWW_BeginProgress` topic returns.

Transaction Type: `POKE`

The *WWW_Exit* Topic

Arguments: None

Transaction Type: `POKE`

The *WWW_GetWindowInfo* Topic

Argument: `Window`

`Window` identifies the browser window for the request. A value of 0xffffffff can be used to get the information from the last active Netscape window.

Returns: `URL, Title`

`URL` is the URL that the window is displaying. The `Title` string is the title of the browser window.

The *WWW_ListWindows* Topic

Argument: `Window`

Returns: An array of window identifiers.

The list is terminated with a value of 0.

The *WWW_OpenURL* Topic

Arguments: `URL, [FileName], Window, Flags, [FormData], [PostDataType], [Server]`

`URL` tells the server the URL to load.

`FileName` is an optional argument that tells Netscape not to display the information but to save it to the specified file name.

`Window` identifies the window that the browser should use to load the URL. As usual, Netscape uses the value 0xffffffff to create a new window if none exists or uses the last active window.

`Flags` sets certain constraints on the loading of the URL. The following are the possible values:

Value	Meaning
0x0	Load the URL normally.
0x1	Do not use the document cache when loading the URL.
0x2	Do not use the image cache when loading the URL.
0x4	Load the URL in the background. (Currently, Netscape ignores this value.)

FormData gives the server the data posted to a form.

PostDataType tells the server the MIME type to use when posting the data. If FormData is provided and PostDataType gives no value, the browser uses the default MIME type of application/x-www-form-urlencoded.

Server is an optional argument that identifies the DDE server that should receive progress messages when the loading begins.

Returns: Window

Window tells the DDE client the window identifier that Netscape uses to load the URL. A value of 0x0 means that the load failed and a value of 0xffffffff means that a Netscape window could not display the URL's MIME type.

The *WWW_ParseAnchor* Topic

Arguments: AbsURL, RelURL

AbsURL is an absolute URL that will be passed to Netscape.

RelURL is a relative URL.

Returns: URL

URL is the fully qualified URL combining the given absolute URL and relative URL.

The *WWW_QueryURLFile* Topic

Argument: FileName

FileName provides the browser with a full path to a local file.

Returns: URL

If Netscape loads FileName during the current session, Netscape returns the URL that caused the file to be loaded.

The *WWW_RegisterProtocol* Topic

Arguments: Server, Protocol

Server identifies the DDE server that should handle the specified protocol.

Protocol tells Netscape which protocol the DDE server should handle. Common values for Protocol include http, ftp, news, and mailto. The protocol does not have to be one that Netscape recognizes, which is quite helpful if you want to use custom protocols.

Returns: Success

Success tells the client whether the registration succeeded. A value of TRUE indicates that all went well, and FALSE means that a DDE server was already registered for the given protocol.

The *WWW_RegisterURLEcho* Topic

Argument: Server

Server identifies the DDE server that should receive the URLs that are being loaded into Netscape.

Transaction Type: POKE

The *WWW_RegisterViewer* Topic

Arguments: Server, MimeType, Flags

Server is the DDE server that receives data when Netscape loads the specified MIME type.

MimeType is the MIME type that the DDE server should handle rather than Netscape.

Flags tells Netscape which of several browser options are available for the WWW_RegisterViewer topic:

Value	Meaning
0x1	Save the data to a temporary file and then have the operating system open the file by using the program registered to its type.
0x2	Determine the file name to use with the topic WWW_QueryViewer. You can combine 0x2 with the flags 0x1 and 0x4. When 0x2 is used, Netscape does not automatically remove the file.
0x4	Use the topic WWW_ViewDocFile to have the DDE server open the temporary file.

Returns: Success

Success is TRUE if successful and FALSE if a viewer for the specified MIME type already exists.

The *WWW_RegisterWindowChange* Topic

Arguments: Server, Window

Server provides Netscape with the name of the DDE server to receive the messages about the changes made to the specified window.

Window is the identifier of the window for which changes should be monitored.

Returns: Window

`Window` is the identifier of the window that is actually being monitored. This identifier usually is the same as the `Window` identifier passed to Netscape. A return value of 0x0 indicates failure because an invalid window identifier was passed to Netscape.

The *WWW_ShowFile* Topic

Arguments: `FileName`, `MimeType`, `Window`, `URL`

`FileName` is the path and name of the file to display.

`MimeType` tells Netscape the MIME type of the file to load. Common values for `MimeType` include image/jpeg, image/gif, text/html and text/plain.

`Window` is the Netscape window identifier for viewing the specified file.

`URL` provides the URL for a file, to enable Netscape to attempt reloads if Netscape cannot open the file for reading.

Returns: `Window`

`Window` returns the identifier of the Netscape window used to display the file. A value of 0x0 indicates that the load failed because of invalid entries for `FileName` or `URL`.

The *WWW_UnRegisterProtocol* Topic

Arguments: `Server`, `Protocol`

`Server` is the DDE server that is no longer to be identified with the specified protocol.

`Protocol` is the protocol that is to be unregistered.

Returns: `Success`

If the value is TRUE, `Success` indicates that server was registered; if the value is FALSE, the server was never registered for the given protocol.

The *WWW_UnRegisterURLEcho* Topic

Argument: `Server`

`Server` is the DDE server that is no longer to be sent the URLs.

Transaction Type: `POKE`

The *WWW_UnRegisterViewer* Topic

Arguments: `Server`, `MimeType`

`Server` is the DDE server currently handling the viewing of the specified MIME type.

`MimeType` identifies the MIME type that Netscape is to unregister.

Returns: `Success`

If the value is TRUE, `Success` indicates that the server was registered for the specified MIME type; if the value is FALSE, `Success` indicates that `Server` was never registered for the `MimeType`.

The *WWW_UnRegisterWindowChange* Topic

Arguments: `Server, Window`

`Server` provides Netscape with the name of the DDE server that is no longer to receive the messages.

`Window` is the identifier of the window for which changes have been monitored.

Returns: `Success`

If the value is TRUE, `Success` indicates that the server was registered to receive the window's changes; a value of FALSE indicates that `Server` was never registered for receiving the `Window`'s changes.

The *WWW_Version* Topic

Argument: `Version`

Navigator ignores the argument `Version`, but you must provide a nonempty string.

Returns: `Version`

`Version` is the version of the API that Netscape uses, *not* the version of the Netscape browser.

The *WWW_WindowChange* Topic

Arguments: `Window, Flags, [X], [Y], [Width], [Height]`

`Window` is the Netscape window that is to be changed.

`Flags` indicates the changes to be made to the window:

Value	Result
0x00000001	Changes the size and/or the position according to the X, Y, `Width`, and `Height` arguments.
0x00000002	Maximizes the window.
0x00000004	Normalizes or returns the window to its default size and position.
0x00000008	Minimizes the window.
0x00000010	Closes the window.

`X` is the new X position for the window.

`Y` is the new Y position for the window.

`Width` is the new width for the window.

`Height` is the new height for the window.

Transaction Type: `POKE`

Detailed Descriptions of the Netscape DDE Client Topics

This section details the topics that a DDE server needs to understand to work with a Netscape browser as a client.

The *WWW_Alert* Topic

Arguments: Message, MessageFlag, ButtonFlag

Message contains the string for display of the message.

MessageFlag identifies the type of the message:

Value	Type of Message
0x0	Error
0x1	Warning
0x2	Question
0x3	Status

ButtonFlag tells the DDE server which buttons the alert message box should display:

Value	Buttons To Display
0x0	OK
0x1	OK and Cancel
0x2	Yes and No
0x3	Yes, No, and Cancel

Returns: Answer

Answer is the response that the topic is returning to the Netscape server:

Value	Response
0x0	The alert was not displayed
0x1	OK
0x2	Cancel
0x3	No
0x4	Yes

The *WWW_BeginProgress* Topic

Arguments: Window, Message

Window tells the DDE server which Navigator window is loading URL data.

`Message` is the initial load message that Netscape provides.

Returns: `Transaction`

`Transaction` is the identifier that the DDE server provides to identify this transaction. Netscape uses the identifier in future messages. A value of 0x0 indicates to Netscape that no further progress topics should be sent to this server.

The *WWW_EndProgress* Topic

Argument: `Transaction`

`Transaction` is the identifier associated with the loading of a particular URL.

Transaction Type: `POKE`

The *WWW_MakingProgress* Topic

Arguments: `Transaction`, `Message`, `Progress`

`Transaction` is the transaction identifier.

`Message` is a message that Netscape provides to indicate the current progress.

`Progress` is a number indicating the amount of progress. This number divided by the number received with the `WWW_SetProgressRange` yields an approximation of the percentage complete.

Returns: `QuitLoading`

`QuitLoading` is a Boolean value that, when set to TRUE, tells the Netscape browser to quit loading the current URL.

The *WWW_OpenURL* Topic

Arguments: `URL`, `[FileName]`, `Window`, `Flags`, `[FormData]`, `[PostDataType]`, `[Server]`

`URL` specifies the URL that the Netscape server provides for the DDE server to load.

When specified, `FileName` is the file into which the DDE server should load the URL.

`Window` identifies the Netscape window making the request.

`Flags` is currently unused and should be 0x0.

`FormData` is the data sent from Netscape to be posted with the URL.

`PostDataType`, when specified, is the MIME type of `FormData`.

`Server` is currently not implemented.

Returns: `Success`

`Success` is an arbitrary number that the DDE server provides. The number indicates success and possibly a window number. A value of 0x0 or 0xffffffff indicates a failure to load the URL.

The *WWW_QueryViewer* Topic

Arguments: URL, MimeType

URL identifies the URL that the browser is loading.

MimeType is the URL's MIME type.

Returns: Filename

Filename is the complete path and file name that Netscape is to use when storing the URL.

The *WWW_SetProgressRange* Topic

Arguments: Transaction, Max

Transaction is the transaction identifier sent with the WWW_BeginProgress topic.

Max is a number that represents the largest value that the WWW_MakingProgress topic would ever return.

Transaction Type: POKE

The *WWW_URLEcho* Topic

Arguments: URL, MimeType, Window, BaseURL

URL is the URL that Netscape just loaded.

MimeType is the URL's MIME type.

Window is the Netscape window identifier that loaded the URL.

BaseURL is the fully qualified URL that leads to this URL being displayed.

Transaction Type: POKE

The *WWW_ViewDocFile* Topic

Arguments: FileName, URL, MimeType, Window

FileName is the path and file name that the DDE server should display.

URL is the URL from which FileName was loaded.

MimeType is the URL's MIME type.

Window is the Netscape window that loaded the URL.

Transaction Type: POKE

The *WWW_WindowChange* Topic

Arguments: Window, Flags, [X], [Y], [Width], [Height]

Window identifies the window that has changed.

Flags identifies the characteristics of the window that have changed:

Value	Meaning
0x00000001	The window's size or position has changed.
0x00000002	The window was maximized.
0x00000004	The window was normalized.
0x00000008	The window was minimized.
0x00000010	The window was closed.
0x00010000	The action occurred while Netscape was exiting.

X is the window's X position.

Y is the window's Y position.

Width is the window's width.

Height is the window's height.

An Example Program That Uses Delphi, Netscape Navigator, and DDE

Part

III

Ch

18

With an understanding of the Netscape browser DDE API, you can now use its capabilities to produce a useful program. You can find the code for the following example program in the companion CD's CHAP18/DDE directory.

The sample DDE program, DDEProj, enables a user to load a URL and control the Netscape browser window's positioning (see Fig. 18.2). Simply by selecting a button, the user can have the browser "stick" to the left, right, top, or bottom of the controlling program. This program uses both transaction types Request and Poke, and demonstrates several useful features of Navigator's DDE interface: the capability to control Navigator's display window and to load URLs.

Listing 18.1 shows the example program's interface section, DDEProj. Because the program's objective is to have the browser follow DDEProj's position, a dynamic method (WMMOVE) that captures WM_Move events is necessary. The program also must track the location at which the Netscape browser is to be placed (Direction) as well as the window identifier provided by Netscape (WindowID).

Listing 18.1   DDEUNIT—the Control Declarations and Variables

```
uses
  SysUtils, WinTypes, WinProcs, Messages, Classes, Graphics, Controls,
  Forms, Dialogs, DdeMan, StdCtrls, ExtCtrls, Buttons;

type
  Directions = ( dUp, dDown, dLeft, dRight );

  TForm1 = class(TForm)
```

continues

Listing 18.1   Continued

```
NetscapeDDE: TDdeClientConv; { Component for DDE conversations }
DownBtn: TBitBtn; { Buttons to control browser placement }
LeftBtn: TBitBtn;
UpBtn: TBitBtn;
RightBtn: TBitBtn;
Bevel1: TBevel; { Gives a 3-D look }
Label1: TLabel; { Description for the buttons }
LoadBtn: TButton; { Button used to load a URL into the browser }
URLEdit: TEdit; { Field to enter the URL }
procedure LoadBtnClick(Sender: Tobject);
    { Called when the user pressed the load button }
procedure FormCreate(Sender: TObject);
    { Called when the form is created. Used for initializing }
procedure DirBtnClick(Sender: Tobject);
    { Called when the arrow buttons are pressed }
procedure FormResize(Sender: Tobject);
    { Called if the user resizes the form }
private
{ Private declarations }
WindowId : LongInt; { Window identifier return by Navigator }
Direction : Directions; { Placement for Navigator's window }
Procedure MoveBrowser;
    { Actually move the browser to its desired position }
Procedure ActivateBrowser; { Wake up the browser }
procedure WMMove( var Message: TWMMove ); message WM_MOVE;
    { Called whenever this form is moved }
public
{ Public declarations }
end;

var
 Form1: TForm1;
```

When the user clicks the Load URL button, the program executes the code shown in Listing 18.2.

Listing 18.2   DDEUNIT—the *LoadBtnClick()* Procedure Executes When the User Clicks the Load URL Button

```
procedure TForm1.LoadBtnClick(Sender: TObject);

begin
{Tells Navigator that you want it to load a URL }
 if NetscapeDDE.SetLink( 'NETSCAPE', 'WWW_OpenURL' )
 then Begin
{ Tells Navigator which URL to load, and to use the last active window }
 NetscapeDDE.RequestData( URLEdit.Text + ',,0xFFFFFFFF,0x1,,,,' );
{ Make sure that you can see the browser window }
 ActivateBrowser;
 End;
end;
```

FIG. 18.2
The DDE example
program in action.

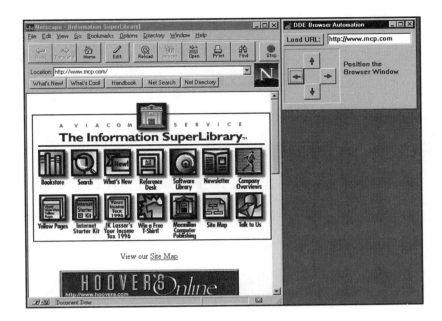

The call to SetLink() actually connects the two programs and tells Netscape what the client wants to talk about. RequestData() tells the server to send the topic-associated data to the client and provides the necessary argument information. The program uses the URLEdit.Text field to build the string to be sent to the Netscape browser. Finally, the program calls the local method, ActivateBrowser (see Listing 18.3).

Listing 18.3   DDEUNIT—the *ActivateBrowser* Procedure Ensures That the Browser Window Is Visible

```
procedure TForm1.ActivateBrowser;

Type
 LongPtr = ^LongInt;

Var
 Window : LongInt;
 Result : LongPtr;

Begin
{ Tell Navigator that you want to make a browser window
  active and visible }
 If NetscapeDDE.SetLink( 'NETSCAPE', 'WWW_Activate' )
 Then Begin
{ Activate the last active window }
 Result := LongPtr( NetscapeDDE.RequestData( '0xffffffff,0x0' ) );
 WindowId := Result^;
```

continues

Listing 18.3 Continued

```
{ If Navigator returned a valid window ID, enable all the arrow buttons }
  UpBtn.Enabled := WindowId <> -1;
  DownBtn.Enabled := WindowId <> -1;
  LeftBtn.Enabled := WindowId <> -1;
  RightBtn.Enabled := WindowId <> -1;
{ Move the browser }
  MoveBrowser;
  End;
End;
```

An interesting aspect of the ActivateBrowser procedure is that the value returned from RequestData() is actually a pointer to a long integer. Usually, this value is treated as a pChar, but not all servers return just strings. By casting pointers, you can receive many types back from RequestData() other than just a pChar. The final operation of ActivateBrowser is to call MoveBrowser (see Listing 18.4).

N O T E Because Delphi expects to return only a pChar from RequestData. To return a pointer to additional data types, a small change to DDEMAN.PAS is required. The method TDdeClientConv.RequestData needs some minor modifications. Without these modifications, the sample program can still load URLs but cannot control the window.

To make the necessary modification, you change the following code:

```
Result := StrAlloc(StrLen (PData) + 1);
             StrCopy (Result, pData);
```

Replace this code with the following:

```
Result := StrAlloc( Len );
Move( pData^, Result^, Len );
```

Listing 18.4 DDEUNIT—the *MoveBrowser* Procedure Positions the Browser Window

```
procedure TForm1.MoveBrowser;

Var
  NewX, NewY, NewWidth, NewHeight : Integer;

Begin
{ If you don't have a valid window ID, exit }
  If WindowId <= 0
  Then
  exit;
  .
  . {Code for figuring out where to place the browser}
  .
{Normalize the window in case it's minimized}
  if NetscapeDDE.SetLink( 'NETSCAPE', 'WWW_WindowChange' )
```

```
Then
NetscapeDDE.PokeData( IntToStr( WindowId ) + ',0x00000004', '' );

{ Tell Navigator that you are going to change
  the size and/or position of its window }
  if NetscapeDDE.SetLink( 'NETSCAPE', 'WWW_WindowChange' )
  Then
{ Here you build and send the string that tells Navigator
  which window and the size and position of the window }
  NetscapeDDE.PokeData(
  IntToStr( WindowId ) + ',' +
  '0x00000001' + ',' +
  IntToStr( NewX ) + ',' +
  IntToStr( NewY ) + ',' +
  IntToStr( NewWidth ) + ',' +
  IntToStr( NewHeight ),
  '' );

End;
```

`MoveBrowser` calculates the browser's placement, sends a command to Netscape to normalize its window, and finally changes the browser window's placement. To send the window-positioning commands, you use `PokeData()`. The first call to `PokeData()` does not send any of the optional arguments for `WWW_WindowChange`, but the second call sends them all.

In summary, the DDE interface into Netscape's browsers enables you to control many of the physical aspects of the Netscape windows. The DDE API also enables a DDE client to monitor and control some of the tasks that the browser usually handles. Where the DDE API is lacking, the OLE Automation API picks up some of the slack. The DDE interface does a nice job of enabling a programmer to control a visible browser window, but if having a viewable browser is unwarranted, your API should be the OLE Automation interface.

Netscape Browser Control with OLE Automation and Delphi

The OLE Automation interface into the Netscape browser enables you to use Navigator without the user being aware that any Netscape tools are loaded. Therefore, the controlling program can use Navigator's Internet capabilities to pull in data and then handle the display of data itself. The interface allows the programmatic control and access to Hypertext Transport Protocol (HTTP), File Transfer Protocol (FTP), newsgroups, and custom data types. With Navigator's help, newsgroup readers and FTP management programs are just a few lines of code away.

For Delphi users, OLE Automation uses the familiar property/method to access the OLE objects. Therefore, controlling Netscape is as easy as setting Netscape variables (properties) and calling methods. Before Delphi 2.0, the prospect of using OLE Automation in a Delphi program was unappealing because of the amount of work required. Fortunately, Delphi 2.0 adds several language features and hooks that make OLE Automation quite easy to use.

The language feature that does much of the magic is the `Variant` data type. This data type actually enables the program to figure out and convert data types at run time. This violates many of the tenants of Pascal, but is a necessary addition to the language.

Before writing any programs, you must first understand Netscape Navigator's OLE Automation interface.

Understanding Netscape's OLE Automation API

The following descriptions of the OLE Automation API for Netscape are presented as Delphi declarations for ease of use and reference.

Function **BytesReady** : ShortInt;

After the browser successfully gathers data with a call to `Open`, data becomes available for the program to receive. `BytesReady` tells the program how much data, in bytes, the `Read` method is ready and waiting to read.

Procedure **Close**;

The `Close` procedure disconnects the program and the OLE Automation object.

> **CAUTION**
>
> You should call the `Close` method even if the call to `Open` fails. This ensures proper clean up.

Function **GetContentEncoding** : String;

`GetContentEncoding` returns the loaded data's MIME encoding. This enables the program to decode the data in whatever manner is necessary. An empty string represents no encoding.

Function **GetContentLength** : Integer;

Theoretically, `GetContentLength` returns the total number of bytes that the current URL will load. If the server does not return an accurate number, `GetContentLength` is inaccurate. You should use the returned number only for approximation purposes.

Function **GetContentType** : String;

If `GetContentType`'s value is an empty string, the MIME content is unknown; otherwise, `GetContentType` returns the MIME type.

Function **GetErrorMessage** : String;

`GetErrorMessage` returns an error message that Netscape generates. This message can vary among versions or across platforms, so don't count on its value. A call to `GetStatus` determines whether there is an error message to retreive.

```
Function GetExpires : String;
```

The `GetExpires` function returns an expiration date for the content. If the browser doesn't provide an expiration date, `GetExpires` returns an empty string.

```
Function GetFlagFancy FTP : Boolean;
```

FTP listings can contain either the file names alone or an expanded version that contains each file's size and date. If `GetFlagFancy` returns TRUE, the FTP listing contains the expanded version of the data.

```
Function GetFlagFancyNews : Boolean;
```

A newgroup might not contain a detailed description. If `GetFlagFancyNews` returns TRUE, only the groups with the description are listed; otherwise, all newsgroups are listed.

```
Function GetFlagShowAllNews : Boolean;
```

If `GetFlagShowAllNews` returns TRUE, all newsgroups are listed; otherwise, only those that contain unread messages are listed.

```
Function GetLastModified : String;
```

The `GetLastModified` function returns the last date and time that the loaded data was modified.

```
Function GetPassword : String;
```

`GetPassword` returns the last password set by a call to `SetPassword`.

```
Function : GetServerStatus : ShortInt;
```

The `GetServerStatus` function returns the current server status. You should call `GetServerStatus` only as a follow-up to `GetStatus` when that function returns an error. `GetServerStatus` error codes are server- and protocol-specific.

```
Function GetStatus : Integer;
```

`GetStatus` returns the current load's status. The possible return values can be ORed together:

Value	Meaning
0x0	There are no problems.
0x1	The server requested a user name.
0x2	The server requested a password.
0x100	Netscape is busy.
0x200	A server error occurred. Call `GetServerStatus` for details.
0x400	A Netscape internal load error has been generated.
0x800	Use `GetErrorMessage` to return Netscape's error message.

```
Function GetUserName : String;
```

`GetUserName` returns the user name set with last call to `SetUserName`.

```
Function IsFinished : Boolean;
```

The IsFinished function returns TRUE if the last load has completed.

```
Function Open( URL : pChar; Method : ShortInt; PostData : pChar;
    PostDataSize : Integer; PostHeaders : pChar ) : Boolean;
```

The Open() function requests that Netscape load the given URL and returns TRUE if successful. You can find details about failure by calling GetStatus. The function's arguments are as follows:

URL is the requested URL

Method is 0 (GET), (POST), or (HEAD).

PostData is the data to be posted.

PostDataSize is the length of PostData.

PostHeaders are additonal headers separated by carriage return and line feed pairs.

```
Function Read( Var Buffer : String; BytesToRead : ShortInt ) : SmallInt;
```

After Netscape successfully loads some data, you can call Read() to transfer that data from Netscape to the calling program. If Read() returns –1, there is no more data to read from Netscape; a return value of 0 means that currently there is no more data and that any other value is the number of bytes that Netscape actually placed in the buffer. The Buffer argument is a pointer to a buffer that is at least BytesToRead long.

```
Function Resolve( BaseURL, RelativeURL : pchar ) : String;
```

Resolve() returns an absolute URL given a base URL and a relative URL.

```
Procedure SetFlagFancyFTP( FancyOn : Boolean );
```

If the SetFlagFancyFTP procedure's FancyOn argument is TRUE, Netscape attempts to return FTP listings that contain additional information other than just the file names.

```
Procedure SetFlagFancyNews( FancyOn : Boolean );
```

If SetFlagFancyNews()'s FancyOn argument is TRUE, Netscape attempts to return only the newsgroups that contain descriptions; otherwise, Netscape returns all newgroups.

```
Procedure SetFlagShowAllNews( AllNews : Boolean );
```

If the SetFlagShowAllNews() procedure's AllNews argument is TRUE, Netscape returns all news messages and not just those that haven't been read.

```
Procedure SetPassword( Password : pChar );
```

SetPassword() sends the Password argument's value to servers requesting a password. A NULL string erases the currently set password.

```
Procedure SetUserName( UserName : pChar );
```

The SetUserName() procedure sends the value in UserName to servers requesting a user name. A NULL string erases the currently set user name.

Using Netscape's OLE Automation API

Once you understand the Netscape Network OLE Automation API, you can quickly and easily write a useful program. This section's demonstration program shows how to apply the OLE Automation API. You can find the complete code for this application in the companion CD's CHAP18/OLE directory.

The sample program loads the Netscape Network OLE object and enables the user to load a URL and view it with a `RichEdit` text control. Figure 18.3 shows the application in action, and Listing 18.5 shows the interface section for the OLE Automation sample program.

N O T E Several features were added to Delphi 2.0 for OLE Automation, so the following code and descriptions are valid only for Delphi 2.0. ▮

FIG. 18.3

The Netscape OLE Automation demonstration program in action.

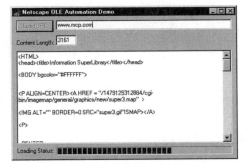

Part
III

Ch
18

Listing 18.5 OLEUNIT—the Interface Section for the OLE Automation Sample Program

```
uses Windows, Classes, Dialogs, Forms, Controls,
  StdCtrls, ComCtrls;

type
  TForm1 = class(TForm)
{ Button that is pressed to load a URL }
  LoadURLBtn: TButton;
{ Field to write in the desired URL }
  URL: TEdit;
{ The approximate length of the URL that is being loaded.
  Navigator provides this field's value. }
  Length: TEdit;
{ Shows the load status visually }
  LoadStatusBar: TProgressBar;
{ Where the loaded URL is displayed }
  URLData: TRichEdit;
{ Labels for the components }
  URLLbl: TLabel;
  LoadLbl: TLabel;
```

continues

Listing 18.5   Continued

```
{ Method that is called when LoadURLBtn is pressed }
 procedure LoadURLBtnClick(Sender: TObject);
{ Method called when the form is created }
 procedure FormCreate(Sender: TObject);
 public
{ Variable used to access the OLE Automation object}
 Navigator : Variant;
{ Variables used to parse the incoming URL }
 LeftOver, Buffer : String;
{ Has the URL finished loading? }
 Finished : Boolean;
{ Method to convert the raw data from Netscape to something viewable }
 Procedure BufferToRichEdit;
 end;

var
 Form1: Tform1;
```

The most noteworthy item in the OLE Automation program's interface section is the declaration of Navigator as type Variant, which will become your OLE Automation object. The compiler has the Huge Strings option enabled, so the strings, Buffer and LeftOver, can be quite large. You can view and change the compiler settings by selecting Options from the Project menu and then selecting the Compiler tab.

The program first must attempt to create the OLE Automation object. The FormCreate() procedure performs this task (see Listing 18.6).

Listing 18.6   OLEUNIT—the *FormCreate()* Method Creates the OLE Automation Object

```
procedure TForm1.FormCreate(Sender: TObject);
begin
 try
 { Load and connect to the Netscape Network OLE Automation object }
Navigator := CreateOleObject( 'Netscape.Network.1' );
 except
{ Display a message if unable to load the Automation object }
 ShowMessage( 'Unable to start the Netscape Navigator' );
{ Disable the LoadURL button if you failed to start Navigator}
 LoadURLBtn.Enabled := False;
 end;
end;
```

When Netscape is installed, it registers the name Netscape.Network.1 with Windows. This enables Windows to load the appropriate OLE object when CreateOLEObject() is called. If all goes well, FormCreate() links to the Automation object. If something goes wrong, a message displays and the Load URL button is disabled.

The program's most interesting method is LoadURLButtonClick(), which is the procedure that makes the demonstration program a well-behaved one (see Listing 18.7).

Listing 18.7 OLEUNIT—the *LoadURLButtonClick()* Procedure

```
procedure TForm1.LoadURLBtnClick(Sender: TObject);

Const
 BuffSize = 512;

var
 BytesRead, ContentLength, TotalRead : Integer;

begin
{ Display a wait cursor while the URL is loading }
 Cursor := crHourGlass;
{ Initialize variable that will be referenced later }
 LeftOver := '';
 Finished := False;
{ Because you are already loading a URL, disable the load button
  in case the user gets impatient }
 LoadURLBtn.Enabled := False;
{ Zero out the URL length variable }
 ContentLength := 0;
{ Clear the URL length field that the user sees }
 Length.Text := '';
{ Set the status bar to the beginning }
 LoadStatusBar.Position := 0;
{ Clear out the area in which you are displaying the URL }
 URLData.Lines.Clear;

{ Can you access the OLE Automation object? }
 If Navigator.Open( URL.Text, 0, '', 0, '' )
 Then begin
{ Set your string's length to the maximium number of characters your
  buffer can hold }
 SetLength( Buffer, BuffSize );
{ Read from the OLE object any available characters
  from the loading URL }
 BytesRead := Navigator.Read( Buffer, BuffSize );
{ Continue reading until there is no more data to read }
 While BytesRead <> -1
 Do Begin
{ If you haven't displayed the length of the URL,
  ask the Automation server for an approximate length }
 If ( ContentLength = 0 )
 Then Begin
 ContentLength := Navigator.GetContentLength;
{ Display the result of the query for the user to see }
 Length.Text := IntToStr( ContentLength );
 End;
 If BytesRead <> 0
 Then Begin
{ Set the length of your buffering string
```

continues

Listing 18.7   Continued

```
    to the number of characters read }
  SetLength( Buffer, BytesRead );
   Inc( TotalRead, BytesRead );
  { Convert your buffer string to something viewable }
   BufferToRichEdit;
   If ContentLength <> 0
   Then
  { Update your load status bar. }
   LoadStatusBar.Position := TotalRead * 100 Div ContentLength;
   End;
  { Enable the program to repond to user events
    even while you are loading a URL }
   Application.ProcessMessages;
   SetLength( Buffer, BuffSize );
   BytesRead := Navigator.Read( Buffer, BuffSize );
   End;
   Finished := True;
   Buffer := '';
   BufferToRichEdit;
   End;
   Navigator.Close;
   Cursor := crDefault;
   LoadURLBtn.Enabled := True;
  end;
```

The LoadURLButtonClick() procedure first displays a wait cursor and disables the Load URL button. The program does not want the user to lose patience and try and load something twice. Instead, the program asks the Netscape OLE Automation object to load whatever URL is contained in the URL edit box. If the load succeeds, the program polls the OLE object for data to be read. If data is found, the program checks how many bytes the total load will be. This number is used to approximate the load status. After reading the data into the string Buffer, the program parses it and then places it in the RichEdit control. The program finally checks whether there is more data to be read; if none remains, the program closes the connection to the OLE object and restores the cursor.

Although this program seems basic, it demonstrates two important aspects of the OLE Automation API: controlling the OLE object and capturing data from the OLE object.

From Here...

This chapter has shown several methods of controlling and using the Netscape Navigator from another program. Because the technology changes so rapidly, checking the Netscape Web site (**http://www.netscape.com**) is probably worthwhile. Further chapters of interest include the following:

■ Chapter 9, "Developing SMTP and POP Mail Clients," explains the types of data that Navigator can retrieve and display.

- Chapter 11, "Building a UUEncoder/Decoder," provides the information that you need to add UUEncoding and decoding to both the DDE and OLE Automation sample programs.
- Chapter 16, "Building a Web Server with Delphi," provides an understanding of the HTML codes. By decoding the HTML codes in the OLE Automation sample, you can get a rudimentary custom browser up and running quite quickly.

Part
III

Ch
18

Appendixes

Internet Applications Command Sets

Just about all of the current crop of Internet applications use a text-based set of commands to perform all their communications. The client sends a command request to the server, and the server responds with the command's results. The command sets that are available for each of the applications that you examined extend far beyond the few commands that you implemented in any of this book's examples. You need to know all the commands available for each of these applications, as well as the possible responses that you might receive from the server. This appendix lists the command sets that you use for the following Internet application protocols:

- File Transfer Protocol (FTP)
- Simple Mail Transport Protocol (SMTP)
- Post Office Protocol (POP)
- Network News Transport Protocol (NNTP)
- Hypertext Transport Protocol (HTTP) ■

The Basic FTP Commands

The FTP commands are passed from the client to the server over the command connection. These are all text-based commands that a user sitting at a dumb terminal can enter using a command-line implementation of an FTP client. Likewise, the responses that the server returns are all text-based, humanly readable replies.

All FTP commands are terminated with the standard carriage-return and newline character combination (#13#10). The response to each of these commands contains a three-digit number as the first piece of information in the reply. The three digits are coded to indicate the nature of the success or failure, as well as the nature of the command.

The first digit of the response code indicates the nature of the reply. Table A.1 lists the values for the first digit.

Table A.1   The Values for the First Digit of FTP Response Codes

Value	Meaning
1	Positive initial response. The requested command is being initiated, and on completion of the command another response code should be received indicating the command's final success or failure.
2	Positive completion response. The requested command has been successfully completed.
3	Positive temporary response. The requested command is all right, but additional information or actions are needed from the client.
4	Negative completion response. The requested command did not succeed or did not execute. The client is encouraged to attempt the command again.
5	Permanent negative completion response. The requested command did not and will not succeed. The client is discouraged from attempting this command again.

The second digit in the response codes indicates the functional area in which the command succeeded or failed. Table A.2 lists these values.

Table A.2   The Values for the Second Digit of the FTP Response Codes

Value	Meaning
0	Syntax. These responses refer to syntax errors or are used as generic OK responses.
1	Information. These responses are replies to requests for information.
2	Connections. These responses refer to the control and data connections.

Value	Meaning
3	Authentication and accounting. These responses are replies for the login process and accounting procedures.
4	Unspecified.
5	File system. These responses indicate the status of the server file system and the requested file transfers or other file system action.

App
A

The third digit in the response codes provides a finer degree of specificity to the responses.

Access Commands

The first set of commands to examine consists of those that connect and log in to the FTP server.

Connecting to the FTP Service   The first command is not really a command, but actually the response that the server sends to the client on connecting to TCP port 21. If the server is busy and has many active connections, it might refuse the connection (most FTP servers limit the number of simultaneous connections that they service). If everything is fine, and the server is running with sufficient available connections, you should receive a response code of 220, letting you know that you are connected and should proceed with the login process. Table A.3 lists these connection reply codes.

Table A.3   Connection Reply Codes

Code	Meaning
120	The service will be ready in a specified number of minutes.
220	The service is ready for a new user connection.
421	The service is unavailable, so the control connection is closing.

ACCT—Account   The ACCT command specifies an account to be used for the FTP session. This account is separate from the user name used in the login process, but can control accounting and access information. The following is the syntax for the account command:

```
ACCT account-information #13#10
```

Table A.4 lists the possible responses.

Table A.4   ACCT Command Reply Codes

Code	Meaning
202	This site does not implement the command.
230	The user is logged in.

continues

Table A.4 Continued

Code	Meaning
421	The service is unavailable, so the control connection is closing.
500	Syntax error. The command was not recognized.
501	Syntax error in the command arguments or parameters.
503	Bad command sequence.
530	The user is not logged in.

CDUP—Change to Parent Directory   This command is a special case of the CWD command. You use it to move up one directory in the file system on the FTP server. This command simplifies the implementation of automated FTP client applications for dealing with different file system syntaxes. The syntax for this command is as follows:

CDUP#13#10

Table A.5 lists the possible responses.

Table A.5 _CDUP_ Command Reply Codes

Code	Meaning
200	OK (the generic positive command response).
421	The service is unavailable, so the control connection is closing.
500	Syntax error. The command was not recognized.
501	Syntax error in the command arguments or parameters.
502	The command is not implemented.
530	The user is not logged in.
550	The requested action was not taken (the file was not found or access has been denied).

CWD—Change Working Directory   This command changes the current directory on the FTP server. The argument to this command is a path name specifying a directory or other system-dependent file system designator. The syntax for the change directory command is as follows:

CWD _pathname_ #13#10

Table A.6 lists the possible responses.

Table A.6 *CWD* **Command Reply Codes**

Code	Meaning
250	The requested action completed.
421	The service is unavailable, so the control connection is closing.
500	Syntax error. The command was not recognized.
501	Syntax error in the command arguments or parameters.
502	The command is not implemented.
530	The user is not logged in.
550	The requested action was not taken (the file was not found or access has been denied).

PASS—Password   The PASS command passes the appropriate password to the FTP server for the specified user name. If the user name is anonymous, the password is usually your electronic mail (e-mail) address. The command's syntax is as follows:

PASS *password* #13#10

Table A.7 lists the possible responses.

Table A.7 *PASS* **Command Reply Codes**

Code	Meaning
202	This site does not implement the command.
230	The user is logged in.
332	You need an account to log in.
421	The service is unavailable, so the control connection is closing.
500	Syntax error. The command was not recognized.
501	Syntax error in command arguments or parameters.
503	Bad command sequence.
530	The user is not logged in.

SMNT—Structure Mount   This command mounts a different file system data structure on the server. The argument is the path name specifying a directory to be mounted. The syntax for this command is as follows:

SMNT *pathname* #13#10

Table A.8 lists the possible responses.

Table A.8   *SMNT* Command Reply Codes

Code	Meaning
202	This site does not implement the command.
250	The requested action has completed.
421	The service is unavailable, so the control connection is closing.
500	Syntax error. The command was not recognized.
501	Syntax error in the command arguments or parameters.
502	The command is not implemented.
530	The user is not logged in.
550	The requested action was not taken (the file was not found or access has been denied).

USER—User Name   This command initiates the FTP server's login process. You send this command with the user name to be used when logging in. If the server allows anonymous FTP logins, the user name is anonymous. If anonymous logins are not allowed, you must use a valid user (account login) name. The following is the command's syntax:

```
USER username #13#10
```

Table A.9 lists the command's possible responses.

Table A.9   *USER* Command Reply Codes

Code	Meaning
230	The user is logged in.
331	The user name is okay, but the password is needed.
332	You need an account to log in.
421	The service is unavailable, so the control connection is closing.
500	Syntax error. The command was not recognized.
501	Syntax error in the command arguments or parameters.
530	The user is not logged in.

Logout Commands

The next two commands end an FTP session. Each allows the server to continue with any file transfers that are currently in progress. If the control connection is unexpectedly closed, the server aborts any file transfers currently in progress.

QUIT—Logout   The QUIT command terminates the user login and causes the server to terminate the command connection. If any file transfers are taking place, they continue until completion. The command's syntax is as follows:

```
QUIT#13#10
```

Table A.10 lists the possible responses.

Table A.10   *QUIT* Command Reply Codes

Code	Meaning
221	The connection is closing.
500	Syntax error. The command was not recognized.

REIN—Reinitialize   The reinitialize command terminates the user login while keeping the command connection open. The client can then issue another USER command to log in again, using a different account, to perform additional file transfers. Any file transfers that are in process when this command is issued continue until completion. The command's syntax is as follows:

```
REIN#13#10
```

Table A.11 lists the possible responses.

Table A.11   *REIN* Command Reply Codes

Code	Meaning
120	The service will be ready in the number of minutes specified.
220	The service is ready for a new user or connection.
421	The service is unavailable, so the control connection is closing.
500	Syntax error. The command was not recognized.
502	The command is not implemented.

Transfer Parameter Commands

The transfer parameter commands specify the parameters—the data types, transmission modes, data connection ports and addresses, and so on—to be used in the various file transfers that are to follow. You should use these commands after the user logs in to the server and before any file transfers are requested. You can reissue these commands and alter them for each file transfer that is to occur during a session.

MODE—Transfer Mode   MODE is another command that you will rarely need (because most FTP implementations support only the default stream mode). You use MODE to switch between stream (S), block (B), and compressed transfer modes. This command's syntax is as follows:

MODE *mode-code* #13#10

Table A.12 lists the possible responses.

Table A.12   *MODE* Command Reply Codes

Code	Meaning
200	OK (the generic positive command response).
421	The service is unavailable, so the control connection is closing.
500	Syntax error. The command was not recognized.
501	Syntax error in the command arguments or parameters.
504	The command is unavailable for the requested parameter.
530	The user is not logged in.

PASV—Server Passive Mode   The PASV command requests the server to enter passive mode, in which the client can initiate the data connection. The response (assuming that it was valid and that 227 was the returned response code) contains the Internet address and TCP port that the client is to use when making this connection. The server address is in the same format as the PORT command uses. The PASV command's syntax is as follows:

PASV#13#10

Table A.13 lists the possible responses.

Table A.13   *PASV* Command Reply Codes

Code	Meaning
227	Entering passive mode (address and port number for data connection). The server then waits for the client to initiate the data connection.
421	The service is unavailable, so the control connection is closing.
500	Syntax error. The command was not recognized.
501	Syntax error in the command arguments or parameters.
502	The command is not implemented.
530	The user is not logged in.

PORT—Client Data Port Address   The PORT command tells the server which Internet address and TCP port to use for the data transmission connection. By default, the server connects to the client using the same address and port as the client's command connection. You issue this command to give the server a different address or port for the data transmission. The server attempts to connect to the specified address and port. If the client, rather than the server, is to initiate the data connections, you should issue the PASV command rather than the PORT command. PORT parses the 32-bit Internet address and 16-bit TCP port into eight-bit values and then passes these values as a series of numbers separated by commas. The syntax for this command is as follows:

```
PORT h1,h2,h3,h4,p1,p2 #13#10
```

For example, if the client wants the server to connect to the TCP port 39, and the client's Internet address is 128.19.4.32, the client would send the command as follows:

```
PORT 128,19,4,32,0,39
```

where h1 through h4 are the client's Internet address, and p1 and p2 are the port number to use. Before you issue this command, the client socket to use for the data connection must be bound to this address and port.

Table A.14 lists the possible responses.

Table A.14   *PORT* Command Reply Codes

Code	Meaning
200	OK (the generic positive command response).
421	The service is unavailable, so the control connection is closing.
500	Syntax error. The command was not recognized.
501	Syntax error in the command arguments or parameters.
530	The user is not logged in.

***STRU*—File Structure**   You are unlikely to need this command, which specifies the file structure to use in the transfer (such as file, record, or page structure). Most of the file transfers that you must perform will use the default (file) structure. This command is a holdover from the days when most systems exchanged files with vastly different file structures. Such file structures, however, no longer differ so significantly. This command's syntax is as follows:

```
STRU structure-code #13#10
```

The following are the structure codes that you use:

Code	Meaning
F	File (no internal structure)
R	Record structure
P	Page structure

Table A.15 lists the possible responses.

Table A.15 *STRU* **Command Reply Codes**

Code	Meaning
200	OK (the generic positive command response).
421	The service is unavailable, so the control connection is closing.
500	Syntax error. The command was not recognized.
501	Syntax error in the command arguments or parameters.
504	The command is unavailable for the requested parameter.
530	The user is not logged in.

TYPE—Data Type The TYPE command specifies the data type to use in the file transfer. The two data types that you must implement are A (ASCII) and I (Image). The A can be followed by formatting specifications (such as nonprint, Telnet format, and carriage control), but is not necessary (or recommended) that you include these formatting specifications. The command's syntax is as follows:

```
TYPE type-code #13#10
```

Table A.16 lists the possible responses.

Table A.16 *TYPE* **Command Reply Codes**

Code	Meaning
200	OK (the generic positive command response).
421	The service is unavailable, so the control connection is closing.
500	Syntax error. The command was not recognized.
501	Syntax error in the command arguments or parameters.
504	The command is unavailable for the requested parameter.
530	The user is not logged in.

File Action Commands

You use the following set of FTP commands to perform various actions on files. You also use these commands to retrieve, send, and move (rename) files, as well as to enable the client to perform some rudimentary file system organization on the server. Most of the commands that involve transferring data between the client and server systems over the data connection return two sets of responses. The first response tells the client that the server is about to start the transfer and open the data connection (or that the client should now open the data connection). The second response tells the client that the transfer has completed or failed and that the data connection should now be closed.

ABOR—Abort Transfer   This command aborts the previous command and any file transfer that might be in progress because of the previous command. If the previous command has been completed, the ABOR command has no effect. If a data transfer is in progress when you issue this command, it aborts the transfer and closes the data connection. The command connection, however, remains open.

If a file transfer is in progress when you issue this command, it terminates the data transfer and returns a 426 reply code to indicate that the data transfer terminated abnormally. Next, the server sends a 226 reply to the client to indicate that the ABOR command completed successfully. This command's syntax is as follows:

```
ABOR#13#10
```

Table A.17 lists the possible responses.

Table A.17   ABOR Command Reply Codes

Code	Meaning
225	The data connection is open, but no transfer is in progress.
226	The data connection is closing because the transfer completed or succeeded.
421	The service is unavailable, so the control connection is closing.
500	Syntax error. The command was not recognized.
501	Syntax error in the command arguments or parameters.
502	The command is not implemented.

ALLO—Allocate Storage Space   Some FTP servers require the ALLO command to reserve the specified storage space for the file that is about to be transferred. This command's argument is an integer that specifies the number of bytes to reserve. If the server uses a record or page structure, this command should also pass the number of records or pages to reserve. The command's syntax is as follows:

```
ALLO bytes-to-reserve[ R records-to-reserve ]#13#10
```

Table A.18 lists the possible responses.

Table A.18   ALLO Command Reply Codes

Code	Meaning
200	OK (the generic positive command response).
202	The site does not implement the command.
421	The service is unavailable, so the control connection is closing.

continues

Table A.18   Continued

Code	Meaning
500	Syntax error. The command was not recognized.
501	Syntax error in the command arguments or parameters.
504	The command is unavailable for the requested parameter.
530	The user is not logged in.

APPE—Append to the File (on the Server)   This is a third form of the STOR (send) command. This form takes a file name with the command. When the server receives the file over the data connection, the command's action depends on whether a file with that name already exists. If a file exists with the specified name, this command appends the new file to the existing file. If there is no file with the specified name, the server creates a new file. This command's syntax is as follows:

```
APPE file/pathname#13#10
```

Table A.19 lists the possible responses.

Table A.19   *APPE* Command Reply Codes

Code	Meaning
110	Restart marker reply. This code is returned when restarting an interrupted file transfer in midfile.
125	The data connection is already open and starting the transfer.
150	The file is ready and about to open a data connection.
226	The data connection is closing because the transfer completed or succeeded.
250	The requested action is completed.
421	The service is unavailable, so the control connection is closing.
425	The data connection cannot be opened.
426	The data connection is closed, so the transfer was aborted.
450	The file is unavailable, so the requested action was not taken.
451	Local processing error. The requested action was aborted.
452	Insufficient storage space. The requested action was not taken.
500	Syntax error. The command was not recognized.
501	Syntax error in the command arguments or parameters.

Code	Meaning
502	The command is not implemented.
530	The user is not logged in.
532	You need an account to store files on the server.
550	The requested action was not taken (the file was not found or access has been denied).
551	The requested action was aborted because the page type is unknown.
552	The action was aborted because it exceeded the storage allocation.
553	The requested action was not taken because the file name is not allowed.

***DELE*—Delete File**   This command deletes a file on the FTP server file system. The capability for the client to execute this command depends on the access permissions available on the FTP server for the user account that the client is using. The client application should double-check with the user before issuing this command request to the server. This command's syntax is as follows:

```
DELE file/pathname#13#10
```

Table A.20 lists the possible responses.

Table A.20   *DELE* Command Reply Codes

Code	Meaning
250	The requested action has completed.
421	This service is unavailable, so the control connection is closing.
450	The file is unavailable, so the requested action was not taken.
500	Syntax error. This command was not recognized.
501	Syntax error in the command arguments or parameters.
502	This command is not implemented.
530	The user is not logged in.
550	The requested action was not taken (the file was not found or access has been denied).

LIST—List the Current Directory Contents   This command requests that the server send a list of the current (or specified) directory's contents to the client over the data connection. This data transfer should use an ASCII transfer data type. The directory contents are formatted using the server system formatting. If the server is a UNIX system, the directory listing contains the permission flags for each of the files and directories, but if the server is a Windows NT system, the listing looks more like a DOS directory listing. The LIST command's syntax is as follows:

LIST[*pathname*]#13#10

Table A.21 lists the possible responses.

Table A.21   *LIST* Command Reply Codes

Code	Meaning
125	The data connection is already open and starting the transfer.
150	The file is ready and about to open a data connection.
226	The data connection is closing because the transfer completed or succeeded.
250	The requested action has completed.
421	The service is unavailable, so the control connection is closing.
425	The data connection cannot be opened.
426	The data connection is closed, so the transfer was aborted.
450	The file is unavailable, so requested action was not taken.
451	Local processing error. The requested action was aborted.
500	Syntax error. The command was not recognized.
501	Syntax error in the command arguments or parameters.
502	The command is not implemented.
530	The user is not logged in.

MKD—Make Directory   This command creates a directory on the server file system. MKD can take either an absolute or relative path name as its argument. The capability to create a directory is limited by the access rights allocated to the user login that the client uses when issuing this command. The MKD command's syntax is as follows:

MKD *pathname*#13#10

Table A.22 lists the possible responses.

Table A.22   *MKD* Command Reply Codes

Code	Meaning
257	The directory name was created or is current.
421	The service is unavailable, so the control connection is closing.

Code	Meaning
500	Syntax error. The command was not recognized.
501	Syntax error in the command arguments or parameters.
502	The command is not implemented.
530	The user is not logged in.
550	The requested action was not taken (the file was not found or access has been denied).

NLST—List the Current Directory Contents (Names Only)   This command works just like the LIST command, except that the transferred data contains only file names. NLIST does not return any other miscellaneous information. This command's syntax is as follows:

NLST[*pathname*]#13#10

Table A.23 lists the possible responses.

Table A.23   *NLST* Command Reply Codes

Code	Meaning
125	The data connection is already open and starting the transfer.
150	The file is ready and about to open a data connection.
226	The data connection is closing because the transfer completed or succeeded.
250	The requested action has completed.
421	The service is unavailable, so the control connection is closing.
425	The data connection cannot be opened.
426	The data connection is closed, so the transfer was aborted.
450	The file is unavailable, so the requested action was not taken.
451	Local processing error. The requested action was aborted.
500	Syntax error. The command was not recognized.
501	Syntax error in the command arguments or parameters.
502	The command is not implemented.
530	The user is not logged in.

PWD—Print Working (Current) Directory   This command retrieves the name and path of the current working directory on the FTP server. The command's syntax is as follows:

PWD#13#10

Some FTP clients use the following alternative syntax:

XPWD#13#10

Table A.24 lists the possible responses.

Table A.24 *PWD* **Command Reply Codes**

Code	Meaning
257	The directory name was created or is current.
421	The service is unavailable, so the control connection is closing.
500	Syntax error. The command was not recognized.
501	Syntax error in the command arguments or parameters.
502	The command is not implemented.
550	The requested action was not taken (the file was not found or access has been denied).

REST—Restart File Transfer   This command specifies a block marker within a file to be used as the starting point when the file transfer is initiated. REST does not start the file transfer; you should use the RETR command to start the transfer. The REST command causes the server to skip the portion of the file preceding the specified block marker after initiating the transfer. You can use this command to restart a file transfer that was interrupted part of way through it. The REST command's syntax is as follows:

REST *block-marker*#13#10

Table A.25 lists the possible responses.

Table A.25 *REST* **Command Reply Codes**

Code	Meaning
350	The requested action is pending because further information is required.
421	The service is unavailable, so the control connection is closing.
500	Syntax error. The command was not recognized.
501	Syntax error in the command arguments or parameters.
502	The command is not implemented.
530	The user is not logged in.

RETR—Retrieve File   This command requests that the server send a particular file to the client. The command's syntax is as follows:

RETR *file/pathname* #13#10

Table A.26 lists the possible responses.

Table A.26 *RETR* Command Reply Codes

Code	Meaning
110	Restart marker reply. This code is returned when restarting an interrupted file transfer in midfile.
125	Data connection is already open and starting the transfer.
150	The file is ready and about to open a data connection.
226	The data connection is closing because the transfer was complete or successful.
250	The requested action is completed.
421	The service is unavailable, so the control connection is closing.
425	The data connection cannot be opened.
426	The data connection is closed, so the transfer is aborted.
450	The file is unavailable, so the requested action was not taken.
451	Local processing error. The requested action was aborted.
500	Syntax error. The command was not recognized.
501	Syntax error in the command arguments or parameters.
530	The user is not logged in.
550	The requested action was not taken (the file was not found or access was denied).

RMD—Remove Directory   This command removes a directory from the server file system. RMD can take either an absolute or relative path name as its argument. The capability to delete a directory is limited by the access rights allocated to the user login that the client uses when issuing this command. The syntax for this command is as follows:

RMD *pathname*#13#10

Table A.27 lists the possible responses.

Table A.27 *RMD* Command Reply Codes

Code	Meaning
250	The requested action has completed.
421	The service is unavailable, so the control connection is closing.
500	Syntax error. The command was not recognized.

continues

Code	Meaning
Table A.27	**Continued**
501	Syntax error in the command arguments or parameters.
502	The command is not implemented.
530	The user is not logged in.
550	The requested action was not taken (the file was not found or access has been denied).

RNFR—Rename File From   The RNFR command is the first half of the two commands that move or rename a file on the server file system. This is the first command to issue, specifying the current path and name of the file to be moved, immediately followed with the RETO command, to specify the new path and name of the file. The syntax for RNFR is as follows:

RENF *file/pathname*#13#10

Table A.28 lists the possible responses.

Code	Meaning
Table A.28	**RNFR Command Reply Codes**
350	The requested action is pending because further information is required.
421	The service is unavailable, so the control connection is closing.
450	The file is unavailable, so the requested action was not taken.
500	Syntax error. The command was not recognized.
501	Syntax error in the command arguments or parameters.
502	The command is not implemented.
530	The user is not logged in.
550	The requested action was not taken (the file was not found or access has been denied).

RNTO—Rename File To   The RNTO command is the second of the two commands that move or rename a file on the FTP server file system. This command is immediately preceded by the RNFR command. RNTO specifies the new name and/or path to use for the file specified in the RNFR command. The syntax for the RNTO command is as follows:

RNTO *file/pathname*#13#10

Table A.29 lists the possible responses.

Table A.29 *RNTO* Command Reply Codes

Code	Meaning
250	The requested action has completed.
421	The service is unavailable, so the control connection is closing.
500	Syntax error. The command was not recognized.
501	Syntax error in the command arguments or parameters.
502	The command is not implemented.
503	Bad command sequence.
530	The user is not logged in.
532	You need an account to store files on the server.
553	The requested action was not taken because the file name is not allowed.

STOR—Store (Send) File   This command tells the server that the client wants to send it a file. The file name passed with the command is the file name to be given to the file on the server file system. If a file already exists with the given name, and the user has access permissions, the new file being transferred from the client erases and replaces the file on the server. The command's syntax is as follows:

```
STOR file/pathname #13#10
```

Table A.30 lists the possible responses.

Table A.30 *STOR* Command Reply Codes

Code	Meaning
110	Restart marker reply. This code is returned when restarting an interrupted file transfer in midfile.
125	Data connection is already open and starting the transfer.
150	The file is ready and about to open a data connection.
226	The data connection is closing because the transfer completed or succeeded.
250	The requested action is completed.
421	The service is unavailable, so the control connection is closing.
425	The data connection cannot be opened.
426	The data connection is closed, so the transfer was aborted.
450	The file is unavailable, so the requested action was not taken.

continues

Table A.30	Continued
Code	**Meaning**
451	Local processing error occurred. The requested action was aborted.
452	Insufficient storage space. The requested action was not taken.
500	Syntax error. The command was not recognized.
501	Syntax error in the command arguments or parameters.
530	User is not logged in.
532	You need an account to store files on the server.
551	The requested action was aborted because the page type is unknown.
552	The action was aborted because it exceeded the storage allocation.
553	The requested action was not taken because the file name is not allowed.

STOU—Store (Send) with a Unique File Name   This command is the same as the STOR command, except that the server creates a unique name to be given to the file (no file name is passed with the command). The syntax for this command is as follows:

STOU#13#10

Table A.31 lists the possible responses.

Table A.31	*STOU* Command Reply Codes
Code	**Meaning**
110	Restart marker reply. This code is returned when restarting an interrupted file transfer in midfile.
125	The data connection is already open and starting the transfer.
150	The file is ready and about to open a data connection.
226	The data connection is closing because the transfer completed or succeeded.
250	The requested action is completed.
421	The service is unavailable, so the control connection is closing.
425	The data connection cannot be opened.
426	The data connection is closed, so the transfer was aborted.
450	The file is unavailable, so the requested action was not taken.
451	Local processing error. The requested action was aborted.
452	Insufficient storage space. The requested action was not taken.
500	Syntax error. The command was not recognized.

Code	Meaning
501	Syntax error in the command arguments or parameters.
530	The user is not logged in.
532	You need an account to store files on the server.
551	The requested action was aborted because the page type is unknown.
552	The action was aborted because it exceeded the storage allocation.
553	The requested action was not taken because the file name is not allowed.

Miscellaneous and Informational Commands

This last set of commands retrieves information about the server status, operating system, and implementation-specific options and commands. You will rarely use this set of commands within an FTP client application; they are more likely to be used by a user during an interactive (command-line driven) FTP session.

HELP—**Help**   Usually, a user issues the HELP command during an interactive, command-line FTP session. The command returns help information on the available commands or on a specific command. The HELP command's syntax is as follows:

```
HELP[ command-string ]#13#10
```

Table A.32 lists the possible responses.

Table A.32   *HELP* Command Reply Codes

Code	Meaning
211	The system status or a help reply.
214	A help message.
421	The service is unavailable, so the control connection is closing.
500	Syntax error. The command was not recognized.
501	Syntax error in the command arguments or parameters.
502	The command is not implemented.

NOOP—**No Operation**   This command gets an OK response from the server. NOOP does not affect any actions or commands that were entered previously or subsequently. You can use NOOP as a "keep alive" command to ensure that the command connection remains active. The command's syntax is as follows:

```
NOOP#13#10
```

Table A.33 lists the possible responses.

Table A.33   *NOOP* Command Reply Codes

Code	Meaning
200	OK (the generic positive command response).
421	The service is unavailable, so the control connection is closing.
500	Syntax error. The command was not recognized.

***SITE*—Site Parameters**   This command provides services specific to the server implementation. The services that use this command are unique for each system and necessary for that implementation, but not universal for all systems and thus not part of the specification. To get information on which services are available through this command on a specific server, use the HELP command in a command-line, interactive FTP session. The SITE command's syntax is as follows:

SITE *service-string*#13#10

Table A.34 lists the possible responses.

Table A.34   *SITE* Command Reply Codes

Code	Meaning
200	OK (the generic positive command response).
202	The command is not implemented at this site.
500	Syntax error. The command was not recognized.
501	Syntax error in the command arguments or parameters.
530	The user is not logged in.

***STAT*—Status**   The status command enables the server to respond with the status of a file transfer (if one is in progress) or a file specified as a command parameter. The STAT command's syntax is as follows:

STAT[*file/pathname*]#13#10

Table A.35 lists the possible responses.

Table A.35   *STAT* Command Reply Codes

Code	Meaning
211	The system status or a help reply.
212	The directory status.
213	The file status.

Code	Meaning
421	The service is unavailable, so the control connection is closing.
450	The file is unavailable, so the requested action was not taken.
500	Syntax error. The command was not recognized.
501	Syntax error in the command arguments or parameters.
502	The command is not implemented.
530	The user is not logged in.

SYST—Server System Type This command finds out which type of operating system the server is running. The reply contains one of the system names contained in the current version of the "Assigned Numbers" document (RFC 1700). This command's syntax is as follows:

SYST#13#10

Table A.36 lists the possible responses.

Table A.36 *SYST* Command Reply Codes

Code	Meaning
215	The system type name.
421	The service is unavailable, so the control connection is closing.
500	Syntax error. The command was not recognized.
501	Syntax error in the command arguments or parameters.
502	The command is not implemented.

SMTP Commands

The basic SMTP conversation consists of a series of commands that the SMTP client issues to the server. The server responds with a numeric response code, followed by a textual message. The numeric response codes consist of three digits, the first of which indicates the command's success or failure. Table A.37 lists the meanings of the code's first digit.

Table A.37 First Digits for SMTP Response Codes

First Digit	Meaning
1	Positive preliminary reply. The command was accepted, but is waiting for confirmation commands from the client.
2	Positive completion reply. The command succeeded.

continues

Table A.37 Continued	
First Digit	**Meaning**
3	Positive intermediate reply. The command was accepted, but is waiting for further information from the client.
4	Transient negative completion reply. The command was rejected, but the client should attempt the command again.
5	Permanent negative completion reply. The command was rejected.

The second digit of the response codes specifies the category of the response (see Table A.38).

Table A.38 Second Digits for SMTP Response Codes	
Digit	**Meaning**
0	Syntax
1	Information
2	Connections
5	Mail system

The third digit provides a finer gradation in the meaning for each of the response categories.

Connecting to the SMTP Server To initiate an SMTP session, the SMTP client establishes a connection with the SMTP server using TCP port 25. On establishing a connection, the client receives a response code that indicates whether the SMTP server can accept the connection and open a new session, or if the service is temporarily unavailable (see Table A.39).

Table A.39 Response Codes for a Connection to an SMTP Server	
Code	**Meaning**
220	The service is ready.
421	The service is unavailable.

DATA This command tells the server that the text that follows this command is the mail message to deliver to the specified recipient. The mail message text should be formatted according to the Internet Message Format (RFC 822) and should end with a single period preceded and followed by the carriage-return/line-feed end-of-line marker common to most Internet applications. This command should initially receive a 354 response code. The client should then send the message, to which the server will probably respond with a 250 response code. The DATA command's syntax is as follows:

```
DATA#13#10
```

Table A.40 lists the possible responses.

Table A.40   *DATA* Command Reply Codes

Code	Meaning
250	The requested action has completed.
354	Start the mail input, ending with <CRLF>.<CRLF>.
421	The service is not available.
451	The action was aborted because of a local processing error.
452	The action was not taken because the disk lacks sufficient storage space.
500	Syntax error. The command was unrecognized.
501	Syntax error in the parameters or arguments.
503	Bad sequence of commands.
552	The action was aborted because it exceeded the storage allocation.
554	The transaction failed.

***EXPN*—Expand**   The EXPN command performs the same function as the VRFY command, but is used to verify mailing lists. If EXPN is passed a valid mailing list name, the server returns the user names and addresses of the recipients listed in the mailing list. The EXPN command's syntax is as follows:

EXPN *mailing-list-name*#13#10

Table A.41 lists the possible responses.

Table A.41   *EXPN* Command Reply Codes

Code	Message
250	The requested action has completed.
421	The service is not available.
500	Syntax error. The command is unrecognized.
501	Syntax error in the parameters or arguments.
502	The command is not implemented.
504	The command parameter is not implemented.
550	The action was not taken because the mailbox is unavailable (not found).

HELO   The HELO command initiates the SMTP conversation. The client system name accompanies the command to establish the client's identity with the server. The server usually replies with a response code of 250, followed with the server's name. HELO should be the first command that an SMTP client issues after establishing a connection with an SMTP server. The command's syntax is as follows:

HELO *client-name*#13#10

Table A.42 lists the possible responses.

Table A.42   *HELO* Command Reply Codes

Code	Meaning
250	The requested action has completed.
421	The service is unavailable.
500	Syntax error. The command is unrecognized.
501	Syntax error in the parameters or arguments.
504	The command parameter is not implemented.

HELP   The user issues the HELP command usually during an interactive, command-line SMTP session. The command returns help information on all available commands or a specific command. The HELP command's syntax is as follows:

HELP[*command-string*]#13#10

Table A.43 lists the possible responses.

Table A.43   *HELP* Command Reply Codes

Code	Message
211	System help is ready.
214	A help information message.
421	The service is unavailable.
500	Syntax error. The command is unrecognized.
501	Syntax error in the parameters or arguments.
502	The command is not implemented.
504	The command parameter is not implemented.

MAIL   This command initiates a mail message and tells the server who is sending the message. The address passed with this command is always the address of the message's originator, although the address might also list several intermediate hosts (if the message is taking several hops on its way to the recipient). The syntax for the MAIL command is as follows:

MAIL FROM: *originator-name@originator-host*#13#10

Table A.44 lists the possible responses.

Table A.44 *MAIL* Command Reply Codes

Code	Meaning
250	The requested action has completed.
421	The service is unavailable.
451	The action was aborted because of a local processing error.
452	The action was not taken because the disk lacks sufficient storage space.
500	Syntax error. The command was unrecognized.
501	Syntax error in the parameters or arguments.
552	The action was aborted because it exceeded the storage allocation.

NOOP—No Operation   NOOP retrieves an OK response from the server. The command does not affect any actions or commands previously or subsequently entered. You can use NOOP as a "keep alive" command to ensure that the command connection remains active. The command's syntax is a follows:

NOOP#13#10

Table A.45 lists the possible responses.

Table A.45 *NOOP* Command Reply Codes

Code	Message
250	The requested action has completed.
421	The service is unavailable.
500	Syntax error. The command is unrecognized.

QUIT   The QUIT command tells the server that the client has no more transactions to issue, and that the connection should be closed. The server responds with OK and then closes the connection. The command's syntax is as follows:

QUIT#13#10

Table A.46 lists the possible responses.

Table A.46 *QUIT* Command Reply Codes

Code	Message
221	The service is closing the connection.
500	Syntax error. The command is unrecognized.

RCPT—Recipient   This command informs the server of who is the message's intended recipient. If the message is to go to multiple recipients, there might be more than one destination mailbox, separated by commas. The syntax for the RCPT command is as follows:

```
RCPT TO: recipient-name@recipient-host[, recipient-name@recipient-host,
    ...]#13#10
```

Table A.47 lists the possible responses.

Table A.47   *RCPT* Command Reply Codes

Code	Meaning
250	The requested action has completed.
251	The user is not local, so the message is being forwarded to *server-name*.
421	The service is unavailable.
450	The action was not taken because the mailbox is unavailable.
451	The action was aborted because of a local processing error.
452	The action was not taken because the disk lacks sufficient storage space.
500	Syntax error. The command is unrecognized.
501	Syntax error in the parameters or arguments.
503	Bad sequence of commands.
550	The action was not taken because the mailbox was unavailable (not found).
551	The user is not local, the client should try connecting to *server-name*.
552	The action was aborted because it exceeded the storage allocation.
553	The action was not taken because the mailbox syntax (name) is incorrect.

RSET—Reset   This command aborts the current mail transaction, discarding any sender, recipient, or message data. RSET clears and resets all buffers and state tables. The command's syntax is as follows:

```
RSET#13#10
```

Table A.48 lists the possible responses.

Table A.48   *RSET* Command Reply Codes

Code	Message
250	The requested action has completed.
421	The service is unavailable.

Code	Message
500	Syntax error. The command was unrecognized.
501	Syntax error in the parameters or arguments.
504	The command parameter is not implemented.

SAML—Send and Mail   The SAML command is like the SOML command, except that SAML always delivers the mail message to the recipient's mailbox, even if the command succeeds in sending the message to the recipient's terminal screen. The SAML command's syntax (like that of SEND and SOML) is as follows:

SAML FROM: *originator-name@originator-host*#13#10

Table A.49 lists the possible responses.

Table A.49   *SAML* Command Reply Codes

Code	Message
250	The requested action has completed.
421	The service is unavailable.
451	The action was aborted because of a local processing error.
452	The action was not taken because the disk lacks sufficient storage space.
500	Syntax error. The command was unrecognized.
501	Syntax error in the parameters or arguments.
502	The command is not implemented.
552	The action was aborted because it exceeded the storage allocation.

SEND   This command is used in place of the MAIL command. The SEND command sends the mail message not to the user's mailbox, but to the terminal screen of the user's current session. You use SEND if you need to send a critical message to the system administrator. If the administrator were actively logged into the mail server, you could send the message directly to his or her computer screen. If the user is not actively logged in to the mail server, or if the user is not accepting terminal messages, the server returns a 450 response code to the RCPT command that should follow the SEND command. The SEND command uses the same syntax as the MAIL command:

SEND FROM: *originator-name@originator-host*#13#10

Table A.50 lists the possible responses.

Table A.50   *SEND* Command Reply Codes

Code	Meaning
250	The requested action has completed.
421	The service is unavailable.
451	The action was aborted because of a local processing error.
452	The action was not taken because the disk lacks sufficient storage space.
500	Syntax error. The command is unrecognized.
501	Syntax error in the parameters or arguments.
502	The command is not implemented.
552	The action was aborted because it exceeded the storage allocation.

SOML—Send or Mail   The SOML command behaves like the SEND command, with one exception: If the recipient's terminal screen cannot display the mail message, the recipient's mailbox automatically receives the message. Like the SEND command, the SOML command uses the same syntax as the MAIL command:

```
SOML FROM: originator-name@originator-host#13#10
```

Table A.51 lists the possible responses.

Table A.51   *SOML* Command Reply Codes

Code	Message
250	The requested action has completed.
421	The service is unavailable.
451	The action was aborted because of a local processing error.
452	The action was not taken because the disk lacks sufficient storage space.
500	Syntax error. The command was unrecognized.
501	Syntax error in the parameters or arguments.
502	The command is not implemented.
552	The action was aborted because it exceeded the storage allocation.

TURN   The TURN command reverses the roles of the client and server systems. TURN tells the server to take on the role of the sender, and the client takes on the role of the recipient. You can use this command to receive any mail messages that you want to send from the server to the client without waiting for the server to initiate an SMTP session with the client. The TURN command's syntax is as follows:

```
TURN#13#10
```

Table A.52 lists the possible responses.

Table A.52 *TURN* Command Reply Codes

Code	Message
250	The requested action has completed.
500	Syntax error. The command is unrecognized.
502	The command is not implemented.
503	Bad sequence of commands.

N O T E Neither the SMTP command set nor the SMTP communications model has a login command. Therefore, any SMTP client can connect to any SMTP server and send mail messages. This leaves the Internet mail system vulnerable to some abuse, by enabling any user to send mail with a fictitious return address (or someone else's real return address). At one time, this vulnerability was the basis of a rumor suggesting that the Netscape Navigator had a security bug. In reality, however, the vulnerability is a security flaw in the SMTP model's design and implementation.

VRFY—Verify   The VRFY command asks the server to verify that the specified recipient is a valid user on the server system. You use this command before initiating a new mail message using the MAIL, SEND, SOML, or SAML commands. The VRFY command's syntax is as follows:

VRFY *user-name or user-address*#13#10

Table A.53 lists the possible responses.

Table A.53 *VRFY* Command Reply Codes

Code	Message
250	The requested action has completed.
251	The user is not local, so the action is being forwarded to *server-name*.
421	The service is unavailable.
500	Syntax error. The command is unrecognized.
501	Syntax error in the parameters or arguments.
502	The command is not implemented.
504	The command parameter is not implemented.
550	The action was not taken because the mailbox was unavailable (not found).
551	The user is not local, so the client should try connecting to *server-name*.
553	The action was not taken because the mailbox syntax (its name) was incorrect.

SMTP Extensions

Internet mail has been using SMTP as the primary transport protocol for many years. As with anything that has been in use for that long, there have been various extensions to the basic protocol. Although none of the extensions to the protocol has been popularized across all SMTP implementations, one extension (documented in RFC 1651) has been standardized to enable the SMTP client to learn which extensions are available on any SMTP server.

This new command, EHLO, is used in place of the HELO command and uses the same syntax. If the server does not support any SMTP extensions, it replies with a 500 response code, signifying that the server did not recognize the command. Otherwise, the server responds with a 250 response code and, if any extensions are supported, multiple lines listing the supported extensions, one to a line, with each line starting with the 250 response code.

N O T E   For the available SMTP extensions, examine the index of RFCs in Appendix C, "RFC Standards Documents," to find the appropriate documentation. Each RFC's title indicates whether the RFC covers SMTP extensions. ■

POP Commands

The POP command set is a small but functional set of commands. The designers decided to keep the session dialog box as simple as possible, determined which functions were absolutely necessary to provide the necessary services needed, and then added a few more functions to provide other desirable services. The designers also decided to provide an extremely simple set of response codes that might be returned to these commands.

POP Response Codes

Most programmers are interested in two basic response states: whether a command succeeded or not. Knowing the exact reason that a command failed might be nice, but doesn't make much difference in determining an appropriate reaction for a client application when its commands fail. With this in mind, the designers of the POP protocol decided to limit the response codes to only two that are sent in response to any of the POP commands:

Code	Meaning
+OK	The command succeeded.
–ERR	The command failed.

These two response codes are followed by a textual message giving any additional information that might be important to the client application or the application user. In these messages, you find the reason that a particular command failed.

Authorization State Commands

On connecting to a POP server, the connection enters the authorization state. To proceed any further, the client must provide the server with a valid mail account ID and password.

On successfully passing the account authorization, the server places the specified mailbox into an exclusive lock state. This prevents any modification of the messages until the server enters the update state. If the server cannot place the account mailbox into an exclusive lock state, the authorization fails and the connection cannot enter the transaction state.

PASS—Password   The PASS command provides the POP server with the appropriate password for the user account specified with the USER command. If the server responds with an error, either the password was wrong or the account mailbox could not be locked. The PASS command's syntax is as follows:

PASS *account-password*#13#10

QUIT   The QUIT command is considered to be both an authorization state and a transaction state command. If you issue this command during the authorization state, the session ends and the connection is severed. If you issue this command during the transaction state, the session closes and the server enters the update state. The command's syntax is as follows:

QUIT#13#10

USER   The USER command provides the POP server with a valid account ID. The server responds with a success reply if the account exists, or an error if the account does not exist. The syntax for this command is as follows:

USER *account_id*#13#10

This command can be issued only while the connection session is in the authorization state after receiving the POP server greeting, or after an unsuccessful USER or PASS command (if the server did not sever the connection).

Transaction State Commands

After the authorization state passes and the mailbox is opened and locked, the session enters the transaction state. This is the state in which the client can issue commands to get information on messages, retrieve messages, or delete messages.

DELE—Delete   The DELE command marks a specific message as deleted, but only until the server enters the update state. Because the deletion is not made until the end of the session, the surrounding messages are not renumbered and the RSET command can undelete all deleted messages (during the session in which they were deleted). The client must supply a valid message number with the DELE command. The command's syntax is as follows:

DELE *message-number*#13#10

LIST   The LIST command retrieves information about the size of a specific message or all the messages. If a message number is passed, the server responds with a single line. The message information is supplied as two numbers: the message number (even if the client supplied the message number) and the message size. If no message number is supplied, the server responds with a multiple-line response, with each message listed on successive lines and ending with the message-termination marker (a period) preceded and followed by a carriage-return/ line-feed character combination. This command's syntax is as follows:

LIST[*message-number*]#13#10

***NOOP*—No Operation**   The NOOP command gets an OK response from the server. You can use this command to keep a session alive. NOOP's syntax is as follows:

```
NOOP#13#10
```

***RETR*—Retrieve**   The client issues the RETR command to retrieve a specific message from the server. The client must supply a valid message number with this command (the message number cannot refer to a deleted message). The server responds by sending the message text, terminating the message with the standard message-termination marker (a single period) preceded and followed by the carriage-return/line-feed combination. RETR's syntax is as follows:

```
RETR message-number#13#10
```

***RSET*—Reset**   The RSET command unmarks any messages that have been marked for deletion during the current session. This command unmarks *all* messages that have been marked for deletion. RSET cannot be passed a message number to undelete a specific message. The command's syntax is as follows:

```
RSET#13#10
```

***STAT*—Status**   The STAT command gets a snapshot of the mailbox. The server replies to this command with the number of messages in the mailbox (except for those that were deleted during the session) and the mailbox's size (in octets or bytes), separated by spaces. The STAT command's syntax is as follows:

```
STAT#13#10
```

The server responds with a reply such as the following:

```
+OK 5 240#13#10
```

This response indicates that the mailbox has five messages with a combined size of 240 bytes.

The Update State

After the client issues the QUIT command from the transaction state, the server enters the update state. In this state, any message marked for deletion is removed and cannot be undeleted. The server then releases the exclusive-access lock that it had placed on the mailbox, so that the mailbox can be updated with any new messages that are received. If a session terminates without issuing the QUIT command from the transaction state, the update state is never entered and no messages are deleted.

Optional POP Commands

The previous commands are specified as a minimal POP server implementation. Three additional commands are recommended but purely optional for the server. These commands give the POP client greater flexibility while maintaining a simple server implementation.

***APOP*—Log In with the Encrypted Password**   An alternative to the USER and PASS commands, the APOP command takes two parameters: the account ID and the account password in an encrypted form. On connecting to the POP server, the server returns a greeting that includes a timestamp. This timestamp applies the MD5 algorithm (defined in RFC 1321) to encrypt the password. This method of POP authentication is recommended for client applications that connect frequently or regularly to a POP mail server, to minimize the passing of unencrypted passwords between the client and server. For further information on this command, see RFC 1725. The APOP command's syntax is as follows:

```
APOP account-id encrypted-password#13#10
```

TOP—the Top Lines of a Message   The TOP command retrieves the header section, and a specified number of lines of the body of a particular message. You can use this command to provide the user with a list of message headers, along with the first few lines of the message, without incurring the overhead of retrieving the entire message for all messages in the mailbox. The TOP command's syntax is as follows:

```
TOP message-number  number-of-body-lines-to-return#13#10
```

UIDL—Unique ID Listing   The UIDL command gets a unique and persistent message ID for one or all messages in the account mailbox. The server generates the message ID, which must be preserved across sessions. This unique message identification provides the client with the capability to track which messages have already been retrieved and which are new, regardless of how many messages have been deleted. The normal message numbers always begin with 1 and are sequential through all the messages currently in a mailbox. Therefore, if message 2 is deleted during a session, that session's message 3 becomes the next session's message 2. For this reason, maintaining a persistent message ID is important. The response to this command is formatted the same as the response to the LIST command, except that the format includes the unique ID rather than the message size. The UIDL command's syntax is as follows:

```
UIDL[ message-number ]#13#10
```

NNTP Commands

RFC 977 defines the NNTP protocol as a series of text-based commands, sometimes with a parameter but often without. In this RFC, 119 is the default socket (TCP) port to be used for the NNTP protocol. The RFC also defines the types of responses that can be returned for each of the various commands. The RFC specifies that you terminate all commands with a carriage-return and newline character combination.

N O T E   Among the commands defined are several that are used to exchange articles between news servers. This book does not cover any of these commands. If after reading this book you want to build your own Usenet news server, you will want to be aware of these commands. For a thorough explanation of them, read RFC 977 before building your Usenet news server. ▪

Valid responses to the NNTP commands consist of two parts: a status code and a textual explanation. The explanation is not specified, so each news server developer can customize it. The status codes, however, are carefully designated.

Each status code is designated with a three-digit number separated from the rest of the message with a space. The first digit of the code indicates the success or failure of the command to which it is responding. Table A.54 lists these codes.

Table A.54   The First Digit of NNTP Status Codes

Digit	Meaning
1	Informational message.
2	The command succeeded.
3	The command has succeeded so far, so continue with the rest of it.
4	The command was correct, but couldn't be performed.
5	The command was incorrect.

The second digit in the status code indicates the function response category (see Table A.55).

Table A.55   The Second Digit of NNTP Status Codes

Code	Meaning
0	Connection, setup, and miscellaneous messages.
1	Newsgroup selection messages.
2	Article selection messages.
3	Distribution function messages.
4	Posting messages.
8	Nonstandard extension messages.
9	Debugging output messages.

The third digit indicates the specific response within the various areas that the first two digits specify. The status codes that can be returned are defined with the commands for which they might be returned. For example, when you first connect to a Usenet news server on port 119, the server automatically sends you a response code of 200 or 201 followed by a short message. Another possible response to the connection is a code of 502, specifying that permission has been denied to your connection. For a listing of all the possible response codes, see RFC 977, section 4.7.2. Table A.56 lists the response codes for a news server connection.

Table A.56   The Response Codes to an NNTP Connection

Code	Meaning
200	The news server is connected, so posting is allowed.
201	The news server is connected, but posting is not allowed.
502	Permission to connect was denied.

ARTICLE   ARTICLE is the STAT, HEAD, and BODY commands combined into a single command. The ARTICLE command is accompanied by a article designator (either the article number or article ID). If the article specified is valid, ARTICLE returns the entire article (including both the header and body sections) and sets the current article pointer. As with the HEAD and BODY commands, a line consisting of a single period followed by the end-of-line marker (the carriage-return/line-feed character combination) indicates the end of the article. Table A.57 lists the result codes that ARTICLE returns.

Table A.57   *ARTICLE* Command Reply Codes

Code	Meaning
220	The article exists, and the article's head and body follow this response line.
412	No newsgroup has been joined.
420	No current article has been selected (you didn't issue either the STAT or ARTICLE command).
423	The article number specified was not found.
430	The article specified was not found.

BODY   The BODY command is the corresponding command to the HEAD command. BODY retrieves the text section of the current article. As with the HEAD command, you must specify the current article before issuing the BODY command. Also as with the HEAD command, a single period on a line by itself marks the end of the article text, followed by the carriage-return/line-feed end-of-line marker. Table A.58 lists the possible result codes for BODY.

Table A.58   *BODY* Command Reply Codes

Code	Meaning
222	The article exists, and the article body follows this response line.
412	No newsgroup has been joined.
420	No current article has been selected (you didn't issue either the STAT or ARTICLE command).

GROUP The GROUP command joins a particular newsgroup. The syntax for the command is as follows:

```
GROUP newsgroup
```

where *newsgroup* is the group to be joined. If the specified group exists on the news server, it responds with code 211, followed by the number of articles in the group, the first and last article numbers in the group, and the group name. If the specified newsgroup does not exist on the server, it responds with code 411, which specifies that no such group exists. To join a particular group before the client can get a listing of articles, or the text of any articles in the newsgroup, you must issue this command. Table A.59 lists the result codes that the server might return in response to a GROUP command.

Table A.59 *GROUP* **Command Reply Codes**

Code	Meaning
211	The specified group was selected.
411	No such group exists on this news server.

HEAD The HEAD command retrieves the header section from the current article. Like the NEXT and LAST commands, HEAD does not take any arguments, so you must call STAT or ARTICLE at least once to set the current article initially (after the current article has been set, the NEXT and LAST commands might have been used to navigate to the current article on which the HEAD command is being used). After HEAD retrieves the article header, the command can parse the header for such information as the author, the subject, and the date of submission. Table A.60 lists the result codes that the server returns.

Table A.60 *HEAD* **Command Reply Codes**

Code	Meaning
221	The article exists, and the article head follows this response line.
412	No newsgroup has been joined.
420	No current article has been selected (you didn't issue either the STAT or ARTICLE command).

The lines of the article header are separated by the carriage-return/line-feed character combination. The end of the article header is specified by a line that consists of a single period followed by the carriage-return/line-feed characters.

LAST The LAST command is the same as the NEXT command, except that LAST navigates backward through the articles in the newsgroup. As with the NEXT command, you have to issue either the STAT or ARTICLE command before using the LAST command. Also, the LAST command does not return any text, so you have to use the HEAD and BODY commands to retrieve the text associated with the new current article. Table A.61 lists the result codes that the LAST command returns.

Table A.61   *LAST* Command Reply Codes

Code	Meaning
223	The article exists.
412	No newsgroup has been joined.
420	No current article has been selected (you didn't issue either the STAT or ARTICLE command).
422	This newsgroup has no previous article (the current article is the first article).

LIST   The LIST command retrieves a list of the newsgroups that are available on the news server to which you are connected. The newsgroups are returned, one on a line, with the ending and beginning article numbers and a flag that indicates whether the posting of new messages is allowed for this particular newsgroup. The format used for this information is *group last first permission* followed by a carriage-return character and a line-feed character. The complete syntax for the LIST command is as follows:

LIST#13#10

N O T E   Even if a particular newsgroup specifies that posting is allowed, if the server responds to the initial connection with a status code of 201 (posting not allowed), the server overrides the group's posting permission and denies all client message posting. ▣

After receiving the LIST command, the server responds with a 215 code followed by a seemingly endless list of newsgroups. At last count, there were well over 6,000 newsgroups, so don't issue this request unless you have time to wait. The list of newsgroups, if you make it all the way to the end, is terminated by a line of text that consists of a single period (.) followed by the carriage-return/newline character combination.

The response to the LIST command is the code 215, which indicates that a list of newsgroups follows.

NEXT   The NEXT command repositions the current article pointer to the next article in the newsgroup. To initialize the current article position, you must issue a STAT or ARTICLE command before issuing the NEXT command. Like the STAT command, the NEXT command does not return any text, so you must use either the HEAD or BODY commands to retrieve the text associated with the current article. Table A.62 lists the response codes that the NEXT command returns.

Table A.62 *NEXT* **Command Reply Codes**

Code	Meaning
223	The article exists.
412	No newsgroup has been joined.
420	No current article has been selected (you didn't issue either the STAT or ARTICLE command).
421	This newsgroup has no next article (the current article is the last one).

NEWGROUPS The NEWGROUPS command is similar to the LIST command. NEWGROUPS returns all the new newsgroups created since the date and time specified with the command. The complete syntax for the command is as follows:

NEWGROUPS *date time* [GMT] [*distributions*]

where *date* is in the format *YYMMDD* and *time* is in the format *HHMMSS*. The last two digits of the year are used, and the nearest century is assumed (for example, *95* indicates 1995, and *10* indicates 2010). The time is specified in 24-hour notation, with the time assumed to be the local server's time zone unless GMT is designated (indicating that the time specified is to be evaluated as Greenwich Mean Time).

The *distributions* parameter is an optional list of distribution categories, separated by commas and enclosed in angled brackets (<>). This limits the new newsgroups to those that fall within the distribution groups specified by this list (for example, <comp> limits the new groups to those that fall in the comp distribution groups, such as **comp.lang.c++** and **comp.os.linux**).

The NEWGROUPS command is responded to with the status code 231 (which indicates that a list of newsgroups is to follow), followed by a list of newsgroups in the same format that the LIST command uses. As with the LIST command, the list of newsgroups is terminated by a line that consists of a single period.

POST Clients issue the POST command to tell the news server that they want to post an article to one or more newsgroups. A client doesn't have to have joined a newsgroup before issuing this command. The article header specifies the newsgroups into which the article is to post. The news server determines the newsgroups into which to post by examining the header section after receiving the article.

On receiving the POST command, the server responds with either code 340, to tell the client to proceed with sending the article, or code 440, to indicate that posting is not allowed (if the news client software maintains whether the news server allows posting, which can be determined from the welcome message received on connecting to the server, the client application can prevent the user from reaching the point at which the 440 code is returned). After receiving the entire article, the server responds with either a code 240, to indicate that the article was submitted successfully, or 441, to indicate that the posting failed.

Before sending the article, the news client must format the message according to RFC 1036. Therefore, the client must fill in the user's name and address, the subject, and any other important information. Also, the client software must end the message with the standard end-of-message marker (a line consisting of a single period).

> **N O T E** Most Usenet readers enable the user to reply to the current article. To do so, the user simply issues a standard POST command and fills in the current article ID in the Reply To header field. ▨

Table A.63 lists the response codes that the news server might return to POST.

Table A.63   *POST* Command Reply Codes

Code	Meaning
240	The article was posted successfully.
340	Proceed with sending the article to be posted.
440	The posting is not allowed.
441	The posting failed.

QUIT   The QUIT command tells the news server that the client will not issue any more commands, and that the server can thus terminate the connection. If the client does not issue this command, the server should detect the disconnection and gracefully close its end of the session.

STAT   The STAT command sets the current article pointer to a specific article within a newsgroup. The news server maintains a current article marker for each NNTP session in progress. By issuing the STAT command with a specific article number or article ID, the current article marker (on the server) is repositioned to the specified article. The command's syntax is as follows:

STAT number

STAT ID

where number is the article number and ID is the article ID. STAT does not return any text, so you have to request it separately. Table A.64 lists the possible responses to the STAT command.

Table A.64   *STAT* Command Reply Codes

Code	Meaning
223	The specified article exists.
412	No newsgroup has been joined.
423	The specified article number was not found.
430	The specified article was not found.

If you want to get a listing of the article headers in a particular newsgroup, you must use the STAT command to set the starting article number. You then can use the STAT command to navigate through the rest of the articles, or use the NEXT command to sequence through the articles.

The HTTP Command Set

Hypertext Transfer Protocol (HTTP) is the communication protocol used in the communications between Web browsers and Web servers. HTTP differs greatly from the Hypertext Markup Language (HTML), which is used to build Web pages. Web browsers use the HTTP protocol to request objects (files) from Web servers.

The HTTP commands consist of fewer commands than the command sets of the other Internet applications. The HTTP commands all follow the same basic syntax: a command (or method), followed by the URL on which to perform the specified task, and then possibly the HTTP version number. Therefore, the simple request form uses the following syntax:

`COMMAND URI #13#10`

The following is an example of the simple request syntax:

`GET /index.html#13#10`

And the full request uses the following syntax:

`COMMAND   URL   ProtocolVersion #13#10`

The following is an example of the full request syntax:

`GET http://home.netscape.com/ HTTP/1.0#13#10`

The HTTP Response Codes

If you use the simple request syntax, you do not receive any response codes in the server's reply. Therefore, because you used the simple HTTP request syntax to build the Web robot example in Chapter 15, "Building a Web Robot To Verify Link Integrity," the robot receives no response codes. If you use the full request syntax, however, you should receive an informational header for each of your requests that contains a numeric response code that you can interpret to determine the degree of success or failure. The response codes use a three-digit numbering sequence similar to that described for previous Internet applications in this appendix.

The first digit in the response code indicates the class of response (see Table A.65).

Table A.65   The Significance of the First Digit in HTTP Response Codes

Code	Meaning
1	Informational. The HTTP 1.0 specification does not use informational response codes. Therefore, there are no 100 series response codes.

Code	Meaning
2	Success. The command was received, understood, and accepted.
3	Redirection. You have to take further action to complete the request.
4	Client error. The request contains bad syntax or otherwise cannot be fulfilled.
5	Server error. The server failed to fulfill an apparently valid request.

Unlike in previous applications, the second and third digit of this code does not have any specific significance. Table A.66 lists all the possible HTTP response codes.

Table A.66   The List of HTTP Response Codes

Code	Meaning
200	OK.
201	Created.
202	Accepted.
204	No content.
301	Moved permanently.
302	Moved temporarily.
304	Not modified.
400	Bad request.
401	Unauthorized.
403	Forbidden.
404	Not found.
500	Internal server error.
501	Not implemented.
502	Bad gateway.
503	Service unavailable.

The Basic HTTP Commands

The HTTP specification has three basic commands, plus several more that have been specified and are in some stage of moving from draft recommendation to specification status. Some of the extension commands are used primarily for maintaining Web pages, and these commands will probably be used increasingly as more browsers have built-in editing capabilities.

GET   The GET command tells the HTTP server to return the file, object, or data identified by the URL or Uniform Resource Identifier (URI) passed as an argument. If the URI refers to a data-producing script or application, this command returns that script's or application's data results, not the script itself.

You can pass GET with an If-Modified-Since header field, turning the command into a conditional GET. This enables a browser to cache pages and resources, retrieving new copies only when they have been updated. This caching reduces the network traffic and can increase connection transfer speed (especially if you are using a Point-to-Point Protocol [PPP] or Serial Line Internet Protocol [SLIP] connection). For more information on how to cache pages and resources until they have been refreshed on the server, see the HTTP 1.0 specification, which is available through the World Wide Web Consortium home page (**http://www.w3.org/**).

HEAD   The HEAD command is similar to GET, except that HEAD returns only the HTTP headers, and not any of the document body. No conditional modifiers are available for the HEAD command.

POST   The POST command submits new files, data, or messages to the server. You can use this command to post a message to a bulletin board or newsgroup, send results from a form, or submit data for a database operation. The URI that the POST command specifies determines how to process the information that the server receives.

The Extended HTTP Commands

The extensions to the HTTP protocol are not available everywhere. They are in various states of becoming standardized, and might not become part of the official standard until HTTP version 2.0 is finalized. You cannot depend on finding any HTTP server that supports these commands, and they might not remain as part of the HTTP specification. The current version of the HTTP working draft is available from the HTTP Working Group at **http://www.w3.org/** or **http://info.cern.ch/**.

CHECKIN   The CHECKIN command replaces the specified object and releases any locks that the CHECKOUT command has placed on the object. The draft specification might replace CHECKOUT and CHECKIN with GET and PUT to make the code control functionality work more like CVS rather than RCS.

CHECKOUT   The CHECKOUT command is similar to the GET command, but includes the additional functionality of locking the object so that other users cannot update it. This command provides a kind of version control into the HTTP specification.

DELETE   The DELETE method requests that the server delete the objects specified by the URL. This command makes the specified URL invalid.

LINK   The LINK command requests that the server link object header information with a specified object without altering the object's content. You can use this command to alter the object's header information without changing the document body.

PUT   The PUT command enables the client to store the enclosed document body section in the specified URL. You can use this command to update existing URLs with new HTML pages. The specified URL must already exist; PUT cannot create new URLs.

SHOWMETHOD   This command returns a description of a given method when you apply that method to a specific object. You use this command when multiple methods are available for a specific object, to enable the client to understand the object interface sufficiently to interact with it.

SPACEJUMP   The SPACEJUMP command is similar to the TEXTSEARCH command in that SPACEJUMP is a flag that indicates whether the GET command can be used with a derived URL. The server is passed a GET command with a set of coordinates (such as on an imagemap) for the server to determine where the client is supposed to go.

TEXTSEARCH   The TEXTSEARCH command returns a flag that indicates whether the search form of the GET command is available. The client then issues a GET command with the appropriate search information.

UNLINK   The UNLINK command removes the specified header information from the specified object. ●

The Internet Message Format

The Internet Message Format, described in Request for Comment (RFC) 822, is a simple format in which information needed for transporting and delivering the message is embedded in a message header that is separated from the message body by an empty line. The header section includes several lines that consist of a field title followed by a colon (:), a space, and the value. As is typical in most Internet messages, a carriage-return/newline character combination (#13#10) terminates the lines of text. A header field uses the following basic syntax:

```
Header Field Name: Value#13#10
```

Applications use the information in the header section to route the message to the appropriate recipient, or to reply to the appropriate sender. The header section often includes information about how to display or interpret the message's contents. ∎

SMTP Mail Headers

RFC 822 defines the Simple Mail Transport Protocol (SMTP) header fields. In fact, these are the only header fields that this RFC defines; all others are defined in the RFCs (or other specification documents) that specify the application's protocol. The SMTP header fields are easily broken up into distinct functional areas based on the function that each field serves. The header fields need not be in the order defined in this section, and you need not include all of them to make a valid and operational SMTP header.

Originator Fields

The originator fields designate the origins of the message. This origin includes the person who sent the message, the computer from which the message was sent, and the address to which replies should be sent.

The From Field   The From field designates the message's originator. The field should contain a machine-readable user address (as in `From: davischa@onramp.net`). This address is not necessarily that of the message's sender, but is the person, system, or process that entered the message. The full name of the sender might appear at the end of the field, enclosed in parentheses (as in `From: davischa@onramp.net (Davis Chapman)`).

Examples:

```
From: davischa@onramp.net
```

```
From: davischa@onramp.net (Davis Chapman)
```

Added by: the user.

The Sender Field   The Sender field designates the message's sender when that sender is not the person, process, or system that originally entered the message. If the sender is not the same as the message's originator, the Sender field must be present. The sender must designate a single person or process that is responsible for sending the message. If a process generates a message, the Sender field should designate the person responsible for the process.

Example:

```
From: theboss@here.com
Sender: davischa@onramp.net
```

Added by: the user or client application.

The Reply-To Field   The Reply-To field designates any mailboxes to which to send responses. This field is significant when mailboxes other than those of the sender or originator should receive the responses. You see this header field most often when an application rather than a person generates the message.

Example:

```
Reply-To: billg@microsoft.com
```

Added by: the user or a message-creating application.

The Receiver Fields

The Receiver fields deliver the message to the appropriate mailbox or process.

The To Field   The To field contains the addresses of the primary recipients. The user can list multiple recipients, separated by commas.

Examples:

```
To: nobody@nowhere.org
```

```
To: nobody@nowhere.org, somebody@somewhere.edu
```

Added by: the user.

The CC Field   The CC (carbon copy) field contains the address of secondary recipients. Like the To field, the CC field can contain multiple addresses, separated by commas.

Examples:

```
CC: somebody@somewhere.org
```

```
CC: nobody@nowhere.org, somebody@somewhere.edu
```

Added by: the user.

The BCC Field   The BCC (blind carbon copy) field contains the addresses of any additional recipients for the message. Copies of the message that you send to the primary and secondary recipients do not include this header line. Some systems include this line only in the author's copy. This header field is used for sending copies of a message to someone whom you don't want any of the message's other recipients to know about.

Example:

```
BCC: billg@microsoft.com
```

Added by: the user.

Reference Fields

The Reference fields identify the message, as well as any other messages that the message references.

The Message-ID Field   The Message-ID field contains a unique identifier that the originating machine generates. This identifier is intended for use not by the human recipient, but by the applications responsible for sending and receiving the message. Each version of a message should have a unique message ID, with no duplicates. This ID usually consists of the date and time that the message was generated, combined with the machine name and possibly another number generator to guarantee uniqueness.

Example:

```
Message-ID: <311519D5.F5D@onramp.net>
```

Added by: the server.

The In-Reply-To Field   The In-Reply-To field contains the message IDs of any previous messages to which this message is a response. This field can contain multiple message IDs separated by commas. The angle brackets in this and subsequent fields mark the beginning and ending of the message IDs. The brackets are a required part of the specification.

Example:

```
In-Reply-To: <310E8844@whitehouse.gov>
```

Added by: the client application.

The References Field   The References field contains the message IDs of any previous messages that this message references. This field can contain multiple message IDs separated by commas.

Examples:

```
References: <31104857.A7A@onramp.net>

References: <31104857.A7A@onramp.net>, <27362773.BR@pionet.net>
```

Added by: the client application.

The Keywords Field   The Keywords field contains keywords or phrases that identify the message's contents. The field can contain multiple words and phrases separated by commas.

Example:

```
Keywords: Delphi, Programming, Internet
```

Added by: the user.

Trace Fields

The Trace fields identify the path that the message has taken to arrive at its destination. These fields are added by the servers, never by the client applications.

The Return-Path Field   The final transport system that delivers the message to its recipient adds the Return-Path field, which contains the route that the message has taken on its way from the originating system to the recipient system.

Example:

```
Path: davischa@onramp.net
```

Added by: the server.

The Received Field   Each transport system through which the message travels adds the Received field. This information is often used to trace transport problems.

Example:

```
Received: from host (localhost [127.0.0.1]) by mlm.InterNex.Net
(8.7.1/8.7.1) with SMTP id HAA10170; Sun, 18 Feb 1996 07:53:43 GMT
```

Added by: the server.

Other Fields

The other fields in the header have no single purpose as a group, but instead have individual purposes.

The Date Field   The Date field contains the time and date that the message originated. The Internet message date format is as follows:

```
[day, ]date> time
```

The day is a three-character abbreviation of the day of the week. The date is in the following format:

```
DD MMM YY
```

The month is a three-character abbreviation of the month of the message's origination. The time portion is in the following format:

```
HH:MM[:SS] timezone
```

HH, *MM*, and *SS* are each two digits designating the hour, minute, and second, respectively, that the message originated. The time zone is a three-character abbreviation of the time zone in which the preceding date and time originated.

Example:

```
Date: Sun, 18 Feb 1996 01:37:01 GMT
```

Added by: the client application or the server.

The Subject Field   The Subject field briefly summarizes the message's contents. The message's originator usually creates the summary.

Example:

```
Subject: Internet Book Progress
```

Added by: the user.

The Comments Field   The Comments field enables users to add comments to the message without disturbing the message body's contents.

Example:

```
Comments: This message doesn't really deal with the current progress of
the Internet programming book
```

Added by: the user.

The Encrypted Field   The Encrypted field indicates whether the message body is encrypted, and if so, which encryption scheme was used. In the value portion of this field, the first value indicates the software that performs the encryption, and the second (optional) value helps the user select the proper decryption key (for example, the public portion of a public key encryption).

NOTE Because a message's header portion must remain unencrypted (for delivery purposes), complete message privacy is not possible. Message recipients, addresses, and subject lines remain unencrypted and thus readily available for unencrypted viewing. ■

Example:

```
Encrypted: PGP 123456
```

Added by: the client application.

Extended Fields

The Internet Message Format has been extended with additional header fields to handle additions to the message format, most notably the Multipurpose Internet Multimedia Extensions (MIME). These fields are limited in that they cannot begin with X- without conflicting with user-defined fields. This section describes some of these extensions.

The MIME-Version Field   The MIME-Version field indicates which version of the MIME protocol was used to construct the message.

Example:

```
MIME-Version: 1.0
```

Added by: the client application.

The Content-Transfer-Encoding Field   The Content-Transfer-Encoding field is a modifier of the message's media type. This modifier indicates which type of encoding was performed on the message and thus which decoding you must perform on the message to restore its initial state.

Example:

```
Content-Transfer-Encoding: 7bit
```

Added by: the client application.

The Content-Type Field   The Content-Type field indicates the message media type (such as text/plain or multipart/mixed).

Example:

```
Content-Type: text/plain; charset=US-ASCII
```

Added by: the client application.

User-Defined Fields

The Internet Message Format allows users to add user-defined header fields. These header fields always begin with X- followed by the field name.

Example:

```
X-Mailer: Delphi SMTP Mailer v1.0
```

Added by: the client application.

Usenet News Headers

The Usenet message headers serve the same function as the mail message headers. Many of the headers are identical to and use the same syntax as their SMTP equivalents.

The Required Header Fields

The required header fields are on every message that you find posted to any newsgroup on the Internet. The posting person or process supplies most of these fields, but the transport systems add a couple.

App

B

The From Field   A Usenet header's From field is the same as in the SMTP definition, with an additional formatting option. The sender's full name can appear as the main portion of the field, followed by the address within angle brackets (as in From: Davis Chapman <davischa@onramp.net>).

Examples:

```
From: davischa@onramp.net
```

```
From: davischa@onramp.net (Davis Chapman)
```

```
From: Davis Chapman <davischa@onramp.net>
```

Added by: the user.

The Date Field   The Date field is the same as in the SMTP definition.

Example:

```
Date: Sun, 18 Feb 1996 01:37:01 GMT
```

Added by: the client application or the server.

The Newsgroups Field   The Newsgroups field is the list of newsgroups to which the message is to be posted. The field can contain multiple newsgroups separated by commas. The listed newsgroups must be existing newsgroups; you cannot create new newsgroups by listing them in this field. Invalid newsgroups included in this field are ignored, because they might be valid newsgroups on a different news server.

Example:

```
Newsgroups: ab.politics, alt.politics.media
```

Added by: the user.

The Subject Field   The Usenet header's Subject field is the same as in the SMTP definition.

Example:

```
Subject: Book Ideas
```

Added by: the user.

The Message-ID Field   The Usenet header's Message-ID field is the same as in the SMTP definition.

Example:

```
Message-ID: <4g0asu$3db@news.innet.com>
```

Added by: the server.

The Path Field   The Path field is much like the Return-Path field in the SMTP header definitions. It shows the path that the message took to arrive at the current news server. Each transport server through which the message passes adds and appends this field. The user or client application does not have to supply this field.

Example:

```
Path: news.onramp.net!news.sprintlink.net!news.us.world.net
```

Added by: the server.

Optional Headers

The optional headers provide for various functionality in addition to the basic newsgroup functionality.

The Reply-To Field   The Reply-To field is similar to the SMTP field of the same name. This field contains the address of the recipient of any electronic mail (e-mail) responses to the message. If this field does not exist, e-mail responses are sent to the address in the From field.

Example:

```
Reply-To: davischa@onramp.net
```

Added by: the user.

The Sender Field   This Usenet header field is the same as in the SMTP definition.

Example:

```
Sender: davischa@onramp.net
```

Added by: the user.

The Followup-To Field   The Followup-To field is a cross between the Newsgroups and Reply-To fields. It is a list of newsgroups to which any responses are to be posted. If you omit this field, the responses will be posted to the newsgroups listed in the Newsgroups field. If the keyword poster is in this field, posted replies are not allowed and responses are instead e-mailed to the message submitter.

Example:

```
Followup-To: <4g0asu$3db@news.innet.com>
```

Added by: the client application.

The Expires Field   The Expires field is a date in the Internet message date format. The field specifies the suggested expiration date of the message. If you omit this field, the local expiration date is used. This field is rarely used and its use is discouraged unless the topic has a natural expiration date. You should instead enable local administrators to manage the expiration date of messages according to local policies that often are established on a basis of available disk space or other system performance limitations.

Example:

```
Expires: Mon, 19 Feb 1996 12:00:00 CST
```

Added by: the user.

The References Field   This Usenet header field is the same as in the SMTP definition.

Example:

```
References: <4g0asu$3db@news.innet.com>
```

Added by: the client application.

The Control Field   The Control field indicates that the message is a control message not intended for users to read. Control messages are messages to the host systems through which they pass.

Example:

```
Control: cancel <4g0asu$3db@news.innet.com>
```

Added by: the client application.

The Distribution Field   The Distribution field limits the distribution of a Usenet message to certain systems. The message is posted to the newsgroups listed on the Newsgroups header field, but is sent only to those systems that subscribe to the newsgroups listed on the Distribution field. Suppose, for example, that you want to post an advertisement to sell a car. You might want to limit the message's distribution to systems within a limited geographic area. To do so, you specify in the Distribution field newsgroups that begin with a state identifier (such as tx, la, ny, and nj).

Example:

```
Distribution: tx, la, ok
```

Added by: the user.

The Organization Field   The Organization field identifies the organization to which the sender belongs. For example, if you were posting a listing as a representative of a corporation or association, you would include in the Organization field the name of the corporation or association.

Example:

```
Organization: Hackers Anonymous
```

Added by: the user.

The Keywords Field   This Usenet header field is the same as in the SMTP definition.

Example:

```
Keywords: Delphi, Programming, Internet
```

Added by: the user.

The Summary Field   The Summary field should contain a brief summary of the message. This field's contents are most often used as part of a follow-up message.

Example:

```
Summary: A collection of possible book ideas
```

Added by: the user.

The Approved Field   The Approved field is required for any message posted to a moderated newsgroup. The newsgroup moderator adds the field, which contains the moderator's e-mail address. Certain control messages also require this field.

Example:

```
Approved: moderator@newshost.com
```

Added by: the user or the administrator.

The Lines Field   The Lines field contains the number of lines in the message body.

Example:

```
Lines: 52
```

Added by: the client application.

The Xref Field   The Xref field is used on local systems only and should never be transmitted. The field lists the newsgroups on the local server in which the message is posted, and the message number in each of those newsgroups.

Example:

```
Xref: onramp ab.politics:564 alt.politics.media:1465
```

Added by: the server.

HTTP Headers

The HTTP headers are not used for routing purposes, but instead for exchanging information between the client and server processes. HTTP 1.0 adopted this format; before this release, no message headers were used to exchange needed information. The HTTP message headers include such information as the type and size of the requested object, whether the object was modified since the last retrieval, or whether to restore the object from cache to reduce transfer time.

Request Headers

The request headers enable the client to pass additional information to the server about the request and the client itself.

The From Field   The From field is much the same as it is in the SMTP and Usenet headers. The field contains the address of the person using the client process. The requesting header includes this field only with the user's approval. For security reasons, a site might not include this field. The field should be easy to disable, because inclusion in the header might conflict with the user's privacy interests or the site's security policy.

Example:

```
From: davischa@onramp.net
```

Added by: the client application.

The If-Modified-Since Field   The client uses the If-Modified-Since field with the GET command to make the object retrieval conditional. If the object was not modified since the specified date (in the Internet message date format), the client should restore from cache. If the object was modified since the specified date, the object is returned.

Example:

```
If-Modified-Since: Sun, 18 Feb 1996 14:52:34 CST
```

Added by: the client application.

The Referer Field   The Referer field contains the URL of the source from which the request URL was obtained. If the URL was not obtained from a source that has its own URL (for example, if the user typed the URL), the Referer field should not be sent. The server can use this field to build a list of sites that are linked to the requested URL.

Example:

```
Referer: http://rampages.onramp.net/~davischa/index.html
```

Added by: the client application.

The User-Agent Field   The User-Agent field specifies the client application that is making the request. This field is not required, but is recommended. You can use this field for statistical purposes or to tailor the server responses according to the client application's limitations.

Example:

```
User-Agent: Delphi Web Browser v1.0
```

Added by: the client application.

Response Headers

In the response header fields, the server sends information about itself to the client.

The Location Field   The Location field specifies the exact location (URL) of the requested object. For example, if you request the World Wide Web Consortium's home page (**http://**

App

B

www.w3.org/), you receive a response that contains a Location field that specifies the returned page as **http://www.w3.org/pub/WWW/**.

Example:

```
Location: http://www.w3.org/pub/WWW/
```

Added by: the server.

The Server Field   The Server field contains information about the software that the server uses to handle the request. By capturing this information and maintaining statistics on the server manufacturers, you can produce statistical information on the market share for each of the server vendors.

Example:

```
Server: Delphi Web Server v1.0
```

Added by: the server.

The WWW-Authenticate Field   The server returns the WWW-Authenticate field with a 401 (unauthorized) response message. The field contains at least one challenge that indicates the authentication scheme and parameters applicable to the request URL. This challenge is a signal from the server that the client application needs to pass the Authenticate header field in subsequent requests as specified in the following note.

N O T E   In this instance, the challenge is a message that tells the client application what to send to the server with the Authentication field. The challenge can be a simple indication of the encryption method to use, or what information the user must supply. The challenge consists of the following:

- The authentication scheme used
- The realm or domain in which the authentication credentials can be used
- Any parameters that must be passed with the credentials

The HTTP 1.0 specification documents the "basic" authentication scheme, but a site can implement any authentication scheme desired. ▧

Example:

```
WWW-Authenticate: Basic realm="BRBA"
```

Added by: the server.

General Headers

The general headers apply to both the request and response headers. They do not apply to the requested object, but to the transmitted message.

The Date Field   The Date field contains the date and time when the message was sent. This date format follows the Internet message date format used in the SMTP and Usenet News message headers.

Example:

```
Date: Sun, 18 Feb 1996 01:37:01 GMT
```

Added by: the client application or the server.

The MIME-Version Field   The MIME-Version field indicates which version of the MIME protocol was used to construct the message. HTTP is not a MIME-compliant protocol, so this field is not a required message header. This field should be used only when the message is MIME-compliant, but is often used indiscriminately. For this reason, you cannot count on this field indicating MIME-compliance accurately.

Example:

```
MIME-Version: 1.0
```

Added by: the client application or the server.

The Pragma Field   The Pragma field includes implementation-specific directives that might apply to any recipient along the request/response chain. The most frequently used Pragma field directive is `no-cache`, which informs any middleman servers (any server through which your requests are being passed as they are routed across the Internet) not to serve the request from any cache that they might be holding, but instead to pass the request to the intended server or client and then refresh the requested object from the original server. Pragma field values are implementation-specific and rarely standardized. The `no-cache` pragma directive is the only standardized directive commonly used.

Example:

```
Pragma: no-cache
```

Added by: the client application or the server.

Entity Headers

The entity headers contain information about the object being sent in the message body. The server's response to a client's request usually includes these header fields, but a client's request might include the fields.

The Allow Field   The Allow field specifies which methods the server supports. The client can still try a method that the Allow field does not specify.

Example:

```
Allow: GET, HEAD
```

Added by: the client application or the server.

The Authorization Field   The client uses the Authorization field to pass the appropriate credentials to the server after receiving a 401 (unauthorized) response message. The HTTP 1.0 specification available from the World Wide Web Consortium (**http://www.w3.org/**) describes the authorization process in detail.

Example:

```
Authorization: Basic QWxhZGRpbjpvcGVuHNIc2FtZQ==
```

Added by: the client application.

The Content-Encoding Field   The Content-Encoding field is a modifier of the object's media type. The field indicates the type of encoding that has been performed on the object, and thus what decoding must be performed on the object to restore its initial state.

Example:

```
Content-Encoding: x-gzip
```

Added by: the server.

The Content-Length Field   The Content-Length field specifies the requested object's size.

Example:

```
Content-Length: 2315
```

Added by: the server.

The Content-Type Field   The Content-Type field indicates the requested object's media type (for example, text/html, image/gif, and image/jpeg).

Examples:

```
Content-Type: text/html
```

```
Content-Type: image/gif
```

Added by: the server.

The Expires Field   The Expires field indicates a date and time after which the requested object is out-of-date. Client applications should not cache the specified object beyond the specified expiration date.

Example:

```
Expires: Mon, 19 Feb 1996 12:00:00 CST
```

Added by: the server.

The Last-Modified Field   The Last-Modified field gives the date (in Internet message date format) when the requested object was last modified. If the client has a copy of the object cached on the local computer that is older than the date that the Last-Modified field specifies, that copy is out-of-date and the server should refresh it.

Example:

```
Last-Modified: Sun, 18 Feb 1996 11:32:45 CST
```

Added by: the server. ●

RFC Standards Documents

In the last few years, the Internet has gone through a phase similar to that of personal computers in the late 1970s and early 1980s. Back then, you could build a state-of-the-art computer in your living room using a soldering gun, a screwdriver, a television set, and a few handfuls of electronic parts. A camaraderie among hobbyists developed as everyone enjoyed building the newest models and arguing over which one was better.

Today, a similar environment exists in the Internet community. For the cost of a computer and a telephone call, you can participate in designing the latest in software programs or communications protocols. And, instead of attending monthly meetings at a local college, you can join a newsgroup and interact with fellow enthusiasts on a daily basis.

You can download source code from an FTP site and port the latest UNIX program to Windows or OS/2. *You* can be the trailblazer; you don't have to wait for someone else to create a program that you want.

One reason that the Internet has grown so quickly is its foundation in public-domain protocols. Every protocol used on the Internet is available for your inspection. You can implement the protocols in any computer language and sell or give away any programs that you create based on those protocols. However, if you use any public-domain source code, remember to give proper credit to the original programmers.

A series of notes called *Request for Comment* notes, or *RFC* notes for short, document the protocols. The RFC Editor (**rfc-editor@isi-edu**) maintains the notes. The RFC notes are archived at **ds.internet.edu**. This archive is duplicated—or *mirrored*—by computer sites all over the world.

This appendix shows you how to request the RFC documents by e-mail and lists the RFC document titles so that you can peruse them at your leisure. ■

RFC Documents Online

Most, if not all, of the RFC documents are available by e-mail from the InterNIC Directory and Database Services server. This book's companion CD includes a copy of every RFC released up to the date of publication. However, the Internet changes so rapidly that you should know how to find out whether new RFCs have been published or old ones updated.

The easiest way to check for such changes is to get the updated RFC Index by e-mail. If you are interested in a new or updated document, you simply send an e-mail message requesting it.

Requesting the RFC Index

You can request the RFC Index by sending an e-mail message to **mailserv@ds.internic.net**. Leave the subject line blank and send the message:

```
document-by-name rfc-index
```

Figure C.1 shows you what the request looks like when you make it through the Netscape Mail program.

FIG. C.1
How to request the RFC index.

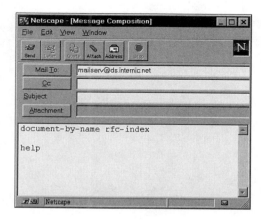

TIP To get more information about how to use the InterNIC server, send the message help, as shown in Figure C.1.

Figure C.2 shows you what the response from the InterNIC server looks like when the request is made using the Netscape mail program. Of course, you can request and receive the information using any mail program.

FIG. C.2

The reponse to a request for the RFC Index.

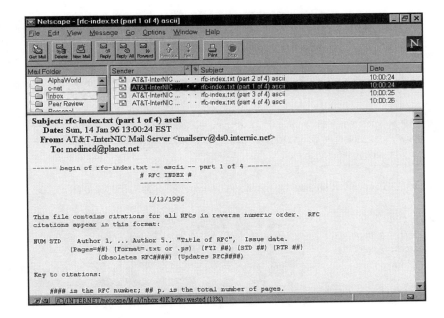

Notice that the server sends the index as four separate documents that do not necessarily arrive in numeric order. Each part of the response is 64K or less.

Requesting an RFC Document

To request RFC documents, send an e-mail message to **mailserv@ds.internic.net**. Leave the subject line blank and send the message

```
document-by-name rfcNNNN
```

where *NNNN* is the number of the RFC document that you want. You can request multiple documents by including more than one line in the message or separating the document names with commas, as in the following example:

```
document-by-name rfcNNNN, rfcYYYY
```

Figure C.3 shows you what the request looks like when you make it using the Netscape Mail program.

FIG. C.3

How to request a
single RFC document
and multiple RFC
documents.

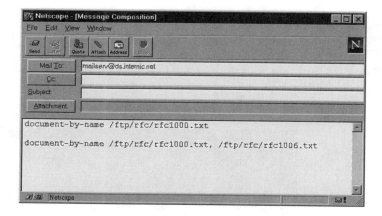

 TIP   When requesting an RFC document, you must specify its full path name. If you are unsure of the full
path name, try using **/ftp/rfc/rfcNNNN.txt,** where *NNNN* is the number of the RFC document that you
want.

Figure C.4 shows the response to requesting RFC1000 and RFC1009.

FIG. C.4

The response to an RFC
document request.

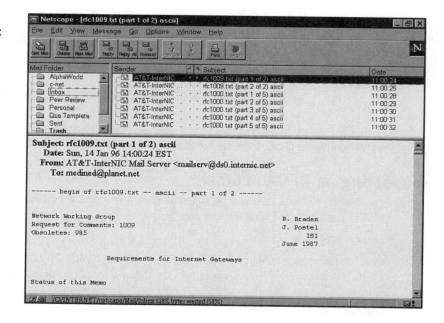

Searching the RFC Documents

If you have a Web browser that supports forms and an Internet connection, you can use the searchable index at the following address:

```
http://ds.internic.net/ds/dspg1intdoc.html
```

> **NOTE** If you aren't sure whether your browser supports forms, simply connect to the Web site and see what happens. If your screen looks similar to Figure C.5 and you see an input text field, your Web browser does indeed support forms. If not, consider changing browsers. ▦

With this index, you can look through all the online RFC document for a specific word or words.

Figure C.5 shows what the request looks like when you make it using the Netscape Mail program.

FIG. C.5

How to search the RFC documents.

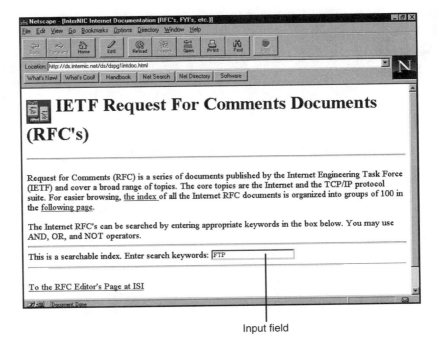

Input field

To use the searchable index, connect to the Web site, enter the search words into the input field, and then press Enter. The Web server then searches through its database of RFC documents and returns a list of documents that match your search words.

Figure C.6 shows the results of searching for the word *FTP*.

FIG. C.6

The results of searching the RFC documents for the string *FTP*.

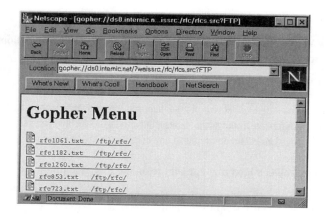

The next section looks at the STD documents, which are RFC documents that have completed the approval process and are considered standards.

Standards Documents

Table C.1 lists the official standards documents for the Internet. These protocols and processes have made it though the full cycle of review as described in Chapter 7, "Internet Development Standards."

Table C.1 Internet Standards Documents

Standard Number	Title	Author(s)	Date	File Information	See Also
0001	Internet Official Protocol Standards	J. Postel	November 11, 1995	38 pages	RFC1880
0002	Assigned Numbers	J. Reynolds & J. Postel	October 1994	TXT=458,860 bytes	RFC1800
0005	Internet Protocol	J. Postel	September 1981	TXT=241,903 bytes	RFC0791, RFC0950, RFC0919, RFC0922, RFC792, RFC1112
0006	User Datagram Protocol	J. Postel	August 1980	TXT=5,896 bytes	RFC0768
0007	Transmission Control Protocol	J. Postel	September 1981	TXT=172,710 bytes	RFC0793
0008	Telnet Protocol	J. Postel & J. Reynolds	May 1983	TXT=44,639 bytes	RFC0854, RFC0855

Standard Number	Title	Author(s)	Date	File Information	See Also
0009	File Transfer Protocol	J. Postel & J. Reynolds	October 1985	TXT=148,316 bytes	RFC0959
0010	Simple Mail Transfer Protocol	Various	November 6, 1995		RFC1870, RFC1869
0011	Format for Electronic Mail Messages	D. Crocker	August 1982	TXT=124,861 bytes	RFC0822, RFC1049
0012	Network Time Protocol	D. Mills	September 1989	TXT=193 bytes	RFC1119
0013	Domain Name System	P. Mockapetris	November 1987	TXT=248,726 bytes	RFC1034, RFC1035
0014	Mail Routing and the Domain System	C. Partridge	January 1986	TXT=18,182 bytes	RFC0974
0015	Simple Network Management Protocol	J. Case, M. Fedor, M. Schoffstall, & J. Davin	May 1990	TXT=72,876 bytes	RFC1157
0016	Structure of Management Information	M. Rose & K. McCloghrie	May 1990	TXT=82,279 bytes	RFC1155, RFC1212
0017	Management Information Base	K. McCloghrie & M. Rose	March 1991	TXT=142,158 bytes	RFC1213
0018	Exterior Gateway Protocol	D. Mills	April 1984	TXT=63,836 bytes	RFC0904
0019	NetBIOS Service Protocols	NetBIOS Working Group	March 1987	TXT=319,750 bytes	RFC1001, RFC1002
0020	Echo Protocol	J. Postel	May 1983	TXT=1,237 bytes	RFC0862
0021	Discard Protocol	J. Postel	May 1983	TXT=1,239 bytes	RFC0863
0022	Character Generator Protocol	J. Postel	May 1983	TXT=6,842 bytes	RFC0864

App
C

continues

Table C.1 Continued

Standard Number	Title	Author(s)	Date	File Information	See Also
0023	Quote of the Day Protocol	J. Postel	May 1983	TXT=1,676 bytes	RFC0865
0024	Active Users Protocol	J. Postel	May 1983	TXT=2,029 bytes	RFC0866
0025	Daytime Protocol	J. Postel	May 1983	TXT=2,289 bytes	RFC0867
0026	Time Server Protocol	J. Postel	May 1983	TXT=3,024 bytes	RFC0868
0027	Binary Transmission Telnet Option	J. Postel & J. Reynolds	May 1983	TXT=8,965 bytes	RFC0856
0028	Echo Telnet Option	J. Postel & J. Reynolds	May 1983	TXT=10,859 bytes	RFC0857
0029	Suppress Go Ahead Telnet Option	J. Postel & J. Reynolds	May 1983	TXT=3,712 bytes	RFC0858
0030	Status Telnet Option	J. Postel & J. Reynolds	May 1983	TXT=4,273 bytes	RFC0859
0031	Timing Mark Telnet Option	J. Postel & J. Reynolds	May 1983	TXT=7,881 bytes	RFC0860
0032	Extended Options List Telnet Option	J. Postel & J. Reynolds	May 1983	TXT=3,068 bytes	RFC0861
0033	Trivial File Transfer Protocol	K. Sollins	July 1992	TXT=24,599 bytes	RFC1350
0034	Routing Information Protocol	C. Hedrick	June 1988	TXT=91,435 bytes	RFC1058
0035	ISO Transport Service on Top of the TCP (Version 3)	M. Rose & D. Cass	May 1978	TXT=30,662 bytes	RFC1006
0036	Transmission of IP and ARP over FDDI Networks	D. Katz	January 1993	TXT=22,077 bytes	RFC1390

Standard Number	Title	Author(s)	Date	File Information	See Also
0037	An Ethernet Address Resolution Protocol	David C. Plummer	November 1982	TXT=21,556 bytes	RFC0826
0038	A Reverse Address Resolution Protocol	Ross Finlayson, Timothy Mann, Jeffrey Mogul, & Marvin Theimer	June 1984	TXT=9,345 bytes	RFC0903
0040	Host Access Protocol Specification	Bolt, Beranek, and Newman	August 1993	TXT=152,740 bytes	RFC1221
0041	Standard for the Transmission of IP Datagrams over Ethernet Networks	C. Hornig	April 1984	TXT=5,697 bytes	RFC0894
0042	Standard for the Transmission of IP Datagrams over Experimental Ethernet Networks	J. Postel	April 1984	TXT=4,985 bytes	RFC0895
0043	Standard for the Transmission of IP Datagrams over IEEE 802 Networks	J. Postel & J. Reynolds	August 1993	TXT=34,359 bytes	RFC1042
0044	DCN Local-Network Protocols	D. L. Mills	August 1993	TXT=65,340 bytes	RFC0891
0045	Internet Protocol on Network System's HYPERchannel: Protocol Specification	K. Hardwick & J. Lekashman	August 1993	TXT=100,836 bytes	RFC1044
0046	Transmitting IP Traffic over ARCnet Networks	D. Provan	August 1993	TXT=16,565 bytes	RFC1201
0047	Nonstandard for Transmission of IP Datagrams over Serial Lines: SLIP	J. L. Romkey	August 1993	TXT=12,578 bytes	RFC1055

App
C

continues

Table C.1 Continued

Standard Number	Title	Author(s)	Date	File Information	See Also
0048	Standard for the Transmission of IP Datagrams over NetBIOS Networks	L. J. McLaughlin	August 1993	TXT=5,579 bytes	RFC1088
0049	Standard for the Transmission of 802.3 Packets over IPX Networks	L. J. McLaughlin	August 1993	TXT=7,902 bytes	RFC1132
0050	Definitions of Managed Objects for the Ethernet-like Interface Types	F. Kastenholz	July 1994	TXT=39,008 bytes	RFC1643
0051	The Point-to-Point Protocol (PPP)	W. Simpson, editor	July 1994	TXT=151,158 bytes	RFC1661, RFC1662

FYI Documents

A group of documents exists that doesn't make protocol specifications but instead explains some features of the Internet and how to use them. These documents are known as *FYIs* (*for your information*). You can find these FYIs on the companion CD-ROM, and Table C.2 lists the specifics of the FYIs.

Table C.2 FYI Documents

Document Number	Title	Author(s)	Date	File Format/ Size	See Also
0001	FYI on FYI: Introduction to the FYI Notes	G. S. Malkin & J. Reynolds	March 1990	TXT=7,867 bytes	RFC1150
0002	FYI on a Network Management Tool Catalog: Tools for Monitoring and Debugging TCP/IP Internets and Inter-connected Devices	R. Enger & J. Reynolds	June 1993	TXT=308,528 bytes	RFC1470

Document Number	Title	Author(s)	Date	File Format/ Size	See Also
0003	FYI on Where To Start: a Bibliography of Internetworking Information	K. L. Bowers, T. L. LaQuey, J. Reynolds, K. Roubicek, M. K. Stahl, & A. Yuan	August 1991	TXT=67,330 bytes	RFC1175
0004	FYI on Questions and Answers— Answers to Commonly Asked "New Internet User" Questions	A. Marine, J. Reynolds, & G. Malkin	March 1994	TXT=98,753 bytes	RFC1594
0005	Choosing a Name for Your Computer	D. Libes	August 1991	TXT=18,472 bytes	RFC1178
0006	FYI on the X Window System	R. W. Scheifler	January 1991	TXT=3,629 bytes	RFC1198
0007	FYI on Questions and Answers: Answers to Commonly Asked "Experienced Internet User" Questions	G. S. Malkin, A. N. Marine, & J. Reynolds	February 1991	TXT=33,385 bytes	RFC1207
0008	Site Security Handbook	J. P. Holbrook & J. Reynolds	July 1991	TXT=259,129 bytes	RFC1244
0009	Who's Who in the Internet: Biographies of IAB, IESG, and IRSG Members	G. Malkin	May 1992	TXT=92,119 bytes	RFC1336
0010	There's Gold in Them Thar Networks! or Searching for Treasure in All the Wrong Places	J. Martin	January 1993	TXT=71,176 bytes	RFC1402
0011	A Revised Catalog of Available X.400 Implementations	A. Getchell & S. Sataluri, editors	May 1994	TXT=124,111 bytes	RFC1632

continues

Table C.2   Continued

Document Number	Title	Author(s)	Date	File Format/ Size	See Also
0012	Building a Network Information Services Infrastructure	D. Sitzler, P. Smith, & A. Marine	February 1992	TXT=29,135 bytes	RFC1302
0013	Executive Introduction to Directory Services Using the X.400 Protocol	C. Weider & J. Reynolds	March 1992	TXT=9,392 bytes	RFC1308
0014	Technical Overview of Directory Services Using the X.400 Protocol	C. Weider, J. Reynolds, & S. Heker	March 1992	TXT=35,694 bytes	RFC1309
0015	Privacy and Accuracy Issues in Network Information Center Databases	J. Curran & A. Marine	August 1992	TXT=8,858 bytes	RFC1355
0016	Connecting to the Internet— What Connecting Institutions Should Anticipate	ACM SIGUCCS	August 1992	TXT=53,449 bytes	RFC1359
0017	The Tao of IETF —A Guide for New Attendees of the Internet Engineering Task Force	The IETF Secretariat & G. Malkin	November 1994	TXT=50,477 bytes	RFC1718
0018	Internet Users' Glossary	G. Malkin & T. Parker	January 1993	TXT=104,624 bytes	RFC1392
0019	FYI on Introducing the Internet—a Short Bibliography of Introductory Internetworking Readings	E. Hoffman & L. Jackson	May 1993	TXT=7,116 bytes	RFC1463

Document Number	Title	Author(s)	Date	File Format/ Size	See Also
0020	FYI on "What Is the Internet?"	E. Krol & E. Hoffman	May 1993	TXT=27,811 bytes	RFC1462
0021	A Survey of Advanced Usages of X.00	C. Weider & R. Wright	July 1993	TXT=34,883 bytes	RFC1491
0022	FYI on Questions and Answers— Answers to Commonly Asked "Primary and Secondary School Internet User" Questions	J. Sellers	February 1994	TXT=113,646 bytes	RFC1578
0023	Guide to Network Resource Tool	EARN staff	March 1994	TXT=235,112 bytes	RFC1580
0024	How To Use Anonymous FTP	P. Deutsch, A. Emtage, & A. Marine	May 1994	TXT=27,258 bytes	RFC1635
0025	A Status Report on Networked Information Retrieval: Tools and Groups	J. Foster	August 1994	TXT=375,469 bytes	RFC1689, RTR0013
0026	K-12 Internetworking Guidelines	J. Gargano & D. Wasley	November 1994	ASCII= 66,659 bytes, PS=662,030 bytes	RFC1709
0027	Tools for DNS Debugging	A. Romao	November 1994	TXT=33,500 bytes	RFC1713
0028	Netiquette Guidelines	S. Hambridge	November 20, 1995	21 pages	RFC1855

App
C

Current RFC Documents

Table C.3 contains a list of current RFC documents. This shortened list reflects the most current RFCs available. The table doesn't include any RFCs marked as "Obsolete." The RFCINDEX.HTM hypertext file on the companion CD-ROM, however, contains full references to all the RFCs currently available.

Table C.3 Current RFC Documents as of January 13, 1996

RFC Number	Title	Author(s)	Date	File Format/ Size
1887	An Architecture for IPv6 Unicast Address Allocation	Y. Rekhter & T. Li	January 4, 1996	25 pages
1886	DNS Extensions To Support IP Version 6	S. Thomson & C. Huitema	January 4, 1996	5 pages
1885	Internet Control Message Protocol(ICMPv6) for the Internet ProtocolVersion 6 (Ipv6)	A. Conta & S. Deering	January 4, 1996	20 pages
1884	IP Version 6 Addressing Architecture	R. Hinden & S. Deering	January 4, 1996	18 pages
1883	Internet Protocol, Version 6 (Ipv6) Specification	S. Deering & R. Hinden	January 4, 1996	37 pages
1882	The 12-Days of Technology before Christmas	B. Hancock	December 26, 1995	5 pages
1881	IPv6 Address Allocation Management	I. IESG	December 26, 1995	2 pages
1880	Internet Official Protocol Standards	J. Postel	November 29, 1995	38 pages
1871	Addendum to RFC 1602— Variance Procedure	J. Postel	November 29, 1995	4 pages
1870	SMTP Service Extension for Message Size Declaration	J. Klensin, N. Freed, & K. Moore	November 6, 1995	9 pages
1869	SMTP Service Extensions	J. Klensin, N. Freed, M. Rose, E. Stefferud, & D. Crocker	November 6, 1995	11 pages
1868	ARP Extension—UNARP	G. Malkin	November 6, 1995	4 pages
1867	Form-Based File Upload in HTML	E. Nebel & L. Masinter	November 7, 1995	13 pages
1866	Hypertext Markup Language—2.0	T. Berners-Lee & D. Connolly	November 11, 1995	77 pages

RFC Number	Title	Author(s)	Date	File Format/ Size
1864	The Content-MD5 Header Field	J. Myers & M. Rose	October 24, 1995	4 pages
1863	A BGP/IDRP Route Server Alternative to a Full Mesh Routing	D. Haskin	November 20, 1995	16 pages
1862	Report of the IAB Workshop on Internet Information Infrastructure, October 12-14, 1994	M. McCahill, M. Schwartz, K. Sollins, T. Verschuren, & C. Weider	November 3, 1995	27 pages
1861	Simple Network Paging Protocol—Version 3 —Two-Way Enhanced	A. Gwinn	October 19, 1995	23 pages
1860	Variable Length Subnet Table for Ipv4	T. Pummill & B. Manning	November 20, 1995	3 pages
1859	ISO Transport Class 2 Non-use of Explicit Flow Control over TCP RFC1006 Extension	Y. Pouffary	November 20, 1995	8 pages
1858	Security Considerations for IP Fragment Filtering	P. Ziemba, D. Reed, & P. Traina	November 25, 1995	10 pages
1857	A Model for Common Operational Statistics	M. Lambert	November 20, 1995	27 pages
1856	The Opstat Client— Server Model for Statistics Retrieval	H. Clark	October 20, 1995	21 pages
1855	Netiquette Guidelines	S. Hambridge	October 20, 1995	21 pages
1854	SMTP Service Extension for Command Pipelining	N. Freed & A. Cargille	October 4, 1995	7 pages
1853	IP in IP Tunneling	W. Simpson	October 4 1995	8 pages
1852	IP Authentication Using Keyed SHA	P. Metzger & W. Simpson	October 2, 1995	6 pages

continues

App

C

Table C.3 Continued

RFC Number	Title	Author(s)	Date	File Format/ Size
1851	The ESP Triple DES—CBC Transform	P. Metzger, P. Karn, & W. Simpson	October 2, 1995	9 pages
1850	OSPF Version 2 Management Information Base	F. Baker & R. Coltun	November 3, 1995	80 pages
1848	MIME Object Security Services	S. Crocker, N. Freed, J. Galvin, & S. Murphy	October 3, 1995	48 pages
1847	Security Multiparts for MIME:Multipart/ Signed and Multipart/ Encrypted	J. Galvin, S. Murphy, S. Crocker, & N. Freed	October 3, 1995	11 pages
1846	SMTP 521 Reply Code	A. Durand & F. Dupont	October 2, 1995	4 pages
1845	SMTP Service Extension for Checkpoint/Restart	D. Crocker, N. Freed, & A. Cargille	October 2, 1995	8 pages
1844	Multimedia E-Mail Agent Checklist (MIME) User	E. Huizer	August 24, 1995	8 pages
1843	HZ—a Data Format for Exchanging Files of Arbitrarily Mixed Chinese and ASCII Characters	F. Lee	August 24, 1995	5 pages
1842	ASCII Printable Characters-Based Chinese Character Encoding for Internet Messages	Y. Wei, Y. Zhang, J. Li, J. Ding, & Y. Jiang	August 24, 1995	5 pages
1841	PPP Network Control Protocol for LAN Extension	J. Chapman D. Coli, A. Harvey, B. Jensen, & K. Rowett	September 29, 1995	66 pages
1838	Use of the X.500 Directory to Support Mapping between X.400 and RFC 822 Addresses	S. Kille	August 22, 1995	8 pages

RFC Number	Title	Author(s)	Date	File Format/ Size
1837	Representing Tables and Subtrees in the X.500 Directory	S. Kille	August 22, 1995	7 pages
1836	Representing the O/R Address Hierarchy in the X.500 Directory Information Tree	S. Kille	August 22, 1995	11 pages
1835	Architecture of the Service	P. Deutsch, R. Schoultz, P. Faltstrom, & C. Weider	August 16, 1995	41 pages
1834	Whois and Network Information Lookup Service Whois++	J. Gargano & K. Weiss	August 16, 1995	7 pages
1833	Binding Protocols for ONC RPC Version 2	R. Srinivasan	August 9, 1995	14 pages
1832	XDR: External Data Representation Standard	R. Srinivasan	August 9, 1995	24 pages
1831	RPC: Remote Procedure Call Protocol Specification Version 2	R. Srinivasan	August 9, 1995	18 pages
1830	SMTP Service Extensions for Transmission of Large and Binary MIME Messages	G. Vaudreuil	August 16, 1995	8 pages
1829	The ESP DES-CBC Transform	P. Metzger, P. Karn, & W. Simpson	August 9, 1995	10 pages
1828	IP Authentication Using Keyed MD5	P. Metzger & W. Simpson	August 9, 1995	5 pages
1827	IP Encapsulating Security Payload (ESP)	R. Atkinson	August 9, 1995	12 pages
1826	IP Authentication Header	R. Atkinson	August 9, 1995	13 pages
1825	Security Architecture for the Internet Protocol	R. Atkinson	August 9, 1995	22 pages

App C

continues

Table C.3   Continued

RFC Number	Title	Author(s)	Date	File Format/ Size
1824	The Exponential Security System ESS: an Identity-Based Cryptographic Protocol for Authenticated Key-Exchange EISS—Report 95/4	H. Danisch	August 11, 1995	21 pages
1823	The LDAP Application Program Interface	T. Howes & M. Smith	August 9, 1995	22 pages
1822	A Grant of Rights To Use a Specific IBM Patent with Photuris	J. Lowe	August 14, 1995	2 pages
1821	Integration of Real-time Services in an IP-ATM Network Architecture	M. Borden, E. Crawley, B. Davie, & S. Batsell	August 11, 1995	24 pages
1819	Internet Stream Protocol Version 2 (ST2)—Protocol Specification Version ST2+	L. Delgrossi & L. Berger	August 11, 1995	109 pages
1818	Best Current Practices	J. Postel, T. Li, & Y. Rekhter	August 4, 1995	3 pages
1817	CIDR and Classful Routing	Y. Rekhter	August 4, 1995	2 pages
1816	U.S. Government Internet Domain Names	Federal Networking Council (FNC)	August 3, 1995	8 pages
1815	Character Sets ISO-10646 and ISO-10646-J-1	M. Ohta	August 1, 1995	6 pages
1814	Unique Addresses Are Good	E. Gerich	June 22, 1995	3 pages
1813	NFS Version 3 Protocol Specification	B. Callaghan, B. Pawlowski, & P. Staubach	June 21, 1995	126 pages
1812	Requirements for IP Version 4 Routers	F. Baker	June 22, 1995	175 pages
1810	Report on MD5 Performance	J. Touch	June 21, 1995	7 pages

RFC Number	Title	Author(s)	Date	File Format/ Size
1809	Using the Flow Label Field in Ipv6	C. Partridge	June 14, 1995	6 pages
1808	Relative Uniform Resource Locators	R. Fielding	June 14, 1995	16 pages
1807	A Format for Bibliographic Records	R. Lasher & D. Cohen	June 21, 1995	16 pages
1806	Communicating Presentation Messages: the Content-Disposition Header	R. Troost & S. Dorner	June 7, 1995	8 pages
1805	Location-Independent Data/Software Integrity Protocol	A. Rubin	June 7, 1995	6 pages
1804	Schema Publishing in X.500 Directory	G. Mansfield, P. Rajeev, S. Raghavan, & T. Howes	June 9, 1995	10 pages
1803	Recommendations for an X.500 Production Directory Service	R. Wright, A. Getchell, T. Howes, S. Sataluri, P. Yee, & W. Yeong	June 7, 1995	8 pages
1802	Introducing Project Long Bud: Internet Pilot Project for theDeployment of X.500 Directory Information in Support of X.400	H. Alvestrand, K. Jordan, S. Langlois, & J. Romaguera	June 12, 1995	11 pages
1801	MHS Use of the X.500 Directory To Support MHS Routing	S. Kille	June 9, 1995	73 pages
1798	Connectionless Lightweight Directory Access Protocol	A. Young	June 7, 1995	9 pages
1797	Class A Subnet Experiment	IANA	April 25, 1995	4 pages

App
C

Converting from C and C++ to Object Pascal

A paradox exists for developers. Managers hear how new tools make programming so easy that anyone can write an application, while the developer thinks "Yeah, but will the application work consistently and quickly?" This places the developers in a precarious situation in which they want their applications to work well and fast and are willing to invest the extra time and effort that C and C++ require, yet their managers want users to have all the latest advantages—*now!* Delphi answers most of the developers concerns about rapid application development (RAD) while giving management the application that it wants as quickly as possible. Switching to Delphi, however, can mean an abrupt change and a steep learning curve if you haven't seen any Pascal code in years. This appendix is intended to help you face switching to Delphi to leverage your knowledge of C and C++ for Object Pascal. ■

Conversion Considerations

Every day, developers rewrite and port existing applications to take advantage of new operating systems and computer hardware. Before undertaking such a challenge, the development team must consider its approach. Many teams choose to port with the same language. At first glance, this approach makes sense. The team is generally familiar with the language and should easily adapt to the new environment. Unfortunately, especially in the case C and C++, this approach does not always work. Simply moving from Windows 3.1 to Windows 95 alone can present many unforeseeable problems. Horror stories abound from developers who have been forced to move from DOS to Windows. Although C and C++ are fantastic for developing system and utility functions, using them for your total application development is much like building a car by hand: You might build a fabulous car, but few people will be able to afford it. Delphi provides familiarity with language (nearly all Computer Science college students learn Pascal) while adding a few new arguments to the fire. One such argument is that the users are unconcerned with the underlying code and worry about functionality only—whether the application can help them with their job. Tools such as Delphi encapsulate the user interface, leaving the programming team free to focus attention on the application's logic. At the same time, Delphi provides native compilation that yields much faster speeds than most of its fourth-generation language (4GL; C, COBOL, are considered 3GL, or third-generation languages) competitors. This appendix does not fully discuss the issue (which is far beyond its scope), but further discussion is often held under a less-than-formal arrangement in many of the Internet newsgroups (such as **comp.lang.pascal.borland**).

Language Semantics

After deciding to move to Delphi (and Object Pascal), you need a general understanding of the differences and similarities between C, C++, and Object Pascal. Tables D.1 and D.2 list most of the operators, keywords, and internal types that exist within each language and their accompanying uses.

Table D.1   Operators

Group	Symbol	Example	Language C/C++	Pascal	Purpose
Assignment	:=	X := Y		✓	Left assignment operator.
	=	X = Y	✓		Left assignment operator.
Arithmetic	+	X = 1 + 2	✓	✓	Adds.
	+=	X += 2	✓		Adds. The example results in X being equal to the sum of X and 2.

Group	Symbol	Example	Language C/C++	Pascal	Purpose
	-=	X -= 3	✓		Subtracts. The example results in X being equal to the difference of X and 2.
	-	X = 3 - 1	✓	✓	Subtracts. Preincrement or postincrement by 1.
	++	(++)X(++)	✓		
	--	(--)X (--)	✓		Subtracts. Predecrement or postdecrement by 1.
	%	X = Y % 2	✓		Modulus.
	mod	X := Y mod 2		✓	Modulus.
	*	X := Y * 3	✓	✓	Multiplier.
	/	X = Y / 3	✓	✓	Division.
	div	X = X div 3		✓	Division.
Relational	=	If X = Y Then		✓	Is equal to.
	==	if(X==Y)	✓		Is equal to.
	<=	If X <= Y Then	✓	✓	Is less than or equal to.
	>=	If X >= Y Then	✓	✓	Is greater than or equal to.
	<>	If X <> Y Then		✓	Is not equal to.
	!=	if(x!=y)	✓		Is not equal to.
	Not	If Not X Then		✓	Logical negation.
	!	if(!x)	✓		Logical negation.
	And	If X AND Y Then		✓	Logical And.
	&&	if(x && y)	✓		Logical And.
	Or	If X or Y Then		✓	Logical Or.
	!!	if(x ¦¦ y)	✓		Logical Or.
	Xor	If X Xor Y		✓	Exclusive Or.
Pointer	@	@X		✓	Returns the address of a variable.
	&	&X	✓		Returns the address of a variable.

continues

Table D.1   Continued

			Language		
Group	Symbol	Example	C/C++	Pascal	Purpose
	^	`^X`		✓	Pointer dereferencing.
	*	`*X`	✓		Pointer dereferencing.
Language modifiers	`/*` `*/`	`/* This is a comment */`	✓		Multiline comments.
	`//`	`//This is a comment`	✓	✓	Single-line comments (for Delphi 2.0 only).
	`(*` `*)`	`(*This is a comment *)`		✓	Multiline comments.
	`{` `}`	`{ This is a comment }`		✓	Multiline comments.
	`[]`	`X[1]`	✓	✓	Array indexes.
	`{`	`if(x){`	✓		Block specification.
	`}`	`...` `};`			
	begin end	`If X Then begin ... end;`		✓	Block specification.
	;	`while(X);`	✓	✓	Line termination.

Table D.2   Reserved Words

		Language		
Reserved Word	Example	C/C++	Pascal	Purpose
As	`<Instance> As <Type>`		✓	Performs a typecast, if valid. An exception is raised if the typecast is invalid.
asm	`asm {...}` `asm ... end`	✓	✓	Declares inline assembler.

Reserved Word	Example	Language C/C++	Pascal	Purpose
array	`X : array[1..10]` `of Integer`		✓	Declares a Pascal style array.

case
of
else
	`Case X Of`
	`    1:`
	`else`
	`    ...`
	`end`
			✓	Selects from multiple result possibilities.

switch
case
default
	`switch(x){`
	`    case 1:`
	`    ...`
	`    default`
	`};`
		✓		Selects from multiple result possibilities.

class	`class X` `X = Class()`	✓	✓	Specifies a class definition.
const	`const X`	✓	✓	Notifies the compiler that a variable should not be modified.
do ... while	`do {...} while X`	✓		Loops while the expression is true, and executes blocked code at least once.
Repeat ... until	`repeat Inc(X)` `until X = 100`		✓	Loops while the expression is true, and executes blocked code at least once.
Exports	`exports <function` `list>;`		✓	Lists functions to be exported within an application.
file	`X = File`		✓	Specifies a file handle.

for ... to ...
downto
	`For X := 1 to 10`
	`For X := 10`
	`downto 1`
			✓	Loops the specified number of iterations.

for	`for(x=1;x<10;x++)`	✓		Loops the specified number of iterations.

App
D

continues

Table D.2 Continued

Reserved Word	Example	C/C++	Pascal	Purpose
friend	friend MyClass;	✓		Indicates that another class has full access rights to the one in which the identifier appears.
function	Function Foo() as Integer		✓	Declares a function.
goto	goto try_again	✓	✓	Causes program execution to jump to the given label.
If ... Then Else	IF X Then Else		✓	Causes blocked code to execute when the expression evaluates to True.
if ... else	if(x){...} else{...}	✓		Causes blocked code to execute when the expression evaluates to True.
implementation			✓	Notifies the compiler of where bodies of functions are held.
inherited	inherited;		✓	Calls the ancestor object.
inline		✓		Specifies that the code should create a function call.
initialization			✓	Specifies a block of code that should be executed when a module is loaded.
interface			✓	Identifies the portion of a module that will be accessible from other applications.
is	If X is Obj Then		✓	Returns True when variable is of Obj type.

		Language		
Reserved Word	**Example**	**C/C++**	**Pascal**	**Purpose**
label	label X;		✓	Defines a placement marker.
library			✓	Causes the creation of a DLL.
nil			✓	Refers to a pointer variable without a value.
procedure			✓	Declares a procedure that does not return a value.
program	program KillerApp		✓	Declares a program name.
property	property X: Integer read GetX write SetX;		✓	Identifies a property and access methods.
raise	raise EOutOfResources	✓		Raises a program exception.
record	Rec = Record ... End;		✓	Defines a Pascal structure.
set	tSet = Set Of 0..9		✓	Specifies a set of finite, defined members.
static	static int nRef	✓		Indicates that the variable does not lose value when the block is exited.
Struct	struct mnystruct { ...};	✓		Declares a data structure.
try	try { foo(); }	✓	✓	Begins an exception block.
type			✓	Indicates the beginning of a user-defined type.
typedef	typedef struct Test {...};	✓		Indicates the beginning of a user-defined type.

App
D

continues

Table D.2   Continued

Reserved Word	Example	Language C/C++	Pascal	Purpose
unit			✓	Indicates the beginning of a Pascal code module.
uses	Uses System		✓	Indicates which units this unit will call.
var			✓	Indicates the beginning of a variable-declaration block.
with			✓	Indicates that the following code references a specific object.

Modifying Structures and Classes

One of the first places you will want to look is the structures and classes. Although the concepts behind the creation of data types are similar, several pitfalls await.

Structure Definitions   In most applications, the structures remain unchanged when applied to a Pascal record. However, you have to consider some changes before moving structures that depend on C quirks. For example, one quirk arises when a character array is the last member in a structure. When you allocate more memory for the structure than is required, you know that memory is available for your character array. Unlike standardized C, Object Pascal is not required to support the capability to append data to a structure. The lack of guaranteed support can cause many hard-to-find bugs and memory leaks. Specifically, many of Delphi's memory-allocation routines insert an unsigned integer in front of the allocated memory that indicates the allocated block's size. Overwriting this integer can cause your application to see too little or too much available memory, resulting in improper deallocation and wild pointers. Many C++ programmers have already discovered similar problems when converting C structures to C++ classes when the v-table is accidentally overwritten.

Class Definitions   However, you have to give the classes considerable rethought before you begin the conversion process. In most applications, changes to the way that you define classes are pervasive.

Another pitfall for C++ conversions is the implementation of template-based classes. Object Pascal does not use templates, so converting applications that previously used a template facility within C++ will require more effort. Making each template instance type-safe requires a manual process. The Standard Template Library is such a recent addition to the C++ language that it is unlikely to be an immediate threat to most conversions. However, duplicating the library's functionality in Object Pascal is a chore.

Similarly, many older C++ applications use a port of the NHIL class library. Originally created in SmallTalk and used extensively in C++ applications, this class library defines a series of data-manipulation classes such as bags and linked lists. The C++ applications then used multiple inheritance to extend the class libraries further. Object Pascal does not use multiple inheritance, so this fundamental difference creates a major hurdle for most conversion processes.

```
//C++ Code with multiple inheritance
class MyBase1
{
public:
   int A;
};

class MyBase2
{
public:
   int B;
};

class MyClass : MyBase1, MyBase2
{
public:
   int C;
};

//Invalid Object Pascal Code
Type
   TMyClass = class(TMyBase1, TMyBase2)
      public:
      C : Integer;
   End;
```

To help you overcome these pitfalls, Object Pascal provides code that is arguably easier to maintain, debug, and read after the conversion is complete. To replace multiple inheritance trees, you will probably want to use embedded classes, if possible. Try not to confuse embedded classes with nested classes—the class definition does *not* occur within another class. Instead, an embedded class is instantiated as a member within another class. To handle indirection of unknown classes, you can use TClass, which is a ClassOf TObject. Some implementations of multiple inheritance fall easily into this conversion, but others do not. Whenever you find that you are spending a lot of time recreating inheritance trees because of multiple inheritance, you should consider starting fresh.

Many C++ applications use overloaded operators such as the increment (++) and decrement (--) operators. The Object Pascal designers took another approach by creating functions that mimic most of those operators. In C++, new is actually an operator that you can overload, but in Object Pascal, new is a global function. Similarly, instead of overloading the assignment operator to handle logical copies rather than the default bitwise copy, you overload the Assign method.

Overloading the Assign method can actually be helpful in that you might sometimes prefer either bitwise or logical copies in the same application. A good example is in TFont. A bitwise copy of a font object can result in its untimely release on destruction and a guaranteed General Protection Fault (GPF) error. The GPF occurs because the bitwise copy duplicates properties like the device context handle. If you were copying the font for use on another window, when the other window closes, the TFont reference is destroyed and the handles are released. The next access to that TFont attempts to write to a device context that has been released. TPersistent first defines the Assign method, so if you are using a variable not declared as a descendant of TPersistent, the compiler will not locate the method. Similar approaches are taken throughout Object Pascal.

Converting Functions and Variables

When you convert C and C++ functions to Object Pascal, what initially seems apparent can cause compilation errors or incorrect execution for various reasons. Unfortunately, some of the Pascal and Object Pascal language semantics are less than intuitive for many C++ programmers. For example, it is not readily apparent how you would initialize all the elements in an array variable within Object Pascal. The method Pascal provides is not altogether pretty either. For example, compare the following statements. Here's the C/C++ version:

```
int x[] = {0,1,2,3,4,5,6,7,8,9,10};
```

And here is the Pascal version:

```
Type
     MyArray = Array[0..10] of Integer;
Const
     InitArray : MyArray = (0,1,2,3,4,5,6,7,8,9,10);
```

You might also notice that in the preceding C instance, you can later modify the values of each item in the array at run time. In the Pascal version, however, you cannot. Having to declare initialized arrays as constant initially seems to be a hindrance, but you don't often initialize arrays when you don't intend for them to be constant, even if you neglect to declare them as such.

Pointer referencing and dereferencing sometimes can also be fairly unintuitive and difficult to learn in Pascal. In fact, learning pointers can be easier in C, particularly if using pointers is part of your assembler experience. When declaring a pointer in Pascal, you do so by using a predefined type such as PChar or by entering the ^ symbol before the type name, as in the following example:

```
Type
     PMyType = ^Char;
Var
MyPointer1 : PMyType;
MyPointer2 : ^Char;
```

The two variables, MyPointer1 and MyPointer2, are exactly the same. As in C, you can reference an array as a pointer. Therefore, you can pass the preceding example of InitArray as a pointer. In Object Pascal, you dereference a pointer by placing the ^ character *after* the variable that you want to reference (as in X := Y^; Y^ := X;). In contrast, you place C's * character *before* the variable that you are referencing (as in X = *Y; *Y = X).

Compared to converting variable definitions, converting functions is relatively straightforward. However, always keep in mind the method that you are using to pass the variables. The keyword Var is used in several possible ways in the function declaration. When the Var keyword appears with a type, it is passed by reference (as in C++ when you precede the identifier with the & character).

If the Var keyword appears in an Object Pascal function definition without a type, it is passed by reference but must be cast to a valid type before your code can perform any operations on it. This Object Pascal convention is more flexible than its C++ counterpart, but also more dangerous. An untyped variable in Object Pascal is fairly synonymous with that of C's infamous void pointer. In Object Pascal, any variables declared in the parameter list that are not accompanied by the Var keyword are passed by value, so changes to the variable are made to a copy of the original parameter but not to the actual parameter. As in C++, this can become confusing when the changes are made to a variable that a pointer references. When you pass a pointer by value, you pass a copy of the variable's address, and the original data immediately reflects any modifications to the data residing in this address.

Unlike C and C++, Object Pascal does not contain the keyword return. Therefore, you must return values from a function by assigning the value to the function name just before exiting the function. Visual Basic programmers are familiar with this technique. You use the function name to store the current return value and later reference that stored value if necessary. Unfortunately, having a function name on the right-hand side of an assignment can result in recursion if the function has no arguments. To help you avoid recursion, Object Pascal provides an implicit variable, Result. You can assign the Result variable to and from a function as necessary with no threat of recursion. The following two examples are the same:

```
Function MyFunc(X : Integer) : Integer;
begin
   MyFunc := X * 12;
end;

Function MyFunc(X : Integer) : Integer;
begin
   Result := X * 12;
end;
```

However, another problem then becomes apparent to programmers who are accustomed to returning immediately: How do you leave a function or procedure without using mountains of If Then statements? Object Pascal provides the keyword Exit to alleviate this problem. Exit instructs the code pointer to leave the currently executing block. As in C, if the Exit (return) statement is in the main program, the program halts. If the Exit statement is in a procedure or function block, control passes back to immediately after the function call. Note that if you modify the Borland-provided example code for the Exit procedure to appear as in the following example, the code that writes the *y* never executes because the Exit call forces an immediate return:

```
procedure WasteTime;
begin
```

```
        begin
            repeat
                //return to the calling procedure
                //   when a key is pressed
                if KeyPressed then Exit;
                Write('x');
            until False;
        end;
        //The following will not execute
        WriteLn('y');
end;
```

C/C++ Sample Application Sources

Converting existing applications is not easy, but can be quite rewarding. By doing so, you can provide access to functionality and memory spaces previously unavailable. In the 32-bit world, fault tolerance and high performance issues also come to play, making a strong argument for all developers to move their applications forward. Unfortunately, available information is sometimes limited.

You can acquire sample C and C++ code from several sources. The *Microsoft Systems Journal, Dr. Dobbs Journal,* and other magazines have FTP sites available on the Internet as **ftp:// ftp.microsoft.com**, **ftp://ftp.mv.com/pub/ddj**, and so on. Check your favorite magazine for information on an FTP site near you. One of the best places to find helpful information is in such newsgroups as **comp.lang.***. Newsgroups exist for both Delphi and C++. In these newsgroups, you can also find database information, neural net algorithms, employment, and more—all at your fingertips. ●

Browsing the CD-ROM

This appendix describes the contents of the CD-ROM included with your copy of *Building Internet Applications with Delphi 2*. The CD includes all the code samples used in the book, so that you can examine, modify, and experiment with the full source code. The CD also includes the full text of all currently available Requests for Comments (RFCs) so that you can read the complete specifications that the book references (as well as those that the book does not reference). Along with these standards documents, the CD includes the full specification document for Windows Sockets (WinSock) 1.1 and 2.0 (the CD also includes the WinSock 1.1 specifications as a Windows Help file).

Also included on the CD is a collection of shareware, freeware, and demonstration Delphi components that you can use to build Internet (and non-Internet) applications. Most of these components are limited-functionality samples of commercial Delphi components packages. If you like what you see in one sample, and it falls in line with components that you need, contact the developers for the full-fledged versions. Along with these components is a collection of shareware and freeware Internet applications and utilities. You can examine these to see what other developers have done, and develop ideas of what new Internet applications need to be created. ■

What Is Shareware?

Much of the software on the CD is *shareware*. Shareware was developed as an alternative to traditional methods of software distribution. You can try a shareware software package for a trial period (usually 30 days) before paying for it. Initially, few programs were available in the shareware market, and they were distributed mainly through local bulletin board systems.

With the vast popularity of the Internet and the ease of connecting to File Transfer Protocol (FTP) sites, the quantity and quality of shareware have improved dramatically.

The retail distribution channels are just starting to offer a large number of Internet applications. Most of the commercial activity is focusing on suites of applications that include Telnet, FTP, electronic mail (e-mail), Gopher, and a Web browser. However, there still are plenty of opportunities to create new programs that expand the market and make a profit.

Most of the software on the CD includes some type of file (or instructions in the software itself) that tells you how to register the software. *Remember that you're obligated to register any shareware software that you plan to use regularly.* You gain many benefits by registering the shareware:

- You have a clean conscience, knowing that you've paid the author for the many hours that he or she spent to create such a useful program.

- You might enjoy additional benefits, such as technical support from the author, a printed manual, or additional features that are available only to registered users. Consult the individual programs for details about the bonuses you might receive for registering.

- Registering puts you on the author's mailing list so that you keep up-to-date about new versions of the software, bug fixes, compatibility issues, and so on. Again, the benefits of registration vary from product to product. Some authors even include in the cost of registration a free update to the next version.

- If the license agreement states that you must pay to continue using the software, you violate the license if you don't pay. In some cases, unregistered use may be a criminal offense. Wise individuals, corporations, and businesses register shareware to avoid any chance of legal problems.

NOTE   Several of the authors and companies that provided software for this CD-ROM requested that this book include a notice of their copyright, shareware agreement, or license information. The lack of such a statement printed in this book doesn't indicate that the software isn't copyrighted or doesn't have a license agreement. See the text or help files for specific copyright or licensing information. ■

Getting Updates for Software

The documentation that accompanies the programs on the CD-ROM usually tells you where to find updated versions. However, continually monitoring 10 or 20 FTP sites for new versions isn't exactly easy.

Que has come up with a solution: a special FTP site at which this book's readers can get new versions of the CD's software. As soon as Que receives an update, it's posted on the FTP site and you can download the update by anonymous FTP. The FTP address for this site is **ftp.mcp.com** (*MCP* stands for Macmillan Computer Publishing, the company that owns Que).

Also, Macmillan maintains several mailing lists to notify subscribers automatically when programs are updated. By pointing your Web browser at **http://www.mcp.com/**, choosing Reference Desk, and then selecting Information SuperLibrary Reports, you'll learn how to subscribe to the various mailing lists. Choose one that fits your needs.

> **N O T E** Many of the authors and companies asked that this book include an e-mail or postal address at which readers can contact them. If you don't find a specific e-mail address listed in the book, you can find an e-mail address for nearly every program on the CD in the program's documentation, in the program itself (often by choosing the Help menu's About command), or on the Web pages that describe the applications on the CD. ▨

Installing Software from the CD-ROM

Before using any software on the CD, you must install it. Many of the programs come with their own installation program. If a program includes an installation program, the program's description on the Web page gives you the directions that you need to install the program.

If a program doesn't have an installation program, the installation process is straightforward:

1. Create on your hard drive a folder for the software.

> **T I P** It's a good idea to create one main folder (such as \INTERNET) in the root of your hard drive for all your Internet software, and then create subfolders for individual programs in that folder. This keeps your hard drive's root folder less cluttered.

2. Copy all the files and subfolders from the program's folder on CD to the folder that you created on your hard drive. Remember to reset the Read Only attribute after copying the files. After switching to the folder (using the DOS CD command) that contains the newly copied files, type the following command, which uses the DOS ATTRIB function to reset the Read Only attribute from all the files in a folder:

   ATTRIB –r *.*

> **N O T E** Each application on the CD has an associated Web page. Before installing an application, you might want to check the application's Web page for any late-breaking news. You can also find special installation instructions on this Web page. You can read the Web pages by starting at the home page of \APPCD.HTM on the CD. ▨

3. After copying all the files, create an icon for each program that you plan to run in Windows. An easy way to do so is to drag the program file from the folder on your hard drive under My Computer to your desktop or the folder in which you want to place the icon.

App
E

You might try creating a program group to hold all your Internet program icons.

That's all there is to installing any programs that do not include an installation program. Repeat these steps for any software that you want to install.

Delphi Components

This section describes the Delphi components and add-ons that the CD includes. Most of these components are reduced-functionality versions of much larger commercial Delphi add-ons.

WebHub

WebHub is a Delphi Common Gateway Interface (CGI) framework that enables you to snap together dynamic, database-driven Windows Web site applications instantly. The CD includes a freeware version complete with source code. This version offers much less functionality than the commercial set of Delphi CGI components. You can purchase the commercial version for $665.

WebHub dramatically expands your Web site's performance and functionality. Its commercial version enables you to do the following:

- *Get creative with WebHub's page-oriented publishing paradigm.* WebHub recognizes that Web sites consist of pages, that pages consist of sections, and that sections consist of reusable "chunks." These chunks can be anything from Hypertext Markup Language (HTML) to an action component that builds a grid or faxes a message. WebHub adds structure in the right places, freeing you to focus on the more creative aspects of your applications.

- *Leverage teamwork.* HTML artists can focus on page layout; Delphi programmers can concentrate on programming. WebHub's advanced macro syntax enables the HTML artist to reach inside the Delphi .EXE and publish various properties—from an edit box's text to a TStringList on the surfer's private session object. Delphi developers can program action components such as data grids, interactive outlines, and e-mail while an HTML artist activates the components.

- *Easily access surfer data.* You needn't provide any custom programming to track surfers and their data, because WebHub automatically tracks this information. This greatly facilitates data entry for the programmer—and the surfer.

- *Distribute processing.* WebHub queues page requests across multiple .EXEs on the same machine, and in Maître d'Hub mode, even directs surfers to other machines within a cluster. For high traffic sites with large media files, WebHub offers media cycling—a novel yet simple way to pull files off multiple machines.

- *Build relevant Java applets.* You can open up an infinite range of possibilities to serve surfers. WebHub cooperates with Java applets by passing them surfer data as needed. Use WebHub for database connectivity, and use Java for custom, client-side user-interface solutions.

WebHub is available in both 16- and 32-bit commercial versions and supports Netscape, WebSite, and Spry Web servers.

As Richard Gorman, Borland's Vice President of Products, says, "Delphi developers who need to build database-driven Web sites today should turn to WebHub for innovative, high-performance applications." For more information on the commercial version of WebHub, point your Web browser to **http://super.sonic.net/ann/delphi/cgicomp/**.

The Business Object Architecture

The CD includes a demonstration version of the Business Object Architecture. Delphi developed this client/server development tool for creating database-enabled Web sites. All layout, application logic, and data definitions are defined and manipulated in the tool's graphical, WYSIWYG (What You See Is What You Get)-integrated development environment.

Business Object Architecture is a product of Moai Technologies, Inc. Other products from Moai include the following:

- TMoaiImage, a Delphi component for displaying .GIFs (with transparency) and JPEGs.
- TMoaiText, a Delphi component for minimalist rich-text editing that supports font size, boldface, italics, and underlining. TMoaiText is a suitable component for displaying Web browser text.

For more information on these and other products from Moai Technologies, visit **http://www.moai.com/**.

Network Collection Kit v1.0

The CD also includes a demonstration version of the Network Collection Kit, which is a library of Internet functionality compiled into a simple-to-use library. The library has the following main features:

- Complete WinSock support. You can create WinSock-compliant client/server applications.
- A single function that enables your application's users to browse networks and select the machine that is the server. You don't have to remember Internet Protocol (IP) addresses or machine names.
- Easy management of Internet e-mail. With the Business Object Architecture, managing e-mail has never been easier. The library offers complete support for sending and receiving Internet e-mail.
- A Multipurpose Internet Multimedia Extensions (MIME) module. You can prepare MIME-compliant messages, including file attachments.
- A Simple Mail Transport Protocol (SMTP) module. With this module, you can send e-mail across the Internet.
- A Protocol-to-Protocol version 3 (POP3) module. You can retrieve e-mail and then use the MIME parsing module to extract messages and file attachments.

App

E

■ Base64 encoding and decoding support. The library automatically encodes and decodes files for you.

The library can help you develop WinSock and Internet applications efficiently. The application program interface (API) is quite simple to use and well documented in a Windows help file. For more information on the Network Collection Kit or any other products from Sapient Technology, Inc., visit Sapient's Web page at **http://www.xmission.com/imagicom/**.

The Silverware Communications Tool Kit

The CD includes a Windows help file for the Silverware Communications Tool Kit, which provides full serial communications functionality for use in many programming languages, including Delphi. This easy-to-use toolkit's features include the following:

■ Multilanguage support

■ Reliability (the toolkit doesn't use WM_COMMNOTIFY)

■ Intelligent high-level dialog box functions

■ File transfers

■ Examples for every language

■ Device-independence (beyond COM2)

■ Extensive online help

■ Auto dialer

■ SmartModem support

■ Demonstation programs

■ No royalties

■ Free technical support

■ A comprehensive function return code system

■ Timer functions

■ Low- and high-level control

■ Professional documentation

■ Consistent naming

Most Windows programming languages can use the library, which is implemented as a dynamic link library (DLL). For more information, visit **http://rampages.onramp.net/~silver/**.

Youseful Delphi Components

The CD includes a shareware version of the Youseful Delphi Components, which are a set of over 15 native Delphi VCL components that you use as building blocks to create installation programs for your own programs. You first install the components into Delphi, and then create a new project. Each component represents a different installation functionality; for example, the TInstallAlias component represents the installation of an alias. Just drag and drop the components that you want onto your main form and then set the properties. Then when you double-click the TInstall component, it builds the installation files for you, using compression and more.

Using the Youseful Delphi Components to customize your installation is simple. Each component represents a different installation function, and each of these components publishes many events to which you can attach your own event handlers. You don't have to learn any new language, because you use the native Delphi.

For more information on the Youseful Delphi Components, visit the Web page at **http://ourworld.compuserve.com/homepages/whitewb**.

The PowerTCP Libraries

The PowerTCP Libraries enable Delphi programmers to create Transmission Control Protocol/Internet Protocol (TCP/IP) applications. Components in the library provide the following:

- Low-level TCP/IP client/server functions
- FTP
- Telnet
- VT220 emulation

The PowerTCP Libraries provide a complete set of high-level TCP/IP protocol functions that you can quickly add to any Delphi application. Use PowerTCP to minimize completion time and interoperability problems for your next TCP/IP development project.

Using the PowerTCP Libraries, you can quickly write custom networking applications without writing any socket library code—Dart Communications' experienced network programming staff handles the details. For more information concerning PowerTCP, install the libraries and read the file INSTCOMP.WRI.

For more information on PowerTCP or any other products from Dart Communications, visit its Web page at **http://www.dart.com/**.

App

E

InfoPower

InfoPower provides database developers with the most powerful suite of native Delphi VCL data-aware components available. InfoPower components are fully integrated with Delphi and link directly into your .EXE files—royalty free.

InfoPower includes a full-featured, data-aware, three-dimensional (3-D), multitable grid with optional fixed columns, cell color control, title alignment, and more. InfoPower's grid enables you to display the data in your tables as check boxes, combo boxes, or table-populated combo boxes (which are great for table lookups), or you can display your own custom dialog box.

Your application's users will also love InfoPower's collection of dialog boxes, including an incremental search dialog box that makes it easy to find related records of interest, a table lookup dialog box for lookups and fills, a locate dialog box for pattern searches, and a pop-up, resizable memo field editor.

With InfoPower, you can give your application's users the power to select a table's active index, incrementally search for a value contained in the active index, create live, editable views of tables filtered by any field, and much more, by simply dragging and dropping an InfoPower component onto your form.

For more information on InfoPower or any other products from Woll2Woll Software, visit its Web page at **http://www.woll2woll.com/**.

HTMLViewer

HTMLViewer is a set of shareware Delphi components for creating Web browsers and HTML editors with Delphi. These components and their full-featured commercial versions are available from NetMasters, L.L.C. Among the components available are TDelphiCGI, TDelphiMIME, and THTMLViewer.

TDelphiCGI provides the following:

- Quick creation of Common Gateway Interface (CGI) applications for Windows 95/NT servers
- Utilization of all existing Delphi knowledge
- Dynamic creation of HTML documents
- Expanding creation of robust Web-based database applications
- Easy Web-enabling of your applications
- Implementation of components that is as easy as placing them on a form (really!)
- Quick creation of HTML 1.0 and 2.0 documents
- Fast, easy connection to Delphi data sources
- Easy access to all form and server variables
- Full WinCGI 3.0 compliance
- Collection of user demographics
- The price of $299 for the package, including source code

TDelphiMIME provides the following:

- Rapid MIME transfer implementation from any streamed data source
- An alternative data stream for better system utilization
- Advanced functionality for professional developers
- Integration of binary objects such as images, video files, audio files, Java objects, Java scripts, VRML, and applications
- Custom MIME types, including compressed and encrypted data
- Unlimited connections
- Data warehousing for the Web
- A price of $299 for the package, including source code
- A price of $499 for the CGI/MIME combination package, including source code

`THTMLViewer` provides the following:

- Rapid HTML display implementation from files or text streams
- Fast rendering of HTML for help files, MultiMedia viewers, and Web browsers
- Advanced functionality for professional developers
- Customizable event handlers for `OnHotspotClick`, `OnBitmapRequest`, `OnFormSubmit`, `OnHistoryChange`, `OnHotspotCover`, and `OnProcessing`
- The `ViewImages` property
- Automatic scroll bars
- Launching of other functions and applications from hotspots
- Loading of files and triggering of events from your Delphi application
- Dynamic creation of form files and linking of such files to the BDE for truly modular programming
- Full control over font size, color, and style
- A price of $199 for the package, including source code

Internet Tools

This section describes the many Internet applications that the CD includes. These applications are grouped by subject so that you can quickly find the programs that you need.

Connection Software

This category of software enables you to make the physical connection to the Internet through a phone line or a local area network (LAN).

Core Internet-Connect v2.0 Trial Version   Core Internet-Connect provides WinSock and TCP/IP for networks and is designed to help users connect. The program also is designed for developers who want to build other TCP/IP applications. On the companion CD, you can find Core Internet-Connect at \WEBPAGES\APPS\INETCON2.HTM and \APPS\CONNECT\INETCON2.

N O T E   This package contains the Internet-Connect Trial Copy program. Internet-Connect is developed and marketed by Core Systems, 245 Firestone Drive, Walnut Creek, CA 94598, (510) 943-5765. ▓

Crynwr Packet Drivers   Crynwr is a collection of drivers that most DOS-based (and some Windows-based) Internet applications require. The collection serves as an interface between established network software and packet-based Internet connections. These archive files include a wide range of drivers for most popular network packages, such as Novell NetWare and Artisoft LANtastic. The CD also includes source code for each driver. You can find Crynwr on the companion CD at \WEBPAGES\APPS\CRYNWR.HTM and \APPS\CONNECT\CRYNWER.

NetDial   NetDial is an Internet dial-up program with many features. NetDial can call, connect to your Internet host, log you in, and run your TCP/IP program at the click of a mouse. Other features include baud-rate support of up to 256K baud, as many as 99 redial attempts, automatic dialing on startup, sound support, support for up to five separate configurations, a cumulative timer window (which tracks all time online), a built-in call log viewer/editor, support for as many as five startup programs on startup, and additional modem support. You can find NetDial at \WEBPAGES\APPS\NETDIAL.HTM and \APPS\CONNECT\NETDIAL.

Slipper/CSlipper v1.5   Slipper/CSlipper version 1.5 is a DOS-based replacement application for SLIP8250. Slipper and CSlipper provide Internet connections through a packet-driver interface. Both applications are small and command-line-driven. You can find Slipper and CSlipper at \WEBPAGES\APPS\SLIPPR.HTM and \APPS\CONNECT\SLIPPTR.

Trumpet WinSock v2.0b   Trumpet WinSock is the most widely used shareware WinSock package. The software supports modem and network connections. This version features firewall support and improved scripting and routing capabilities. You can find Trumpet WinSock at \WEBPAGES\APPS\TWSK20B.HTM and \APPS\CONNECT\TWSK20B.

N O T E   The Trumpet WinSock is now distributed as shareware. You can use the Trumpet WinSock program for 30 days to evaluate its usefulness. If you determine at the end of this evaluation period that you're satisfied with the product, you must register it.

Trumpet WinSock v2.0b has a Send Registration option that automatically posts encrypted credit-card details to Trumpet Software International. To take advantage of this feature, open the File menu and choose Register. ▦

E-Mail and Accessories

E-mail is one of the most popular features on the Internet. You'll be sending much mail, so choose a program with which you feel comfortable.

Eudora v1.4.4   The Eudora e-mail package offers many features. It supports private mailboxes, reply functions, periodic mail checking, and many more features that make this software one of the best mail packages on the market. For a detailed exploration of this product and Internet e-mail, see *Using Eudora* by Dee-Ann and Robert LeBlanc (Que, 1995). You can find Eudora at \WEBPAGES\APPS\EUDORA.HTM and \APPS\EMAIL\EUDORA.

N O T E   You can get information about Eudora 2, the program's commercial version, on the Web page for Qualcomm's QUEST group. The Uniform Resource Locator (URL) is **http://www.qualcomm.com/quest/QuestMaln.html**. Alternatively, you can get information about the commercial version by sending e-mail to **eudora-sales@qualcomm.com** or by calling (800) 2-EUDORA—that is, (800) 238-3672. ▦

Pegasus Mail   Pegasus Mail is a powerful, easy-to-use e-mail program. Several add-ins for Pegasus make it easier to send attachments of popular document types, such as Word Pro and Word for Windows. One add-in, Mercury (a mail transport system), is included in the

\APPS\EMAIL\PEGASUS\MERCURY folder. Pegasus is free software that you can use without restriction. You can find Pegasus at \WEBPAGES\APPS\PEGASUS.HTM and \APPS\EMAIL\PEGASUS.

RFD Mail   RFD Mail is a Windows offline mail reader that supports many online services, including CompuServe, Delphi GEnie, MCI Mail, World UNIX, the Direct Connection, MV Communications, Panix, the Well, the Portal System, NETCOM, CRL, INS, and the Internet Access Company. The program's other features include support for scripts, an address book, folders with drag-and-drop and search capability, backup and restore capability, polling, and multiple signature blocks. You can find RFD Mail at \WEBPAGES\APPS\RFDMAIL.HTM and \APPS\EMAIL\RFDMAIL.

WinSMTP   WinSMTP is a mail server, or *daemon*. It sends and receives SMTP mail and also acts as a POP3 mailbox. If you have a Serial Line Internet Protocol (SLIP) account, your provider holds your mail for you in a mailbox that you can reach with SMTP or POP3. By using WinSMTP, you can have multiple users on your site without buying multiple accounts from your Internet service provider. Also, you can administer mailing lists and debug mail clients that you are writing. The registered version includes several enhancements, such as a Finger server. You can reach the author, Jack De Winter, at **wildside@wildside.kwnet.on.ca**, and more information is also available at **http://wildside.kwnet.on.ca**. You can find WinSMTP at \WEBPAGES\APPS\WINSMTP.HTM and \APPS\EMAIL\WINSMTP.

Transfer Pro   Transfer Pro is a Windows-based shareware tool that enables you to send text, application data, messages, images, audio, video, executable files, and other data types by e-mail, using the latest MIME 1.0 standards specified in RFC 1341. The program supports UU and XX encoding and decoding. You can find Transfer Pro at \WEBPAGES\APPS\XFERPRO.HTM and \APPS\EMAIL\XFERPRO.

WinMIME   WinMIME includes some utilities that are useful with .WAV and .GIF attachments. The program records or plays MIME attachments. WinMIME provides no documentation, but if you play around with the program a bit, you'll get the hang of it. You can find WinMIME at \WEBPAGES\APPS\WINMIME.HTM and \APPS\EMAIL\WINMIME.

Finger and WHOIS Applications

You use Finger and WHOIS applications to get information about a user.

Cfinger v1.1   Cfinger is a truly Windows-based application that enables you to select users with a mouse click. The application can use any WHOIS database and enables you to search the results of its searches. You can find Cfinger at \WEBPAGES\APPS\CFINGER.HTM and \APPS\FINGER\CFINGER).

Finger 1.0   Finger 1.0 is a simple Finger client written for Borland C++ 3.1 using the ObjectWindows Libraries (OWL). The CD includes this program's source code. The documentation is rather sketchy, but such a simple application doesn't require extensive documentation. You can find Finger at \WEBPAGES\APPS\FINGER10.HTM and \APPS\FINGER\FINGER10.

App

E

WinWHOIS   WinWHOIS is an easy-to-use, Windows-based WHOIS search front-end application. The program keeps a log of responses, so you can copy and paste an address if you find what you are looking for. You can find WinWHOIS at \WEBPAGES\APPS\WINWHOIS.HTM and \APPS\FINGER\WINWHOIS.

WinSock Finger Daemon   WinSock Finger Daemon is a Windows Finger server that you can set up to deliver information about multiple users on the same machine or for a single user. This server runs on your machine to deliver information about you. You can find WinSock Finger Daemon at \WEBPAGES\APPS\WFNGRD.HTM and \APPS\FINGER\WFNGRD.

N O T E   Jim O'Brien of Tidewater Systems wrote this software. The CD's inclusion of WinSock Finger Daemon does not grant a license for continued use. ■

FTP Clients

You use file-transfer clients to download files from FTP sites.

WS_FTP   The WS_FTP client is extremely easy to use. It comes preconfigured with many popular FTP sites, and you can add more. WS_FTP also supports advanced features such as firewalls. The CD includes 16-bit and 32-bit versions. You can find WS_FTP at \WEBPAGES\APPS\WS_FTP.HTM, \APPS\FTP\WS_FIP16, and \APPS\FTP\WS_FTP32.

WinFTP   The WinFTP client is based on WS_FTP but includes some additional features. With the history dialog box, you can select a folder that you've already visited without having to traverse the entire folder tree. Among many other features, the client provides filters that enable you to search for specific file types, such as *.TXT or *.ZIP, in the local and remote hosts. The CD includes 16-bit and 32-bit versions. You can find WinFTP at \WEBPAGES\APPS\WINFTP.HTM and \APPS\FTP\WINFTP.

WFTPD v2.0   WFTPD is the first shareware FTP server (*daemon*) written specifically for WinSock. An FTP server enables your machine to be an FTP site, so that users can point their client programs to your site and download files from it. WFTPD supports anonymous access, access from Mosaic, Netscape, other World Wide Web (WWW) browsers, folder-based per-user security, and configurable onscreen and to-file logging. You can find WFTPD at \WEBPAGES\APPS\WFTPD and \APPS\FTP\WFTPD.

N O T E   The registered version, which costs $15, includes the following features:

- No limit on the number of GETs or PUTs per login or per run of the program.
- Customizable greeting and farewell messages. (The unregistered version has fixed messages that identify your site as using unregistered shareware.) ■

The supplied help file includes most of the information that you need to use this product, but you can address additional inquiries to the author, Alun Jones, at **alun@texis.com**, or fax them to (512) 346-2803.

Gopher

Gopher clients enable you to search for information stored on Gopher servers.

Gopher for Windows   The Chinese University of Hong Kong created Gopher for Windows, which is a simple little Gopher client. If you're looking for something fancy, this program might not be the ticket for you. If you want something fast and simple, though, this program is the perfect Gopher client. You can find Gopher for Windows at \WEBPAGES\APPS\WGOPHER.HTM and \APPS\GOPHER\WGOPHER.

Hampson's Gopher v2.3   Hampson's Gopher is a small, yet powerful, Windows-based Gopher client that enables a user to search the many Gopher servers scattered around the Internet. Extensive help is available in the application. You can find Hampson's Gopher at \WEBPAGES\APPS\HGOPHER.HTM and \APPS\GOPHER\HGOPHER.

N O T E   FTP Software has licensed version 2.4 of Hampson's Gopher, so it is no longer available for free distribution. ▨

Go4Ham   Go4Ham is a Gopher server that enables your site to be a Gopher site. Users throughout the Internet can then access your Gopher documents by using any Gopher client. You can find Go4Ham at \WEBPAGES\APPS\GO4HAM.HTM and \APPS\GOPHER\GO4HAM.

HTML Conversion

Some documents that you want to publish on the Web might already exist in another format. The HTML conversion applications in this section enable you to convert documents to the HTML format for use on the Web.

RTF to HTML   RTF to HTML is a utility for converting documents from rich text format (RTF) to HTML. RTF is a format that many word processors—including Word for Windows—can import and export. The package also includes a Word for Windows 2.0 template for writing HTML. You can find RTF to HTML at \WEBPAGES\APPS\RTF2HTML.HTM and \APPS\HTML\RTF2HTML.

Tex2RTF   Tex2RTF is a handy utility for converting LaTeX files to HTML in Windows. (The utility can also convert LaTeX to the Windows Help file format.) The LaTeX format is popular for files created in print and online, and is also a common language used for technical documents. This program has a good help system that you should read through to help you make the most of the utility. You can find Tex2RTF at \WEBPAGES\APPS\TEX2RTF.HTM and \APPS\HTML\TEX2RTF.

HTML Editors

HTML documents are the heart of the Web. Whether you're creating a Web site for a major corporation or just putting up a few personal pages, you'll need an HTML editor or translator. The applications in this section are stand-alone editors for creating HTML documents.

HTML Assistant for Windows   HTML Assistant for Windows is a simple shareware HTML document editor. You implement most of the program's commands by using a huge toolbar.

App

E

The program is a good editor for small documents, but this version limits file size to 32K. (A professional version that loads larger documents is available; see the help file for ordering information.) One neat feature is the program's capability to convert files that contain URLs (for example, Cello bookmarks and Mosaic .INI files) to HTML documents that any Web browser can read. You can find HTML Assistant for Windows at \WEBPAGES\APPS\HTMLASST.HTM and \APPS\HTML\HTMLASST.

HTMLed HTMLed is a powerful shareware HTML document editor. The interface features an easy-to-use toolbar, and the abundant and clear menus make it easy to find the features that you need. You can find HTMLed at \WEBPAGES\APPS\HTMLED.HTM and \APPS\HTML\HTMLED.

HTML Writer HTML Writer is a stand-alone HTML authoring program. The program's extensive set of menu options enables you to insert most HTML tags. HTML Writer has a nice toolbar for implementing many HTML tags. Another good feature is the support of templates, which you can use to design and create HTML documents with a consistent look and feel. You can find HTML Writer at \WEBPAGES\APPS\HTMLWRIT.HTM and \APPS\HTML\HTMLWRIT.

SoftQuad HoTMetaL SoftQuad HoTMetaL is a freeware full-featured, professional-quality HTML editor for Windows. With this program, you can edit multiple documents at the same time, use templates to ensure consistency among documents, and use the powerful word-processor-like features to perform such actions as search and replace. You can find SoftQuad HoTMetaL at \WEBPAGES\APPS\HOTMETAL.HTM, \APPS\HTML\HOTMETAL, and \WWW\HOTMETAL.

The commercial version, HoTMetaL PRO, includes the following new features:

- A cleanup filter called TIDY for any invalid legacy HTML files
- Bitmapped graphics inline in your documents
- Macros to automate repetitive tasks and reduce errors
- Rules checking and validation to ensure correct HTML markup
- A built-in graphical table editor
- The capability to fix invalid HTML documents and import them (with the Interpret Document command)
- A URL editor
- Full table and forms support
- Macro creation and editing support
- Document-validation commands
- Support for Microsoft Windows Help
- A printed manual and access to support personnel
- Home-page templates
- Editing tools
- Spell checking

- A thesaurus
- Full, context-sensitive search-and-replace capability

N O T E You can order a copy of HoTMetaL PRO from SoftQuad for $195. ■

WebEdit v1.0c   The WebEdit editor enables you to edit multiple documents at once and provides a clean, simple interface that hides the editor's powerful features. You can find WebEdit at \WEBPAGES\APPS\WEBEDIT.HTM and \APPS\HTML\WEBEDIT.

HTML Editors for Microsoft Word

The template files in this section work with Microsoft Word for Windows (versions 2 and 6). If you like the Microsoft Word editing environment, try some of these templates. Essentially, they enable you to insert HTML codes into any new or existing Word document.

ANT_HTML   ANT_DEMO.DOT is a template that works in Word for Windows 6.*x* and Word 6.*x* for the Macintosh to help you create hypertext documents. You can insert HTML codes into any new or existing Word document or into any ASCII document. You can find ANT_HTML at \WEBPAGES\APPS\ANT.HTM and \APPS\HTML\ANT_DEMO.

ANT_DEMO is a demonstration version of the ANT_PLUS conversion utility and the ANT_HTML package. ANT_HTML and ANT_PLUS work in all international versions of Word 6.*x*.

N O T E Jill Swift copyrighted ANT_HTML.DOT and ANT_DEMO.DOC in 1994. For more information, contact Jill Swift, P.O. Box 213, Montgomery, TX 77356, or **jswift@freenet.fsu.edu**. ■

GT_HTML   GT_MTML is another Word 6.*x* template for creating HTML documents. Only a few HTML tags are currently supported, but they are the most common tags and should be useful for many basic HTML documents. You can find GT_HTML at \WEBPAGES\APPS\GT_HTML.HTM and \APPS\HTML\GT_HTML.

HTML Author   HTML Author is another template for creating HTML documents in Word for Windows 6.*x*. You can find HTML Author at \WEBPAGES\APPS\HTMLAUTH.HTM and \APPS\HTML\HTMLAUTH.

N O T E Grahame S. Cooper copyrighted the HTML Author software and its associated manual in 1995. You can copy and use them as long as you don't modify them (other than to change the paragraph styles).

The HTML Author software is provided as is, without warranty or guarantee. Neither Cooper nor the University of Salford accept any liability for errors or faults in the software or any damage arising from the use of the software.

You can obtain new versions and updates of the software from the University of Salford at the following Web address:

http://www.salford.ac.uk/docs/depts/iti/staff/gsc/htmlauth/summary.html ■

App

E

WebWizard   WebWizard is another HTML authoring system that works as a template in Word for Windows 6.*x*. The system adds a new toolbar with some HTML commands and adds a new WebWizard menu to the menu bar when loaded. You can find WebWizard at \WEBPAGES\APPS\WEBWIZA.HTM and \APPS\HTML\WEBWIZA.

Miscellaneous Applications

The applications listed in this section enable you to track IP addresses, talk to someone else over the Internet, keep your system time correct, and keep organized.

IP Manager   IP Manager helps you keep track of IP addresses, ensures that you don't have duplicate addresses, and even launches FTP and Telnet sessions. You can find IP Manager at \WEBPAGES\APPS\IPMGR.HTM and \APPS\MISC\IPMGR.

This trial version is limited to only 25 devices. You can try IP Manager for 21 days. If at the end of the trial period you decide not to buy IP Manager, you should delete it.

Internet VoiceChat   Internet VoiceChat (IVC) enables two users connected to the Internet to talk to each other by way of their PCs. The program requires both PCs to have sound cards, microphones, and speakers. You can find Internet VoiceChat at \WEBPAGES\APPS\IVC.HTM and \APPS\MISC\IVC.

The current version of IVC doesn't transmit the conversation in real time. It waits for a pause (such as the pause at the end of a sentence) and transmits the whole phrase at once. A SLIP connection doesn't affect audio quality, but you can choose a lower sampling rate to speed transmission. Even so, the sound should be telephone quality or better. See the IVC.FAQ file for more information about using this interesting application.

If you use Trumpet WinSock, be sure to upgrade to Version 2.0b, because IVC isn't compatible with earlier versions.

NOTE   Richard L. Ahrens copyrighted Internet VoiceChat in 1994. You can use IVC's unregistered version on an evaluation basis for no more than 30 days. Continued use after the 30-day trial period requires registration, which is $20 for individual users. Site licenses are negotiable. When you register, you get additional features, such as answering-machine and fax modes. Contact the author at 7 Omega Court, Middletown, NJ 07748. ▪

Name Server Lookup   Name Server Lookup is a simple but powerful utility for looking up information about a specific machine or domain on the Internet. The program reports the numeric IP address and other information for the site or machine name. You can find Name Server Lookup at \WEBPAGES\APPS\NSLOOKUP.HTM and \APPS\MISC\NSLOOKUP.

Sticky   Sticky is an interesting application that enables you to post little "sticky notes" on other users' computers by using the Internet. You can create a small database of other users to which to send these notes. The CD provides Sticky at \WEBPAGES\APPS\STICKY.HTM and \APPS\MISC\STICKY.

Time Sync   Time Sync version 1.4 is a Windows-based application designed to synchronize your PC's clock with the time on a UNIX host. This program, which relies on an established WinSock connection, is written in Visual Basic. You can find Time Sync at \WEBPAGES\APPS\TSYNC.HTM and \APPS\MISC\TSYNC.

U2D   The handy U2D program converts UNIX text-file line endings to DOS text-file format. All you have to do to process a file (or files) is to drag them from File Manager to the U2D icon. You can find U2D at \WEBPAGES\APPS\U2D.HTM and \APPS\MISC\U2D.

WebWatch   WebWatch, an Internet utility from Specter, Inc., enables you to track changes in selected Web documents. WebWatch generates a local HTML document containing links to only those documents updated after the given date. You use this local file to navigate to the updated documents, using any Web browser. You can find WebWatch at \WEBPAGES\APPS\WEBWATCH.HTM and \APPS\MISC\WEBWATCH.

In a typical scenario, you set the anchor document (the local file, parsed for your URLs) to your Netscape BOOKMARK.HTM file and the result file (the file in which the program generates its output) to your home page. Your home page thus always contains links to the fresh, "must-see" documents, and you still can use your bookmarks in the usual way.

The CD-ROM contains a prerelease limited edition of WebWatch. The full, final release enables you to use your "last visit" date as Netscape stores it, instead of having to specify a general "update" date. The final release also doesn't limit the number of URLs that you can visit in one run.

To learn more about WebWatch, visit the following address:

> **http://www.specter.com/users/janos/webwatch/index.html**

You can download your free evaluation copy of the final release from the following address:

> **ftp://ftp.specter.com/users/janos/webwatch/wwatch10.zip**

Windows Sockets Host   Windows Sockets Host is a simple utility that determines a host computer's name based on a dotted-decimal IP address, or vice versa. You can find Windows Socket Host at \WEBPAGES\APPS\WSHOST.HTM and \APPS\MISC\WSHOST.

App
E

Windows Sockets Net Watch   Windows Sockets Net Watch makes active checks on Internet hosts that are listed in its database file. This checking is useful for monitoring whether a host is functioning. This program is designed to work on any WinSock DLL, but the documentation has some notes on which WinSocks it works well on and the ones with which it has problems. You can find Windows Sockets Net Watch at \WEBPAGES\APPS\WSWATCH.HTM and \APPS\MISC\WS_WATCH.

Windows Sockets Ping   Windows Sockets Ping is an uncomplicated Windows application that tests an Internet connection. Its author wrote the program to test whether his two computers were connected on the Internet; you can use it to do the same thing. The archive includes the source code, and the author grants you permission to alter it. The CD includes Windows 3.1 and Windows NT versions. You can find Windows Sockets Ping at \WEBPAGES\APPS\WSPING.HTM and \APPS\MISC\WS_PING.

N O T E   Because Windows Sockets Ping uses nonstandard WinSock calls, this application might not run on every WinSock stack. ■

WSArchie   Archie clients enable you to connect to an Archie server and search for a file. Most programs come preconfigured with the locations of several servers; try to choose a server near you. When a search succeeds, you can simply click the file to start downloading.

WSArchie is a WinSock-compliant Archie program that enables you to connect to an Archie server and search for a file by using the familiar Windows interface. You can configure WSArchie to transfer files directly from the list of found files so that you don't have to open your FTP client manually and then reenter the address and directory information. You can find WSArchie at \WEBPAGES\APPS\WSARCHIE.HTM and \APPS\ARCHIE\WSARCHIE.

WSIRC   WinSock Internet Relay Chat (WSIRC) provides a real-time way to converse with one or more people by computer over the Internet. Whatever you type, everyone else sees. Not much software is available for the PC for IRC, but this program is very good.

This product is available in three versions: a freeware version, a shareware version that provides more functions when registered, and retail versions for personal and corporate use. The program's author also can custom-design an IRC client for special needs.

The CD includes both the freeware and shareware versions. In this release, the shareware version has all the features enabled, but only for a limited time; after 30 days, you must register the shareware version to continue using it. The freeware version has no such limitations. You can find WSIRC at \WEBPAGES\APPS\WSIRC.HTM and \APPS\IRC\WSIRC.

Newsreaders

Although many ways are available for reading Usenet newsgroups, a dedicated reader usually makes reading faster and easier.

NewsXpress   NewsXpress is one of the latest Windows newsreaders, and is quickly becoming quite popular. It has all the features found in the leading newsreaders but provides a more pleasant interface. You can find NewsXpress at \WEBPAGES\APPS\NXPRESS.HTM and \APPS\NEWS\NXPRESS.

Paperboy v2.05   Paperboy is a Windows-based offline newsreader. Host programs such as UQWK create packets in the Simple Offline Usenet Packet (SOUP) format. This newsreader can accept these packets from the host and download them to your PC. You can find Paperboy at \WEBPAGES\APPS\PBOY205.HTM and \APPS\NEWS\PAPERBOY.

Trumpet Newsreader   Trumpet is a full-featured shareware WinSock newsreader for Windows. You can use Trumpet to perform all the expected functions, such as reading, posting, and replying (as a follow-up post or by e-mail). You also can save messages and decode attached files. You can find Trumpet at \WEBPAGES\APPS\WTWSK.HTM and \APPS\NEWS\WTWSK.

 N O T E   Three other versions of this software are available for other types of Internet connections. All these versions are similar in function to the WinSock version:

- WT_LWP requires Novell LWP DOS/Windows and is located in the folder \APPS\NEWS\WT_LWP.

- WT_ABI requires the Trumpet terminate-and-stay-ready (TSR) TCP stack and is located in the folder \APPS\NEWS\WT_ABI.
- WT_PKT works with a direct-to-packet driver (internal TCP stack) and is located in the folder \APPS\NEWS\WT_PKT.

WinNews Server You can use the WinNews Server application to collect news so that several different users at your site can read without downloading each article repeatedly. You can also use this server to test your news client. The CD includes an early beta copy of the software; the product should be significantly improved by the time this book reaches the shelves. You can reach the author, Harold Bunskoek, at **cis@cis.iaf.nl**. The CD provides WinNews Server at \WEBPAGES\APPS\WINNEWS.HTM and \APPS\NEWS\NNTP.

WinVN Newsreader WinVN is a full-featured, public-domain WinSock newsreader for Windows. The WinVN program and Usenet newsgroups are discussed in detail in *Using UseNet Newsgroups*, published by Que Corporation. You can find WinVN at \WEBPAGES\APPS\WINVN16.HTM and \APPS\NEWS\WINVN16.

YARN YARN is a freeware, offline program for Usenet mail and news. It runs in DOS 3.0 or higher, but does not run in Windows. Host programs such as UQWK create packets in the SOUP format. This newsreader can accept these packets from the host and download them to your PC. YARN accepts these packets, and performs better than the common QWK format readers for Usenet use because it preserves more of the unique Usenet header information when posting replies. You can find YARN at \WEBPAGES\APPS\YARN.HTM and \APPS\NEWS\YARN.

Telnet

Telnet enables you to log in to a remote server and use a text-based terminal session. It's one of the simplest interfaces to a remote computer over the Internet.

COMt COMt is a shareware program that enables a standard Windows-based communication program to act as a Telnet client in a TCP/IP environment. The program enables you to use your communications program's more powerful features in a Telnet session. You can find COMt at \WEBPAGES\APPS\COMT.HTM and \APPS\TELNET\COMT.

EWAN In a typical setting, EWAN is used primarily for Telnet; you can save configurations for several different Telnet sites. The program supports a capture log, and you can perform the usual copy-and-paste operations from the text to the capture log. You can find EWAN at \WEBPAGES\APPS\EWAN.HTM and \APPS\TELNET\EWAN.

TekTel TekTel is a simple Telnet application with Textronix T4010 and VT100 emulation. The program is a little rough around the edges, but functional. The CD includes the Visual Basic source code. You can find TekTel at \WEBPAGES\APPS\TEKTEL.HTM and \APPS\TELNET\TEKTEL.

YAWTELNET   YAWTELNET (Yet Another Windows Socket Telnet) is a freeware Telnet client designed specifically to work well with Mosaic. Many of the menu commands aren't functional, but you can select text in the active window and copy it to another application. You can find YAWTELNET at \WEBPAGES\APPS\YAWTEL.HTM and \APPS\TELNET\YAWTEL.

 N O T E Hans van Oostrom copyrighted YAWTELNET in 1994. Refer to LICENSE.TXT in the \YAWTEL folder for complete copyright information. ■

Web Browsers

Most of the Web browsers have recently become commercialized. You can still find shareware versions of Windows-based browsers on the Web. However, commercial browsers are incorporating all the newest features.

Lynx   Lynx is a Web client for DOS machines. The program is an alpha release that doesn't currently support forms. One positive feature is that Lynx opens each URL that you access in a separate window, which enables you to have several documents open at once. The program also has support for displaying inline images. You can find Lynx at \WEBPAGES\APPS\LYNX.HTM and \APPS\WWW\LYNX.

SlipKnot   SlipKnot is a graphical Web browser specifically designed for Microsoft Windows users who have UNIX shell accounts with their service providers. SlipKnot's primary feature is that it doesn't require SLIP, PPP, or TCP/IP services. It also provides background retrieval of multiple documents and storage of complete documents on users' local hard disks. You can find SlipKnot at \WEBPAGES\APPS\SLIPKNOT.HTM and \APPS\WWW\SLIPKNOT.

Web Servers

The programs in this section enable your Windows-based PC to act like a Web site that other Web browsers can access.

Web4Ham   Web4Ham is a Web server for Windows. The program enables your Windows PC to act like a Web site that other Web users can access with any Web client software. You can find Web4Ham at \WEBPAGES\APPS\WEB4HAM.HTM and \APPS\WWW\WEB4HAM.

Windows HTTPD v1.4   Windows HTTPD is a Web server for Windows that has extensive online documentation in HTML format. This small, quick server offers such features as form support, image mapping, and folder-level security. You can find Windows HTTPD at \WEBPAGES\APPS\WHTTPD.HTM and \APPS\WWW\WHTTPD.

Web Accessories

The applications in this section help you with your Web surfing by enabling you to launch other applications or store URLs for future reference.

Launcher   Launcher is a neat freeware utility that enables you to launch a Windows application from a link in a Web browser such as Mosaic. This feature enables you to open an application (such as WordPerfect or Excel) without having to create a link to a particular document. The CD-ROM supplies the source code. You can find Launcher at \WEBPAGES\APPS\LAUNCHER.HTM and \APPS\WWW\LAUNCHER.

URL Grabber Demo   Have you ever read an article in a Usenet newsgroup or an e-mail message and noticed a URL that you wanted to save for further reference? Although you can copy and paste the URL into a browser and then save it in a hotlist or bookmark, the handy URL Grabber utility makes this process even easier. The URL Grabber toolbar enables you to grab URLs from documents as you read them and then save a collection of addresses as HTML documents that you can open in any Web browser. You then have a Web document that contains all the links to the URL addresses that you saved, enabling you to jump to those URLs quickly and easily. This demonstration version limits you to grabbing three addresses each time that you run the program. You can find the URL Grabber at \WEBPAGES\APPS\GRABDEMO.HTM and \APPS\WWW\GRABDEMO.

Useful Utilities

This section describes the many utility applications that the CD includes. This eclectic mix of programs includes graphics and sound editors, compression software, and other useful utilities. Although you are unlikely to use all these programs, you should find at least one that you can use.

Compression Software

To save on download time over the Internet and disk space on servers, most applications are compressed into archives. The applications in this section help you decompress these archives so that you can run the applications that you have downloaded.

ArcMaster   ArcMaster is a handy utility for compressing and decompressing files using many popular compression formats. The utility supports .ZIP, .LHZ, .ARJ, and other formats. You must have the file compression/decompression utilities for each of these formats, because ArcMaster is just a front-end that makes it easier to use the DOS utilities. ArcMaster supports drag-and-drop, enables you to manipulate compressed files conveniently, and converts files from one compression format to another. You can find ArcMaster at \WEBPAGES\APPS\ARCMASTR.HTM and \APPS\COMPRESS\ARCMASTR.

ArcShell   ArcShell is a Windows shell for .ZIP, .LHZ, .ARC, and .ARJ compression files. You must have the file compression/decompression utilities for each of these formats, because ArcShell is just a front-end that makes it easier to use the DOS utilities. You can find ArcShell at \WEBPAGES\APPS\ARCSHELL.HTM and \APPS\COMPRESS\ARCSHELL.

Drag and Zip   Drag and Zip is a set of utilities that turns the Windows 3.1 File Manager into a file manager for creating and managing .ZIP, .LHZ, and .GZ files. With its built-in routines to zip and unzip files, Drag and Zip makes it quite easy to compress files into .ZIP files and to extract compressed files from .ZIP files, from any Windows File Manager that supports drag-and-drop. Drag and Zip also supports use of copies of PKZIP, LHA, and GUNZIP to manage compressed files. The utility includes a built-in virus scanner that you can use to scan the files

App
E

in the compressed file for possible viruses. You can find Drag and Zip at \WEBPAGES\APPS\DRAGZIP.HTM and \APPS\COMPRESS\DRAGZIP.

WinZip v5.6   WinZip is a Windows ZIP archive-managing program that no Internet user should be without. This application provides a pleasant graphical interface for managing many archive-file formats, such as .ZIP, .ARJ, .ARC, and .LZH. WinZip enables you to open text files from an archive directly to the screen so that you can read a file in an archive without actually extracting it. You can find WinZip at \WEBPAGES\APPS\WINZIP.HTM and \APPS\COMPRESS\WINZIP.

Version 5.6 adds support of archives using the GZIP, TAR, and Z formats common on the Internet. You can now manage these files just as easily as ZIP files. You often find files on the Internet that were stored as TAR files and then compressed with GZIP or Z. WinZip handles these multiple formats with no problems. This support is unique among the other ZIP file utilities discussed in this appendix.

Zip Manager   Zip Manager is a stand-alone Windows ZIP utility. You don't have to have PKZIP and PKUNZIP to use Zip Manager, which sets it apart from most other Windows-based ZIP utilities. Zip Manager is 100-percent PKZIP 2.04-compatible, and the compression utilities are designed especially for Windows. ZMZIP and ZMUNZIP are built in to Zip Manager. You can find Zip Manager at \WEBPAGES\APPS\ZIPMGR.HTM and \APPS\COMPRESS\ZIPMGR.

Zip Master   Zip Master is another Windows ZIP utility that doesn't require that you also have PKZIP or PKUNZIP. You can use Zip Master to add to, freshen, or update existing ZIP files; create new ZIP files; extract from or test existing ZIP files; view existing ZIP file contents; and perform many other functions. You can find Zip Master at \WEBPAGES\APPS\ZIPMASTR.HTM and \APPS\COMPRESS\ZIPMASTR.

File Readers: Postscript, Sound, Images, and Video

If you frequently download graphics, sound, or specially formatted files, you need software to view, listen, or otherwise manipulate these files.

Media Blastoff   The Media Blastoff viewer supports several popular graphics formats as well as sound and movies. The file formats probably most useful to you with the Internet are .GIF, .AVI, and .WAV. You can find Media Blastoff at \WEBPAGES\APPS\BLASTOFF.HTM and \APPS\READERS\BLASTOFF.

GhostView v1.0   You can use GhostView version 1.0, a Windows 3.1 application, to view printer files that conform to GhostScript 2.6 or later standards. GhostScript is an interpreter for the PostScript page-description language that many laser printers use. You can also use GhostView to print GhostScript-embedded documents. The archive includes the application's source code. GhostView is the interpreter that the National Center for Supercomputing Applications (NCSA) recommends for use with Mosaic for viewing PostScript files with GhostScript. You can find GhostView at \WEBPAGES\APPS\GSVIEW.HTM and \APPS\READERS\GSVIEW.

Jasc Media Center   If you have many multimedia files that you've collected from the Web, you'll find this utility useful for keeping them organized. It supports 37 file formats, including

.GIF, JPEG, MIDI, .WAV, and .AVI. You can use unsupported formats if you have an external file filter for them. The CD provides Jasc Media Center at \WEBPAGES\APPS\JASC.HTM and \APPS\READERS\JASCMEDI.

PlayWave   PlayWave is a simple Windows application for playing .WAV sound files. The program requires fewer mouse clicks for playing .WAVs and can be set to loop a .WAV file continuously. You can find PlayWave at \WEBPAGES\APPS\PLAYWAVE.HTM and \APPS\READERS\PLAYWAV.

PlayWave's author states that this application might not work on all systems. To use PlayWave, open the View menu, choose Options under My Computer, and use the File Types sheet to associate .WAV files with PlayWave, not the Sound Recorder. Then, when you double-click .WAV file names, you invoke PlayWave, not the Sound Recorder. To use PlayWave with your Web browser, designate it as the viewer for .WAV files; then, when you download a .WAV format sound, PlayWave will start.

VuePrint   VuePrint is a graphics viewer that opens, saves, and prints graphics in JPEG and .GIF formats, as well as several other popular formats. It includes a screen saver that displays collections of these file formats. VuePrint also has a built-in UUEncoder and UUDecoder, which makes the viewer an all-in-one graphics solution for most of your Internet graphics needs. You can find VuePrint at \WEBPAGES\APPS\VUEPRINT.HTM and \APPS\READERS\VUEPRINT.

WinECJ   WinECJ is a fast JPEG viewer. It can open multiple files and includes a slide-show presentation mode. You can find WinECJ at \WEBPAGES\APPS\WINECJ.HTM and \APPS\READERS\WINECJ.

WPlany   The WPlany sound utility plays sound files through a Windows .WAV output device (such as a SoundBlaster card). NCSA recommends WPlany for use with Mosaic. The program supports several sound-file formats (including most formats that are used on the Internet) and is quite easy to use. However, after WPlany begins to play a sound file, you can't stop it, so you must let it play to completion. You can find WPlany at \WEBPAGES\APPS\WPLANY.HTM and \APPS\READERS\WPLANY.

App
E

File Encryption Software

If you have sensitive information that you want to send to someone over the Internet, you need an encryption program to ensure that unauthorized individuals cannot read your documents. This section describes two encryption applications that provide this protection.

Crip for Windows   Crip for Windows is a Windows-based text-encryption program for use over the Internet. It has options for dealing with PC line feeds in files that are sent over the Internet. (See the README file for information on these options.) You can find Crip for Windows at \WEBPAGES\APPS\CRIP.HTM and \APPS\ENCRYPT\CRIPWIN.

Enigma for Windows   The Enigma for Windows file-encryption program supports the Data Encryption Standard (DES) used by many United States government agencies. Although the program isn't designed for sending encrypted messages by Internet e-mail, you can use it to transfer files through any protocol that supports binary transfer. You can encrypt files on an FTP site, send encrypted files as attachments to e-mail using UUEncode or MIME, or make encrypted files available through the Web as links from an HTML document.

Enigma isn't a public key system, so you use the same password to encode and decode files. This limits Enigma's security for Internet usage, because anyone receiving a file must know your password. You can find Enigma for Windows at \WEBPAGES\APPS\ENIGMA.HTM and \APPS\ENCRYPT\ENIGMA.

Picture Conversion and Manipulation Software

In addition to applications or text information files, the Internet offers a wealth of images in many different formats. These applications help you convert images to a format that you can use.

Image'n'Bits   Image'n'Bits is a graphics manipulation and conversion utility. The program supports .BMP and .GIF as well as other formats. Image'n'Bits also offers such special effects as dithering, pixelizing, and solarizing. If you're working with artistic images or photographs as Web images, this program is quite useful. You can find Image'n'Bits at \WEBPAGES\APPS\IMA.HTM and \APPS\CONVERT\IMA.

Murals   Murals enables you to use JPEG and .GIF images as wallpaper directly, without converting them to .BMP format. This capability saves you a great deal of disk space. You can find Murals at \WEBPAGES\APPS\MURAIS.HTM and \APPS\CONVERT\MURALS.

Paint Shop Pro   Paint Shop Pro is a powerful graphics viewing and editing utility. It supports about 20 different graphics file formats, including the .GIF and JPEG formats commonly found on the Web. Paint Shop Pro has a host of features for editing and manipulating graphics, and rivals commercial packages with its number and variety of filters and special effects. The utility also includes a screen-capture program. You can find Paint Shop Pro at \WEBPAGES\APPS\PAINTSHP.HTM and \APPS\CONVERT\PAINTSHP.

WinJPEG   WinJPEG is a Windows-based graphics-file viewer and converter. You can read and save TIFF, .GIF, JPEG, .TGA, .BMP, and .PCX file formats with this viewer/converter. WinJPEG has several color-enhancement and dithering features that enable the user to alter a graphics file slightly. The program also supports batch conversions and screen captures. You can find WinJPEG at \WEBPAGES\APPS\WINJPEG.HTM and \APPS\CONVERT\WINJPG.

WinLab   WinLab is a powerful graphics viewer and editor. In addition to its image-processing features, WinLab has built-in TWAIN and network support and a WinSock-compliant application for sending and receiving images. You can find WinLab at \WEBPAGES\APPS\WINLAB.HTM and \APPS\CONVERT\WINLAB.

Grabbit Pro   If you're putting Web pages together for software documentation, you'll find the Grabbit Pro Windows screen-capture utility to be an invaluable aid in creating pages with embedded screen shots. (Grabbit Pro doesn't save files in .GIF format, so if you want to use saved images as inline images, you must convert them by using one of the other conversion utilities discussed in this section.) The CD includes both Windows 3.1 and Windows NT versions of

Grabbit Pro, which you can find in \WEBPAGES\APPS\GRABPRO.HTM and \APPS\CAPTURE\GRABPRO.

UUEncode/UUDecode Software

UUEncoding converts binary files (programs and archives) to text so that they can be transmitted over the Internet in messages. After receipt, the message files must be converted back (UUDecoded) to their original binary form.

Batch UUD for DOS   As its name implies, Batch UUD for DOS is a batch UUDecoder that runs in DOS. With UUD, all you have to do is type **UUD *.*** in DOS or choose the File menu's Run option in Windows to decode all saved files in UUEncoded format. The program is smart, as well: By alphabetizing all entries, UUD can make a logical guess at the order of split files. You can find Batch UUD for DOS at \WEBPAGES\APPS\BATCHUUD.HTM and \APPS\UUENCODE\BATCHUUD.

Extract v3.04   Extract is a Windows application for encoding and decoding UU-embedded files. You can find Extract at \WEBPAGES\APPS\EXTRACT.HTM and \APPS\UUENCODE\EXTRACT.

N O T E   Extract's documentation is slightly outdated. The author requests that you send e-mail regarding the program to **dpenner@msl.cuug.ab.ca**. ■

UUCode   UUCode is a Windows-based application that decodes UUEncoded files sent over the Internet in messages. This application also UUEncodes a binary file so that you can insert it into a message and send the file over the Internet in the message. The program's configuration options include file overwriting, default file names, and status messages. You can find UUCode at \WEBPAGES\APPS\UUCODE.HTM and \APPS\UUENCODE\UUCODE.

WinCode   WinCode is a great utility for UUEncoding and UUDecoding files. Two of its useful features are its effortless multiple file handling and its capability to tie its menus to other programs. The program decodes many poorly encoded files that other decoders can't handle. You can find WinCode at \WEBPAGES\APPS\WINCODE.HTM and \APPS\UUENCODE\WINCODE.

App
E

Internet Documents

The \DOCS folder and its subfolders contain quite a bit of information. A description of all the files is beyond the scope of this section. Explore the \DOCS folder to find some of the more esoteric files.

Frequently Asked Questions (FAQs) (\DOCS\FAQ)

The CD includes some Frequently Asked Questions (FAQ) documents. FAQ documents exist for nearly every subject that is related to the Internet, and plenty more that have nothing to do with the Internet itself, but are popular with Internet users. The CD includes the following FAQs:

■ Emily Postnews answers your questions on netiquette (EMILYPST.PAQ)

■ How to find the right place to post (FINDPOST.FAQ)

■ The "good net-keeping seal of approval" for Usenet software (GNKSA.TXT)

■ How to create a new Usenet newsgroup (HOWCREAT.FAQ)

■ Internet Relay Chat (IRC) frequently asked questions (IRC.FAQ)

■ IRC Undernet frequently asked questions (IRC.UND1 FAQ and IRC.UND2 FAQ)

■ Answers to frequently asked questions about Usenet (NETFAQ.FAQ)

■ Hints on writing style for Usenet (NETSTYLE.FAQ)

■ Introduction to **news.announce** (NEWSANCE.FAQ)

■ Introduction to the ***.answers** newsgroups (NEWSANSW.FAQ)

■ A primer on how to work with the Usenet community (NEWSPRIM.TXT)

■ Rules for posting to Usenet (NEWSRULE.FAQ)

■ Usenet software: history and sources (NEWSSOFt.FAQ)

All FAQs are updated regularly. Check the *Newsgroups:* header in these postings and look in those groups for more recent copies before acting on the information that you find in them. Thousands of FAQs are posted to the Usenet group **news.answers** every month.

List of FTP Sites (\DOCS\FTPSITES)

This folder contains several files that list FTP sites. Each site listing includes the country of origin, a comment about the site, and the types of files that the site holds.

FYIs (\DOCS\FYI)

An FYI (*for your information*) document is published strictly for its information content. The document isn't meant to be a standard. FYIs tend to be less technical than RFCs or STDs.

Provider List (\DOCS\PROVIDER)

This folder contains several text files listing companies and providers that supply a constant Internet connection. Many sites listed in these text files also have dial-up access to the Internet. The provider lists present information about each site, such as contact name, phone number, Internet address, and system information. The lists arrange each site by region. The provider lists include lists of Internet providers in the United States, Africa, Asia, Australia, Canada, the former Soviet bloc, Latin America, the Middle East, and Western Europe. InterNIC compiles and maintains the lists.

STDs (\DOCS\STD)

An STD document is an RFC document that has been accepted as a standard. STDs tend to be technical.

RFCs (\RFC)

The RFC documents are the working notes of the committees that develop the protocols and standards for the Internet. The documents are numbered in the order in which they were released. Any skipped numbers represent RFCs that are outdated, were replaced by newer ones, or were never issued. The CD Home Page (APPCD.HrM) gives you various ways to view the RFC list. In addition to sorting the RFC by author and number, you can view some humorous RFCs, which have been highlighted in their own section.

Many RFCs are rather dry reading, and some are almost impenetrably dense. However, they define the specification for the part of your software that talks to the Internet, so they are "must" reading for you. ●

Index

X-Y-Z

Check out Que® Books on the World Wide Web
http://www.mcp.com/que

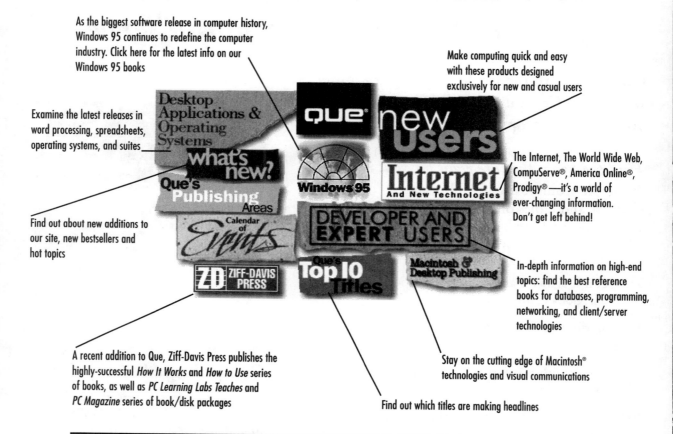

As the biggest software release in computer history, Windows 95 continues to redefine the computer industry. Click here for the latest info on our Windows 95 books

Make computing quick and easy with these products designed exclusively for new and casual users

Examine the latest releases in word processing, spreadsheets, operating systems, and suites

The Internet, The World Wide Web, CompuServe®, America Online®, Prodigy® —it's a world of ever-changing information. Don't get left behind!

Find out about new additions to our site, new bestsellers and hot topics

In-depth information on high-end topics: find the best reference books for databases, programming, networking, and client/server technologies

A recent addition to Que, Ziff-Davis Press publishes the highly-successful *How It Works* and *How to Use* series of books, as well as *PC Learning Labs Teaches* and *PC Magazine* series of book/disk packages

Stay on the cutting edge of Macintosh® technologies and visual communications

Find out which titles are making headlines

With 6 separate publishing groups, Que develops products for many specific market segments and areas of computer technology. Explore our Web Site and you'll find information on best-selling titles, newly published titles, upcoming products, authors, and much more.

- Stay informed on the latest industry trends and products available
- Visit our online bookstore for the latest information and editions
- Download software from Que's library of the best shareware and freeware

Complete and Return this Card
for a *FREE* Computer Book Catalog

Thank you for purchasing this book! You have purchased a superior computer book written expressly for your needs. To continue to provide the kind of up-to-date, pertinent coverage you've come to expect from us, we need to hear from you. Please take a minute to complete and return this self-addressed, postage-paid form. In return, we'll send you a free catalog of all our computer books on topics ranging from word processing to programming and the internet.

Mr. ☐   Mrs. ☐   Ms. ☐   Dr. ☐

Name (first) ☐☐☐☐☐☐☐☐☐☐☐☐☐ (M.I.) ☐   (last) ☐☐☐☐☐☐☐☐☐☐☐☐☐☐☐☐

Address ☐☐☐☐☐☐☐☐☐☐☐☐☐☐☐☐☐☐☐☐☐☐☐☐☐☐☐☐☐☐☐

☐☐☐☐☐☐☐☐☐☐☐☐☐☐☐☐☐☐☐☐☐☐☐☐☐☐☐☐☐☐☐

City ☐☐☐☐☐☐☐☐☐☐☐☐☐☐☐☐☐☐   State ☐☐   Zip ☐☐☐☐☐   ☐☐☐☐

Phone ☐☐☐   ☐☐☐   ☐☐☐☐   Fax ☐☐☐   ☐☐☐   ☐☐☐☐

Company Name ☐☐☐☐☐☐☐☐☐☐☐☐☐☐☐☐☐☐☐☐☐☐☐☐☐☐☐☐☐

E-mail address ☐☐☐☐☐☐☐☐☐☐☐☐☐☐☐☐☐☐☐☐☐☐☐☐☐☐☐

1. Please check at least (3) influencing factors for purchasing this book.

Front or back cover information on book .... ☐
Special approach to the content .... ☐
Completeness of content .... ☐
Author's reputation .... ☐
Publisher's reputation .... ☐
Book cover design or layout .... ☐
Index or table of contents of book .... ☐
Price of book .... ☐
Special effects, graphics, illustrations .... ☐
Other (Please specify): _____ ☐

2. How did you first learn about this book?

Saw in Macmillan Computer Publishing catalog .... ☐
Recommended by store personnel .... ☐
Saw the book on bookshelf at store .... ☐
Recommended by a friend .... ☐
Received advertisement in the mail .... ☐
Saw an advertisement in: _____ ☐
Read book review in: _____ ☐
Other (Please specify): _____ ☐

3. How many computer books have you purchased in the last six months?

This book only .... ☐   3 to 5 books .... ☐
2 books .... ☐   More than 5 .... ☐

4. Where did you purchase this book?

Bookstore .... ☐
Computer Store .... ☐
Consumer Electronics Store .... ☐
Department Store .... ☐
Office Club .... ☐
Warehouse Club .... ☐
Mail Order .... ☐
Direct from Publisher .... ☐
Internet site .... ☐
Other (Please specify): _____ ☐

5. How long have you been using a computer?

☐ Less than 6 months   ☐ 6 months to a year
☐ 1 to 3 years   ☐ More than 3 years

6. What is your level of experience with personal computers and with the subject of this book?

	With PCs	With subject of book
New	☐	☐
Casual	☐	☐
Accomplished	☐	☐
Expert	☐	☐

Source Code ISBN: 0-7897-0732-2

7. Which of the following best describes your job title?

Administrative Assistant .... ☐
Coordinator .... ☐
Manager/Supervisor .... ☐
Director .... ☐
Vice President .... ☐
President/CEO/COO .... ☐
Lawyer/Doctor/Medical Professional .... ☐
Teacher/Educator/Trainer .... ☐
Engineer/Technician .... ☐
Consultant .... ☐
Not employed/Student/Retired .... ☐
Other (Please specify): _____ ☐

8. Which of the following best describes the area of the company your job title falls under?

Accounting .... ☐
Engineering .... ☐
Manufacturing .... ☐
Operations .... ☐
Marketing .... ☐
Sales .... ☐
Other (Please specify): _____ ☐

9. What is your age?

Under 20 .... ☐
21-29 .... ☐
30-39 .... ☐
40-49 .... ☐
50-59 .... ☐
60-over .... ☐

10. Are you:

Male .... ☐
Female .... ☐

11. Which computer publications do you read regularly? (Please list)

_____
_____
_____
_____
_____
_____
_____
_____
_____
_____

Comments: _____
_____
_____

Fold here and scotch-tape to mail.